Verdict

Verdict

Assessing the Civil
Jury System

Robert E. Litan

editor

The Brookings Institution
Washington, D.C.

Copyright © 1993
THE BROOKINGS INSTITUTION
1775 Massachusetts Avenue, N.W., Washington, D.C. 20036

Library of Congress Cataloging-in-Publication data

Verdict : assessing the civil jury system / [editor], Robert E. Litan.
    p.   cm.
    Includes bibliographical references and index.
    ISBN 0-8157-5282-2 (cl : alk. paper)—ISBN
0-8157-5281-4 (pa : alk. paper)
    1. Jury—United States.   I. Litan, Robert E.
KF8972.A5V47   1993
347.73'0752—dc20
[347.307752]   93-9389
                                                        CIP

9 8 7 6 5 4 3 2 1

The paper used in this publication meets the minimum
requirements of the American National Standard for
Information Sciences—Permanence of paper for Printed
Library Materials, ANSI Z39.48-1984

Foreword

THE RIGHT to a jury trial in civil cases is enshrined in the Seventh Amendment to the Constitution and has long been a feature of the American system of civil justice. In recent years, however, the workings of the jury system—in both civil and criminal cases—have become the subject of public discussion, if not controversy.

In this volume, edited by Brookings senior fellow Robert E. Litan, a group of prominent legal scholars, practitioners, and judges report their findings about how the civil jury system is working and what, if any, changes might improve it. The chapters in this volume were originally prepared for a joint project and symposium that Brookings conducted with the American Bar Association's Litigation Section in June 1992. A summary of that symposium was presented in *Charting a Future for the Civil Jury System,* published by Brookings in December 1992.

In contrast to the earlier report, which reflected the consensus views of the more than one hundred participants at the symposium, this volume presents the findings and views of the individual authors. As a result, the disagreements are sharper and some of the recommendations are more far-reaching. Nevertheless, there is strong agreement among the authors in this volume that resolving disputes through jury trial remains an important and valuable mechanism that should be preserved and strengthened.

Emily Chalmers, James Schneider, Deborah Styles, and Theresa Walker edited the manuscript. David Bearce, Laura Kelly, and Alison Rimsky verified its content; Susan Woollen prepared it for typesetting; and Julia Petrakis constructed the index. Anita Whitlock provided administrative assistance.

The overall project on the civil jury system, of which the publication

of this volume marks the completion, was supported financially by Aetna
Life & Casualty Company; Ford Motor Company; the Foundation for
Change; the General Electric Foundation; Popham, Haik, Schnobrich
& Kaufman, Ltd.; and Jenner & Block. This publication is also the
second volume sponsored by the new Brookings Center for Law,
Economics and Politics, directed by Litan. This Center has received
financial support from the Crum & Forster Inc.; Honeywell, Inc.; the
Reinsurance Association of America; the Starr Foundation; the State
Farm Insurance Companies; and Union Carbide Corporation.

The views expressed here are those of the authors and should not be
attributed to the trustees, officers, or staff members of the Brookings
Institution, or to the employers, sponsors, or funders of individual
authors.

BRUCE K. MACLAURY
President

Washington, D.C.
May 1993

Contents

Tables

Figure

Verdict

CHAPTER ONE

Introduction

Robert E. Litan

T HE AMERICAN SYSTEM of civil justice, much admired around the world, in recent years has become the subject of great controversy at home. Indeed, the workings of the civil justice system even became an issue in the 1992 presidential campaign.

Complaints focus on both substance and procedure. The nation's tort laws that provide compensation to injured parties, for example, have come under attack for discouraging socially worthwhile innovation. Defenders of the tort system assert that liability rules must be stringent to deter firms and individuals from selling risky products or otherwise behaving in an unsafe manner. Many states have so far sided with the critics, at least to some degree, by modifying their liability laws in some fashion in recent years. At the federal level, however, Congress has so far rejected various proposals for tort reform.

On procedural issues, the situation has been somewhat different. Perhaps surprisingly, the antagonists in the tort reform debate—the plaintiffs' and defendants' bar, the insurance industry, the manufacturing sector, and the public interest community—generally have agreed that the civil justice system is too expensive and too slow. In 1990 Congress, in recognition of that reality, enacted legislation requiring federal district courts to develop and then implement plans to reduce delay and transactions costs for litigants. Only a relatively few states, however, seem to have taken a similarly strong interest in procedural reform.

Brookings has taken part in the debates on both the substantive and procedural aspects of the civil justice system. In 1988 and again in 1991, the institution published edited volumes about the workings and effects of the nation's liability laws.[1] And in 1990, a task force convened by Brookings published a report on the delay and transactions costs in the federal courts whose recommendations were largely incorporated in the Civil Justice Reform Act of 1990.[2]

This book continues the work of the Brookings Institution in civil justice by focusing on an important subject that has both substantive and procedural aspects: the use of juries to resolve civil disputes. In fact, the right to a jury trial in civil actions for damages is so important that it is enshrined in the Seventh Amendment to the U.S. Constitution and in similar provisions in most state constitutions.

Nevertheless, the jury system too has attracted criticism. Some of those worried about the excesses of the tort system, for example, have argued that juries are incapable of understanding complex issues and are often biased against such deep pocket defendants as insurance companies, large companies, or physicians. Others have expressed concern that the rules of civil procedure are too stilted and impede jurors' understanding of issues. Still others are troubled about the rules governing the selection of juries. Perhaps the most damning public criticisms of the jury system— in a criminal trial, to be sure, but one with much broader implications— followed the verdict in the first Rodney King police brutality case in Los Angeles in 1992, where because of the widely shown videotape of the critical events at issue in the trial, millions of Americans found themselves unable to understand the jury's acquittal.

In short, given the apparent misgivings about aspects of the civil jury system, the time is ripe for a scholarly reexamination of the civil jury. In this book a distinguished group of academic scholars and judges do that by assessing various aspects of the civil jury system.

Chapter 2 begins by describing the history of the jury as a decisionmaker in both civil and criminal matters. Chapters 3 and 4 present competing views of the objectives of the jury system and whether, and to what extent, actual practice meets those objectives. Chapters 5 through 8 describe what is known about how juries work and what attitudes lawyers, judges, litigants, former jurors, and the public at large hold about the system. Chapters 9 through 14 present a wide range of recommendations for improving the jury system or changing it in a way that, in the opinion of some authors, would further the broader objectives of the justice system. Chapter 15 closes by placing the discussion of the jury in a broader context of how society resolves or manages civil disputes.

The idea for this project originated in discussions among this author, Brookings senior staff member Warren Cikins, and two recent chairmen of the American Bar Association's Section on Litigation, Ted Tetzlaff and

G. Marc Whitehead, who reported the section's interest in cosponsoring a symposium on the subject. An advisory group of approximately thirty distinguished legal practitioners helped select the authors of the chapters that follow. It was agreed that the authors of these chapters would present drafts to the symposium, which was held in June 1992 and attended by more than one hundred attorneys, judges, academic scholars, and representatives of users of the judicial system, including businesses, insurance companies, and public interest organizations. The product of that symposium was a report published by Brookings in December 1992, *Charting a Future for the Civil Jury System.*

Readers of that report will detect a number of differences from the views presented here. Broadly speaking, many of the authors in this volume seem more willing to entertain fundamental changes to the jury system than the participants in the symposium, who strongly defended the jury as an institution but who also agreed that jury trials and selection procedures could be improved to some degree.

More than twenty-five years ago, Harry Kalven and Hans Zeisel of the University of Chicago published what continues to stand as the preeminent study of the jury system.[3] This book does not pretend to update or augment that effort. However, all of the authors in the following chapters approached the subject matter of the civil jury in a similar spirit, with an open mind as to how the jury functions and whether certain features of the civil jury system should be modified or reformed.

The History of the Civil Jury

The American jury system, like that of the common law more generally, has its roots in England. In its original form, juries were used by the Crown to gather information for prosecuting alleged criminals. Later, juries evolved as decisionmakers in both criminal and civil contexts. In the process, juries moved from being handmaidens of royal authority to bulwarks of liberty, acting as a means for ordinary citizens to resist excessive demands by government. In their capacity as jurors, ordinary citizens essentially could make legal doctrine. In principle, of course, jurors made law only for the cases before them. But in the process of reaching their verdicts—deciding, for example, what is or is not reasonable conduct—juries could and did make precedent-setting decisions that affected private behavior throughout society.

In chapter 2 Stephan Landsman explains how the jury system in the United States has evolved. As in England, the views of the American system have also undergone change.

In colonial times, jury service was common for community residents and viewed as an essential instrument of governance and a strongly unifying experience for those who served. That view was a key reason why the right to a jury trial was included in the Constitution. After the revolution, however, the view of the jury gradually changed: juries were no longer seen as a means of governing, but instead as essential bodies for counterbalancing the growing power of judges and the fear that that power could be abused. Indeed, as the country matured during the nineteenth century, power shifted away from juries to judges, who increasingly controlled the procedures and outcomes of disputes and criminal trials. Nonetheless, the jury still continued to be an important force in shaping common law, especially for tort actions, or when individuals sought compensation for the injuries they alleged were caused by other individuals or corporations.

The jury as an institution came under strong attack in the early years of the twentieth century, with opponents challenging its composition, procedures, and even its right to exist. These criticisms stimulated a series of empirical studies of the ways juries worked, which ultimately only enhanced the jury's reputation.

In short, Landsman explains, the jury of today has a mixed heritage. On the one hand, juries have been assigned a wide range of tasks, including the assessment of business morality, protection of the consuming public, the definition of key Constitutional rights, and the determination of questions of life and death in criminal cases. On the other hand, the jury system continues to be the target of reform proposals. Some of these have already been adopted: in many jurisdictions, juries can be fewer than twelve persons in size, unanimous verdicts are not required, questioning of jurors (during voir dire) has been limited, and the right of the parties to make peremptory challenges (where no reason need be given) has been restricted.

Landsman concludes his historical overview with a warning. The civil jury as an institution is not invincible, as demonstrated by the fact that it disappeared in England (where it was born) in the years between the First World War and the depression. If the jury in the United States is not to suffer the same fate, Landsman argues, its importance to democratic values must be appreciated and significantly broader reform efforts resisted.

As we shall soon see, this view is not shared by all of the authors in this project. Some believe that fundamental reforms are desirable, if not essential. But there is broad agreement among all of the authors that the jury still has and will continue to have an important role to play in the American system of civil justice.

Competing Views of the Civil Jury

It is often said that where one sits determines where one stands. By the same token, one's views about the efficacy or desirability of the jury system depend significantly on the purposes one believes the jury is supposed to fulfill. In this spirit, chapters 3 and 4 present very different perspectives on the objectives and achievements of the civil jury as an institution. Subsequent chapters contain more detailed discussions of the empirical evidence relating to many of the claims advanced in chapter 3 by Marc Galanter and chapter 4 by George Priest.

To set the stage, it is useful to describe the essential features of the civil jury. Typically, it consists of twelve persons (but in many jurisdictions, juries as small in size as six are permitted), all ordinary citizens and generally not legal professionals (although most jurisdictions allow attorneys to serve), chosen randomly; sitting discontinuously (that is, dispersing after the case is over), and, in the words of George Priest, "aresponsible" in the sense that juries decide cases without having to give reasons, while their verdicts are largely invulnerable to review. The critical question to which both Galanter and Priest address themselves is how such a system of decisionmaking can be justified.

Marc Galanter takes up the defense by making the distinction already made between two functions of the jury system: to decide specific cases, and to collectively generate a body of legal knowledge and doctrine that underpins the American system of "litigotiation." Galanter uses the latter term because relatively few of the cases filed actually are decided by juries but instead are settled by negotiation between the parties.

Galanter's reading of the substantial accumulated body of jury research is that juries have been found to do a good job of deciding cases. Jurors are as conscientious and able to recall evidence as judges. Jurors and judges also agree about as often as one could reasonably expect given the often complex matters juries are asked to resolve. Although some evidence shows that jury outcomes are affected by the identities of the litigants, Galanter finds little support for the notion that juries are biased against deep pocket defendants. On the whole, Galanter finds the evidence supporting juries as decisionmakers somewhat remarkable, given that the cases that make it to trial are those in which the facts and the law are most strongly in dispute.

At the same time, however, the fact that the fraction of cases decided by juries has fallen in recent years—from about 5 percent of federal cases in 1961 to just 2 percent in 1991—is the reason why Galanter concentrates on the norm-setting or signaling function that juries collectively perform. He observes that jury decisions affect private behavior through many channels: through the judicial apparatus and related reporting services, attorneys, word-of-mouth discussions by jurors of their experiences, academic publications, and perhaps most importantly through reporting by the mass media. As the share of cases decided by juries falls—and even more importantly, as the number of jury verdicts declines relative to the population as a whole—jury outcomes increasingly are transmitted to the public not through jurors but through the other channels.

Galanter suggests that little is known about how individuals form beliefs about the jury system or its outcomes, let alone how these factors affect the litigotiation process. He points to evidence that lawyers display persistent and sizable variability and error in their readings of the potential outcomes of jurors' decisionmaking. Among other things, Galanter believes this is because of a media bias that overstates the number and size of jury verdicts: only large verdicts tend to be newsworthy, thus distorting perceptions by lawyers and the public of likely outcomes.

The jury system, of course, has its monetary and nonmonetary costs. The latter include some variance in verdicts pertaining to similar cases, which sends blurry signals to private actors. Nevertheless, in Galanter's view, the benefits of the jury system outweigh the costs. The jury promotes democratic values and helps legitimate judicial outcomes. But for Galanter a key advantage is the jury's strongly positive impact on the litigotiation system. The amateurism and transience of juries, which some find to be vices, Galanter argues are their virtues. Because juries have neither experience nor institutional responsibilities, they respond to the case at hand, free of the biases and hardened attitudes that can all too easily develop among professionals seeing similar cases day in and day out. The freshness of jury decisions helps ensure that legal norms are aligned with emerging community values and understandings.

George Priest advances a very different perspective on the civil jury system in chapter 4 by attempting to match specific types of civil cases with the various justifications that have been advanced for having juries, rather than judges, decide these disputes. He concludes that while, in principle, many types of civil cases satisfy these criteria, in practice only a small proportion of the millions of the civil cases that are filed each year do so.

For example, Harry Kalven, one of the most prominent academic defenders of the jury system, argued that a group of representatively chosen laypersons was appropriate for deciding disputes whose resolution required the application of some "community sense of values." Cases meeting this standard include those involving claims of defamation and cases requiring complex societal value judgments, such as wrongful death actions for homemakers or children (whose activities are not measured by the market, as is the case for working men and women), or perhaps tort cases in which victims have suffered extreme pain and suffering.

Jury decisionmaking in civil cases can also be justified as a means of preserving democratic values. A similar argument justifies jury decisionmaking in criminal cases. Priest suggests that condemnation actions, or civil suits against the police or other governmental agencies, would satisfy this criterion for upholding democracy.

Harry Kalven also defended the discontinuous nature of jury service on the grounds that juries serve as a "lightning rod for animosity." Such a characteristic is helpful, he argues, in cases involving great public controversy since juries can render a decision and then their members can return to anonymity. In contrast, if permanently appointed judges were to decide these delicate questions, they might long remain an object of controversy.

Priest argues that the most difficult characteristic of the civil jury to defend is its "aresponsibility"—that is, its freedom from explaining or justifying decisions, as well as its insulation from effective review (except in cases of serious error). Nevertheless, Yale Law School Dean Guido Calabresi has defended this characteristic in cases requiring "tragic choices," such as the determination of which individual best deserves a scarce dialysis machine or resuscitator. In such instances, requiring statements of the standards by which decisions are made in individual cases (one individual is younger than another and therefore should be first in line to receive the treatment) may be destructive of larger social values (all citizens deserve equal treatment).

A final defense of jury decisionmaking as an institution is that jury service gives citizens important lessons in civic virtues and in the law itself. This feature of the jury system, which de Tocqueville championed as "wonderfully effective in shaping a nation's judgment and increasing its natural lights," is continuously bolstered by post-trial interviews of jurors.

Priest then asks how relevant each of these various justifications is for the actual casework of the modern civil jury. He attempts to supply answers by examining empirical evidence of civil jury experience in the metropolitan Chicago civil courts over a twenty-one-year period ending in the mid-1980s. He finds that in only a few of these disputes are any of the various justifications met.

For example, less than 2 percent of the Chicago jury trials involved defamation or wrongful death of nonmarket participants, or two of the categories of cases most likely to satisfy Kalven's "community values" justification for jury decisionmaking. Expanding as widely as possible the other category of such cases, those with difficult judgments on pain and suffering, adds another 16 percent to the total. Still another 5 percent represents cases implicating governmental power. In all, the cases meeting what Priest believes are the most important types of specific matters where jury decisionmaking can be justified, constituted less than one-quarter of all the cases tried by Chicago juries during this period.

What, then, were these juries doing most of the time? In almost two-thirds of the cases, they were resolving disputes deriving from routine auto accidents causing routine injuries. Priest notes that slightly over half of the Chicago juries spent their time on cases in which the most serious claimed injury was a strain, bruise, fracture, or dislocation.

Priest also finds that the number of Chicago citizens able to learn about civic virtues was very limited. Whereas in de Tocqueville's day, the typical citizen may have served on a jury every 3 or 4 years, in Chicago during the two decades that Priest examined, a citizen faced the likelihood of jury service once every 260 years. The odds of serving on a case requiring application of community values or the exercise of governmental power were much smaller, only once over 1,252 years.[4]

In short, Priest questions whether the civil jury is appropriate for resolution of the types of disputes that currently dominate its caseload. Moreover, he wonders whether the features of the civil jury that ensure its democratic character—namely, its composition of lay persons with little experience in the law, chosen randomly—increase uncertainty about outcomes and thus impair the ability of parties in routine and nonroutine cases to settle out of court. If true, then the congestion that now prevents a large proportion of cases from ever reaching a jury is, at least in part, a product of the jury system.

The Empirical Evidence

Generally speaking, the other authors do not address the implied criticism of the jury system represented in Priest's essay. For that matter, few of the critics of the jury system rest their attacks on the grounds that Priest advances. Instead, the critiques relate to the competence, rationality, and other characteristics of jurors. These issues and others are taken up in chapters 5 through 8, which summarize the empirical evidence related to how juries function and how various individuals and groups view the jury system.

Characteristics of Jury Decisions

Robert MacCoun begins in chapter 5 by reviewing what can be learned about jury decisions themselves, based on a combination of statistical studies of jury verdicts, post-trial juror interviews, "shadow" jury studies, and mock jury experiments.

Despite great variation across jurisdictions, several findings about jury verdicts stand out (although they are open to multiple interpretations). Plaintiffs prevail somewhat more than half of the time, typically between 55 and 65 percent. But perhaps contrary to widespread belief, defendants usually win in medical malpractice and product liability cases in particular. Median awards have generally been stable in auto cases, but such awards have grown in product liability and medical malpractice. Mean awards are much higher than median awards and have grown at a faster pace owing to the increase in million-dollar awards. However, about 20 percent of all awards—and an even higher percentage of large dollar awards—are reduced by post-trial activities (appellate decisions and settlements). Despite the attention they receive, punitive awards are still rare.

Some evidence shows that jurors frequently fail to understand the judge's instructions. At the same time, the instructions may not be that important to the outcome since jurors tend to determine liability by constructing plausible stories that appear to make sense of the evidence. To some extent, jurors' common-sense judgments appear to correspond to the common law of torts. MacCoun finds some evidence, however, that jurors' judgments on liability are influenced by plaintiffs' injuries, contrary to the law's intent.

Jurors take many approaches to computing damages. Some reach their results by systematic calculation; others appear to set the figure in more arbitrary fashion. Many jurors set some kind of anchor to the damage award and then make adjustments. Researchers still have little idea, however, of how "blindfolding the jury" to various factors (such as whether the plaintiff has insurance) influences their awards.

MacCoun reports that evidence clearly shows that jurors in the minority tend to eventually conform to the majority's view. Jurors appear to compromise among themselves to determine the size of the award, although the process is rarely one of explicit averaging. There is some evidence that final awards are larger than jurors' initial opinions, suggesting that awards grow during deliberation. Jury size and the assigned decision rule (whether or not the verdict must be unanimous) do not appear to influence the direction of verdicts, but they may affect the amount.

MacCoun also reports that jurors are often vulnerable to various extralegal influences that may bias their verdicts. For example, several studies have documented that juries treat corporations differently than individual defendants, not because they have deep pockets, but because jurors find it easier to sanction an impersonal organization than an individual for misconduct.

Finally, in comparison to cases decided by judges, juror-awarded damages tend to be higher and more variable. At the same time, however, plaintiffs win some types of tort cases more frequently in bench trials than in jury trials, a pattern that may arise because of differences in the types of cases that are tried by judges and juries. Still, judges appear to agree with about 80 percent of jury verdicts, although juries tend to be more generous about damages than judges.

Jury Decisionmaking in Complex Cases

Much of the criticism about jury performance stems from charges that lay jurors are ill equipped to decide the outcomes of complex cases, or those with intricate scientific, statistical, or economic issues. In chapter 6, Richard Lempert assesses the evidence on jury decisionmaking in these matters.

Lempert finds that a combination of experimental and anecdotal evidence supports the view that juries can and often do a good job of resolving complex cases, a view seconded by Jonathan Casper in chapter 13. Typically, juries follow the leads of their most knowledgeable members. There is also some evidence that jurors can understand the basic features of complex statistical evidence, such as models using regression techniques.

To be sure, Lempert identifies some complex litigations where the jury verdicts seem mistaken, but in most of these situations, there is little reason to believe that the complexity of a particular matter was responsible for the jury's errors. Serious mistakes by the attorney for the losing side or by the judge were more apt to affect verdicts. And when juries appear to be at fault for misplaced verdicts, the principal culprit seems to be the trouble the jury had in understanding the legal instructions, a problem that is found in complex and noncomplex cases.

Less information is available about how judges rather than juries perform in complex cases, but Lempert reports anecdotal evidence suggesting that complexity can pose as substantial problems for rational judicial factfinding as it can for jury decisionmaking. That is, there is no guarantee that judges will decide complex matters wisely. Interestingly, the case studies suggest that when judges seem to be most capable of handling trials involving complex issues, juries perform best.

Attitudes toward the Jury

The attitudes of the public, the litigants, judges, attorneys, and former jurors toward the jury system are important because they influence how the system operates. For example, potential litigants and their attorneys decide whether or not to press or settle their claims based, in part, on how they think juries might react to them. Judges must determine what guidance and instructions to give to the jury in individual cases, an assessment that depends on their views of the jury and its competence. In society at large, the prospect of jury decisions may deter risky behavior or influence technological innovation. And finally, like other political institutions, the jury system must have the support of the citizenry if it is to function effectively. For if the jury as an institution is not perceived as a legitimate means of resolving disputes, then the public will not accept its verdicts.

In chapter 7, Valerie Hans surveys what is known about the attitudes toward the jury system held by key groups. She begins by outlining the strong public support for the jury, as reflected in opinion poll data. At the same time, most of the public believes that a litigation explosion has occurred, that jury awards have increased in recent years, and that civil justice costs are high. Some of these views are correlated with attitudes toward the jury. For example, those who believe in a litigation explosion are more likely than those who believe otherwise to perceive that jury awards are excessive. More generally, while most members of the public express concern about high jury awards, they also rank other factors—such as undeserving plaintiffs and refusals by insurance companies to settle deserving claims—above the jury as important reasons for rising lawsuit costs.

Despite the many cases that are tried before juries, most individuals obtain their information about the courts and the jury from the media rather than from direct experience as jurors. While the public is not well informed about the operations of the courts and legal system, people seem somewhat more knowledgeable about the jury system in particular. Little is known about how direct and indirect experiences with the legal system work together with exposure to media information to create perceptions of the jury.

National and regional surveys also show that trial judges endorse the jury system. Significantly, judges agree with civil jury outcomes in the vast majority of cases, modifying awards in only a few trials. Hans reports that judges confirm Lempert's finding that juries perform well in cases with complex technical, scientific, and business issues, and therefore judges endorse the continuation of trial by jury in such cases. In fact, judges are more willing to limit the right to a jury trial in minor cases involving small sums of money—or, as Priest finds, most of the cases that dominate the judicial calendar—than in complex civil cases. At the same time, only a minority of judges favor a "major" reform of the civil jury system.

Limited evidence exists on the view of attorneys toward the jury system, but what is available suggests that they have significant misconceptions about certain features of the system. In particular, Hans notes that attorneys often believe that the civil jury is pro-plaintiff in tort cases, which as MacCoun discusses, is most likely to be true only when plaintiffs are severely injured. Some scholars have argued that mistaken perceptions about jury tendencies are detrimentally affecting settlement strategies, suggesting that more precise information about jury decisionmaking is desirable, a suggestion endorsed by Marc Galanter in his chapter.

The few systematic studies of litigants' opinions toward the jury system vary significantly, with some showing strong endorsement of the jury and others showing a divergence of opinion. The writings and advertisements of representatives of business and insurance, in particular, reflect their concerns, as potential defendants, about unreasonable jury awards. In contrast, injured parties who have retained an attorney are more likely to believe that jury awards are reasonable.

Finally, Shari Diamond in chapter 8 reviews what is known about how jurors view the system. The attitudes of jurors are important, Diamond argues, for several reasons: jurors who have negative experiences in court are likely to make every effort to avoid jury service in the future and to encourage their friends and neighbors to do the same; in addition, the impressions of jurors are important in helping shape the views of society on the civil justice system generally and thus on the respect citizens have for the law.

Diamond observes that the limited available evidence strongly suggests that most jurors find their service a positive experience; this view is true even among jurors who initially were reluctant to serve. Even less is known about why jurors feel the way they do, but Diamond reports that the factor most strongly noted by jurors was how well they were treated when they were processed, that is, how long they had to wait and generally were treated; but even this factor accounted for less than 1 percent of the variation in ratings of jurors' satisfaction.

Jurors do complain about some aspects of jury service. About one-fifth of jurors, according to the survey evidence, resent the personal questions asked of them during the voir dire, or the selection process. Many jurors complain about the repetition of evidence, and many report being frustrated that rules of evidence seem arbitrarily to exclude certain evidence they believe would be important. Some jurors also report being confused by disorganized presentation of trial exhibits, suggesting a need for counsel to present exhibits and testimony in an organized fashion to facilitate comprehension by jurors. Many jurors have also reported difficulty understanding judicial instructions, and there is ample evidence that instructions are often unnecessarily incomprehensible. Jurors also express some frustration about the minimal guidance they are given in computing damage awards. Many of the issues about which jurors complain are the subject of reform proposals.

Much controversy has arisen in recent years over whether expert testimony unduly sways jurors. Diamond's view of the evidence is that most jurors do not naively and uncritically accept expert testimony, find expert testimony useful in reaching their decisions, and have less trouble than may be commonly believed understanding such testimony.

Finally, Diamond suggests that the evidence in the civil arena runs somewhat counter to the conventional wisdom from the criminal arena that jurors make up their minds before jury deliberation begins. In fact, deliberations may change the outcome in as many as 30 percent of civil cases.

Recommendations

In chapters 9 through 14 a group of academic scholars and judges present various recommendations for changing and, in their opinion, improving the civil jury system. Certain authors of the earlier chapters also supported certain reforms.

Peter Schuck in chapter 9 suggests that two broad objectives motivate proposals for reform. One is to reduce the administrative costs and delay that frustrate plaintiffs and defendants alike. Schuck argues, however, that these costs are not that large and, to some extent, are offset by the social benefits of the jury system.

A second reform objective is to reduce the jury's irrationality. Some critics believe juries reach inconsistent decisions in some cases that have similar fact patterns. These decisions do not pertain so much to verdicts in routine cases—to which juries and judges overwhelmingly tend to agree—but to damage awards and to verdicts in complex cases. Some defenders of the current system do not find such outcomes disturbing. For example, Jonathan Casper argues that while the desire to obtain rational and predictable jury verdicts is understandable, it is also an unattainable goal given the inherent uncertainty in the factfinding process, whether the decisionmaker is judge or jury. Many participants in the June 1992 symposium also questioned whether consistency of awards, and their effects on private behavior, should even be an objective of the civil justice system. In their view, the importance of the system is in providing a mechanism for bringing to bear community values on each case that is heard and to legitimate the results, whatever they may be. The jury system is such a mechanism.

Nevertheless, to critics, the problem of inconsistent verdicts—within and across jurisdictions—sends confusing signals to the public about what behavior is to be expected and, in the process, leads to inefficiency and arguably undermines respect for the legal system. Schuck concedes the presence of inconsistency but questions how much of a deleterious effect it has actually had on various forms of private behavior. Moreover, he argues that the media have exaggerated the outlying damage awards and given the mistaken impression that such aberrations are the norm. Schuck questions whether moving from jury to bench trials would reduce some of the inconsistencies in jury decisions and awards that now exist.

Schuck still considers various suggestions for reforming the jury system. To reduce administrative costs, he suggests that filing fees be raised for parties who demand a jury trial in order to cover the full net social cost of such trials. This proposal would reduce the demand for trials and promote settlement. In order to ensure continued access to the jury trial system for low-income individuals, Schuck would provide special fee waivers under certain conditions.

Schuck concentrates most of his attention, however, on reforms designed to reduce aberrant jury outcomes. The proposals he and several others consider can be classified in much the same way as was done during the June 1992 jury symposium.

First, the more modest reform suggestions call for various procedural changes designed to improve jurors' comprehension. The underlying rationale, of course, is that the better jurors understand the evidence in the context of the applicable legal standard, the more rational and defensible the verdicts will be.

Second, the more far-reaching recommendations call for narrowing the discretion of juries, altering jury size, and changing the decision rules for reaching verdicts, all with the aim of preventing aberrant verdicts.

Third, some observers believe that certain types of cases warrant special treatment and should not be subjected to decisionmaking by a jury.

Fourth, others would change the way juries are chosen, largely to ensure that they are more representative of the communities in which trials take place.

In general, those who advocate the various suggestions briefly summarized below seem to feel more strongly that the current system requires improvement than did the participants at the symposium that produced *Charting a Future for the Civil Jury*, whose members strongly endorsed the effectiveness of the current jury system but nevertheless supported, in varying degrees, enhancements to the system. Significantly, however, substantial overlap recurs between the list of recommendations endorsed by the authors in this volume and those supported, or at least mentioned, in the symposium report.

Improving Juror Comprehension

Most of the suggestions found in chapters 10 through 13 focus on changes in trial procedures and techniques that would improve the ability of jurors to understand the law and the evidence. Many of these suggestions are aimed at trial judges, others at the attorneys.

For example, Stephen Saltzburg in chapter 10 recommends that jurors be allowed to take notes; to ask questions in writing (to be posed by the judge) of witnesses; and to discuss the case during the trial. He believes that lawyers can contribute most to the jurors' comprehension by using visual exhibits to the greatest extent possible. He suggests that courts liberally encourage the use of videotaped depositions of important witnesses not available for trial (rather than having the deposition transcript just read to the jury) and other videotaped evidence and computer-generated reenactments.

Saltzburg also argues that judges can and should facilitate jurors' comprehension. To further this objective, he urges judges to be more aggressive in pushing opposing attorneys to present at trial only the truly disputed facts and issues in a case. Saltzburg would allow judges to penalize parties who engage in a pattern of denying facts not really in dispute by limiting that party's evidence, or after a verdict has been returned, to hold a hearing for the purpose of considering sanctions against such parties. Saltzburg also urges that judicial instructions to juries be vastly simplified to be cleansed of legal jargon and to be as case specific as possible. And he would urge judges to be more aggressive in screening expert and scientific evidence to ensure that jurors will understand it.

Judge Lee Sarokin and Thomas Munsterman in chapter 11 point out that several of the suggestions for improving juror comprehension advanced by Saltzburg and others are already in use in various federal and state courts around the country. However, if they are not in use, Sarokin and Munsterman urge that they should be. Thus, they agree with Saltzburg and others that jurors be allowed to take notes, ask questions, hear mini-summations throughout the trial from the attorneys (which would help jurors understand what they already have heard and will hear next), and receive notebooks with all exhibits clearly marked. They would also have judges give the jurors general legal instructions at the beginning of the trial, and not just at the end, while giving the juries written copies of both to facilitate their deliberations. And, they would limit the time each side has to present evidence.

Judge William Schwarzer and Alan Hirsch express concern that current evidentiary rules preclude too much relevant information from juries on the grounds that it may result in "unfair prejudice, confusion, or misleading the jury." Originally, only potentially inflammatory evidence, such as bloody shirts or shocking photographs, were excluded on this ground (under Rule 403 of the Federal Rules of Evidence). Today, the authors observe, some judges are excluding expert testimony on this ground, a tendency they believe denies the jury its right to assess the relevance of evidence on its own. Accordingly, they urge that judges be more sparing in invoking Rule 403. More generally, Schwarzer and Hirsch warn that by excluding evidence of such matters as the parties' insurance coverage, the availability of treble damages in antitrust cases, the rights of prevailing parties to attorneys' fees, the taxability of awards, settlement offers, and actual settlements involving some of the parties, the law treats jurors condescendingly and allows them to reach conclusions and make decisions on the basis of incomplete information.

Both Jonathan Casper in chapter 13 and Richard Lempert (chapter 6) are more cautious about such reforms as note-taking, allowing jurors to ask questions, preinstructing juries, and providing juries with written copies of the judge's instructions. In their view, the evidence is not yet sufficient to establish that these reforms would improve jurors' comprehension. However, Lempert observes that those who have been exposed to these reforms—judges, lawyers, and jurors—seem to like them, and with the exception of note-taking, believe they are likely to help. Casper takes a more skeptical view, warning of the unintended consequences of adopting major reforms. Indeed, if juries and judges agree about 80 percent of the time—as Kalven and Zeisel's study suggested—why make major changes? In the end, both Casper and Lempert cautiously call for further experimentation with new procedures designed to improve jurors' comprehension, but they urge at the same time that the effects of any experiments be carefully studied.

Narrowing Juror Discretion and Other Structural Reforms

For those who believe that jury verdicts and awards are excessively variable or random, more far-reaching reforms designed to limit or at least inform the discretion of juries may be the only appropriate response. Peter Schuck considers proposals of this genre in chapter 9: changing substantive legal doctrines to make outcomes more certain, requiring juries to defer to the judgments of others (such as upholding genuinely consensual, informal contracts and exempting from liability certain products approved as safe by regulatory agencies), allowing juries to award damages only within the bounds of a schedule (perhaps based on the age of the plaintiff and severity of the injury, or, alternatively, upholding their awards so long as they explain their deviation from historically determined range of awards); asking juries to hand down special verdicts on specific sub-issues rather than just an ultimate yes or no verdict; and diverting certain categories of disputes to nontrial mechanisms of resolution.

Schuck holds out little promise for the first option, namely, changes in substantive legal doctrines. If juries are as biased or error-prone as critics charge, their answers under the new doctrines may be no better than their answers under the old. In any event, Schuck interprets the failure of Congress to enact tort reform legislation during the 1980s when the so-called liability crisis was at its peak as strong evidence that meaningful changes in substantive civil law doctrines designed to narrow jury discretion are not likely to occur (at least at the federal level). Schuck nevertheless favors experimenting with the scheduling of damages or with requirements that juries explain "deviant" awards. In his view, such approaches would preserve, but guide, the discretion of jurors and make damage awards more predictable, facilitating insurance coverage of products and services and encouraging negotiated settlements. Meanwhile, Saltzburg and Sarokin and Munsterman favor the use of special verdicts, jury interrogatories, and the use of bifurcation (deciding liability issues before damages, or vice versa) in complicated cases when a decision on one or a few issues may obviate the need for trying others. Casper is much more cautious about the use of these techniques, and Lempert points out that devices like special verdicts may share the vices of poorly drafted instructions.

Several authors also considered changes in the jury's structure that might lead to more predictable outcomes. Schuck and Galanter urge that jury size be expanded beyond the six persons that are now used for juries in many jurisdictions. Both believe that larger juries are less likely to produce aberrant results. However, both also suggested that experiments be run with juries of different size rather than choosing any number arbitrarily.

Moving Cases Outside the Jury System

An even more controversial way of providing more predictable outcomes in civil disputes is to channel more of them outside the jury system. The movement in some jurisdictions toward more intensive use of alternative dispute resolution (ADR) procedures—including arbitration and mediation—is one way this can be accomplished. No-fault automobile accident law can also be viewed as a device for doing so, as can replacement of jury trials with trials by judges or administrative law judges for certain types of claims.

Of these alternatives, only the first and the third have been extensively tried. ADR is now perhaps the nonjury technique used most often.

Administrative procedures are also used to resolve disputes over social security claims and certain civil rights matters. Peter Schuck nevertheless doubts whether much public support exists for moving further away from the jury trial as a means of dispute resolution; if anything, he finds that public attitudes, as evidenced by recent legislative developments, more strongly favor an expansion of the jury's role rather than its limitation.

Juror Representativeness, Selection, and Service

Finally, several of the authors addressed the representativeness and selection of juries. The objective here is both to ensure that verdicts are better informed by the values of the community in the case, and that those summoned to jury service do not face discrimination in the courthouse itself.

Toward this end, Saltzburg in his chapter urged eliminating automatic exemptions from jury while making jury service more palatable. Thus, Saltzburg would ask all citizens to designate one to two weeks every several years when they would be available for jury service, so that all would know well in advance when they might be called. And, he urges that courts schedule their trials more flexibly, perhaps from late afternoon through early evening, in order to accommodate individuals who work. Indeed, jurors might even be given exhibits and videotapes of depositions to view at home over weekends to reduce the time required in court. Furthermore, Saltzburg urges courts to develop systems for backing up each judge so that cases are not postponed because a particular judge might not be available.

Sarokin and Munsterman also call for a narrowing, if not elimination of, exemptions from jury service. They would reduce the length of jury service, increase jury pay, and eliminate the use of alternate jurors. They also suggest, as does Barbara Babcock in chapter 14, that attorneys make opening statements not just to the final jury members who may be chosen for service in a particular trial, but to the entire panel of potential jurors (the venire), a procedure they suggest would make it easier for jurors to disclose any biases that may prevent them from serving.

Both Saltzburg and Babcock expressed concern about the use of peremptory challenges (those for which no reason need be given) to exclude certain jurors from service. Under recent case law, jurors cannot be eliminated on racial grounds. Babcock shows the astonishing lengths to which the Supreme Court seems willing to go to ensure representative juries, both in civil and criminal matters. Babcock, however, would extend the logic of the Court's analysis of racially motivated peremptory challenges to the exclusion of women from juries, which she believes the Court should also prohibit. Babcock's analysis would seem to call into question the wisdom of retaining peremptory challenges, a view adopted by Sarokin and Munsterman in their chapter, but she concludes otherwise and defines a standard by which peremptory challenges can still be retained, while outlawed when they are motivated by racial or sexual discrimination.

Schwarzer and Hirsch take a somewhat different approach toward jury selection and service. They place less weight on ensuring that juries are representative of local communities than on ensuring that jurors with appropriate employment or educational backgrounds be chosen to hear particular cases (especially those involving complex issues). Thus, they would allow each party to select a given number of prospective jurors, subject to challenges only for cause. They would also authorize judges to establish minimum standards for service, to actually select a few of the most qualified jurors, or at least strike the least qualified members from the venire.

Concluding Thoughts

Chapters 2 through 14 concentrate on the role of the jury in civil litigation. In the concluding chapter, Judith Resnik takes a broader view by discussing several developments in the federal arena that point to a declining faith in "factfinding" in trials featuring live testimony, and the growing preference for resolving disputes through streamlined trials or negotiation. While some may find this trend desirable or even inevitable given the millions of cases that reach the civil docket each year, Resnik argues otherwise, claiming that in the rush to settle disputes or to economize on live testimony, the social advantages of adjudication may be lost.

Resnik points to various developments that have contributed to this trend. The Civil Justice Reform Act of 1990, which urges the reduction of expense and delay in the federal courts, in her view gives an impetus to disposing of cases by settlement and thus necessarily degrades the importance of live testimony in court. A recent amendment to Rule 63 of the Federal Rules of Civil Procedure (FRCP) allows greater freedom for one judge to substitute for another (a move supported by Saltzburg), a change which Resnik also believes devalues the role of factfinding.

Similarly, she argues that a proposed amendment to Rule 43 of FRCP would allow the direct examination of witnesses to be submitted by written report in nonjury trials, a step that would eliminate much live testimony from the courtroom.

Resnik also points to significant changes in the factfinders themselves: increasingly, the federal courts make use of agency findings, magistrates, and bankruptcy courts to resolve matters. The Federal Courts Study Committee also calls for the delegation of factfinding power to other agents rather than to judges appointed and confirmed under Article III of the Constitution. And the increasing share of cases in the federal courts involving many parties—especially the large-scale "tort" cases—has intensified the interest of judges in resolving disputes through negotiation rather than trial.

Whether or not one agrees with Resnik's view of recent trends, there is little dispute among the authors in this book that much more information is needed to assess fully how the civil jury has been functioning in the United States. Thus, Galanter and others, including the participants in the June 1992 jury symposium, call for improved efforts at collecting data on verdicts and damage awards on a consistent basis in all jurisdictions so that the public and the policymakers can have a better understanding of the outcomes and effects of the jury system. In the meantime, the chapters that follow present and discuss what evidence has been adduced thus far, and how aspects of the jury system might be changed to improve its performance.

Notes

1. See Robert E. Litan and Clifford Winston, eds., *Liability: Perspectives and Policy* (Brookings, 1988); and Peter W. Huber and Robert E. Litan, eds., *The Liability Maze: The Impact of Liability Law on Safety and Innovation* (Brookings, 1991).

2. Brookings Task Force on Civil Justice Reform, *Justice for All: Reducing Costs and Delay in Civil Litigation* (Brookings, 1990).

3. Harry Kalven and Hans Zeisel, *The American Jury* (University of Chicago Press, 1966).

4. Since the period that Priest examined, Chicago has adopted the one day/one trial method of jury service supported in the symposium report, which should have resulted in more widely distributed jury service throughout the population in the county. To this extent, reforms in the jury system may be able to address some of the criticisms of the jury system that Priest advances.

CHAPTER TWO

The History and Objectives
of the Civil Jury System

Stephan Landsman

"T HE PURPOSE of the jury trial in . . . civil cases [is] to assure a
fair and equitable resolution of factual issues."[1] With these words, Justice
Byron White of the United States Supreme Court in 1973 set about
dismantling one of the structures integral to the Anglo-American civil
justice process for more than 700 years—trial by a jury of twelve. Rather
than considering the rich and varied history or multiplicity of functions
served by the jury throughout its evolution, the Court was content to
assign to it a single procedural purpose. In doing so, White or his fellow
justices resorted to the sort of reductionist strategy all too often employed
in interpreting the Seventh Amendment's mandate that "in suits at
common law, where the value in controversy shall exceed twenty dollars,
the right to trial by jury shall be preserved."[2]

Most frequently, the Court's reductionism has taken a historical form,
deciding questions about the applicability or appropriateness of challenged
jury procedures simply by ascertaining whether they were in use in
English common law courts in 1791.[3] In the last several decades the
Court has augmented this historical approach with a functional analysis
that attempts to resolve questions by arbitrarily assigning the jury a
single narrow purpose and judging all questions of the appropriateness
of procedures, like reduced jury size, in light of that purpose. This was
precisely what the Court did in *Colgrove* when it confined juries to the
single objective of factfinding and then approved federal juries as small
as six persons on the theory that they can find facts as well as larger

This article is dedicated to the memory of Robert Hanley (1924–91), a lawyer who
knew a thing or two about juries.

juries.[4] These techniques have stripped the jury mechanism of the variety and dynamism that marked its development for more than nine centuries.

The Court's rationale for denying the complex history and functions of the jury is not clear. What seems likely, at least in cases like *Colgrove*, is that reductionism has been used to marginalize the jury, rendering it less important and, therefore, more easily amenable to reform. Such reductionism is tempting, because it also makes the crafting of decisions far simpler by obviating the need to sort out the ambiguities of a history that has as many strands as there were original colonies and as many interpretations as there were members of the committee that drafted the Seventh Amendment. Yet, reductionism's strength is also its weakness. By defining the complexity and mutability of the jury out of existence, reductionism robs us of a thorough appreciation of the institution's past service, present value, and future potential.

Removing the reductionist blinders and surveying the history and objectives of civil jury trial reveal that the jury has been anything but an unchanging fixture of courtroom procedure. Its most pronounced characteristic has been its adaptability. In its earliest form, the jury served royal objectives as an inquisitorial mechanism devoted to gathering data such as that recorded in William the Conqueror's *Domesday Book*. Somewhat later it took on the trappings of an executive agency, enforcing a myriad of policies in the king's name and adjudicating a broad range of disputes. The jury's association with state authority and rule continued through the centuries. As early as the reign of the Tudors, however, and far more pronouncedly in the time of the Stuarts, it became a bulwark of liberty that offered a way for citizens to resist excessive governmental demands.

The American jury, too, has gone through a host of changes. It is said to have been the essential instrument of governance in colonial times and to have provided one of the few experiences common to virtually every colonist. With the coming of the conflicts that led to the Revolution, the jury was transformed into an expression of American concerns about judicial independence and democratic government. Later, during the formative period of the Republic, the jury came to be viewed as the essential counterbalance to the threat of excessive judicial power.

As the country matured during the nineteenth century, authority shifted away from the jury toward the rapidly professionalizing judiciary. As judges became increasingly powerful, the jury seemed to take on the character of an anchor, tethering the law to a sometimes neglected humanity and common sense. While the expansion of judicial power in the 1800s resulted in a narrowing of the scope of jury decisions, the jury came out of that epoch a still-vital institution whose control over a range of issues—especially in tort litigation—had, if anything, been enhanced.

In the years following the turn of the century, the jury was subjected to some of the sharpest criticism in its long history. Its opponents challenged its composition, its procedures, and its very right to exist. These criticisms inspired a series of pathbreaking empirical studies that ultimately enhanced the jury's reputation. Thus, the jury has arrived in the late twentieth century with a mixed heritage. On the one hand, it is a reinvigorated body that has been assigned a myriad of vital tasks that include assessing business morality, protecting consumers, and defining a number of constitutional rights, as well as determining questions of life and death in capital criminal cases. On the other hand, it has become the target of numerous reform proposals, some of which have been adopted (for example, shrinking the size of juries; doing away with the unanimity requirement; narrowing voir dire, or preliminary examination of jurors; and restricting the exercise of peremptory challenges). Other reform proposals have the potential to undermine the integrity of the institution (most particularly accepting the idea that there are cases too complex for the jury to handle).

This chapter surveys the historical evolution of the jury. It should be noted that piecing together an outline of the jury's story has not been a simple task, as few scholars in recent times have devoted their attention to the history of the jury. There is little primary source research, especially on the activities and verdicts of American juries during the last 300 years. The bits and pieces strung together here have been culled from the works of writers preoccupied with other questions, such as the early development of the judiciary,[5] the birth and growing pains of American legal doctrine,[6] the transformation of tort law in the nineteenth century,[7] and modern social science analyses of jury behavior.[8] Why there has been so little study of jury records is hard to say. Perhaps historians, like the members of the Supreme Court, have found it easier to rely on reductionist models than to delve into long-forgotten court records. The present discussion only begins consideration of many of the issues and, because of the meager sources available, must be considered extremely tentative in its conclusions.

The Rise of The Civil Jury

The rise of the jury in both England and America has been inextricably intertwined with the creation and defense of fundamental rights. This section explores the complex story of the jury's growth and especially its association with the assertion of political and civil rights.

The English Background

The exact roots of the jury are a matter of substantial scholarly uncertainty. Orthodox opinion, supported by the writings of legal scholars such as Frederic Maitland and James Thayer, has held that the jury is a Norman import, brought to England by William the Conqueror and his followers after their victory at Hastings in 1066.[9] More recent scholarly work by John P. Dawson and others has shifted attention to the Anglo-Saxon antecedents of Norman jury procedure.[10] While modern legal thinkers have not generally asserted that the jury is actually an Anglo-Saxon institution, some have persuasively contended that important precursors to the jury existed in England before the time of the Norman conquest and are likely to have played a significant part in inducing Englishmen to place their trust in the jury trial mechanisms eventually put forward by the Angevin kings.

One thing that does seem relatively clear from accounts of the early history of the jury is that the Normans were willing to press a rudimentary form of trial by jury into service in order to secure their administrative hold on lands they had seized by force. These early juries were bodies of citizens summoned by royal command to testify about property arrangements, local customs, and taxable resources in each neighborhood of the realm. One product of their testimony was the *Domesday Book*; another was the most efficient administrative infrastructure in Europe. The critically important aspects of this early jury procedure were its reliance on royal authority, its compulsory nature, its practice of gathering information from a group of local men, and its movement away from older, indigenous approaches that allowed litigants to settle disputes by either ordeal or combat. These characteristics would remain important facets of the jury's operations for centuries.

The jury continued to function primarily as an administrative mechanism until the reign of Henry II, who came to the throne in 1154. By a series of statutory enactments, or assizes, Henry transformed the jury into a genuine instrument of justice.[11] Maitland suggests that Henry initially used jury trials to establish a procedure for adjudicating the complaints of tenants who claimed to have been "disseised, that is dispossessed, of [their] free tenement unjustly and without judgment."[12] The new remedy, known as the "assize of novel disseisin," offered claimants in such circumstances an alternative to trial by combat: they could submit their claims to a jury of at least arguably knowledgeable local citizens. The technique was "fully organized" by 1179 and became an overwhelming success, establishing a procedural pattern that was repeatedly copied over the course of the next century to address different sorts of legal claims.[13] The reasons for its popularity were neatly summarized by the early treatise writer known as Glanvill:

> It so well cares for the life and condition of men that every one may keep his rightful freehold and yet avoid the doubtful chance of the duel, and escape that last penalty, an unexpected and untimely death, or, at least, the shame of enduring infamy in uttering the hateful and shameful word [craven] which comes from the mouth of the conquered party with so much disgrace, as the consequence of his defeat. This institution springs from the greatest equity. Justice, which, after delays many and long, is scarcely ever found in the duel, is more easily and quickly reached by this proceeding. The assize does not allow so many essoins[14] as the duel; thus labor is saved and the expenses of the poor reduced. Moreover, by as much as the testimony of several credible witnesses outweighs in courts that of a single one, by so much is this process more equitable than the duel. For while the duel goes upon the testimony of one sworn person, this institution requires the oaths of at least twelve lawful men.[15]

The jury grew for two reasons other than its popularity with litigants. In 1215, Pope Innocent III and the Fourth Lateran Council prohibited ecclesiastical officiation in trials by combat and ordeal. This step effectively undermined the existing procedural alternatives to the jury and opened the way for its rapid expansion. Dawson has argued that the jury's increased popularity may also be traced to the economic benefits it offered the Crown.[16] The jury procedure placed most of the judicial system's work in the hands of unpaid local citizens. While a small number of professional judges was necessary to supervise the process, most duties were handled by men who did not have to be maintained at the king's expense, making it possible to manage a great deal of judicial business for which substantial fees could be charged with only a modest royal investment. The arrangement was doubly attractive to fiscally hard-pressed medieval English monarchs because it generated revenue while at the same time sustaining a highly centralized form of government.

It has been repeatedly suggested that in these early days, jurors functioned essentially as witnesses. There is a good deal of evidence in twelfth- and thirteenth-century jury practice to support such a contention. William Forsyth, in his 1852 treatise, points out that Glanvill describes the jury's obligation to report to the judges any case in which all the jurors are ignorant of the facts. In such cases, "others were chosen who were acquainted with the facts in dispute."[17] Only in a setting where jurors are the key source of information does such a procedure make sense.

The primary method of reviewing jury verdicts and reversing their results in these early days was attaint, which Thayer found mentioned in cases as early as 1202.[18] Attaint involved a rehearing of the original evidence by a second jury, twice the size of the first and made up of presumably knowledgeable local citizens. If this second jury concluded that the first had erred, the verdict would be overturned and each of the original jurors condemned to the most severe punishment, on the theory that perjury had been committed. As Forsyth concludes: "Originally a wrong verdict almost necessarily implied perjury in the jurors. They were witnesses who deposed to facts within their knowledge, about which there could hardly be the possibility of error."[19]

Further support for the hypothesis that the earliest jurors served primarily as witnesses may be gathered from the treatment accorded witnesses to the signing of legal documents in medieval times. When a deed or similar document was at issue, witnesses who had attested to its solemnization by appending their signatures to it generally had to be produced at trial. At the end of the presentation of evidence these witnesses would be combined with the jury and all would deliberate together to decide the case.[20] This amalgamation suggests a parity of function consistent with the assumption that jurors and witnesses performed a similar task.

While the deed witnesses presumably had information to provide to the court, individual jurors might or might not be well informed about the facts of the case. To encourage jurors to increase their value as witnesses, procedures required that the sheriff provide their names at least six days before the trial so that the parties could "inform" them of pertinent facts.[21] By the same token, adjudicatory procedures were arranged so that jurors would at least feel some duty to investigate the questions to be tried.[22] All this pushed the jurors in the direction of the witnessing function.

Yet the jury was never simply a collection of witnesses. Dawson has ably pointed out the weaknesses of the witness hypothesis, most particularly its failure to account for the facts that jurors were never all expected to be eyewitnesses and that they were always required to enter into a collective verdict.[23]

Eventually, English procedure cut the ties that bound jurors to the witnessing role. Perhaps the most significant single step in this direction was the development in the mid-1500s of the requirement that jury verdicts be unanimous. While the unanimity requirement may, on the surface, seem unrelated to the witness hypothesis, a deeper examination suggests otherwise. Genuine witnesses are likely to disagree among themselves, but when they are compelled, like jurors, to harmonize their views into one conclusive verdict, the individual witnessing function must inevitably be subordinated to the group's need for consensus.

John Dawson argues that the step toward unanimity was taken by English judges so that they could "divest themselves of any duty to assemble or appraise the evidence. The factfinding function was imposed instead on groups of laymen, whose ignorance was disguised by a group verdict and whose sources of knowledge the judges refused to examine." [24] The reasons for this move are not easy to identify. The willingness of litigants to accept juries rather than judges as factfinders seems to have been one of the likely causes along with the tremendous savings in time and money achieved by relying on juries rather than magistrates.[25]

The connection between witnessing and jury service was further eroded as the mixed juror/witness panel, attaint procedure, and juror knowledge requirement were altered or abandoned. Perhaps the earliest of these mechanisms to yield was the combined juror/witness jury panel. Thayer quotes Chief Justice Thorpe as declaring in a 1349 case that

> Witnesses should say nothing but what they know as certain, i.e., what they see and hear. If a witness is returned on the jury, he shall be ousted. A challenge good as against a juryman is not good against a witness. If the witnesses and the jury cannot agree upon one verdict, that of the jury shall be taken, and the defeated party may have the attaint against the jury.[26]

Thayer has suggested that by the early 1500s the separation of witnesses from the jury was probably complete in all cases.[27] Attaint died out as a method of review by the early sixteenth century. In 1565 Sir Thomas Smith, a widely quoted observer of the judiciary, remarked on the fact that attaint was no longer really in use.[28] Finally, although jurors with independent knowledge of the facts were hypothesized as a possibility as late as 1670, when Chief Justice Vaughan made reference to them in *Bushel's Case*,[29] but by 1682 it had become a punishable offense to contact or inform jurors of anything regarding an impending trial.[30]

Perhaps as important as the decline of the jury's witnessing function was the rise of in-court testimony as the basis for arriving at a decision. While the precise moment of the shift to testimonial presentations in open court may be impossible to fix, such presentations clearly came to dominate courtroom procedure during the fifteenth and sixteenth centuries. John Fortesque's *De Laudibus Legum Anglie*, written in approximately 1470, describes a judicial process that relied on the presentations of witnesses in open court, although juror knowledge of the facts might still play a part.[31] Thomas Green, in his seminal research on the criminal jury, has noted the influx of a great flood of new testimonial evidence during the middle years of the sixteenth century.[32] Statutes requiring the testimony of one or more witnesses began to appear during the 1500s and made in-court inquiry essential in some cases.[33] Throughout this era, barriers to live testimony were slowly being dismantled.[34] The end of the process probably came in the mid-1600s with procedures that isolated jurors from outside influences, requiring that cases be decided on the basis of what was presented in open court.

The early history of the English jury is remarkable not only because of the jury's ongoing ability to adapt to new and different needs, but because of its contribution to the establishment of certain fundamental principles of democratic governance. These principles, and the jury itself, would come to play a critical part in the tumultuous events leading to the fall of the Stuarts, the rejection of absolute monarchy, and the rise of parliamentary government.

From its earliest days the British jury was called upon to perform a wide range of tasks and, as I have noted, its unpaid labors made possible a higher degree of royal control than was possible elsewhere in Europe at the time. Yet, as Dawson has pointed out, relying on the jury and other lay decisionmakers (such as justices of the peace) had the unanticipated effect of "train[ing] English society, through its local leadership, in the skills and the practices of self-government."[35] Over the course of 600 years, English jurymen learned to govern themselves, developing traditions of independence from central bureaucratic authority.[36] During the struggle for political liberty in the seventeenth century, this background had a profound impact on Englishmen's views and their willingness to fight for what they perceived to be their rights.

The jury was also responsible for bringing into government the "middling sort," who, over time, would become the bedrock of English political democracy. Stephen Roberts has pointed out that, in the 1600s, "the jury was the most representative institution available to the English people."[37] How it became so is not hard to imagine. Beginning early in the jury's history, the wealthy attempted to avoid jury service by placing others on the panels in their stead.[38] Thus, men of modest property holdings became the mainstay of the jury system. While many observers complained in the sixteenth and seventeenth centuries that such jurors were not "sufficient freeholders," it is clear that the yeomanry formed the social backbone of the country's jury system.[39] This development effectively drew an expanding group of citizens into governance and distributed power more broadly through at least the upper economic strata of English society. It is understandable that such an arrangement might have alarmed England's most highly placed citizens.

The jury became even more important as the volume of litigation soared in the sixteenth and seventeenth centuries. In the thousand-person village of Earls Colne, for example, more than 200 legal actions were brought between the years 1589 and 1593.[40] In such a context, jurors occupied a critical place in the social regulatory framework. The fact that the "middling sort" could hold this position demonstrates the access they were gaining to the power that would serve as a basis for the development of political independence. William Blackstone aptly summarized the role these middle-class men soon came to play:

A competent number of sensible and upright jurymen, chosen by lot from among those of the middle rank, will be found the best investigators of truth; and the surest guardians of public justice. For the most powerful individual in the state will be cautious of committing any flagrant invasion of another's right, when he knows that the fact of his oppression must be examined and decided by twelve indifferent men, not appointed till the hour of trial; and that, when once the fact is ascertained, the law must of course redress it. This therefore preserves in the hands of the people that share, which they ought to have in the administration of public justice, and prevents the encroachments of the more powerful and wealthy citizens.[41]

In the seventeenth century the Stuart kings increasingly sought to intrude upon these and other traditional arrangements concerning the exercise of governmental power.[42] The predictable response from juries was a rising tide of resistance. John Beattie, a modern historian specializing in seventeenth- and eighteenth-century legal practice, has declared that "the late seventeenth century was the heroic age of the English jury, for in the political and constitutional struggles of the reigns of Charles II and James II, trial by jury emerged as the principle defense of English liberties."[43]

One of the most important moments for the jury came in 1670, when the Quakers William Penn and William Mead were prosecuted for preaching in public.[44] A jury of twelve Londoners refused to convict them, despite the strongest sort of judicial pressure. The judge then fined and jailed the jurors, including one Edward Bushel, who not only refused to pay his fine but initiated a habeas corpus proceeding challenging the legality of his incarceration. In a precedent-setting ruling Sir John Vaughan, Chief Justice of Common Pleas, barred the jailing or fining of jurors for anything but overtly corrupt behavior.[45] Vaughan's ruling sharply curtailed judicial control over the jury.

Alarmed by the *Bushel* ruling, the judiciary sought, especially in seditious libel cases, to narrow the options available to jurors by tightly circumscribing the questions they were asked to decide. These efforts were undermined in 1688 in the *Seven Bishops Case*, when another courageous London jury acquitted seven Anglican bishops of seditious libel for signing a letter opposing the reading in their churches of James II's second *Declaration of Indulgences*. The acquittal of the bishops has been viewed as the true beginning of the Glorious Revolution[46] and had the effect of catapulting the jury to popularity "as a bulwark of liberty, [and] as a means of preventing oppression by the Crown."[47] The many treatises extolling the jury that then came onto the market had a profound influence on eighteenth-century American as well as English views about jury trial.[48]

The jury became a defender of rights not only in criminal but in civil cases. During the 1760s John Wilkes, a member of Parliament, engaged in a series of radical political actions that included publishing a broadsheet, the *North Briton*, in which Wilkes appeared to charge the king with lying about peace negotiations then underway with France. Although Wilkes was quickly arrested and charged with seditious libel, the case was soon dismissed on a rather technical point involving parliamentary privilege. Wilkes immediately began a damages action for false arrest, trespass, and theft of personal papers. In the ensuing trial a jury awarded him the extraordinary sum of £1,000 in damages against a number of government officials, including Lord Halifax.[49] This decision, which included substantial punitive damages, is generally agreed to have been the first occasion on which "punitives" were awarded. The jury's power to protect the rights of citizens in civil cases was emphasized by Chief Justice Camden, who declared that the jury has the authority "to give damages for more than the injury received. Damages are designed not only as a satisfaction to the injured person, but likewise as a punishment to the guilty, to deter from any such proceeding for the future, and as a proof of the detestation of the jury to the action itself."[50]

From the era of the Glorious Revolution to the time of Wilkes's struggles, the jury was the very essence of liberty, a fundamentally democratic institution that served as a check on the tyrannical and oppressive power of government.

The American Reception

The jury came to America with the earliest settlers. The 1606 charter given by James I to the Virginia Company has been read as incorporating the right to jury trial. By 1624 juries were an option in all civil and criminal cases in Virginia.[51] The Massachusetts Bay Colony followed a similar pattern. Jury trials were introduced there in 1628, and jury procedure was codified in the Massachusetts Body of Liberties in 1641.[52] The Colony of West New Jersey followed suit in 1677, as did Pennsylvania under William Penn in 1682. Eventually, all the colonies embraced trial by jury.

From early in colonial history the jury played a critical role. Focusing on developments in Massachusetts, William Nelson, has concluded that in prerevolutionary days the jury was the central instrument of governance.[53] Its wide-ranging activities contrast starkly with the circumscribed operations of both the royal executive and the colonial legislature. It would appear that Massachusetts juries occupied a position strikingly similar to that held by juries in medieval England. They were the chief assessors of legal claims and primary enforcers of legal rights for their communities. Nelson argues that it was the objective of seventeenth- and early eighteenth-century Massachusetts juries to maintain the economic and social stability of colonial society by enforcing a rather strict code concerning the payment of debts and acting as moral watchdogs.[54]

Nelson concludes that Massachusetts juries had vast authority and independence in the colonial era. He bases his argument on the observation that juries seem, like their forebears in the Glorious Revolution, to have had power over questions of law as well as fact.[55] Their freedom in this regard was arguably enhanced by the fact that trials were always conducted before panels of three judges, each free to state his own view of the law in closing instructions, a technique that provided jurors with as many as three different versions to choose from. The jurors' critical assessment of the law was further encouraged by the trial attorneys, who were permitted to argue legal questions in their closing arguments. It is legitimate to surmise that, in such a setting, the jury had broad control over legal as well as factual issues and was the dominant player in the courtroom process.

Despite the appeal of these arguments, caution should be used in determining whether the jury actually held sway over the adjudicatory process. A range of restraints were in place that could have restricted jury power, including rules of evidence that strongly encouraged jurors to see themselves as bound to make their decision solely on the basis of oath-supported testimony;[56] a shared set of religious and social values so strong and pervasive that it undoubtedly served to limit a jury's freedom of action; a small caseload that offered juries few opportunities to exercise their power; and a judiciary that included locally prominent figures[57] capable of exercising some degree of influence over their neighbors and acquaintances serving as jurors. If English experience is any guide, such judges could prove extremely skillful in controlling juries.[58] In Massachusetts it seems likely that some sort of balance was maintained between judges and juries: they were expected to prevent each other from exercising arbitrary power or ignoring the needs of society.

The Massachusetts arrangement may not have been typical. In his study of Virginia, A. G. Roeber has concluded that real power was wielded in the colony's early days by lay justices of the peace.[59] Whatever the situation in individual states, however, historical evidence makes it clear not only that people throughout America were preoccupied with safeguarding the jury but that they relied on the jury to restrain government. In 1735 John Peter Zenger was charged with seditious libel for accusing the Governor of New York, William Cosby, of corruption, misfeasance, and usurpation of the right to jury trial. The case was tried to a jury that was instructed by the judge to convict if it found the defendant had published the words in question—a matter clearly established by the proof. Zenger's attorneys, however, argued that the jury was free to reject the judge's instructions if it found the journalist's charges true. When the jury acquitted Zenger, it helped to establish several critical propositions: that the press should be free to criticize the government, that truth should be a defense against libel charges, and that jurors can consider questions beyond those narrowly presented to them by judges. The case also made it clear that colonial juries, like their English counterparts, were fully capable of defending fundamental rights.[60] While Zenger's was a criminal case, its repercussions were felt in all sorts of colonial jury proceedings.

When the right to a jury trial was threatened, citizen reaction was generally swift and hostile, especially in New York, where, on several occasions, the royal governors tried to institute or expand juryless chancery proceedings.[61] One dramatic clash occurred in 1727, when the legislature passed a resolution condemning both Governor William Burnet and the chancery court because of a fee schedule the governor had attempted to impose in chancery cases. Another took place in the 1730s, when New York Chief Justice Lewis Morris, who had denied Governor William Cosby's motion to have a case concerning the governor's salary heard in a nonjury forum, was removed from office. Shortly thereafter Cosby manipulated his powers in the chancery court to enter a ruling on a land claim in favor of certain of his allies. This so-called affair of the "oblong tract" caused Cosby to be publicly compared to Lord Chancellor George Jeffries, who, during the last years of the Stuart monarchy, abused his powers by undermining the municipal charters of communities opposed to the king. When Governor Cosby died in 1736, the dispute cooled, but the threat of juryless trials—especially in cases concerning titles to land (a question seen at the time as involving the paramount political right)—was a source of continuing anxiety to New Yorkers.

Through the succeeding decades jury caseloads appeared to grow. Roeber reports that in Virginia between 1750 and 1774 jury trials increased dramatically. This was most particularly true with respect to actions to recover debts, which had generally been resolved by summary judgment until the 1750s when jurors became increasingly likely to be sympathetic to debtors.[62] A shift away from the sort of social control manifest in early colonial court actions was under way, and the jury seemed to be one of the agents of change helping to introduce new values into law and society.

In the 1760s the struggle over jury rights expanded to the admiralty and vice admiralty courts, forums used by British royal officials to enforce the Navigation Acts and other laws designed to control colonial commerce.[63] These juryless courts usually dealt with criminal matters such as smuggling and failure to pay customs duties, but they could and did deprive colonists of civil jury trials, especially with respect to the seizure of vessels and conversion of cargoes.[64] The denial of the right to trial by jury was a strong irritant in relations between America and Britain and featured prominently in formal colonial complaints in the 1760s and 1770s. In a clear challenge to the Stamp Act, which denied that right, the resolutions of the Stamp Act Congress of 1765 specifically declared that "trial by jury is the inherent and invaluable right of every British subject in these colonies."[65]

From the 1760s until the Revolution the jury came, in the colonial mind, to represent the most effective means available to secure the independence and integrity of the judicial branch of government. It was precisely for this reason that the British authorities increasingly sought either to control or to avoid jury adjudications. The fight over jury rights was, in reality, the fight for American independence and served to help unite the colonies.

In 1773 a dispute erupted when the British authorities insisted that they, rather than the Massachusetts colonial legislature, should control judicial salaries.[66] Their actions created a clear threat to judicial independence and led to a call that Massachusetts judges resign rather than accept the new arrangement. Four judges refused royal salaries, and when a fifth, Chief Justice Peter Oliver, accepted, the legislature voted to impeach him. Although the British governor blocked the impeachment, jurors around the colony refused to participate in Judge Oliver's trials. Their actions demonstrated colonial resolve on the issue of judicial independence and the role of jurors as spokesmen for the colony.

In the mid-1770s a series of American congresses protested the oppressive behavior of British authorities in enforcing the so-called Intolerable Acts and similar measures. These congresses repeatedly supported the right to trial by jury in both civil and criminal cases and excoriated royal administrators for tampering with that right. The First Continental Congress in 1774 specifically targeted a series of acts that sought to move certain categories of cases from American to English courts, as well as royal regulations that interfered with the selection of jurymen in Massachusetts. The fifth resolution of the congress stated, "The respective colonies are entitled to the common law of England, and more especially to the great and inestimable privilege of being tried by their peers of the vicinage according to the course of that law."[67]

Concern about jury trials was reiterated by the Second Continental Congress, whose Declaration of Causes and Necessities of Taking Up Arms, issued in July 1775, specifically challenged Parliament's passage of statutes "extending the jurisdiction of admiralty and vice admiralty beyond their ancient limits [and] depriving [the colonies] of the accustomed and inestimable privilege of trial by jury, in cases affecting both life and property."[68] The work of the congresses culminated in the Declaration of Independence, which included the denial of "the benefits of trial by jury" as one of the grievances leading to the creation of the independent United States.[69]

For obvious reasons juries were exceedingly popular with the drafters of the new state constitutions. Virginia set the pattern in 1776 by specifically including both civil and criminal jury trial in its Bill of Rights, and the majority of other states quickly followed suit. In fact, as one historian notes, "the right to trial by jury was probably the only one universally secured by the first American state constitutions."[70] It has been hypothesized that a shared allegiance to the right to trial by jury played an important part in drawing the new nation closer together.[71] The jury appealed to citizens and leaders alike, not only because of the role it played in furthering the cause of the Revolution, but because of its fundamentally participatory approach to justice.

In the early 1780s democratic aspirations led Americans to fashion state governments in which the legislature was preeminent and the national government little more than a loose confederacy. As Alexander Hamilton pointed out, there was at that time an "extreme jealousy of power."[72] The new arrangement, however, did not prove satisfactory, and many Americans began to suspect that their interests were not sufficiently protected, especially the right to property. A fear that anarchy would overwhelm the nation was heightened by a series of events that took place between 1784 and 1787. In that period authorities in North Carolina and Rhode Island began manipulating currencies to assist debtors. In one instance, Rhode Island's Supreme Court ruled in favor of a creditor who refused to accept depreciated paper currency; the court was promptly censured and the judges replaced.[73] In Massachusetts taxpayers began the open revolt that became known as Shays' Rebellion and was widely, though mistakenly, believed to have threatened the very foundation of order in New England.[74]

This background is important to understanding how the civil jury, which had been the most popular vehicle of courtroom justice in the period leading up to and including the Revolution, could be completely ignored by the drafters of the Constitution in 1787.

The Jury and the Constitution

Those who came together in Philadelphia to draft a new plan of government were overwhelmingly creditor-oriented nationalists.[75] Deeply troubled by recent events in the country, they were committed to the creation of a strong national government that could put an end to the threat of anarchy and spent most of their time fashioning the executive and legislative branches of this new, stronger central government.

Matters concerning the judiciary "ran a poor third as a focus of interest," and the civil jury was mentioned only twice, on September 12 and 15, 1787.[76] These two brief discussions resulted in the decision to refrain from mentioning the civil jury in the Constitution's text, because, the delegates said, "the Representatives of the people may be safely trusted in this matter," and numerous drafting problems made inclusion of a civil jury guarantee impossible.[77] The Constitution, without any guarantee of right to trial by jury in civil cases, was transmitted to the Continental Congress on September 17, 1787.

While it is not at all likely that the drafters intentionally set out to exclude the civil jury from America's courts, its omission from the Constitution signaled a profound shift in the way an exceedingly powerful segment of society had come to view the right to a jury trial in civil cases. Most of those who have examined the question have concluded that the claims about drafting difficulties were disingenuous and that what was really involved was a growing belief that the jury had only a modest part to play in the governance of postrevolutionary America.[78] There were at least three major reasons for this view. First, since the British government no longer controlled the judiciary, juries were not essential to counterbalance biased judges. Second, the Revolution had resulted in democratically elected legislatures, and jury review or nullification of laws enacted by such bodies raised troubling questions about respect for democracy. Third, jury decisions were bound to be ad hoc and, quite frequently, anticreditor. If America's financial system was to be rendered sound, it was arguably necessary to curtail jury action in favor of more predictable and consistent rulings protecting investors.[79]

As part of a larger effort to defend the Constitution as originally written, Alexander Hamilton, on behalf of the so-called Federalists, produced his famous analysis of the jury.[80] He assured his readers that the omission of the civil jury was not intended as an attempt to abolish jury trials and went on to extol the jury's virtues in the following terms: "The friends and adversaries of the plan of the convention, if they agree in nothing else, concur at least in the value they set upon the trial by jury; or if there is any difference between them it consists in this: the former regard it as a valuable safeguard to liberty; the latter represent it as the very palladium of free government."[81] He then proceeded, however, to set forth the Federalist view that there is no "inseparable connection between the existence of liberty and the trial by jury in civil cases." He followed this with a reductionist analysis of the jury's functioning, concluding that its only special value is as a hedge against judicial corruption and that it is inappropriate in cases touching on international relations, such as those involving seized ships, and equity, which he considers problems too "nice and intricate" for common folk.[82]

Hamilton sought to place the institution under the absolute control of the federal legislature and saw no need for it other than to restrain judicial venality. The response to these ideas was emphatically negative. In fact, the Antifederalists, who were challenging the appropriateness of the Constitution as a whole, treated the absence of a civil jury guarantee as sufficient grounds to oppose the adoption of the document. In responding to Hamilton and other critics of the jury, they stressed three points: first, the jury was the best available means of thwarting unpopular laws enacted by an insensitive national legislature; second, it provided a method of protecting debtors from inflexible rules in the regulation of commerce; and third, it could rein in corrupt or overactive judges.[83]

All the Antifederalists' arguments were motivated by a pervasive concern to ensure that the courts were not allowed to become the exclusive province of the judges. They were driven, at least in part, by the fear of a federal judiciary modeled upon the famous English judge, Lord Mansfield, whose "habit of controlling juries does not accord with the free institutions of this country."[84] In addition, the Antifederalists believed that juries could loosen the grip of the law, nullifying or refashioning it in appropriate cases. Judges, as prisoners of the letter of the law and the attitudes of their profession, were in no position to do these things. The Antifederalists frequently cited with approval Blackstone's famous statement:

> The impartial administration of justice, which secures both our persons and our properties, is the great end of civil society. But if that be

entirely entrusted to the magistracy, a select body of men, and those generally selected by the prince or such as enjoy the highest offices in the state, their decisions, in spite of their own natural integrity, will have frequently an involuntary bias towards those of their own rank and dignity: it is not to be expected from human nature, that *the few* should be always attentive to the interests and good of *the many*.[85]

It was the jury rather than the judges that could serve the interests of democracy and inject the values of the "many" into judicial proceedings.

The result of the Antifederalist agitation was a call by at least seven of the states ratifying the Constitution for a new amendment that would secure the right to jury trial in civil cases. While the Antifederalists failed in their campaign to prevent the adoption of the Constitution, they were the "generative force behind the seventh amendment [and] their arguments should be given due weight in determining the purpose behind [it]."[86]

The text of the amendment proved less difficult to draft than Hamilton had supposed. In order to encompass the great range of jury practices then operative in America, the drafters couched the amendment in broad terms.[87] This was in accord with earlier Antifederalist arguments that had rejected contentions about drafting difficulties by stressing the utility of "reference . . . to the common law of England, which obtains through every state."[88]

The triumph of the right to trial by jury in civil cases was reflected not only in the Seventh Amendment but in the Judiciary Act of 1789 as well. That act held equitable jurisdiction, that is, jurisdiction over questions not requiring a jury hearing, tightly in check and emphasized remedies at law with their concomitant jury trial. This is not surprising in light of the fact that the act was being drafted at precisely the same moment the Seventh Amendment was making its way through Congress.[89] The act also reflected the Antifederalist program by restraining the power of appeals courts to review factual questions determined by a jury.

The Jury as Compromise

The jury, which had served as a symbol of democracy and restraint on judicial power in the Antifederalist campaign against the Constitution, took on a somewhat different role in American society between 1790 and 1810. It became an instrument of compromise that tempered both the ardent Federalist desire for a strong judiciary and the Republican radicals' thirst for a simplified law without courtrooms or lawyers. Experiences in Pennsylvania, Massachusetts, and on the national level all illustrate the general direction of developments.

In 1800 a strong-willed Federalist Pennsylvania state court judge named Alexander Addison barred one of his fellow judges, a Republican, from answering Addison's statement to a grand jury concerning the merits of the recent election of a Republican governor. This act, repeated several months later, provoked the Pennsylvania Legislature to impeach Addison. At the subsequent trial before the state Senate, during which Addison continued his "insolent, arrogant and overbearing conduct," he was convicted and removed from office.[90]

Addison was the archetypal overzealously political judge, all too ready to interfere with the jury. His removal symbolized the broadly shared belief that such conduct was unacceptable interference with the jury, especially when cast in political terms, and would not be tolerated. Addison's removal opened up the possibility of a partisan review of the performance of all sitting judges. Although Pennsylvania's Republican legislators flirted with this idea, they eventually seemed to settle on a compromise that left judicial independence intact as long as it was not used to pursue overtly political objectives.

Pennsylvania's jury system came under attack not only from high-handed judges but from Republican radicals as well. With the espoused goal of freeing the people from lawyers and law courts, this group sought to remove as much litigation as possible from traditional courts, drastically modify courtroom procedure, and utilize arbitration whenever possible. This program became an important issue in the hard-fought 1805 election campaign between radicals and more moderate Republicans. When the moderates won, the traditional system of an independent judiciary working in tandem with juries was retained. In these political contests, as in the Addison affair, the jury was viewed as occupying a middle ground: it was the compromise that allowed the two sides to coexist.

The dispute in Massachusetts focused specifically on jury power, in particular on the question of whether the jury had the right to decide matters of law as well as fact.[91] Traditionally, Massachusetts juries had been free to disregard a judge's instructions and bring in a general verdict that conflicted with the court's views of doctrine. Federalists in the state had long been pushing for a more efficient judicial system which, among other things, would curtail the jury's power in this regard. In 1803 Supreme Court Justice Theodore Sedgwick concretized Federalist objectives by calling for the adoption of judicial circuit riding, limitations on appeals, and an end to the practice of permitting juries to interpret the law. Sedgwick argued, "In all instances where trial by jury has been practiced, and a separation of the law from the fact has taken place, there have been expedition, certainty, system and their consequences, general approbation. Where this has not been the case, neither expedition, certainty nor system has prevailed."[92]

The legislature quickly enacted the circuit-riding system and other procedures, but Federalists and Republicans came into sharp conflict over limitations on the jury's power to interpret the law. The Republicans saw this change as ceding additional power to a judiciary that was already too powerful. They countered the Federalist proposals by arguing for a substantial expansion of the jury's authority, including the freedom to question witnesses and the right to bring in any decision without the prospect of reversal. This last proposal was viewed by some as a challenge to the maintenance of any fixed law. Massachusetts moderates eventually resolved this conflict by reaffirming the independence of the judiciary and insisting that juries retain the sort of powers they had previously held. Again, the traditional jury was a key element in the compromise.

The pattern of conflict and compromise was acted out even more dramatically on the federal level. The election of Jefferson in 1800 sent shock waves through the Federalist establishment. Seeking to secure their power in the overwhelmingly Federalist judicial branch, the lame duck Federalist Congress enacted the Judiciary Act of 1801 and several other pieces of legislation. These intensely partisan acts created posts designed to be hurriedly filled by the outgoing Federalist administration and altered a variety of procedural and jurisdictional requirements in ways advantageous to Federalist constituencies.

These steps were a direct challenge to the Jeffersonian Republicans and immediately provoked a crisis. Eventually, President Jefferson decided to pursue the constitutionally questionable course of repealing the legislation. At the same time he refused to grant outstanding commissions to those in line for appointment under the Federalists' enactments. This provoked the famous constitutional challenge decided in *Marbury* v. *Madison*.[93] Chief Justice John Marshall fashioned a decision that emphasized the judiciary's authority to review the constitutionality of legislation but yielded to the Republicans on the specific question of Marbury's commission, averting a direct confrontation between the judiciary and the executive. In avoiding a constitutional confrontation, the two sides seemed to strike a bargain. The Republicans appeared to be willing to recognize the independence and power of the judiciary as long as the judges agreed to refrain from using their position to seek clearly partisan political objectives.[94]

This modus vivendi seemed to come apart with the impeachment of John Pickering, a mentally unbalanced federal judge from New Hampshire. Pickering was ousted after a heated Senate debate questioning whether mental incompetence amounted to one of the "high Crimes and Misdemeanors" listed in the Constitution as the only legitimate grounds for removal.[95] In Pickering's case a majority of senators eventually took a broad view of the impeachment power.

Partly on the strength of this expansive interpretation, the Congress almost immediately turned its attention to another Federalist judge, Supreme Court Justice Samuel Chase, who was charged with overtly partisan behavior. All seven articles of impeachment focused on his bias. One concentrated on an inappropriately political charge Chase delivered to a grand jury in Baltimore, while the other six focused on his partisan conduct in the treason trial of John Fries and the seditious libel trial of James Callender. In the Fries case, Chase was accused of stifling the defense attorneys by issuing a preemptive legal opinion that prevented them from arguing certain questions of law to the jury. This led counsel to withdraw from the proceedings in protest. Chase then announced he would act as the defendant's counsel, but his closing remarks favored the prosecution, reminding the jury that Fries had been previously tried and convicted—despite the fact that the earlier conviction had been reversed on appeal.[96] Fries was once again convicted of treason and sentenced to death.

The defense lawyers' main objective during the trial of journalist James Callender was to challenge the constitutionality of the Sedition Act under which he was charged.[97] Again, Chase preemptively intervened, barring Callender's attorneys from presenting certain evidence or arguing the law to the jury; like Fries' counsel, Callender's defense lawyers chose to resign rather than comply with Chase's ruling, resulting in a lopsided trial and Callender's conviction. Chase's real offense in both these cases was having invaded the province of the jury, most particularly by removing certain legal issues from their purview.[98] By acting as he did he opened himself to charges of judicial oppression. He was likened to Lord Chancellor Jeffries and accused of having trespassed on territory set aside for the jury in such celebrated cases as Zenger and the Seven Bishops. Chase's impeachment trial in the Senate had the effect of underscoring the continuing importance of the jury as adjudicator of law as well as fact. Although Chase himself was acquitted, the compromise that recognized jury power was reiterated.

In *Democracy in America*, Alexis de Tocqueville concludes that the American jury of the 1830s was a fundamentally "political institution," whose primary function was to place political power in the hands of the governed.[99] Putting his finger on the essence of the Jeffersonian compromise, he observed that "in no country are the judges so powerful as where the people share their privileges."[100]

The high drama of the Jeffersonian period eventually gave way to more mundane and materialistic times in which the jury's freedom was significantly altered. A number of historians have concluded that the ever more forceful demands of merchants, bankers, and industrialists for a more predictable (and perhaps sympathetic) system inevitably led to the curtailment of the jury's power, especially with respect to the making of law.[101] Some of the changes, as well as some limitations to the "curtailment hypothesis" will be explored in the next two sections. What follows will not be a systematic tracing of the history of the jury over the last 150 years, but rather an examination of several critical moments in that history—moments that reveal both change and continuity.

The Jury as Anchor in a Sea of Shifting Doctrine—Tort Law in the Nineteenth Century

The nineteenth century has been described as a time of great judicial "ingenuity." Legal historians have stressed the idea that throughout the century judges were busy creating new legal doctrine in a number of areas, including tort.[102] Many of the new tort rules have been said to reflect the perceptions of the judges—who frequently saw the needs of the industrialists as paramount—rather than more liberal and humanistic views. In such a context, it is not surprising that judges frequently criticized the jury and were inclined to take ever more forceful steps to control it. But while judicial action restraining the jury in tort cases was an important part of the nineteenth century story, it was not the whole tale. There was appreciable resistance to change by jurors, and, throughout the period, juries kept the law from completely abandoning notions of common decency and fairness. Shortly after the turn of the century, the backlash against one-sided and harsh tort doctrines resulted in a renewed reliance on the jury to humanize the law, a trend that has continued to the present day.

Foremost among the substantive tort principles created by the judiciary to control the jury was the doctrine of contributory negligence. This rule, in its most rigorous form, requires that a plaintiff found to have contributed, even in the slightest degree, to her or his injury be denied all redress.

The doctrine was treated as neither new nor special when it made its first appearance in the 1809 English case of *Butterfield* v. *Forrester*.[103] Why it received so little attention is something of a mystery. It has been suggested that the court had no intention of creating a new broad-ranging doctrine but was simply reiterating traditional or even medieval notions about liability in cases involving a sequence of wrongful acts.[104] Be that as it may, during the 1800s the doctrine grew into the foremost barrier to recovery in tort cases. Contributory negligence serves as an effective barrier in tort cases because it shifts the focus of judicial attention from the defendant's liability to the plaintiff's conduct. The plaintiff must prove that certain self-protective measures were taken (such as stopping, looking, and listening before crossing a railroad track). If the plaintiff cannot provide such proof, the judge, as a matter of law, may dismiss the case without its ever being considered by the jury. Alternatively, the judge may sharply narrow the jury's deliberations by giving the strictest sort of judicial instructions focusing on the plaintiff's failure of proof.

In 1946 Professor Wex Malone wrote what has generally been treated as the definitive history of the rise of contributory negligence in America.[105] He focused his study on the growth of the doctrine in New York State, one of the early industrial leaders of the nation.

The doctrine was first applied in New York in 1829 but grew slowly, appearing in only four appellate decisions in twenty years.[106] Between 1850 and 1860, however, contributory negligence was relied upon in a dozen decisions, nine of them after 1855. The doctrine's use tripled in the next decade and doubled in the one after that. Malone argues that the reason for the dramatic upsurge in the use of contributory negligence was "a seething, although somewhat covert, dissatisfaction over the part [judges and lawyers] felt the jury was destined to play in . . . cases against corporate defendants."[107]

During the nineteenth century, the judiciary increasingly seemed to believe that the jury was incapable of comprehending the new industrial reality. Judges began to assume that jurors were irremediably biased against all corporate defendants. The courts' analysis was neatly summarized by Judge Barculo in *Haring* v. *New York and Erie Railroad*:

We can not shut our eyes to the fact that in certain controversies between the weak and the strong–between an humble individual and a gigantic corporation, the sympathies of the human mind naturally, honestly, and generously, run to the assistance and support of the feeble, and apparently oppressed; and that compassion will sometimes exercise over the deliberations of a jury, an influence which, however honorable to them as philanthropists, is wholly inconsistent with the principles of law and the ends of justice. There is, therefore, a manifest propriety in withdrawing from the consideration of the jury, those cases in which the plaintiff failed to show a right of recovery.[108]

Juries came to be viewed as mere *"assistants* of the courts, whose province it is to aid them in the decision of disputed questions of fact."[109] The purpose of such a reductionist declaration, which would be used to confine the jury to a subordinate place in the litigation process, is clear. The doctrine that enforced this subordination was contributory negligence, which ceded the judge broad powers to remove cases from jury consideration. Thus empowered, the judge could steer the case as he believed the needs of society demanded.

There were, however, substantial weaknesses in the contributory negligence doctrine. First, the rule was premised on the questionable notion that jurors, as lay individuals, indiscriminately favor plaintiffs in tort cases. In his empirical examination of actual jury decisions in Alameda County, California, between 1880 and 1900, Lawrence Friedman found that, while jurors did tend to favor plaintiffs, they did not do so "crudely or inevitably"; rather, they appeared to exercise careful and discriminating judgment.[110] This behavior cannot have differed markedly from that of New York juries and must have weakened the New York judges' arguments against the jury.

Second, classical contributory negligence doctrine provided virtually no impetus for improvements in safety. For example, although railway air brakes were invented in 1868, they were not generally adopted by the railroad industry until legislation was passed compelling installation in the mid-1880s.[111] One likely reason for the delay was restrictive tort doctrines such as contributory negligence.

Contributory negligence was also troublesome because it placed in the judge's hands an extremely broad power "to accept or reject jury participation at [his] pleasure."[112] This unbridled discretion was as potentially lawless and unpredictable as anything a jury might do on its own. In an effort to restrain this power in cases involving the railroads, which made up the bulk of tort actions, certain rules were developed. These called for rejection of railroad liability for accidents in rural settings, where people were assumed to have a clear view of trains approaching intersections, but allowed cases to go to the jury in urban environments.[113] The intellectual poverty of this mechanical approach, premised on nothing more than geography, is obvious.

Perhaps the most troubling thing about contributory negligence was the way it dehumanized the law by attempting to drive the jury from the tort process. Nineteenth-century tort doctrine became an inflexible set of rules that rendered issues such as powerlessness, corporate oppression, and compassion unimportant as the judges pursued allegedly majestic "principles of law."[114] John Noonan has movingly pointed out the terrible human toll that is taken when judges hiding behind such "masks," ignore human considerations and the harm legal doctrines can inflict in the name of an abstract and often insidious set of principles.[115]

To argue, as Malone did, that judicial authority triumphed through application of the doctrine of contributory negligence misses the most important chapter of the story. Contributory negligence was not society's last word on torts; in fact, the doctrine fell into progressively greater disfavor, and the jury was eventually restored to its earlier level of participation in the tort process. Indeed, the jury may never have been banished to the degree Malone suggests. In states other than New York, including New Hampshire and California, there is evidence that contributory negligence was a relatively disfavored doctrine in the late nineteenth century that did not regularly result in shutting the jury out of the process.[116]

Whatever hold the doctrine had had on the law began to loosen in earnest by the early 1900s. Seymour Thompson, in his 1901 *Commentaries on the Law of Negligence*, called contributory negligence "cruel and wicked" and said it "shocks the ordinary sense of justice of mankind."[117] In 1908 Congress enacted the Federal Employers' Liability Act (FELA) which barred contributory negligence in cases involving a wide range of railway workers. Under the FELA, juries awarded damages in liability cases based on the doctrine of comparative negligence, which permitted partial recovery for a plaintiff who had shared fault for the injury. In 1910 Mississippi began using that approach as the basis for all personal injury lawsuits. Use of this doctrine increased slowly until the 1970s, when its popularity soared; today, more than forty states have some form of comparative negligence rule.[118]

As significant as the shift to comparative negligence was the judiciary's growing reliance on jurors to ameliorate the consequences of harsh tort doctrines. Judges permitted jurors to whittle away at the contributory negligence rule. Writing in 1938 about an offshoot of the contributory negligence doctrine, Fleming James, Jr., said, "The real solution for the present lies in the jury and in the approval of simpler and vaguer formulas in the instructions to the jury."[119] Trial judges occasionally even acknowledged their use of this strategy, as did Boston Federal District Judge Charles Wyzanski, Jr., who in 1952 candidly declared that "juries are the device by which the rigor of the law is modified pending the enactment of a new statute."[120] Judges, Wyzanski said, could not do the job themselves because their hands were tied by outmoded but still binding legal rules.

In these ways the jury was restored to prominence. Ironically, it may be because of contributory negligence that the jury regained center stage in the tort process. Critics have decried this result, but, for the present, it appears that the jury is viewed as the most effective instrument to assure the humanity and sensibility of tort law. Judicial hegemony produced harsh and dubious doctrine, and that experience seems to have provided a lesson in the limits of judicial wisdom and the value of citizen participation.

The Jury and the Rhetoric of Efficiency

As judges began to retreat from the doctrine of contributory negligence and the jury to reassume its earlier responsibilities in civil litigation, another challenge was gaining prominence. This critique focused not on the jury's role in any substantive area of law, but on its inefficiency. One of the first twentieth-century critics to sound this theme was Alfred Coxe. In the first volume of the *Columbia Law Review* in 1901 he challenged the jury, most particularly in civil cases, as an inefficient mechanism in need of substantial overhaul.[121] While Coxe acknowledged the jury's ability to resolve factual questions, he believed it was incapable of addressing truly complex matters. He pointed to the unanimous decision rule as a substantial deterrent to effective adjudication and stressed the need to improve the quality of the jury pool, or venire. His comments are striking not only because of their contemporary sound but because of the absence of any empirical grounding for either his criticisms or proposed solutions. The jury's flaws were assumed to be self-evident (as were appropriate reforms), and rhetoric was apparently viewed as ample justification for change.

The rhetoric of efficiency was taken up and amplified over the succeeding thirty years. A brief survey of the *Index to Legal Periodical Literature* suggests that the number of articles criticizing the efficiency of the jury grew from approximately sixteen between 1899 and 1906 to thirty-nine between 1924 and 1932.[122] One of the leading critics of this era was Professor Edson Sunderland of the University of Michigan Law School. In his seminal 1915 article "The Inefficiency of the American Jury," Sunderland argued that trial judges should be granted the power to comment extensively during closing remarks on the quality and implications of the evidence presented in their courtrooms.[123] This approach, widely relied on in English practice, had been sharply curtailed in America on the theory that it allowed excessive judicial intrusion into the jury's province.

Sunderland contended that such comments could substantially improve efficiency by reducing the time needed to select jurors and present the evidence and by giving the court an opportunity to correct errors that might otherwise lead to appeals and new trials. This theory is predicated on the judge's ability to guide jurors with his observations. Sunderland argued that the jury would not lose its independence but rather would remain a free agent that could never be forced into a decision against its will.[124] Sunderland made no effort to present empirical justification for these assertions. Faced with the objection that judicial commentary is inconsistent with the jury's political role as check on the judiciary, Sunderland adopted a reductionist strategy, claiming that in a democracy the jury has little political significance and that its only real job is to resolve properly questions of fact—an approach strikingly similar to that adopted sixty years later by Justice Byron White in *Colgrove* v. *Battin.*

Sunderland revisited the jury issue on several occasions over the next ten years. He campaigned for the use of special verdicts, which he presented as a means of curtailing jury authority by requiring jurors to detail the basis for their decisions.[125] In 1926 he specifically returned to the theme of inefficiency repeating almost verbatim his article from ten years earlier.[126] Interestingly, in a new section of this cobbled-together article, he attacked various rules of evidence and called for empirical data to justify regulations that seemed to him premised "upon the merest speculation."[127] Unfortunately, he did not apply the same standard to his own criticism of the jury or his assertions about the benefits of judicial commentary.[128]

Sunderland's articulation of a selective empirical concern in his 1926 article should not come as a complete surprise. In certain legal circles in the 1920s, a decided shift away from a rhetorical and formalist approach to the law was under way.[129] The legal realist movement was taking hold, perhaps inspired by Oliver Wendell Holmes, who had declared, "The life of the law has not been logic; it has been experience."[130] The realists wanted to study how the law really operates and to usher in a new era of reform premised upon their findings. As several prominent realists put it, "The reformers have failed because the necessary basic research has been lacking. . . . We regard facts as the prerequisites for reform."[131]

Empirical work was begun on a number of topics, including the efficiency of the jury. One of the centers of this activity was Yale Law School, where Charles E. Clark was at work. Clark was no friend of the jury. In a 1923 article he had opined,

Jurists of experience find little to say in support of the delays, the expense, and the aleatory results of trial by jury. In England it is being more and more restricted. Its real advantage seems to be a kind of safety valve for the judicial system. It relieves the judges of the burden and the odium of deciding close questions of fact in cases, such as personal injury actions, where the feelings of litigants are apt to run high.[132]

In 1927 Clark and a number of Yale colleagues began an examination of cases filed in the New Haven Superior Court. Their objective was "to substitute for the vague generalizations of the older economists and philosophers concrete information based on adequate statistical information" and to use this as a springboard to reform.[133]

By 1934 Clark and coauthor Harry Shulman had amassed a data base of more than 23,000 cases stretching between 1919 and 1932. On the strength of this data base, they set out to survey the value of the jury. In "Jury Trial in Civil Cases—A Study in Judicial Administration," they argued that their findings provided empirical justification for criticisms of the efficiency of the jury.[134] They found that, although juries were used in only 4 percent of civil cases, these cases consumed as much as 44 percent of aggregate civil trial time; that the vast preponderance of jury cases were clustered in the auto negligence area; and that juries consumed the time of substantially more than twelve jurors, leading to higher costs for the state. On the basis of these findings, the researchers concluded,

> Whatever the political, psychological or jurisprudential values of the jury as an institution may be, its use in the civil litigation covered by this study is certainly not impressive. The picture seems to be that of an expensive, cumbersome and comparatively inefficient trial device employed in cases where exploitation of the situation is made possible by underlying rules. Persuasive reasons are found in the facts set forth for the definite limitation of the right of jury trial to the role of safety valve; and for the greater use of the summary judgment in the debt cases, the requirement of substantial jury trial fees, and the reduction in the number of jurors required for a petit jury to nine or even six.[135]

It is difficult to see these arguments as convincing, since the data are not tightly focused on jury operations but rather incorporate such cases as a small part of a larger data base. Many of the statistically based insights are, at best, marginally significant, and the authors fail to consider the role of the jury either as trend-setter or political mechanism. Clark and Shulman in fact stacked the debate by adopting a reductionist strategy that excluded consideration of the great variety of functions served by the jury. They also failed to determine whether their data were typical of the broader American scene. In fact, in 1930, Professor Silas Harris of Ohio State Law School had pointed out that the Connecticut data were seriously skewed because juries there were atypically antiplaintiff in their orientation owing to the impact of an idiosyncratic 1854 jury selection law that compelled the impaneling of a superabundance of conservative rural veniremen. This, in turn, discouraged plaintiffs from opting for the jury with the same frequency noted in other jurisdictions.[136] All these factors pointed up the need for a broader research effort capable of looking beyond raw court statistics and focusing on more than a single locale. Unfortunately, by the mid-1930s the empirical efforts of the realist movement had begun to falter. Their failure to yield substantial support for reform and the considerable expense involved in the effort put a damper on further inquiry.[137]

Large-scale research on the jury resumed in the 1950s when Hans Zeisel, Harry Kalven, and the University of Chicago Jury Project turned their attention to the subject. The project focused on particular localities, such as Manhattan's congested courts, as well as surveying the nation at large through a series of samples. Both juror and judge case assessments were collected and analyzed to generate information about the jury's internal workings and its reliability.[138] In their first book-length monograph which focused on the question of delay, Zeisel and his colleagues found that, while jury trials are approximately 40 percent longer than bench trials, the cost of the jury system is more than justified by the values it introduces into the trial process. The researchers outlined a series of case and trial management techniques as the most promising avenues for addressing the problem of delay in jury trials.[139]

Another of the project's key findings was that the judge and jury agree about trial outcome approximately three quarters of the time.[140] This level of agreement compares favorably with that of other sorts of decisionmakers in American society, including diagnostic physicians and psychiatrists as well as grant evaluators for the National Science Foundation.[141] Kalven and Zeisel conducted a range of sophisticated analyses that led them to conclude that the jury generally "follows the evidence and understands the case."[142] The project's findings established a strong empirical defense of the jury trial. George Priest, commenting in 1990, concluded,

> Over the past quarter century . . . support for the civil jury has become nearly unanimous. In large part, the overwhelming modern belief in the importance of the civil jury can be attributed to the influential work of the University of Chicago Jury Project led by Harry Kalven and Hans Zeisel. In its time, the Kalven-Zeisel Jury Project was the most ambitious empirical study of jury decisionmaking that had ever been attempted. As a result of their extensive empirical analysis, the authors claimed that the civil jury was a superior institution for adjudicating disputes involving complex societal values, that the jury served as an important instrument of popular control over law enforcement, and that the jury brought a superior sense of social equity to the decisionmaking process. Indeed, the authors interpreted their empirical findings to confirm simultaneously each of these assertions.[143]

While Priest's views on the uncritical reception of the jury can be challenged in light of both Supreme Court decisions such as *Colgrove* v. *Battin* and the continuing rhetorical attacks on the jury, Kalven and Zeisel did shift the debate into the empirical realm and force policy makers to begin at least thinking about social science analysis.

The Jury Redux

The late twentieth-century jury stands in the unenviable position of being condemned on a regular basis because it must decide the most difficult questions to come before the courts. Oliver Wendell Holmes neatly captured its predicament when he declared

> I confess that in my experience I have not found juries specially inspired for the discovery of truth. I have not noticed that they could see further into things or form a saner judgment than a sensible and well trained judge. I have not found them freer from prejudice than an ordinary judge would be. Indeed one reason why I believe in our practice of leaving questions of negligence to them is what is precisely one of their greatest defects from the point of view of their theoretical function: that they will introduce into their verdict a certain amount— a very large amount, so far as I have observed—of popular prejudice, and thus keep the administration of the law in accord with the wishes and feelings of the community. Possibly such a justification is a little like that which an eminent English barrister gave me many years ago for the distinction between barristers and solicitors. It was in substance that if law was to be practiced somebody had to be damned, and he preferred that it should be somebody else.[144]

Today, juries are regularly asked to review the propriety of business transactions of the most ambiguous and troubling sort. It was to a jury that the Pennzoil Corporation turned when Texaco tampered with a lucrative deal involving the Getty Oil Company. From the beginning, the behavior of the principals in this affair had been riddled with the shoddiest practices, including bad faith bargaining, destruction of evidence, and apparent efforts to buy influence.[145] The jury in the case rendered one of the largest, most widely discussed, and most sharply criticized verdicts in American history.

What is most striking about this case is the amount of power that was vested in the jury and the abysmal failure of every other participant in the process to behave in a responsible manner, including the corporate players, the lawyers representing the parties, and even the judiciary, which was tainted by the appearance of impropriety. Whether the jury acted well or badly, it was all that society had left in a transaction gone desperately wrong. While the verdict raises many difficult questions, it may not be entirely out of line to suggest that the presence of juries in similar cases could circumscribe the damage that is being done to our corporate and financial infrastructure.

Judicial management of negligence litigation in the nineteenth century eventually led to a liberalization of the jury's role in twentieth century tort cases. Modern juries have been asked to handle questions that affect the lives and health of countless Americans. In the absence of any other remedial mechanism, citizens exposed to toxic substances and victims of defective products have turned to the jury. Jury decisions in these areas have been far from ideal, but they have at least offered plaintiffs a hearing and a response.

Among the most interesting jury decisions have been those involving smokers and the tobacco companies. Juries have generally rejected smokers' claims, viewing the voluntary actions of the plaintiffs as a barrier to recovery. The difficulty faced by jurors in these cases is powerfully dramatized by the declaration of one of their number in the recently concluded case of Rose Cipollone. After the conclusion of that case, the first in which any award was made to a smoker, juror Ralph Eliseo plaintively asked, "Why do I have to have the responsibility of deciding if a person was responsible for smoking, was responsible for their own death? If Rosie knew she was smoking a bad product why didn't she stop? I didn't think it was fair that she put this burden on me." [146] Yet Eliseo and his fellow jurors did shoulder the burden, as jurors have been doing for hundreds of years. And their behavior in products cases like those involving tobacco suggests more thoughtful and measured consideration than is available elsewhere in the system.

Juries in our day have also been asked to rule on matters of the greatest constitutional gravity. Of course, this is clearest in the criminal setting, where the Supreme Court has emphasized the value of having juries decide the question of life or death in capital cases. But it is also true in the civil arena. In defamation cases such as that between Ariel Sharon, the Israeli politician, and *Time* magazine, juries have been asked to decide the limits of freedom of the press and the nature of the public's right to be informed. They have generally handled such matters with great sensitivity. In the Sharon case, the jury harshly criticized *Time* but recognized the strictness of the constitutional limit on libel. [147] As in the time of Peter Zenger, the jury stood ready to sort out issues vital to a free society while respecting the principle of free expression.

Conclusion

Examples like the Pennzoil, Cipollone, and Sharon cases may prove very little by themselves. Equally, examples of the worst juror errors prove very little. More than a hundred years ago, Forsyth cautioned against "arguments by anecdote." As he put it, "It would not be difficult for an opponent of the system to cite ludicrous examples of foolish verdicts, but they would be a very unfair sample of the average quality; and nothing can be more unsafe than to make exceptional cases the basis of legislation."[148] The jury is not a simple device, and an appreciation of its history can only be gained if reductionist thinking is avoided.

History teaches that the jury has been protean, repeatedly adapting to the needs of changing times. It was an engine of inquisition for William I but a bulwark of resistance to James II. Understanding this changing organ of government requires continuing the empirical work begun by Kalven and Zeisel almost forty years ago. It is no coincidence that serious modern discussions on the jury regularly include social scientists, as well as lawyers.

That the civil jury is not invincible is demonstrated by its disappearance in England over the course of the twenty years between World War I and the Great Depression. Having done without the jury for more than a decade, fundamentally because of the exigencies of the war and its aftermath, solicitors and barristers got out of the habit of jury litigation.[149] If the American jury is not to suffer the same fate, we must be sensitive to de Tocqueville's observation:

> The institution of the jury, if confined to criminal causes, is always in danger; but when once it is introduced into civil proceedings, it defies the aggressions of time and man. . . . The jury, and more especially the civil jury, serves to communicate the spirit of the judges to the minds of all the citizens; and this spirit, with the habits which attend it, is the soundest preparation for free institutions. It imbues all classes with a respect for the thing judged and with the notion of right. If these two elements be removed, the love of independence becomes a mere destructive passion. It teaches men to practice equity; every man learns to judge his neighbor as he would himself be judged. And this is especially true of the jury in civil causes; for while the number of persons who have reason to apprehend a criminal prosecution is small, everyone is liable to have a lawsuit. . . . It invests each citizen with a kind of magistracy; it makes them all feel the duties

which they are bound to discharge towards society and the part which they take in its government. By obliging men to turn their attention to other affairs than their own, it rubs off that private selfishness which is the rust of society.[150]

If we do not heed this advice we are likely to lose one of the most flexible and democratic of governing devices. Our loss could not be measured in terms of the jury's past service alone. We would also be deprived of the adaptations yet to be fashioned in response to the ever changing needs of society.

Notes

1. *Colgrove* v. *Battin*, 413 U.S. 149, 157 (1973).
2. Ibid.
3. There is ample historical justification for focusing on English common law practice in 1791 in interpreting the scope of the Seventh Amendment. See note 88 and the accompanying text. But this approach has all too frequently led the courts to ignore the dynamic nature of the jury trial right and become preoccupied with the demonstrable presence or absence of a challenged procedure at one specific moment in time. See Charles W. Wolfram, "The Constitutional History of the Seventh Amendment," *Minnesota Law Review*, vol. 57 (March 1973), pp. 744–45. An example of this tendency is the Supreme Court's ruling in *Dimick* v. *Schiedt*, 293 U.S. 474 (1935).
4. For another example see *Tull* v. *U.S.*, 481 U.S. 412, 425–27 (1987).
5. See, for example, Stephen B. Presser, *The Original Misunderstanding: The English, the Americans, and the Dialectic of Congressional Jurisprudence* (Durham, N.C.: Carolina Academic Press, 1990).
6. See, for example, William E. Nelson, *Americanization of the Common Law: The Impact of Legal Change on Massachusetts Society* (Harvard University Press, 1975).
7. See, for example, Wex S. Malone, "The Formative Era of Contributory Negligence," *Illinois Law Review*, vol. 41 (July–August 1946), pp. 151–82.
8. See, for example, Harry Kalven, Jr., and Hans Zeisel, *The American Jury* (Little, Brown, 1966).
9. Frederick Pollock and Frederick W. Maitland, *The History of English Law before the Time of Edward I*, 2 vols. (Cambridge University Press, 1895), vol. 1, p. 72; and James B. Thayer, *A Preliminary Treatise on Evidence at the Common Law* (Little, Brown and Company, 1898), p. 50.
10. John P. Dawson, *A History of Lay Judges*, (Harvard University Press, 1960), p. 120.
11. Patrick Devlin, *Trial by Jury* (London: Stevens and Sons, 1956), p. 7.
12. Pollock and Maitland, *The History of English Law*, vol. 1, p. 125.
13. Dawson, *A History of Lay Judges*, p. 121.
14. Dawson defines essoins as "excuses for non-attendance." *A History of Lay Judges*, p. 295.
15. The passage from Glanvill is cited and translated in Thayer, *A Preliminary Treatise*, p. 42, n.1.
16. Dawson, *A History of Lay Judges*, pp. 293–94.

17. William Forsyth, *History of Trial by Jury* (New York: B. Franklin, originally published 1852, reprinted 1971), p. 105.

18. Thayer, *A Preliminary Treatise*, p. 143.

19. Forsyth, *History of Trial by Jury*, p. 152.

20. Thayer, *A Preliminary Treatise*, pp. 97–102.

21. As late as 1427, these procedures were still being codified as law. Thayer, *A Preliminary Treatise*, p. 92.

22. Pollock and Maitland, *The History of English Law*, vol. 2, p. 627.

23. Dawson, *A History of Lay Judges*, pp. 123–25. In the criminal setting, recent study has disclosed that jurors were frequently drawn from a wide geographical area (a majority lived more than five miles from the scene of the crime) and were unlikely to be true witnesses. Bernard W. McLane, "Juror Attitudes toward Local Disorder: The Evidence of the 1328 Lincolnshire Trailbaston Proceedings," in *Twelve Good Men and True: The Criminal Trial Jury in England, 1200–1800*, edited by J. S. Cockburn and Thomas A. Green (Princeton University Press, 1988), pp. 56–57.

24. Dawson, *A History of Lay Judges*, p. 126.

25. Pollock and Maitland, *The History of English Law*, vol. 2, pp. 620–25; and Dawson, *A History of Lay Judges*, p. 128.

26. Quoted in Thayer, *A Preliminary Treatise*, p. 101.

27. Thayer, *A Preliminary Treatise*, p. 102.

28. Thomas Smith, *De Republica Anglorum* (Barnes and Noble, originally published 1583, reprinted 1972), p. 111.

29. 124 Eng. Rep. 1006 (C.P., 1670). It is, however, generally agreed that Vaughan was being purposefully anachronistic when he spoke. Thomas A. Green, *Verdict according to Conscience: Perspectives on the English Criminal Trial Jury, 1200–1850* (University of Chicago Press, 1985), pp. 242–45; John H. Langbein, "The Criminal Trial before the Lawyers," *University of Chicago Law Review*, vol. 45 (Winter 1978), pp. 284–300.

30. Lloyd E. Moore, *The Jury: Tool of Kings, Palladium of Liberty* (W. H. Anderson Company, 1973), p. 70.

31. John Fortesque, *De Laudibus Legum Anglie* (Cambridge University Press, 1942) (S.B. Chrimes edition), pp. 58–63.

32. Green, *Verdict according to Conscience*, pp. 105–52.

33. Thayer, *A Preliminary Treatise*, p. 179.

34. Ibid., pp. 125–36. I am referring to barriers such as charges of maintenance and conspiracy.

35. Dawson, *A History of Lay Judges*, p. 134.

36. Green, *Verdict according to Conscience*, p. 105.

37. Stephen K. Roberts, "Juries and the Middling Sort: Recruitment and Performance at Devon Quarter Sessions, 1649–1670," in Cockburn and Green, *Twelve Good Men and True*, p. 182.

38. Statutes from 1285 and 1293 (during the reign of Edward I) point out the efforts made by the wealthy to avoid jury service. Thayer, *A Preliminary Treatise*, p. 90.

39. P. G. Lawson, "Lawless Juries? The Composition and Behavior of Hertfordshire Juries, 1573–1624," in Cockburn and Green, *Twelve Good Men and True*, p. 124 and 133.

40. Alan Macfarlane, *Reconstructing Historical Communities* (Cambridge University Press, 1977), p. 183.

41. William Blackstone, *Commentaries on the Laws of England* (Garland Publishing, originally published 1783, reprinted 1978), vol. 3, p. 380.

42. Green, *Verdict according to Conscience*, p. 105.

43. "London Juries in the 1690s," in Cockburn and Green, *Twelve Good Men and True*, p. 214.

44. For a description of Penn and Mead's trial see Green, *Verdict according to Conscience*, pp. 221–36.

45. Ibid., pp. 236–64.

46. Ibid., pp. 262–63, 320–21.

47. Austin W. Scott, "Trial by Jury and the Reform of Civil Procedure," *Harvard Law Review*, vol. 31 (March 1918), p. 676.

48. For example, "The Englishman's Right," "The Guide to English Juries," and "The Security of Englishmen's Lives." See Scott, "Trial by Jury," pp. 676–78.

49. 98 Eng. Rep. 489 (C.P., 1763).

50. 98 Eng. Rep. 489–99. Wilkes's case and his ongoing conflicts with the British administration were a matter of keen interest in the American colonies. In the early 1770s South Carolina went so far as to provide Wilkes with monetary support for one of his political campaigns. John Brewer, "The Wilkites and the Law, 1763–74: A Study of Radical Notions of Governance," in John Brewer and John Styles, eds., *An Ungovernable People: The English and Their Law in the Seventeenth and Eighteenth Centuries* (Rutgers University Press, 1980), pp. 139–40.

51. Harold Hyman and Catherine Tarrant, "Aspects of American Trial Jury History," in Rita James Simon, ed., *The Jury System in America* (Sage Publications, 1975), pp. 24 and 25.

52. Massachusetts Body of Liberties, paragraph 29 reproduced in Richard L. Perry and John C. Cooper, eds., *Sources of Our Liberties: Documentary Origins of Individual Liberties in the United States Constitution and Bill of Rights* (Chicago: American Bar Foundation, 1959), p. 151.

53. Nelson, *Americanization of the Common Law*. My analysis of prerevolutionary Massachusetts is based upon Nelson's work.

54. Ibid., pp. 45–47.

55. Ibid., p. 3.

56. Ibid., pp. 24–26.

57. Ibid., p. 33.

58. J. S. Cockburn, *A History of English Assizes 1558–1714* (Cambridge University Press, 1972), pp. 122–24.

59. A. G. Roeber, *Faithful Magistrates and Republican Lawyers: Creators of Virginia Legal Culture, 1680–1810* (University of North Carolina Press, 1981).

60. Paul Finkelman, "The Zenger Case: Prototype of a Political Trial," in Michal R. Belknap, ed., *American Political Trials* (Greenwood Press, 1981), pp. 21–42.

61. Stanley N. Katz, "The Politics of Law in Colonial America: Controversies over Chancery Courts and Equity Law in the Eighteenth Century," in Donald Fleming and Bernard Bailyn, eds., *Law in American History* (Harvard University Press, 1980). My analysis of the New York chancery disputes is based upon Katz's work.

62. Roeber, *Faithful Magistrates and Republican Lawyers*, p. 128.

63. Hyman and Tarrant, "Aspects of American Trial Jury History," p. 29.

64. Wolfram, "The Constitutional History of the Seventh Amendment," pp. 654–55 n. 47.

65. Resolutions of the Stamp Act Congress, 1765, paragraph 7, in Perry and Cooper, *Sources of Our Liberties*, pp. 267, 270.

66. Hyman and Tarrant, "Aspects of American Trial Jury History," p. 29.

67. Declaration and Resolves of the First Continental Congress, 1774, Resolution 5, in Perry and Cooper, *Sources of Our Liberties*, pp. 281–82, 288.

68. Declaration of the Causes and Necessity of Taking up Arms, 1775, Ibid., p. 296.

69. Declaration of Independence, 1776, Ibid., p. 320.

70. Leonard W. Levy, *Legacy of Suppression: Freedom of Speech and Press in Early American History* (1960 reprint, Belknop Press of Harvard University Press), p. 281, quoted in Wolfram, "The Constitutional History of the Seventh Amendment," p. 655.

71. Hyman and Tarrant, "Aspects of American Trial Jury History," p. 30.

72. Alexander Hamilton, *The Papers of Alexander Hamilton*, Harold C. Syrett, ed., vol. 2 (Columbia University Press, 1961–87), p. 649, quoted in Forrest McDonald, *Novus Ordo Seclorum* (University Press of Kansas, 1985), p. 2.

73. McDonald, *Novus Ordo Seclorum*, p. 156.

74. McDonald, *Novus Ordo Seclorum*, pp. 176–78.

75. Wolfram, "The Constitutional History of the Seventh Amendment," pp. 675–77; and McDonald, *Novus Ordo Seclorum*, pp. 185–86.

76. Edith G. Henderson, "The Background of the Seventh Amendment," *Harvard Law Review*, vol. 80 (December 1966), p. 292.

77. The quote, delivered by Mr. Gorham on September 12, 1787, was originally reported in James Madison, *Debates in the Federal Convention*. See Henderson, "The Seventh Amendment," pp. 293–94.

78. Henderson, "The Seventh Amendment," pp. 293–94.

79. McDonald, *Novus Ordo Seclorum*, pp. 41 and 290–91.

80. Alexander Hamilton, James Madison, and John Jay, *The Federalist*, no. 83 (Mentor Books, originally published 1788, reprinted 1961).

81. Ibid., p. 499.

82. Hamilton, "no. 83," pp. 499 and 505.

83. Wolfram, "The Constitutional History of the Seventh Amendment," pp. 673–710.

84. Comment by a Virginia judge in *Hague* v. *Stratton*, 8 Va. (4 Call) 84, 85 (1786), quoted in Morton J. Horwitz, *The Transformation of the American Law 1780–1860* (Harvard University Press, 1977), p. 142.

85. Blackstone, *Commentaries on the Laws of England*, vol. 3, p. 379.

86. Wolfram, "The Constitutional History of the Seventh Amendment," p. 673.

87. Henderson, "The Seventh Amendment," p. 336.

88. "A Democratic Federalist," *Pennsylvania Packet*, October 23, 1787, quoted Ibid., p. 297.

89. Charles Warren, "New Light on the History of the Federal Judiciary Act of 1789," *Harvard Law Review*, vol. 37 (November 1923), p. 54.

90. Richard E. Ellis, *The Jeffersonian Crisis: Courts and Politics in the Young Republic* (Oxford University Press, 1971), pp. 157–83, especially p. 165. My analysis of the Pennsylvania conflicts is based upon Ellis' work.

91. Ellis, *The Jeffersonian Crisis*, pp. 184–229. My analysis of the Massachusetts conflicts is based upon Ellis' work.

92. Ellis, *The Jeffersonian Crisis*, p. 190.

93. 1 Cranch 137, 2 L.Ed. 60 (1803).

94. Ellis, *The Jeffersonian Crisis*, p. 69.

95. Ellis, *The Jeffersonian Crisis*, pp. 69–75.

96. Presser, *The Original Misunderstanding*, pp. 110–13. My analysis of Chase's impeachment is based on the outstanding work of Professor Presser.

97. Ibid., p. 137.

98. Ibid., p. 18.

99. Alexis de Tocqueville, *Democracy in America* (Knopf, originally published 1830, reprinted 1945), p. 291.

100. Ibid., p. 297.

101. Nelson, *Americanization of the Common Law*, p. 8: Horwitz, *The Transformation of American Law*, pp. 140–41.

102. See Horwitz, *The Transformation of American Law*; and Nelson, *Americanization of the Common Law*.

103. 103 Eng. Rep. 926 (K.B. 1809).

104. Fleming James, Jr., "Last Clear Chance: A Transitional Doctrine," *Yale Law Journal*, vol. 47 (March 1938), pp. 704–05.

105. Wex Malone, "The Formative Era of Contributory Negligence," *Illinois Law Review*, vol. 41 (July–August 1946), pp. 151–82.

106. Ibid., p. 153.

107. Ibid., p. 155.

108. 13 Barb. 2 (N.Y. 1853), p. 15, quoted in Malone, "The Formative Era of Contributory Negligence," p. 158.

109. *Ernst v. Hudson River Railroad Company*, 24 How. Prac. 97 (N.Y. 1862) quoted in Malone, "The Formative Era of Contributory Negligence," p. 159 (emphasis in original).

110. Lawrence M. Friedman, "Civil Wrongs: Personal Injury Law in the Late 19th Century," *American Bar Foundation Research Journal*, vol. 1987, p. 375.

111. Malone, "The Formative Era of Contributory Negligence," p. 161.

112. Ibid., p. 169.

113. Ibid., pp. 169–72.

114. See text accompanying note 120.

115. John T. Noonan, *Persons and Masks of the Law: Cardozo, Holmes, Jefferson and Wythe as Makers of the Masks* (Farrar, Straus and Giroux, 1976), pp. 19–20.

116. Gary T. Schwartz, "Tort Law and the Economy in Nineteenth-Century America: A Reinterpretation," *Yale Law Journal*, vol. 90 (July 1981), pp. 1744–45, 1751–52.

117. Seymour D. Thompson, *Commentaries on the Law of Negligence in All Relations* (Indianapolis: Bowen Co., 1901), vol. 1, pp. 168–69, quoted in Friedman, "Civil Wrongs," p. 357.

118. W. Page Keeton, gen. ed., *Prosser and Keeton on the Law of Torts*, 5th ed. (West Publishing Co., 1984), p. 471.

119. James, "Last Clear Chance," p. 723.

120. Charles E. Wyzanski, Jr., "A Trial Judge's Freedom and Responsibility," *Harvard Law Review*, vol. 65 (June 1952), p. 1286.

121. Alfred C. Coxe, "The Trials of Jury Trials," *Columbia Law Review*, vol. 1 (May 1901), pp. 286–97.

122. In the 1899 to 1906 period there were 96 articles in the *Index* section entitled "Jury." Of these 66 were neutral, irrelevant, or unavailable. In the 1924 to 1932 period there were 184 articles in the appropriate section. Of these 128 were neutral, irrelevant, or unavailable. It is likely that because of the problem of unavailability the data set forth in the text undercount the number of efficiency-concerned jury-critical articles in each period. However, the ratio between the two periods would not appear likely to change dramatically on the basis of the unavailable material.

123. Edson R. Sunderland, "The Inefficiency of the American Jury," *Michigan Law Review*, vol. 13 (February 1915), pp. 302–16.

124. Ibid., pp. 309–10.

125. Edson R. Sunderland, "Verdicts, General and Specific," *Yale Law Journal*, vol. 29 (January 1920), p. 253.

126. Edson R. Sunderland, "The Problem of Trying Issues," *Texas Law Review*, vol. 5 (December 1926), pp. 18–40.

127. Ibid., p. 22.

128. Sunderland eventually gathered data on jury operations. These appear in a speech he gave in 1937. Edson R. Sunderland in "Trial by Jury," *University of Cincinnati Law Review*, vol. 11 (March 1937), pp. 120–31.

129. Wallace Loh has provided a fine brief definition of formalism. He says formalism

"conceived of law as a closed, deductive body of logically ordered rules." Wallace Loh, *Social Research in the Judicial Process: Cases, Reading, and Text* (Russell Sage Foundation, 1984), p. 612.

130. Oliver W. Holmes, *The Common Law* (Little, Brown and Company, 1881), p. 1.

131. Quoted in John H. Schlegel, "American Legal Realism and Empirical Social Science: From the Yale Experience," *Buffalo Law Review*, vol. 28 (Summer 1979), p. 468.

132. Charles E. Clark, "Union of Law and Equity and Trial by Jury Under the Codes," *Yale Law Journal*, vol. 32 (May 1923), p. 711.

133. Charles E. Clark, "Fact Research in Law Administration," *Mississippi Law Journal*, vol. 1 (January 1929), pp. 324–44.

134. Charles E. Clark and Harry Shulman, "Jury Trial in Civil Cases—A Study in Judicial Administration," *Yale Law Journal*, vol. 43 (April 1934), pp. 867–85.

135. Ibid., p. 884.

136. Silas A. Harris, "Is the Jury Vanishing?" *New York University Law Quarterly Review*, vol. 7 (March 1930), pp. 657–73.

137. Schlegel, "American Legal Realism," p. 572.

138. Kalven and Zeisel, *The American Jury*, pp. 33–54.

139. Hans Zeisel, Harry Kalven, Jr., and Bernard Buchholz, *Delay in the Court* (Little, Brown, 1959), pp. 8–18, especially p. 9.

140. Kalven and Zeisel, *The American Jury*, p. 56.

141. Shari Diamond, "Order in the Court: Consistency in Criminal-Court Decisions," in C. Jones Sheirer and Barbara L. Hammonds, eds., *The Master Lecture Series, Psychology and the Law*, vol. 2 (American Psychological Association, 1983).

142. Kalven and Zeisel, *The American Jury*, p. 149.

143. George L. Priest, "The Role of the Civil Jury in a System of Private Litigation," *University of Chicago Legal Forum*, vol. 1990, p. 162.

144. Oliver Wendell Holmes, "Law in Science and Science in Law," *Harvard Law Review*, vol. 12 (1899), pp. 443, 459–60.

145. Thomas Petzinger, Jr., *Oil and Honor: The Texaco-Pennzoil Wars* (Putnam, 1987).

146. Steven Brill, *Trial by Jury* (Simon and Schuster, 1989), p. 416.

147. Brill, *Trial by Jury*, p. 132.

148. Forsyth, *History of Trial by Jury*, p. 376.

149. Devlin, *Trial by Jury*, p. 133.

150. de Tocqueville, *Democracy in America*, p. 295.

CHAPTER THREE

The Regulatory Function
of the Civil Jury

Marc Galanter

T HE CIVIL JURY is largely an American institution.[1] Are we the last
to discard an obsolete institution? Or do we know something other
countries do not know? To decide whether civil juries are a good thing,
one has to ask what juries are supposed to do. I would answer
that basically they do two things. Distributively, they decide cases.[2]
Collectively, they generate a body of knowledge that fuels the American
system of "litigotiation." I use this neologism as a reminder that this is
a system in which only a minority of eligible claims are made and only
a minority of these proceed to disposition by trial; the vast majority are
resolved by settlement, abandonment, or ruling at an earlier stage.[3] It is
important to recall that America does not have two systems, one of
litigation and one of negotiation, but a single system of "litigotiation"—
that is, of contesting claims in the vicinity of courts, where recourse to
the full process of adjudication is an infrequent occurrence but at every
stage an important option and threat.

In the aggregate, juries provide signals or markers by which legal
actors form estimates of what other juries will do and on that basis make
decisions and formulate policies about claims, offers, settlements, and
trials, and even about preclaim investments in safety, disclosure, and so
forth. Thus the impact of the small number of jury trials is vastly
disproportionate to their number. One can apply to the civil jury Harry
Kalven's and Hans Zeisel's observation about the criminal jury:

at every stage of this informal process of pre-trial dispositions . . .
decisions are in part informed by expectations of what the jury will
do. Thus, the jury is not controlling merely the immediate case before
it, but the host of cases not before it which are destined to be disposed

of by the pre-trial process. The jury thus controls not only the formal resolution of controversies . . . but also the informal resolution of cases that never reach the trial stage. In a sense the jury, like the visible cap of an iceberg, exposes but a fraction of its true volume.[4]

To shift metaphors, one can visualize the jury as part of a system of "bargaining in the shadow of the law." The jury casts a shadow across the wider arena of claims, maneuvers, and settlements by communicating signals about what future juries might do. Of course, the jury is not the only source of these predictive shadows, which are cast not only by legal decisions but also by cost, delay, risk, party capability, and so forth.[5]

The transmission and reception of these signals is a crucial aspect of the jury. As an institution, the reality of juries includes the images of them held by lawyers, judges, insurers, litigants, and wider audiences. Juries are present as a threat and as a supply of markers, both variously interpreted. Hence what gives rise to these interpretations is part of the jury process; what changes these interpretations is as crucial as changes in jury behavior.

These threat and signal functions of the jury derive from the position of the jury in our legal system. In other modes of lay participation in the legal process—for example, justices of the peace and neighborhood dispute centers—the popular element is cast as alternative or auxiliary to the qualified professional court. If things are not resolved in the initial stages, there is recourse to the professionals.[6] But the jury is located toward the "top" of the system rather than the bottom; the professionals work in the shadow of the amateurs. If a case involves a sharp contest of claims and elicits heavy investment, it moves to the jury not away from it. And the professionals are committed to defer to the jury, according its decisions some, often considerable, finality.

The salience of the jury's second function can be realized through a little thought experiment. Imagine a system of disputing in which not only juries but judges, courtrooms, lawyers, court reporters, experts, and parties' time and appetites for vindication were present in inexhaustible supply, so that each case proceeded through the full process to decision by a jury. In such a world, juries would not have this second, regulatory function and could be evaluated solely on their merits as deciders of each case.

But in a world of shortages, transaction costs, and risk aversion, trials and juries are few compared with the number of disputes. Hence, evaluation of the civil jury involves more than the question "are juries

Table 3-1. *Trials as Percentage of Civil Terminations, U.S. District Courts, Selected Years, 1961–91*

Terminations	1961	1970	1980	1988	1991
Total civil terminations[a]	50,490[b]	79,466	154,985	238,140	211,040
Total trials	5,553	7,975	10,091	11,618	8,427
Percentage of terminations that are trials	11.0	10.0	6.5	4.9	4.0
Total jury trials	2,585	3,409	3,920	5,920	4,294
Percentage of trials that are jury trials	46.6	42.7	38.8	51.0	51.0
Percentage of terminations that are jury trials	5.1	4.3	2.5	2.5	2.0

Source: Administrative Office of the U.S. Courts, *Annual Reports*, (1961, 1970, 1980, 1988, 1991), table C-4.
a. Land condemnation cases excluded.
b. Transferred and consolidated cases excluded.

good deciders of cases?" It also entails a second question: Is the system of civil juries a good means of regulating the system of "litigotiation"? In theory these are independent: one might be answered affirmatively and the other negatively. I propose to focus on the second question because it is more neglected and because, as I shall argue, it is more consequential. But before one can assess the jury's performance, it is important to have some sense of the institutional presence of the civil jury.

Incidence and Distribution of Jury Trials

Relative to the tens of millions of claims made each year or the millions of filings, the number of jury trials is exceedingly small. Overall, they take place in less than 1 percent of cases terminated in state courts and in 2 percent of terminations of federal courts (table 3-1, table 3-2).[7] Jury presence varies from field to field. Tort cases go to juries more frequently than cases in other fields.[8] Within the tort field, patterns of jury invocation differ from topic to topic. In medical malpractice, for example, verdicts made up 3 to 4 percent of paid claims.[9] In the state courts of general jurisdiction for which data are available, the portion of contract cases disposed by jury trial ranges from 0.3 percent to 1.4 percent (table 3-3). In the federal courts, apart from torts (4.3 percent), only civil rights (4.5 percent), antitrust (5.0 percent), and "other diversity" (4.3 percent) had jury trials in more than 2 percent of dispositions in 1991 (table 3-4).

Overall there are more than 50,000 civil jury trials each year in the

Table 3-2. *Civil Jury Trials, by State and Subject Matter, 1988*

Type	Number of jury trials	Percentage of total jury trials	Number of dispositions	Jury trials as percentage of dispositions
Florida Circuit Court				
Tort	1,575	67.9	33,411	4.7
Contract	448	19.3	54,529	0.8
Property	98	4.2	51,062	0.2
Other[a]	200	8.6	101,765	0.2
Total	2,321	100.0	240,767	1.0
Hawaii Circuit Court				
Tort	31	55.4	1,635[b]	1.9
Contract	8	14.3	1,554[b]	0.5
Property	1	1.8	247[b]	0.4
Other	16	28.6	5,039[b]	0.3
Total	56	100.1[c]	8,475[b]	0.7
Massachusetts Superior Court				
Tort[d]	406	77.9	17,767	2.3
Contract	78	15.0	5,646	1.4
Property[e]	37	7.1	33,915	0.1
Total	521	100.0	57,328	0.9
Minnesota District Court				
Tort	481	60.4	10,807	4.5
Contract	122	15.3	8,899	1.4
Property	81	10.2	17,353	0.5
Other	113[f]	14.2	40,940	0.3
Total	797	100.1[c]	77,999	1.0
Texas District Court				
Tort	1,592	46.8	40,674	3.9
Contract	535	15.7	55,878	1.0
Property	9	0.3	439	2.1
Other	1,266	37.2	127,450	1.0
Total	3,402	100.0	224,441	1.5
Washington Superior Court				
Tort	501	82.8	10,888	4.6
Contract	51	8.4	13,237	0.4
Property	19	3.1	13,192	0.1
Other	34	5.6	19,843	0.2
Total	605	99.9[c]	57,160	1.1

Source: National Center for State Courts, *Annual Report, 1988* (Williamsburg, Va., 1988), part 2, table 2.
a. "Other" includes miscellaneous civil cases.
b. All case types exclude some cases reported as reopened prior cases.
c. Does not equal 100 percent because of rounding.
d. Does not include data from Boston Municipal and District Court departments.
e. Real property rights disposed data do not include summary process and civil cases from the Housing Court Department.
f. Does not include estate cases.

Table 3-3. *Disposition of Contract Cases in State Courts of General Jurisdiction and in Federal District Courts, 1988*

Location and court	Number of contract dispositions	Number of contract trials[a]	Contract trials as percentage of contract dispositions	Total number of civil jury trials[b]	Number of contract jury trials	Contract jury trials as percentage of all civil jury trials	Jury trials as percentage of contract dispositions	Jury trials as percentage of contract trials
Federal District Court	65,303[c]	2,507[d]	3.8	5,920	1,126	19.0	1.7	44.9
Federal District Court, diversity only	32,990	2,048	6.2	3,051	1,014	33.2	3.1	49.5
Florida Circuit Court	54,529	2,306	4.2	2,321	448	19.3	0.8	19.4
Hawaii Circuit Court	1,554	27	1.7	56	8	14.3	0.5	29.6
Massachusetts Superior Court	5,646	580	10.3	521	78	15.0	1.4	13.4
Minnesota District Court	8,899	496	5.6	797	122	15.3	1.4	25.0
Texas District Court	55,878	5,332	9.5	3,402	535	15.7	1.0	10.0
Washington Superior Court	13,237	452	3.4	605	51	8.4	0.4	11.3
Wisconsin Circuit Court	64,340	1,632	2.5	1,076	203	18.9	0.3	12.4

Sources: Administrative Office of the U.S. Courts, *Annual Reports* (1988), table C-4; and National Center for State Courts, *Annual Reports* (1988), part 2, table 2.
a. A nonjury trial is counted when first evidence is introduced or first witness is sworn.
b. A jury trial is counted at jury selection, empaneling, or when a jury is sworn.
c. Includes recovery cases.
d. A trial is counted when a case terminates during or after trial.

Table 3-4. *Civil Jury Trials in U.S. District Courts, 1991*

Type	Number of jury trials	Percentage of total jury trials	Number of terminations	Jury trials as percentage of terminations
Tort	1,956	45.6	45,357	4.3
Civil rights	845	19.7	18,828	4.5
Contract	686	16.0	34,756	2.0
Prisoner petitions	311	7.2	40,776	0.8
Other federal question	126	2.9	10,177	1.2
Labor (FLSA, LMRA & labor litigation)	94	2.2	13,847	0.7
Intellectual property	68	1.6	5,240	1.3
Real property	39	0.9	9,414	0.4
Tax	53	1.2	2,683	2.0
Antitrust	29	0.7	583	5.0
Bankruptcy	16	0.4	4,611	0.3
Other U.S.	21	0.5	4,115	0.5
Forfeiture (other than liquor)	38	0.9	5,443	0.7
Social security	2	0	7,366	0
Recovery	2	0	7,311	0
Other diversity	5	0.1	115	4.3
Constitutionality of state statute	2	0	245	0.8
Other local	1	0	93	1.1
Total	4,294	100.0	211,040	2.0

Source: Administrative Office of the U.S. Courts, *Annual Report* (1991), table C-4.

United States, compared with 200,000 civil cases in the federal courts and over 9 million in state courts of general jurisdiction.[10]

In many state courts, the civil jury is overwhelmingly a tort institution. Available statewide figures for courts of general jurisdiction in nine states show the tort portion of civil jury trials ranging from 46 percent to 82 percent: the median percentage of tort juries was 67.3 percent (table 3-5). Contract cases are usually the next largest portion of jury trials—from 8 percent to 19 percent (median 15.3 percent) in the seven courts of general jurisdiction for which statewide data exist (table 3-3).[11]

The most detailed picture of juries in a single state is E. Patrick Hubbard's study of South Carolina, which collected information on verdicts in twenty-six of the state's forty-six counties, containing 80 percent of its population and accounting for 80 percent of case filings, for 1976 to 1985.[12] In South Carolina over two-thirds of all jury verdicts were in tort cases: of these more than 40 percent were in motor vehicles cases, 3 percent in products liability cases, 3 percent in medical malpractice

Table 3-5. Disposition of Tort Cases in State Courts of General Jurisdiction and in Federal District Courts, 1988

Location and court	Number of tort dispositions	Number of tort trials[a]	Tort trials as percentage of tort dispositions	Number of civil jury trials[b]	Number of tort jury trials	Tort jury trials as percentage of all civil jury trials	Jury trials as percentage of tort dispositions	Jury trials as percentage of tort trials
Federal District Court	44,145	3,517[c]	8.0	5,920	2,549	43.1	5.8	72.5
Federal District Court, diversity only	30,172	2,408	8.0	3,051	1,994	65.4	6.6	82.8
California Superior Court	103,822	4,031	3.9	n.a.	1,610	n.a.	1.6	39.9
Florida Circuit Court	33,411	1,903	5.7	2,321	1,575	67.9	4.7	82.8
Hawaii Circuit Court	1,635	46	2.8	56	31	55.4	1.9	67.4
Massachusetts Superior Court	17,767	1,155	6.5	521	406	77.9	2.3	35.2
Michigan Circuit Court	35,531	1,159	3.3	1,318[d]	1,020	77.4	2.9	88
Minnesota District Court	10,807	1,755	16.2	797	481	60.4	4.5	27.4
Ohio Court Of Commons Pleas[e]	29,302	2,128	7.3	1,391	936	67.3	3.2	44
Texas District Court	40,674	5,461	13.4	3,402	1,592	46.8	3.9	29.2
Washington Superior Court	10,888	700	6.4	605	501	82.8	4.6	71.6
Wisconsin Circuit Court	16,949	928	5.5	1,076	692	64.3	4.1	74.6

Sources: Administrative Office of the U.S. Courts, *Annual Report* (1988), table C-4; and National Center for State Courts, *Annual Report* (1988), part 2, table 2.

n.a. Not available.

a. A nonjury trial is counted when first evidence is introduced or first witness is sworn.
b. A jury trial is counted at jury selection, empaneling, or when a jury is sworn, except as noted.
c. A trial is counted when a case terminates during or after trial.
d. A jury trial is counted at verdict or decision.
e. Disposition data exclude wrongful death torts.

Table 3-6. Change in Composition of Civil Jury Trials (major categories only) in U.S. District Courts, 1961–91

	1961		1970		1980		1988		1991	
	Number of jury trials	Percentage of total jury trials	Number of jury trials	Percentage of total jury trials	Number of jury trials	Percentage of total jury trials	Number of jury trials	Percentage of total jury trials	Number of jury trials	Percentage of total jury trials
Tort	2,102	81.3	2,593	76.1	2,169	55.3	2,549	43.1	1,956	45.6
(Diversity)	...	...	(1,968)	(57.7)	(1,699)	(42.6)	(1,994)	(34.1)	(1,592)	(37.1)
Contract	302	11.7	459	13.5	686	17.5	1,126	19.2	686	16.0
(Diversity)	...	...	(416)	(12.2)	(649)	(16.6)	(1,014)	(17.3)	(610)	(14.2)
Tax	55	2.1	83	2.4	63	1.6	47	0.8	53	1.2
Real property	40	1.5	36	1.1	24	0.6	52	0.9	39	0.9
Labor	24	0.9	32	0.9	98	2.5	135	2.3	94	2.2
Antitrust	17	0.7	27	0.8	74	1.9	38	0.6	29	0.7
Civil rights	6	0.2	97	2.8	520	13.3	1,213	20.5	845	19.7
Intellectual property	4	0.2	9	0.3	37	0.9	105	1.8	68	1.6
Prisoner petitions	0	0	9	0.3	97	2.5	336	5.7	311	7.2
Local jurisdiction	n.a.	n.a.	226	6.6	26	0.7	13	0.2	14	0.3
(Tort)	...	...	(195)	(5.7)	(14)	(0.4)	(9)	(0.2)	(8)	(0.2)
(Other)	...	...	(31)	(0.9)	(12)	(0.3)	(4)	(0.1)	(6)	(0.1)
Total jury trials[a]	2,585	...	3,409	...	3,920	...	5,920	...	4,294	...

Source: Administrative Office of the U.S. Courts, *Annual Reports* (1961, 1970, 1980, 1988, 1991), table C-4.
n.a. Not available.
a. Totals are for jury trials in all categories, not just those listed.

cases, and 5 percent in premises liability cases. Most of the remainder—over 20 percent—were contracts cases.

In the federal courts, the distribution of civil juries is somewhat different.[13] In 1991 there were 4,294 civil cases terminated by jury trial (table 3-4)—of these 1,956 (45.6 percent) were tort cases. Another 845 were civil rights cases (19.7 percent), and 686 were contracts cases (16 percent). The proportion of tort cases has fallen dramatically from 81.3 percent in all civil jury trials in 1961 to 45.6 percent thirty years later (table 3-6). There were actually fewer tort jury trials in the federal courts in 1991 (1,956) than there were in 1961 (2,102)—a decrease of 7 percent. But in this same thirty-year period the number of nontort juries increased by 384 percent, from 483 to 2,338. Unfortunately there is no comparable information about the number and composition of jury trials in state courts.

The number of jury trials in federal courts (2,585 in 1961, 4,294 in 1991) increased more slowly than the total number of cases, so that jury trials as a portion of all terminations fell from 5.1 percent in 1961 to a historic low of 2.0 percent in 1991.

Federal courts loom larger on the map of jury trials—and thus of symbols and signals—than the distribution of civil litigation would suggest. Federal courts handle only 2 percent of all the civil cases in American courts of general jurisdiction, but they hold a much higher portion of jury trials—perhaps 10 percent in 1988. And given the greater preponderance of torts in state court jury trials, the federal courts are the scene of an even higher percentage of nontort civil jury trials—perhaps over 15 percent.

The Jury as Decisionmaker

Whether juries are good deciders of cases is a more complicated question than it may first appear. There are many dimensions of goodness to be considered and weighted. Beyond this, the question is ambivalent. Does it refer to the cases that contemporary civil juries actually decide? Or does it ask whether there is some population of cases that juries are ideally suited to decide? Does it refer to juries as presently constituted, regulated, and instructed or to some ostensibly improved sort of juries? And of course such a question inescapably entails comparison of juries as decisionmakers with the other institutions that might be deployed in their stead: judges or arbitrators or bureaucrats or mediators. This requires consideration of how these alternative devices actually work. For it is important to avoid false comparisons between the idealized institutions that inhabit the pages of proposals and the flawed and imperfect institutions that populate the real world.

I shall give this series of questions short shrift in order to focus on the jury's neglected second function as regulator. I justify this emphasis as a counterbalance to the copious attention given the good-decider question. Michael Saks recently observed that "we know more about jury decision-making than about any other aspect of the legal process."[14] The already sizable literature on this topic is further enriched by many of the papers in this volume. So I shall touch here on only a few aspects of the good-decider question (which I take in the limited sense of asking how real world juries as presently arranged compare with real world alternatives as they now function).

The literature, on the whole, converges on the judgment that juries are fine decisionmakers.[15] They are conscientious, collectively they understand and recall the evidence as well as judges, and they decide on the basis of the evidence presented.[16]

Juries decide cases pretty much (but not too much) along the same lines as judges. It is often assumed that juries are more prone than judges to find liability. A preliminary report from the University of Chicago Jury Project a generation ago found that juries held defendants liable in 55 percent of personal injury cases. Judges reported that they would have found liability in 54 percent of those cases. Judges and juries agreed on liability in 79 percent of the cases, and the disagreements were approximately even—that is, in 10 percent of cases the judges would have found liability where juries did not and in 11 percent of the cases the judges would not have found liability where juries did.[17] This rate of agreement compares favorably with the consistency achieved by other pairs of decisionmakers engaged in complex human judgments. Shari Diamond compiled for comparison a set of representative studies of consistency among judges faced with complex clinical judgments in individual cases where the decisonmaker had to "evaluate and combine incomplete or potentially unreliable information to reach a decision."[18] Table 3-7, adapted from Diamond, includes the University of Chicago Jury Study criminal jury findings, which are comparable to the civil jury findings noted above.

The limited divergence of judge and jury comports with the finding of Kevin Clermont and Theodore Eisenberg that federal court judges decide in favor of plaintiffs in a higher proportion of cases than do juries,

Table 3-7. *Frequency of Consistency between Judges on Complex Decisions*

Decisionmakers	Stimulus	Decision	Agreement between two judges
NSF versus NAS peer reviewers	150 grant proposals submitted to NSF	To fund or not to fund (half funded by NSF)	75%
7 employment interviewers	10 job applicants	Ranked in top 5 or in bottom 5	70%
4 experienced psychiatrists	153 patients interviewed twice, once by each of 2 psychiatrists	Psychosis, neurosis, character disorder	70%
21–23 practicing physicians	3 patient-actors with presenting symptoms (doctors could request further information and could order and receive test results)	Diagnosis: correct, incorrect	67%, 77%, 70%
3,576 judge-jury pairs	3,576 jury trials	Guilty or not guilty	78%
12 federal judges	460 presentence reports (at sentencing council)	Custody or no custody	80%
8 federal judges	439 presentence reports (at sentencing council)	Custody or no custody	79%

Source: Shari Seidman Diamond, "Order in the Court: Consistency in Criminal-Court Decisions," in C. James Scheirer and Barbara L. Hammonds, eds., *The Master Lecture Series: Psychology and the Law*, vol. 2 (Washington: American Psychological Association, 1983), pp. 124–25.

a result they attribute to biased selection based on misattribution to juries of pro-plaintiff bias.[19]

There is a widespread belief that jurors are biased against corporations and other defendants with deep pockets. But the patterns of jury response are more complex. In studies by the Institute for Civil Justice, litigant identity did have an effect on outcomes, but it operated on two tiers. Contrary to common lore, businesses and government units were, on the whole, more successful with juries than were individuals.[20] In cases involving ordinary injuries, government and corporate defendants were no more likely to be found liable than other defendants. "But when they were sued by plaintiffs with severe, permanent injuries, corporations were found liable more often than other defendants," and they usually paid larger awards, and these patterns have remained constant over two decades.[21] The differential is commonly attributed to the presence of deep corporate pockets, an explanation that fails to account for the favorable treatment of corporations in ordinary cases.[22] A recent study of juror response to personal injury claims by individuals against corporate defendants described jurors as highly suspicious of the motivations and deservingness of plaintiffs and found "little evidence of tough standards and punitiveness" toward corporations.[23]

A related notion is that jurors are excessively generous. Awards in jury cases are, on the whole, higher than those in cases tried by judges. In a study of tort dispositions in twenty-four metropolitan trial courts in one month of 1988, the median jury award was $26,500 and the median bench trial award was $8,500.[24] Obviously, there is a strong selection bias; that is, the cases that go to juries are not comparable to those tried by judges. Comparing jury verdicts with judges' "shadow verdicts" in the same cases, the University of Chicago Jury Project found jury damage awards in the 1960s about 20 percent higher than judges would have awarded—although judges reported that they would have made higher awards in a significant minority of cases.[25] Recent surveys of judges give no indication that judges and juries have diverged in the thirty years since then. Only 6 percent of the judges in the 1987 *National Law Journal* survey thought jury awards had been excessive "in many cases."[26] And in the Harris judges' poll, only 5 percent of federal judges and 4 percent of state judges reported that they had reduced jury damage awards more than five times in the previous three years.[27] Indeed, some recent evidence suggests that jurors are less generous with compensation than judges or arbitrators.[28] In any event, one could as readily indict jurors for undercompensation as for the opposite. Larger verdicts typically fall short of covering the plaintiff's full economic losses.[29]

The performance of juries as decisionmakers is particularly remarkable because there is reason to think that the cases submitted to juries are selected because they are particularly difficult and ambiguous. Compared to other decisionmakers, Michael Saks reminds us, the jury, uniquely, has to "deal with a body of cases from which the easiest 80–95 percent have been removed. . . . Other decisionmakers have the luxury of the full range of their cases, which makes higher concordance rates easier to attain."[30]

Learning about Juries

Is the jury a good means of regulating the system of litigotiation? Here the "jury" needs to be distinguished from the general architectural features of the system so that one does not inadvertently attribute to the jury effects that are produced by these other features and thus overestimate the potential effects of modifications in the role of the jury. Among the features that frame the jury as we know it are the following.

—A system with many lawyers relative to the number of judges.

—An adversary system with a private market in lawyers, who exhibit strong ties to clients and seek to maximize the interests of those clients.

—A judicial "plant" capable of full-blown processing of only a small minority of disputes that reach the legal system.

—A system of bargained outcomes in which most cases are resolved by negotiation between disputants rather than by the authoritative decision of a judge; such settlements are officially commended and encouraged.

—A system in which actors strategize about settlements in the light of their expectations, including expectations of future involvement with the system and available knowledge about the probable outcome of official decisions.

—The knowledge about probable outcomes available to disputants includes a stock of ostensibly applicable rules and a body of commentary on them; authoritative discursive applications of these rules in some contested cases—that is, judicial opinions—and commentary on them.[31] It also includes information about nondiscursive decisions in specific cases (such as sentencing and jury verdicts). And it includes information about settlements and policies that reflect participants' expectations about these decisions.

—The information that is broadcast is incomplete and unrepresentative; it is subjected to many baffles and filters. For example, case reports are selected by judges and publishers, jury verdicts are selected by media appeal and the exigencies of reporter services, and information about settlements is filtered by the strategic considerations of parties.[32]

In assessing the performance of the jury as a source of signals that regulate the litigotiation system, I assume that the jury and rival devices will be functioning in a system more or less like the one sketched here. I take these features as given for the present discussion of possible reform, although some features may be more malleable than others.

How does the jury fit into this system? The small fraction of cases that are tried by juries not only distributes a sizable portion of the compensation paid to plaintiffs but also provides the signals that influence the outcome of a vastly larger number of cases settled or abandoned without trial. In his classic study of automobile injury settlements, H. Laurence Ross found that the "basis of settlements in serious cases seems on both sides to be an estimate of the likely recovery of the claimant before a jury. . . . Both sides come to this estimate by comparing a given case in its many dimensions against other, similar, cases, that have gone to trial."[33] Reference to jury value was more attenuated in the evaluation of smaller, routine claims, where potential trial was rendered improbable by the transaction costs, but even here "the relevance of jury value [was] generally admitted."[34]

The relative importance of juries as transmitters of signals rather than as deciders of cases seems to have increased.[35] Filings and dispositions have increased more rapidly than jury trials.[36] Jury trials in the federal courts increased from 2,585 in 1961 to 4,294 in 1991 (table 3-1) but make up a declining portion of total terminations. The percentage of cases terminated by jury trial dropped from 5.1 percent in 1961 to 2.0 percent in 1991.[37] Although the evidence is spotty, there appears to be a comparable relative decline in cases terminated by jury trials in state courts.[38] But absolutely, there are more trials, more relevant markers and symbols, more information, and more problems of retrieving, collating, and interpreting these signals.

This minority of tried cases casts a major part of the law's shadow; however, the shadow is not simply the product of what juries do. It is affected by the process of creating and communicating and extracting knowledge about what juries do. The shadow depends on what the disputants, lawyers, judges, mediators, parties, potential parties, and so forth think juries will do. (The discussion here focuses on lawyers, who form the majority of those who self-consciously deploy jury knowledge, but the observations that follow apply, with appropriate modification, to others as well.) Presumably, their expectations are derived in some measure from what they think juries have done and their understanding of why. How are the responses—partly shrouded by secrecy—of a multitude of dispersed juries crystallized into usable knowledge?

Information about juries and the assumptions and theories that inform such assessments reaches legal actors through a number of channels.

Personal Experience

Lawyers rely on their own experience with juries. Because only a small portion of cases are tried, the fund of experience of settled cases is far larger than experience with tried cases. Recall that there are roughly twice as many lawyers as there were just twenty years ago, but there are probably not appreciably more civil jury trials. Because the profession has grown rapidly, lawyers are on the average younger and have fewer years of experience in practice.[39] Lawyers probably have, per capita, less experience with jury trials as participants. Assuming that there are more than 50,000 civil jury trials each year and assuming (generously) that each jury trial engages four lawyers, every lawyer would participate in a jury trial less than once in three years—if jury trials were evenly spread among lawyers, which of course they are not. But even trial specialists have a limited fund of first-hand jury experience. A recent survey found that the median career number of trials was fifty-one for a population of plaintiff and defense lawyers whose median involvement with litigation was fourteen years.[40] For all but a few lawyers, experience with juries is more mediated, more indirect, more vicarious. The shadow of the jury is viewed less through the lenses of personal experience and more through other media.[41]

Oral Culture

Probably the major medium through which the signals of jury propensities are transmitted remains the oral culture of the lawyers and other "regulars."[42] This culture includes a great deal of lore about juries and about particular kinds of jurors. Not much is known about the way that lawyers combine this with information from other sources.

This oral culture may be undergoing changes as the structure of law practice changes. There are many more lawyers; as noted earlier, they are younger and have fewer years of experience than their predecessors of twenty-five years ago; they practice in larger units, and more of them are more specialized. Since the number of those practicing in most localities and specialties has increased, it seems likely that more of their encounters with opposing lawyers are with lawyers not previously known to them. One might anticipate, then, that the oral culture would rely less on implicit understandings and reference to shared experience.

Judges and Other Settlement Brokers

Many trial judges have more experience with juries than all but a few lawyers. Over the past generation, judges have become more active in promoting settlements, which has come to be seen as a respectable and commendable part of judicial work.[43] Judges—and other court personnel such as magistrates, clerks, and special masters—have devised and adopted many innovative techniques for promoting settlements.[44] These efforts tend to be more intense when an eventual trial would be by jury because judges feel more inhibited about aggressive settlement efforts when they might end up trying the cases themselves.[45] Hence the settlement discourse of judges contains considerable lore about juries. Many judges are confident that they know "what a case is worth" and how juries will react to its various features.

However, judges' usable direct experience of civil juries may be limited. There are fewer than ten civil jury trials per judge annually in the federal system, and their features vary sufficiently to render elusive any useful generalizations. In any event, lawyers seem to welcome settlement promotion by judges. One poll of lawyers reported that 73 percent believed judges should push for settlements; only 20 percent were opposed.[46] Lawyers with cases in the four federal districts studied by Wayne Brazil overwhelmingly believed that such judicial intervention would significantly improve the prospects for achieving settlement; they especially approved judicial settlement efforts in jury matters and credited them with greater effectiveness in that setting.[47]

Intensified promotion of settlement by judges works a curious distortion of jury signals. More than thirty years ago Harry Kalven, noting the ability of the jury to blend conflicting considerations, observed that "the function of the jury in the end may be not to adjudicate the case, but, as it were, to settle it vicariously."[48] Today, judges eager to promote settlements undertake to provide what is in effect a vicarious jury verdict. This is formalized in the curious device known as a summary jury trial, in which a group of jurors drawn from the jury panel listens to summary presentations by both sides and provides an advisory response.[49] By cutting such corners as witness' testimony, the summary jury trial attempts to unlock early a genuine and direct jury signal. In judicial settlement conferences, on the other hand, judges often respond to comparably incomplete presentations by proffering their reading of what a jury might do. Such readings are based on the judge's experience, as lawyer and judge, with juries, garnished by an admixture of "jury knowledge" from various oral and published sources.

Another variant on these devices for delivering the jury signal is the voluntary jury-determined settlement, in which the parties have set limits on the range of the jury's award through a high-low agreement. The parties retain control over the process and the jury issues a binding verdict after an abbreviated trial. Reversing the sequence of the summary jury trial, here the jury makes the final cut within the parameters established by the settlement. But like the summary jury trial, the jury-determined settlement confines the jury's role to dispute settlement and attenuates its broader signaling function.[50]

Appellate Courts and Official Reporting

Some information about what juries do is carried in law reports, typically in opinions about jury awards that were challenged as excessive or not justifiable on the basis of the evidence. In the course of describing the leeways that trial judges and appellate courts will allow juries, these reports, and the legal publications summarizing and collating them, provide a picture of what juries do. Until the publication in the late 1980s of after-the-verdict research, these materials were the principal basis for ascertaining the relation of verdicts to actual payouts.[51]

Jury Verdict Reporting Services

National and local services compile and distribute information about jury verdicts. These services differ in scope, sources, comprehensiveness, detail, frequency, and depth of analysis. Local services approach comprehensive coverage, while the national Jury Verdict Research is more selective.[52] JVR aims to include "significant" or "important" verdicts, and it makes "every effort to collect reliable information on all million-dollar verdicts."[53] This selectivity, combined with its computational practices, means that JVR's portrayal of jury awards emphasizes the high end of the range.[54] Presumably these services are used differently by various participants in different kinds of cases. There are only a few glimmerings of the patterns of use. H. Laurence Ross found that jury verdict reports, routinely consulted by attorneys, "were seldom used by [insurance company] claims men [adjusters]." Daniels noted other uses of these reporters: by a judge, for example, to inform pre-trial conferences and by a lawyer to "cool out" overly optimistic clients.[55]

Specialized Trade Sources

These sources, including handbooks, specialized litigation reporters, practitioner journals, continuing education seminars and other presentations range from coverage that is more technical and systematic than the jury verdict services to presentations that are only a step removed from the informal oral culture of lawyers. One subcategory of particular interest is the flow of information, written and oral, along the specialized networks for information sharing and, sometimes, for strategic coordination that have grown up among lawyers engaged with particular kinds of cases. Examples include the networks among plaintiffs' lawyers in asbestos, DES, and formaldehyde cases.[56]

Jury Consulting

In the past two decades jury research commissioned for use in individual cases has grown.[57] This research takes a number of forms, including community surveys and focus groups to identify favorable jurors and appealing themes for presentation; videotaping and interviewing jurors in mock trials; and shadow juries who observe trials and are debriefed daily.[58] Since use of these techniques is costly, they are confined mostly to sizable civil cases, but they have been used in some criminal trials involving rich or visible defendants. It has been estimated that in 1989 there were 300 businesses in the trial consultant field.[59] Lawyers who use them obtain new information, of varying quality, and presumably some of this spills back into lawyers' lore about juries.

Mass Media

One should be wary of underestimating the extent to which legal professionals draw on the mass media, not only for specific items of information, but by absorbing general orientations for interpreting such information. Current discourse about the litigation explosion and the liability crisis, for example, displays a complex linkage between mass media and presentations in specialist forums. Thus "horror stories," often originating with professionals, are popularized by the mass media and return to be incorporated in discourse among professionals.[60] Even purportedly analytic findings may be adopted uncritically from the media.[61] The media therefore help determine which aspects of legal activity languish in obscurity and which gain wide currency and are used to interpret the legal world.[62] Daniels points out that the media, "especially the national media, and legal elites rely on each other and on the national [jury verdict] reporters for information. This leads to an emphasis on the unusual cases and those with high awards, which then are treated as if they are representative of all cases."[63] Media influence varies from setting to setting: for legal professionals, as for others, general estimates of conditions will more closely track media accounts than will their judgments in familiar contexts.[64]

Popular Culture

Lawyers and other civil justice regulars share in the popular culture about juries—the beliefs and expectations about juries that circulate among nonprofessionals. Fed by the mass media on one side and the lawyers' oral culture on the other, the popular legal culture carries stories and adages about juries' role and performance. It is not known how much participation in more specialized occupational discourse displaces these popular perceptions.[65]

Research

Research such as that of the University of Chicago Jury Project, psychological studies of jury decisionmaking, and the reports of the Institute for Civil Justice is creating a systematic and cumulative portrait of jury behavior. This constitutes a kind of learning about juries that had not previously been available. Results of this research can be expected to feed back through specialist presentations and mass media into the pool of knowledge employed by various legal actors.[66]

The legal world as a whole has opened up remarkably in recent years. We have enormously expanded our knowledge of the world of American law since the days of the University of Chicago Jury Project. A tradition of sustained, systematic, cumulative research has been institutionalized in universities, research institutes, journals, and scholarly associations. A richer, more detailed picture of legal institutions also comes from more detailed, intrusive, investigative reporting about law in the general press, and the emergence of a new kind of trade press within the legal world.[67]

Barriers of secrecy have fallen. Core legal activities are more accessible—as dramatized by laws mandating open meetings, the Freedom of Information Act, and televised courtroom proceedings. The old presumptions of confidentiality have given way to a presumption favoring free flow of information: thus the growth of the practice of permitting jurors to be interviewed after the verdict and the occasional court-sponsored debriefing.[68] In 1955, after the Chicago jury researchers were censured for tape-recording actual jury deliberations with judicial and counsel permission, over thirty jurisdictions enacted prohibitions of jury tapping.[69] In contrast, in 1986 the filming and television broadcast of an actual jury deliberation passed with little comment.[70] Exposure that is unremarkable now was unthinkable just a generation ago. Everything points to overcoming the barriers that made research with real juries forbidding.

Conclusion

As the structures of professional life are altered, the sources of information about juries are changing. With fewer jury trials relative to the total number of cases and to the number of lawyers, lawyers have less direct personal experience with juries; new channels of information proliferate, making available a flow that is both richer and harder to interpret. Improved education, greater specialization, the nationalization of law practice, the upgrading of the plaintiffs' bar—all change the ways in which this information is processed. The arrival of voluminous and detailed systematic research on juries means that there is both more good and more bad jury information around. To their skill in doping out juries, lawyers now must add skill in doping out research.

The Quality of "Jury Knowledge"

In visualizing the role of the jury in the litigation process, I have had recourse to familiar metaphors: the iceberg or pyramid of cases, of which fully adjudicated cases form the visible peak, and the idea that most cases are resolved by bargaining in the shadow of the jury. Each implies that throughout the pyramid or realm of shadows the construction of cases and the negotiation of settlements are guided by the visible stratum of authoritative decisions, including those of juries. This image of hierarchic control is typically reinforced by assumptions that legal actors are rational, resource-maximizing decisionmakers, that they possess accurate knowledge of what juries and judges might do, and that these expectations dominate or control their actions. Thus, with adjustments for the inevitable noise and for transaction costs, the bargaining process accurately transmits the authoritative decisions in a few cases into outcomes in the vast majority of them. In this model of hierarchic control, if outcomes at the base of the iceberg appear arbitrary or capricious, the suspicion arises that these qualities infect the decisionmaker at the top—in this instance, the jury.

Is the hierarchic control model accurate? Does the process produce outcomes that accurately reflect what juries would do? How much distortion is present? The literature provides only a few tantalizing hints. Patricia Danzon, who is sanguine about the rationality of participants and the efficiency of the tort system, estimates that "some 39 to 53 percent of [medical malpractice] claims that are dropped [without payment] would in fact have won if pressed to verdict" and 23 to 43 percent of claims that received a settlement would not have won at verdict.[71] She presents these estimates as evidence that there are stable and predictable relations between potential verdicts and settlement outcomes. The presence of false negatives and false positives on such a scale is troubling. It suggests that the signals provided by verdicts are accompanied by a tremendous amount of noise or are overwhelmed by other factors.

Very little is known about the process by which information about juries is disseminated and images and beliefs formed, and about how these interact with other factors in the settlement process. Danzon's aggregate analysis may be supplemented by several studies that illuminate the way jury knowledge is used in the evaluation of individual cases.

A provocative experiment conducted by Gerald Williams dramatically showed the complexity and variability of the process of translating information about what juries do into assessments of what a case is worth. Williams reported that he

obtained the cooperation of 40 practicing lawyers in Des Moines, Iowa, who agreed to be divided into 20 pairs and to prepare and undertake settlement negotiations in a personal injury case. Approximately two weeks in advance of the negotiations, the attorneys were randomly assigned to represent either the plaintiff or the defendant (as counsel for the insurance company). Attorneys assigned to represent the plaintiff were given identical case files, as were attorneys assigned to the defense. Under the facts, it was assumed the case arose in Iowa, Iowa law applied, and if the case went to trial it would be tried to a jury in Des Moines, Iowa. To assure comparability of predicted jury awards, photocopies of comparable jury awards from the Des Moines area were included in the case files for both sides, [and] participating lawyers were informed that results of the negotiations would be published, with attorney names attached, among the participants at the workshop. This meant the attorneys had their professional reputations riding on the outcomes.[72]

After the attorneys negotiated their settlements, fourteen of the twenty

Table 3-8. *Results of Experimental Negotiation by Des Moines Attorneys*

Attorney pair	Plaintiff's opening demand	Defendant's opening demand	Settlement
1.	$ 32,000	$10,000	$18,000
2.	50,000	25,000	No settlement
3.	675,000	32,150	95,000
4.	110,000	3,000	25,120
5.	Not reported	Not reported	15,000
6.	100,000	5,000	25,000
7.	475,000	15,000	No settlement
8.	180,000	40,000	80,000
9.	210,000	17,000	87,000
10.	350,000	48,500	61,000
11.	87,500	15,000	30,000
12.	175,000	50,000	No settlement: narrowed to $137,000–$77,000
13.	97,000	10,000	57,500
14.	100,000	. . .	56,875
		Average settlement:	47,318

Source: Gerald R. Williams, *Legal Negotiations and Settlement* (West, 1983), p. 7.

pairs were willing to submit a signed statement of results. Williams gives us the striking results in table 3-8.

Both demands and outcomes ranged widely among these experienced lawyers, who were equipped with the same information about jury verdicts. Although one can imagine various threats to the validity of these results—for example, sampling bias or varying amounts of experience with personal injury cases—they nevertheless strongly suggest that information about what juries have done in "comparable cases" can interact with other factors to produce great variation in lawyers' responses to a case.

The amount of variance in Williams's experiment may be accentuated by two departures from real life. Although Williams's subjects conscientiously applied themselves to the files, they may have curtailed the usual practice of consultation, declining to burden colleagues with a simulation. If so, the situation involved a shift for many participants from colleague consultation to jury verdict reports as the primary basis for case valuation. Could it be that the former would generate greater consensus on valuation than the latter?

Another important element missing in the Williams's simulation was the alternative of the trial. In a real life bargaining situation, the alternative to successful settlement negotiations is a trial, viewed by most lawyers most of the time as a costly, risky, disruptive, and onerous undertaking. In the simulation the risk of this outcome was absent. The only penalty for failure to settle was a possible and marginal loss of face before the researcher. With the sanction for failure thus reduced, many lawyers may have been inclined to act more optimistically, exposing themselves to greater risk of disagreement than when a situation contained real sanctions for failure to agree.

The "trial as the alternative" element was very much present in Philip Hermann's early 1960s study, which compared verdicts in 443 back and neck injury cases with the final demands and offers of plaintiffs and defendants. Only one-sixth of the demands and offers fell within 25 percent of the verdict. Hermann concluded that "the guessing is equally wild on the part of both attorneys and the insurance companies."[73]

Douglas Rosenthal's analysis of the settlement of personal injury cases in New York in the 1960s retains the "same case" quality of the simulation, while providing a realistic context and comparison with the real world outcome. Five experts were asked to estimate what each of fifty-nine actual settled cases was worth in terms of settlement at various stages and jury award. Panelists tended to agree about the relative value of the cases. But Rosenthal observed that the "considerable variation among panelists with respect to each case does not accord with the widespread assumption that experts will tend to reach a consensus on the value of any particular case."[74] The panel average was then compared to the actual settlement. Actual settlements ranged from more than twice the panel consensus to just one-sixth of it. The median recovery was about 75 percent of the panel evaluation for the corresponding stage. About 40 percent of recoveries were for less than two-thirds of the panel valuation.[75]

What are we to make of this persistent and sizable variability and error in lawyers' readings of potential outcomes? Is it the result of the capriciousness of juries? Or does it point to problems in the formation and use of knowledge about juries? Or do the sources of error lie outside juries in other features of the litigation process?

Contemporary critics of the jury blame this disarray on the capriciousness and unpredictability of the jury.[76] But one should take pause, for the Institute for Civil Justice studies, Danzon's study, and others provide evidence of massive stability and consistency in jury decisionmaking. This steadiness is particularly impressive in view of the selection factors that deliver to juries only the most difficult-to-decide cases and the increased diversity of the juries themselves. Over the past generation, there has been a striking change in the composition of juries as jury rolls have expanded by the inclusion of more women and minorities, and by the curtailment of automatic or easy excusal for various occupational groups.[77]

Yet there is a widespread perception that juries are less stable and predictable than they once were. Unlike many such perceptions of decline, this one may have some foundation. It may be that jury stability has been compromised by the innovation of using smaller juries and less demanding decision rules,[78] practices guaranteed to produce greater variability in jury verdicts.[79] Although there is some uncertainty about the magnitude of such effects, it may well be that it is sufficient to aggravate the sense of unpredictability and danger that besets players in the liability game.

Even complete and accurate information about what juries have done would be very difficult to apply, since everything depends on judgments of similarity and difference in the cases and estimates of the range of jury variation in responding to them. In fact, the information received through the various channels is incomplete, conflicting, and of very mixed quality. And the daunting task of interpretation is rendered especially perilous by features of the setting in which this information is generated and used.

The literature of cognitive psychology catalogs a number of factors that lead to biased inferences and judgments about uncertain events.[80] For example, decisionmakers often ignore relevant baseline information, misattributing representativeness to data. The frequency of easily remembered events is exaggerated, leading to overestimation of risk from publicized hazards relative to less visible ones.[81] "Vivid information, that is, concrete, sensory and personally relevant information, may have a disproportionate impact on beliefs and inferences."[82] Furthermore, biased receptiveness to confirming evidence makes people excessively confident of the accuracy of their knowledge.[83] It has been suggested that these cognitive infirmities afflict juries and judges.[84] They seem especially applicable to the users of jury knowledge, who draw conclusions about the characteristics of large populations on the basis of incomplete and biased samples.

Using jury knowledge is a complex interpretive undertaking, involving assessments of the comparability of earlier and later cases, of the location of specific verdicts along the range of expectable jury responses, and of the scope, slope, and speed of trends in jury behavior. It is an undertaking ideally suited for the appearance of the kinds of flawed intuitive judgment described in the cognitive psychology literature. Even those in possession of a great deal of accurate information may make spurious inferences about the patterns of jury response.

The setting in which jury knowledge is used lacks some of the checks that might minimize these cognitive slips. Bargaining in the shadow of jury verdicts involves constant estimates of imponderables, and only intermittent opportunities for feedback to check the accuracy of these estimates. Law and economics scholars liken litigation decisions to investment decisions, such as the decision to purchase or sell stock, the accuracy of which can be checked against changes in the market price. Because most cases end in settlement, however, the accuracy of the great majority of readings by legal actors are never tested. Like the participants in Williams's mock negotiations, each negotiator can go away thinking that he or she performed well—an impression that other actors have a strategic interest in fostering. The opportunities for learning are quite skewed. Lawyers' estimates that are excessively favorable to their own clients encounter challenge and testing more often than estimates that were too "pessimistic." Hence lawyers typically experience "correction" only at the optimistic end of the scale.[85] Because the feedback is biased, the accumulation of experience does not improve the accuracy of the readings.[86]

The distortions that result from the micropolitics of settlement interact with distortions that result from the social organization of jury knowledge.[87] A number of mutually reinforcing factors conspire to institutionalize the overestimation of jury awards. Plaintiffs' lawyers exaggerate the size of claims for tactical and promotional purposes, especially in tort cases. Recoveries are only a fraction of demands.[88] Large demands are newsworthy—as are large verdicts—but plaintiff losses and reductions of awards are rarely news. Widely circulated horror stories recount, with fictitious embellishments, ludicrous claims and outlandishly large awards.[89] The market for tales of stonewalling resistance and Scrooge-like offers is more restricted. Stephen Daniels found that the national jury verdict reporters tended to replicate and feed the bias of the popular press: "All are highly selective and the picture they present is biased toward the unusual situation and the large award (the ones that attract attention); and for some . . . there is a very real plaintiff victory bias because of the reliance on . . . lawyer self-reporting of cases."[90]

Skewed feedback and media bias interact to produce systematic overestimation of the frequency and magnitude of jury verdicts not only in wider publics but among those whose attentiveness or expertise might be thought to make them more accurate observers. Overestimation of recoveries is found among lawyers generally and among experienced trial specialists as well as among doctors and legislators.[91] There is some suggestive evidence that judges tend to overestimate the amounts that juries will award.[92] One experienced observer, the head of Jury Verdict Research and a former personal injury defense lawyer, reported a similar tendency among insurers:

> Representing insurance carriers, it has always surprised me how the evaluations of value of similar injury claims varied so widely among different companies, even for claims which they see with frequency, such as cervical strain. Of course, all claim executives believe their evaluations are sound because they have been evaluating claims for many years. Their "experience" may be simply repeating the same evaluation philosophy—often far from the reality of what juries are really awarding. Unfortunately for their companies, they often believe that juries award larger verdicts than they really do. I am continually amazed at the numerous settlements for far greater amounts than could be reasonably expected for a similar case by a jury. . . . It is obvious that the insurance carrier's representatives were influenced by the high verdict awards reported by the news media.[93]

The presence of systematic misperceptions of jury performance is indirectly but dramatically displayed in Kevin Clermont's and Theodore Eisenberg's recent analysis of differences in outcomes between judge and jury trials. Comparing outcomes of cases tried to judges and to juries in federal district courts from 1979 to 1989, they found that, contrary to the lore of lawyers and observers, plaintiffs won a higher portion of the cases tried before judges. They explain this result by the skewed mix of cases that reach judges and juries, which is in turn driven by "misinformed bargaining" based on "persistent misperceptions" of the characteristics of juries as decisionmakers. These misperceptions persist because they draw on enduring cultural stereotypes; evidence that could be used to refine them is difficult to assemble and assess; and "many lawyers prefer to rely on personal experience and anecdote."[94]

Maintaining the Integrity of the Legal Process

The costs and disadvantages of the jury—expense, administrative cumbrousness, majoritarian bias, variance, inconsistency, blurry signals—might be thought to argue in favor of letting some other decisionmakers—judges or arbitrators or bureaucrats—make the determinations presently entrusted to juries. But such a conclusion can follow only from a comparative analysis of institutional alternatives.[95] It is not sufficient to ascertain that juries have deficiencies as well as virtues; one must weigh those against the virtues and deficiencies of the likely alternative institutions. Unfortunately, less is known about the performance of those alternatives than about juries, so that a comprehensive systematic comparison is not possible.

Nevertheless there is some evidence that the cognitive disarray that pervades our system of litigotiation is not traceable to the fact that the signals are broadcast by juries rather than professional decisionmakers. Several studies of settings in which decisionmakers were not juries but judges portray a similar regime of indistinct and distorted signals that are often lost or misread. For example, studies of personal injury settlements in England, where there are no juries in such cases, show a process pervaded by a sense of uncertainty about what judges will do.[96] In a revealing American study, Howard Erlanger, Elizabeth Chambliss, and Marygold Melli conducted in-depth interviews with thirty lawyers involved in twenty-five settled cases of divorce involving minor children in Dane County, Wisconsin. Regarding child support and property divisions, they observed, "Several of the lawyers we interviewed report that they have difficulty discerning court standards and that they cannot predict the outcomes of court processes. . . . Even the lawyers in our sample who do think there are set standards and who do say they can predict outcomes differ in their opinion of the content of those court standards; obviously, they cannot all be correct."[97] Unclear signals about outcomes can flourish when decisions are entirely in the hands of professionals. Departure from the orderly hierarchy conveyed by the pyramid or iceberg images with their suggestion that the "visible cap" of verdicts "controls" the larger settlement arena is not necessarily a function of the presence of the jury. That is, legal actors read jury signals badly not because juries are bad signalers but because the signals in many sectors of the litigotiation system are blurred and distorted by the cognitive, contextual, and media biases reviewed in the previous section.

In any event, comparisons of costs are incomplete without consideration of the corresponding benefits. Do juries have advantages that commend them over professional decisionmakers, whether judges or bureaucrats or arbitrators? I shall put aside arguments about the role of the civil jury in the larger political system (by providing civic education and by legitimizing the judicial process) in favor of arguments for the more proximate effects of the jury on the litigotiation process itself.

The shape of that process is invisibly but massively influenced by the presence of the jury institution. The use of the jury requires a concentrated trial rather than a discontinuous one.[98] The tendency of American civil procedure toward diffusion into serial proceedings—discovery, motions, hearings, pretrial conferences, and so forth—is limited by the exigencies of physically assembling and insulating the jury to hold a concentrated, continuous trial.[99] This in turn radiates influence back to earlier stages of the process. For example, since there can be no interruptions to pursue new evidentiary leads, all potentially relevant information must be gathered beforehand to permit uninterrupted presentation within the fixed time frame of the continuous trial.

The presence of the trial as an uninterrupted plenary event requiring a closure of case development, massive commitment of resources, and acceptance of risks by all actors, makes it a formidable threat. It is a threat that is difficult to use but it drives the bargaining that lies at the heart of the litigotiation system.[100]

The costs of the jury are associated with its amateurism and its transience, but these are also the source of important virtues. The jury is lay or amateur in two senses. Its members are not professionals or experts who possess special knowledge of legal norms or of the realm of facts in question. Nor do jurors decide cases for a living: they are transients who remain citizens rather than workers in the litigation shop, and they don't do it recurrently or often.[101] Jurors have neither a communicated tradition of work to draw upon nor a web of reciprocal relations with other actors in the system. Unlike those who work in the system, they have no continuing relations with other actors to maintain nor any shared patterns of accommodating the law to institutional exigencies. The absence of experience and continuity means they do not become jaded or lapse into the typifications and routines that envelop the regulars.[102]

By providing fresh individualized responses impervious to customary patterns and knowing expectations, the jury helps preserve the decision process from being swallowed up by the surrounding bargaining process. Marygold Melli, Howard Erlanger, and Elizabeth Chambliss observed that in the child support arena they explored (where there were no juries) there was a

question of who is in fact casting the shadow of the law. The expectation of what a particular judge would set for child support had to be determined from the cases in his or her court—most of which involved settlements. The shadow of the law, therefore, was cast by the agreements of the parties. It seems that, rather than a system of bargaining in the shadow of the law, divorce may well be one of adjudication in the shadow of bargaining.[103]

The regime they describe features a spiral of attribution in which supposedly autonomous decisionmakers take cues from other actors who purport to be mirroring the decisions of the former.[104] A similar dissolution of legal standards is evident in Janet Cooper Alexander's description of securities class actions as "a world where all cases settle." In such a world, "it may not even be possible to base settlements on the merits because lawyers may not be able to make reliable estimates of expected trial outcomes. . . . There is nothing to cast a shadow in which the parties can bargain."[105] Judges preside over routine settlements that reflect not legal standards but the strategic position of the repeat players:

> because securities class actions rarely if ever go to trial, settlement judges, like lawyers, have little relevant experience to draw on other than their knowledge of settlements in similar cases . . . their role becomes not to increase the accuracy of settlements, but to provide an impetus to reach *some* settlement. In the absence of information about how similar cases fared at trial, settlement judges could be an important force in maintaining a "going rate" approach to settlements.[106]

Judith Resnik found, in the prevalence of consent decrees in which judges in effect delegate official power to the negotiators before the bench, another example of the supposedly central and independent formal process of adjudication becoming subordinated to the supposedly penumbral process of bargaining that surrounds it.[107]

Juries impede the collapse of individualized decisionmaking into the stereotyping, cooperation and trade-offs of routine processing that "favors status quo distributions of wealth and power, gives repeat players an advantage, and encourages stereotypical settlements in which bargainers smooth over or ignore the idiosyncratic features of individual claims."[108] In doing so, the jury helps retain the salience of the substantive morality embodied in the law—and helps align that morality with the emergent moral sense of the community or communities.[109] In a system in which issues of culpability are typically effaced in settlement and routine processing, it is a good thing that at the end of the day there is recourse to a forum that can respond to the particulars in terms of moral conviction undiluted by the constraints of institutional priorities or career concerns.

From the point of view of regulating the litigotiation process, the major offset to a net increase in blurrier signals or other disadvantages of the jury is the advantage of a fresh response less mediated by institutional concerns and more resonant with the emerging moral sense of community. I make no claim to know the magnitude of these beneficial effects, but it is my sense as an observer of the process that they are sufficiently in evidence that other means of addressing the disadvantages of the jury should be tried before measures that reduce its incidence or its decisional mandate.

I have argued that much of the apparent capriciousness and unpredictability that disturbs the jury's critics has its source not only in the performance of the jury but in the general features of the litigotiation system, including the way that "jury knowledge" is organized and used. The jury's contribution to these discomforts of the system can be addressed by several kinds of measures:

—structural changes to reduce variance, such as larger juries with strict decision rules, and

—reforms that improve the quality of jury response, such as permitting note-taking and questioning by jurors, providing understandable instructions and better information to make damage calculations

Beyond these it is important to upgrade the quality of jury knowledge by breaking the feedback loops that project distorted signals. Since less is known about jury knowledge than about juries, ideas about how to accomplish this are necessarily tentative.

—One line that seems promising is to improve the collection and compilation of information about juries and to develop reliable indicators to trace the contours and trends of jury decisions.

—Another is to develop knowledge about the way that actors construct "jury knowledge" out of this information and the way they employ this knowledge in the litigotiation process.[110]

—The simulation techniques, with their capacity for controlled variation, that have played such an important role in research on jury decisionmaking, may be equally fruitful in teaching us about jury knowledge. Imagine, for example, an experimental "duplicate bridge" negotiation between lawyers, like that devised by Williams in which information on the actions of previous juries was systematically varied.[111]

—One particularly significant inquiry into the impact of jury knowledge is the effect of the jury knowledge that jurors themselves bring into the process and the problem of upgrading or constraining that knowledge.

Jurors themselves may be affected by views of what jurors generally do and by other information about the civil justice system. We are only beginning to get a sense of the complex effects of this feedback loop on patterns of jury awards. A 1986 survey of 213 Seattle jurors found that they greatly overestimated the frequency of million dollar damage awards and that the greater they believed the frequency of million dollar awards to be, the *higher* the damages they awarded in a mock trial. Paradoxically, most of these jurors attributed their sense that jury awards were too high to the news media while agreeing that the media tended to exaggerate the number of high awards.[112] Interviewing 141 Delaware jurors who had sat in tort cases involving a business, Valerie Hans and William Lofquist concluded that the jurors they interviewed were "quite cognizant of other civil juries, real and apocryphal. Their concerns about deep pockets, the litigation crisis, and the integrity of plaintiffs were implicitly and explicitly linked to the presumed excesses of antecedent juries . . . jurors often viewed themselves as responsible for returning moderation and good judgment to the civil justice system."[113] But in this study, stronger juror perceptions of a litigation explosion were correlated with *lower* awards.[114]

For a long time the policy discourse about civil justice proceeded at some remove from the formation of the beliefs and understandings that jurors injected into the system. One of the distinctive features of the present period of heated concern about civil justice is the systematic attempt to harness jury sentiments to stances in the policy debate.[115] Once this loop has been established, it raises the tricky questions whether, to preserve the integrity of the jury as a regulatory mechanism, jurors should be given an accurate picture of what earlier juries have done, or whether the ban on communicating with jurors should be extended to restrict propaganda aimed to influence the jury pool.[116]

I think that an emphasis on restricting propaganda aimed at jurors is misguided. Even apart from First Amendment problems, it strikes me that such targeted commercial speech is only a small part of the system of information about the civil justice system. A far larger and more influential stream runs through the media and the popular culture that feeds on them. The real problem is not that there are distorted pictures out there but that there is so little reliable, comprehensive, and comprehensible stuff to compete with them. Knowledge about civil justice matters is pitifully thin and inadequate. Legal professionals, as guardians of the civil justice system, have a collective responsibility to promote an appreciation of its accomplishments and its problems. This entails a joint responsibility to contribute to a cumulative and reliable body of knowledge about the system. We have come a long way with research on the jury as decisionmaker; it is time to begin to seriously to address our ignorance of the larger role of the jury as regulator of the litigotiation process. This requires that we build institutions to monitor and understand that process.

Notes

1. See Marc Galanter, "The Civil Jury as Regulator of the Litigation Process," *University of Chicago Legal Forum*, vol. 1990, pp. 201–71, especially p. 202.

2. Technically, they influence the outcome of cases by deciding certain disputed "issues of fact" in a way that is binding on the trial judge and appellate courts, subject to limited powers to set aside or modify the verdict because of prejudice, excessiveness, or being against the weight of the evidence—and subject to the power of the parties to negotiate a postverdict settlement with an eye to the possibilities just mentioned.

3. Numerically, trials provide only a minority of authoritative decisions by courts. Analyzing 1,649 cases in federal and state courts in five localities, Herbert M. Kritzer found that 7 percent terminated through trial, but another 24 percent terminated through some other form of adjudication—for example, arbitration, dismissal on the merits, or decision on a significant motion that led to settlement. See *The Justice Broker: Lawyers and Ordinary Litigation* (Oxford University Press, 1990), pp. 73–76. Default judgments have been omitted from this computation.

4. Harry Kalven, Jr., and Hans Zeisel, *The American Jury* (Little, Brown, 1966), pp. 31–32.

5. The "bargaining in the shadow" image is set out in Robert H. Mnookin and Lewis Kornhauser, "Bargaining in the Shadow of the Law: The Case of Divorce," *Yale Law Journal*, vol. 88 (April 1979), pp. 950–97; the elaboration can be found in Marc Galanter, "Justice in Many Rooms: Courts, Private Ordering and Indigenous Law," *Journal of Legal Pluralism and Unofficial Law*, vol. 19 (1981), pp. 1–48.

6. Compare the persistent reports from civil law and socialist countries with "mixed" tribunals that lay judges are dominated by the professionals: Robert M. Hayden, "Who Wants Informal Courts? Paradoxical Evidence from a Yugoslav Attempt to Create Workers' Courts for Labor Cases," *American Bar Foundation Research Journal*, vol. 1985 (Spring 1985), pp. 293–314; Gerhard Casper and Hans Zeisel, "Lay Judges in the German Criminal Courts," *Journal of Legal Studies*, vol. 1 (January 1972), pp. 135–92; Kalman Kulcsar, *People's Assessors in the Courts: A Study on the Sociology of Law*, trans. Patricia Austin (Budapest: Akademiai Kiado, 1982); Erhard Blankenburg, Ralf Rogowski, and Siegfried Schonholz, "Phenomena of Legalization: Observations in a German Labour Court," *European Yearbook in Law and Sociology*, vol. 1978 (The Hague: Martinus Nijhoff Publishers, 1979), p. 33; and John P. Richert, *West German Lay Judges: Recruitment and Representatives* (University Presses of Florida, 1983).

7. Comprehensive data on jury trials in courts of general jurisdiction are available for six states for 1988. Jury trials as a percentage of overall civil dispositions ranged from 0.7 percent in Hawaii to 1.5 percent in Texas (see table 3-2).

8. In every state court system for which 1988 statewide data are available, juries were

found most frequently in tort cases—from 1.6 percent of tort dispositions in the California Supreme Court to 4.7 percent in the Florida Circuit Court (see table 3-5). These tort juries make up a smaller portion of all the tort *claims* disposed of, since many claims do not show up as filings. Verdicts were returned in about 1 percent of a large sample of paid liability claims in automobile insurance cases in 1977. James K. Hammitt, and colleagues analyzed verdicts in a nationwide sample of over 20,000 automobile insurance claims closed with some payment by twenty-nine insurers during a two-week period in 1977. They report that "verdicts were returned in only about 200 cases." James K. Hammitt and others, *Automobile Accident Compensation* (Santa Monica: Rand Institute for Civil Justice, 1985), p. 753.

9. Patricia Munch Danzon reports that 7 percent of her sample of 6,000 malpractice claims closed in 1974 and 1976 were tried to verdict: *Medical Malpractice: Theory, Evidence, and Public Policy* (Harvard University Press, 1985), p. 32.

10. The estimate of annual civil jury trials is based on the following calculation. According to the National Center for State Courts there were 20,597 civil jury trials in 1988 in the courts of general jurisdiction in the twenty-four states (and the District of Columbia) for which data were available. This figure is rough because small claims trials are included in the totals of a few states, and a few others leave out property and other case categories. But if we assume that these more or less cancel one another out and that these jurisdictions, which taken together contained 43 percent of the nation's population, were representative, there would have been a total of 47,900 jury trials in state courts of general jurisdiction in 1988. In that year the federal courts held 5,920 jury trials, so the grand total would be 53,820 plus the jury trials held in courts of limited jurisdiction. Compare John Guinther's estimate of 45,000 to 75,000 civil jury trials annually in state courts: *The Jury in America* (Facts on File, 1988), p. 167. For state courts of general jurisdiction, see *State Court Caseload Statistics: Annual Report 1990* (Williamsburg, Va.: National Center for State Courts, 1992), p. 10. The comparable figures for 1988 were roughly 250,000 in the federal courts and 8 million in the state courts. I am indebted to Dr. Brian J. Ostrom of the National Center for State Courts for his helpfulness in analyzing the state data.

11. Property cases are the scene of the next largest, but far smaller, number of jury trials. In the six state courts of general jurisdiction for which data are available, property jury trials range from 0.3 percent to 10.2 percent of all jury trials (table 3-3). For six states a rough picture can be assembled of how all civil jury trials are distributed by subject matter (table 3-2).

12. F. Patrick Hubbard, "'Patterns' in Civil Jury Verdicts in the State Circuit Courts of South Carolina: 1976–85," *South Carolina Law Review*, vol. 38 (Summer 1987), pp. 699–754. Additional data from the study may be found in F. Patrick Hubbuard, *South Carolina Civil Jury Verdict Research Project: Report on Findings* (South Carolina Law Institute, 1986). Unlike the studies by the Institute of Civil Justice and by Stephen Daniels, which rely on published jury verdict reports, and unlike the reports by the National Center for State Courts, which are aggregates derived from recorded filing data, the South Carolina study was based on examination of individual case files in the county courthouses.

13. The federal figures are for terminations; but some state figures and the ICJ studies are based on a count of all jury trials commenced and include dropouts—directed verdicts, dismissals, settlements—and hung juries. See Audrey Chin and Mark A. Peterson, *Deep Pockets, Empty Pockets: Who Wins in Cook County Jury Trials* (Santa Monica: Rand Institute for Civil Justice, 1985), pp. 21ff.

14. Michael J. Saks, "Do We Really Know Anything about the Behavior of the Tort Litigation System—and Why Not?" *University of Pennsylvania Law Review*, vol. 140 (April 1992), p. 1235.

15. Valerie P. Hans and Neil Vidmar, *Judging the Jury* (Plenum Press, 1986); Valerie

P. Hans, "Jury Decision Making," in Dorothy K. Kagehiro and William S. Laufer, eds., *Handbook of Psychology and Law* (Springer-Verlag, 1992), pp. 56–76; Reid Hastie, Steven D. Penrod, and Nancy Pennington, *Inside the Jury* (Harvard University Press, 1983); and Saul M. Kassin and Lawrence S. Wrightsman, *The American Jury on Trial: Psychological Perspectives* (Bristol, Pa.: Hemisphere Publishing, 1988).

16. Michael J. Saks, *Small-group Decision Making and Complex Information Tasks* (Washington: Federal Judicial Center, 1981); Richard O. Lempert, "Civil Juries and Complex Cases: Let's Not Rush to Judgment," *Michigan Law Review*, vol. 80 (November 1981), pp. 68–132; and Christy A. Visher, "Juror Decision Making: The Importance of Evidence," *Law and Human Behavior*, vol. 11 (March 1987), pp. 1–17.

17. Harry Kalven, Jr., "The Dignity of the Civil Jury," *Virginia Law Review*, vol. 50 (October 1964), p. 1065. Jury verdicts were compared with responses of judges who were asked to report "how he would have decided the case had it been tried to him alone" (p. 1063).

18. Shari Seidman Diamond, "Order in the Court: Consistency in Criminal-Court Decisions," in C. James Scheirer and Barbara L. Hammonds, eds., *The Master Lecture Series: Psychology and the Law*, vol. 2 (Washington: American Psychological Association, 1983), pp. 119, 124–25.

19. Kevin M. Clermont and Theodore Eisenberg, "Trial by Jury or Judge: Transcending Empiricism," *Cornell Law Review*, vol. 77 (July 1992), pp. 1124–77. They compare outcomes of cases tried to judges and to juries in federal district courts from 1979 to 1989. I discuss their interpretation of these results later.

20. Chin and Peterson, *Deep Pockets, Empty Pockets*, p. 25.

21. Chin and Peterson, *Deep Pockets, Empty Pockets*, pp. 42–43, 44.

22. An interesting alternative to the deep pocket theory–that the public holds corporations to a higher standard of behavior than it does individuals and thus attributes to corporations inexcusable recklessness in situations where an individual would be judged less harshly—is suggested by Valerie P. Hans and H. David Ermann, "Responses to Corporate Versus Individual Wrong-doing," *Law and Human Behavior*, vol. 13 (June 1989), pp. 151–66.

23. Valerie P. Hans and William S. Lofquist, "Jurors' Judgments of Business Liability in Tort Cases: Implications for the Litigation Explosion Debate," *Law & Society Review*, vol. 26, no. 1 (1992), p. 101.

24. David B. Rottman, "Tort Litigation in the State Courts: Evidence from the Trial Court Information Network," *State Court Journal*, vol. 14 (Fall 1990), pp. 4–18.

25. Kalven, "The Dignity of the Civil Jury," p. 1065.

26. Ellen L. Rosen, "The View from the Bench: A National Law Journal Poll," *National Law Journal* (August 10, 1987), p. S8.

27. Louis Harris and Associates, Inc. for Aetna Life and Casualty, *Judges' Opinions on Procedural Issues: A Survey of State and Federal Trial Judges Who Spend at Least Half Their Time on General Civil Cases*, no. 874017 (1987), p. 87.

28. Kevin M. Clermont and Theodore Eisenberg, "Trial by Jury or Judge: Transcending Empiricism," *Cornell Law Review*, vol. 77 (July 1992), pp. 1124–77; and Neil Vidmar, "Medical Malpractice Juries," *Duke Law Magazine*, vol. 9 (Summer 1991), p. 12.

29. Elizabeth M. King and James P. Smith, *Computing Economic Loss in Cases of Wrongful Death* (Santa Monica, Calif.: Rand Institute for Civil Justice, 1988).

30. Saks, "Do We Really Know Anything," pp. 1235–37.

31. It is worth reminding ourselves that authoritative statements are not the only possible way officials can give such guidance—they can publish abstract essays or illustrative examples rather than case reports.

32. Lauren K. Robel, "The Myth of the Disposable Opinion: Unpublished Opinions and Government Litigants in the United States Courts of Appeals," *Michigan Law Review*,

vol. 87 (April 1989), pp. 940–62; William L. Reynolds and William M. Richman, "An Evaluation of Limited Publication in the United States Courts of Appeals: The Price of Reform," *University of Chicago Law Forum*, vol. 48 (Summer 1981), pp. 573–631; Daniel N. Hoffman, "Non-Publication of Federal Appellate Court Opinions," *Justice System Journal*, vol. 6 (Fall 1981), pp. 405–34; and Stephen Daniels, "Civil Juries, Jury Verdict Reporters, and the Going Rate," paper prepared for the 1986 annual meeting of the Law and Society Association.

33. H. Laurence Ross, *Settled Out of Court: The Social Process of Insurance Claims Adjustments* (Chicago: Aldine, 1970), pp. 114–15. Ross emphasizes that "jury value and settlement value are not the same thing," since the latter incorporates discounts for the costs and risks avoided. In his study, it was the claimant "who yields [the] discount for settlement" (p. 115). Ross's field work was conducted in the mid-1960s, so there is a question of whether the patterns he reported still obtain.

34. Ross, *Settled Out of Court*, p. 112. In his study of personal injury claims in New York City, Douglas E. Rosenthal reports that the "going values are based on prior settlements, recent jury verdicts obtained by the attorney and his associates in similar types of cases and some rules-of-the-game, such as the rule that a fair settlement in a strong case should not depart too greatly from a figure that reflects the victim's out-of-pocket expenses multiplied by three." *Lawyer and Client, Who's in Charge?* (N.Y.: Russell Sage Foundation, 1974), p. 36.

35. See, for example, Richard O. Lempert, "More Tales of Two Courts: Exploring Changes in the 'Dispute Settlement Function of Trial Courts,'" *Law & Society Review*, vol. 13 (Fall 1978), pp. 91–138, on the shift in mode of court contribution to dispute settlement.

36. Indeed, the absolute number of jury trials has fallen in at least some jurisdictions. Thus in San Francisco there were fewer than half as many jury trials in 1980-84 as in 1960–64. In Cook County the number of jury trials was about the same. Mark A. Peterson, *Civil Juries in the 1980s: Trends in Jury Trials and Verdicts in California and Cook County, Illinois* (Santa Monica: Rand Institute for Civil Justice, 1987), p. 6.

37. Administrative Office of the United States Courts, *Annual Report* (1940), p. 39; (1970), p. 245a; and (1991). This includes terminations "during or after trial," so it includes cases that were settled after trial had begun.

38. See, for example, Lawrence M. Friedman and Robert V. Percival, "A Tale of Two Courts: Litigation in Alameda and San Benito Counties," *Law & Society Review*, vol. 10 (Winter 1976), p. 288; Stephen Daniels, "Continuity and Change in Patterns of Case Handling: A Case Study of Two Rural Counties," *Law & Society Review*, vol. 19, no. 3 (1985), pp. 381–420; and Wayne McIntosh, "150 Years of Litigation and Dispute Settlement: A Court Tale," *Law & Society Review*, vol. 15, nos. 3–4 (1980-81), pp. 838–39. Compare Peterson, *Civil Juries in the 1980s*, p. 6.

39. "The median age of lawyers dropped from forty-six years in 1960 to thirty-nine years in 1980. Lawyers under thirty-six made up 24 percent of the lawyer population in 1960 and 39 percent in 1980." Barbara A. Curran, "American Lawyers in the 1980s: A Profession in Transition," *Law & Society Review*, vol. 20, no. 1 (1986), p. 23. Of all lawyers practicing in 1980, 42 percent had been admitted after 1970 (p. 25).

40. Defense Research Institute, *Civil Litigation in State Courts: Perspectives on the Process and Preferences for Reform* (Chicago: February 1992), section H, pp. 11–12.

41. However, the personal experience of a small minority of lawyers has been enriched in recent years through freer postverdict interviewing of jurors.

42. When asked how they arrived at their initial evaluation of their most recently resolved case, fewer than one-quarter of the respondents to an unpublished *Wisconsin Law Review* survey reported using jury verdict reports, while 70 percent relied heavily on consultations with other attorneys in their own firms. Report on file with the author.

43. Marc Galanter, "The Emergence of the Judge as a Mediator in Civil Cases," *Judicature*, vol. 69 (February-March 1986), pp. 257–62.

44. Marc Galanter, "A Settlement Judge, not a Trial Judge: Judicial Mediation in the United States," *Journal of Law & Society*, vol. 12 (Spring 1985), pp. 1–18. Data on the prevalence of judicial settlement activities are summarized on p. 7. The following discussion is in terms of judges' efforts to promote settlement, but applies with some adaptation to the other categories of intervenors as well.

45. For example, Judge Hubert L. Will counseled newly appointed judges, "I have no hesitation in rolling up my sleeves and going the whole way in an analysis of a jury case. I have some reservations about non-jury cases, but, if asked by counsel to participate, I will do so. You have to be more careful, and you have to indicate the possibility that you'll transfer the case to another judge for trial." Hubert L. Will, Robert R. Merhige, Jr., and Alvin B. Rubin, "The Role of the Judge in the Settlement Process," *Federal Rules Decisions*, vol. 75 (Sept. 13–18, 1976), p. 211.

46. Paul Reidinger, "The Litigation Boom," *American Bar Association Journal*, vol. 73 (February 1987), p. 37.

47. Wayne D. Brazil, *Settling Civil Suits: Litigators' Views About Appropriate Roles and Effective Techniques for Federal Judges* (Chicago: American Bar Association, 1985), pp. 40, 63, 73.

48. Harry Kalven, Jr., "The Jury, the Law, and the Personal Injury Damage Award," *Ohio State Law Journal*, vol. 19 (Spring 1958), p. 177.

49. Thomas D. Lambros and Thomas H. Shunk, "The Summary Jury Trial," *Cleveland State Law Review*, vol. 29 (1980), pp. 43–57; Thomas D. Lambros, "The Summary Jury Trial and Other Alternative Methods of Dispute Resolution: A Report to the Judicial Conference of the United States Committee on the Operation of the Jury System," January 1984, *Federal Rules Decisions*, vol. 103, pp. 461–518; and Thomas D. Lambros, "The Summary Jury Trial—An Alternative Method of Resolving Disputes," *Judicature*, vol. 69 (February–March 1986), pp. 286–90. Results are evaluated in M. Daniel Jacoubovitch and Carl M. Moore, *Summary Jury Trials in the Northern District of Ohio* (Washington: Federal Judicial Center, 1982); Richard Posner, "The Summary Jury Trial and Other Methods of Alternative Dispute Resolution: Some Cautionary Observations," *University of Chicago Law Review*, vol. 53 (Spring 1986), pp. 366–93; and James J. Alfini and others, *Summary Jury Trials in Florida: An Empirical Assessment* (Tallahassee: Florida Dispute Resolution Center, 1989).

50. Neil Vidmar and Jeffrey Rice, "Jury-Determined Settlements and Summary Jury Trials: Observations about Alternative Dispute Resolution in an Adversary Culture," *Florida State University Law Review*, vol. 19 (Summer 1991), pp. 89–103.

51. Reported appellate cases are an incomplete source of information about postverdict reductions because they give no information about trial court reductions that are not appealed or about settlements incorporating reductions.

52. Even local services seem to display some bias toward more complete reporting of tort cases than others. Studies based on verdict-reporting services consistently display a higher portion of tort juries than do official state statistics. Perhaps this reflects more user interest in tort cases, where verdicts might reveal recurrent jury propensities, than in contract cases, where damages are more likely to be driven by the particulars of the agreement in question.

53. Jury Verdict Research, *Injury Valuation: Current Award Trends*, vol. 4 (Solon, Ohio, 1986), p. 12. This is not to say that JVR collects only large verdicts. Philip J. Hermann, its president, reports that JVR collects data, mostly from clerks of court, on over 24,000 of an estimated 31,000 personal injury verdicts rendered each year. Telephone interview with Philip J. Hermann, May 11, 1990.

54. Stephen Daniels's study of jury verdicts, based on the local jury verdict services,

observes that "JVR's coverage is highly selective, reporting on what it determines to be precedent-setting verdicts." See Daniels, "Civil Juries," p. 6. See also A. Russell Localio, "Variations on $962,258: The Misuse of Data on Medical Malpractice," *Law, Medicine and Health Care*, vol. 13 (June 1985), pp. 126–28.

55. Ross, *Settled Out of Court*, p. 112; and Daniels, "Civil Juries," pp. 10–11.

56. See generally, Marc Galanter, "Lawyers' Litigation Networks," paper prepared for the Conference on Frontiers of Research on Litigation, September 20, 1985, University of Wisconsin.

57. The origin of so-called scientific jury selection is commonly considered the involvement of sociologist Jay Schulman in the 1972 conspiracy trial of the Berrigan brothers and other Vietnam War opponents. See Hans and Vidmar, *Judging the Jury*, p. 81. In a turnabout, Schulman worked for General Westmoreland in his libel suit against CBS. Emily Couric, "Jury Sleuths: In Search of the Perfect Panel," *National Law Journal*, vol. 8 (July 21, 1986), p. 34. The use of shadow juries dates from a 1977 IBM antitrust case: Stephen J. Adler, "Consultants Dope Out the Mysteries of Jurors for Clients Being Sued," *Wall Street Journal*, October 24, 1989, pp. A1, A10.

58. For a profile of these techniques and some of their practitioners, see Couric, "Jury Sleuths." For an assessment of their efficacy, see Hans and Vidmar, *Judging the Jury*, chap. 6; and Hastie, Penrod and, Pennington, *Inside the Jury*, chap. 7.

59. Adler, "Consultants Dope Out the Mysteries of Jurors." A year earlier it was reported that membership of the American Society of Trial Consultants had grown to 150 from 32 in 1982. Doron P. Levin, "Stretching the Limits of the Jury Consulting Game," *New York Times*, July 1, 1988, p. B9.

60. Compare Steven Brill and James Lyons, "Headnotes: The Not-So-Simple Crisis," *American Lawyer* (May 1986), pp. 1, 12–17; Fred Strasser, "1987 Focus on States: Both Sides Brace for Battle," *National Law Journal*, vol. 9 (February 16, 1987), pp. 1, 37, 39; and Robert M. Hayden, "The Cultural Logic of a Political Crisis: Common Sense, Hegemony, and the Great American Liability Insurance Famine of 1986," *Studies in Law, Politics and Society*, vol. 11 (1991), pp. 95–117. See also Stephen Daniels, "The Question of Jury Competence and the Politics of Civil Justice Reform: Symbols Rhetoric and Agenda-Building," *Law and Contemporary Problems*, vol. 52 (Autumn 1989), pp. 269–310. On the role of atrocity stories in legal policy discourse, see Marc Galanter, "Reading the Landscape of Disputes: What We Know and Don't Know (and Think We Know) about Our Allegedly Contentious and Litigious Society," *UCLA Law Review*, vol. 31 (October 1983), p. 64.

61. For example, a major law firm, preparing a report on the liability crisis on behalf of a coalition of "affected organizations," provided the following evidence that "defendants are being exposed to damage awards of increasing and unpredictable amounts. . . . The average verdict in both products liability and medical malpractice cases now exceeds one million dollars, according to preliminary studies by Jury Verdict Research, Inc. See "Sorry Your Policy is Canceled, *Time* 20 (Mar. 24, 1986)." Sidley & Austin, *The Need for Legislative Reform of the Tort System* (Chicago, May 1986), p. 32, note 47.

62. Thus, the media feature stories about the size of product liability judgments derived from JVR reports but omit the qualifications and shortcomings of the data. Compare Localio, "Variations on $962,258," p. 126.

63. Daniels, "Civil Juries," p. 17. Lawyers may be particularly susceptible to believing in this representativeness because legal education consists of a diet of unusual cases that are taken to be typical.

64. There is a whole tradition of research suggesting that media accounts influence societal-level judgments (that is, judgments about patterns and conditions in the larger community) more strongly than they influence personal-level judgment (that is, about the problems and risks that face the respondent). Tom R. Tyler and Fay Lomax Cook, "The

Mass Media and Judgments of Risk: Distinguishing Impact on Personal and Societal Level Judgments," *Journal of Personality and Social Psychology*, vol. 47 (October 1984), pp. 693–708. Thus, researchers have found that concern about crime as a public problem and personal fear of crime are often unrelated, and that judgments about personal risk are influenced primarily by personal experience and experiences conveyed through social networks, not by media reports of crime. Tom R. Tyler and Paul J. Levrakas, "Cognitions Leading to Personal and Political Behaviors: The Case of Crime," in Sidney Kraus and Richard M. Perloff, eds., *Mass Media and Political Thought: An Information Processing Approach* (Beverly Hills: Sage Publications, 1985). Reviewing the literature, Tyler concludes that "mass media reports of crime do not appear to be an important influence on fear of crime. Instead, fear appears to be generated primarily through personal victimization and the experiences of friends and neighbors." Tom R. Tyler, "Assessing the Risk of Crime Victimization: The Integration of Personal Victimization Experience and Socially Transmitted Information," *Journal of Social Issues*, vol. 40 (Spring 1984), p. 31. This same dissociation of social and personal levels of analysis may characterize the professionals who are the audience and source of mass media reports on litigation, juries, and so forth. Perhaps it is the mark of professionals to be able to use the relatively abstract societal-level information about the world in general to form estimates of risk in personal-level situations.

65. For a sense of the carryover of popular views into local legal culture, see David M. Engel, "The Oven Bird's Song: Insiders, Outsiders, and Personal Injuries in an American Community," *Law & Society Review*, vol. 18, no. 4 (1984), pp. 551–82.

66. It is often assumed that insurers, trade associations, or recurrent defendants are possessed of systematic portrayals of trends in jury behavior beyond the public domain knowledge referred to in the preceding discussion. Perhaps there is some closely guarded proprietary information of this type, but the only systematic information circulated under insurance industry auspices is in closed-claim studies. These are aggregate portraits of claims closed and do not contain any analyses of juries. It is my sense that the findings of ICJ's jury research were as new to insurers as to others in the system.

67. Marc Galanter, "The Legal Malaise; or, Justice Observed," *Law & Society Review*, vol. 19, no. 4 (1985), pp. 537–56.

68. Comment, "Public Disclosures of Jury Deliberations," *Harvard Law Review*, vol. 96 (February 1983), pp. 886–906.

69. Kalven and Zeisel, *The American Jury*, pp. vi–vii.

70. Herzberg's *Inside the Jury Room*, broadcast on PBS "Frontline," April 11, 1986.

71. Danzon, *Medical Malpractice*, p. 50; compare p. 43. The derivation of these estimates is explained in Patricia Munch Danzon and Lee A. Lillard, *The Resolution of Medical Malpractice Claims' Modeling the Bargaining Process* (Santa Monica, Calif.: Rand Institute for Civil Justice, 1982), p. 47.

72. Gerald R. Williams, *Legal Negotiations and Settlement* (West, 1983), p. 3.

73. Philip J. Hermann, "Predicting Verdicts in Personal Injury Cases," *Insurance Law Journal*, no. 475 (August 1962), pp. 505–17.

74. Rosenthal, *Lawyer and Client*, p. 202. The makeup of the panel and the method of securing evaluations are described on pp. 202–07.

75. Rosenthal, *Lawyer and Client*, pp. 38, 207.

76. See examples in Galanter, "Jury as Regulator," pp. 207–08.

77. Hans and Vidmar, *Judging the Jury*, chap. 4.

78. *Williams v Florida*, 399 U.S. 78 (1970), established the constitutionality of state juries of fewer than twelve members. By 1976, thirty-eight states had passed legislation specifically authorizing juries of fewer than twelve for civil actions. National Center for State Courts Research and Information Service, *Facets of the Jury System: A Survey*, R0028 (Denver: 1976), pp. 4–5. In Washington State, for example, civil jury trials automatically

began employing six-member juries unless one of the litigants requested a twelve-member jury: *Revised Code of Washington Annotated*, 4.44.120 (West, 1968). See also New Jersey Constitution Article I, and *New Jersey Statutes Annotated*, 2A:80-2 (West, 1976). In *Colgrove* v. *Battin*, 413 U.S. 149 (1973), the Supreme Court held that a six-member civil jury in a U.S. district court does not violate the Seventh Amendment. By 1976, "some 81 of the 94 federal district courts [had] adopted rules reducing the size of juries in civil actions" (*Facets of the Jury System*, p. 5).

The Supreme Court, in *Johnson* v. *Louisiana*, 406 U.S. 356 (1972), and *Apodaca* v. *Oregon*, 406 U.S. 404 (1972), ruled that states need not require jury unanimity. The Court allowed proportions of nine out of twelve in Louisiana and ten out of twelve in Oregon to constitute a majority for a valid verdict. By 1976 "over half the states allow[ed] for non-unanimous verdicts in civil cases" (*Facets of the Jury System*, p. 9).

79. Hans Zeisel, ". . . And Then There Were None: The Diminution of the Federal Jury," *University of Chicago Law Review*, vol. 38 (Summer 1971), pp. 710–24; and Hans Zeisel and Shari S. Diamond, "Convincing Empirical Evidence on the Six Member Jury," *University of Chicago Law Review*, vol. 41 (Winter 1974), pp. 281–95. Zeisel's analysis is qualified and extended by Lempert, who agrees that the decisions of twelve-person juries are "likely to be more consistent across similar cases, and are more representative of the community in that they are more likely to reflect the decisions that would prevail if the entire community could judge the trial for itself." Richard Lempert, "Uncovering 'Nondiscernible' Differences: Empirical Research and the Jury-Size Cases," *Michigan Law Review*, vol. 73 (March 1975), p. 679. Saks views the decline in jury size as the "best explanation" of increased variability of jury awards. Michael J. Saks, "In Search of the 'Lawsuit Crisis,'" *Law, Medicine and Health Care*, vol. 14 (1986), pp. 77–79.

80. Richard E. Nisbett and Lee Ross, *Human Inference: Strategies and Shortcomings of Social Judgment* (Englewood Cliffs, N.J.: Prentice-Hall, 1980); Amos Tversky and Daniel Kahneman, "Availability: A Heuristic for Judging Frequency and Probability," *Cognitive Psychology*, vol. 5 (September 1973), pp. 207–32; Tversky and Kahneman, "Belief in the Law of Small Numbers," *Psychological Bulletin*, vol. 76 (August 1971), pp. 105–10; Kahneman and Tversky, "Subjective Probability: A Judgment of Representativeness," *Cognitive Psychology*, vol. 3 (July 1972), pp. 430–54; Kahneman and Tversky, "On the Psychology of Prediction," *Psychological Review*, vol. 80 (July 1973), pp. 237–51. Much of this literature is usefully assessed in Elizabeth Loftus and Lee Roy Beach, "Human Inference and Judgment: Is the Glass Half Empty or Half Full?" *Stanford Law Review*, vol. 34 (April 1982), pp. 938–56.

81. Loftus and Beach, "Human Inference and Judgment," pp. 944–45.

82. Nisbett and Ross, *Human Inference*, p. 190.

83. Loftus and Beach, "Human Inference and Judgment," p. 946.

84. Molly Selvin and Larry Picus, *The Debate over Jury Performance: Observations from a Recent Asbestos Case* (Santa Monica: Rand Institute for Civil Justice, 1987), p. 46; Loftus and Beach, "Human Inference and Judgment," p. 946; Troyen A. Brennan and Robert F. Carter, "Legal and Scientific Probability of Causation of Cancer and Other Environmental Disease in Individuals," *Journal of Health Politics, Policy and Law*, vol. 10 (Spring 1985), p. 54.

85. Compare Williams's finding, based on a study of Denver and Phoenix attorneys, that the prevalent negotiating style (65 percent of his respondents) is a cooperative rather than an aggressively competitive one, so that opportunities for testing "optimistic" claims are reduced. Williams, *Legal Negotiations and Settlement*, p. 19.

86. Compare Loftus and Beach, "Human Inference and Judgments," p. 955. This bias is one example of a general lack of feedback in settlement behavior, which in turn is one part of a problem of quality control. Concern in recent years about lawyers' competence in the courtroom has eclipsed the question of their performance as negotiators. Unlike the

courtroom, where performance is subject to controls and sanctions as well as observation and comparison, negotiation is unregulated and largely invisible.

87. The strategic character of settlement negotiations and the influence of contextual factors, such as litigant resources, on their course are analyzed in Samuel R. Gross and Kent D. Syverud, "Getting to No: A Study of Settlement Negotiations and the Selection of Cases for Trial," *Michigan Law Review*, vol. 90 (November 1991), pp. 319–93.

88. This is a historic pattern of long standing. Over a ninety-year period in two Massachusetts counties, recoveries amounted to about one-quarter of the *ad damnum*—only 15 percent in tort cases, the yield declining over time. Michael Stephen Hindus, Theodore M. Hammett, and Barbara M. Hobson, *The Files of the Massachusetts Superior Court: An Analysis and A Plan for Action, 1859–1959: A Report of the Massachusetts Judicial Records Committee of the Supreme Judicial Court* (Boston: The Court, 1979), p. 149. For instance, Robert Silverman found of Boston courts in the late nineteenth century, "the sum recovered rarely equaled more than 10 percent of the *ad damnum.*" *Law and Urban Growth: Civil Litigation in the Boston Trial Courts, 1880–1900* (Princeton University Press, 1981), p. 115.

89. See note 60.

90. Daniels, "Civil Juries," p. 14. Compare Localio, "Variations on $962,258," pp. 126–29. Compare the assertion that the English counterpart, *Current Law*, is "low on damages" because of selective reporting by insurance companies. Hazel G. Genn, *Hard Bargaining: Out of Court Settlement in Personal Injury Actions* (N.Y.: Oxford University Press, 1987).

91. Donald R. Songer, "Tort Reform in South Carolina: The Effect of Empirical Research on Elite Perceptions concerning Jury Verdicts," *South Carolina Law Review*, vol. 39 (Spring 1988), pp. 585–605; Rosenthal, *Lawyer and Client*, pp. 23, 202–07.

92. G. Thomas Munsterman, Janice T. Munsterman, and Stephen D. Penrod, *A Comparison of the Performance of Eight- and Twelve-Person Juries* (Arlington, Va.: National Center for State Courts, 1990), pp. 70–72.

93. Philip J. Hermann, *Report to the Subcommittee on Economic Stabilization of the [United States House of Representatives] Committee on Banking, Finance and Urban Affairs: Testimony on the Liability Crisis Focusing on the Facts of the Insurance Crisis*, in HR 241.15.4, Part I *Liability Insurance Crisis* (Solon, Ohio: Jury Verdict Research, August 6, 1986), pp. 22–23.

94. Kevin M. Clermont and Theodore Eisenberg, "Trial by Jury or Judge: Transcending Empiricism," *Cornell Law Review*, vol. 77 (July 1992), pp. 1161, 1170, 1172.

95. Neil Komesar, "In Search of a General Approach to Legal Analysis: A Comparative Institutional Alternative," *Michigan Law Review*, vol. 79 (June 1981), pp. 1350–92.

96. Donald Harris and others, *Compensation and Support for Illness and Injury* (Oxford: Clarendon Press, 1984), p. 98. Hazel Genn, *Hard Bargaining*, p. 75, found that 89 percent of solicitors in her survey agreed that it is difficult to predict how much a judge will award to a successful plaintiff. Compare Clermont and Eisenberg's suggestion that American lawyers misperceive the decisional patterns of judges as well as of juries: "Trial by Jury or Judge," p. 1163.

97. Howard S. Erlanger, Elizabeth Chambliss, and Marygold S. Melli, "Participation and Flexibility in Informal Processes: Cautions from the Divorce Context, *Law & Society Review*, vol. 21, no. 4 (1987), p. 599.

98. Arthur Taylor von Mehren, "The Significance for Procedural Practice and Theory of the Concentrated Trial: Comparative Remarks," in Norbert Horn, ed., *Europaishes Rechtsdenken in Geschichte und Gegenwart*, vol. 2 (München: Beck, 1982), pp. 361, 364.

99. Compare the observation of Jack B. Weinstein and Eileen B. Hershenov on the jury system inhibiting the "procedural swing to equity" in contemporary mass tort litigation. "The Effect of Equity on Mass Tort Law," *University of Illinois Law Review*, vol. 1991, no. 2 (1992), p. 274.

100. H. Laurence Ross, *Settled Out of Court: The Social Process of Insurance Claims Adjustment* (Aldine, 1980), p. 157. Compare, for example, Thomas C. Schelling's observation that threats that cannot be "decomposed into a series of consecutive smaller threats" are harder to make credible. *The Strategy of Conflict* (Oxford University Press, 1963), p. 41. Because this threat is costly to carry out, its value depends on the credibility with which it can be delivered. That in turn varies with the prowess of counsel and the formidability of parties.

101. In earlier eras juries may have lacked this second type of amateurism. Describing jury practice at the Old Bailey from 1675 to 1735, John H. Langbein reported that juries tried scores of cases, often deliberating on them in batches, and typically included many veteran jurors. "The Criminal Trial before the Lawyers," *University of Chicago Law Review*, vol. 45 (Winter 1978), pp. 263, 274–77.

102. The tendency of regulars in the legal process to gravitate into such typifications and routines has been documented in civil claims (see, for example, Ross, *Settled Out of Court*, pp. 134–35) as well as in criminal matters (see, for example, David Sudnow, "Normal Crimes: Sociological Features of the Penal Code in a Public Defender's Office," *Social Problems*, vol. 12 (Winter 1965), p. 255; and Lynn M. Mather, "Some Determinants of the Method of Case Disposition: Decision-making by Public Defenders in Los Angeles," *Law & Society Review*, vol. 8 (Winter 1973), p. 187). G. K. Chesterton endorsed juries because "the horrible thing about all legal officials, even the best, about all judges, magistrates, barristers, detectives, and policemen, is not that they are wicked . . . not that they are stupid . . . it is simply that they have got used to it. . . . They do not see the awful court of judgment; they only see their own workshop." "The Twelve Men," in *Tremendous Trifles* (Philadelphia: Dufour Editions, 1968), p. 56. I am indebted to Justice Shirley S. Abrahamson for drawing my attention to this essay.

Neil Komesar argues that the knowledge accumulated by the regulars absorbs biases from the cumulative efforts of constituency groups to educate them—a subtle, attenuated form of "capture by the regulated." "Injuries and Institutions: Tort Reform, Tort Theory and Beyond," *New York University Law Review*, vol. 65 (April 1990), pp. 27, 42. In this view one of the virtues of the jury is its relative ineducability.

103. Marygold S. Melli, Howard S. Erlanger, and Elizabeth Chambliss, "The Process of Negotiation: An Exploratory Investigation in the Context of No-Fault Divorce," *Rutgers Law Review*, vol. 40 (Summer, 1988), p. 1147.

104. Erlanger, Chambliss, and Melli observe that in such a regime "judges may be following the patterns they see in informal settlements, rather than the other way around; thus instead of 'bargaining in the shadow of the law,' one should refer to 'litigating in the shadow of informal settlement.'" See "Participating and Flexibility in Informal Processes," pp. 599–600.

105. Janet Cooper Alexander, "Do the Merits Matter? A Study of Settlements in Securities Class Actions," *Stanford Law Review*, vol. 43 (February 1991), p. 567.

106. Alexander, "Do the Merits Matter?" p. 566.

107. Judith Resnik, "Judging Consent," *University of Chicago Legal Forum*, vol. 1987, pp. 43–102

108. Robert J. Condlin, "Bargaining in the Dark: The Normative Incoherence of Lawyer Dispute Bargaining Role," *Maryland Law Review*, vol. 51, no. 1 (1992), p. 21. On the "informational poverty of bargaining," see John Roemer, "The Mismarriage of Bargaining Theory and Distributive Justice," *Ethics*, vol. 97 (October 1986), pp. 88, 97, 102; and David Luban, "The Quality of Justice," *Denver University Law Review*, vol. 66, no. 3 (1989), pp. 393–95.

109. In their richly elaborated depiction of English and American legal cultures, Patrick S. Atiyah and Robert S. Summers contrast a more formal, more certain, more predictable, more strictly and evenly enforced English law with a more indefinite and uneven American

counterpart that is more substantive—that is, grounded in the country's moral and policy commitments. They regard the jury as closely associated with the "substantive vision" of law in America. *Form and Substance in Anglo-American Law: A Comparative Study of Legal Reasoning, Legal Theory, and Legal Institutions* (Clarendon Press, 1987), p. 425.

110. This would entail examination both of the cognitive qualities and of the cultural proclivities. Robert M. Hayden, "The Cultural Logic of a Political Crisis: Common Sense, Hegemony, and the Great American Liability Insurance Famine of 1986," *Studies in Law, Politics, and Society*, vol. 11 (1991), pp. 95–117.

111. See the discussion in this chapter of the experiment by Gerald Williams.

112. Edith Greene, Jane Goodman, and Elizabeth F. Loftus, "Jurors' Attitudes about Civil Litigation and the Size of Damage Awards," *American University Law Review*, vol. 40 (Winter 1991), pp. 813, 815.

113. Hans and Lofquist, "Jurors' Judgments of Business Liability in Tort Cases," pp. 111–12.

114. Hans and Lofquist, "Jurors' Judgments," pp. 93–107. This result is compatible with the results of a 1979 experiment by Elizabeth Loftus finding that exposure of subjects to a single insurance advertisement linking soaring insurance costs to inflated jury awards led to significantly lower awards for pain and suffering. "Insurance Advertising and Jury Awards," *American Bar Association Journal*, vol. 65 (January 1979), pp. 68–70.

115. Daniels, "Question of Jury Competence."

116. In October 1992 a Texas trial judge ordered a new trial in a personal injury case in response to claims by a plaintiff that jurors might have been swayed by President Bush's animadversions against trial lawyers and "crazy lawsuits" in his acceptance speech at the Republican convention the night before the jury deliberated and awarded $11,000 to a plaintiff "seeking more than $60,000 in medical expenses for an on-the-job back injury." Ruth Rendon, "Lawyer-Bashing by Bush Gets Man a Second Shot at Lawsuit," *Houston Chronicle*, October 27, 1992, p. A1. Similar questions are raised by campaigns against "lawsuit abuse" that place billboards decrying excessive awards near courthouses. Christi Harlan, "Trial Lawyers Battle Critics in the Courts," *Wall Street Journal*, October 19, 1992, p. B1.

CHAPTER FOUR

Justifying the Civil Jury

George L. Priest

AMONG THE VARIOUS mechanisms and institutions of American democracy, there are two it seems simply unthinkable to criticize: the right to vote and the system of trial by jury, both civil and criminal. Indeed, in drafts of this article written prior to the Rodney King verdict, I took pains to emphasize to readers that my otherwise modest conclusion—that we really ought to study whether trial by jury is appropriate for all civil cases—still stems from a deep devotion to the United States and an unswerving loyalty to the Constitution. This affirmation remains necessary, however, because even the Rodney King verdict does not seem to have greatly affected public devotion to the jury. In fact, in the days after the riots that followed the verdict, the *Wall Street Journal*, in a report on modern racial diversity, concluded almost incredibly, that the one bright spot among governmental institutions in terms of the treatment of blacks was the jury system itself.[1]

The Rodney King verdict, however, should change, or begin to change, public perceptions of jury decisionmaking. Perhaps for the first time in modern history, the King trial allowed the public itself to see much of the evidence against the accused, to evaluate it, and to compare that evaluation with the jury's. Each year, of course, there are many controversial jury decisions in both civil and criminal trials. But the public has never before been able to accurately evaluate the variety of intangible characteristics—context, demeanor, general credibility—that

Some of the discussion and much of the empirical material in this paper derives from a more extensive treatment in George L. Priest, "The Role of the Civil Jury in a System of Private Litigation," *University of Chicago Legal Forum*, vol. 1990. I am grateful to Karen Crocco and Stacie East for research assistance, Paul McGuire for programming help, and the Program in Civil Liability for support.

might have influenced the actual jury to which the case was tried. Thus, despite the many times jury verdicts have seemed at odds with evidence described in the press, the public almost unanimously has deferred to the jury and blamed the press for biased or incomplete coverage. This lack of information, coupled with a tradition of judicial silence and attorney reticence concerning jury decisionmaking, has meant that, in general, the public has had no basis for believing that juries ever make mistakes or are motivated by values other than the search for the truth.

Given the extraordinary reservoir of support for the jury, it is difficult to believe that the Rodney King verdict would put that myth to lie.[2] Perhaps the most that can be expected is some acceptance of the idea that occasionally a jury may stray in its search for truth. To my mind, however, the implications of the Rodney King verdict are far more serious. The King verdict, like the verdicts in state-tried civil rights cases in the 1960s, suggests that our system of largely undisciplined jury decisionmaking may conceal pockets, perhaps chasms, of incomprehension and bias—racial, sexual, or otherwise. It is pleasing to view the juror as a modern-day Henry Fonda from *Twelve Angry Men*, initially modest and unassuming but ultimately transformed by the responsibility placed upon him or her into a person of heroic achievement. At base, there is no foundation for this perception, a perception rejected with respect to other officers of public governance given equal or greater responsibility, who differ from jurors only in that their performance is not shielded from popular view.

The widespread support for the civil jury stems from a variety of sources. First, the jury system seems vaguely tied to the country's history and the revolution, a view encouraged by Alexis de Tocqueville who, regarded the civil jury as quintessential to American democracy. Among academics, support for the civil jury can be attributed in large part to the influence of the work of the famous University of Chicago Jury Project, led by Harry Kalven and Hans Zeisel. In its time, the Kalven-Zeisel Jury Project was the most ambitious empirical study of jury decisionmaking ever attempted.[3] Kalven and Zeisel, strong supporters of the civil jury, found a way to interpret each of their empirical findings as a positive demonstration of benevolent jury operation.[4] Presented in the extraordinary rhetoric of Harry Kalven,[5] their conclusions removed the civil jury from the range of criticism for more than a generation. Perhaps the most important continuing source of support, however, derives from civil jurors themselves who, asked to render decisions of significance, nearly uniformly regard the experience as interesting and important.[6] Yet by far the most important reason for the extraordinary support for the civil jury is not affirmative—that decision by an institution like the jury is compelled by logic or principle—but by the absence of any negatives. Quite unlike any other institution of American government, the civil jury has escaped serious critical inquiry throughout the nation's history.

Again, at the acknowledged risk of being accused of treason, I wish to modestly repair that gap. Far from hostile to the institution of the civil jury, I propose to inquire whether affirmative reasons can be found for supporting both the institution itself and the delegation to it of all civil litigation. The particular characteristics of the civil jury are well known: it comprises twelve people rather than one individual; laypersons, not professionals; they are chosen randomly and "discontinuously," rendering one decision or some limited set of decisions, then dispersing; and they are "aresponsible," deciding without giving reasons and largely invulnerable to review.[7] This paper seeks only to inquire what grounds there are for delegating important questions of public affairs to an institution bearing these particular characteristics.

Most importantly, I wish to examine whether there are principled grounds for the aresponsible character of jury decisionmaking. To my mind, the most unusual characteristic of the jury—and especially the civil jury—is that, in a regime devoted primarily to the principled rule of law, jurors are intentionally allowed to make their decisions without requiring that they be justified or subjected to review, except on grounds of gross error. Our system of government delegates decisionmaking in many contexts to groups of individuals rather than to a single individual. Yet even a court of appeals *en banc*, a congressional committee, or a presidential cabinet is not delegated the authority to proceed without justifying its decisions and subjecting them to further institutional review, prerogatives routinely delegated to a panel of twelve laypersons chosen randomly from the population. The aresponsibility of the civil jury is even more extraordinary given the widespread acceptance that the most distinctive features of the Anglo-American system of law are the discipline and principled constraint that derive from the necessity of explaining and justifying important public decisions. Surely the most important difference between the rule of law in America and the "authority" in Eastern Europe and the former Soviet states is that: in America, the exercise of public authority must be explained and justified, that is, except for decisions by American juries. It is not evident that jury performance might not be substantially improved, without sacrifice to its central features, if jurors were compelled to explain the grounds for their decisions.

As I shall discuss, there are principled grounds for civil jury aresponsibility, though they are limited and relate primarily to particular types of cases that juries sometimes are called upon to decide. The ambition of this paper is to carefully define those grounds and then to determine empirically the extent to which the work civil juries actually do corresponds to them.

Part 1 of the paper addresses the central justifications for the various institutional characteristics of the civil jury and describes the implications of these justifications for the workload of the modern civil jury. Part 2 examines the extent to which a modern urban court system, the Cook County civil courts in the Chicago, Illinois, metropolitan area, performed the functions for which decision by civil jury can be defended. Part 3 addresses the findings and suggests that the civil jury and the delegation to it of all civil cases are difficult to defend and may substantially affect the quality of civil justice in the United States.

The Institutional Characteristics of the Jury and How They Are Defended

Perhaps the most prominent defense of the civil jury as an adjudicative institution is that of Harry Kalven.[8] Kalven defended the civil jury by a process of reverse inference, inquiring which legal issues are best decided by an institution whose principal characteristics are that it is composed of twelve lay citizens, chosen randomly from the population, who decide one case and then disperse. According to Kalven, particular types of disputes will necessarily arise in society that can best be decided by an institution like the civil jury. What are these disputes? According to Kalven they are disputes for which the application of "the community sense of values" is especially important.[9] A civil jury is best suited to resolve such disputes because lay citizens, who are not usually trained in the law, will bring to these cases a closer "feel of the community" and of its standards. Indeed, the professional training and discipline of a trial judge may be counterproductive in deciding such disputes.[10] More generally, according to Kalven, a lay jury may be far more able than a judge to apply societal values broadly, eliminating rigidity in the law.[11]

A jury, unlike a judge or legislature, can "legislate interstitially"—that is, equitably fill in gaps in the legal system—in particular with respect to questions involving complex value judgments.[12]

Other institutional features of the civil jury serve complementary purposes. Selecting jurors randomly rather than taking volunteers or selecting community leaders insures that diverse aspects of community sensibility are considered. The representative and discontinuous character of the jury deflects criticism that might otherwise be damagingly concentrated on a continuously sitting judge.[13] In this way, the jury acts as a "lightning rod for animosity and suspicion" for socially necessary but troubling judgments.[14] Finally, a jury of twelve introduces greater common sense to decisionmaking, since the judgment of twelve persons is very probably superior to the judgment of an individual.[15] According to this view, therefore, a civil jury is most appropriate for issues requiring the application of complex societal values by a group of citizens who, in dispersing, deflect possible antagonism.

A similar view has been elaborated with greater precision by my colleague Guido Calabresi in his prominent book *Tragic Choices*.[16] A tragic choice to Dean Calabresi is a selection, sometimes compelled in a complex society, from among a set of alternatives, all of which are difficult or impossible according to some widely accepted moral vision. For example, the allocation of an insufficient number of kidney dialysis machines compels a tragic choice, because assigning the machine to one patient necessarily implies making the otherwise unacceptable decision to allow patients denied the machine to die from renal failure.[17]

Calabresi argues that the lay jury is an institution particularly appropriate for making tragic decisions of this nature. Calabresi regards the civil jury as prototypical of an agency that is "decentralized" and "representative" as well as discontinuous and aresponsible. The jury is decentralized because it is composed of laypersons; it is societally representative because its members are chosen randomly. On these grounds, the jury possesses an authority and a decisionmaking freedom that are unavailable to other potential adjudicative institutions.[18] Calabresi argues that together these features allow the civil jury to render decisions in tragic circumstances in a way impossible for professional, continuous, or more formally responsible governmental institutions.

The jury's representativeness and lack of responsibility . . . [are] the source of the characteristic and powerful way in which the jury operates: Juries apply societal standards without ever telling us what these standards are, or even that they exist. This is especially important in those situations in which the statement of standards would be terribly destructive.[19]

The Kalven and Calabresi treatments provide the strongest defense for the substantive role of the civil jury as a decisionmaking institution. According to this view, civil juries are appropriate for the reduction of disputes that require the application of complex societal values.[20] Similarly, in cases of extreme sensitivity or controversy, the discontinuous jury may better appear as society's voice, and, when decisions are extremely difficult and require judgments inherently impossible to defend—deciding that one person rather than another should live, for example—the decisionmaking authority should operate aresponsibly, without offering reasons and, *a fortiori*, not subject to review since there are no superior grounds or principles from which to review the decision.

Regrettably, Kalven does not pursue his defense of the civil jury with much rigor in his discussion of the cases that juries actually do decide. Kalven claims vaguely that the civil jury's feel of the community and sensitivity to social situations is important in determining what actions constitute ordinary negligence. On roughly similar grounds, he defends a jury's definition of substantive liability in defamation disputes, presumably because the jury can better evaluate the impact of a defamatory statement on an individual's reputation within the community.[21] Cases of this nature may justify convening a group of laypersons and, perhaps, selecting them randomly, but they do not explain the need for the limited jury tenure. That is, cases involving routine negligence or even defamation would not seem to require "a lightning rod for animosity." Moreover, it is difficult to see why disputes of this nature are so inherently difficult that they require that a jury be freed from providing reasons for its decision or from appellate review.

Kalven gives greater attention to the civil jury as an institution for determining damages. He admits that most calculations of damages in personal injury cases consist of routine summing up of the basic damages elements: medical expenses, lost income, and pain and suffering. He argues strongly, however, that decision by civil jury is needed when any of these damages elements involves a complex societal value judgment. He claims, for example, that the calculation of pain and suffering damages in disfigurement cases requires a feel of the community and sensitivity to social situations. He emphasizes that there are other cases in which the calculation of economic loss may be inherently difficult, such as where the victim had no market earnings, giving as examples a housekeeper or a child, especially when the child has been killed and the normal standard for wrongful death awards—loss of support—seems inappropriate.[22]

Calabresi's treatment of the role of the civil jury adds greater precision to this argument. His best and most frequent example of the defensible role of the lay jury—the allocation of kidney dialysis machines—is today, however, most commonly filled by special juries convened to advise hospitals, not by civil trial juries. But Calabresi's emphasis of the special role of the lay jury in rendering decisions in tragic circumstances seems to express more carefully what Kalven had in mind in his reference to the jury's role in decisions involving complex value judgments, where application of the community sense of values is important. Perhaps an illustration of the Kalven-Calabresi point is the calculation of pain and suffering damages for victims who have suffered catastrophic loss. In these cases, assigning a cash value to the loss necessarily implies an evaluation of the "value" of life or a substantial portion of life. In such cases, it may well be argued that the decision of a civil jury is institutionally superior to that of a judge for precisely the reasons Kalven and Calabresi give. The judgment is made by a group of lay citizens with a discontinuous existence, acting without formal responsibility, and more sensitive to the value the community places on human life. Kalven's examples of the social judgments inherent in calculating the value of lost productivity to housekeepers or children are also closely consistent with this interpretation.

In this view, the civil jury is a superior adjudicative institution for defining liability and evaluating damages when complex or conflicting societal values are involved. Many aspects of a factfinder's work in civil litigation require judgments that are in some sense difficult, either because there is no empirical or conceptual basis for them (such as pain and suffering) or because they involve projections into the future (such as lost income or medical costs). According to the Kalven-Calabresi approach, however, it is not the difficulty of a judgment per se that commends the institution of the civil jury, but the appropriateness of resolving the difficult judgment by the application of broad societal values. Where broad or conflicting societal values are involved, an institution with the characteristics of a civil jury may be especially important.

A second substantive defense of civil jury decisionmaking has received less attention but can be constructed by comparing the roles of the civil and criminal juries. The criminal jury has long been defended as a democratic political institution that protects citizens from arbitrary or unlawful state prosecution. The civil jury might be expected to serve a complementary function, first, in suits where the government exercises authority through civil litigation—such as property condemnation actions—and, second, in suits where the government is a defendant in suits brought by citizens claiming to have been harmed by governmental action. In this respect, the role of the civil jury must surely have increased over time as governmental immunities have been waived or restricted and as courts have expanded opportunities for citizen suits for violations of the requirement that government actions comply with due process of law. Of probably greatest modern significance are suits claiming damages for false arrest, false imprisonment, or assault by a law enforcement officer. In contexts such as these, the democratic features of jury selection provide a forum in which the civil jury's determination of liability or measurement of damages discipline and constrain arbitrary or unlawful behavior by government employees or agencies.

The final function attributed to the civil jury—also the most vague and least amenable to precise analysis—is the role of civil jury service in educating citizens about the operation and importance of the rule of law. The celebration of the jury's role in achieving this end derives from de Tocqueville who, summing up his study *Democracy in America,* concluded that "the main reason for the practical intelligence and the political good sense of the Americans is their long experience with juries in civil cases." De Tocqueville's admiration for civil jury service was unbounded: "civil juries . . . instill some of the habits of the judicial mind into every citizen"; "[spread] respect for the courts' decisions and for the idea of right throughout all classes"; "teach men equity in practice"; "make all men feel that they have duties toward society and that they take a share in government"; and "are wonderfully effective in shaping a nation's judgment and increasing its natural lights." [23]

Since de Tocqueville, the importance of the civil jury's role in educating citizens has been endorsed by virtually all commentators, even those seemingly hostile to the jury. [24] Some have complained that this method of education comes at too high a cost in terms of productivity, [25] but the point does not contest the existence of educative benefits. Moreover, as I have mentioned, almost all studies of juror reaction to civil jury service show that individuals believe the experience is important and educational. [26]

Of course, there are limitations to this defense as well. Providing widespread lessons in the civic virtues may explain random selection and service on only a single jury, which spread the experience among the greatest number of Americans. Training in the civic virtues would not explain, however, exempting juries from providing reasons for their decisions or from some form of appellate review. Indeed, the stronger argument would seem to be that civic education could be enhanced if jurors were obliged to explain their decisions and if the decisions were reviewed by some appellate board—just as tests are reviewed by teachers—in order to refine the civic lesson.

To my knowledge, these justifications represent the only efforts made thus far to defend the civil jury. To summarize, there are three principal justifications for the institution of the civil jury:

—To resolve cases requiring the application of complex societal values, especially where statement of the values applied is inherently difficult or problematic;

—To resolve cases involving some political dimension, such as the affirmative applications of state authority (property condemnation actions) or suits seeking redress for governmental exercise of authority; and

—As an institution for civic education in the virtues of the rule of law.

The next section presents empirical evidence on the extent to which the actual role of the jury in modern civil adjudication corresponds to these justifications.

The Workload of Civil Juries

The following tables report work of Cook County civil juries from 1959 to 1979. The data were compiled from the *Cook County Jury Verdict Reporter*, a weekly newsletter describing all cases tried to juries in the Cook County courts.[27] The tables report both total numbers of cases and total juror time (in days) for specific types of civil cases, those involving complex societal values and those involving the exercise of governmental power. The last part of this section addresses the significance of jury service as a civic experience. To my knowledge, there are no comparable studies describing the civil jury caseload in detail and certainly none that examine how much time jurors spend on different types of cases.

Some aggregate figures suggest the magnitude of civil jury responsibilities. During the twenty-one years covered by the sample, jurors resolved

Table 4-1. *Juror Time in Damages Cases Involving Complex Values, Cook County, Illinois, 1959–79*

Type of case	Number of cases	Mean trial length, days	Total juror days	Percent of total
All cases	16,984	3.8	769,188	100.00
(1) Libel	24	4.7	1,344	0.17
(2) Slander	18	3.3	720	0.09
Personal injury				
(3) Quadriplegic	17	12.7	2,592	0.34
(4) Hemiplegic	5	8.8	528	0.07
(5) Permanent brain damage	128	8.7	13,416	1.74
(6) Permanent total disability	67	7.4	5,988	0.78
(7) Amputation, arm	17	10.6	2,160	0.28
(8) Amputation, hand	14	7.6	1,284	0.17
(9) Amputation, leg	37	9.9	4,380	0.57
(10) Amputation, foot	5	5.8	348	0.05
(11) Loss, one eye	65	6.3	4,908	0.63
(12) Loss, two eyes	10	10.4	1,248	0.16
(13) Paralysis, arm	14	6.6	1,116	0.15
(14) Paralysis, hand	5	9.2	552	0.07
(15) Paralysis, leg	3	6.7	240	0.03
(16) Paralysis, two legs	6	4.3	312	0.04
(17) Fracture, head	287	5.0	17,172	2.23
(18) Fracture, neck	54	5.1	3,312	0.43
(19) Scarring, head	29	39.3	13,680	1.78
(20) Scarring, face	151	3.5	6,276	0.82
(21) Facial cut	353	3.3	13,932	1.81
(22) Burn, entire body	24	6.2	1,776	0.23
(23) Death, child	152	4.8	8,772	1.14
(24) Death, housekeeper	5	5.4	324	0.04
(25) Death, student	9	3.8	408	0.05
(26) Death, retiree	5	2.4	144	0.02
(27) Death, unemployed	1	6.0	72	0.01
(28) Loss, consortium	248	5.1	15,192	1.98

Source: Derived by author from the *Cook County Jury Verdict Reporter.*

16,984 cases.[28] These cases required jurors to sit, in aggregate, 769,188 juror days. At 250 working days per year, civil jurors in Chicago spent well over 3,000 working years (an average of 142 juror working years per year) adjudicating civil disputes.

Cases Involving Complex or Conflicting Societal Values

Table 4-1 lists all the types of cases from the sample that might be characterized as involving issues that require the jury to apply complex or conflicting societal values when evaluating damages. The cases are listed by categories of injuries. The columns show the total number of such cases resolved by civil juries over the period, the average trial length in days for each type of case,[29] the aggregate time jurors spent on such cases, and the percentage of total juror time spent deciding each type of case. Rows 1 and 2 describe libel and slander cases that Kalven thought particularly appropriate for civil jury resolution, believing that the jurors would be sensitive to the effect of the defendant's act on the plaintiff's reputation in the community.[30]

The rest of the table describes cases sent to juries involving serious personal injury short of death, where setting a dollar amount for the loss might require a judgment on the value of life or some significant feature of life.[31] For almost all of these types of cases, the aggregate proportion of juror time was relatively small. The greatest proportion of juror time was spent in cases involving claims of head fractures, facial cuts, scarring of the head, and permanent brain damage.

Rows 23–27 show cases involving the deaths of individuals without market incomes. As I have noted, Kalven believed that the civil jury is superior to a judge for calculating damages in these cases because the jurors can better define society's views of the value of the victims' productivity losses.[32] Though Kalven only applied his analysis to cases involving the death of housekeepers and children, I have broadened the category to include all victims without market incomes.[33] Row 28 describes cases involving claims of loss of consortium (an action by the spouse of a victim for the spouse's loss because of the injury to the victim), included because of the complicated societal judgment required in valuing damage to a relationship. The 15,192 juror days, or 1.98 percent of total juror time, devoted to these cases is surely an exaggeration, however, since consortium actions are usually joined with the action of the principal victim, and I am not able to determine how much trial or deliberation time was allocated to just the consortium count.

The most striking feature of table 4-1, of course, is the relatively small amount of juror time devoted to cases involving complex or conflicting damages value judgments. Again, the data presented in this table were those most faithfully corresponding to the types of cases that Kalven and Calabresi suggested might implicate complex or conflicting societal values—cases for which the special characteristics of the civil jury—nonprofessional, representative, discontinuous, and aresponsible—are most justified. Yet only six of the twenty-eight types of cases demanded more than 1 percent of the Chicago juries' aggregate time. Undoubtedly, the small numbers of cases reported reflect—fortunately—that the number

Table 4-2. *Juror Time in Most Frequent Damages Cases,*
Cook County, Illinois, 1959–79

Type of case	Number of cases	Mean trial length, days	Total juror days	Percent of total
All cases	16,984	3.8	769,188	100.00
Fracture, one leg	1,184	4.3	60,936	7.92
Whiplash	1,739	2.9	60,216	7.83
Strain, back	1,807	3.0	36,780	4.78
Strain, neck	899	3.2	34,356	4.47
Fracture, back	588	4.9	32,784	4.26
Fracture, one arm	475	4.1	23,028	2.99
Fracture, head	287	5.0	17,172	2.23
Fracture, one foot	322	4.2	16,044	2.09

Source: Derived by author from the *Cook County Jury Verdict Reporter.*

of catastrophic or serious personal injuries occurring in society is small.[34] In addition, of course, the more precisely the categories are differentiated, the smaller the percentages will appear. Yet adding all of the categories (including those that are overinclusive) in table 4-1 together reveals that civil juries spent just 15.88 percent of time on cases that might involve complex or conflicting value judgments in determining damages.

If cases involving complex societal values are a relatively small proportion of the civil jury caseload, where does the jury spend its time in determining damages. Table 4-2 includes those injuries for which such determinations required the greatest percentage of juror time.[35] The categories of inquiries are arranged in descending order according to the number of juror days required for each. I report all individual injury categories requiring more than 2 percent of total juror time.

Row 1 shows that the type of injury on which jurors spent the greatest amount of time was a single broken leg: 60,936 juror days (equal to 244 juror years), over the 21-year period. Whiplash cases were actually more numerous than single broken leg cases but required slightly less total juror time: 60,216 juror days (241 juror years). Other fracture cases as well as cases involving neck and back strains were also numerous,[36] but the only potentially serious injury among the group was head fractures, which required only about sixty-nine juror years.

The disaggregated character of the specific injuries in tables 4-1 and 4-2, however, disguises certain features of the allocation of juror time. In table 4-3, I have attempted to combine specific case categories into more generic injury types to present a broader perspective. Rows 1–10 of the table 4-3 list cases in which the calculation of damages might

Table 4-3. *Juror Time in Damages Cases, Summary, Cook County, Illinois, 1959–79*

Type of case	Number of cases	Mean trial length, days	Total juror days	Percent of total
All cases	16,984	3.8	769,188	100.00
Complex values				
(1) Libel, slander	42	4.1	2,064	0.26
(2) Quadriplegic, hemiplegic, permanent damage	217	8.6	22,524	2.93
(3) Loss, any body part or organ	304	6.7	24,276	3.16
(4) Paralysis, any body part	44	6.6	3,468	0.45
(5) Head or neck fractures[a]	341	5.0	20,484	2.66
(6) Head or face scars or cuts	747	4.7	41,940	5.45
(7) Nerve damage, any body part	194	4.1	9,576	1.24
(8) Burn, entire body	24	6.2	1,776	0.23
(9) Death, all nonmarket	172	4.7	9,720	1.26
(10) Loss, consortium	248	5.1	15,192	1.98
Total rows 1–10	. . .	. . .	. . .	19.62
Truly routine damages				
(11) Fractures[b]	3,686	4.3	189,228	24.60
(12) Strain, sprains	2,405	3.1	89,064	11.58
(13) Whiplash	1,739	2.9	60,216	7.83
(14) Bruises	1,204	2.9	42,084	5.47
(15) Cuts[c]	412	3.3	16,416	2.13
(16) Dislocations	194	4.4	10,020	1.30
Total rows 11–16	. . .	. . .	. . .	52.91

Source: Derived by author from the *Cook County Jury Verdict Reporter.*
a. Row 5 includes head fractures reported in table 4-2, row 7.
b. Not including head and neck fractures.
c. Not including head and facial cuts.

involve complex or conflicting societal values, while rows 11–16 illustrate truly routine damages categories.

Row 1, for example, adds together the case categories of the sample dealing with the necessity of evaluating reputation within the community. Row 2 shows a summary of cases involving catastrophic injury, including quadriplegia and hemiplegia, cases in which the victim was rendered comatose, and claims of permanent brain damage or permanent total disability. Rows 3–6 extend substantially beyond the injury categories reported in table 4-1 in order to dispel concerns that the categories listed earlier were underinclusive of cases involving complex or conflicting societal values. Again, some categories are overinclusive of issues that could potentially involve complex or conflicting societal evaluations; over 20 percent of juror time in nerve damage cases, for example, involved claims of some form of nerve damage to one hand or one arm.

Individuals will interpret differently the meaning of "complex and conflicting societal values," but the figures listed here are certainly overestimations. For example, it is not clear that Kalven's view of the important role of the civil jury as a "lightning rod for animosity" or Calabresi's advocacy of the importance of the civil jury in contexts of "tragic" judgments can be extended to the eighty-two cases involving amputation of a finger or part of a finger or to the fourteen cases involving claims of shoulder paralysis.

Finally, below row 10, I have added together the proportions of jury time spent on all of the injury categories that might conceivably implicate complex or conflicting societal values with respect to damages calculation. Again, this total acknowledges that the categories have been defined overinclusively to sketch the outer bound of juror responsibility for complex value determinations. In sum, jurors in Chicago spent 19.62 percent of time on complex value damages judgments.

Rows 11–16, by contrast, show the time spent by civil juries determining damages at the other end of the injury spectrum, the truly routine injuries. For consistency, these categories, too, have been expanded beyond the categories of the single most frequent injuries presented in table 4-2. (For example, row 11 includes, besides leg, back, arm, and foot fractures, all cases involving bone fractures other than those of the head and neck.) This half of table 4-2 shows that civil juries spent 24.60 percent of their time measuring damages in fracture cases, over double the amount of time spent on the theoretically complex value cases. Jurors spent another 11.58 percent of their time on cases in which strains or sprains were the most serious reported injury. Indeed, if the time spent on whiplash cases is added to the total spent on cases involving strains and sprains, the total is only slightly less than the total for all the cases that arguably could involve complex value judgments. In addition, juries spent large amounts of time evaluating even more routine injuries such as bruises, cuts, and dislocations.

Table 4-2 shows that civil juries in Chicago devoted overwhelming amounts of time to evaluating injuries that are truly routine. More specifically, juries spent twelve times as much time on bruises as on paralysis and about four times as much on strains and sprains as on all catastrophic injuries. Juries also spent more time on cases in which the most serious claimed injury was a dislocation than on all cases involving death to nonmarket participants. The most frequently litigated injury, fractures, required 96 times the hours devoted to libel and slander; 55 times those spent on paralysis; 19 times those evaluating death to nonmarket participants; 8 times those required for catastrophic injury; and 7 times those needed for amputation or loss of a body organ.

Compare in aggregate the two ends of the injury spectrum: Chicago civil juries spent 19.62 percent of their time in evaluating damages in cases that arguably could involve complex or conflicting societal values. In contrast, they spent 52.91 percent of their time on routine injuries.

Cases Involving Governmental Power

The second principal justification of the civil jury is that it serves— like the criminal jury—as a democratic counterforce to the state in civil actions involving the exercise of governmental power. Though there has been little effort in the civil jury literature to specify the precise nature of the disputes for which the civil jury might serve this role, I have attempted in table 4-4 to collect all cases fitting this description. Rows 1–4 present all cases involving direct exercise of police power.[37] In rows 5–12, I expand the definition of governmental power to include all cases in which some governmental unit was a party to the litigation.[38]

Though the most persuasive justification of the civil jury as a democratic counterforce focuses on the casetypes presented in rows 1–4, civil jury decisionmaking is clearly appropriate for any case in which some governmental agency is a party litigating against a citizen. Although the democratic features of the jury are arguably less crucial in cases involving private security guards, I have included the category because of the police-like character of the underlying dispute. The figures in rows 5–11 overstate total governmental litigation—perhaps substantially— because the individual cases overlap. In many cases, citizen-plaintiffs sue more than one governmental entity in the same case. For example, there is substantial overlap between rows 5 and 6, which show cases involving suits against an individual police officer as well as against the police department instructing or monitoring the officer. Note that rows 5–11 include virtually all the cases reported above in rows 1–4.[39]

Rows 9–11 present claims against broader political entities. These suits, typically, are brought for injuries suffered on poorly maintained sidewalks or streets or in public parks or forest preserves. It is not

Table 4-4. *Juror Time in Cases Involving Government Power, Cook County, Illinois, 1959–79*

Type of case	Number of cases	Mean trial length, days	Total juror days	Percent of total
All cases	16,984	3.8	769,188	100.00
(1) Malicious prosecution	39	3.3	1,536	0.20
(2) False arrest	102	3.4	4,200	0.55
(3) False imprisonment	8	3.6	348	0.05
(4) Assault by police	19	5.6	1,284	0.17
Governmental litigation Government as defendant (categories overlap)				
(5) Police officer	75	4.5	4,056	0.53
(6) Police department	30	5.6	2,016	0.26
(7) Fire department	17	4.5	924	0.12
(8) Private security guard	21	4.6	1,164	0.15
(9) All city of Chicago	425	4.4	22,308	2.90
(10) All Cook County	11	3.5	468	0.06
(11) All State of Illinois	4	8.5	408	0.05
Government as plaintiff				
(12) All government as plaintiff[a]	14	3.8	636	0.08

Source: Derived by author from the *Cook County Jury Verdict Reporter.*
a. Category includes the two condemnation cases tried to juries over the period.

immediately obvious that the political content of a typical pothole case or a "slip and fall" at a streetcorner should compel the convening of a representative, discontinuous, aresponsible adjudicative institution, but I include them to sketch the upper boundary of cases involving governmental power.

The striking feature of table 4-4 is the infrequency of occasions on which the civil jury is compelled to resolve cases involving the exercise of governmental power. Cases involving claims of malicious prosecution, false arrest or imprisonment, and assault by a police officer required, in aggregate, only 0.97 percent of civil jury time. Cases in which some governmental employee or agency was a party-litigant, again in aggregate, required only 4.15 percent of civil jury time. At the maximum, if all malicious prosecution and false arrest cases are added to the governmental party cases—resulting in yet another overinclusive category—the total is only 4.9 percent.

Which types of disputes take up most of civil juries time? Table 4-5 shows those cases that required the greatest proportion of the Chicago

Table 4-5. *Juror Time in Most Frequent Types of Cases, Cook County, Illinois, 1959–79*

Type of case	Number of cases	Mean trial length, days	Total juror days	Percent of total
All cases	16,984	3.8	769,188	100.00
(1) Auto collision, intersection	4,352	3.3	173,616	22.57
(2) Auto rear-end	2,968	3.3	115,824	15.06
(3) Auto-pedestrian	1,552	4.0	74,112	9.64
(4) Auto, guest action	688	3.6	31,728	4.12
(5) Auto head-on	492	4.2	24,912	3.24
(6) Auto-cycle	408	3.7	18,240	2.37
Total auto	11,545	3.5	485,904	63.17
(7) Action against property owner	1,613	3.8	73,020	9.49
(8) Job-site, third-party action	767	5.7	52,488	6.82
(9) Product liability	553	6.0	39,876	5.18
(10) Common carrier, alighting-jerking	576	3.3	23,424	3.05
(11) Malpractice	328	5.7	22,380	2.91

Source: Derived by author from the *Cook County Jury Verdict Reporter.*

civil juries' effort. I have segregated the categories as narrowly as the data will allow in order not to exaggerate the figures. Row 1 shows that civil juries spent 22.57 percent of their time, equal to 173,661 days (695 juror years), on cases involving auto collisions at intersections. Row 2 shows that rear-end auto collision cases required 15.06 percent of total civil jury time, equal to 115,824 juror days (463 juror years). Suits by pedestrians hit by autos required 9.64 percent of juror time (row 3); guest actions, 4.12 percent (row 4); head-on collision cases, 3.24 percent (row 5); and collisions between autos and motorcycles or bicycles, 2.37 percent (row 6). Just below row 6, I have added together all the time juries devoted to auto accident cases. In aggregate, civil juries in Chicago spent 63.17 percent of their total time resolving auto accident cases, an investment that equals 1,943 juror years. In contrast, juries spent only 845 juror years deciding all other types of liability cases (rows 7–11).

A comparison of tables 4-4 and 4-5 shows a striking difference between the relative investment of civil juror effort in cases involving governmental power and in more routine societal disputes. Apparently civil juries spend 75 times evaluating rear-end collisions as they do deciding cases of malicious prosecution; 24 times as much time on auto guest actions as on assaults by the police; 65 times as much time on head-on collisions as on claims of false imprisonment. Indeed, the magnitude of these differences is astounding. Juries expend over 15 times as much effort on auto accident cases alone as on all cases in which any governmental agency or employee is a party to the litigation.

Even in absolute terms, the numbers are overwhelming. In terms of juror years, during the twenty-one years of the Chicago sample, civil juries spent almost seven centuries resolving cases involving auto collisions at intersections, over four and one-half centuries resolving rear-end collisions, and over a century and a quarter on auto guest actions brought by passengers against drivers. Almost incredibly, the civil jury spent almost two millennia (1,943 juror years) on aggregate auto accident cases.

The role of the civil jury as a democratic counterforce in cases involving governmental power is trivial in comparison, suggesting that the occasions when civil juries are actually employed in a political role are very limited in our society. Though the period of the sample (1959–79) perhaps does not accurately represent the current extent of suits against government agencies, especially because I report only state court and not federal civil rights actions, the comparison is still extraordinary. Twenty-one years of false arrest, false imprisonment, and assault actions against the police required no more than 16.8, 1.4, and 5.1 juror years, respectively. At the maximum, all cases involving governmental power (table 4-4, rows 1, 2, and 5–12) required less than 8 percent of the time jurors invested in auto accident cases.

Civil Jury Service as Civic Education

The third principal justification for the institution of the civil jury is that jury service provides practical instruction in the operation of the rule of law in a democratic society. The educative effects of jury service were invoked at the country's founding in support of both the Seventh Amendment to the Constitution and those state constitutional provisions guaranteeing a right to a civil jury.[40] Perhaps more importantly, civil jury experience was later celebrated (in de Tocqueville's highly influential study of the United States) as central to the political genius of American society.[41] Indeed, in the civil jury literature over the years, the educative function of the civil jury has been used effectively to trump any skepticism about the jury, perhaps because the implied result of jury experience—increased civic responsibility—can be thought to be of nearly infinite value in a democracy. Whatever the reason, there has been little effort over the years either to measure with any precision how jury service alters people's commitment to democracy or to compare jury service to other civic experiences or educational mechanisms for improving citizenship.

Although no data are available to evaluate the extent to which civil jury experience enhances civic responsibility, it is possible to examine the potential scope of the effect. Based on observations from his travels in America in the early 1830s, de Tocqueville reported that civil jury service was required just frequently enough to educate all American citizens, but not so frequently that it became burdensome. According to de Tocqueville, "The jurors being very numerous, each citizen's turn to serve hardly comes more than once in three years."[42] Though somewhat ambiguous, this estimate in reduced form suggests that the probability of civil jury service during any one year for an average citizen in de Tocqueville's time was somewhere between 0.25 and 0.33.

I have gathered comparable figures for citizens in Chicago during the period of the study (table 4-6). It shows the number of jury trials in Cook County during each year and the number of sitting jurors. Although some recent accounts have emphasized that large numbers of citizens are at some time called for jury service, it is unclear whether reporting for service provides a civic education equivalent to that offered by actual deliberation and judgment.[43] Thus, column 2 reports the number of jurors actually rendering a verdict. According to Max Sonderby, founder of the *Cook County Jury Verdict Reporter*, individual jurors served for a two-week period during the years reported here. During the 1960s, Sonderby reports, it was not uncommon for a single individual to serve on more than one jury, but during the 1970s service on a jury would excuse a citizen from further service.[44] To err on the high side, I have not factored in multiple service.

In Cook County, civil jurors are chosen from the lists of registered voters. Column 3 shows the number of registered voters during each year constituting the pool of available jurors.[45] Finally, column 4 derives the probability of civil jury service for each year by dividing the number of jurors by the number of registered voters. Thus, for example, in 1959, voters faced the prospect of serving once every 377.5 years; in 1960, once every 454.1 years. As noted, I ignore multiple jury service, so the probabilities reported in column 4 are overestimates.

The magnitude of the educative effect of civil jury service has changed substantially since de Tocqueville's time. Americans may have served on juries once every three or four years in the 1830s, but the opportunities

Table 4-6. *Probability of Jury Service, Cook County, Illinois, 1959–79*

Year	Jury trials	Total jurors	Registered voters	Probability of jury service each year
1959	534[a]	6,408	2,418,907	0.0026
1960	487	5,844	2,653,804	0.0022
1961	583	6,996	2,552,014	0.0027
1962	614	7,368	2,430,107	0.0030
1963	1,045	12,540	2,414,834	0.0052
1964	914	10,968	2,663,693	0.0041
1965	849	10,188	2,663,693	0.0038
1966	1,078	12,936	2,506,298	0.0052
1967	1,121	13,452	2,522,560	0.0053
1968	1,175	14,100	2,633,036	0.0054
1969	928	11,136	2,562,160	0.0043
1970	915	10,980	2,444,841	0.0045
1971	1,041	12,492	2,455,047	0.0051
1972	894	10,728	2,810,618	0.0038
1973	892	10,704	2,810,618	0.0038
1974	820	9,840	2,548,280	0.0039
1975	861	10,332	2,574,454	0.0040
1976	691	8,292	2,703,176	0.0031
1977	627	7,524	2,865,174	0.0026
1978	746	8,952	2,530,253	0.0035
1979	581[a]	6,972	2,554,118	0.0027
Average	. . .	. . .	. . .	0.0038

Sources: Number of jury trials and total jurors was derived by author from the *Cook County Jury Verdict Reporter.* The number of registered voters was derived from Chicago and Cook County Boards of Election Commissioners. I am grateful to Donna McNamara of the Chicago Board of Election Commissioners and Peter J. Johnen, chief of administrative services for the chief judge, Circuit Court of Cook County, for compiling these data.

a. Extrapolated from part-year results.

for civic education are dramatically lower today in modern urban jurisdictions such as Chicago. Chicago voters faced the greatest likelihood of civil jury service in 1968: once every 186.7 years. On average, for the 21-year period, Chicago jurors faced an annual probability of civil jury service of 0.0038, equal to service once every 260.2 years. Those extremely diligent citizens who registered to vote during each of their years of eligibility faced a probability of serving on a civil jury of roughly 8 percent by age 40, 16 percent by age 60, and 20 percent at some point during their lifetimes.

The striking feature of table 4-6 is how relatively few citizens experience the civic educational effect of jury service. Cook County is one of the largest metropolitan areas in the United States; its total population during the years of the study exceeded 5 million.[46] Yet on average, fewer than 10,000 citizens per year served on civil juries. In the year with the greatest number of trials, 1968, only 14,100 citizens served on civil juries.

Of course, there is every reason to believe that the civic training provided by jury service has an impact beyond the actual jurors themselves as citizens relate their jury experiences to family and friends. But even if we imagine that this ripple effect triples the educative effects of jury service, no more than 40,000 Chicago citizens in any year of the twenty-one years studied were beneficiaries of this civic education—a figure that represents approximately 1.5 percent of the average number of registered voters and 0.76 percent of the Cook County population.

Moreover, proponents of the educative aspects of the civil jury have tended to regard all jury service as equivalent in terms of the civic education it provides. It is worthwhile in this regard, however, to reconsider the kinds of cases on which civil juries spend their time. It is not clear that, regardless of subject matter, all disputes possess identical educative opportunities in the civic virtues.

Surely the strongest case for jury service as civic education can be made for disputes involving exercise of the police power: false arrest or imprisonment, assault by a police officer, malicious prosecution, and possibly condemnation actions. But these cases take up only 0.97 percent of civil juror time (table 4-4). An argument, though less strong, can be raised that jurors learn about civic responsibility from all cases in which a government entity is a party, though again, this position seems strained with respect to cases involving potholes and "slip and falls" in public parks. Adding these disputes to the police power disputes gives no more than 4.9 percent of aggregate juror time, however, (table 4-4). Similarly, many cases that at first appear to involve complex or conflicting societal values can be expected to provide some form of civic education. But many of these cases involve little more than the evaluation of enormous pain and suffering—perhaps heart-rending, even tragic—but more educative of the vagaries of life than of the role of a citizen in a democracy.

Even if all these disputes do provide civic education, they make up less than 25 percent of the civil jury's burden. Measured in terms of numbers of jurors sitting on such cases, rather than of aggregate juror time, during the 21-year period of the study an average of only 1,755 jurors annually deliberated on disputes involving governmental power or complex societal values (tables 4-3 and 4-4). Again, tripling this number to account for the ripple effect on friends and relatives, no more than 5,265 Cook County citizens in any year were beneficiaries of the civic education of civil jury service—some 0.2 percent of the average number of registered voters and 0.1 percent of the Cook County population. Chicago citizens registered to vote during every year of eligibility faced a 5 to 6 percent chance of serving on a jury during their lifetimes in a civil dispute involving governmental power or complex societal values.

Can We Justify Juries for All Civil Litigation?

Part 3 shows that, if we take the justifications for decision by civil jury seriously, it is very hard to defend the largest portion of the work that the modern civil jury actually does. Below is a systematic summary of the characteristics of the civil jury, evaluated for their appropriateness to the different forms of litigation:

—*Lay, not professional; twelve persons, not one; chosen randomly from the population*. Kalven and Calabresi provide a powerful defense of the lay and representative characteristics of the civil jury, viewing them as important to the resolution of cases involving complex societal values for which no professional training is readily available. Convening a decisionmaking unit of twelve laypersons chosen randomly from the citizenry may be justified for the 19.62 percent of the cases involving complicated damages issues. Similarly, a civil jury with these characteristics may be justified for the 4.9 percent of the cases in which governmental power is an issue.[47] It is very difficult, however, to defend an institution of this nature for the resolution of the routine kinds of injuries and accidents that comprise the bulk of the civil jury's work. For example, what good reasons are there for convening twelve citizens to determine damages in the 52.91 percent of civil cases where the most serious injury suffered by the plaintiff was a cut, fracture, strain or bruise? What possible reason is there to insist on having "a feel of the community" in the 63.17 percent of the caseload involving automobile collisions?

—*Sitting discontinuously: dispersing after a single decision*. Kalven and Calabresi defend the discontinuous character of civil jury decisionmaking by invoking concerns about the animosity or hostility that might be directed at a single decisionmaker resolving highly controversial disputes. Without a case-by-case review of the litigation in the Chicago courts, it is difficult to know how many cases between 1959 and 1979 generated public attention of this nature, with one exception. During the period under study, a Chicago civil jury ruled on an action brought by dependents of Black Panther leader Fred Hampton, who was killed by Chicago police in a controversial 1969 raid on his apartment. Clearly, a case this controversial may best be decided by a group of citizens who can reacquire anonymity by dispersing after the decision.

How many cases of this nature are likely to arise in our civil courts? It is very hard to believe that any but the most extraordinary of, say, auto collision cases would involve controversy of this nature. Even cases involving complicated damage assessments are not likely to generate the kind of public notoriety that would require Kalven's "lightning rod" release mechanism. Again, while notorious cases can be imagined, it is difficult to justify assembling a jury in more than a minuscule portion of civil cases on the grounds of this concern.

—*"A responsible," deciding without giving reasons and insulated from review absent gross error.* Kalven did not seriously defend the extraordinary freedom from justification that our legal system affords the civil jury, though he implied that some decisions—such as the evaluation of extreme pain and suffering damages—may simply not be amenable to justification in terms of logic or reason. Calabresi presents a more compelling defense for this freedom: cases in which it might be possible to define the reasons underlying the decision—that is, the adjudicator can explain why one decision rather than another has been made—but in then stating the reason would be destructive of broader social values. The best example is the unavoidable life and death choice between two applicants for a kidney dialysis machine. A jury might be able to explain the specific reason that led it to choose one applicant over the other, but making those reasons public may conflict with the more general societal norm of treating all citizens equally.[48]

It is difficult to identify any set of cases delegated to civil juries that fully meet the criteria set forth by Kalven and Calabresi. Even in cases involving pain and suffering damages, a jury must make a decision regarding liability. There are no grounds that justify exempting the jury from giving reasons for its decision, even if the jurors cannot articulate in terms of principle why it chose one dollar amount over another as a measure of pain and suffering. In the American system of justice, providing reasons for a decision serves not only to explain reasoning, but to ensure consistency. A jury (or any other decisionmaker) may not be able to justify in terms of logic the award of a certain dollar figure for pain and suffering, but it could justify the award in terms of consistency with other verdicts in similar contexts. Difficulty in providing specific reasons need not be translated into a relaxation of the demands of consistency.

Calabresi's example of the destructive effects of providing reasons seems incongruous when considered in light of the day-to-day work of the civil jury. A civil jury never makes life and death decisions but merely awards or refuses to award monetary damages to one claimant or another. It is difficult to imagine any context in which a civil jury's definition of the grounds for its decision would be destructive of larger values of the society.

The issue of more extensive review of jury decisions by some appellate body is somewhat more complicated. Perhaps it can be argued that appellate review is pointless in the case of decisions for which there is essentially no basis—such as the measurement of pain and suffering. Again, however, in a legal regime in which consistency of outcome across citizens is valued, the review of civil jury decisionmaking would contribute to a just result. Finally, for cases involving governmental power, it may be believed that more extensive review of jury decisions could be seen as counterproductive, since the appellate courts constitute part of the government whose actions juries restrain. However, the number of cases involving governmental power that are tried to civil juries is very small. In the period of my study, the total was 4.9 percent (table 4-4).

—*Training in the civic virtues.* Although there have been some criticisms of the civil jury as a decisionmaking institution, it has been most commonly conceded that the limitations of the jury system are outweighed by the educative benefits to society (as emphasized by de Tocqueville) and to individuals (as shown by juror polls). Regrettably, however, here too it is clear that the magnitude of civic training provided by jury service is minimal; the proportion of the population in a major urban jurisdiction that can ever be expected to serve on a jury or learn vicariously from another's service is very small.

As de Tocqueville traveled around the country in the early decades following the revolution, civil jury service may well have contributed significantly to citizen identity with the nation and commitment to its democratic management. At a time when democracy remained a theory and there was little formal education, the experience of civil jury service may have been a very effective mechanism for imparting societal norms and providing training in the operation of the laws.

But times have surely changed. Democracy is no longer an unknown and untried technique of political organization. There are many existing sources of education in civic responsibility, from the public schools that make it part even of the traditional elementary curriculum to the media, both inconceivable to de Tocqueville. Throughout the history of our nation, no one has had sufficient interest to attempt a study of the way civil jury service changes people's values or perceptions in comparison to other training mechanisms. De Toqueville's hypothesis is proven by nothing more than assertion.

Some Further Concerns about Civil Jury Decisionmaking

I have presented what are, to my mind, substantial grounds for believing that the role of the civil jury must be reconsidered, and we must rethink how appropriate it is as an institution in our broader system of justice. Most important, I have suggested that it is very hard to defend the delegation to the jury of all civil litigation rather than (following Canada's example) some smaller set of disputes for which the jury's characteristics as a decisionmaker are better designed.

As described earlier, however, the extraordinary public endorsement of the civil jury stems less from the affirmative understanding that its characteristics as well suited to the tasks that our system assigns it than from what appears to be an absence of negative implications that might compel a rethinking of the civil jury's role. Indeed, to many, the fact that the United States has retained the civil jury is happily contrasted to the broad elimination of the institution in Britain and the restrictions imposed on it in Canada as an example of the superior U.S. commitment to democracy—without any sacrifice to the system of justice.

My empirical findings, however, begin to suggest that delegating all civil cases to juries may well have substantial negative implications that have not been seriously addressed in the modern literature on civil juries. The single most important finding is the sheer magnitude of the cases involving purely routine accidents and injuries that reach civil juries. The Chicago experience suggests that, though proportions and types of cases may vary across jurisdictions, civil juries in the United States are saddled with an extraordinary burden of resolving the routine.

Why do so many cases involving routine injuries and routine accidents reach civil juries? The question is an important one, given the seemingly endemic problem of delay in civil trials, especially in urban jurisdictions such as Chicago.[49] As is well known, delays in litigation in the United States chiefly afflict civil jury calendars.[50] In the Chicago courts during the period of study, for example, the average time from suit to trial was 4.71 years, and from incident to trial 5.68 years.[51] In the ten years since, delay in civil trials in Chicago has grown worse.[52]

Under the American system of civil procedure, trial by jury can be requested by either plaintiff or defendant. Disputes will be referred to the civil jury calendar whenever either litigant believes that decision by jury will be more favorable than decision by judge. Put conversely, the only cases that will not be referred to the civil jury calendar are cases in which both parties believe, necessarily for opposite reasons, that decision by judge will be more favorable than decision by jury. This point alone suggests why, in most jurisdictions, overwhelming proportions of tort cases are referred to the jury calendar.[53]

Referring a case to the civil jury calendar, however, is only the first step. The most important factor in determining which cases actually reach civil juries is the success of the parties' settlement negotiations prior to trial. By far the largest majority of civil disputes are settled before they are litigated. In the Cook County courts during the period of study, typically only 2 to 4 percent of disputes were ever tried to juries.[54] All the rest were settled on terms mutually more favorable to the parties than the expense of an actual civil trial would have been.

Disputes will be settled or litigated depending upon whether the difference in the parties' settlement offers is greater or less than the combined costs of trial.[55] The difference in the parties' settlement offers, in turn, will be determined by the stakes in the case and predictions concerning the outcome of a trial.[56] Thus, of cases on the jury calendar, those most likely to proceed to trial will be those in which the stakes are very high, those for which the outcome is highly uncertain, or both.

This method of choosing trial or settlement presents a much different picture of how cases are delegated to the civil jury than might be imagined from the literature justifying the institution. In our system of private litigation, disputes are delegated to civil juries not on the grounds that the jury is the most appropriate decisionmaking institution because the disputes implicate complex societal values or political issues. Instead, disputes are delegated to the civil jury because the parties' settlement offers diverge. In turn, parties' settlement offers diverge because the underlying uncertainty over the outcome overwhelms the potential savings in litigation costs.

The large personal injury caseload of the civil jury does not result from the simple fact that juries are likely to be more sympathetic than judges toward injured victims.[57] Plaintiffs expecting more sympathy from a jury than from a judge will surely place their cases on the civil jury calendar. But the decision to litigate or settle is necessarily a cooperative one. Defendants are equally aware that a jury may be sympathetic to the plaintiff. Large numbers of routine personal injury cases reach juries because litigants have different expectations concerning the extent of jury sympathy; thus, settlement demands and offers diverge, precluding resolution of the case without a trial.

Of course, in all jurisdictions, disputes will arise that involve issues of sufficient importance to the parties that settlement is not available on any terms.[58] For all other disputes, however, the chief determinants of settlement versus trial are the stakes of the case, uncertainty over the outcome, and litigation costs. Disputes involving very high stakes as well as disputes involving complex legal or factual issues are likely to be pressed to trial because of consequent differences in settlement offers. Cases involving routine injuries (and thus routine damages) or routine accidents (and thus routine issues of liability) are far more likely to be settled, because differences in the expected outcome are likely to be less. For a routine case to proceed to trial, the level of uncertainty about the outcome must be exceedingly high.

Why then do so many cases involving routine accidents and injuries reach juries in Chicago? The Chicago courts are dominated by routine litigation, most probably, because the difficulty of predicting how Chicago juries will decide these cases makes it impossible for the parties to agree on a settlement amount to save litigation costs. Is Chicago likely to differ from other jurisdictions in terms of the volume of routine civil jury litigation? Under the American system, which does not limit the right to trial by jury, the volume of routine cases in various jurisdictions will differ only as they differ in terms of the stakes of cases, the predictability of jury decisions, or the magnitude of litigation costs. There is little reason to believe that litigation costs are lower in Chicago to justify an exceptionally high level of routine litigation. There is just as little reason to believe that Chicago cases are atypical in terms of the amount at stake. Indeed, since delay in the tort system encourages settlement by reducing the potential value of a jury verdict, and since the Chicago courts are among the most congested in the country, theoretically Chicago should have a lower proportion of routine litigation than less congested jurisdictions.[59] Chicago is likely to differ from other jurisdictions in terms of routine cases only if Chicago juries are inherently less predictable.[60]

The source of the great volume of routine litigation is the institution of the civil jury itself. The civil jury is an engine of uncertainty. Each of the principal institutional characteristics of the civil jury impairs the efforts of private litigants to settle and leads to the predominance of routine disputes in the civil jury caseload. Decision by lay citizens rather than professionals increases the uncertainty of outcome. Random selection of citizens increases the uncertainty of outcome. The discontinuous nature of decision by any single jury and the failure of the jury to explain or justify its decision precludes a careful estimate of the outcome based upon past behavior and, thus, increases the uncertainty of outcome. One may readily endorse that it is crucial for our democratic system to convene a group of twelve citizens, chosen randomly from the population, who sit discontinuously rather than professionally and decide aresponsibly, for the resolution of disputes involving complicated societal values or political issues. But each of these characteristics is antagonistic to the private resolution of routine disputes.

The extensive delay in the civil trial system in Chicago necessarily derives from the sheer volume of disputes involving routine accidents and injuries that proceed to trial. Large urban jurisdictions like Chicago are characterized by an enormous inflow of civil litigation that must ultimately be processed through a narrow bottleneck of civil juries. For example, during the period of study, on average over 41,000 cases remained pending each year on the civil jury calendar, and over 10,000 new cases were filed each year.[61] Chicago civil juries were able to process on average roughly 800 of these cases per year (table 4-6). All the rest had to either settle out of court or wait for trial, generating the average 4.71 years from suit to trial. Since then, the problem has become worse. In 1989 in Cook County, over 67,000 cases were pending on the civil jury calendar, and 25,000 new cases were filed during the year. The Cook County courts were able to process only 728 jury trials.[62]

Many commentators have criticized the extent of civil court congestion, principally from a concern about process. They find it unseemly that a Chicago complainant must wait, on average, six years to reach a jury. The costs of civil trial delay are substantially more tangible, however. The Illinois courts do not award prejudgment interest. As a consequence, at a modest 7 percent discount rate, the average six-year delay in 1989 in Chicago between suit and trial effectively reduces the present value of a complainant's judgment or settlement by 33 percent.[63] Thus, a victim who has suffered $100,000 in damages prior to suit receives only a present value of $66,634 upon a civil jury's vindication of the victim's rights. These figures show how heavily dependent our civil litigation system is on the private settlement of disputes. Indeed, although the lengthy delay in the Chicago courts seems extreme, it is as low as it is only because 96 to 98 percent of disputes settle out of court. The only way to significantly affect the level of litigation delay in a major urban jurisdiction like Chicago is to increase the rate of civil settlement.

Thus, the most promising prospect for reducing delay in the civil courts is constraining the jurisdiction of the civil jury. If civil jury jurisdiction were limited to those cases involving complex or conflicting societal values, political issues, or the government as plaintiff or defendant—even if the categories were defined expansively—the problem of civil jury delay would be reduced dramatically. As I have tried to show, cases involving complex or conflicting societal values—defined broadly— make up at the maximum 19.62 percent of the cases that reach civil juries. Cases where governmental power is an issue—again defined broadly—are at most 4.9 percent of the civil jury cases. Together these categories of cases constitute less than one-quarter of the current civil jury burden. It follows directly that, without change, our current jury apparatus could handle all these cases and still see a dramatic reduction in the extent of litigation delay.[64]

Restricting the jurisdiction of the civil jury, however, will not eliminate routine cases but only shift them from the jury to the bench trial calendar. There is no point to the shift unless there are reasons to believe that it will reduce delay. There are strong reasons to think so. Kalven and Zeisel estimate that trial by judge would be 40 percent faster than trial by jury, but this effect is hardly the more important one.[65] The principal benefit of shifting routine litigation from the civil jury to the bench calendar is that the shift is likely to increase the settlement rate dramatically. The important issue here is not whether judges process cases more rapidly than juries, but whether judges are more predictable than juries. To the extent that they are, disputes are more likely to be settled rather than pressed to trial and the backlog of pending lawsuits to decline.

Each of the differences between the characteristics of the civil jury and the civil judge suggest that the shift of routine litigation to the judicial calendar will increase predictability and promote settlement. The judge is a professional, not a lay citizen. The judge sits continuously, and his or her previous decisions—especially if accompanied by written or oral opinions that explain and justify them—provide a guide for predicting future decisions. It follows necessarily that the prospect of decision by judge will increase settlements and reduce trials. Of course, it also follows, though necessarily to lesser extent, that if juries were required to issue opinions or even special verdicts, settlements would also increase and court delay decline.

Some commentators have disparaged the civil settlement process, extolling the societal values of authoritative judge or jury decisionmaking.[66] These values are surely important. But in the context of a judicial system that in 1989 was burdened with 67,000 pending and 25,000 new cases, the idea that all disputes should be tried to a verdict is unrealistic. Our society necessarily must rely on the private settlement process for the resolution of civil litigation. First, restricting the jurisdiction of the civil jury to cases for which jury resolution can be defended—cases involving complex or conflicting societal values or political content—and, second, requiring juries to explain the grounds for their decisions, will reduce the extent of civil court congestion. There is little clear social purpose in convening twelve randomly chosen citizens to resolve a rear-end accident case in which the most serious injury is a bruise or fracture. Litigants most commonly proceed to trial by jury in routine cases, not because of some individual or societal conception that trial by jury will fulfill a fundamental social objective, but because differences in their expectations of the jury's decision are too great to allow them the settlement which they most probably prefer.

Only further study will show how much the delay in civil trials can be eliminated by a selective, rather than a universal, delegation of cases to the jury or by more systematic jury opinions or special verdicts. But the costs of our current system of universal delegation are potentially very serious. However substantial the merits of the institution of the civil jury in terms of citizen involvement and training in the civic virtues, the aggregate charge of 33 percent of loss against all of Cook County's litigants—the 67,000 with cases pending in 1989 and the 25,000 with newly filed disputes—cannot be dismissed on the basis of myths and homilies.

Notes

1. Ellen Joan Pollack and Stephen J. Adler, "Justice for All? Legal System Struggles to Reflect Diversity, But Progress Is Slow," *Wall Street Journal*, May 8, 1992, p. 1.

2. Indeed, there have been vigorous efforts to reinterpret the Rodney King tape to justify the jury's decision. See Roger Parloff, "Maybe the Jury Was Right," *American Lawyer*, vol. 14 (June 1992), p. 7.

3. For a bibliography of the Chicago Jury Project, see Harry Kalven, Jr., and Hans Zeisel, *The American Jury* (Little, Brown, 1966), pp. 541–45.

4. For example, Kalven and Zeisel's most important finding was that judges agreed on

outcomes reached by both civil and criminal juries in roughly 80 percent of cases and disagreed in about 20 percent, a finding invoked in support of the jury by many participants in this symposium: Kalven and Zeisel, *American Jury*, p. 58; and Harry Kalven, Jr., "The Dignity of the Civil Jury," *Virginia Law Review*, vol. 50 (October 1964), pp. 1055, 1064–65. Kalven and Zeisel interpreted the 80 percent agreement as confirming evidence of the overall aptitude of lay jury decisionmaking and the 20 percent disagreement as confirming evidence of the jury's role as a democratic counterforce to state authority: Kalven and Zeisel, *American Jury*, pp. 494–97; and Kalven, "Dignity of the Civil Jury," pp. 1064–66. Kalven and Zeisel also found that civil juries awarded damages greater by 20 percent, on average, than judicial awards, which they interpreted as confirming evidence of the jury's comparatively greater sense of equity. Kalven, "Dignity of the Civil Jury," pp. 1065–66. Kalven and Zeisel did not attempt to show carefully that the 20 percent rate of disagreement between judges and juries occurred either in criminal cases involving controversial prosecutions or in civil cases involving the exercise of state authority. Nor did they show that the 20 percent greater civil damages occurred in cases in which some greater public than judicial equity was arguably appropriate. Finally, they never attempted to explain their incredible finding of nearly equivalent judge-jury agreement in civil and criminal cases. The finding suggests either some deeper interactive relationship between judge and jury or some feature of judge questionnaire response. In more typical social science research, disparities with outcomes of the magnitude of 20 percent are regarded as sufficiently significant to warrant intensive examination.

5. See, for example, Harry Kalven's description: "The jury is almost by definition an exciting and gallant experiment in the conduct of serious human affairs." ("Dignity of the Civil Jury," p. 1055).

6. The Chicago Jury Project studied civil juror reactions. Kalven, again with brilliant effect, reported the results as confirming that, despite lost wages and occasional complaints about inefficient administration, civil jury service was "very often a major and moving experience in the life of the citizen-juror" (Kalven, "Dignity of the Civil Jury," p. 1062).

7. The terms "discontinuous" and "aresponsible" are taken from the helpful discussion of the institution in Guido Calabresi and Philip Bobbitt, *Tragic Choices* (W.W. Norton, 1978), pp. 57–64.

8. Harry Kalven, Jr., "The Jury, the Law, and the Personal Injury Damage Award," *Ohio State Law Journal*, vol. 19, no. 1 (1958), pp. 158, 161; and Kalven, "Dignity of the Civil Jury," pp. 1055, 1058, 1061–68.

9. Kalven, "Damage Award," p. 161.

10. Kalven, "Dignity of the Civil Jury," p. 1058; and Kalven and Zeisel, *American Jury*, pp. 7–9.

11. Kalven and Zeisel, *American Jury*, pp. 8–9.

12. Kalven, "Damage Award," p. 161; and Kalven and Zeisel, *American Jury*, pp. 8–9.

13. A good example from the criminal context of the form of focused, lingering hostility avoided by jury decisionmaking might be the notoriety that attended Judge Irving Kaufman throughout his career as a consequence of his presiding over the Rosenberg trial.

14. Kalven and Zeisel, *American Jury*, p. 7; and Kalven, "Dignity of the Civil Jury," p. 1062.

15. Kalven, "Dignity of the Civil Jury," p. 1067; and Kalven and Zeisel, *American Jury*, p. 8. Moreover, twelve persons are less corruptible than one person. "Dignity of the Civil Jury," p. 1062. Kalven's formulation has had exceptional influence on the current understanding of the role of the jury. See, for example, Fleming James, Jr., and Geoffrey C. Hazard, Jr., *Civil Procedure*, 3d ed. (Little, Brown, 1985), pp. 428–29 (adopting the Kalven formulation of the justification of the civil jury in its entirety).

16. Calabresi and Bobbitt, *Tragic Choices*.

17. Ibid., pp. 17–19, 186–89.

18. Ibid., pp. 57–64.

19. Ibid., pp. 17–19, 186–89, 57–64.

20. See text preceding note 23 for a discussion of the civil jury as a democratic counterforce in civil disputes involving the government and text at notes 23–26 as a mechanism for instilling civic virtue.

21. Kalven, "Dignity of the Civil Jury," pp. 1058, 1071–72.

22. See generally, Kalven, "Damage Award," pp. 160–61, 167–69.

23. Alexis de Tocqueville, *Democracy in America*, ed. J. P. Mayer (Anchor Books, 1969), pp. 274–75.

24. See, for example, Charles P. Curtis, "The Trial Judge and the Jury," *Vanderbilt Law Review*, vol. 5 (February 1952), pp. 150, 157; and Dale W. Broeder, "The Functions of the Jury: Facts or Fictions?" *University of Chicago Law Review*, vol. 21 (Spring 1954), pp. 419–21 (accepting educative role but arguing that it comes at the expense of litigants who deserve professional judgments). Note, however, that Broeder's criticism of the jury appears disingenuous, written as a "devil's advocate" exercise to summon all possible criticisms of the jury. Broeder was a prominent contributor to the University of Chicago Jury Project.

25. Donald L. Martin, "The Economics of Juror Conscription," *Journal of Political Economy*, vol. 80 (July–August 1972), pp. 680–702.

26. Kalven, "Dignity of the Civil Jury," p. 1062.

27. The data were collected by the author with support from the Rand Corporation's Institute for Civil Justice. For a detailed description of the data, see Mark A. Peterson and George L. Priest, *The Civil Jury: Trends in Trial and Verdicts, Cook County, Illinois, 1960–1979*, R-2881-ICJ (Santa Monica: Rand Institute for Civil Justice, 1982).

28. The full sample includes 17,478 cases. Cases dismissed or resolved by motion after a jury was convened are excluded.

29. The underlying data report only the dates trial began and the jury verdict was rendered. I report the difference. Thus the trial length calculation includes the time required for jury deliberation; I am not able to distinguish trial from deliberation time. This method exaggerates the length of part-day trials. I attempted to test for the reporting problem by subtracting separately one and two days from each case. The relative proportions of time for the various case categories reported in the tables were not substantially affected by these adjustments. Thus I report the full difference.

30. Kalven, "Dignity of the Civil Jury," p. 1071.

31. For each case, the injury listed was described as the most serious injury that the plaintiff suffered.

32. See notes 31–32; and Kalven, "Damage Award," pp. 161, and 167–69.

33. My expanded definition may be too broad. Note that cases involving the death of retirees (row 26) require on average only 2.4 days, less than the average for the sample as a whole. Though such individuals lacked market incomes at the time of death, they did have previous market experience that may perhaps have made it easier to gauge the economic loss suffered by dependents. Thus, the complex value judgments necessary in cases involving the death of children or housekeepers may not have been necessary here.

34. Of course, not all catastrophic injuries nor deaths to nonmarket participants will generate litigation.

35. Again, I report for each case only the most serious injury claimed by the plaintiff.

36. Whiplash reported in row 2 is a neck and back strain suffered in a rear-end accident. The neck and back strains reported in rows 3 and 4 were suffered in other kinds of accidents.

37. The malicious prosecution and false arrest categories are overinclusive. Although such actions are most typically brought against the police, some are brought against

institutions such as stores or restaurants that summon the police, and still others, against private citizens.

38. Note that I do not present separately the two property condemnation cases litigated to juries over the period.

39. The only possible exception is suits for false arrest or malicious prosecution against private parties in which the police were not joined as defendants.

40. See generally, Paul B. Carrington, "The Seventh Amendment: Some Bicentennial Reflections," *University of Chicago Legal Forum*, vol. 1990, pp. 33–86.

41. De Tocqueville, *Democracy*, pp. 270–76.

42. De Tocqueville, *Democracy*, Appendix I, R, p. 729.

43. Stephen J. Adler and Wade Lambert, "More Americans Are Called for Jury Duty," *Wall Street Journal*, July 10, 1990, p. B8 (reporting Defense Research Institute study claiming 45 percent of U.S. adults have been called at least once for jury duty, though only 17 percent have ever begun a trial).

44. Personal communication.

45. I am grateful to Donna McNamara of the Chicago Board of Election Commissioners and Peter J. Johnen, chief of administrative services for the chief judge, Circuit Court of Cook County, for compiling these data.

46. The Cook County population in 1960 was 5.13 million; in 1970, 5.49 million; and in 1980, 5.25 million. Bureau of the Census, *U.S. Census, 1980* (Department of Commerce).

47. Again, both of these figures are overestimates, perhaps substantial. See notes 33, 37, and 39.

48. Even Calabresi's tragic judgment example is not without controversy. That is, in a society committed to the rule of law, why shouldn't a jury have to explain and justify that it is choosing to allocate machines to the young over the old, to the relatively healthy over the unhealthy, to parents over the childless?

49. See George L. Priest, "Private Litigants and the Court Congestion Problem," *Boston University Law Review*, vol. 69 (May 1989), pp. 527–29.

50. See, for example, Thomas Church, Jr., and others, *Justice Delayed: The Pace of Litigation in Urban Trial Courts* (Williamsburg, Va.: National Center for State Courts, 1978), tables 2.1 and 2.4 (showing jury delay roughly four to five times greater in civil than criminal courts).

51. Priest, "Congestion," p. 532.

52. According to Max Sonderby, Cook County Jury Verdict Reporter, the current suit-to-trial delay in Chicago is over six years. Telephone interview, July 13, 1990. The increase in congestion in Chicago led Cook County, Illinois, Chief Judge Harry G. Comerford to inform the Cook County Board in 1989 that "he needs 130–140 new courtrooms, at a cost as high as $500 million, and 50–60 more judges because of mushrooming caseload," Charles Mount, "5 Counties Cut Court Backlogs," *Chicago Tribune*, May 30, 1989, sec. 2, p. 1. I am grateful to Geoffrey P. Miller for this information. Very recently, there have been reductions in delay in the Cook County courts, chiefly because of recent changes in jurisdictional amounts. As with earlier changes of this nature, the reduction in delay is likely to be temporary. See generally, Priest, "Congestion."

53. For estimates of the proportion of judge versus jury litigation, see Hans Zeisel, Harry Kalven, Jr., and Bernard Bucholz, *Delay in the Court* (Little, Brown, 1959), p. 88.

54. Priest, "Congestion," p. 540, table 1.

55. William M. Landes, "An Economic Analysis of the Courts," *Journal of Law and Economics*, vol. 14 (April 1971), pp. 61–107.

56. For a more precise description of the trial-settlement decision process, see George L. Priest and Benjamin Klein, "The Selection of Disputes for Litigation," *Journal of Legal Studies*, vol. 13 (January 1984), p. 1.

57. Though, holding other factors constant, any institutional feature that increases the chance of plaintiff's success will increase the likelihood of litigation by increasing the expected value of the case to both parties.

58. Some, though probably not all, of political content litigation is of this character. For example, the NAACP is not likely to settle *Brown* v. *Board of Education*, though an individual citizen may be very willing to accept a monetary settlement from a police department.

59. Zeisel and others, *Delay*, p. xxi, note 1; and Priest, "Congestion."

60. Chicago, of course, is a city with a diverse population, but more diverse than other large cities? The question deserves further study.

61. Derived from *Annual Reports of the Administrative Office of the Illinois Courts, 1959–79*.

62. I am grateful to Max Sonderby and Rich Atkins of the Cook County Court Administrator's Office for these figures. For more recent trends, see note 52. Note that the simple number of cases filed and pending ignores multiple plaintiffs, and so is a substantial understatement.

63. The settlement amount, of course, will be determined with reference to the expected judgment should the case go to trial and so will also be reduced by expected delay. See Priest and Klein, "Selection of Disputes."

64. This is true even when the rate of litigation versus settlement of such cases increases because of the reduction in delay. See Priest, "Congestion."

65. Zeisel and others, *Delay*, pp. 78–79.

66. See generally Owen M. Fiss, "Against Settlement," *Yale Law Journal*, vol. 93 (May 1984), pp. 1073–90.

CHAPTER FIVE

Inside the Black Box: What Empirical Research Tells Us about Decisionmaking by Civil Juries

Robert MacCoun

CRITICS CONTEND that awards by civil juries are often excessive, unpredictable, and inequitable; that many civil cases are too complex for lay jurors to handle; and that civil-jury trials take too long and cost too much. Others challenge the validity of these claims and defend the jury's role in American civil justice. This controversy is not new; many of the same issues have been debated for decades.[1] What may be new is the increasing role of empirical research on jury behavior.

The need for systematic research on the behavior of civil juries becomes more pressing when policymakers contemplate proposals for modifying the civil-justice system.[2] Many proposals for reform are predicated on untested—and often implicit—hypotheses about the effects that new rules and procedures will have on decisionmaking by juries. Earlier empirical research has demonstrated how tort reforms can have unintended effects when policymakers fail to anticipate the behavior of jurors, lawyers, and litigants.[3] Although critics tend to focus on the *outcomes* of jury decisionmaking—liability verdicts and damage awards—effective evaluation and implementation of policy also require an understanding of the *process* of jury decisionmaking. For example, when we require juries to itemize awards for compensatory damage, do they calculate damages one item at a time, or do they start with a total award and then "work backward," dividing that lump sum among the items? The process

This chapter was prepared with support from the Rand Institute for Civil Justice and a grant from the Law and Social Science Program of the National Science Foundation. Debra August provided valuable research assistance. Some material in this chapter has been revised, updated, and extended from my earlier paper, "Getting Inside the Black Box: Toward a Better Understanding of Civil Jury Behavior" (Santa Monica: Rand Institute for Civil Justice, 1987).

that juries follow is likely to determine whether or not the policy has its intended effect on compensatory awards.[4]

This chapter discusses the potential contribution to the policymaking process of systematic empirical research on the behavior of civil juries. It opens with a discussion of the hazards of relying on anecdote, personal experience, or media coverage to infer general principles of jury performance. It provides a brief primer on methods of jury research, with an emphasis on their comparative strengths and weaknesses. Some readers may prefer to skip this section and get to the findings, but I recommend against that strategy—*caveat emptor*! The next section summarizes some of the major patterns in liability, compensatory, and punitive jury judgments documented by archival analyses by researchers at the Institute for Civil Justice (ICJ), the American Bar Foundation (ABF), and elsewhere. The following sections attempt to explain how civil juries reach such judgments, drawing most heavily on research on mock jurors and describing the effects of extralegal variables on jury judgment. The final section compares the jury with its alternatives and offers some general conclusions.

Some important topics are not covered in this chapter. The focus is on personal injury torts because that is where the research attention has been. As a result, the chapter gives scant attention to questions of jury behavior in other areas of civil litigation, such as contracts. This chapter addresses only peripherally the emerging literature on complex litigation and the jury because that important topic is ably addressed in the chapter by Richard Lempert in this volume.[5]

The Hazards of Casual Induction

Anecdotes and apocryphal tales about jury behavior circulate in most courthouses, and in recent years they have dominated the civil-jury debate.

The Media Provides a Biased Sample of Jury Verdicts

The popular media—and all too often the specialized legal media— fuel the discussion of the civil jury. Understandably, the media seem to be attracted to the occasional civil-jury verdict that seems unusually large (more than $10 billion to Pennzoil), unusually small ($1 to the U.S.

Football League), or just plain unusual ($988,000 to a woman who alleged that a hospital CAT scan prevented her from using her psychic powers). As described, these verdicts usually seem outrageous, often suggesting that the jury in question was irrational, incompetent, or hopelessly prejudiced. No doubt some juries do make egregious errors. But can we rely on these anecdotes to infer general principles of jury performance? Are such incidents truly indicative of a wider problem in jury decisionmaking? As in the old party game Telephone, these stories tend to become grossly distorted in the telling and retelling. Few people ever bother to examine the actual details of the cases in question; those who do sometimes find that the verdicts in question seem more reasonable. Citizens who are dissatisfied with legal decisions have revised their evaluations after reviewing more of the evidence presented at trial.[6]

A more fundamental problem is that these stories in no way constitute a random sample of jury verdicts and are therefore unlikely to tell us anything about the more general distribution of jury verdicts or the performance of jurors.[7] Psychological research has documented our pervasive reliance on an *availability heuristic*—we tend to overgeneralize from outcomes that are vivid, recent, or memorable.[8] This heuristic is often adaptive, but it can lead us to overestimate the likelihood of salient events—accidents, tornadoes, homicides, terrorist incidents—while underestimating less vivid events—stomach cancer, stroke, asthma, emphysema. Thus, the media may inadvertently lead us to overestimate the frequency of jury trials, the likelihood of plaintiff victories, and the magnitude of awards; the result may be biased decisionmaking by manufacturers, insurers, attorneys, plaintiffs, and potential claimants.[9]

Jury Verdicts Provide a Biased Sample of Litigation

A further complication is that jury verdicts in no way constitute a representative sample of legal disputes. Most observers of legal culture recognize that most potential grievances never become lawsuits and that more than 90–95 percent of lawsuits never reach the jury.[10] This fact is often forgotten, or its implications for legal policy are overlooked, but it does not trivialize jury verdicts.[11] As Marc Galanter has pointed out, settlement negotiations take place "in the shadow of the jury," as litigants and their attorneys attempt to anticipate how a jury would respond to their dispute.[12] Thus, knowledge of jury verdicts serves a bellwether function, providing a crude indicator of "the going rate" in case value.

Economic models of the settlement process suggest that as a consequence of this bellwether function, juries will tend to get the hardest cases; the easy, lopsided cases will tend to settle prior to trial.[13] This tendency makes it hazardous to draw certain tempting inferences from patterns in data on jury verdicts, although some research methods are more vulnerable to this problem than others. In fact, one of the more provocative settlement models, the model described by George Priest and Benjamin Klein, predicts that jury verdicts will tend to favor plaintiffs about 50 percent of the time, regardless of prevailing legal standards or any biases in jury behavior, because informed, rational litigants will already have taken those factors into consideration in their settlement decisions.[14] If this prediction were true, patterns of jury verdicts would tell us nothing whatsoever about jury behavior. But this 50:50 prediction is based on certain assumptions about litigant rationality, risk aversion, and relative stakes that may be incorrect, and, as we shall see, the prediction is refuted by much of the available data.[15] Nevertheless, for our purposes, the important point of these settlement models is that patterns of jury verdicts may be the product of litigant behavior in addition to (or instead of) jury behavior.

Methods for Studying Jury Behavior

An obvious way to investigate jury behavior is to observe deliberating juries and to document the content of their deliberations. This approach was attempted in the mid-1950s as part of the Chicago Jury Project, a major research program undertaken at the University of Chicago. Having secured the court's permission, researchers eavesdropped on the deliberations of several federal juries, without the participants' knowledge. This endeavor was quickly aborted, however, when congressional inquiries resulted in legislation prohibiting attempts to monitor ongoing jury deliberation.[16] Since then, juries have deliberated in private.[17]

Legislation mandating jury secrecy creates difficulties for researchers because it places the behavior of juries inside a "black box." We can observe what goes into the box (the events at trial), and we can observe what comes out of the box (jury verdicts), but we don't really know what's going on *inside* the box. This problem has forced social scientists to explore alternative methods for studying juries. The major empirical research techniques include archival analyses, post-trial interviews, the use of shadow juries, field experiments, and mock-jury experiments.[18]

Archival Analysis

Although jury deliberation takes place behind closed doors, we can still learn a great deal by studying case characteristics and jury verdicts—the inputs and outputs of jury deliberation. Mark Peterson and his colleagues at the ICJ pioneered this archival approach with a series of statistical analyses of civil jury verdicts in California and in Cook County, Illinois.[19] In these studies, civil-jury verdicts and case characteristics are identified from the published Jury Verdict Reporters (since courts rarely record such data systematically), coded, aggregated, and then analyzed statistically. The major strength of this approach is that it allows identification of aggregate patterns and longitudinal trends in liability judgments and in compensatory and punitive damage awards. These archival studies have had a major effect on the policy debate by challenging some claims about trends in tort verdicts.

The archival method is a correlational approach: using statistical analyses, it identifies reliable relationships between certain characteristics of litigants or cases and jury verdicts. For example, Peterson and Audrey Chin found that in the 1960s and 1970s in Cook County, the size of jury awards was related to certain characteristics of the plaintiff and of the defendant. For example, under certain conditions, juries tended to award more money in trials to individual plaintiffs when the defendant was a corporation than when the defendant was an individual. It is tempting to infer a causal link in these relationships. We may hypothesize that juries make corporations pay more because they are thought to have deeper pockets, a causal hypothesis that casts doubt on the equitability of jury awards. Chin and Peterson acknowledge that other factors might account for this apparent effect of corporate identity. Unfortunately, the limitations of their jury-verdict data base prevented them from examining such factors in their analyses. This is an inherent drawback of the archival approach: archival sources of data rarely include measures of all the variables in which the analyst might be interested. In general, the archival approach is better suited to describing the effects of jury deliberation than to explaining how and why juries reach their judgments. As we will see, research using other methodologies suggests that factors other than deep pockets probably *do* explain the bias toward individual rather than corporate defendants.

Post-trial Interviews

Although we cannot observe juries as they deliberate, jury secrecy legislation is somewhat less restrictive with regard to interviews with jurors after the deliberations. Social scientists, legal scholars, and many journalists have taken this approach.[20] Post-trial interviews with jurors provide eyewitness evidence regarding the deliberation process. Like eyewitness testimony during a trial jurors' post-trial accounts are vulnerable to error and distortion, and similar caveats apply.[21] Jury deliberation is typically a complex emotional experience, and jurors' verdicts can have profound moral and political implications. Thus, jurors may distort or revise their recollections, whether consciously or unconsciously, in order to justify their decisions or to cast their behavior in a more favorable light. A great deal of information may be rapidly forgotten, and jurors' explanations of why they did what they did should be taken with a grain of salt. Psychological research has demonstrated that people (experts and otherwise) have a very limited ability to describe accurately their own judgment processes.[22] Finally, some post-trial juror interviews are case studies of a particular (and often controversial) jury trial. As a result, they presumably tell us more about that particular jury than about generic deliberation experiences.

Shadow Juries

A shadow jury is a group of citizens, selected to mimic the demographic characteristics of an actual jury, who sit in a courtroom and observe a trial.[23] The jurors are interviewed for their reactions to trial events, and they can be asked to deliberate as if they were actually trying the case, although this feature of the method is apparently neglected in some applications. Like scientific jury selection, shadow juries are typically used as an adversarial consulting tool to assist attorneys in preparing and conducting a trial. They can also, however, be used as a research tool. For example, Hans Zeisel and Shari Diamond assessed the effectiveness of voir-dire strategies by comparing a jury's verdict to the judgments of a shadow jury composed of jurors who were excused on peremptory challenges.[24]

Studies of shadow juries allow researchers to examine how other juries might try the same case. One drawback of this method is that shadow jurors—unlike actual jurors—are aware that their judgments have no legal consequences. This characteristic is also shared by mock jurors and will be discussed in more detail below. Practical limitations govern the number of shadow juries that can be studied in any given trial. First, trials can last many days, with constant delays and interruptions, making it very expensive to pay shadow jurors for their time, and courtrooms rarely have the seating capacity to permit a large number of shadow juries to observe a case. Finally, these studies are often undermined when the litigants settle a case before the conclusion of a trial.[25] Because of these problems, shadow juries are rarely used in jury research.

Field Experiments

The archival, post-trial interview, and shadow jury methods have a common limitation: they study trials as they naturally occur in the legal system, therefore limiting our ability to draw causal inferences about the effects on jury behavior of variables that are relevant to policy. If a sufficiently large number of cases is sampled, and enough information is known about each case, one can attempt to control statistically for the effects of the many variables that naturally occur in the legal environment, but statistical control leaves causal questions unanswered. Causal variables are policy levers; if we understand them, we can successfully design or implement new policies, but if we fail to understand them, our policies may have undesirable effects or no effect at all.

The experimental method is the most powerful research tool for identifying causal variables.[26] In the experimental approach, a variable of interest is systematically varied while holding all other variables constant in order to identify its effects. The key to experimentation is random assignment of juries to experimental conditions. Despite their great potential, field experiments involving jury trials have rarely been conducted in the past because of the difficult ethical and legal questions they raise.

Randomized field experimentation on juries should be most feasible when policymakers wish to test a proposed reform relating to jury conduct prior to its implementation; any inequities to litigants due to random assignment to policies are likely to be minimal; or potential inequities to litigants can be remedied at the conclusion of the experiment. Two recent field experiments on juries apparently met these criteria.[27] The Judicial Council of the State of Wisconsin wanted to evaluate two new statutes permitting members of the jury to take notes and the use of supplemental written jury instructions and two other techniques of interest: juror questioning of witnesses and pre-trial instructions. Trial judges permitted the researchers randomly to assign jury trials to different combinations of courtroom techniques. These studies are rare examples of the successful implementation of a randomized field experiment on juries. Because of the enormous obstacles to field experimentation on juries, jury researchers often use an alternative experimental strategy, the mock-jury simulation experiment.

Mock Juries

The mock-jury simulation method is an active research tradition in the social sciences—in fact, it is the most commonly used tool for studying jury behavior.[28] Hundreds of mock-jury simulation studies have been published since the early 1970s.[29] Diamond and Jonathan Casper conducted a recent study that is a good example.[30] They recruited more than 1,000 prospective jurors from a jury pool in Cook County, Illinois. The jurors were shown an hour-and-fifteen-minute videotaped simulation of all the key elements of an antitrust trial, reenacted in a courtroom by a professional actors.[31] Jurors then rendered verdicts, either individually or in one of seventy different six-person juries.

What did the researchers gain by this artificial procedure that they couldn't have gained by examining actual jury verdicts, interviewing actual jurors, or seating a shadow jury in the courtroom during the actual trial? Quite a lot. Although the mock-jury technique is artificial, its artificiality endows it with a number of virtues.

First, the mock-jury methodology permits the use of the experimental method while avoiding many of the logistical obstacles to field experiments. For example, Diamond and Casper were interested in the effects of judicial instructions regarding the trebling of awards in private antitrust litigation. This factor could be studied using archival comparisons of actual jury awards before and after the practice of instructing the jury about trebling was discontinued in the mid-1970s. Any differences in outcomes, however, could be attributable to differences in the types of cases brought to these juries, in other changes in law or procedure during that time, or in more general trends in jury behavior. Diamond and Casper were able to avoid this uncertainty by randomly assigning mock jurors to one of six variations in judicial instructions in the same case; the variations involved whether jurors were told of the trebling rule, admonished not to let it influence their award, or given an explanation for the rule. Moreover, the mock-jury approach made it feasible to examine how a large number of juries would try the same case, which made it more sensitive to the effects of the experimental factors under study. Their results suggested trebling instructions tend to reduce awards and that admonitions from the judge are ineffective.

A second advantage of the mock-jury method is that it gives researchers a better idea of what goes on inside the black box. Mock-jury deliberations can be observed or videotaped to permit a systematic analysis of the decisionmaking process.[32] A third advantage is that the mock-jury method permits almost unlimited variation in legal procedures and rules and in the testimony or characteristics of trial participants under study, including variations that would be all but impossible to explore in actual trials. This means that it can be used to assess the effects of proposed reforms before they are implemented. Thus, the mock-jury method is *not* simply a substitute for observations of actual jury deliberations. Even if jury deliberations were opened to public scrutiny, studies of mock juries would remain an important research tool.

Nevertheless, the artificial nature of the approach has led critics to question the extent to which we can confidently generalize its results to actual jury verdicts.[33] The most obvious of the many differences between mock juries and actual trials is that mock (and shadow) jurors know that their judgments will not have serious consequences (beyond contributing to the scientific study of juries). Research on this question has yielded contradictory results, with studies finding the verdicts of mock criminal jurors sometimes harsher, sometimes more lenient, and sometimes no different from the verdicts of jurors who are—or believe that they are— actually trying a case.[34] Thus, mock-jury verdicts do not appear to have an inherent, systematic pattern of bias. In carefully conducted simulation studies, mock jurors report that they take their task quite seriously, and their behavior usually attests to that fact; mock jurors will often deliberate for hours without any financial incentives to do so, and mock jurors have been known to become quite emotional when defending their positions. Another concern involves the reliance on college students as mock jurors, but research indicates that students and adults eligible for jury duty provide quite similar judgments.[35] Investigators can never guarantee that the results of a simulation study will generalize to actual juries. Nevertheless, simulation experiments are a major tool in most basic and applied sciences. When the objective is to estimate precisely the magnitude of trends and patterns in actual jury trials, the archival

Table 5-1. Comparison of Empirical Methods for Studying Jury Behavior

Method	Permits replication across trials?	Permits replication across juries per trial?	Permits control over trial attributes?	Permits control over juror attributes?	Provides deliberation-process data?	Realism of trial and decision consequences?	Practical drawbacks or limitations?
Archival analyses	Yes	No	Statistical control only	Statistical control if attributes are known	No	Trial and consequences are real	Limited by availability and quality of archival data
Post-trial interviews	Yes, if multiple trials are studied	No	Statistical control if multiple trials	Statistical control	Indirectly through juror reports	Trial and consequences are real	Juror reports may be distorted or incomplete
Shadow jury	Yes, but usually one trial only	Yes, but practical limit on number	Limited experimental or statistical control	Limited experimental or statistical control	Yes, if shadow juries deliberate	Real trial, mock verdicts	Expensive; trials often end prematurely
Field experiment	Yes	No	Experimental and statistical control	Experimental and statistical control	No, unless combined with post-trial interviews	Trial and consequences are real	Difficult to obtain court and litigant permission
Mock-jury experiment	Yes, but practical limit on number	Yes	Experimental and statistical control	Experimental and statistical control	Yes	Realism of trial varies, mock verdicts	Difficult to simulate lengthy trials

method is more appropriate. The role of mock-jury experimentation is to explain the processes underlying those patterns.

Comparison of Methods

Table 5-1 compares the five major empirical methods for studying jury behavior. As in most policy research, the choice of jury research methods involves inevitable trade-offs. Each of the major empirical methods in table 5-1 has certain advantages but also certain limitations. None of the methods described here is necessarily preferable to the others in an absolute sense; instead, the relative strengths and weaknesses of each approach determine what it can and cannot contribute to the research question of interest. In general, our understanding of any phenomenon is enhanced by convergent findings from alternative methodologies.[36] Moreover, the use of multiple methods can lead to discoveries that would be overlooked if we were able to rely solely on a single favored research method.

Describing Jury Verdicts

I will only briefly review the major descriptive findings on patterns of civil-jury verdicts over time and across jurisdiction and type of case. I can readily summarize general patterns, but the existing literature is not large, and the reader who would like more detail is advised to consult the relevant studies, which provide detailed tables of outcomes for specific types of case, configurations of parties, years, and jurisdictions.[37] One should bear in mind, however, that much of the literature is rapidly growing out of date; we know relatively little about more recent trends since 1985.[38] My focus is on verdicts, but these studies should also be consulted for data on the prevalence of litigation more generally, or jury trials specifically.

Liability Patterns

The Priest-Klein model discussed earlier predicts that selection pressures in the settlement process will result in cases that go to jury trial being won by plaintiffs approximately 50 percent of the time.[39] But archival studies actually find considerable variation in the likelihood of a plaintiff victory (win rate) across jurisdictions, across case types, and over time.[40] For example, Stephen Daniels and Joanne Martin found win rates ranging from 40 percent to 79 percent across forty-three sites in ten states. The rates were below 50 percent in four sites and above 65 percent in three sites. For thirty sites, however, the rate fell in the range of 55 percent to 65 percent.[41] Win rates are generally lower for cases involving medical malpractice and product liability than for cases of automobile negligence.[42] A number of different studies indicate that the liability rate for medical malpractice cases is around 33 percent.[43] Some evidence suggests that the liability rate has increased with the introduction of pure comparative-negligence rules, although it is difficult to estimate unambiguously the effects of changes in legal doctrine using archival jury data.[44] Evidence for an increase in the likelihood of plaintiff victories is mixed; some jurisdictions, such as Cook County, Illinois, experienced an increase in the early 1980s, but other jurisdictions remained stable or even had decreases.[45] In the federal courts, Theodore Eisenberg and James A. Henderson, Jr., show a 24 percent decline in the plaintiff success rate in cases of product liability between 1979 and 1989.[46]

Compensatory Damages

Any discussion of trends in compensatory damages must begin with a brief primer in basic statistics, because the distinction between the *mean*, *median*, and *expected* awards turns out to be critical to the debate on tort reform. The mean ("the average") is the sum of all compensatory damages awarded in a category (jurisdiction, year, case type), divided by the number of compensatory damage awards. It is a common measure of central tendency in statistics, but it is very sensitive to outliers; a few very high damage awards can greatly inflate the mean well above what most plaintiffs ever receive. The median award (sometimes called "the typical award") is the 50th percentile of the award distribution; in other words, 50 percent of all awards were larger than the median, and 50 percent were smaller. The expected award is the average award multiplied by the plaintiff victory rate; it is the best measure of a plaintiff's expected outcome at trial. The expected award will be smaller than the mean award because many plaintiffs fail to win damages.

Since the pioneering study done by Mark Peterson and George Priest, the general finding has been that the median compensatory damage award is much smaller than the mean award, because the occasional very large award inflates the mean.[47] The median award was below $50,000 in twenty-nine of forty-three sites in the ABF data base and about $30,000 for tort cases in the 1989 NCSC sample. Both sources show that medical malpractice and product liability awards are rarer, but higher.[48] Peterson and Michael Shanley found that about 20 percent of all awards are changed by post-trial activities at the level of the trial court or the appellate court; overall, defendants in their study actually paid only 71 percent of the amount the jury awarded, and reductions were greatest among the largest awards.[49]

In their review of the ICJ data on San Francisco and Cook counties, Deborah Hensler and her colleagues argued that while median awards in auto cases remained generally stable between 1960 and 1984, median awards in product liability and medical malpractice increased over that period, and mean awards grew sharply in all three categories.[50] Much of the growth in mean awards was attributable to growth in million-dollar awards, but while million-dollar awards accounted for the majority of total dollars awarded by juries, they occurred less than 4 percent of the time in Cook County and 6 percent of the time in San Francisco.[51] When considering these trends, it is important to recognize that *describing* trends in awards doesn't *explain* them. While it is possible that they represent real changes in jury generosity, it is arguably more likely that they represent changes over time in the behavior of litigant or attorney and the mix of local cases, new legal theories, new trial strategies (for example, "day-in-the-life" videos), rising medical costs, and so on.[52]

Punitive Damages

Several recent studies of punitive damages point to a common conclusion: Despite the attention they receive, punitive damages are infrequent, and in personal injury cases, they are very rare.[53] Daniels and Martin found that fewer than 5 percent of money damage cases in their sample included punitives—about 9 percent of all the cases where plaintiffs prevailed. For personal injury cases, Peterson and his colleagues found fewer than three a year in Cook County, and fewer than one a year in San Francisco, with no increase over a twenty-five-year period. After an exhaustive search, Michael Rustad was able to locate only 355 punitive damage awards in product liability cases in the United States between 1965 and 1990.

Like compensatory awards, median and mean punitive awards differ dramatically. For example, among punitive awards for personal injury in the ICJ sample, San Francisco had a median of $72,000 and a mean of $231,000; Cook County a median of $6,000 and a mean of $498,000.

Again, the means are grossly inflated by a few outliers. Of the twenty sites in the ABF sample that had at least ten punitive awards, fifteen had a median below $40,000. The GAO and Rustad studies suggest that product liability cases have disproportionately large punitive awards, reporting medians of $400,000 and $625,000, respectively. But the Peterson, GAO, and Rustad studies all indicate that as many as half of all punitive awards are reduced or eliminated in post-trial proceedings, most often for the largest awards. The net effect is that defendants in the aggregate pay only about 50–60 percent of the punitive amounts awarded by juries.

The Bronx Jury and Other Jurisdictional Variations

One of the striking findings in the ABF sample is the high degree of variation among jurisdictions in jury verdicts.[54] Much of this variation is to be expected by chance, but there do appear to be stable differences for some counties. Consider, for example, Bronx County, New York. In the ABF sample, Bronx County had a plaintiff victory rate of 72 percent, with significantly higher awards (some California jurisdictions were also high outliers).[55] Does this indicate that Tom Wolfe was correct in asserting that "the Bronx Jury is a vehicle for redistributing the wealth"?[56] Perhaps. Using multivariate analyses, Daniels argued that "local socioeconomic or environmental factors provide the primary explanation" for cross-site variations in medical malpractice, although it should be noted that 68 percent of this variance remained unexplained by his model.[57] Brian Ostrom and his colleagues found marginally significant state-by-state differences in awards after controlling for litigant configuration, type of tort, method of disposition, and time for disposition.[58] But before we can conclude that interjurisdictional variation is attributable to true differences in jury generosity, we must control for a broader array of potential cross-site differences in the behavior of litigant and attorney, the mix of local cases, medical costs, and so on. In the absence of such analyses, interpreting cross-site differences is hazardous.

Explaining Jury Verdicts

Variation among jurors within a venire is also very difficult to predict or to explain using broad sociodemographic factors.[59] Intuition and courtroom folklore suggest that personal characteristics of jurors might predispose them toward certain types of verdicts.

Jury Selection

Practicing attorneys usually have their own pet theories and rules of thumb for selecting jurors. Plaintiffs' attorney Melvin Belli, for example, has argued that "women are too brutal" and "accountants are too stingy" to make favorable jurors for plaintiffs.[60] But systematic experiments suggest that attorneys may not be capable of accurately selecting favorable jurors—their choices are no more accurate than if they simply tossed a coin.[61]

It isn't clear that social scientists can do any better, however. Trial consultants often use "scientific jury selection" techniques in an attempt to replace these informal voir-dire strategies with systematic social science methods, including survey research and statistical analyses. Nevertheless, a large body of systematic empirical research has called into question the efficacy of both traditional and scientific jury selection strategies.[62] In general, the demographic characteristics, personality traits, and general attitudes of jurors have weak and unreliable effects on verdicts. Many of the effects that are occasionally found are statistical artifacts due to capitalization on chance variation and are therefore difficult to replicate. This does not mean that the idiosyncrasies of particular jurors never influence verdicts in particular cases or that jurors are basically inter-changeable. Rather, it is extremely difficult to predict a juror's preference for a verdict based on the kind of personal characteristics that can be observed prior to a trial.[63]

Defenders of the scientific approach to jury selection argue that under certain conditions it can have a significant effect on the outcome of a trial.[64] For example, it appears to be quite useful in bringing about a change in venue or venire, and it is more likely to be effective in trials involving controversial issues where relevant attitudes can be explored in pre-trial surveys. Consistent with this latter point, some studies show that attitudes toward tort reform are significantly associated with compensatory damage awards in mock-juror research, whereas demographics have little or no reliable association.[65]

Comprehending the Law

A growing body of studies indicates that some jurors may fail to comprehend as much as 50 percent of the judge's instructions regarding the law.[66] Studies show, however, that comprehension levels can be improved significantly through the use of carefully constructed, patterned jury instructions; quantified standards of proof; and additional instructions provided at the beginning of the trial.[67]

Research, such as the Diamond and Casper study mentioned earlier, indicates that the judge's admonitions during trial sometimes fail to have their intended effect. For example, a number of studies suggest that juries are influenced by inadmissible evidence even when they are instructed to disregard it.[68] Not every instance of noncompliance can be explained by noncomprehension, however. On rare occasions, juries have been known to nullify the law intentionally when it conflicts with their standards for fairness.[69]

Meter Reading and Story Telling

Psychologists have developed a number of models of the process by which jurors integrate the evidence presented at trial and produce a verdict. The focus has been on decisionmaking in criminal trials, but many of the same processes are probably at work. A review of the details of all of these models is beyond the scope of this paper.[70] But Lola Lopes has aptly summarized them using two images: The juror as "meter reader" and the juror as "story teller."[71]

Meter-reader models are mathematical models that assume that jurors assign some sort of quantitative value to each item of evidence to represent its probative value for the verdict. The models posit a mathematical rule (such as, Bayes Theorem or weighted averaging) for combining these probative values into a final judgment, which is then compared to a standard of proof. Research to date supports a weighted averaging rule. How would this averaging process take place? Psychologists do not posit that jurors are actually computing a weighted average "in their heads." One plausible way in which an averaging rule would describe the process is for jurors to imagine some sort of continuum of the weight of evidence, ranging from "definitely not liable" to "definitely liable." (This notion of an implicit continuum is captured by the common expression "I'm leaning that way.") Psychologists call this process *anchoring and adjustment*—the juror anchors on some initial value and then adjusts this value in light of each new piece of evidence.[72] At the end of a civil trial, if the perceived weight of the evidence exceeds the preponderance of evidence standard, the juror votes "liable." This model has several implications for liability judgments, which I will only list here: (1) It implies that juror judgments will deviate from normative rules for combining probabilistic data; (2) it implies that jurors may "double count" redundant testimony; (3) it implies that jurors may "tally" evidence without carefully considering the implications one item has for the relevance or credibility of another item; and (4) it implies that jurors may think in simple, unidimensional terms rather than considering the separate legal elements of the verdict, such as intent or foreseeability.[73]

The story-teller model is an alternative theoretical perspective that shows great promise for understanding juror decisionmaking.[74] To summarize a complex theory briefly, the story-teller model proposes that jurors cognitively represent trial evidence by constructing a narrative story that integrates testimony and facilitates recall. Jurors then attempt to match the story to available verdict categories, selecting the verdict that provides the best fit.[75] Recent research has been supportive of the model in criminal cases, but its implications for liability judgment have not been examined in detail. Like the averaging model, the story-teller model suggests that jurors may deviate from normative principles of probability theory, but it also suggests that jurors will be more sensitive to interdependencies among items of evidence and to the legal elements that compose the operative definition of negligence.

I suspect that the meter-reader model and the story-teller model are each valid, but each characterizes a different aspect of civil-jury decisionmaking. The story-teller model seems to capture the reasoning that underlies most liability decisions. On the other hand, the anchor-and-adjustment process seems to characterize better how jurors evaluate damages and, perhaps, some purely statistical evidence. These arguments are elaborated in the next two sections.

Determining Liability

A key feature of the story construction process is the assessment of causation and responsibility, a process psychologists have studied for many years under the rubric "attribution theory."[76] Attribution research attempts to describe how people explain their world and to evaluate the implications of these explanations for subsequent judgments, emotions, and actions. Initially, attribution theory focused almost exclusively on the attribution of *causality*; humans were construed as "intuitive scientists," drawing causal inferences via the configuration and covariation in time and space of events in the social world. But it soon became apparent that people's attributions regularly departed from this normative scientific model.[77] By coincidence, in 1980 two theoretical essays independently advanced an alternative model characterizing all humans as "intuitive lawyers," based in part on the legal philosophy outlined in the classic work *Causation in the Law* by H. L. A. Hart and Tony Honoré.[78] From this perspective, lay attributions of *responsibility* are distinguished from attributions of causality; personal causation is seen as necessary, but not always sufficient, for moral liability.[79] Thus, perceivers do not always hold actors responsible for the outcomes their actions have caused.

The common law outlines a number of additional considerations for inferring guilt or liability given an inference of causality, such as foreseeability, intent, coercion, capacity, and duty. Hart and Honoré argue that these legal concepts are derived from common sense. Thus, one objective of contemporary attribution research is to test this alleged fit between the explicit legal model and the implicit lay model(s) of responsibility.[80] For example, do perceptions of foreseeability and intent have consistent effects on lay judgments of responsibility? Do jurors understand and apply legal criteria for liability verdicts? How is liability allocated among multiple parties? How are these judgments converted into percentage terms when special verdicts are required?

The mock-jury approach is especially well suited to exploring attributional processes in liability decisions, but relatively few such studies have taken place to date. For example, Edward Green manipulated the precautions taken by the defendant, the degree of risk, and the extent of injuries in a negligence case to explore how jurors assess "reasonable conduct."[81] Green found that mock jurors ignored the extent of injuries but were sensitive to the risk and precaution factors. In a series of studies, Joel Johnson and Jerome Drobny have demonstrated a *contiguity effect*, whereby experimental manipulations of the temporal proximity between an act and a plaintiff's injuries influenced perceptions of the negligence of both the defendant and the plaintiff; specifically, delay reduced the perceived negligence of the defendant, while increasing the perceived negligence of the plaintiff.[82] Ewart Thomas and Mary Parpal manipulated the foreseeability and intentionality of the actions of the plaintiff and defendant in four different civil suits and found that mock jurors tended to attribute less liability to the defendant than a pure comparative negligence rule would predict.[83]

Recent attributional work describes how observers isolate a single cause among a complex field of conditions preceding an undesired outcome, suggesting that observers place special emphasis on conditions that deviate from the normal state of affairs in some way.[84] Related research on counterfactual reasoning suggests that when harm befalls a victim under abnormal conditions, observers feel greater sympathy.[85]

For example, several recent studies suggest that jurors might recommend greater compensation for a victim when they can readily imagine an alternative scenario in which the victim would not have been harmed; the latter study also indicated that the perpetrator of the accident was seen as more negligent.[86] Another recent study provided evidence that jurors favored the plaintiff in a medical malpractice case, despite a strong evidentiary case for the defendant physician, when testimony under cross-examination raised the counterfactual question, "if only he had ordered the mammogram."[87] This effect was eliminated in a follow-up experiment, when the defense attorney in the mock trial clarified that a mammogram was not dictated by the applicable standard of practice.

Research on trial cognition in felony cases indicates that certain logical and probabilistic inconsistencies are attenuated when the legal decisionmaker's task is broken down into a series of subdecisions.[88] A similar process may be triggered by the use of *special interrogatories* in civil cases, which decompose the liability decision in a step-by-step fashion. To date, only one study has investigated this procedure, finding no effect on liability or on total award, but an effect on the apportionment of the award across compensatory and punitive damages, with a greater fraction apportioned to compensatory damages in the special interrogatory condition.[89]

In a typical tort trial, the jury receives evidence pertaining to both liability and damages prior to deliberation. A key policy question is whether jurors are capable of evaluating liability independent of damages. Psychological research on distributive justice suggests that there are multiple, often conflicting norms of fairness.[90] One such norm is equity, or proportionality, which suggests that resources should be allocated in proportion to contributions or efforts. A pure comparative negligence standard can be thought of as a proportionality model. According to this norm, victims should be compensated in proportion to contribution to injuries—in other words, to fault. Jurors operating under the equity norm would need to allocate fault before determining damages.

But another prominent norm is *need*—allocate more to those who need more. A concern for the plaintiff's need might subtly influence jurors' evaluations of liability. To date, jury research provides mixed evidence for an association between the severity of an injury and liability. I recently asked members of a local jury pool to rank various goals for civil verdicts; the most popular goal was that "the one at fault should pay" (equity norm), followed by "deterring negligent conduct," "compensating the plaintiff" (need norm), and then "punishing the defendant."[91]

But jurors may say one thing and do another, either consciously or unconsciously. What about jury behavior?

Some studies have failed to find an association between the severity of an injury and liability, while other studies provide some support.[92] Interestingly, a rare comparison of decisionmaking by judges and by college students found no differences between groups; in each population, perceived blameworthiness of offenders was a function of an intent-only rule for some respondents, but an intent-plus-damages rule for others, suggesting that at least some respondents—even judges—may consider damages when evaluating liability.[93] Additional evidence to support the idea that damages affect liability comes from a recent mock-jury study of unitary and bifurcated trials, in which liability was found for 100 percent of the mock juries in the unitary conditions, but for only 72 percent in the bifurcated conditions, where liability was determined prior to testimony on damages.[94]

Compensatory Damages

The size, equitability, and predictability of civil damage awards appear to be the most salient issues in the civil-jury debate.[95] Participants and observers often find the "black box" dilemma especially frustrating here, and this frustration is enhanced by occasional anecdotes that suggest arbitrary or irrational behavior. For example, Harry Kalven describes a jury that allegedly decided that the defendant was liable, estimated the plaintiff attorney fees, and then multiplied that estimate by ten to derive a damage award![96]

Kalven argues that "it is a major characteristic of the jury's approach to damages that it does not much concern itself with the damage components as an accountant might but searches rather for a single sum that is felt to be appropriate."[97] But in a case study based on post-trial interviews, jurors told Molly Selvin and Larry Picus that they determined each separate component of each plaintiff's damages and then totaled them.[98] Jane Goodman, Edith Greene, and Elizabeth Loftus found that jurors varied in the computational strategies they adopted: 31 percent used a simple multiplicative strategy to estimate lost future income; 26 percent used a similar strategy but adjusted the result upward or downward to reflect other factors; 15 percent made more sophisticated exponential computations to account for changes in potential income over time; and 27 percent simply selected an award recommendation without explicit computations.[99] This study examined only individual decisionmaking. Computational strategies in group deliberation are discussed below.

Evidence from post-trial interviews with civil jurors suggests that the ad damnum—the plaintiff's requested damage award—might serve as a reference point for the jury's calculations.[100] This is interesting in light of the earlier discussion of the anchor-and-adjustment strategy (the meter-reader model). Research in cognitive psychology suggests that when making quantitative decisions, people often use a specific salient number as an anchor or starting point; new information may then lead to adjustments away from this anchor, but the size of the anchor influences the range into which the final decision falls.[101]

Attorneys are believed to exploit this phenomenon by exaggerating the ad damnum.[102] A mock-jury study reported by J. J. Zuehl provides some evidence for this anchoring effect, while suggesting some boundary conditions on its influence.[103] Mock juries tried a personal injury case in which the ad damnum was systematically varied. Each jury received one of four different damage requests: $10,000, $75,000, $150,000, or a request for "substantial compensation" with no specific dollar amount mentioned. Zuehl reports that the ad damnum appeared to set an upper boundary; juries often adjusted downward, but only three juries exceeded the ad damnum request, and all three were in the $10,000 condition. When a precise dollar amount was requested, 50 percent of the damage awards matched that request exactly. As the amount requested increased, compliance with the ad damnum decreased, from 70 percent in the $10,000 condition to 29 percent in the $150,000 condition. The average awards in the three exact request conditions were $18,000, $62,800, and $101,400, with an average award of $74,600 in the substantial compensation condition.

A more recent mock-jury study examined the effects of a defense "counter-anchor."[104] In one condition, neither side cited a specific compensatory damage recommendation. In a second condition, a plaintiff's expert recommended $719,354, while the defense attorney recommended $321,000. In a third condition, the defense recommendation came from an expert, rather than from the attorney. Jurors awarded more money in the plaintiff-expert-only condition than in the counterexpert condition, suggesting that the defense recommendation was more influential when it came from an expert than from the defense attorney. Awards were smallest when neither side had an expert and no ad damnum was presented. The study provided additional support for the role of anchoring effects in juror judgment. In the plaintiff-expert-only condition, 37 percent of the mock jurors awarded $719,354 exactly; in the two-expert condition, 21 percent awarded the plaintiff recommendation, and 20 percent awarded the defendant recommendation. The authors found little evidence that jurors tried to split the difference; instead, they favored one expert or the other. But this study only examined the awards of individual jurors. Below, I consider the possibility of compromise awards resulting from deliberation processes.

Further evidence for anchoring and adjustment comes from a recent study of the effects of consolidating plaintiffs in mass tort trials.[105] Mock juries heard a plaintiff's case separately or in a consolidated trial with three other plaintiffs; the study also varied whether one plaintiff was an outlier (a very severely injured plaintiff). The study found that the outlier received higher awards when tried alone, suggesting that in the consolidated trial the less severe cases pulled down the value of the outlier's case. In the consolidated trial, the outlier tended to raise the value of the awards to other plaintiffs.[106] These results suggest the kind of weighted averaging that the anchor-adjustment strategy produces.

Many states use special or itemized verdict formats in which juries are told to break down personal injury awards into a series of elements or components. The assumption underlying this proposal is that it will make juries more publicly accountable and will inform the judge and the public as to the basis of the decision, paving the way for appeals or remittitur. The process is hypothesized to make jurors comply with Kalven's "accountant" model, by making a decision about the value of a claim for each element and then adding them up at the end. Kalven's alternative hypothesis is that juries may determine their award holistically, and then work backward using arithmetic to determine the components.[107] As far as the judge or the public is concerned, the jury will seem to have followed a very rational piecemeal accounting process, when in fact, the jury did something very different. If this is the case, then itemization will not reduce inflated awards, and any post-trial activities will be based on misleading information.

The limited empirical evidence to date provides some support for the use of special or itemized verdicts. In Zuehl's study of the effects of the ad damnum, mock juries were randomly assigned to one of three verdict formats: a global general verdict format, an itemized special verdict format, or a control condition in which no particular verdict format was required. Zuehl found that the ad damnum had the greatest effect on awards in the control condition and the least effect in the special-verdict condition. The ability of special verdicts to mitigate extralegal biases in the awards process has not been established, however. For example, if certain extralegal factors heighten the sympathy that jurors feel for the plaintiff, will itemization make it more difficult for them to increase the award, or will they simply inflate one or more of the damage components? This issue could be explored by manipulating extralegally biasing factors (such as defendant attractiveness) in a mock-jury study.

Some of the major policy questions regarding civil-jury awards involve the so-called "silent instructions"—also known as "blindfolding the jury."[108] Traditionally, jury instructions have not told jurors whether or how to consider the implications of attorney fees, taxes, insurance, interest rates, or potential reductions on appeal when computing damage awards. Evidence from archival analyses, post-trial interview studies, and mock-jury experiments indicates that juries often take such considerations into account.[109] Sometimes this occurs explicitly; on other occasions, such considerations might have an indirect influence through the personal preferences of some of the jurors. Thus, in the absence of explicit instructions, the effects of these factors are likely to be inconsistent, haphazard, and sometimes contrary to the intentions of the law.[110] Mock-jury or field experiments should be conducted to examine the effects of explicit instructions regarding these factors.[111]

Group Deliberation

A number of mock-jury studies, and at least one post-trial interview study of actual jurors have examined the relationship between the distribution of verdict preferences among individual jurors prior to deliberation and the jury's final verdict.[112] In general, there is a strong strength-in-numbers effect—that is, the verdict favored by a majority of the jury at the onset of deliberation usually prevails. The movie *Twelve Angry Men*, in which Henry Fonda portrayed a lone juror who converted an eleven-juror majority from conviction to acquittal, made for compelling drama, but research suggests that such occurrences are truly exceptional. Minority factions, especially minorities of one, rarely prevail in jury deliberations. In the criminal realm, advocates of acquittal appear to be somewhat more influential in deliberation; this phenomenon is usually labeled a *leniency bias*. This asymmetric pattern of influence appears to be a consequence of the reasonable-doubt standard; the leniency effect disappears when mock juries are asked to apply the preponderance-of-evidence standard to a criminal case.[113] Since the preponderance-of-evidence standard is typically used in civil trials, we would not expect a similar pattern of asymmetric influence. Consistent with this argument, Kalven and Zeisel found that when judges and juries disagreed, criminal juries were more lenient than judges, but civil juries were equally likely to favor either party.[114]

Unlike decisions of guilt (and, perhaps, liability), the determination of damages permits the possibility of compromise.[115] Thus, the determination of damages might be predicted by the average of jurors' preferred damage awards, with jurors' preferences carrying equal weight or perhaps varying in weight as a function of their persuasiveness, prestige, or other social characteristics.[116] After observing numerous mock juries, Kalven's impression was that some juries compute such an average but later modify it during deliberation, while other juries resort to it after other attempts at consensus fail.[117] Note, however, that a weighted-average rule might accurately describe a jury award even if the jury never explicitly computed an average.[118]

A phenomenon called group polarization is one of the most reliable findings in research on small-group behavior.[119] In general, when a bipolar issue is under consideration (guilt vs. innocence, pro or con, conservative or liberal), group discussion tends to shift both individual and group judgments in the direction of the average prediscussion opinion—for example, slightly cautious groups become more cautious, and slightly risky groups become more risky. If the group has no dominant preference either way, then group polarization will not occur. Are civil-jury awards influenced by such an effect? If so, it might help to explain why observers occasionally feel that jury awards are excessive. The theoretical basis for such a prediction is not clear, however. Polarization occurs when the topic under discussion falls on a bipolar continuum with a midpoint, and it is difficult to conceptualize monetary awards in such terms.

Nevertheless, mock-jury research has identified some extremity shifts for civil damages. For example, in his study of ad damnum effects, Zuehl reports that average jury awards exceeded the average recommendations of jurors before deliberations in all four ad damnum conditions. Another experiment involving an antitrust suit found that average mock-jury awards were significantly larger than average predeliberation awards; in fact, majorities were more likely to favor the defendant than the plaintiff at the outset of deliberation.[120] In another experiment, mock jurors' punitive damage recommendations became more extreme following deliberation under unanimity but not under majority rule, but there was no extremity shift for compensatory damages in either condition.[121]

Analyses of deliberation indicated that discussion of punitive damages was characterized by personal values and pressures for conformity, whereas discussion of compensatory damages was characterized by references to testimony and by inferences drawn from the evidence. The investigators argue that under a nonunanimous decision rule, jurors with extremely punitive recommendations may be ignored.

Mock-jury studies provide an opportunity to see how multiple juries would decide the exact same case: in general, considerable inconsistency exists among juries.[122] From a research perspective, this inconsistency is "error variance," making it difficult to model the deliberation process; from a policy perspective, it raises concerns about the fairness of jury verdicts. But two caveats are in order. First, trial simulations in most mock-jury experiments are intentionally designed to be somewhat ambiguous. Second, the key policy question (which I address below) is whether judges are any more consistent than juries. Considerable evidence points to consistency among judges as well, at least in criminal cases.[123]

Jury Size and Decision Rule

In the 1970s, a number of Supreme Court decisions paved the way for reductions in jury size (*Ballew* v. *Georgia*, 1978; *Williams* v. *Florida*, 1970) and the jury's required decision rule for consensus (*Apodaca et al.* v. *Oregon*, 1972; *Johnson* v. *Louisiana*, 1972). Since then, many studies using a variety of methods have examined the effects of jury size and decision rule.[124] Although some studies have found differences in the verdicts rendered by smaller or nonunanimous juries, these results can typically be explained by other factors. For example, some archival studies have failed to account for differences in the types of cases brought to traditional or nontraditional types of juries. More carefully controlled studies have not found differences in the rates of criminal conviction, although there may be effects on civil-jury awards.[125] It is quite possible that the reduction in jury size has made awards more variable and therefore less predictable.[126]

Jury size and decision rules have a number of other important effects on jury performance. For example, smaller juries are less likely to represent a cross section of the community. In addition, jury studies suggest that smaller and nonunanimous juries recall less evidence, deliberate more quickly and less thoroughly than their traditional counterparts, but—perhaps as a consequence—are less likely to hang. Importantly, citizens perceive twelve-person and unanimous juries to be significantly fairer than smaller, nonunanimous juries.[127] Now evidence suggests that reductions in jury size do not actually produce significant reductions in court costs and trial duration—the original motivation for the modification.[128] I believe that the accumulated evidence supports a return to the twelve-person jury requirement, and perhaps the unanimity requirement as well, although I think the case for the latter is stronger in criminal cases.

Extralegal Influences

Critics of the jury system occasionally claim that jury verdicts are more likely to be driven by whim, prejudice, or emotion than by the hard facts of the case. Indeed, considerable evidence suggests that jurors are susceptible to the effects of such extralegal factors as the physical characteristics of litigants, the presence and content of pre-trial publicity, and inadmissable evidence.[129] Deliberation seems to attenuate these extralegal biases in clear cases, but it can actually amplify them in very close cases.[130] The effect of extralegal factors on jury judgments should not be exaggerated. In general, the strength of the evidence presented at trial appears to be a major—perhaps the most important—determinant of the jury's verdict.[131] If one party presents a stronger body of evidence, the jury's verdict will probably reflect that fact. Nevertheless, these extralegal factors are relevant to the question of jury impartiality and the fairness of jury verdicts. They also provide insights into the motives of jurors, which are important if we are to promote fairer verdicts.

Most research on extralegal biases has examined criminal trial settings. One exception, which I discuss below, is the effect identified by Chin and Peterson of defendant identity on verdicts. Another exception is an interesting line of research on the effects of decedent gender on juror awards in wrongful death litigation; this work suggests that jurors—both male and female—not only award significantly more when the decedent was a male, but actually use different computational strategies for male and female decedents.[132]

Recall that in their archival analysis of jury verdicts in Cook County, Chin and Peterson found that after controlling for injuries, juries awarded significantly more money in cases with corporate or government defendants than in cases with individual defendants.[133] This effect has been replicated by other archival analyses.[134] This effect is widely described as a "deep pocket" effect, but, as we shall see, it is better characterized as a "corporate identity effect." The inference is that jurors award more because defendants with extensive financial assets—deep pockets—can afford to pay more. In essence, the notion is that jurors are driven by the need norm of distributive justice, rather than by the equity norm.

The effect is open to alternative explanations, however. It could be an artifact of differences in legal standards, conduct of parties, or settlement practices. Indeed, one hypothesis is that the effect is more attributable to attorney selection of cases than to juror generosity.[135] If so, it should disappear when these factors are held constant in a mock-jury setting. Nevertheless, several mock-jury studies have conceptually replicated the corporate identity effect.[136] For example, Valerie Hans and David Ermann created a brief trial summary in which several workers incurred permanent lung damage following exposure to a toxic substance during a landscaping job. Students read one of two versions of the case in which the defendant was described either as "Mr. Jones" or as "the Jones Corporation." This simple manipulation influenced both liability and damage judgments. The corporation was held liable for significantly more claims than the individual, and awards against the corporation were significantly larger than awards against the individual in each category of damages: hospital bills, doctor bills, and especially "pain and suffering." Hans and Ermann point out that this pattern of verdicts might not require an inference that the corporate defendant has deeper pockets than the individual defendant.

In a recent series of studies, I tested the deep-pockets explanation for these results, and my results cast doubt on the explanatory role of defendant wealth.[137] My strategy for testing the deep pockets argument is to construct fictional personal injury cases in which I can plausibly describe the defendant as being a relatively poor blue-collar individual, a corporation, or an individual with wealth equivalent to that of the corporation. The deep pockets hypothesis suggests that liability and awards should be greater for the corporation and for the wealthy individual than for the poor individual. But I've found that jurors treat wealthy and poor individuals the same, despite the fact that they believe the wealthy individual has adequate financial resources for compensating the plaintiff. Instead, liability and awards tend to be greater for the corporation than for either individual, suggesting that some other difference between corporations and individuals drives the effect.[138]

Hans and Ermann suggest that apparent deep pocket results can also be explained by an alternative-standard hypothesis: citizens might hold organizations to more stringent standards of conduct and responsibility than they apply to individual defendants, so the same action is evaluated differently depending on the defendant's identity. I would argue that this hypothesis is consistent with an extension of the "reasonable person standard" used in tort law.[139] W. L. Prosser and W. P. Keeton define this notion as "a personification of a community ideal of reasonable behavior, determined by the jury's social judgment."[140] Interestingly, they point out that the reasonable person's physical attributes should match those of the actor in question; thus, a blind actor should be evaluated relative to what the jury would expect of a reasonable blind person. This suggests that the jury should adopt a "reasonable corporation" standard when evaluating a corporate defendant, and a "reasonable government" standard when evaluating a government standard. The alternative-standard hypothesis is consistent with the argument that the general social and legal trend throughout this century has been toward stricter standards of liability, especially for businesses.[141] A variation on this hypothesis is that jurors hold corporations to the same standard but think that corporations are more likely to fall short—to cut corners in the interest of profits. Alternatively, it may simply be easier for jurors to sanction an impersonal aggregate entity than a flesh-and-blood (or in the mock context, paper-and-pencil) person. Future research will have to sort out these alternatives.

Comparing Juries to Other Legal Factfinders

Several legal scholars have pointed out that the appropriate standard by which to evaluate the quality of jury performance is not some absolute benchmark of perfection, but rather the performance of the most likely alternative factfinder, the trial judge.[142] Or, to extend this argument, the arbitrator, or the expert tribunal. In this section, I will review the limited research that is available on this question.

One approach is to compare verdicts in bench trials and in jury trials. David Rottman's recent study of state courts found that across all tort cases, mean and median awards were larger for juries than for judges.[143] Moreover, awards were considerably more variable in jury trials than in bench trials. Rottman did not attribute these results to judge-jury differences in decisionmaking, however; he argued that the differences are probably attributable to differences in case factors that determine litigants' choice of forum. In another study, Donald Wittman compared jury and arbitration awards and found that juries were more variable than arbitrators.[144] Like Rottman, he noted that forum selection processes could make juries look more unpredictable even if, ceteris paribus, they were equally consistent.

A fascinating new study by Kevin Clermont and Theodore Eisenberg contrasts plaintiff win rates in federal civil bench trials and in federal civil jury trials.[145] The authors argue that their data refute both popular and academic views. The popular view is that juries are pro-plaintiff, suggesting that the ratio of plaintiff victories at bench trial and jury trial ("the win ratio") should be greater than 1.00. The academic view, following the Priest-Klein logic, is that this win ratio should equal 1.00 because of selection processes at work in litigant bargaining. In fact, Clermont and Eisenberg found that the win ratio was 1.15 for motor vehicle torts, 1.71 for products liability torts, and 1.72 for medical malpractice torts. In other words, plaintiffs won more cases before judges than before juries.[146] Does this mean that juries actually have a pro-defendant bias in civil cases? Like Rottman and Wittman, Clermont and Eisenberg point out that such results could be caused by the case selection processes that determine whether a case is settled, taken to a judge, or taken to a jury. They raise three possibilities: same treatment but different cases; different treatment but same cases; or different treatment and different cases. Their analyses argue for the latter, but they acknowledge that these results are not yet fully understood.

One way of getting around the selection problem is to examine how juries and other factfinders decide the same cases. Kalven and Zeisel's seminal University of Chicago Jury Project compared the verdicts of juries with the verdicts that trial judges reported they would have rendered had they tried the case.[147] Kalven and Zeisel found that judges agreed with the jury's verdict about 80 percent of the time and that judges were as likely to agree with juries in complex cases as in simpler ones. In the cases where both agreed that the defendant was liable, 23 percent of the time the jury awarded more, 17 percent of the time the judge said he would have awarded more, and only 4 percent of the time were they in close agreement. On average, the jury awards were 20 percent higher than those the judges would have recommended. Juries found against corporations only 2 percent more often than did judges, but when corporations were liable, juries awarded 25 percent more.[148] One drawback of this study is that judges did not render their verdict recommendations prior to learning the jury's verdict; it is possible that their responses partially reflect their attitudes toward the jury system in addition to their evaluation of the cases at hand.[149]

Wittman tried to control for selection processes by examining awards in trials de novo where juries tried previously arbitrated cases; he found that juries were still less consistent than arbitrators. Of course, a trial de novo will differ in many ways from an arbitration hearing, even for the same case. A much stronger test is to have different decisionmakers evaluate the same body of evidence. For example, Neil Vidmar and Jeffrey Rice asked eighty-nine jurors and twenty-one arbitrators to assess noneconomic damages for the same medical malpractice case.[150] They found no significant differences between juror and arbitrator awards—if anything, the median juror awards were somewhat smaller. Moreover, questionnaire responses suggested that jurors and arbitrators used very similar reasoning processes in determining their awards.

Two recent studies have directly compared decisionmaking by college students and trial judges in the same fictitious cases. One study, discussed earlier, found no differences between these groups in evaluations of blameworthiness, although legal liability judgments were not assessed.[151] In a recent set of experiments on the evaluation of statistical evidence, Gary Wells found a remarkable convergence of liability verdicts for college students and trial judges. Students and judges not only responded almost identically to the same evidence; they also reacted almost identically to experimental *variations* in the evidence.[152] Wells found that many judges demonstrated fallacious statistical reasoning of the sort that has been documented with students and other populations.

A limitation of many of these studies is that they rarely compare the processes by which juries, judges, and arbitrators make decisions. This makes it difficult to draw any inferences about factfinding competence from their findings, for agreement rates tell us nothing about relative or absolute accuracy. Future research might overcome this limitation by assessing factfinding performance using direct measures of accuracy, such as the amount and accuracy of evidence recalled, comprehension of expert testimony, and so forth. Although we know that jurors can make mistakes, no solid evidence suggests that they are less competent than judges as factfinders, and juries might conceivably be more competent at some tasks.[153]

Some readers will greet with some skepticism the notion that juries might outperform judges. After all, judges are drawn from a more restrictive population than jurors, they are specially trained in the law, and they quickly accumulate a great deal more trial experience than most jurors are ever likely to get. But unlike judges (in the typical bench trial), jurors perform in groups rather than individually. Social psychologists have been comparing individual and group performance for decades, and considerable evidence shows that groups outperform individuals on a variety of intellectual tasks, including recall of factual material, generation of solutions to problems, and correction of errors.[154] Of course, these studies typically compared the average performance of individuals and groups sampled from the same population, which is analogous to comparing a single juror to a group of jurors or a single judge to a group of judges. Nonetheless, the heterogeneity of the jury might be a benefit in complex cases. Juries might actually be better suited than judges for coping with some dimensions of complex litigation.[155]

Conclusions

The debate over civil-jury performance has relied too heavily on speculation, hearsay, and circumstantial evidence. Throughout this paper, I have argued that systematic empirical research is needed if policymakers are to draw sound conclusions about proposals for modifying the civil jury system. I believe that the research I've reviewed here can provide readers with a more informed perspective on civil-jury behavior, but most of the research on the topic has only been conducted in the past decade— much of it in the past five years. A great deal remains to be learned.

A reasoned evaluation of civil-jury performance should be premised on explicit performance criteria. Scholars have identified a variety of standards that legal experts and lay citizens have used to evaluate jury performance.[156] I have summarized and integrated these criteria in figure 5-1.

These criteria aren't completely independent of each other; instead, they are loosely coupled. For example, high accuracy would seem to imply high consistency (but only if we know which cases to compare), whereas high consistency needn't imply high accuracy. Factfinding competence and impartiality are presumably prerequisites for accuracy, but we can rarely assess decision accuracy directly; indeed, if we knew the right verdict, we wouldn't need a jury.[157] Thus, we use other criteria as imperfect proxies for accuracy. When the correct answer isn't known, citizens tend to evaluate legal decisions in terms of the apparent fairness of the procedures that produced them.[158]

Little consensus exists regarding the relative importance and appropriateness of these criteria. In fact, this disagreement over criteria character-

Figure 5-1. *Criteria for Evaluating the Jury System*

Representativeness
Representation of an approximate cross section of the community
Representation and expression of a diversity of viewpoints
Impartiality
No extralegal biases in deliberation
No systematic patterns of extralegal bias in verdicts
Legal competence
Comprehension of relevant laws and legal standards
Compliance with relevant laws and legal standards
Factfinding competence
Thorough and accurate recollection of evidence
Logical coherence of inferences drawn from the evidence
Accuracy of decision
Attribution of guilt or liability supported by evidence
Plausible calculation of economic damages in civil litigation
Consistency of decision
Consistency across jury verdicts in similar cases
Consistency across jury verdicts in different jurisdictions
Dispute resolution
Perception by the disputants that the decision process was fair
Acceptance of the decision by the disputants
Legitimacy
Public perception that jury composition and verdicts are fair
Educative function and sense of efficacy derived from participation
Efficiency
Reasonable duration of trial
Reasonable expense of trial

izes a great deal of the civil-jury controversy. In this chapter, I have reviewed evidence on many of these criteria, but the data cannot provide a conclusive verdict—nor would my readers accept one as valid. Empirical research is an essential input to the evaluation process, but the process is itself a judgment task, not unlike the task of the jury in many ways.

Given what we know so far, what's my scorecard for figure 5-1? This is a judgment call involving some speculation beyond existing data, but based on what we now know, I would give judges the edge on legal competence and efficiency, but juries the edge on representativeness, dispute resolution, and legitimacy.[159] Factfinding competence, decision consistency, and decision accuracy are uncertain, but I would expect groups to outperform individuals, the average judge to outperform the average juror, and the appropriate expert to outperform the average judge and the average juror. Thus juries should outperform jurors, judicial panels should outperform judges, and expert panels should outperform lone experts, but it is anybody's guess how juries stack up against lone experts or lone judges. *Impartiality* is a question mark. I've cited evidence that jurors are vulnerable to extralegal biases, but we know that judges are also vulnerable in this regard, even with the best of intentions.[160]

What's the bottom line? Should we abolish or curtail the civil-jury system? As I've argued, the existing data cannot speak for themselves. We still know too little to make an informed judgment. Even if we knew more, the conclusion would depend on one's ranking of the criteria, deciding which are absolutely crucial and which might be traded off against each other. Different people will provide different rankings. Are we fiddling while Rome burns? Fiddling, perhaps, but I don't see that Rome *is* burning—I don't see compelling evidence that the civil-jury system is fatally flawed. It is unrealistic to expect perfection from any legal factfinding procedure. Indeed, the choice among legal decisionmakers probably involves inevitable trade-offs among social desiderata. If so, we should make sure that our choices are well informed.

Notes

1. For a view of the debate thirty years ago, see Milton D. Green, "Juries and Justice—The Jury's Role in Personal Injury Cases," *University of Illinois Law Forum*, vol. 1962 (Summer 1962), pp. 152–71; and Harry Kalven, Jr., "The Dignity of the Civil Jury," *Virginia Law Review*, vol. 50 (October 1964), pp. 1055–75. For a much longer view, see Stephan Landsman's chapter in this volume.

2. See President's Council on Competitiveness, *Agenda for Civil Justice Reform in American* (August 1991); American Bar Association, *ABA Blueprint for Improving the Civil Justice System* (February 1992); Brookings Task Force on Civil Justice Reform, *Justice for All: Reducing Costs and Delay in Civil Litigation* (Brookings, 1989); *Reporter's Study: Enterprise Responsibility for Personal Injury* (American Law Institute, April 1991); and *Who Should Be Liable? A Guide to Policy for Dealing with Risk* (Committee for Economic Development, 1989).

3. See James K. Hammitt, Stephen J. Carroll, and Daniel A. Relles, "Tort Standards and Jury Decisions," *Journal of Legal Studies*, vol. 14 (December 1985), pp. 751–62; and Robert J. MacCoun, "Unintended Consequences of Court Arbitration: A Cautionary Tale from New Jersey," *Justice System Journal*, vol. 14 (1991), pp. 229–43.

4. See Harry Kalven, Jr., "The Jury, the Law, and the Personal Injury Award," *Ohio State Law Journal*, vol. 19 (Spring 1958), pp. 158–78.

5. I also recommend Joe S. Cecil, Valerie P. Hans, and Elizabeth C. Wiggins, "Citizen Comprehension of Difficult Issues: Lessons from Civil Jury Trials," *American University Law Review*, vol. 40 (Winter 1991), pp. 727–74.

6. For some examples, see Stephen Daniels, "The Question of Jury Competence and the Politics of Civil Justice Reform: Symbols, Rhetoric, and Agenda-Building," *Law and Contemporary Problems*, vol. 52 (Autumn 1989), pp. 269–310; and Loretta J. Stalans and Shari Seidman Diamond, "Formation and Change in Lay Evaluations of Criminal Sen-

tencing: Misperception and Discontent," *Law and Human Behavior*, vol. 14 (June 1990), pp. 199–214.

7. For example, the *ABA Journal* has an annual listing of the year's ten largest jury verdicts. While a sample size of ten is better than a sample size of one, it clearly falls far short of an adequate statistical sample. Surely no lawyer or executive would grant credence to a public opinion or marketing survey based on only ten responses. Daniel Bailis and I are conducting a statistical content analysis of media reporting of civil-jury verdicts to assess the degree of accuracy or of distortion of liability patterns.

8. See Paul Slovic, Baruch Fishchoff, and Sarah Lichtenstein, "Facts versus Fears: Understanding Perceived Risk," in Daniel Kahneman, Paul Slovic, and Amos Tversky, eds., *Judgment under Uncertainty* (Cambridge University Press, 1982).

9. See Donald R. Songer, "Tort Reform in South Carolina: The Effect of Empirical Research on Elite Perceptions Concerning Jury Verdicts," *South Carolina Law Review*, vol. 39 (Spring 1988), pp. 585–605; and James N. Dertouzos and Lynn A. Karoly, *Labor Market Responses to Employer Liability* (Santa Monica: Rand Institute for Civil Justice, 1992). Note that even if liability risks were perceived accurately, highly risk-averse decisionmakers might continue to focus on the high end of the risk distribution; see James G. March and Zur Shapira, "Managerial Perspectives on Risk and Risk Taking," *Management Science*, vol. 33 (November 1987), pp. 1404–18.

10. William L. F. Felstiner, Richard L. Abel, and Austin Sarat, "The Emergence and Transformation of Disputes: Naming, Blaming, Claiming," *Law & Society Review*, vol. 15 (1980–81), pp. 631–54; Deborah R. Hensler and others, *Compensation for Accidental Injuries in the United States* (Santa Monica: Rand Institute for Civil Justice, 1991).

11. MacCoun, "Unintended Consequences."

12. Marc Galanter, "Jury Shadows: Reflections on the Civil Jury and the 'Litigation Explosion,'" in Morris S. Arnold and others, *The American Civil Jury* (Washington: Roscoe Pound American Trial Lawyers Foundation, 1987), pp. 15–42; and Marc Galanter, "The Civil Jury as a Regulator of the Litigation Process," *University of Chicago Legal Forum*, vol. 1990, pp. 201–71.

13. These models are reviewed by Robert D. Cooter and Daniel L. Rubinfeld, "Economic Analysis of Legal Disputes and Their Resolution," *Journal of Economic Literature*, vol. 27 (September 1989), pp. 1067–97.

14. George L. Priest and Benjamin Klein, "The Selection of Disputes for Litigation," *Journal of Legal Studies*, vol. 13 (January 1984), pp. 1–55.

15. For example, Donald Wittman, "Is the Selection of Cases for Trial Biased?" *Journal of Legal Studies*, vol. 14 (January 1985), pp. 185–214; and Theodore Eisenberg, "Testing the Selection Effect: A New Theoretical Framework with Empirical Tests," *Journal of Legal Studies*, vol. 19 (June 1990), pp. 337–58. A weakness of the Priest-Klein and similar models is their neglect of *noneconomic* considerations in litigant decisionmaking; see Robert MacCoun, E. Allan Lind, and Tom Tyler, "Alternative Dispute Resolution in Trial and Appellate Courts," in Dorothy K. Kagehiro and William S. Laufer, eds., *Handbook of Psychology and Law* (Springer-Verlag, 1992), pp. 95–118; and Hensler and others, *Compensation for Accidental Injuries*.

16. Harry Kalven, Jr., and Hans Zeisel, *The American Jury* (Little, Brown, 1966), pp. vi–vii; and Enid Campbell, "Jury Secrecy and Contempt of Court," *Monash University Law Review*, vol. 11 (December 1985), pp. 165–200. The advantages and disadvantages of jury secrecy are considered in "Public Disclosures of Jury Deliberations," *Harvard Law Review*, vol. 96 (February 1983), pp. 886–906.

17. The Public Broadcasting Service television documentary "Frontline: Inside the Jury Room" (April 11, 1986) provided a rare exception to this secrecy by videotaping an actual criminal jury deliberation in a trial court in Wisconsin.

18. An additional approach is the use of formal modeling and computer simulation; it

is a powerful analytic method but does not produce empirical data on jury behavior. See Steven Penrod and Reid Hastie, "Models of Jury Decisionmaking: A Critical Review," *Psychological Bulletin*, vol. 86 (May 1979), pp. 462–92; and Reid Hastie, Steven Penrod, and Nancy Pennington, *Inside the Jury* (Harvard University Press, 1983).

19. The ICJ's archival work on juries is summarized in Deborah R. Hensler and others, *Trends in Tort Litigation: The Story Behind the Statistics* (Santa Monica: Rand Institute for Civil Justice, 1987). Stephen Daniels and Joanne Martin at the American Bar Foundation (ABF) have another major program of archival jury research that is reviewed in this paper. The ICJ data is more useful for describing variation over time, while the ABF data is more useful for describing variation across jurisdictions. More recently, the National Center for State Courts has assembled a sample of verdicts from twenty-seven state trial courts in 1989; it is also reviewed in this paper.

20. See Campbell, "Jury Secrecy"; also note, "Public Disclosures"; Valerie P. Hans and William S. Lofquist, "Jurors' Judgments of Business Liability in Tort Cases: Implications for the Litigation Explosion Debate," *Law & Society Review*, vol. 26 (February 1992), pp. 85–116; Elizabeth F. Loftus, Jane Goodman, and Edith Greene, *Jury Comprehension in Complex Cases: Report of the Special Committee of the ABA Section on Litigation* (American Bar Association, 1990); John Guinther, "The Jury in America," in *American Civil Jury*, pp. 45–67; Molly Selvin and Larry Picus, *The Debate Over Jury Performance: Observations from a Recent Asbestos Case* (Santa Monica, Calif.: Rand Institute for Civil Justice, 1987); Arthur D. Austin, *Complex Litigation Confronts the Jury System: A Case Study* (University Publications of America, 1984); and C. L. Hinchcliff, "Portrait of a Juror: A Selected Bibliography," *Marquette Law Review*, vol. 69 (Summer 1986), pp. 495–514.

21. See Loftus and others, *Jury Comprehension*, p. 4.

22. Richard Nisbett and Lee Ross, *Human Inference: Strategies and Shortcomings of Social Judgment* (Prentice Hall, 1980), chap. 9.

23. Donald E. Vinson, "The Shadow Jury: An Experiment in Litigation Science," *American Bar Association Journal*, vol. 68 (October 1982), pp. 1243–46. In a more sophisticated variant called the *alternate jury method*, potential jurors watch the trial without knowing whether they will be on the true jury or the alternate jury, and in some cases may even deliberate without knowing for sure; see Loftus and others, *Jury Comprehension*.

24. Hans Zeisel and Shari S. Diamond, "The Effect of Peremptory Challenges on Jury and Verdict: An Experiment in a Federal District Court," *Stanford Law Review*, vol. 30 (February 1978), pp. 491–531.

25. This became a major problem for the recent American Bar Association study of jury comprehension; see Loftus and others, *Jury Comprehension*, p. iii.

26. Thomas D. Cook and Donald T. Campbell, *Quasi-Experimentation: Design and Analysis Issues for Field Settings* (Houghton-Mifflin, 1979).

27. Larry Heuer and Steven D. Penrod, "Increasing Jurors' Participation in Trials: A Field Experiment with Jury Notetaking and Question Asking," *Law and Human Behavior*, vol. 12 (September 1988), pp. 231–62; and Larry Heuer and Steven Penrod, "Instructing Jurors: A Field Experiment with Written and Preliminary Instructions," *Law and Human Behavior*, vol. 13 (December 1989), pp. 409–30.

28. The term *mock jury* is occasionally used to describe a very different technique—the use of groups of citizens who view an abbreviated case and then deliberate in order to help attorneys prepare for a trial. In this paper, the mock-jury method will be used to refer to mock jury research experiments rather than to adversarial trial techniques.

29. Valerie P. Hans and Neil Vidmar, *Judging the Jury*; (Plenum Press, 1986); and Robert MacCoun, "Experimental Research on Jury Decisionmaking," *Science*, vol. 244 (June 5, 1989), pp. 1046–50.

30. Shari Seidman Diamond and Jonathan D. Casper, "Blindfolding the Jury to Verdict Consequences: Damages, Experts, and the Civil Jury," Working Paper 9127, American Bar Foundation, 1991.

31. Why didn't they use a videotape of an actual trial? First, the sheer length of many actual trials makes them impractical for use in mock-jury research, where tens of different juries try the same basic case. And reenacted trials allow the researcher to construct and manipulate trial events for experimental purposes.

32. For a good example, see Hastie and others, *Inside the Jury*.

33. This issue is debated in the special issue of *Law and Human Behavior* on research methodology, vol. 3, no. 1/2 (1979).

34. See Hastie, Penrod, and Pennington, *Inside the Jury*, p. 41.

35. For example, Robert J. MacCoun and Norbert L. Kerr, "Asymmetric Influence in Mock Jury Deliberation: Jurors' Bias for Leniency," *Journal of Personality and Social Psychology*, vol. 54 (January 1988), pp. 21–33.

36. See Cook and Campbell, *Quasi-Experimentation*.

37. Most of what we know about actual patterns of jury verdicts comes from work by Mark Peterson and colleagues at Rand's ICJ and Stephen Daniels and Joanne Martin at the ABF. The ICJ findings are described in Mark A. Peterson and George L. Priest, *The Civil Jury: Trends in Trials and Verdicts, Cook County, Illinois, 1960–1979* (Santa Monica: Rand Institute for Civil Justice, 1982); Michael G. Shanley and Mark Peterson, *Comparative Justice: Civil Jury Verdicts in San Francisco and Cook Counties, 1959–1980* (Santa Monica: Rand Institute for Civil Justice, 1983); Mark Peterson, *Compensation of Injuries: Civil Jury Verdicts in Cook County* (Santa Monica: Rand Institute for Civil Justice, 1984); Audrey Chin and Mark Peterson, *Deep Pockets, Empty Pockets: Who Wins in Cook County Jury Trials* (Santa Monica: Rand Institute for Civil Justice, 1985); Mark Peterson, *Civil Juries in the 1980s: Trends in Jury Trials and Verdicts in California and Cook County, Illinois* (Santa Monica: Rand Institute for Civil Justice, 1987); Mark Peterson, Syam Sarma, and Michael Shanley, *Punitive Damages: Empirical Findings* (Santa Monica: Rand Institute for Civil Justice, 1987); and Michael Shanley and Mark Peterson, *Posttrial Adjustments to Jury Awards* (Santa Monica: Rand Institute for Civil Justice, 1987). The ABF research is described in Stephen Daniels and Joanne Martin, "Jury Verdicts and the 'Crisis' in Civil Justice," *Justice System Journal*, vol. 11 (Winter 1986), pp. 321–48; Stephen Daniels, "Tracing the Shadow of the Law: Jury Verdicts in Medical Malpractice Cases," *Defense Law Journal*, vol. 40 (July 1991), pp. 415–49; and Stephen Daniels and Joanne Martin, "Myth and Reality in Punitive Damages," *Minnesota Law Review*, vol. 75 (October 1990), pp. 1–64. Studies by other investigators are cited later. The estimates presented here vary somewhat across studies because of some mix of differences in the sampling of time periods, sites, and case types.

38. This should change in the very near future. Both the ICJ and the jury-verdict data bases are currently being updated and geographically broadened. A recent study by the National Center for State Courts (NCSC) presents data on all tort verdicts in twenty-seven state courts during three months in 1989; see Brian Ostrom, David Rottman, and Roger Hanson, "What Are Tort Awards Really Like? The Untold Story from the State Courts," National Center for State Courts, Arlington, Va., 1992. Theodore Eisenberg and James A. Henderson, Jr., present analyses of trends in product liability verdicts in the federal courts between 1978 and 1989; see "Inside the Quiet Revolution in Products Liability," *UCLA Law Review*, vol. 39 (April 1992), pp. 731–810.

39. Priest and Klein, "Selection of Disputes."

40. See Eisenberg, "Testing the Selection Effect."

41. Daniels and Martin, "Jury Verdicts." The NCSC study of tort cases found a rate of 54 percent across five state courts during 1989; see Ostrom and others, "Tort Awards."

42. Daniels and Martin, "Jury Verdicts"; Ostrom and others, "Tort Awards"; and Peterson, *Civil Juries in the 1980s*.

43. About 32 percent in Daniels, "Tracing the Shadow of the Law," p. 423; 33 percent for Randall R. Bovberg and others, "Juries and Justice: Are Malpractice and Other Personal Injuries Created Equal?" *Law and Contemporary Problems*, vol. 54 (Winter 1991), p. 22; 29 percent in Ostrom and others, "Tort Awards"; and 19 percent in Thomas B. Metzloff, "Resolving Malpractice Disputes: Imaging the Jury's Shadow," *Law and Contemporary Problems*, vol. 54 (Winter 1991), p. 50. Peterson reports higher rates in Cook County (including Chicago) in the 1980s; see *Civil Juries in the 1980s*, p. 17.

44. Peterson, *Civil Juries in the 1980s*; Daniels and Martin, "Jury Verdicts"; Hammitt, Carroll, and Relles, "Tort Standards"; and Stuart Low and Janet Kiholm Smith, "The Relationship of Alternative Negligence Rules to Litigation Behavior and Tort Claim Disposition," *Law and Social Inquiry*, vol. 17 (Winter 1992), pp. 63–87.

45. See Peterson, *Civil Juries in the 1980s*; and Daniels and Martin, "Jury Verdicts"; note that both sets of data end their coverage at 1985.

46. Theodore Eisenberg and James A. Henderson, Jr. "Inside the Quiet Revolution in Products Liability," *UCLA Law Review*, vol. 39 (April 1992), pp. 731–810.

47. Peterson and Priest, *The Civil Jury*.

48. Daniels and Martin, "Jury Verdicts"; and Ostrom and others, "Tort Awards." Ostrom and others report medians of $250,000 and $215,000 for medical malpractice and product liability awards, respectively. A recent Government Accounting Office study of product-liability verdicts in five states during 1983–85 found mean and median awards of $845,000 and $157,000, respectively; see *Product Liability: Verdicts and Case Resolution in Five States*, GAO/HRD-89-99 (September 1989).

49. Shanley and Peterson, *Posttrial Adjustments*; see also Ivy E. Broder, "Characteristics of Million Dollar Awards: Jury Verdicts and Final Reimbursements," *Justice System Journal*, vol. 11 (Winter 1986), pp. 349–59; and Government Accounting Office, *Product Liability*, chap. 3.

50. Hensler and others, *Trends in Tort Litigation*. Henderson and Eisenberg's study suggests that mean product-liability awards in the federal courts peaked in 1986 and declined somewhat thereafter; see "Inside the Quiet Revolution," p. 765.

51. Peterson, *Civil Juries in the 1980s*.

52. On this latter point, I highly recommend Michael J. Saks, "Do We Really Know Anything about the Behavior of the Tort Litigation System—and Why Not?" *University of Pennsylvania Law Review*, vol. 140 (April 1992), pp. 1147–1292.

53. Peterson and others, *Punitive Damages*; Daniels and Martin, "Myth and Reality in Punitive Damages"; General Accounting Office, *Product Liability*; and Michael Rustad, *Demystifying Punitive Damages in Products Liability Cases: A Survey of a Quarter Century of Trial Verdicts* (Roscoe Pound Foundation, 1991).

54. See also Government Accounting Office, *Product Liability*, pp. 25–26.

55. Daniels and Martin, "Jury Verdicts"; and Daniels, "Tracing the Shadow of the Law."

56. Tom Wolfe in *The Bonfire of the Vanities* (Farrar, Strauss, Giroux, 1987); see also Arthur S. Hayes, "Bronx Cheer: Inner-City Jurors Tend to Rebuff Prosecutors and to Back Plaintiffs," *Wall Street Journal* (March 24, 1992), p. 1.

57. Daniels, "Tracing the Shadow of the Law," p. 32.

58. Ostrom and others, "Tort Awards," p. 21.

59. I limit my discussion, however, to the composition of the jury, not the jury pool. For research on the latter, see Joe S. Cecil, E. Allan Lind, and Gordon Bermant, *Jury Service in Lengthy Civil Trials* (Washington: Federal Judicial Center, 1987); and Hiroshi Fukurai and Edgar W. Butler, "Organization, Labor Force, and Jury Representation:

Economic Excuses and Jury Participation," *Jurimetrics Journal of Law, Science and Technology*, vol. 32 (Fall 1991), pp. 49–69.

60. Solomon M. Fulero and Steven D. Penrod, "Attorney Selection Folklore: What Do They Think and How Can Psychologists Help?" *Ohio Northern University Law Review*, vol. 17 (Spring 1990), pp. 229–53.

61. Norbert L. Kerr and others, "On the Effectiveness of Voir Dire in Criminal Cases with Prejudicial Pretrial Publicity: An Empirical Study," *American University Law Review*, vol. 40 (Winter 1991), pp. 665–701; and Reid Hastie, "Is Attorney-Conducted Voir Dire an Effective Procedure for the Selection of Impartial Juries?" *American University Law Review*, vol. 40 (Winter 1991), pp. 703–26. Of course, attorneys have other objectives for voir dire besides identifying favorable jurors.

62. Shari Seidman Diamond, "Scientific Jury Selection: What Social Scientists Know and Do Not Know," *Judicature*, vol. 73 (December–January 1989), pp. 178–83; Steven Penrod and Daniel Linz, "Voir Dire: Uses and Abuses," in Martin F. Kaplan, ed., *The Impact of Social Psychology on Procedural Justice* (C. C. Thomas, 1986), pp. 135–63; Hastie, Penrod, and Pennington, *Inside the Jury*, chap. 7; Hans and Vidmar, *Judging the Jury*, chaps. 4–6; and the special issue of *Forensic Reports*, vol. 3, no. 3 (1990).

63. In general, psychologists have found that such variables in individual differences are more successful at predicting broad patterns of behavior than at predicting any single behavior, such as voting for a verdict. See Mark Snyder and William Ickes, "Personality and Social Behavior," in Gardner Linzey and Elliot Aronson, eds., *Handbook of Social Psychology*, 3d ed., vol. 2 (Random House, 1985), pp. 883–947. Of course, attorneys are usually interested in predicting a fairly limited number of behaviors during voir dire.

64. R. S. Tindale and D. H. Nagao, "An Assessment of the Potential Utility of 'Scientific Jury Selection': A 'Thought Experiment' Approach," *Organizational Behavior and Human Decision Processes*, vol. 37 (June 1986), pp. 409–25; and Gary Moran, Brian L. Cutler, and Elizabeth Loftus, "Jury Selection in Major Controlled Substance Trials: The Need for Extended Voir Dire," *Forensic Reports*, vol. 3 (1990), pp. 331–48.

65. Jane Goodman, Elizabeth Loftus, and Edith Greene, "Matters of Money: Voir Dire in Civil Cases," *Forensic Reports*, vol. 3 (1990), pp. 303–29; and Edith Greene, Jane Goodman, and Elizabeth Loftus, "Jurors' Attitudes About Civil Litigation and the Size of Damage Awards," *American University Law Review*, vol. 40 (Winter 1991), pp. 805–20. See also Kalven, "The Dignity of the Civil Jury," p. 174. Interestingly, Greene and others found that jurors who believed million-dollar awards were common tended to give larger awards, not smaller, suggesting that some tort reform advertisements may have had unintended consequences.

66. Hans and Vidmar, *Judging the Jury*, chap. 8; A. Elwork and Bruce D. Sales, "Jury Instructions," in S. M. Kassin and L. S. Wrightsman, eds., *The Psychology of Evidence and Trial Procedure* (Sage, 1985), pp. 280–91; and Phoebe C. Ellsworth, "Are Twelve Heads Better than One?" *Law and Contemporary Problems*, vol. 52 (Autumn 1989), pp. 205–24.

67. Elwork and Sales, "Jury Instructions"; Heuer and Penrod, "Instructing Jurors"; Vicki L. Smith, "Impact of Pretrial Instruction on Jurors' Information Processing and Decision Making," *Journal of Applied Psychology*, vol. 76 (April 1991), pp. 220–28; Lynne Forster Lee, Irwin A. Horowitz, and Martin J. Bourgeois, "Juror Competence in Civil Trials: The Effects of Preinstruction and Evidence Technicality," *Journal of Applied Psychology* (forthcoming); and Dorothy K. Kagehiro, "Defining the Standard of Proof in Jury Instructions," *Psychological Science*, vol. 1 (1990), pp. 194–200.

68. For example, William C. Thompson, Geoffrey T. Fong, and D. L. Rosenhan, "Inadmissible Evidence and Juror Verdicts," *Journal of Personality and Social Psychology*, vol. 40 (March 1981), pp. 453–63; and Jonathan D. Casper, Kennette Benedict, and Jo

Perry, "Juror Decision Making, Attitudes, and the Hindsight Bias," *Law and Human Behavior*, vol. 13 (September 1989), pp. 291–310.

69. Richard L. Weiner and others, "The Social Psychology of Jury Nullification: Predicting When Jurors Disobey the Law," *Journal of Applied Social Psychology*, vol. 21 (September 1991), pp. 1379–1401; and Irwin A. Horowitz and Thomas E. Willging, "Changing Views of Jury Power: The Nullification Debate, 1787–1988," *Law and Human Behavior*, vol. 15 (April 1991), pp. 165–82.

70. These models are reviewed by MacCoun, "Experimental Research on Jury Decision Making," and by Nancy Pennington and Reid Hastie, "Juror Decision-Making Models: The Generalization Gap," *Psychological Bulletin*, vol. 89 (March 1981), pp. 246–87.

71. Lola Lopes, commentary at the Juror Decisionmaking Conference, Northwestern University, May 11, 1986.

72. See Robin M. Hogarth and Hillel Einhorn, "Order Effects in Belief Updating: The Belief-Adjustment Model," *Cognitive Psychology*, vol. 24 (January 1992), pp. 1–55.

73. See MacCoun, "Experimental Research on Jury Decision Making"; and Pennington and Hastie, "Juror Decision-Making Models."

74. Nancy Pennington and Reid Hastie, "A Cognitive Theory of Juror Decision Making: The Story Model," *Cardozo Law Review*, vol. 13 (November 1991), pp. 5001–39; "Evidence Evaluation in Complex Decision Making," *Journal of Personality and Social Psychology*, vol. 51 (August 1986), pp. 242–58; "Explanation-Based Decisionmaking: Effects of Memory Structure on Judgment," *Journal of Experimental Psychology: Learning, Memory, and Cognition*, vol. 14 (July 1988), pp. 521–33; "Explaining the Evidence: Tests of the Story Model for Juror Decisionmaking," *Journal of Personality and Social Psychology*, vol. 62 (February 1992), pp. 189–206; and W. Lance Bennett and Martha S. Feldman, *Reconstructing Reality in the Courtroom: Justice and Judgement in American Culture* (Rutgers University Press, 1981).

75. Vicki L. Smith, "Prototypes in the Courtroom: Lay Representations of Legal Concepts," *Journal of Personality and Social Psychology*, vol. 61 (December 1991), pp. 857–72.

76. See Fritz Heider, *The Psychology of Interpersonal Relations* (Wiley, 1958); Edward E. Jones and Kenneth E. Davis, "From Acts to Dispositions: The Attribution Process in Person Perception," in Leonard Berkowitz, ed., *Advances in Experimental Social Psychology*, vol. 2 (Academic Press, 1965), pp. 219–66; Harold H. Kelley, "Attribution Theory in Social Psychology," in D. Levine, ed., *Nebraska Symposium on Motivation* (University of Nebraska Press, 1967), pp. 192–238; Hillel J. Einhorn and Robin M. Hogarth, "Judging Probable Cause," *Psychological Bulletin*, vol. 99 (January 1986), pp. 3–19; and Patricia W. Cheng and Laura R. Novick, "Covariation in Natural Causal Induction," *Psychological Review*, vol. 99 (April 1992), pp. 365–82.

77. Nisbett and Ross, *Human Inference*.

78. Frank D. Fincham and J. M. Jaspars, "Attribution of Responsibility: From Man the Scientist to Man as Lawyer," in Leonard Berkowitz, ed., *Advances in Experimental Social Psychology*, vol. 13 (Academic Press, 1980), pp. 81–138; V. Lee Hamilton, "Intuitive Psychologist or Intuitive Lawyer? Alternative Models of the Attribution Process," *Journal of Personality and Social Psychology*, vol. 39 (November 1980), pp. 767–72; and Herbert L. A. Hart and Tony Honoré, *Causation in the Law* (Oxford University Press, 1959).

79. Of course the law also defines exceptions in which actors are liable for outcomes they did not cause directly, including strict liability and vicarious liability.

80. Kelly G. Shaver, *The Attribution of Blame: Causality, Responsibility, and Blameworthiness* (Springer-Verlag, 1985); and V. Lee Hamilton and Joseph Sanders, *Everyday Justice: Responsibility and the Individual in Japan and the United States* (Yale University Press, 1992).

81. Edward Green, "The Reasonable Man: Legal Fiction or Psychosocial Reality," *Law & Society Review*, vol. 2 (February 1968), pp. 241–57.

82. Joel T. Johnson and Jerome Drobny, "Proximity Biases in the Attribution of Civil Liability," *Journal of Personality and Social Psychology*, vol. 48 (February 1985), pp. 283–96; and Joel T. Johnson and Jerome Drobny, "Happening Soon and Happening Later: Temporal Cues and Attributions of Liability," *Basic and Applied Social Psychology*, vol. 8 (September 1987), pp. 209–34. See also Einhorn and Hogarth, "Judging Probable Cause."

83. Ewart A. C. Thomas and Mary Parpal, "Liability as a Function of Plaintiff and Defendant Fault," *Journal of Personality and Social Psychology*, vol. 53 (November 1987), pp. 843–57.

84. Cheng and Novick, "Covariation"; and Einhorn and Hogarth, "Judging Probable Cause." See also Hart and Honoré, *Causation in the Law*; and John L. Mackie, *The Cement of the Universe: A Study of Causation* (Clarendon Press, 1974).

85. Daniel Kahneman and Dale T. Miller, "Norm Theory: Comparing Reality to Its Alternatives," *Psychological Review*, vol. 93 (April 1986), pp. 136–53; and Dale T. Miller, William Turnbull, and Cathy McFarland, "Counterfactual Thinking and Social Perception: Thinking about What Might Have Been," in M. Zanna, ed., *Advances in Experimental Social Psychology*, vol. 23 (Academic Press, 1990), pp. 305–31.

86. Dale T. Miller and Cathy McFarland, "Counterfactual Thinking and Victim Compensation: A Test of Norm Theory," *Personality and Social Psychology Bulletin*, vol. 12 (December 1986), pp. 513–19; and C. Neil Macrae, "A Tale of Two Curries: Counterfactual Thinking and Accident-Related Judgments," *Personality and Social Psychology Bulletin*, vol. 18 (February 1992), pp. 84–87. Another recent study failed to find the effect. Jane Goodman, Edith Greene, and Elizabeth F. Loftus, "Runaway Verdicts or Reasoned Determinations: Mock Juror Strategies in Awarding Damages," *Jurimetrics Journal of Law, Science and Technology*, vol. 29 (Spring 1989), pp. 285–309.

87. Martin J. Bourgeois, Irwin A. Horowitz, and Lynne Forster Lee, "The Effects of Technicality and Access to Trial Transcripts on Verdicts and Information Processing in a Civil Trial," *Personality and Social Psychology Bulletin* (forthcoming).

88. David A. Schum and Anne W. Martin, "Formal and Empirical Research on Cascaded Inference in Jurisprudence," *Law & Society Review*, vol. 17 (November 1982), pp. 105–51.

89. Elizabeth C. Wiggins and Steven J. Breckler, "Special Verdicts as Guides to Jury Decisionmaking," *Law and Psychology Review*, vol. 14 (Spring 1990), pp. 1–41.

90. Morton Deutsch, "Equity, Equality, and Need: What Determines Which Value Will Be Used as the Basis for Distributive Justice?" *Journal of Social Issues*, vol. 31 (Summer 1975), pp. 137–49; and Jennifer L. Hochschild, *What's Fair? American Beliefs about Distributive Justice* (Harvard University Press, 1981).

91. Robert J. MacCoun (unpublished data, Rand, 1991).

92. Green, "The Reasonable Man," p. 246; Peterson, *Compensation of Injuries*, p. 41; Thomas and Parpal, "Liability as a Function of Plaintiff and Defendant Fault," pp. 851–52; and Bovbjerg and others, "Juries and Justice."

93. Edmund S. Howe and Thomas C. Loftus, "Integration of Intention and Outcome Information by Students and Circuit Court Judges: Design Economy and Individual Differences," *Journal of Applied Social Psychology*, vol. 22 (January 1992), pp. 102–16.

94. Irwin A. Horowitz and Kenneth S. Bordens, "An Experimental Investigation of Procedural Issues in Complex Tort Trials," *Law and Human Behavior*, vol. 14 (June 1990), pp. 269–85. Although plaintiffs fared better on liability in the unitary condition, they fared better on damages in the bifurcated condition; awards were significantly lower in unitary trials than in bifurcated trials where liability was found.

95. I limit my discussion to compensatory rather than punitive damages, because we

currently know very little about punitive damage judgments. Some variables that might be examined include award recipient (plaintiff versus charitable fund), nature of defendant conduct, severity of harm, extent of risk of harm (broad or limited), and the wealth and identity of the defendant. My colleagues and I at the ICJ plan to examine some of these effects in a mock-jury experiment.

96. Kalven, "Dignity of the Civil Jury," p. 1069.

97. Kalven, "The Jury, The Law," p. 161.

98. Selvin and Picus, *Debate over Jury Performance.*

99. Goodman, Greene, and Loftus, "Runaway Verdicts."

100. Dale W. Broeder, "The University of Chicago Jury Project," *Nebraska Law Review,* vol. 38 (May 1959), pp. 744–60.

101. Kahneman, Slovic, and Tversky, *Judgment Under Uncertainty*; and Hogarth and Einhorn, "Belief-Adjustment Model."

102. Broeder, "Chicago Jury Project," p. 758.

103. J. J. Zuehl, "The Ad Damnum, Jury Instructions, and Personal Injury Damage Awards," University of Chicago, Department of Sociology, August 4, 1982.

104. Allan Raitz and others, "Determining Damages: The Influence of Expert Testimony on Jurors' Decision Making," *Law and Human Behavior,* vol. 14 (August 1990), pp. 385–95.

105. Irwin A. Horowitz and Kenneth S. Bordens, "The Effects of Outlier Presence, Plaintiff Population Size, and Aggregation of Plaintiffs on Simulated Civil Jury Decisions," *Law and Human Behavior,* vol. 12 (September 1988), pp. 209–30.

106. The study also found that defendant negligence increases as a function of the size of the nontrial plaintiff population.

107. Kalven, "The Jury, The Law," p. 161; Goodman, Greene, and Loftus, "Runaway Verdicts," found that about 27 percent of the mock jurors in their sample arrived at a global damage award without explicit computations.

108. Kalven, "The Jury, The Law," p. 163; Shari Seidman Diamond, Jonathan D. Casper, and Lynne Ostergren, "Blindfolding the Jury," *Law and Contemporary Problems,* vol. 52 (Autumn 1989), pp. 247–67; Diamond and Casper, "Blindfolding the Jury."

109. Hammitt, Carroll, and Relles, "Tort Standards"; Broeder, "Chicago Jury Project"; Selvin and Picus, *Debate over Jury Performance*; Goodman, Greene, and Loftus, "Runaway Verdicts"; Raitz and others, "Determining Damages"; and Diamond and Casper, "Blindfolding the Jury."

110. Hammitt, Carroll, and Relles, "Tort Standards."

111. See Diamond and Casper, "Blindfolding the Jury."

112. MacCoun, "Experimental Research on Jury Decision Making"; Hastie and others, *Inside the Jury*; Penrod and Hastie, "Models of Jury Decision Making"; and Kalven and Zeisel, *American Jury.*

113. MacCoun and Kerr, "Asymmetric Influence."

114. Kalven and Zeisel, *American Jury.*

115. Guinther, "Jury in America," p. 53; and Diamond and Casper, "Blindfolding the Jury."

116. Cheryl C. Graesser, "A Social Averaging Theorem for Group Decisionmaking," in N. H. Anderson, ed., *Contributions to Information Integration Theory* (Academic Press, 1982).

117. Kalven, "The Jury, The Law," p. 177.

118. Penrod and Hastie, "Models of Jury Decision Making."

119. Daniel J. Isenberg, "Group Polarization: A Critical Review and Meta-Analysis," *Journal of Personality and Social Psychology,* vol. 50 (June 1986), pp. 1141–51; and David G. Myers and Helmut Lamm, "The Group Polarization Phenomenon," *Psychological Bulletin,* vol. 83 (July 1976), pp. 602–27.

120. Diamond and Casper, "Blindfolding the Jury."

121. Martin F. Kaplan and Charles E. Miller, "Group Decision Making and Normative Versus Informational Influence: Effects of Type of Issue and Assigned Decision Rule," *Journal of Personality and Social Psychology*, vol. 53 (August 1987), pp. 306–13.

122. See discussion by Horowitz and Bordens in "Experimental Investigation of Litigation in Complex Tort Cases," p. 284.

123. See Shari Seidman Diamond, "Order in the Court: Consistency in Criminal-Court Decisions," in C. James Scheirer and Barbara L. Hammonds, eds., *Psychology and the Law: The Master Lecture Series*, vol. 2 (Washington: American Psychological Association, 1983), pp. 123–46.

124. See reviews by Hastie, Penrod, and Pennington, *Inside the Jury*; and Norbert L. Kerr and Robert J. MacCoun, "The Effects of Jury Size and Polling Method on the Process and Product of Jury Deliberation," *Journal of Personality and Social Psychology*, vol. 48 (February 1985), pp. 349–63.

125. Kaplan and Miller, "Group Decision Rule."

126. Saks, "Behavior of the Tort Litigation System," pp. 1269–71; Hans and Vidmar, *Judging the Jury*, p. 167; and Diamond, "Order in the Court," pp. 132–34. The argument is based on statistical sampling theory, but the analogy between empaneled juries and random samples is an imperfect one. Though it is a plausible hypothesis, it requires more rigorous testing than it has received to date.

127. Robert MacCoun and Tom R. Tyler, "The Basis of Citizens' Perceptions of the Criminal Jury: Procedural Fairness, Accuracy, and Efficiency," *Law and Human Behavior*, vol. 12 (September 1988), pp. 333–52.

128. Peter W. Sperlich, ". . . And Then There Were Six: The Decline of the American Jury," *Judicature*, vol. 63 (January 1980), pp. 262–79; and G. Thomas Munsterman, Janice T. Munsterman, and Steven D. Penrod, *A Comparison of the Performance of Eight- and Twelve-Person Juries* (Williamsburg, Va.: National Center for State Courts, 1990).

129. Hans and Vidmar, *Judging the Jury*, chap. 9; Frank C. Dane and Lawrence S. Wrightsman, "Effects of Defendants' and Victims' Characteristics on Jurors' Verdicts," in Norbert L. Kerr and Robert M. Bray, eds., *The Psychology of the Courtroom* (Academic Press, 1982), pp. 83–118; John S. Carroll and others, "Free Press and Fair Trial: The Role of Behavioral Research," *Law and Human Behavior*, vol. 10 (September 1986), pp. 187–201; and Thompson, Fong, and Rosenhan, "Inadmissible Evidence."

130. Robert J. MacCoun, "The Emergence of Extralegal Bias during Jury Deliberation," *Criminal Justice and Behavior*, vol. 17 (September 1990), pp. 303–14.

131. Kalven and Zeisel, *American Jury*; Christy A. Visher, "Juror Decision Making: The Importance of the Evidence," *Law and Human Behavior*, vol. 11 (March 1987), pp. 1–17; and Carol M. Werner and others, "The Impact of Case Characteristics and Prior Jury Experience on Jury Verdicts," *Journal of Applied Social Psychology*, vol. 15, no. 5 (1985), pp. 409–27.

132. Jane Goodman and others, "Money, Sex, and Death: Gender Bias in Wrongful Death Damage Awards," *Law & Society Review*, vol. 25, no. 5 (May 1991), pp. 263–85; and Goodman, Greene, and Loftus, "Runaway Verdicts."

133. Chin and Peterson, *Deep Pockets, Empty Pockets*.

134. Bovberg and others, "Juries and Justice," p. 33; Donald Wittman, "The Price of Negligence Under Differing Liability Rules," *Journal of Law and Economics*, vol. 29 (April 1986), pp. 151–63; and Wittman, "The Behavior of Litigants, Juries, and Professional Arbitrators in Civil Cases: An Empirical Study of Comparative Justice and the Issue of 'Deep Pockets,' " paper prepared for the annual meeting of the Law and Society Association, Berkeley, Calif., 1990. See also Brian J. Ostrom and David B. Rottman, "Does Plaintiff and Defendant Status Matter? A Comparison of Outcomes in Tort Litigation," Williamsburg, Va.: National Center for State Courts, 1991. This effect has not been observed

in post-trial interviews—see Guinther, "Jury in America"; and Hans and Lofquist, "Jurors' Judgments of Business Liability"—although the effect could exist without jurors acknowledging or recognizing it.

135. Bovbjerg and others, "Juries and Justice."

136. David T. Wasserman and J. Neil Robinson, "Extra-Legal Influences, Group Processes, and Jury Decision-Making: A Psychological Perspective," *North Carolina Central Law Journal*, vol. 12 (Fall 1980), pp. 96–159; Valerie P. Hans and M. David Ermann, "Responses to Corporate versus Individual Wrongdoing," *Law and Human Behavior*, vol. 13 (June 1989), pp. 151–66; Robert J. MacCoun, "Deep Pockets or Corporate Identity? Understanding the Effects of Defendant Identity on Civil Jury Verdicts," paper prepared for the annual meeting of the Law and Society Association, Amsterdam, June 28, 1991.

137. MacCoun, "Deep Pockets or Corporate Identity?"

138. This corporate identity effect is not robust across all case variations, however; in some situations jurors treat all the defendants the same. I am currently investigating the basis for the effect and the conditions under which it occurs.

139. MacCoun, "Inside the Black Box" (1987).

140. William L. Prosser and W. Page Keeton, *Prosser and Keeton on the Law of Torts*, 5th ed. (West, 1984), p. 32.

141. Valerie P. Hans, "The Jury's Response to Business and Corporate Wrongdoing," *Law and Contemporary Problems*, vol. 52 (Autumn 1989), pp. 177–203.

142. Richard O. Lempert, "Civil Juries and Complex Cases: Let's Not Rush to Judgment," *Michigan Law Review*, vol. 80 (November 1981), pp. 68–132; and Kalven, "Dignity of the Civil Jury."

143. David B. Rottman, "Tort Litigation in the State Courts: Evidence from the Trial Court Information Network," *State Court Journal*, vol. 14 (1990), pp. 4–18. See also Ostrom and others, "Tort Awards."

144. Wittman, "Behavior of Litigants, Juries, and Professional Arbitrators."

145. Kevin M. Clermont and Theodore Eisenberg, "Trial by Jury or Judge: Transcending Empiricism," *Cornell Law Review*, vol. 77 (July 1992), pp. 1124–77.

146. A recent study of tort cases in state trial courts found win rates of 69.6 percent for bench trials and 54.3 percent for jury trials; this translates into a 1.28 win ratio. See Ostrom and Rottman, "Does Plaintiff and Defendant Status Matter?"

147. Kalven and Zeisel, *American Jury*; and Kalven, "Dignity of the Civil Jury."

148. Broeder, "Chicago Jury Project," p. 750. Again, recall that this need not imply a deep pockets bias.

149. See M. H. Walsh, "The American Jury: A Reassessment," *Yale Law Journal*, vol. 79 (November 1969), pp. 142–58; and A. E. Bottoms and M. A. Walker, "The American Jury: A Critique," *Journal of the American Statistical Association*, vol. 67 (1972), pp. 773–79. Peter Blanck has recently outlined a much more sophisticated methodological framework for comparing judge-jury agreement; see "Panel One: What Empirical Research Tells Us: Studying Judges' and Juries' Behavior," *American University Law Review*, vol. 40 (Winter 1991), pp. 775–804.

150. Jeffrey J. Rice and Neil Vidmar, "Non-Economic Damage Awards in Medical Negligence: A Comparison of Jurors and Arbitrators," Duke University Law School, August 1992. Interestingly, Rice and Vidmar found that "nominal" jury awards—calculated by randomly sampling and averaging sets of twelve juror awards—were significantly *less* variable than randomly selected individual arbitrator awards.

151. Howe and Loftus, "Integration of Intention and Outcome Information."

152. Gary L. Wells, "Naked Statistical Evidence of Liability: Is Subjective Probability Enough?" *Journal of Personality and Social Psychology*, vol. 62 (May 1992), pp. 739–52.

153. See Ellsworth, "Are Twelve Heads Better Than One?"

154. See Michael J. Saks, *Small Group Decision Making and Complex Information Tasks* (Washington: Federal Judicial Center, 1981); and Ivan D. Steiner, *Group Process and Productivity* (Academic Press, 1972).

155. See Lempert, "Civil Juries and Complex Cases."

156. See MacCoun, "Getting Inside the Black Box" for an earlier version of this figure. See also D. W. Broeder, "The Functions of the Jury: Facts or Fictions?" *University of Chicago Law Review*, vol. 21 (Spring 1954), pp. 386–424; Hastie, Penrod, and Pennington, *Inside the Jury*; Kalven, "Dignity of the Civil Jury"; MacCoun and Tyler, "The Basis of Citizens' Perceptions"; and Selvin and Picus, *Debate over Jury Performance*.

157. Compliance with the law is not always a prerequisite for accuracy, since some rules of evidence place due process concerns before truth seeking.

158. See E. Allan Lind and Tom R. Tyler, *The Social Psychology of Procedural Justice* (Plenum Press, 1988); MacCoun, Lind, and Tyler, "Alternative Dispute Resolution"; and John Thibaut and Laurens Walker, "A Theory of Procedure," *California Law Review*, vol. 66 (May 1978), pp. 541–66.

159. For evidence that citizens prefer juries to judges, see MacCoun and Tyler, "Basis of Citizens' Perceptions." See also the chapter by Valerie Hans in this volume.

160. For example, there is evidence that judges may be more lenient in sentencing physically attractive criminal defendants; see A. Chris Downs and Phillip M. Lyons, "Natural Observations of the Links between Attractiveness and Initial Legal Judgments," *Personality and Social Psychology Bulletin*, vol. 17 (Ocotber 1991), pp. 541–47; and John E. Stewart, "Defendant's Attractiveness as a Factor in the Outcome of Criminal Trials: An Observational Study," *Journal of Applied Social Psychology*, vol. 10 (July–August 1980), pp. 348–61. Note that groups may or may not be more impartial than individuals, depending on the strength of the evidence, the composition of the group, and the applicable standards of proof; see MacCoun, "Emergence of Extralegal Bias."

CHAPTER SIX

Civil Juries and Complex Cases: Taking Stock after Twelve Years

Richard Lempert

T WELVE YEARS AGO, as the first Reagan administration was coming into office, it appeared that the civil jury, at least in complex cases, might be on the way out. The hostility of Chief Justice Warren Burger toward the civil jury was no secret and the circuit courts were split on the question of whether the Seventh Amendment guarantee of trial allowed an exception for complex cases. The issue was ripe for Supreme Court resolution.[1] Moreover, a body of then-recent scholarship provided the Court with some historical justification for reading a complexity exception into the Seventh Amendment as well as with more modern policy arguments for eliminating the civil jury or dramatically altering its tasks in complex litigation.[2] The Supreme Court did not, however, seize the moment, and the issue remains unresolved. Today most federal courts still feel obligated by the Seventh Amendment to try legal cases to juries no matter what their complexities as long as one party insists.[3]

In failing to act, the Court was acting wisely, or so I argued in an article published in 1981.[4] That article was based on the following premises: first, that the framers of the Seventh Amendment had important and enduring reasons for constitutionalizing the right to trial by jury in civil cases; second, that the claim that a complexity exception was implicit in the Seventh Amendment lacked adequate historical support; and third, that even if the Seventh Amendment contained no complexity exception, Fifth Amendment due process gave civil litigants the right to insist on bench trials if a judge could be expected to decide a litigant's case

Work on this paper was supported by the Cook and Cohn funds of the University of Michigan Law School. I would like to thank Shari Diamond, Phoebe Ellsworth, and Neil Vidmar for their comments on an earlier version of this chapter. I also thank Lisa Bernt for her research assistance and Gail Ristow for her careful reading of the final manuscript.

rationally and a jury, even with the aid of reformed procedures, could not.

I commended judicial inaction on the issue because at the time I wrote the empirical evidence was insufficient to determine whether some cases were so complex that only a bench trial was likely to yield a rational judgment. To prove this, I argued, meant that one would have to show: first, that it was possible to identify a set of cases so complex that juries did not deal rationally with them; second, that such failures of rationality were inherent in the institution of jury trial and not the result of mutable ways of treating jurors or developing cases for trial; and, third, that judges were likely to decide such cases more rationally than juries.[5]

Twelve years have passed since I wrote my article. One might expect that we now have the data needed to determine whether the showings I argued for can be made. If so, perhaps the Supreme Court can give us a sound, empirically based resolution of the "complexity exception" issue that has for so long been on hold. This paper examines the research produced during the past twelve years to see if this is possible. It seeks to determine what we know now that we did not know then about the ability of juries to handle complex cases, about our capacity for improving that ability, and about the ability of judges to improve on jury performance in such cases. It asks whether there is an adequate empirical basis for concluding: that juries can or cannot cope with complex cases; that we can or cannot change the way jury trials are conducted so that rational jury decisionmaking will not be thwarted by complexity; and that judges can cope with complex issues that juries cannot master.

To avoid keeping the reader too long in suspense, let me say at the outset that the answer to each part of this question is no. Such research as has been conducted on these topics is either too flawed or too limited to provide answers with firm enough empirical foundations to justify Supreme Court reliance. Yet we have learned something. To anticipate the discussion that follows, the jury often appears to do surprisingly well in the face of complexity, particularly insofar as complexity is defined by length of trial and the introduction of massive arrays of evidence. We know little about the judge's capacity to cope with complexity, but what we do know gives us no reason to be confident that the judge will do better than the jury. We also lack the kinds of rigorous research needed to argue that reforms in case management or jury practice can solve perceived problems. We are at a point, however, where a number of reforms can be suggested with little risk that they will make things worse and considerable reason to believe they will improve jury performance. Finally, theoretical developments in cognitive and jury psychology suggest a new perspective that we might wish to bring to bear in thinking about the complexity problem. I shall deal with these matters in turn.

Juries and Complex Cases

There are many dimensions to complexity, but one feature that stands out in the discussion of complex cases is protraction. The horrible examples in the literature on complex cases, that is those cases cited as clearly unsuitable for jury trial by those who would abrogate the right to jury trial, are cases that take a long time to try to a verdict. Trial length is important to the argument against jury trial because lengthy trials raise serious problems of juror memory; are associated with massive amounts of information for the jury to comprehend; mean that large numbers of jurors, including a disproportionate number of those most likely to be especially capable, are excused from jury service; and can impose hardships on jurors who do serve, hardships that in theory might interfere with juror performance by causing resentment.

Case Studies

Perhaps because protraction is seen as a central feature of complex litigation, psychologists in their studies of mock juries have seldom focused explicitly on the issue of jury factfinding in complex cases. Instead, most of what we have learned during the past decade about the jury's capacity to cope with complexity is anecdotal; it is based on close attention to jury behavior in particular cases chosen because of their research convenience or celebrity. Table 6-1 identifies and summarizes important characteristics of cases reported in the literature that meet two principal criteria. First, the case had to be one that could be regarded as complex by virtue of either its length or its subject matter. Second, the case description had to focus largely on the jury's performance, and the author's assessment of this performance had to be based at least in part on interviews with some or all of the jurors who participated in the case. While the focus of this paper is on civil trials, cases involving criminal trials are included in table 6-1. Although the legal question regarding the right to jury trial in complex cases may, for constitutional reasons, have a different answer in the criminal context than it has in the civil context, the problems that complexity poses for juror decisionmaking do not necessarily differ with case type.[6]

Serious problems arise from reliance on anecdotal case histories. Cases chosen for study may not be typical of the range of complex cases either in the nature and extent of their complexity or in the ways that judges, jurors, and lawyers reacted to that complexity. Moreover, the case study methodology is not designed to be reproducible. Different authors viewing different cases choose to emphasize different features, and where they do focus on the same issues, standards for judgment may vary. These problems are compounded in the current instance, for many of the studies collected in table 6-1 were reported by journalists and not by social scientists. Not only did these journalists wish to tell a good story, but they were seldom concerned with what their observations could tell us generally about jury behavior in the face of complexity. Nevertheless, I believe that much can be learned from looking at how jurors performed across a range of complex cases. Any conclusions reached on the basis of what we can learn from these cases studies must be tentative, but even tentative knowledge is better than a knowledge vacuum.

Table 6-1 summarizes important features of each of the cases described. Several of the cases are among the most highly publicized and celebrated cases that have been tried in this country in recent years. Other cases are less well known; and a number may be considered run-of-the-mill complex cases. None of the cases appears as formidable for a factfinder as cases like *SCM Corp.* v. *Xerox Corp.* or *Zenith Radio Corp.* v. *Matsushita Elec. Indus. Corp.*, which are the kinds of cases most commonly cited by those arguing for a complexity exception to the Seventh Amendment, but were a complexity exception established, at least some of the listed civil cases might, upon motion of a party, be removed from the civil jury docket.

The case descriptions come from a diverse group of observers. The four cases attributed to the ABA's 1989 report come from a study designed by a team of social scientists and lawyers. The social scientists who were in charge of the data gathering and are, I presume, responsible for the descriptions presented, are Elizabeth Loftus, Jane Goodman, and Edith Greene, Ph.D. psychologists who have written extensively on issues relating to jury trial. Arthur Austin, who described the trial and retrial in the case of *Cleveland* v. *Cleveland Electric Illuminating Company* (C.E.I.), an antitrust case that pitted a city against a privately owned utility, was at the time of his study a Professor of Jurisprudence at Case Western Reserve University. Molly Selvin and Larry Picus, who

Table 6-1. *Characteristics of Complex Cases*

Characteristic	ABA sexual harassment	ABA antitrust	ABA arson
Court	Federal	Federal	Federal
Subject	Sexual harassment	Antitrust—price maintenance conspiracy	Criminal conspiracy to commit arson
Length of trial[a]	4 weeks	9 days	2 weeks
Sources of complexity other than length	3 years of behavior to sort out, 175 exhibits	Unraveling meaning of an intricate chain of business transactions; difficult instructions on conspiracy; use of business jargon	Conspiracy law, complex fact question; five-day recess in midtrial
Jury aids	Note-taking; each side limited to 25 hours of testimony	Special verdict form.[b] Note-taking allowed; preliminary instructions	One juror took notes
Jury size	8	6	12
Inherent difficulty of evidence[c]	Low	Moderate	Low
Jurors who completed college[d]	Not available	0 (estimate)	3–5 (estimate)
Defensibility of verdict	High	High	High
Comment	None	Yes[e]	Yes[f]

Table 6-1 (cont'd)

Characteristic	ABA trade secrets	Pennzoil v. Texaco	Cleveland v. C.E.I. #1
Court	Federal	State	Federal
Subject	Trade secrets and restraint of trade	Tortious interference with contract	Antitrust, attempt to monopolize
Length of trial[a]	6 weeks	4½ months	8 weeks
Sources of complexity other than length	Highly technical testimony, subtle patent issues, law of tortious intereference	Difficult financial analyses and business concepts	Difficult concepts
Jury aids	Preliminary instructions; limits on testimony; note-taking allowed	Special questions posed; juror questions allowed for part of trial	Special interrogatories
Jury size	6	12	6
Inherent difficulty of evidence[c]	High	Liability low	Moderate
Jurors who completed college[d]	2–3 (estimate)	1–3 (estimate)	0
Defensibility of verdict	Moderate[g]	Liability: moderate; damages: low	Low
Comment	Yes[h]	Yes[i]	Yes[j]

Characteristic	Cleveland v. C.E.I. #2	U.S. v. DeLorean (criminal)	U.S. v. GAF Corp.
Court	Federal	Federal	Federal
Subject	Antitrust, attempt to monopolize	Criminal conspiracy	Stock manipulation (criminal)
Length of trial[a]	11 weeks	4 months	6 weeks
Sources of complexity other than length	Difficult concepts	Potentially distracting videotape	Technical financial concepts
Jury aids	Copy of instructions allowed in deliberations; special interrogatories; preliminary instructions summarized issues and defined terms; written final instructions	Written instructions for each juror; note-taking	
Jury size	6	12	12
Inherent difficulty of evidence[c]	Moderate	Low	Low
Jurors who completed college[d]	0	7	0–1
Defensibility of verdict	High	High[k]	Moderate (hung)
Comment	Yes[l]	Yes[m]	Yes[n]

Table 6-1 (cont'd)

Characteristic	California v. Keating	——— v. W.R. Grace & Co.	Charles Newman et al. v. Johns Manville et al.	Micro/Vest v. ComputerLand Corp.
Court	State	Federal	Federal	State
Subject	Violating California Corporations Code and fraud in selling bonds (criminal)	Toxic tort	Products liability (asbestos)	Breach of contract, conversion
Length of trial[a]	10+ weeks	4 months	7 days	8 + weeks[s]
Sources of complexity other than length	Need to understand market in junk bonds and duties of buyers and sellers; evidence entirely circumstantial; multiple counts and plaintiffs	Technical (hydrogeological) conflicting expert testimony	Complex medical issues	
Jury aids		Special interrogatories (poor), trial in phases	Jurors given trial notebooks containing background information; preliminary instructions on some issues; note-taking allowed; four-question verdict form	
Jury size	12	6	6	12
Inherent difficulty of evidence[c]	Moderate	High	Liability: moderately high; damages: low (?)	Low
Jurors who completed college[d]	1	1	Not available	0–3
Defensibility of verdict	High	Low[o]	Liability: high; damages: low[r]	Liability: high; damages: low
Comment	Yes[p]	Yes[q]	Yes[r]	Yes[t]

Sources: For ABA sexual harassment, antitrust, arson, and trade secrets cases: ABA (1989).

Pennzoil v. Texaco: Stephen J. Adler, "How to Lose the Bet-Your-Company Case," *American Lawyer* (January-February 1986), pp. 27–30, 107–10; *Cleveland v. C.E.I. #1* and *Cleveland v. C.E.I. #2*: Arthur D. Austin, *Complex Litigation Confronts the Jury System: A Case Study* (Frederick, Md.: University Publications of America, 1984); *United States v. DeLorean*: Steven Brill, "Inside the DeLorean Jury Room," *American Lawyer* (December 1984), pp. 94–105; *United States v. GAF Corp.*: Alison Frankel, "He Bombed as a Stool Pigeon," *American Lawyer* (May 1989), pp. 34–89; *California v. Keating*: Gay Jervey, "Charlie Keating, Meet Your Peers," *American Lawyer* (March 1992), pp. 100–09; ———— v. *W. R. Grace & Co.*, see Mitchell Pacelle, "Contaminated Verdict," *American Lawyer* (December 1986), pp. 75–80; *Charles Newman et al. v. Johns Manville et al.*: Molly Selvin and Larry Picus, *The Debate over Jury Performance: Observations from a Recent Asbestos Case,* (Santa Monica: Institute for Civil Justice, 1987); and *Micro/Vest v. ComputerLand Corp.*: Claudia Weinstein, "Losing Big at ComputerLand," *American Lawyer* (October 1983), pp. 123–30.

a. In some cases the trial time was given in days or hours. These figures were converted into days or weeks by assuming five hours to a trial day and five days to a trial week.

b. The use of special questions or verdict forms had the potential to complicate the jury's task as well as to ease it.

c. Where a large amount of difficult, unfamiliar scientific information bore on the central issues in the case, technical difficulty is coded as high. Where technical or specialized information seemed somewhat easier to understand, or where full understanding seemed less crucial to correct decisionmaking because the evidence was not so central, because it was redundant with other evidence that was easier to understand, or because a vaguer understanding would suffice, difficulty is coded as moderate or low, depending on how these factors appeared to play out.

d. Where occupational but not educational information was given, I attempted to estimate the number of college-educated jurors on the basis of their occupations.

e. Jurors with good understanding guided the others, some of whom were confused.

f. Jurors requested but could not get a transcript of crucial testimony; they complained of having to reconstruct testimony from memory.

g. Without compromise forced by the holdout, the verdict would have been highly defensible.

h. The most able juror assumed the leadership role. The jury reached a compromise verdict because of one holdout. The lack of indexing made it difficult to find documents in the jury room.

i. The trial had two judges. The first made several mistaken evidentiary rulings that strongly hampered the defense case; the second posed a jury charge that undermined the defendant's position. Defense counsel failed to put on an expert witness to explain a key concept that the jury misunderstood and failed to offer the jury any evidence or argument on the damage issue. The plaintiff's attorney contributed $10,000 to the trial judge's reelection campaign (the judge's largest contribution). He also contributed $10,000 to the judge's administrative judicial superior.

j. The judge seemed biased against the city. The jurors were not properly concerned with the issue of the relevant market. The jurors' attitudes toward the size and identity of the parties affected the verdict. The jurors did not understand the concept of proximate cause and failed to limit certain evidence to impeachment. After an early straw vote, the jury did not function well. The jurors did not understand their instructions, which were given orally in a one-and-a-half hour lecture by the trial judge, but they did seem to understand the conduct testimony.

k. The jury hung five to one against the judge's apparent preferred verdict.

l. Unlike the first case, the judge provided the jury with a written copy of his instructions to use during its deliberations.

m. The judge did an excellent job in keeping things clear and being unbiased. The jury discussed matters thoroughly and systematically; juror mistakes were corrected by other jurors.

n. This was the second mistrial in the case; the first was caused by a prosecutorial failure to disclose an expert's report to the defense. The jury voted in the first half hour, with the jurors split into three groups. Many opinions changed during deliberations. The case turned on credibility issues. The jurors were not moved by a plea to "send a message to government" or by the government pointing out that the defendant's idea of community service was founding the Aspen Junior Golf Foundation.

o. A new trial was needed because special questions were answered inconsistently.

p. The jury did not take an initial vote; the foreman encouraged a general discussion. The jury made a careful analysis of the evidence and the instructions and was not swayed by dislike of one victim. There was a substantial conflict of views. No defense case was presented.

q. The jury interpreted its task in terms of guilt or innocence. The jurors attempted to deal with the evidence systematically and to look at the evidence from both sides. The verdict form had a "not determined" response category, which in effect decided the issue for the defense without the jury knowing it; neither the plaintiff's counsel nor the judge explained that a "not determined" answer was equivalent to a "no." Only one juror—the only college graduate—understood the implications of a "not determined" response. He did not explain this to the others because he liked the result.

r. The authors argue that most damage awards were excessive, but that is because defense counsel never explained that if the plaintiffs had asbestosis the disease would not progress equally in all plaintiffs. The authors also argue that one plaintiff's award was cut back because of his nationality, but the award was still substantial and fair compared with what others received. This plaintiff received the same amount in punitive damages.

s. The case lasted as long as it did because it was tried only four hours a day, four days a week.

t. The defendant intransigently refused to settle. The jurors misunderstood the judge's instructions on damages and misinterpreted the facts. The jury allowed a questionable cause of action to be added, which opened the door to the punitive damages. Crucial evidence on damages was excluded by the trial judge. Not much evidence was offered in support of the plaintiff's punitive damage request, and nothing was offered by the defendant, who simply asked for a zero verdict. The jury incorrectly remembered an instruction on punitive damage.

described *Charles Newman* v. *Johns Manville*, a tort suit to recover for asbestosis, were researchers with the Rand Corporation's Civil Justice Research Institute. The remaining trial descriptions are the work of journalists and free-lance writers, each of whom published in *American Lawyer*, and, in the case of *Pennzoil* v. *Texaco*, a *Wall Street Journal* reporter and a trial juror.

Dealing with Complexity

The first thing to notice about table 6-1 is the range of cases that are arguably complex, particularly if trial length alone indexes complexity. Corporate law violations, toxic torts, conspiracies, stock manipulations, sexual harassment allegations, claims under the antitrust laws, breaches of contract, and matters relating to trade secrets all may give rise to colorable claims of substantial complexity, and this is just a group of cases that happen to have caught the eye of courtroom observers. The point is not a small one. Even though the case for a complexity exception has been made in reference to cases that appear more complex than most of the cases summarized in the table, if a complexity exception were to be created, the potential slippery-slope problem would be substantial. The prospect of lengthy trials and conflicting expert testimony on specialized topics would make most of the cases in the table colorable candidates for the withdrawal of juries. In deciding whether to withdraw juries, substantial judicial discretion would have to be exercised. Even if a trial court stretched that discretion, an appellate court might well be reluctant to reverse given the prospect of an expensive, time-consuming retrial and the difficulties an objector would have in showing that a judge's verdict was unreasonable.

With respect to technical difficulty, two of the cases in table 6-1 seemed to turn largely on evidence so specialized and esoteric that any nonspecialist might have considerable difficulty in understanding. These are the ABA trade secrets case, which involved highly technical testimony about subtle patent issues, and the *W. R. Grace* case, involving epidemiological evidence as well as conflicting expert testimony about difficult issues in hydrogeology. Next highest on this dimension is the liability issue in the *Johns Manville* case, which involved conflicting interpretations of pulmonary and lung-function tests as well as statistical evidence on the association between exposure to asbestos and the development of asbestosis. Cases I have categorized as moderate in their technical complexity are cases that involved unfamiliar business situations such as the need to understand normal practice in the junk-bond market (an issue in *Keating*) or the need to understand economic concepts at issue in antitrust cases such as the need to understand the characteristics of a "relevant geographic market" (an issue in the *C.E.I.* case).

In those cases labeled low in difficulty, esoteric and unfamiliar evidence either figured less prominently in the issues the jury had to resolve or it should have been relatively easy for the jury to understand. Thus, in the sexual harassment case two psychiatrists testified for the plaintiff, but the defense called no expert witnesses and the plaintiff could have made a case for both liability and damages even without the psychiatric testimony. In the *GAF* stock manipulation trial, jurors had to understand how stock trading worked, a matter that most of the jurors in this case found to be difficult "new terrain," but this is the kind of information that many lay jurors would know and that should be relatively easy to explain. The fact that I have rated the evidence in a trial as low in difficulty does not, however, mean that jurors will understand it. In the *C.E.I.* litigation, for example, the concept "natural monopoly" figured prominently in both trials. Compared with other testimony on the issue of monopolization, this concept should have been easy for a jury to understand. Austin's interviews indicate, however, that in two trials only one juror, an alternate, adequately understood the defense's claim of natural monopoly.

One may conclude from looking at these cases that with some frequency trials confront jurors with evidence that only experts have no difficulty understanding. Moreover, even where the evidence should be comprehensible to a jury, jurors chosen in a particular case may not comprehend.

The situation may not be so bleak as this summary suggests, however. Methodologically, these case studies are reconstructions of deliberations, and after the trial (in some of these studies, weeks or months after) jurors may overstate the degree of confusion that existed in the jury room.[7] Moreover, individual jurors who say that "no one understood" an issue may be speaking more for themselves than for others, since those who did understand may not have had the occasion to exhibit their understanding directly to their fellow jurors or, if they attempted to do so, their understanding may not have been clear to the others. In this respect the trials described in the ABA study are particularly important. The ABA study was conducted by trained researchers who both interviewed jurors from the cases they studied and observed the deliberations of alternate jurors who had been on the trial panels. The authors' observed that in almost all cases the juries were led by their most competent members. Neil Vidmar reports a similar observation. In medical malpractice trials he has studied, the most influential jurors understood the evidence. These findings suggest that jurors with poor understandings of key evidence can be guided toward correct verdicts even if their misunderstandings of crucial evidence are never fully clarified.[8] In *W. R. Grace* we see a perverse variant of this: the only juror who apparently understood the full legal implications of the way the jury answered a question on the verdict form kept quiet about what it meant because he liked the result the jury's misinformed answer would yield.

Understanding the Facts

The jury's problems in understanding are compounded by limited juror ability. As the table reveals, many of the juries had few or no members with college educations. Most of the jurors who worked outside the household had blue-collar or clerical jobs. Since education and occupation are correlates of juror competence, some of these juries may have had few people capable of providing intelligent leadership.[9] However, this difficulty is not an intrinsic failure of the jury system. A number of commentators have suggested ways of dealing with this problem, including making it more difficult for the better educated to avoid jury duty or the sitting of full or partial blue-ribbon juries.[10] Moreover, even without changing the conditions of jury duty, highly capable juries may be seated if the lawyers, perhaps urged on by the judge, cooperate and do not routinely exercise their peremptory challenges on those jurors most likely to understand the case. In the *DeLorean* trial, for example, seven college-educated individuals were on the jury, none of them missed a trial day or arrived late, and they performed at the highest level.[11] Similarly, one of the judges interviewed by the ABA researchers reported that in a complex case where both sides wanted an intelligent jury, a highly capable jury was seated and three weeks of trial time was saved because the jurors took depositions home to read after the trial day was over.

A special problem of understanding arises when there is a conflict of expert testimony. The difficulty is that when the two sides provide different interpretations of a situation, a person who previously knew nothing about the issue may have little basis for choosing between them. This is a generic problem with expert testimony that exists almost apart from its inherent degree of complexity.[12] In these circumstances juries seem to rely heavily on other credibility cues (for example, does the expert seem like a hired gun?) as well as on the way in which the evidence fits in with the other elements of the parties' stories. Thus, if as in the *Pennzoil* case a party seems to have acted improperly, the jury is less likely to believe an expert who suggests that technically there was no impropriety despite the appearance than it is to believe an expert who suggests that the action violated commonly understood business norms. It should be recognized that juries commonly decide between conflicting nonexpert testimony on such grounds as well, and to some extent they are celebrated for this. Thus, when a jury hears an eyewitness who places the defendant at the scene of the crime and a defendant's spouse who testifies that the defendant was home at the time of the crime, the jurors weigh the relative credibility of the two witnesses and how their testimony fits into a larger story. They may have no more rational basis for deciding between such witnesses than they do for deciding between two experts who reach opposite conclusions on matters about which the jurors were previously ignorant.

Yet the jury faces problems in dealing with conflicting but unfamiliar expert testimony, whether hard to understand or not, that it does not face to the same degree in dealing with the conflicting testimony of ordinary witnesses. The most important is that experts are selected by the parties to be convincing.[13] In these circumstances, as Samuel Gross points out, the normal cues to credibility are likely to be misleading, for a low credibility expert who testifies in a way that is unlikely to be believed is not likely to be hired.[14] Indeed, one might expect those who know their cases are weak to make the strongest efforts to find experts who appear credible, for if they could not they would be foolish not to settle. At the same time, one should not overdraw the distinction between conflicting expert testimony and the conflicting testimony of ordinary witnesses, for if experts are adept at appearing credible regardless of the credibility of their testimony, ordinary witnesses may appear credible or incredible for reasons that have little or nothing to do with credibility such as apparent confidence or class distinctions in speaking style.[15]

A second problem that distinguishes battles of experts from the conflicting testimony of ordinary witnesses is that we feel that when ordinary witnesses tell conflicting stories, there is little anyone can do but decide instinctively, on the basis of credibility cues and consistency with other evidence, who is telling the truth. With experts one often has the feeling that if only the decisionmaker had sufficient expertise, a correct judgment would be made. This feeling gives rise to proposals for such things as science courts or the use of expert panels to resolve the esoteric scientific issues that arise in litigation.[16] To the extent that the feeling is justified, trying complex cases to juries or even to judges poses a special threat. This is a threat to legitimacy posed by the danger that clearly incorrect decisions will be reached and that these mistakes will become obvious. The threat can easily be exaggerated, however. Where experts differ in complex cases, the differences are usually sincere. Indeed, I would suggest that the more difficult the issue—that is, the harder it is for the lay person to decide which expert's opinion is more credible— the more likely it is that both positions are reasonably maintained. Thus, in the W. R. Grace case, leading experts in hydrogeology differed on whether toxic wastes could pass beneath a river to contaminate a town's wells. While one side is undoubtedly right, it is likely that hydrogeology today cannot tell us which one it is. In these circumstances a jury response downplaying the importance of the evidence, even though it is at the center of the proximate-cause issue, and focusing on other evidence that suggests contamination (how else can an exceptionally high incidence of leukemia be explained) and on the responsibility or irresponsibility of the defendants might be the best we can expect of a decisionmaker, even an expert decisionmaker.[17]

Evaluating Jury Verdicts

The bottom line, and perhaps the best test of whether jury leadership or other factors alleviate individual problems of understanding in complex cases, is the quality of the verdicts that juries return. Here the case studies have an interesting tale to tell. It is summarized in the evaluation of the juries' verdicts from the perspectives of the persons describing the cases.[18] Note first that most jury verdicts seem defensible; they are close to the verdicts that judges would have rendered or they seem fair and reasonable. Also, in cases where the jury had to decide both liability and damages, if the verdict appears mistaken, the holding on damages is more likely to appear unsupported by the evidence than the finding of liability.[19]

Where verdicts are of moderate or low defensibility, the complexity of the jury's factfinding task is not ordinarily at the heart of the problem. This can be best appreciated if we look closely at cases with such verdicts.

First, consider the American Bar Association (ABA) trade secrets case. The verdict is labeled moderately defensible because the judge's comments indicate agreement (though not in so many words) with the jury's finding for the counterclaim plaintiff on one count and with its findings for the counterclaim defendant on several other counts. The judge, however, would have found for the counterclaim plaintiff on two counts where the jury found for the defendant, and he would have granted greater damages than the jury did. Although the ABA trade secrets case is one of the most technically difficult of the cases in table 6-1, the jury's failure to arrive at a more acceptable verdict does not seem to stem from that difficulty. Eleven jurors, including five of the six who decided the case and the six alternates who for purposes of the study deliberated to a decision, shared the judge's verdict preferences. The unsatisfactory nature of the jury verdict stems from a sixth juror who appeared not to understand the judge's instructions and forced a compromise by obstinately holding out for his preferred verdict. Apparently, therefore, the jurors did very well except for the stubborn, uncomprehending juror, a type found regardless of case complexity.[20]

One wonders how such good performance was possible in such a complex case. A clue may be found in the lawyers' comments about some of the most complex evidence. One attorney, suggesting that the jury probably never understood the complex chemistry underlying a zeolite production process, remarked that the plaintiff never attempted to explain the chemistry involved because the case did not require that knowledge. Another lawyer, commenting on laboratory reports and scientific progress reports filled with chemical equations that had been entered into evidence, noted that the reports may have been useful for their bulk because they made it clear how much experimental work had been done month by month. Thus one has a case that in large measure doesn't seem comprehensible to a jury as well as jurors who admit to being mystified by some of the evidence. Yet the jurors' verdict preferences, with one exception, seem eminently sensible because a scientist's understanding of the evidence does not seem essential to the fair disposition of the case.

In the two *C.E.I.* trials that Austin observed, the jury verdicts were inconsistent, with the first jury hanging five to one in favor of the plaintiff City of Cleveland and the second jury finding for the defendant. This inconsistency might suggest jury irrationality, but the indictment is probably mistaken. As Austin points out, the defendant's strategy changed between the two trials so that the different juries were hearing quite different presentations of the evidence. Moreover, one piece of evidence offered at the first trial, which the plaintiff had regarded as its "smoking gun," was ruled inadmissible at the second.

Looking at the *C.E.I.* trials separately, I have rated the verdict at the second trial high on defensibility since the judge appears to have agreed with it, while I rated the hung-jury outcome at the first trial low on defensibility because the vote was five to one away from the direction the judge seems to have thought correct. While the jury's failure to understand some of the concepts and evidence relating to the antitrust issues may have played a part in the jurors' votes, their poor performance, if it was poor, seems attributable to less esoteric reasons. The most important is probably that the jurors failed to limit the plaintiff's smoking-gun evidence—testimony that *C.E.I.* had hired a lawyer to bring in his own name a suit designed to hamper the plaintiff's business—to the impeachment purposes for which it was allowed.[21] The other factors to which Austin attributes the first verdict are the jury's failure to understand certain legal instructions and concepts such as the meaning of proximate cause and the fact that the jury took an early straw vote, after which its deliberations did not function well.

Thus, if the jury did not reach a defensible result in the first *C.E.I.* case, the failure does not seem to have resulted primarily from the case's complexity. Indeed, it is not clear that the case was so complex as to be beyond the ken of a jury. Rather, the first jury, having no college-educated members, seems to have been especially ill-equipped to understand what may in principle have been comprehensible evidence. The second jury, while still failing to understand certain concepts, seems to have better understood the evidence, although this jury too consisted largely of blue-collar workers, none of whom was a graduate of a four-year college. The two juries differed, however, in that the second had several members who had substantial occupational responsibility. The other failures of the first jury, the failure to give proper weight to a limiting instruction and confusion about such concepts as proximate cause, are failures that occur in simple cases as well as in complex ones.[22]

In the *W. R. Grace* case, Mitchell Pacelle suggests that the jury performed poorly since a new trial was needed because of the jury's inconsistent answers to special questions and because in giving an allowed answer to one question the jury did not realize the implications of its answer.[23] Pacelle, however, notes that the question that gave rise to the inconsistent answer was the poorly worded product of a day and a half of legal debating in the judge's chambers. Moreover, when the jury asked the court for help in understanding the question, the judge's remarks were as confusing as the initial question. The jurors, left to their own devices, came up with a reasonable, though incorrect, interpretation of the question and their answer meant a new trial (almost immediately forestalled by a settlement) had to be ordered.

The jurors' other problem in the case was that they responded "not determined" to a special question asking when the W. R. Grace Company had polluted certain wells—not realizing that this answer meant the plaintiffs had not proved an element of their case and so could not recover.[24] The jurors were led to this decision by a verdict form that invited them to answer the question "not determined" without explaining the consequences of such an answer and by the failure of the plaintiff's counsel—to the defense counsel's astonishment—to explain to the jury in closing argument the implications of a not-determined verdict.

The answer "not determined" does not, however, suggest jury incompetence. The *W. R. Grace* case, as appears from the table, contained perhaps the most technical evidence of any of the cases discussed. It would be difficult for any lay person, judges included, to decide between the conflicting expert testimony in the case, and even an expert might have felt that it was impossible to date the start of the contamination to a specific month and year, as the question put to the jury apparently required.[25]

The *Pennzoil* case involved a suit by Pennzoil against the Texaco Corporation for tortiously interfering with an "agreement in principle" that Pennzoil had reached to take over the Getty Oil Company and to purchase the stock in Getty held by the Getty museum. The jury's verdict on liability was probably wrong, and its decisions on both actual and punitive damages appear hugely excessive. Yet the three available reports make it difficult to blame these errors on the jury or on the complexity of the case, even though the jury's apparent failure to understand certain key words—"indemnities" and "agreement in principle"—fostered jury mistakes.

The jury's failure to understand the implications of certain promises of indemnity that Texaco had given the Getty interests played a major role in its decision to award Pennzoil $3 billion in punitive damages, but this failure appears attributable at least in part, however, to the trial judge's decision to exclude evidence of other litigation brought by Pennzoil. This evidence, as Stephen Adler tells us, was the "only one good way for Texaco to convince the jury that Pennzoil could have sued the Getty interests if it had wanted to—indemnities notwithstanding."[26] The problem caused by the exclusion of the "other litigation" evidence was compounded in the deliberations on punitive damages when the jury asked a question bearing on Texaco's possible responsibility for actions of the Getty interests and the defense was content with a reply instructing the jury to reread the instructions. Defense counsel were content with this reply because they believed the instructions contained a sentence telling the jury that the defendant was responsible only for its own actions. The evening after the jury's inquiry, however, the defense counsel discovered that the instructions contained no such sentence, but the judge the next day refused to give the jury a supplementary charge to correct this deficiency.

The $7.53 billion awarded for actual damages was exactly the amount Pennzoil sought. This may well be $7 billion more than the evidence justified, assuming Pennzoil was correct in its liability claim, but it is hard to fault the jury on this issue or to attribute the excess to the complexity of the damage issue. Rather the jury's award reflects the testimony on the damage issue of three Pennzoil witnesses, one of whom had particularly high credibility, and Texaco's decision to put forward no evidence that contradicted this testimony. Thus when the jury deliberated, the only damage evidence before them tended to establish Pennzoil's full claim, and, as a juror pointed out in deliberations, the jury had been instructed to decide the case on the evidence.

On the liability issue it is similarly difficult to attribute the verdict, assuming it was mistaken, to the case's complexity or to the jury's inability to follow the evidence. Rather, jury errors, if they occurred, can be explained by judicial rulings on the admissibility of evidence, the court's charge, which according to both Adler and Thomas Petzinger favored Pennzoil in a variety of ways, and to certain strategic errors of the defense team, such as the failure to offer expert evidence about how the crucial term "agreement in principle" was understood in the business world.[27]

Micro/Vest v. *ComputerLand* was a contract action brought primarily against William Millard, the chief executive officer of ComputerLand, and secondarily against the corporation. It was brought to recover on a clause in a loan agreement that allowed the noteholder to convert the debt into shares of ComputerLand stock, but the plaintiff also sued under a novel theory of conversion that allowed it to claim that dividends owed on the stock allegedly due the noteholders had been tortiously converted to the defendant's own use. This theory was important because it provided a basis for claiming substantial punitive damages. In the *Micro/Vest* case, unlike *Pennzoil*, the jury's verdict on liability appears to have been well-merited; indeed before the trial began defense counsel sent his client a letter warning that "the case was indefensible" and that if he did not settle, he could be "exposed to huge punitive . . . damages." [28]

The award of punitive damages, over $125 million against the two defendants, seems excessive; indeed, it is unclear whether any punitive damages were justified. While part of the reason for the award appears to be that the jury "remembered" an instruction that was never given—that punitive damages had to hurt—this failure of memory does not appear to be the result of massive evidence–the trial on punitive damages followed the return of the general verdict and lasted only a few days—or to evidence that was particularly complex. Indeed, the jury's mistake seems to be the result more of a lack of evidence than of a surfeit. The defense attempted to set an implausibly low value on ComputerLand's net worth and presented no evidence on what Millard was worth. More important, the trial judge excluded evidence of a partial summary judgment that left open the issue the jury had tried; this evidence tended to refute the plaintiff's contention that Millard was using the trial in bad faith to get out of honoring his note. Defense counsel said of this ruling, "It was a devastating setback. I literally sat down stunned." [29] The plaintiff, like the defendant, offered little evidence on the defendant's net worth but was nonetheless allowed to refer to Millard numerous times as a billionaire and to give an estimate of the value of ComputerLand stock. Of course, the trial judge's questionable decision to allow the plaintiff to add a theory of tortious conversion to its contract case made the punitive damage award possible in the first place.

The final case in which the reporter seriously questions the quality of the jury's decisionmaking is the asbestosis case, *Charles Newman et al. v. Johns Manville et al.*, described by Molly Selvin and Larry Picus. [30] This is a case in which three insulators and the wife of an insulator claimed they developed asbestosis as a result of exposure to the defendant's product. These four claimants were bellwether plaintiffs for a group of thirty cases that had been consolidated for trial in a federal district court. The authors point to a number of errors that seem to have infected the verdict, but, as with most of the other verdicts that have been described, it is hard to link the authors' criticisms to a failure to understand the admittedly complex evidence in the case. Two of the authors' complaints concern the jury's failure to follow judicial instructions. One of these instructions was a limiting instruction regarding evidence admissible against only one of ten defendants; another was an instruction on permissible bases of damages. [31] These kinds of failures are found in simple cases as well as in complex cases, and no data suggest that their likelihood increases with the complexity of the case. In the particular context of the *Manville* case, the first error is one that as a matter of psychology may have been difficult or impossible for the jurors to avoid; the second may be the kind of justice-oriented nullification of the law for which some might value the civil jury—akin, for example, to jury awards that take account of the fact that parties will have to pay attorneys' fees.

The third critique that Selvin and Picus make of the *Johns Manville* jury is that the jurors seem to have reduced the amount awarded one plaintiff because he was a Mexican national. The authors suggest the possibility of discriminatory motives. If these existed, they are not a result of complexity, but I doubt the existence of discrimination.[32]

Finally, in one respect the jurors misunderstood the scientific facts. They assumed in their deliberations that the asbestosis afflicting each of the plaintiffs would progress to the point where each would become as sick as the lead plaintiff. Given the nature of asbestosis, however, even if the jurors were correct in accepting the diagnosis of asbestosis as attested by the plaintiffs' doctors, they were almost certainly incorrect in awarding damages with the expectation that each plaintiff would inevitably become seriously disabled by the disease. Again, however, it is hard to fault the jury for the error or to blame it on the complexity of the case. The jurors had been told that asbestosis was a progressive disease, and the defendant never put on a witness to tell the jury of the wide variability in its progression.

When Verdicts Are Mistaken

Considering the group of case studies, we see that complex cases often present evidence that jurors do not fully understand and that juries do not always get things right in reaching their verdicts. At the same time complexity, particularly as operationalized by protraction or large amounts of evidence, is not necessarily confusing. Even when the evidence is quite difficult to follow, jurors may understand much of it and reach verdicts that in retrospect appear both justified and rational. Moreover, when jury verdicts seem mistaken, it is difficult to attribute the mistakes largely to the complexity of the evidence the jurors encountered and to their difficulty in understanding it. Rather, as I read the case studies, erroneous verdicts seem to have two general sources: one is the kinds of factors that can lead jurors astray in ordinary cases and the other is the mistakes of lawyers or of judges.

The most serious problem that jurors encounter in their efforts to get things right appears to be an inability to apply instructions correctly. Yet this difficulty exists whether cases are complex or simple.[33] Moreover, we know how to increase comprehension substantially, but little effort has been made in this direction.[34]

The difficulty that jurors have in understanding instructions poses, however, a special problem in complex litigation that has not heretofore been recognized. A standard way of attempting to aid jurors in complex cases is to break down the jury's decisionmaking task through special verdict forms, special interrogatories, and other such devices, and there is some evidence that jurors find these helpful.[35] These devices are themselves instructions, however, and they carry with them the danger of misunderstanding. The best example of how well-meaning efforts to simplify the jury's task can lead to error occurred when John DeLorean, after his acquittal on drug charges, was tried in Detroit for federal fraud, racketeering, and tax evasion.[36] He was acquitted even though three of the twelve jurors said after the trial that they left the deliberations believing that DeLorean was guilty. The reason for DeLorean's acquittal was a special verdict form that read in part:

> You must remember at all times that the accused cannot be found guilty . . . unless you unanimously find beyond a reasonable doubt that he committed at least two acts of racketeering. You must not only unanimously agree as to which of the eleven specific acts of racketeering were committed, if any, but also which specific subpart of each alleged act was committed. *Without such unanimous agreement, you must find the defendant not guilty* [emphasis added].[37]

The jury, which disagreed about whether DeLorean had committed the requisite two acts of racketeering, returned a unanimous verdict of not guilty on the racketeering charge because the special verdict form seemed to mandate an acquittal if the jury members could not reach unanimous agreement.

In somewhat less dramatic fashion, several of the less defensible verdicts returned in the trials listed in table 6-1 seem to have been similarly affected by the jury's difficulty in dealing with special questions or special verdict forms. In *W. R. Grace*, for example, the jury never knew the consequences of concluding "not determined" on the special verdict form, and they misinterpreted the meaning of another of the special verdict questions. In *Pennzoil*, the wording of eight special questions that the judge posed for the jury was tilted against the defendant.[38] The jury's difficulties in dealing with such devices may, however, be largely avoidable. In several of the cases in which instructions or special questions caused problems, the jurors were aware of a problem and sought clarification by questioning the judge, but the judge usually provided no specific help, instead calling their attention to all or a portion of the instructions that the jury had previously been given. More helpful judicial responses might have avoided error.

A second difficulty the jurors had in some cases was understanding esoteric facts when the parties offered conflicting expert testimony from apparently credible sources. But this too is a problem found in cases that are not generally thought of as complex since it appears associated with a conflict of experts and not with other features that make a case complex. Jane Goodman, Edith Greene, and Elizabeth Loftus questioned trial court judges about the difficulties that jurors had in complex cases. The judges cited as recurrent problems comprehension of medical testimony and the evaluation of damages in complex personal injury cases, particularly in situations when jurors were faced with "reconciling totally conflicting expert testimony from highly qualified medical witnesses."[39] But this kind of conflict often occurs in what are otherwise run-of-the-mill tort cases, the routine fodder of the civil jury.[40] Ironically, conflicting expert testimony, which juries are not well equipped to handle, often does not make a jury's verdict appear irrational since a decision for either party when experts cannot agree often appears reasonable. In *W. R. Grace*, for example, regardless of how the jury decided the contamination issue, an observer cannot conclude that the jury was mistaken on the evidence. The situation is similar with respect to the jury's finding in *Johns Manville* that each of the plaintiffs was suffering from asbestosis. As a juror discussing conflicting medical testimony in another asbestos case said, "the expert testimony was not a real factor in our decision, except in the very backhanded sense that it lent medical credence to any result."[41] Problems attributable to misunderstanding do arise, and the jury can be wrong when it credits less reliable expert testimony over more reliable testimony. At its extreme, this is the so-called "junk science" problem.[42] In none of the cases noted in table 6-1 did the jury seem to prefer less credible scientific evidence over more credible evidence. In the *Pennzoil* case, however, the jury on the liability issue accepted what appears to be an unrealistic view of how the business world viewed an "agreement in principle" to consummate a multibillion-dollar merger.

The jury's action in *Pennzoil*, however, brings us to the second factor that by my reading of the case studies is particularly salient when juries go astray in complex litigation: the mistakes of lawyers and judges. In *Pennzoil*, the judge, "with some exceptions . . . didn't permit the lawyer-witnesses to testify on their understanding of the term 'agreement in principle,'" and Texaco did not produce any expert witness to make the point that an agreement in principle is understood not to be binding.[43] Thus, the jury's mistaken perspective on this issue may plausibly be attributed to the rational weighing of the evidence presented rather than to a failure to comprehend or to appreciate the evidence.[44]

Lawyer mistakes often seem to stem from underestimating the capacity of the jury. In three cases—*Micro/Vest, Pennzoil,* and *Johns Manville*—lawyers did not produce important evidence on damages, probably because they feared that to do so would concede a liability issue they were contesting.[45] In other cases jurors noted, resented, and sometimes drew adverse inferences from attempts to appeal to their emotions. In the ABA trade secrets case, for example, the jurors were not impressed by the cross-defendant's suggestion that a verdict for the cross-plaintiffs might cost 138 New Yorkers their jobs. In *Johns Manville* the jurors were scornful of the lead plaintiff's wife's reference to the fact that the next day was her forty-fifth wedding anniversary. The defendant's attempt in *Micro/Vest* to show the humble background of their client seems to have done more harm than good. As one juror in *Micro/Vest* commented: "The whole case was on the contract, but they kept going back to what he [Millard] did as a child: selling newspapers and such. When you hear seven times what school someone went to, it gets a little old. They got away from what they were really there for."[46]

The set of complex cases I have examined seems to include more arguably mistaken verdicts than one would expect to find in an equivalent number of simpler cases. Given the nonrandom nature of the sample and the number of celebrated cases, it is impossible to say whether judges and lawyers are more likely to err in complex cases than in simpler ones, but it is certainly reasonable to think so. Also mistakes may be more consequential in complex cases than in simple cases because juries in complex cases may be more susceptible to being misled by error. Had the Texaco case been simpler, for example, the jury might not have needed opposing evidence to appreciate the unreasonableness of Pennzoil's demand. Complexity may therefore pose special difficulties for juries in part because of the special difficulties it poses for judges and counsel. As most judges and lawyers realize, complexity is a sign that special care must be taken.

The case studies, examined together, suggest several additional features that bear on a jury's likely performance in complex litigation. Jurors appear to work hard and to take their jobs seriously, sometimes to the point of reading important documents in the case word by word. This observation is confirmed by Gordon Bermant and his coauthors who in examining another set of protracted trials note, "Judges and lawyers are uniformly complimentary of the diligence of the juries in these cases."[47]

—Lawyers seem often to seek less well-educated juries.[48] But when they do not do so, as in the *DeLorean* trial, the jury may include several members with a college education. This is consistent with the findings of a study by Joe Cecil, Allan Lind, and Gordon Bermant.[49] Twenty-two percent of the jurors they interviewed who had served in trials of twenty days or more were college graduates, a proportion that is only 10 percent less than the proportion of college graduates among interviewed jurors who had served in trials of six days or less.

—Juries often include individuals who understand material that most of their fellow jurors do not. These members are particularly important because, as the ABA studies indicate, juries in complex cases tend to follow the lead of their most competent members.

—In several cases where the jury verdict was problematic and the deliberations as reconstructed seemed flawed, an early straw vote was a potential causal factor. Conversely, in several cases that appear to have been well handled by the jury, the foreperson took care to avoid early polarization.

—In some of the trials the judge's attempts to aid the jury through such means as allowing note-taking, allowing the jury to take written copies of instructions to the jury room, furnishing trial handbooks, and the like seem to have helped.

—Length alone does not seem to lead to jury confusion. Juries seem to have few problems in trials that are long but that otherwise have no special sources of complexity. The ABA sexual harassment trial and the *DeLorean* trial are illustrative examples. Conversely, if conflicting technical evidence is presented, a long trial is not necessary for jury confusion. These observations are consistent with the findings of Cecil, Lind, and Bermant. They interviewed ninety-nine jurors who had served in federal trials lasting twenty days or more and eighty-one jurors who had served in federal trials lasting six days or less.[50] They report that 46 percent of the jurors in long trials found that evidence was difficult, but so did 29 percent of the jurors in short trials, a difference smaller than they expected and one that could result if longer trials are more likely than shorter ones to involve issues elucidated by scientific or technical evidence. Their conclusion, like my conclusion from reviewing the case studies, is that "concerns about the unique difficulty of the evidence in protracted civil trials may have been overstated."[51]

To sum up, one must be wary of drawing firm conclusions from a nonrandom sample of cases studies. This is clearly true here, particularly since half the studies I cite were done by journalists not specially concerned with showing how juries deal with complexity as a general matter. Some tentative conclusions appear reasonable, however. First, juries confronted with technical information have problems understanding that information, and if there is conflicting expert testimony, jurors may have the feeling that they do not know whom to believe. Second, juries often seem able to find their way around such confusion and to arrive at appropriate verdicts. Third, when juries make mistakes in deciding complex cases, the mistakes seem more often due to mistakes in understanding judicial instructions or to the errors of the judge or lawyers than they are to the difficulty of understanding the implications of complex or massive amounts of evidence. Complexity may exacerbate the jury's difficulties with instructions or the degree to which juries are likely to be misled by the mistakes of others, but the cases we have considered do not reveal the existence of such effects. *Overall, the sample of cases I have examined provides no empirical support for the claim that there is a denial of the due-process right to a rational decision on the evidence when juries are seated in complex civil cases.* The failure to find a clear link between complexity and a denial of due process is consistent with aggregated data collected by Larry Heuer and Steven Penrod.[52] They report that in 160 federal cases collected so as to oversample complex cases, judges were no more likely to disagree with jury verdicts in complex cases than they were in cases that were shorter or simpler on the law or facts.

Laboratory Research

Turning from case studies to the psychologist's laboratory, we find either more relevant studies than we can deal with or very few. Most studies that bear on the quality of jury factfinding and the influence of particular variables should apply to juries in complex cases in the same way that they apply to juries in simpler cases, and in this sense too many studies qualify. Few studies use as stimuli the factual settings of complex cases or seek to pose for mock jurors the kinds of special problems that are associated with complex cases, and in this sense there is little to canvass. To keep things manageable, I will review only the latter, more relevant, studies.

Before I do, a word about external validity is in order. For obvious reasons, there are no studies that expose mock jurors to the trial lengths or masses of evidence that are common in complex litigation. This, however, may not be as great a threat to our ability to generalize from controlled experiments as one might assume; the case studies suggest that long trials and massive arrays of evidence are not the most important sources of the special difficulties that jurors may encounter in complex litigation. One cannot assume, however, that these factors do not matter. Even if the difference between a taped trial of two to four hours and a trial of a few days does not shake our confidence in our ability to generalize from experimental findings to juror performance in ordinary cases—and the evidence indicates that it should not—the difference between a taped trial of the same length and an actual trial of six weeks to six months may mean that what we learn from a simulation is an unreliable guide to the way an actual jury would act after a long trial. We do not know what weight to give this concern. With stimuli less rich than those of the taped trial, concerns about external validity loom even larger. At the same time, before criticizing a study for not mimicking real-life situations, one must consider the point the study is designed to reveal and the justification for generalizing from it. Realism is not always necessary to generalization.

The first set of psychological studies of potential relevance to the special problems that confront jurors in complex cases concerns the way jurors deal with statistics. Statistical evidence is often found in complex litigation, and people without statistical training frequently find statistics hard to understand. Several researchers have looked at what mock jurors do when confronted with statistical evidence.[53] William Thompson and Edward Schumann identify two fallacies that can deceive jurors when they are confronted with statistics about incidence rates, such as blood type prevalence, that link a defendant to a crime. One, which they call the "prosecutor's fallacy," is to think that the probability of a defendant's guilt can be determined by subtracting the incidence rate of a matching characteristic from one.[54] The other, which they call the "defense attorney's fallacy," is to treat incidence evidence as irrelevant almost regardless of the rarity of the matching characteristic because at most it shows that the defendant falls into a larger group, one of whom is guilty.[55]

In an experiment with student subjects, Thompson and Schumann found that when presented with evidence relating to the probability of a hair match about 25 percent of their subjects fell into one error or the other, and they were about equally divided between the two types of errors. On a jury, particularly a twelve-person jury, such error rates would not be of great concern because it is likely that there would be people present who understood how the evidence should be weighed and that these jurors could explain the weaknesses of the fallacious approaches. Indeed, even if only people making the two types of errors were present on the jury, discussion might reveal why neither position was correct. In a second experiment, however, subjects heard advocates arguing for interpretations of blood type evidence consistent with either the prosecutor's fallacy or the defense attorney's fallacy. In these circumstances, only 22 percent of the subjects rejected both arguments. One would expect actual jurors, most of whom do not have a college education, to do worse in dealing with such statistical arguments than college students serving as experimental subjects.

The relationship between falling prey to a fallacy and reaching an incorrect decision is, however, not clear. This is the somewhat ironic lesson of another study by E. L. Schumann and W. C. Thompson.[56] In this study mock jurors watched a relatively realistic trial simulation on a four-hour videotape. The closing arguments they observed either ignored the blood-type evidence, included a fallacious prosecution argument, included a fallacious defense argument, or included competing fallacious arguments. Only the argument for the prosecutor's fallacy when presented alone had an effect; it increased the conviction rate from about 50 percent to 70 percent and the average estimated probability of guilt to 85 percent. In the other conditions both the rates of conviction and the estimates of average probability of guilt fell. The irony is that given the probability of guilt as estimated by control subjects who received no blood-type evidence, the blood-type evidence should have increased the average probability of guilt to above .90. Only those subjects who fell victim to the prosecutor's fallacy were close!

The tendency of the subjects in the Schumann and Thompson study to underestimate the probative weight of statistical evidence is not surprising. There are good theoretical reasons for expecting statistical evidence to be less influential with factfinders than intrinsically less probative nonstatistical evidence.[57] Other researchers have also found evidence about the statistical incidence of matching blood types to be relatively uninfluential, even when expert statistical testimony is presented explaining its implications.[58]

Some complex cases may well involve incidence statistics of the type that Thompson and Schumann and others have investigated; or perhaps cases that contain such statistics should be considered complex regardless of their other characteristics. The statistics that are involved in most cases conventionally considered complex, however, are somewhat different in nature. They usually consist, as in toxic tort cases, of epidemiological statistics which turn on comparisons between exposed and unexposed populations, or, as in many antitrust and most sex-discrimination law suits, they are the statistics associated with regression analyses. I have been able to find only two studies that deal with such statistics.

Molly Treadway has explored the adequacy of juror intuitions in dealing with evidence such as the four-fold relative-risk tables that epidemiologists use to determine whether a particular condition causes a particular disease.[59] She found that the intuitions of twenty-five subjects who were members of the Baltimore city jury pool were not good. Her subjects were asked to examine two tables, one of which showed a relative risk from exposure of 2.8 and the other a relative risk of 1.01, and to determine from each table (1) whether exposure to a substance increased a person's risk of developing an abnormality, and (2) for any particular person exposed to the substance who had the abnormality, whether it was more likely than not that the substance rather than something else had caused the abnormality. Only 41 percent of the determinations accorded with the answers reached through epidemiological analysis, and only two persons, or 8 percent of the respondents, made all four determinations in accordance with epidemiological reasoning. These results are not encouraging, but they do not adequately address the issue that concerns us. The reason for their inadequacy is that in litigation jurors are not confronted with relative-risk tables and asked for their best interpretation. Rather, the tables are presented by experts who explain what they imply. One would expect instructed jurors to do far better in understanding the implications of the data presented to them than jurors not so instructed.

Shari Diamond and Jay Casper, in a particularly good simulation study, exposed 1,022 Cook County jurors to a seventy-five-minute videotape of the damage portion of a suit brought under the Sherman

Act.[60] The jurors were informed that in the first phase of the trial the defendants had been found to have engaged in illegal price-fixing. As one aspect of this research, they explored the reactions of jurors to competing yardstick and statistical models, two common types of models used to establish damages in such cases.[61] In the various conditions of the experiment, the models were counterbalanced by party and by the amount of damages they implied. The jurors returned individual verdicts following their exposure to the case and then deliberated in seventy six-person juries until verdicts were returned.

The authors did not find that the jurors ignored the statistical expert or that the effects of his testimony were dwarfed by the effects of the more concrete yardstick testimony. Overall, jurors gave somewhat higher awards ($216,515 versus $200,813) when the plaintiff's expert presented a statistical model than when he used a yardstick comparison, but the difference is not statistically significant.[62] The overall influence of the statistical evidence relative to the yardstick evidence appeared to be the result of two competing forces: the statistical expert was seen as more expert than the expert presenting the yardstick model, and this made him more convincing; but the statistical expert's testimony was seen as less clear than the testimony presented by the yardstick expert, and this made him less convincing.[63] Jurors who found the statistical testimony to be similar to the yardstick testimony in clarity expressed a statistically significant difference in awards. When the statistical expert testified for the plaintiff, the mean award was $220,517; when he testified for the defendant; it was $168,223.

The deliberation process had a marked effect on damage awards, as the juries' verdicts averaged about 27 percent higher than the average of their members' predeliberation judgments. This was not due to the effect of outliers, for the correlation across juries of outlier preferences with final verdicts was relatively low while the correlation with each group's mean and median predeliberation preferences was strong.[64] Among jurors the preferences of the foreperson were particularly influential.[65] This is important when we recall from the case studies that juries seem to be most influenced by their most capable members, and we note the tendency for juries to select particularly capable members as forepersons. For example, in the Diamond and Casper study, the 13 percent of the jurors in the pool who had had both some postgraduate education and a statistics course accounted for 36 percent of those persons chosen as forepersons. Moreover, the predeliberation preferences of forepersons with both these characteristics had considerably more influence on final verdicts than the preferences of forepersons who had neither postgraduate education nor a course in statistics.[66] These findings should caution researchers about generalizing from the average individual response to statistical evidence to the response of juries, and they emphasize the way in which the composition of real juries in actual cases may affect how complex evidence influences deliberations.[67]

Overall, Diamond and Casper provide the most resounding support for the capacities of juries dealing with complex issues that can be found in the scientific literature. They write

> The responses to expert testimony we observe . . . suggest that jurors play an active role in assimilating and assessing testimony. Jurors did not simply adopt the view of a witness they rated high on expertise, using apparent expertise as a peripheral cue to conclude that the expert must be correct.[68] Rather, consistent with deeper processing of information which produces attitude change when the listener is highly involved, the jurors appeared to consider and evaluate the content of what the expert was presenting, and were less likely to be persuaded if they did not feel they understood it.
>
> This approach not only suggests active evaluation and perhaps even subtlety in dealing with expert testimony, but it also indicates the care jurors use in evaluating evidence to reach their decisions. When presented with complex statistical testimony, jurors were not simply over-powered by material they did not understand. Rather the persuasive force of such testimony appears to depend in substantial measure on the ability of the expert to express clearly the basis for the conclusions it is being used to support. Our results thus suggest that concerns about jurors' uncritical willingness to accept statistical evidence may be overstated.[69]

Of course, concerns about external validity may limit the real-world implications of Diamond and Casper's research. It may be difficult to make statistical evidence clear when it is embedded in weeks of other evidence or, if trial length is not a problem, when the statistical testimony itself takes hours to deliver, when it is followed by a cross-examination that may take days, when there is competing statistical testimony of a similar type, when one side is using its experts to obfuscate, and when peremptory challenges have been used to strike jurors who know too much about statistics. But even in a worst-case scenario, in which these concerns correctly identify the reality of much modern complex litigation, one may still reasonably conclude from the Diamond and Casper study that jury weaknesses in dealing with the kinds of statistical evidence most commonly associated with complex litigation are not inherent in the institution of the civil jury but are the result of the way in which complex jury trials are managed.

A second body of laboratory studies that may have special relevance to the quality of jury performance in complex cases comprises studies that focus on joinder. These studies matter because one factor that may make for complexity is the joining of parties or counts, as in *Johns Manville*, which involved four bellwether plaintiffs—who would have litigated separately had they not been part of a "case congregation"—and ten defendants, some of whom might not have been involved in every suit had the plaintiffs' cases been tried individually.

Joinder can involve parties, causes of action (counts or charges), or both. Most of the research on joinder in the psychological literature involves the joinder of charges in criminal cases that would not be considered complex.[70] Generally the research shows that a criminal defendant is disadvantaged when charges are joined, but the mechanism by which this occurs is unclear. Three possible mechanisms are: confusion of the evidence (evidence admitted on one charge is remembered as bearing on another charge); accumulation of evidence across charges (evidence admitted on one charge reinforces evidence relevant to another charge); and inferences about the defendant's character (the jury character-izes the defendant with a criminal schema and views the evidence on each charge in that light). The studies designed to elucidate which if any of these mechanisms operate are often limited in their focus and yield inconsistent results.

These mechanisms might all operate in civil cases in which different causes of action are combined, but if they do it is not clear that they should systematically disadvantage one party or the other. In the studies dealing with charge joinder, incriminatory evidence always implicates the defendant. In civil cases, on the other hand, a plaintiff may introduce evidence on several counts suggesting that the defendant was responsible for the plaintiff's injuries, but the defendant may offer evidence on the same counts suggesting that the harm the plaintiff suffered was the plantiff's fault. Also unlike those cases of criminal joinder that have been the subject of psychological research, the crucial evidence offered on one civil count may be admissible on another, as when a jury is charged with deciding whether a defendant is responsible under either a negligence theory or a strict liability theory.

To the extent that evidence in a civil case is admissible on only one count, as when evidence of a plaintiff's contributory negligence is admissible to rebut negligence liability but not strict liability, a jury's failure to apply instructions to limit the influence of the evidence to the one count would not be surprising.[71] The difficulties posed by the added counts are not specific to complex litigation. If, however, the presence of alternative causes of action means that considerably more evidence is presented than when only a single cause of action is alleged and that the trial lasts much longer as a consequence, one might point to alternative causes of action as a source of complexity apart from the danger of legal or evidential confusion. But alternative causes of action are not usually regarded as substantially lengthening trials, and no investigation of the effects of alternative causes of action has tried to simulate what would otherwise be considered a complex case. Instead, it is party joinder that is usually seen as making potentially simple cases complex. Trying the cases of different parties together can involve numerous lawyers, dramatically increase the amount of relevant evidence, and require the jury to link different items of evidence to the cases of one or more of the parties.

Irwin Horowitz and Kenneth Bordens have attempted to study the effects of party joinder in a simulated complex case.[72] They used as a stimulus a four-hour audio tape of a toxic tort trial in which the evidence was intentionally complicated and at times boring. The subjects were 396 jury-eligible men and women, who deliberated in 66 six-person juries. The case involved a large chemical company that had allegedly leaked effluent that entered the food chain and harmed four people who brought suit and unnamed others. Litigation of the plaintiffs' claims raised both negligence and state-of-the-art issues. The researchers were primarily interested in the difference between the verdicts when the cases brought by the four plaintiffs were tried together and the verdicts in these same cases when they were tried separately. Within these conditions, an additional variation contrasted a situation in which plaintiff A was an outlier with respect to the seriousness of her injury (suffering from a rare liver cancer) with a situation in which she was not (suffering from chloracne rather than cancer). The final variable was whether the jurors were told there were twenty-six or "many hundreds" of other victims or whether the existence of other victims was not mentioned.

Overall the data do not suggest that the aggregation of plaintiffs led to confusion. Only the plaintiff with the weakest case, a man who may have continued to eat fish after knowing the food chain was contaminated, was helped by having his case aggregated with the others, and this effect may reflect rational information processing. If the question of whether the plaintiff was responsible for his illness was a close one, the fact that people who clearly weren't responsible for their condition suffered from the contamination is some reason to believe that the plaintiff's suffering was not his fault. The data also show that compensatory damages were not affected, as they should not be, by the presence of an outlier or by the number of other victims; that the greater the responsibility attributed to the defendant, the higher the awards; and that the earlier the date that the jurors thought the defendant should have known about the toxicity of the chemical it was discharging, the higher the awards. Where liability was found, punitive damages were greater if an outlier was part of the aggregate and if there were hundreds of other victims. These results also appear reasonable since punitive damages should reflect the amount and extent of the harm a wrongdoer does.

Two potentially disquieting notes in the study are first a finding that the presence of an outlier is associated with a higher proportion of findings of no liability and second that there is substantial variance across juries in their verdicts. The effect of the outlier in stimulating findings of no liability is associated in the taped deliberations with remarks attributing fault to the outlier. This appears to be a classic "just world" response.[73] The fact that the three juries that blamed the outlier in this way also denied recovery to her coplaintiffs probably reflects the fact that evidence linking the defendant to the coplaintiff's injuries was arguably no stronger, and in one case was clearly weaker, than the evidence linking the defendant to the outlier's injuries. The variance in verdicts and awards is troubling but variance of this sort is probably not peculiar to jury trials.[74] As the authors point out, similar inconsistencies have been found in judicial behavior when matters such as sentencing have been examined, and a recent study suggests that in medical malpractice cases jury verdicts are no less consistent than arbitrators' awards.[75] Moreover, much of the inconsistency in liability verdicts is attributable to those cases where the irrationality of just-world thinking appears to be operating. Inconsistent damage awards may in large measure reflect the fact that the plaintiffs did not request specific amounts of money, so the juries did not have the kinds of anchors and supporting evidence that actual juries often have at trials. Whatever else is happening, the jurors seem not to be misled by the additional complexity of dealing with four plaintiffs rather than one.[76]

Looking at the joinder studies together with the studies of how juries use statistical evidence highlights a number of potential problems posed by the irrationality of some human decisionmaking. The studies do not, however, suggest that juries are likely to be less competent in complex cases than in other cases. Indeed, the more realistic studies, those by Diamond and Casper on statistical evidence and Horowitz and Bordens on joinder, show juries coping rather well with those features that make the decisionmaking tasks posed by the stimulus cases more complex than the decisionmaking tasks that juries encounter in more ordinary litigation.

Judges and Complex Cases

Even if the jury were substantially less able to deal with complexity than it apparently is, due process should not require the abrogation of the Seventh Amendment right to trial by jury unless judges can decide complex cases more rationally than juries can. There is, as we have seen, little systematic empirical evidence that relates to the competence of the jury in complex litigation; virtually none bears on the competence of the judge. Judges have not cooperated in studies of themselves as they decide complex cases; they seldom participate as subjects in simulation studies and have not done so in studies simulating complex litigation; and they seldom grant interviews in which they explain how they understood the evidence in complex cases. Judges do write opinions, but their opinions may provide little insight into the true bases of their decisions. Even where an opinion suggests a mastery of complex materials, the reader cannot know whether the judge has understood the subject, whether the judge *after* reaching a decision relied on a clerk to convey an impression of understanding, or whether the judge and/or the clerk simply copied large passages from the briefs of the side they favored. The evidence on how judges handle complexity is therefore fragmentary. What we can say is that there is no guarantee that a judge can do a better job than a jury; that there are a number of cases in which we would not want to force the parties to a bench trial; and that when the judge is unbiased and capable, parties may be particularly likely to opt for a bench trial, but if they don't there is a better than average chance that the jury will be up to its task.

Linking Judge and Jury

In almost every case study we examined, where the defensibility of a jury verdict was evaluated as low or moderate, those who reported on the trials noted mistakes made by the lawyers and/or the judge. Conversely, in those trials where the jury seemed to perform at its best, like the *DeLorean* trial, the judge seemed to have performed exceptionally well also. This has the ironic implication that were there an exception to the Seventh Amendment for complexity, it is likely that the quality of judge trials would be highest in cases where the jury was likely to do a good job as well, for competent judges can enhance the competence of juries over which they preside. To the extent that the case for a judge trial turns on the assumption of a competent judge, we are assuming the kind of judge most likely to preside over a competent jury.

The apparent link between judicial and jury competence means that if we look at cases where juries are confused or err, there is an above average chance that we will find a judge who is confused or mistaken as well. It is not necessarily true, however, that a judge who gives a jury poor guidance will perform equally poorly as a factfinder. A judge who confuses the jury with an unclear instruction might correctly interpret the law as a trier of fact. A judge whose questionable evidentiary rulings have prejudiced one side's case before the jury might nonetheless find for that side, perhaps influenced by the very evidence that he or she wrongfully excluded and the jury will not hear. By the same token, however, judicial mistakes may signal more general failings. A jury, even one hampered by judicial mistakes, may be better at factfinding than a judge who cannot adequately organize a trial or state a rule of law. Indeed, in some cases the jury's strength of numbers and experience may make it more able in finding facts than even an excellent judge.[77]

Understanding the Evidence

We have no systematic evidence on the capacity of judges to deal with the kinds of evidence that make complex cases difficult, but anecdotal evidence of situations in which judges appear not to have fully comprehended scientific evidence is easy to find. To begin at the top, we have the example of the Supreme Court's opinion in *Williams* v. *Florida*, which took the results of a classic psychological experiment to mean the opposite of what they implied.[78] At the opposite end of the judicial hierarchy, Michael Saks and Richard Van Duizend, who read transcripts of a homicide case that raised definition of death problems, concluded that the prosecution was not as conversant with the medical facts as the defense.[79] Yet the judge, whom they interviewed, praised the prosecutor's preparation and was unimpressed by the defense.

Statistical evidence seems to present courts with recurring problems. Sometimes courts are too ready to receive statistical evidence because they do not realize its weaknesses.[80] On other occasions courts are too reluctant to hear statistical evidence that is essential to understanding the facts before it. In Minnesota, for example, the state legislature had to pass a statute to overturn a Minnesota state supreme court ruling that statistical evidence relating to DNA matches was inadmissible[81] even though such information is essential to estimate the probative value of a DNA match. Some years before in the same state, a trial court made the opposite error. In *State* v. *Carlson*, the court admitted misleading statistical evidence based on an inadequate scientific foundation to show the probative value of a hair match; a man was convicted and sentenced to prison for life perhaps because of it.[82] Both a Federal District Court (*U.S.* v. *Massey*) and an Illinois Trial Court (*U.S. ex Rel. Di Giacomo* v. *Franzen*) made the same error.[83] Other cases in which trial and appellate courts have had varying degrees of difficulty in correctly interpreting statistical evidence are documented by the National Research Council in a report it prepared on statistical evidence in courts.[84]

The recent controversy over DNA evidence also reveals the difficulty that judges can have with scientific information. While one would expect rational decisionmakers to reach the same conclusions on the same evidence, court decisions on the admissibility of DNA evidence have differed, even though the evidence bearing on admissibility was similar. Indeed, in one case a court that refused to admit DNA evidence relied heavily on briefs that had been offered in a case that accepted it.[85] Finally one occasionally encounters cases where judges admit that scientific evidence is beyond them.[86]

The point of all this is not to establish the general inability of judges to cope with scientific evidence. The available anecdotal evidence does not allow us to reach any conclusion about the seriousness of the problems that judges face in dealing with the kinds of evidence that make cases complex or about the abilities of our nation's judges to understand and to decide correctly complex cases. Nor do we even know, except in the rare case, how judges go about deciding the factual issues in complex cases. The anecdotal evidence does mean that just as there are no guarantees that juries will understand the technical evidence in a complex case or decide such cases correctly, so there are no guarantees that judges will get everything right. Nor do we have any firm empirical basis for deciding whether judges will in some sense decide complex cases better than juries do over the long run. The best evidence we have on this count is Larry Heuer and Steven Penrod's finding that judges are no more likely to disagree with jury verdicts when cases are complex than when they are not.[87] This suggests that jury and judge verdicts are not likely to differ over the long run because of factors that distinguish complex cases from simpler ones.

Making Rational Decisions

In short we have no reliable empirical basis for saying that litigants are more likely in judge than in jury trials to receive decisions based on a rational evaluation of the evidence, nor can we reach the opposite conclusion. Perhaps we are on firmest ground when we simply note that modern psychology has demonstrated numbers of ways in which human decisionmakers act irrationally, if consistency in dealing with formally identical problems or scientifically rational models such as Bayes' Theorem are valid standards of rational decisionmaking.[88] Moreover, people sometimes will be influenced by actions or conditions they are not aware of, and they may misattribute their decisions to factors that have not influenced them at all.[89] Even knowing about these dangers does not necessarily provide protection from them. All people have limited capacities, which can lead to problems in understanding difficult, unfamiliar material. Both judges and jurors are human. As factfinders in complex cases, judges and juries are probably more like each other than they are different in dealing with the problems they confront.

Juries, however, may maintain one advantage over judges. This is that in some number of complex cases they are likely to be the fairer decisionmaker, both in appearance and in reality. The *Pennzoil* trial provides a vivid example of why a jury may appear to be and perhaps is a fairer decisionmaker. In *Pennzoil*, two days after Judge Farris was chosen to supervise pre-trial proceedings, Joe Jamail, plaintiff's lead counsel, donated $10,000 to the Farris reelection campaign. Until that time Jamail had given Farris $100.00. Jamail also gave $10,000 to the reelection campaign of the judge who was Farris's administrative superior. Farris, in turn, though one can never know for certain what influenced him, made a number of questionable pre-trial evidentiary rulings that severely hampered the case Texaco wanted to present.[90]

Consider also the work of Bermant and his coauthors. They interviewed lawyers in eleven protracted cases that could have been tried to either a judge or a jury. Their basic finding is not at all surprising: lawyers prefer to try their cases before the factfinder that gives them a better chance of winning. All six attorneys who chose jury trials and said why they did so listed the identity of the judge as the main or the only reason. Four of these attorneys specifically referred to the biases of the judges assigned to hear the case, and bias may have motivated the two who simply gave the judge's identity as their reason for choosing a jury trial. In two of the four cases in which the parties could have forced a jury trial but agreed to a bench trial, the competence and fairness of the judge was mentioned as the most important reason, with one attorney specifically noting that he looked on jury trials as "buffers against incompetent judges."[91]

Several lawyers interviewed by Bermant and his coauthors noted reasons other than bias or judicial competence for wanting or avoiding a jury trial. Chief among these other reasons was a sense of how a client or witnesses would appear to the jury. Two attorneys, both of whom had been forced by their opponents to try their cases to juries, said that they preferred bench trials when their cases were strong and jury trials when their cases were weak, implying that judges are more accurate factfinders than juries.

The comments reported by the Bermant team present a mixed picture. It seems that lawyers view jury trials in protracted cases (and perhaps in all cases) primarily as a protection against judicial bias. But they also see juries as responding to certain "human elements" that judges might ignore, and as less predictable than judges in the sense that a weak case does not necessarily mean defeat. At the same time, where a case is protracted and both lawyers have confidence in the competence and integrity of the trial judge, agreement to waive a jury trial may not be difficult to achieve. Whether the views these lawyers have of the relative merits of juries and judges is accurate is difficult to determine. A considerable body of research indicates that even when aspects of a case might appeal to the prejudices of jurors, unless the case is otherwise close on the facts, the evidence dominates.[92] One might similarly expect judicial biases to be tempered by the weight of the evidence. If so, the choice of a bench trial or a jury trial is more likely to affect the outcome when a case is close on the facts than when the evidence clearly favors one side. In these cases it is most important to avoid a biased judge, or, for that matter, a biased jury.

The right to trial by jury also provides some degree of protection against the managerial judge, a figure that has been both praised and damned in the scholarly literature.[93] The power of a judge bent on settling a case in accord with a personal sense of justice is considerable even if the exercise of this kind of judicial authority may be questioned.[94] In some cases managerial judges have used tactics that parties might perceive as coercive to achieve settlements the judges regarded as fair. It is simply a fact of modern litigation that judges who desire to mold cases to their preferences have substantial power to do so. If a judge who favored a certain result were sure to try the case if a suggested settlement was declined, the judge's power to coerce settlements would truly know no bounds. Thus a right to jury trial in complex cases may be necessary to ensure that the more basic due-process right of a fair trial remains.

To sum up, even if juries cannot resolve complex cases rationally, one cannot be sure that bench trials would improve the situation. Judges, too, make mistakes in dealing with scientific and specialized evidence. Examples of judges who get things wrong when confronted with difficult, unfamiliar evidence are easy to find. We currently have no empirical basis for saying that judges will ordinarily do better than juries in deciding complex cases, nor do we have an adequate empirical basis for reaching the opposite conclusion. In the situation where the judge is most likely to do well—that is, where the judge is known to be both fair and competent—limited anecdotal evidence suggests that the right to a jury trial is most likely to be waived. If there is a jury trial in such instances, other anecdotal evidence suggests that the jury system will function at its best.

If it is difficult to choose between bench and jury trials when rational factfinding is taken as a due-process requisite, it seems easier when the right to an impartial decisionmaker or the right to meaningful trial are the values that due process protects. Here it appears that situations arise where the right to a jury trial in complex litigation is an important guarantor of due process rights.[95]

Procedural Reform

The third point that I made in my 1981 article was that even if juries as now constituted were incapable of rationally deciding complex cases, one should not read a complexity exception into the Seventh Amendment unless the jury's incapacities were inherent in the institution. Before giving up on the jury, I argued, we should be sure that we cannot increase jury competence through changes in the way we handle jury cases. Included among the possible changes I mentioned were rewriting jury instructions to make them more comprehensible, furnishing jurors

220 / *Richard Lempert*

with written copies of the court's instructions, giving jurors pre-instructions, allowing jurors to deliberate on various issues as the case progressed, routinely seating twelve-person juries, furnishing jurors with daily transcripts (as an alternative to another possible reform—juror note-taking), dividing issues for decision, refusing party joinder, providing appointed experts to help the jury understand the testimony of the parties' expert witnesses, removing factual controversies by encouraging stipulations, using masters to clarify particularly difficult issues, sitting partial blue-ribbon juries, and allowing jurors to ask questions. Many commentators have suggested similar reforms as ways of helping juries cope with complexity, and the new *Manual for Complex Litigation* endorses some of these reforms as well.[96] Others have noted the potential for simplifying complex litigation through partial summary judgment and for using special masters to promote coherent case organization or to actively encourage factual stipulations.[97]

The implications of such reforms for jury competence may all, in principle, be examined empirically, but little rigorous social scientific investigation of any of them has been done in the years since I wrote.[98] Among the few suggested reforms that have been the subject of carefully controlled research are pre-instructions, the use of written jury instructions, jury note-taking and jury question-asking.

Pre-instructing the Jury

Research in cognitive psychology suggests that informing a person how to frame information he or she is about to receive can enhance recall and aid in the interpretation of ambiguous material. Thus pre-instructing a jury on case-specific matters might aid it in understanding how evidence fits into a case.[99] Vicki Smith reports partial support for this view. She found that the timing of instructions did not affect the recall of mock jurors for either relevant or irrelevant facts in a homicide case, nor did the timing of instructions affect interpretations of the evidence. Mock jurors instructed both before and after the trial were, however, better able to apply the law to the facts of the case than jurors instructed only after the trial.

Pre-instruction on general matters such as the presumption of inno-cence, burdens of proof, or the limited admissibility of certain evidence could in theory affect how evidence is encoded and in this way could affect verdicts.[100] Heuer and Penrod report a field study in which Wisconsin trial judges agreed to assign cases randomly to a "pre-instruction" or a "no pre-instruction" condition.[101] It appears that pre-instructions did not hurt the trial process and may have helped. Jurors who received pre-instructions reported that the pre-instructions generally helped them in accomplishing such tasks as evaluating the evidence during the trial, applying the law to the facts, and remembering the judge's instructions, but a comparison of their responses with the responses of jurors who had not been pre-instructed does not support their belief that they were better off in these ways than if they had not been pre-instructed. Pre-instructed jurors were, however, more satisfied with the way their trials had been conducted than jurors who had not been pre-instructed, and judges were both less surprised by the verdicts of pre-instructed juries and more satisfied with them. Moreover, lawyers and judges saw pre-instructions as having virtually no disruptive or adverse affects on the jury and as tending to increase the fairness of trials. Thus pre-instructions seemed to have had only positive effects, if they had any effects at all.[102] Since Heuer and Penrod do not report what pre-instructions were given, further work must be done to see whether their findings apply to both case-focused, substantive pre-instructions and to instructions on matters, like burdens of proof, that are common across trials.

Giving Written Instructions

Heuer and Penrod's study of pre-trial instructions also randomized the presentation of written instructions to juries for use during their deliberations. Jurors who received written instructions reported that these instructions helped them in a variety of ways, but their ratings of the helpfulness and understandability of the judge's instructions was no higher than the ratings of those who did not receive written instructions, and jurors who had received written instructions performed no better on a multiple choice test designed to measure comprehension of the judge's instructions than did jurors who received only oral instructions.[103] Neither jury deliberations nor the trial seemed to be affected in other significant ways by written instructions, nor did written instructions seem to function differently in longer cases than in shorter ones. Judges and lawyers generally approved of written instructions, however, and did not see them as causing any significant problems.[104] Because all parties seemed to like written instructions and they seemed to cause no harm, Heuer and Penrod recommend written instructions as a jury reform.

Note-taking and Question-asking

Heuer and Penrod also provide us with the best research to date on the effects of allowing jurors to take notes or to ask questions. They did two field studies of these procedures, one in Wisconsin and one with cooperating federal judges across the nation.[105] The Wisconsin study, like the study of pre-instructions and of written instructions, found that no great benefits but little harm came from these procedures. The national study, however, is more relevant to our concerns since the authors looked specifically at how note-taking and question-asking functioned in complex and in simpler cases. This study involved 103 federal judges who agreed to assign one or two cases on an experimental basis.[106] The authors randomly assigned cases to the experimental conditions, and the judges implemented these assignments either in their next case or, if they were willing to accept two assignments, in both their next case and their next complex case. All told, the authors collected data on seventy-five civil and eighty-five criminal trials.

Based on judicial responses, three dimensions of complexity were defined, one relating most closely to the complexity of the evidence, a second to the quantity of the evidence, and a third to the complexity of the law.[107] On average, the judges seemed satisfied with the jury's performance, rating the jury verdicts in both criminal and civil cases above seven on a nine-point scale with respect to both legal correctness (nine indicating strong agreement that the verdict is legally correct) and their own satisfaction with the verdict (nine indicating very satisfied). A composite of these and two other items reveals that judicial satisfaction with the jury's performance did not vary with the complexity of the case.

Jurors who were allowed to ask questions had significantly higher scores than those not allowed to ask questions with respect to feeling well informed, the perceived ease of reaching verdicts and understanding the law, the perceived helpfulness of the prosecutor and defense counsel, and the certainty that they felt that the verdict was correct.[108] Surprisingly, jurors allowed to take notes reported feeling less well informed than jurors who were not allowed to take notes, and they reported it was more difficult to reach a verdict. Judicial approval of jury verdicts was, however, not affected by either of the two experimental procedures, and this finding does not change with the complexity of the case. Excluding hung juries in criminal cases, judges agreed with the juries' verdicts in about 75 percent of the criminal trials and in about 63 percent of the civil cases. Interestingly, in civil cases judges were considerably more likely to disagree when juries returned defendants' verdicts (52 percent disagreement) than when juries returned plaintiffs' verdicts (29 percent disagreement). Disagreement did not seem to be related to case complexity, to trial procedures, or to their interaction.

A test of interaction effects revealed that jurors found the ability to ask questions increasingly helpful (in the sense that they felt well informed and found it easy to understand the law) as the law became more complex. Permission to ask questions also added more to jurors' confidence in their verdicts as the evidence became more complex. As the amount of information offered at trial increased, however, the chance to ask questions seemed to backfire. With heavy information loads, jurors allowed to ask questions were less likely to feel well informed than jurors not allowed to ask questions and more likely to report difficulty in understanding the law and reaching a verdict. For note-taking the two-way interactions with the legal dimension of complexity are significant but directionally inconsistent; in some situations increasing legal complexity is associated with positive juror evaluations, and in other cases it is associated with negative reports. The most important findings seem to be that as legal complexity increases, note-taking jurors are less likely to feel satisfied with their verdicts and are less certain they have reached the right result than jurors not allowed to take notes.

Heuer and Penrod also examined certain procedures that varied because responding judges handled cases in different ways. They found that an initial juror orientation lecture contributed to juror satisfaction and that the use of special verdict forms increased not only juror satisfaction but also verdict confidence and feelings among jurors that they understood the judge's instructions and were well informed. Judges who commented on the evidence or summarized, on the other hand, left jurors feeling that it was harder to reach a verdict and harder to understand the law, and the closer a judge hewed to pattern verdict instructions, the less confidence jurors had in the verdicts they reached.[109] Judicial satisfaction with jury performance was not, however, affected by the use of any of these four procedures.

These data suggest that jurors feel that they perform better when they can ask questions, when they are given verdict forms, and when they receive an initial orientation. But if juries do perform better with these aids, judges seem not to notice.[110] One might argue that as long as jurors feel they are being helped by certain measures, such measures should be used, and this is what Heuer and Penrod conclude. It is not clear, however, that the juror responses that Heuer and Penrod treat as positive indicators of competence are always that. For example, confidence in a verdict rendered in a close, complex case may be illusory since there may be no verdict in which a factfinder should feel confident. A juror who felt less confident in such a case might have done a more honest job of grappling with the evidence and returned a verdict more likely to be correct. The same could be said about the sense that a verdict is easy. Indeed, certain juror attitudes toward their experiences may have a different normative status depending on whether cases are close on the evidence or easy, and whether they are simple to comprehend or complex. Thus while the Heuer and Penrod study is the best effort to date to shed an empirical light on the usefulness of reforms designed to increase jury competence, their results are inescapably ambiguous, for the normative status of their dependent variables is not completely clear. Perhaps this is the reason that judicial evaluations do not confirm juror reports.

Evaluating Informal Experiments

If there have been few rigorous scientific experiments evaluating proposed jury reforms, there has been no lack of experimentation in a more colloquial sense. We saw, for example, in our case studies that most of the trial judges involved "experimented" with one or more of the procedural reforms that have been commonly suggested. Indeed, some reforms, such as note-taking, may be more the rule in complex cases than the exception.[111] Assessments indicate that when judges try innovative procedures, they seldom find the harms they feared and often perceive benefits.

Leonard Sand and Steven Reiss, for example, persuaded one or more of the twenty-eight judges serving on the Second Circuit in June of 1983 to try one or more of seven "novel" procedures.[112] These procedures included ten minutes of attorney participation in voir dire; individual, private voir dire; pre-instructing the jury; allowing jurors to ask questions; informing jurors they could take notes; providing jurors with a written copy of the charge; and providing jurors with a tape recording of the charge. Sand and Reiss found in almost every instance that if lawyers and judges could be induced to go along with a procedure, a majority, sometimes an overwhelming majority, reacted favorably to it. These findings are consistent with the later work by Heuer and Penrod, who report that those Wisconsin judges, lawyers, and jurors who participated in their field experiments invariably liked the innovative procedures they experienced, and they liked them more and saw fewer problems with them than judges, lawyers, and jurors who had not experienced the procedures but were asked how they thought they would have reacted to them.[113]

Reforms Worth Doing

Having reviewed the evidence, I cannot say that there is an adequate empirical basis for concluding that reforms like those that have been proposed will make juries better factfinders in complex cases. Yet given a wealth of unsystematic experience and some few experiments, it appears likely that most proposed reforms will not be harmful. Indeed, there is reason in common sense, scientific theory, and occasional experience to believe that certain of the suggested reforms will do some good. Where the likelihood of harm is low and the possibility of benefits exists, there is a case for action, as there is when some harm is possible but the likelihood of significant benefits is substantial. I believe that a number of the proposed procedural reforms fit one or the other of these two circumstances. Rather than wait for definitive research, some of the proposed procedural reforms should be instituted now.

Since we are acting without full knowledge, however, we should, in innovating, act to gain knowledge. Ideally, courts would institute any reforms experimentally, but this is unlikely to happen. In default of experimental implementation, there should be a systematic attempt, perhaps under the auspices of the Federal Judicial Center and the National Center for State Courts, to monitor reforms and to systematically canvass reactions to them. Indeed these agencies and other funding sources should make the continued experimental evaluation of such reforms a priority. Many reforms are plausible; I will discuss ten I would like to see.

NOTE-TAKING. Opposing note-taking seems futile because it is already often allowed in complex cases. Note-taking was permitted in a number of our case studies, and in no case in which it was allowed was there a suggestion of any problems. Moreover, a theoretical argument can be made that note-taking will increase juror involvement in the trial and juror performance.[114] The experiment by Heuer and Penrod provides some cause for concern, however. In this experiment note-taking was associated with feeling less well informed and finding it harder to decide on a verdict. These feelings are too consistent with a hypothesized danger of note-taking—the possibility that jurors who take notes will miss information as they try to copy other information down—to be summarily dismissed.[115] Thus, in trials where daily transcripts are being prepared, jurors might be barred from taking notes and instead be furnished with transcripts to use as they see fit. The reactions and performance of jurors furnished with transcripts should be compared with those of jurors in similar trials who instead may take notes.

QUESTION-ASKING. This is the reform most strongly supported by the Heuer and Penrod field experiment, and it seems to be the one most desired by jurors as well.[116] The experimental and anecdotal evidence both suggest that jurors do not abuse question-asking privileges, and questions may give lawyers an idea of how well jurors are following the evidence. It should be noted, however, that the *Pennzoil* judge reversed himself and ceased to allow juror questions part way through the trial.[117] Problems with questioning may have arisen in that trial because the judge permitted jurors to interject questions orally at any point in the testimony simply by raising their hands. When jurors submit written questions after a witness has finished direct or cross-examination, problems are not reported.

PRE-INSTRUCTION. Somewhat less confidently, I suggest that at the outset of complex cases jurors receive a composite of pre-instructions and an orientation lecture. The case for this change is better grounded in theory than in experimental evidence, although some apparently positive effects appeared in the Heuer and Penrod experiment.[118]

Theory suggests that if the jurors are aware of the issues they have to resolve, they may be better able to understand the evidence they receive and to put otherwise confusing evidence in an understandable perspective. Theory coupled with some evidence tells us that instructions concerning how evidence should be coded are better given before evidence is encountered than after the fact. In accordance with these views, jurors should be informed before the trial begins of the legal issues they are expected to resolve and of the major factual disputes between parties. While this is also the stuff of opening statements, an introduction unskewed by partisanship might be a helpful prelude to an exposition by the parties. There is, however, a danger of reversible error here, and a judge should develop such comments carefully in consultation with the parties.

It also makes sense for the judge to pre-instruct the jury, as judges now often do, on what is and is not evidence, on how they should respond to objections, on why discussions occur out of the jurors' hearing or with the jury escorted out of the courtroom, and on similar matters. A potentially important pre-instruction that is commonly given emphasizes that every case has two sides and that the jurors should not discuss the case or make up their minds until they have heard all the evidence. While some people regard such instructions as futile, anecdotal evidence from jurors serving in lengthy trials shows that the temptation to discuss a case as it progresses can be and often is resisted. The effectiveness of the instruction to maintain an open mind is more problematic since jurors admit to leaning toward one side or the other as a case progresses. Perhaps the goal of the instruction to keep an open mind would be better achieved if jurors were told at the outset that when they began deliberations, they should not vote immediately but should together review the evidence in the case. Some of the case studies, consistent with mock-jury research suggest that early voting can lock people into positions and diminish the productivity of deliberations.[119]

It is probably also wise to explain the burden of proof to jurors at the outset and, in a criminal case, to acquaint jurors with the presumption of innocence. The theoretical reason for this is that jurors may engage in "on line" decisionmaking as evidence is received, and if they do, they should at least do so knowing the correct standard. Despite the Saul Kassin and Lawrence Wrightsman study that purports to have shown the virtues of this instruction experimentally, this recommendation is based more on common sense and theory than on experimental evidence.[120]

WRITTEN INSTRUCTIONS. Each juror should receive written copies of the instructions for reference during deliberations.

SIMPLIFICATION. Complex cases should be simplified through pre-trial stipulations, severance of joined claims or counts, partial summary judgment when facts are indisputable, and other methods of limiting issues in dispute. One promising technique is to allow the parties only a limited time to present their cases. Two of the courts in our case studies used this technique to apparently good effect. Where, however, one party's case is inherently more time consuming than the other's, difficult problems of fairness may arise. Also, to promote simplification a court should not allow parties to present technical documents largely to impress jurors with their bulk, as may have occurred in the ABA trade secrets case. If documents are redundant or unnecessary, they should be ruthlessly pared down according to the provisions of Rule 403 of the Federal Rules of Evidence to what is new and essential. If jurors are unlikely to understand certain documents, those documents should not be admitted unless the party offering them offers evidence to aid in their understanding.

TRIAL NOTEBOOKS. Steps should be taken, as they often are today, to ensure that jurors can easily follow documentary evidence. One aid in this respect is the loose-leaf trial notebook that can be added to as exhibits are offered. Such notebooks can include at the outset information about important facts the parties have agreed on. Documentary evidence should be distributed to the jurors so that they can follow it as it is discussed, or visual aids should be used to the same effect. Those documents and exhibits admitted into evidence should be organized and indexed for easy retrieval once the jury has retired to the jury room. The jury should not be given boxes of unorganized exhibits, as has occasionally happened.

SIMPLIFIED INSTRUCTIONS. Legal instructions should long since have been rewritten to foster ease of understanding. In jurisdictions where this has not happened (most places), rewriting should occur.

IMPROVED COMMUNICATIONS. During the deliberations jury questions should be answered in plain language. Juries should not simply be referred back to the instructions. The case studies reveal that such references seldom helped and that without judicial guidance a reasonable interpretation of an instruction could be wrong. Indeed, in several of the cases where the jury verdict seemed to reflect a legal misinterpretation, the jury had realized it was having trouble understanding what the law required and had sought the court's aid in understanding but had not received any. As a corollary to this recommendation, as long as a court's answers to juror questions appear fair and helpful, appellate courts should not reverse trial courts simply because precise legal language was not tracked and an unlikely legal misinterpretation is possible.

ENLARGED JURIES. We saw in a number of cases that jurors tend to follow the lead of their most competent members when cases are complex. Increasing the number of jurors increases the likelihood that one or more jurors will have a good understanding of the law and evidence. In addition, the larger the jury, the better the jury's collective memory is likely to be. The recent amendment to Rule 48 of the Federal Rules of Civil Procedure, which eliminates alternate jurors, should help achieve larger juries since no court will seat only six jurors in a complex case and risk a mistrial should one juror be unable to continue. Courts should routinely seat twelve jurors when cases are likely to be complex. Indeed, in long complex cases where substantial juror attrition is a danger, the court should seek the parties' consent to ignore the limitations of the new rule and seat more than twelve jurors, on the understanding that if more than twelve jurors remain at the end of the trial, excess jurors will be treated as alternates. Juror attrition over the course of a long trial might otherwise dissipate the strengths that larger juries afford or even reduce the jury to fewer than six members, allowing one party to force a mistrial. Twelve-person civil juries should be allowed to return verdicts over the dissent of one or two members. This will minimize hung juries, which are especially costly in lengthy cases, and the excessive influence, as in the ABA trade secrets case, of individual and probably incorrect dissenters. Accepting nonunanimous verdicts in federal civil cases requires the consent of the parties, which a judge should try to secure in advance; allowing nonunanimous verdicts in civil cases without party consent is a matter for Congress's agenda.

JUROR SELECTION. Courts should encourage the selection of competent jurors. The tactical desire to gain a jury that can be fooled deserves no legal respect. The issue is, however, a delicate one, for judicial intervention to ensure juror competence can interfere with a party's right to exercise peremptory challenges. But some interference is tolerable if, as I have argued elsewhere, the peremptory challenge is justified largely as a device to eliminate prejudice that escapes the sieve of the challenge for cause.[121] Encroachments on the peremptory challenge, however, have already been made to forestall racial prejudice, and further encroachments, albeit for good reasons, threaten to reduce the peremptory challenge to a challenge for cause. I do not, therefore, support legal change in this area. Rather, I recommend judicial jawboning. The trial judge should make the desirability of securing a capable jury clear and should urge the attorneys not to challenge those jurors who seem most likely to understand the issues in the case. Where such a juror is challenged, the judge might ask an attorney why the challenged juror was thought undesirable. While an attorney would be free to tell the court there was no reason, few attorneys would want to admit, even implicitly, that they wished to avoid jurors who seemed likely to understand the case. Provisions should also be made to compensate jurors generously in trials that exceed a certain length so that fewer people would seek to be excused where cases are likely to last more than a few weeks.[122]

I could suggest more changes that might be made now, but I suspect these ten are more than are likely to happen in the near future. I believe that each of these suggestions can be plausibly justified based on what we know now, but none is as firmly rooted in reliable research as I would like it to be. For this reason it is essential that the institution of such changes should be the occasion for more study and not a signal that research is no longer needed because reform has occurred.

A New Perspective

I have now canvassed the research done since my first article that bears on the three issues that in my view had to be resolved to support a due-process-based complexity exception to the Seventh Amendment right to jury trial. There has, however, been another development since 1981 in the psychological understanding of jury trials that relates to the likely capacity of juries in complex cases. This is the development of a new model of jury decisionmaking that Nancy Pennington and Reid Hastie, its principal proponents, call the "story model."[123] The story model suggests that jurors try to make sense out of the evidence they are offered by constructing the story that best explains it. It is an exciting and plausible development in the effort to understand jury decisionmaking both in its own right and because it fits in nicely with recent developments in cognitive psychology, where stories are a kind of schema linking people, motives, and actions.[124]

At present the story model has been used largely to explain jury decisions in cases like homicides, where such alternative stories as the premeditated assault and the self-defense story can be plausible explanations for the same array of evidence. The model seems to work well in these settings, and it illustrates how jurors can take evidence and, using various criteria for consistency, try to fit it to one among a stock of stories with which they are already familiar. We also see in the experimental evidence that preexisting story structures can cause jurors to misperceive certain evidence or to recall evidence that was never presented. This is to be expected if stories are a type of schema.

Now consider the complex case. From a story perspective there are two types. First, there are cases in which the evidence that makes a case complex can fit a slot, by which I mean a place that holds a story element, in a story. For example, consider a case like *W. R. Grace*. The plaintiff's main story line is not complex and is readily available to most jurors: two companies carelessly dumped poisonous effluents that reached the water table and percolated to the town's wells that supplied the plantiff's water. The plaintiffs drank the water and became seriously ill.

The easy conclusion is that the defendants are wrongdoers who should pay for the harm their effluents caused.

What makes the case difficult is not the unfamiliarity of the basic story line. Instead, at several points the defendants draw on scientific evidence to argue that connections assumed by the story do not exist. For example, the defendant companies denied that their effluents could reach the town's wells and claimed there was no proof that the effluents were the source of the increased incidence of leukemia in the plaintiff population. Thus, what is complex in the trial involves two story slots that must be filled in for the plaintiffs to recover: there must be a way for the defendants' effluents to reach the town's wells, and there must be a reason to conclude that the effluents caused the plaintiffs' leukemia. The trial is not limited to these issues—the plaintiffs, for example, must prove that the defendants discharged the effluents—but the trial, particularly what is complex about the trial, turns on them.

We can think of the jury's decision regarding how to fill each slot as itself involving a competition among stories. But these competing stories are specialized stories that only scientific experts know well. Invariably, in a case like *W. R. Grace*, the scientists whom the jury hears disagrees. How are jurors to decide between opposing scientific stories if such stories are unfamiliar and the jurors have no set of plausible stories with which to compare the scientific evidence? To what extent will juror decisions reflect the ways in which the parts of the story that they can follow pull them along? Is, for example, the very fact that the plaintiffs in *Grace* are suffering from a feared and esoteric disease likely to lead jurors to believe that the defendants' effluents must have seeped into the town's wells and must have been capable of causing the disease (because otherwise there is no explanation for the evidence before them)? Would a jury that accepted the plaintiffs' expert's scientific story for this reason be acting irrationally? Suppose instead of relying on an unfamiliar scientific story about how effluents travel, a juror instead relies on schemas with which he or she is familiar—like the stereotype that nervousness is associated with lying—to decide which expert's story to accept. Is this an irrational basis for decision?

Is there any reason to believe that the judge in a case like *W. R. Grace* would do a better job than the jury? The judge is likely to have a stock of pollution stories much as the jury does, but the judge, like the jurors, is probably unfamiliar with the stories the scientists tell. Moreover, the trial judge's stories may be different from the jury's stories or at least may be differentially accessible. The unscrupulous plaintiff's attorney story (plaintiff's attorney is known for drumming up litigation) may figure in the judge's evaluation of the evidence when it hardly enters into the jury's. Or the judge may have easy mental access to a story in which potential polluters are more responsible or pollution is less likely to be harmful—access not shared by the jurors. In this situation, whose stock of stories should be brought to bear to help make sense of those aspects of the story—scientific stories within the story—that neither the judge nor the jury understands well? I can not answer questions like these here, but they are worth raising; they suggest a new approach to thinking about how judges and jurors respond to one kind of evidentiary complexity.

Other complex cases viewed from a story perspective are ones in which evidence is not necessarily hard to understand, but jurors are unlikely to be acquainted with the set of stories that most plausibly fit the evidence. The *Pennzoil* and *Micro/Vest* trials furnish examples. The jurors in these cases did not know various story lines that might make sense of facts relating to competing tender offers or business understandings about the terms of loans. In cases like these it is not surprising if jurors are tempted to make sense of the evidence by fitting it to stories they are more familiar with, such as a story of people making ordinary agreements. This tendency can be exacerbated when one side encourages the jury to use its ordinary stock of stories to interpret the facts of a case. This occurred in *Pennzoil*. It was perhaps best revealed in an interchange between the plaintiff's attorney, Joe Jamail, a personal-injury lawyer who ordinarily did no business litigation, and Marty Lipton, a well-known New York takeover lawyer. Jamail asked Lipton whether he was "saying that you have some distinction between just us ordinary people making contracts with each other, and whether or not it's a ten-billion-dollar deal? Is there a different standard in your mind?" Lipton replied, "Yes, indeed." Jim Shannon, who may have been the jury's most influential member recalls, "At that point my jaw just dropped."[125] For a Wall Street lawyer or for most judges (not necessarily the judge in the *Pennzoil* trial), an answer that the standard was the same might have caused jaws to drop.

In these circumstances, are we better off with trial to a jury or to a judge? Despite the *Pennzoil* case, people can learn that stories they have not heard of before are plausible. The entrapment story in *DeLorean* is an example. And in *Pennzoil*, there is no reason to believe that the judge would have decided differently; indeed, a number of his pre-trial evidentiary rulings prevented Texaco from presenting a convincing, gapless version of the story it wanted to tell. Moreover, having access to a story that appears to fit a body of evidence is not always a virtue, for when a story is familiar, evidence may be distorted, overlooked, or even invented where the evidence recalls the story but does not fit it perfectly. The jury's virtue is that different jurors have different preferred stories so the jury collectively is less likely than individual decisionmakers to be misled by the kinds of natural distortions and gap-filling that an available story may stimulate.

I do not pretend to have answers to the questions I pose, nor do I now suggest that the story model provides a new or more adequate answer to the question of whether judges or juries are better situated to decide complex cases. But story-model research does provide a new perspective on the issue; one that I think is worth further thought and exploration.

Conclusion

I began this paper by recalling my earlier article suggesting that three kinds of showings had to be made to justify a Supreme Court holding that due process required a complexity exception to the Seventh Amendment right to jury trial: first, a showing that juries did not decide such cases rationally; second, a showing that changes in the management of juries and cases could not cure identifiable jury deficiencies; and third, a showing that judges would find facts in such cases more rationally than juries.

I then examined the empirical evidence relating to these three issues. Much of the available evidence is unfortunately anecdotal. It is the kind of evidence on which one does not want important policy decisions to turn. To the extent that there is systematic social science knowledge that elucidates these three issues, none of it resolves an issue, and much of it is unclear in its import even if concerns about external validity are discounted. In short, not enough social science research has been done to date to allow us to reach firm conclusions about the capacities of juries and judges to handle complex cases or about the potential improvement in jury capacity afforded by possible reforms.

Thus, I could simply end this paper as I ended my first one, with a call for additional empirical research, an argument that the burden of proving the incapacity of juries in complex cases is on those who would limit the Seventh Amendment right, and a judgment that that burden has not been met.

But there is more to be said. Throughout this review, strengths of the jury emerge. A close look at a number of cases, including several in which jury verdicts appear mistaken, does not show juries that are befuddled by complexity. Even when juries do not fully understand technical issues, they can usually make enough sense of what is going on to deliberate rationally, and they usually reach defensible decisions. To the extent that juries make identifiable mistakes, their mistakes seem most often attributable not to conditions uniquely associated with complexity, but to the mistakes of judges and lawyers, to such systematic deficiencies of the trial process as battles of experts and the prevalence of hard-to-understand jury instructions, and to the kinds of human error that affect simple trials as well. The anecdotal evidence should also remind us that it is difficult to predict which complex cases will trouble juries and which they will handle well.

The import of the experimental literature is similar. Experiments show that some factors that make for complexity, such as the joinder of charges or statistical evidence, can lead to jury mistakes. Yet in the most realistic studies, juries perform surprisingly well. In the study by Diamond and Casper, for example, contrary to what one might predict, regression models were as influential as the more concrete and intuitively understandable yardstick models.[126] In the study by Horowitz and Bordens, joined plaintiffs and scientific evidence caused few problems.[127] Moreover, juries in the Diamond and Casper study, like some of the case-study juries, showed an extraordinary capacity for identifying their most capable members and then letting them lead. This suggests that the challenges that complex cases pose might be met best by the simple expedient of getting more capable people to serve on juries.

The empirical evidence also provides no reason to believe that judges will fare better in the face of complexity than juries, for we have little basis for deciding how judges will do at all. What we have instead are anecdotes that make the point that judges dealing with unfamiliar, technical information can be as confused as we fear similarly situated juries are. The most reasonable conclusion about the relative capacity of juries and judges is probably one that I reached in my earlier article without substantial empirical support and am willing, still without substantial empirical support, to reiterate here: in complex cases we can expect that some judges will be more capable than the average jury, and we can expect that the average jury will be more capable than some judges. But in many cases we will not know in advance whether judge or jury is likely to be the more rational decisionmaker.

With regard to reforms in the management of complex cases and the conduct of jury trials, we live in a world of constantly experimenting judges. The problem is that the experimentation most judges do is uncontrolled, hardly visible, and unsystematic, so we learn almost nothing from it except what we can learn from the fact that great outcries over various novel procedures seem not to have arisen. Given this, I have suggested that we should apply the little we have learned from systematic experimentation, consider what social science theory suggests, add a good dose of common sense, and make those limited changes we think will improve the jury system. We should, however, resolve to study the changes we make so that we will learn if our hunches are right.

For more than a decade now, the fitness of juries to hear complex cases has been on trial. Twelve years ago it was only possible to say that the case against the civil jury had not been proven. While we still do not have a wealth of evidence, there is enough to support a more positive verdict. Based on what we know today, there is no empirical case for a complexity exception to the Seventh Amendment. *Instead the weight of the evidence indicates that juries can reach rationally defensible verdicts in complex cases, that we cannot assume that judges in complex cases will perform better than juries, and that there are changes that can be made to enhance jury performance.* These conclusions will not necessarily be sustained as research proceeds. But they are the best that empirical knowledge today can offer.

Notes

1. Warren Burger, "Remarks: Use of Lay Jurors in Complicated Civil Cases," 1979 annual meeting of Chief Justices; and Peter W. Sperlich, "The Case for Preserving Trial by Jury in Complex Civil Litigation," *Judicature*, vol. 65 (March 1982), pp. 394–415.

2. See, for example, Douglas W. Ell, "The Right to an Incompetent Jury: Protracted Commercial Litigation and the Seventh Amendment," *Connecticut Law Review*, vol. 10 (Spring 1978), pp. 775–800; Thomas M. Jorde, "The Seventh Amendment Right to Jury Trial of Antitrust Issues," *California Law Review*, vol. 69 (January 1981), p. 1; William V. Luneberg and Mark A. Nordenberg, "Specially Qualified Juries and Expert Nonjury Tribunals: Alternatives for Coping with the Complexities of Modern Civil Litigation," *Virginia Law Review*, vol. 67 (June 1981), p. 887; Edward J. DeVitt, "Should Jury Trial Be Required in Civil Cases? A Challenge to the Seventh Amendment," *Journal of Air Law and Commerce*, vol. 47 (Spring 1982), pp. 495–516; and Alvin B. Rubin, "Trial by Jury and Complex Civil Cases: Voice of Liberty or Verdict by Confusion?" *Annals AAPSS*, vol. 462 (July 1982), pp. 87–103.

3. The Supreme Court has never applied the Seventh Amendment to the states so, as a matter of federal constitutional law, state courts are free to eliminate jury trials in civil actions. Many states, however, are bound by their own constitutions to offer jury trials in actions at law.

4. Richard O. Lempert, "Civil Juries and Complex Cases: Let's Not Rush to Judgment," *Michigan Law Review*, vol. 80 (November 1981), pp. 68–132.

5. In a situation where neither judges nor juries could be expected to resolve a matter rationally, the resolution of the issue, as some commentators have suggested, could be vested in some other institution, such as a panel of experts. See Luneberg and Nordenberg, "Specially Qualified Juries," p. 887; and David U. Strawn and G. Thomas Munsterman, "Helping Juries Handle Complex Cases," *Judicature*, vol. 65 (March–April 1982), pp. 444–47. In the setting of a lawsuit, such an alternative institution might be confined by the Constitution to the limited role that due process requires; it might, for example, resolve difficult technical questions that the decisionmaker, whether judge or jury, would then take as proven in deciding a case. Outside that class of actions that are "legal" within the meaning of the Seventh Amendment, a broader role might be accorded expert decisionmakers, as is often done in administrative agencies.

6. The cases included in the table are a sample selected for convenience. Some of them had come to my attention before I wrote this chapter; others were uncovered by a research assistant. When I starting writing the first draft of this chapter, I knew of no other case studies that met the criteria for inclusion. Since completing the first draft, I have learned of several additional case studies that meet my criteria, but including them would lengthen the chapter without changing any of the conclusions supported by the current sample. It is important to recognize that my sample of cases is a nonrandom selection containing a disproportionate number of high-profile cases. The cases were not, however, selected because of their tendencies to prove or to disprove any of the hypotheses examined in this chapter. Indeed, not until I selected and read the cases was I aware of their implications for the issues explored in this chapter. Lisa Bernt, a 1992 graduate of the University of Michigan Law School, checked my summaries of key case characteristics.

7. Of course confusion may also be understated after memories have faded.

8. Neil Vidmar, personal communication, August 10, 1992.

9. Fred L. Strodtbeck, Rita M. James, and Charles Hawkins, "Social Status in Jury Deliberations," *American Sociological Review*, vol. 22 (December 1957), pp. 713–18; and Reid Hastie, Steven D. Penrod, and Nancy Pennington, *Inside the Jury* (Harvard University Press, 1983).

10. Lempert, "Civil Juries and Complex Cases"; Luneberg and Nordenberg, "Specially Qualified Juries"; Mark A. Nordenberg and William V. Luneberg, "Decisionmaking in Complex Federal Civil Cases: Two Alternatives to the Traditional Jury," *Judicature*, vol. 65 (March–April 1982), pp. 421–31; and William W Schwarzer, "Reforming Jury Trials," *Federal Rules Decisions*, vol. 132 (West, 1991), pp. 575–96.

11. Steven Brill, "Inside the DeLorean Jury Room," *American Lawyer*, vol. 6 (December 1984), pp. 94–105.

12. Samuel R. Gross, "Expert Evidence," *Wisconsin Law Review*, vol. 1991 (November–December), pp. 1113–1232.

13. Phoebe C. Ellsworth and Jack G. Getman, "The Use of Social Science in Legal Decision Making," in Leon Lipson and Stanton Wheeler, eds., *Law and the Social Sciences* (Russell Sage Foundation, 1987), pp. 581–636; and Anthony Champagne, Daniel Shuman, and Elizabeth Whitaker, "An Empirical Examination of the Use of Expert Witnesses in American Courts," *Jurimetrics*, vol. 31 (Summer 1991), pp. 375–92.

14. Gross, "Expert Evidence."

15. See Elizabeth F. Loftus and Katherine Ketcham, *Witness for the Defense: The Accused, the Eyewitness, and the Expert Who Puts Memory on Trial* (St. Martin's, 1991);

and E. Allan Lind and William M. O'Barr, "The Social Significance of Speech in the Courtroom," in Howard Giles and Robert N. St. Clair, eds., *Language and Social Psychology* (Baltimore: University Park Press, 1977), chap. 4.

16. James A. Martin, "The Proposed 'Science Court,'" *Michigan Law Review*, vol. 75 (April–May 1977), pp. 1058–91; and Luneberg and Nordenberg, "Decisionmaking in Complex Federal Civil Cases" and "Specially Qualified Juries."

17. This is not, I should note, what the jury did in *Grace*. Their verdict is discussed below. And the evidentiary dispute recounted in the text involved pollution attributed to the Beatrice Company, a codefendant in the case.

18. More precisely, I am giving my subjective view of another observer's subjective view of the quality of the verdict.

19. Since mistakes on damages can be corrected through remittitur either at the trial level or on appeal, such mistakes are not as costly to the efficient administration of justice as mistakes on liability that, if caught, are more likely to require a new trial.

20. This is why I argued in my 1981 article for nonunanimous juries in civil cases.

21. This limitation strikes me as legally questionable, so the jury's performance might be better than the judge's in this case.

22. Robert P. Charrow and Veda R. Charrow, "Making Legal Language Understandable: A Psycholinguistic Study of Jury Instructions," *Columbia Law Review*, vol. 79 (November 1979), pp. 1306–74; Amiram Elwork, Bruce D. Sales, and James J. Alfini, "Juridic Decisions: In Ignorance of the Law or in Light of It?" *Law and Human Behavior*, vol. 1, no. 2 (1977), pp. 163–89; Amiram Elwork, James J. Alfini, and Bruce D. Sales, "Toward Understandable Jury Instructions," *Judicature*, vol. 65 (March–April 1982), pp. 432–43; Hastie, Penrod, and Pennington, *Inside the Jury*; and Phoebe C. Ellsworth, "Are Twelve Heads Better Than One?" *Law and Contemporary Problems*, vol. 52 (Autumn 1989), pp. 205–24.

23. Mitchell Pacelle, "Contaminated Verdict," *American Lawyer*, vol. 8 (December 1986), pp. 75–80.

24. One juror, the jury's only college-educated member, understood the implications of the answer. This juror kept quiet because he was the defendant's strongest proponent within the jury room.

25. This does not mean that the jurors would have been acting irrationally had they realized the consequences of an answer of "not determined" and reported a date. The jurors might reasonably have been confident that by a certain date the contamination had begun and might have noted this date. The question, however, called for the earliest date on which the contamination could, by a preponderance of the evidence, be shown to have happened.

26. Stephen J. Adler, "How to Lose the Bet-Your-Company Case," *American Lawyer*, vol. 8 (January–February 1986), p. 107.

27. Adler, "How to Lose the Bet-Your-Company Case"; and Thomas Petzinger, Jr., *Oil and Honor: The Texaco-Pennzoil Wars* (Putnam, 1987).

28. Claudia Weinstein, "Losing Big at Computerland," *American Lawyer*, vol. 7 (October 1985), p. 127.

29. Ibid.

30. Molly Selvin and Larry Picus, *The Debate over Jury Performance: Observations from a Recent Asbestos Case* (Santa Monica: Rand Institute for Civil Justice, 1987).

31. The authors' description of the deliberations is based on one collective interview held several months after the trial had ended. Research on limiting instructions suggests that the admitted role of the forbidden evidence may have loomed larger at the time of the interview, when the limiting instructions may have been forgotten, than it would have had the interview immediately followed the trial. The reason is not that jurors are unaffected by evidence that they are instructed not to consider or to consider only for a limited

purpose, but rather that jurors often act during their deliberations as if they will not be improperly influenced. Thus, if we may rely on studies of mock juries, when a juror mentions evidence the jury has been instructed not to consider, another juror often points out that the evidence is not to be considered, and the information receives no further overt attention. Nevertheless, such evidence may have the effects the instructions were designed to eliminate. Valerie P. Hans and Anthony N. Doob, "Section 12 of the Canada Evidence Act and the Deliberations of Simulated Juries," *Criminal Law Quarterly*, vol. 18 (March 1976), pp. 235–53; and Jonathan D. Casper, Kennette Benedict, and Jo. L. Perry, "Juror Decisionmaking, Attitudes and the Hindsight Bias," *Law and Human Behavior*, vol. 13 (September 1989), pp. 291–310. What may have happened over time is that the jurors forgot they were not supposed to consider certain evidence and accurately reported the effects that evidence had on them, even though at the time these effects would have seemed insubstantial to one observing the jury deliberation. This possibility seems more plausible with respect to the documents that were improperly used against defendants other than the one charged with their production than it does in the case of the jury's apparent defiance of the judge's instructions not to make awards for past medical damages. On the damage issue the jurors reported a formula they used, something they seem unlikely to misremember, and the formula awarded money for past medical expenses contrary to the judge's instructions.

32. Not only did the jurors have reason to believe that the plaintiff's future earnings might be diminished by the likelihood he would return to Mexico, but the adjustment made was not great and avoided a situation in which this plaintiff would have been awarded more than a plaintiff who was far sicker than he was, albeit with a shorter life expectancy. Moreover, when punitive damages were apportioned, the Mexican plaintiff received $1 million, the same as each of the other plaintiffs.

33. Charrow and Charrow, "Making Legal Language Understandable"; Elwork and others, "Juridic Decision"; Elwork, Alfini, and Sales, "Toward Understandable Jury Instructions"; Hastie, Penrod, and Pennington, *Inside the Jury*; and Ellsworth, "Are Twelve Heads Better Than One?"

34. Charrow and Charrow, "Making Legal Language Understandable"; Elwork, Alfini, and Sales, "Toward Understandable Jury Instructions"; Bruce D. Sales, Amiram Elwork, and James J. Alfini, "Improving Comprehension for Jury Instructions," in B. D. Sales, ed., *Perspectives in Law and Psychology*, vol. 1 (Plenum Press, 1977); and J. Alexander Tanford, "Law Reform by Courts, Legislatures, and Commissions Following Empirical Research on Jury Instructions," *Law & Society Review*, vol. 25 (February 1991), pp. 155–75.

35. Larry Heuer and Steven Penrod, "Trial Complexity: A Field Investigation of Its Meaning and Its Effects," unpublished manuscript.

36. Carolyn M. Howell, "*United States* v. *DeLorean*: The Case of the Confused Jury," *Detroit College of Law Review*, vol. 1988 (Spring), pp. 97–118.

37. Ibid., p. 101, n. 27.

38. Adler, "How to Lose the Bet-Your-Company Case."

39. Jane Goodman, Edith Greene, and Elizabeth F. Loftus, "What Confuses Jurors in Complex Cases," *Trial*, vol. 21 (November 1985), p. 66.

40. Gross, "Expert Evidence."

41. Goodman, Greene, and Loftus, "What Confuses Jurors," p. 68.

42. Peter W. Huber, *Galileo's Revenge: Junk Science in the Classroom* (Basic Books, 1991).

43. Adler, "How to Lose the Bet-Your-Company Case," p. 30.

44. James Shannon, *Texaco and the $10 Billion Jury* (Prentice-Hall, 1988).

45. The fear is not irrational. Haney has shown that jurors who have observed the death-qualification process have attitudes toward the case that are more consistent with a

willingness to convict than the attitudes of those who have not witnessed it. Craig Haney, "The Biasing Effect of the Death-Qualification Process," *Law and Human Behavior*, vol. 8 (June 1984), pp. 121–32. At least part of the explanation for this is that the jurors assumed that unless the judge and lawyers thought the defendant was guilty of a capital offense, there would be no death qualification. A defense counsel might similarly fear that a jury would regard the presence of evidence contesting damages as an acknowledgement that the plaintiff's position on liability deserved to prevail. Nevertheless such an attitude on the part of jurors would be only one factor that would affect their weighing of the evidence on liability, and it is unlikely to matter as much as evidence more directly related to liability. The potential costs of not presenting damage evidence are often so substantial that it is foolish to withhold such evidence for strategic reasons.

46. Claudia Weinstein, "Losing Big at ComputerLand," p. 127.

47. Gordon Bermant and others, *Protracted Civil Trials: Views from the Bench and the Bar* (Washington: Federal Judicial Center, 1981), p. 52.

48. Ell, "Right to an Incompetent Jury."

49. Joe S. Cecil, E. Allan Lind, and Gordon Bermant, *Jury Service in Lengthy Civil Trials* (Washington: Federal Judicial Center, 1987).

50. Ibid.

51. Ibid., p. 38.

52. Heuer and Penrod, "Trial Complexity."

53. William C. Thompson, "Are Juries Competent to Evaluate Statistical Evidence?" *Law and Contemporary Problems*, vol. 52 (Autumn 1989), pp. 9–41.

54. If the defendant has the same blood type as the perpetrator of the charged crime and that blood type is found in 10 percent of the population, a juror caught in the prosecutor's fallacy would conclude that since there is a 10 percent probability that the defendant would have the blood type if he were innocent, there must be a 90 percent chance that the defendant is guilty. William C. Thompson and Edward L. Schumann, "Interpretation of Statistical Evidence in Criminal Trials: The Prosecutor's Fallacy and the Defense Attorney's Fallacy," *Law and Human Behavior*, vol. 11 (September 1987), pp. 167–88.

55. If the defendant and perpetrator have a blood type that they share with 1 percent of the population, one who falls prey to the defense attorney's fallacy would reason that in a city of 1,000,000 people probably 10,000 people share the blood type in question, so the evidence has almost no incriminatory value.

56. E. L. Schumann and W. C. Thompson, "Effects of Attorneys' Arguments on Jurors' Interpretation of Statistical Evidence," paper presented at the meetings of the Law and Society Association, 1989.

57. Michael J. Saks and Robert F. Kidd, "Human Information Processing and Adjudication: Trial by Heuristics," *Law & Society Review*, vol. 15, no. 1 (1980–81), pp. 123–60.

58. David L. Faigman and A. J. Baglioni, "Bayes' Theorem in the Trial Process: Instructing Jurors on the Value of Statistical Evidence," *Law and Human Behavior*, vol. 12 (March 1988), pp. 1–17.

59. Molly Treadway, "An Investigation of Juror Comprehension of Statistical Proof of Causation," poster presented at a biennial meeting of the American Psychology-Law Society, Williamsburg, Va., 1990.

60. Shari Seidman Diamond and Jonathan D. Casper, "Blindfolding the Jury to Verdict Consequences: Damages, Experts, and the Civil Jury," *Law & Society Review*, vol. 26, no. 3 (1992), pp. 513–63.

61. Yardstick models are nonstatistical. They use comparative data from similar firms which did business in competitive markets at the time of the defendant's anticompetitive activity and are based on the premise that the difference in prices paid or profits made by

the benchmark firms and the plaintiff is a good measure of the excess costs imposed on or profits lost by the plaintiff company. While valid comparisons are difficult to obtain, the approach is the kind of concrete, common-sense approach that one would expect a jury to understand intuitively and to appreciate easily. Regression models involve time series analyses of pricing patterns before, during, and sometimes after the price-fixing agreement. The model used in the experiment involved a statistical projection, based on performance before price-fixing, of the price the plaintiff would have paid had there not been a price-fixing agreement. Jurors are not accustomed to dealing with regression models, and one would expect that they would find statistical modeling difficult to understand.

The other aspect of this study, which I shall not discuss, concerned the implications of informing jurors that awards in suits brought under the Sherman Act are trebled.

62. Whether he offered a statistical model or a yardstick model, the plaintiff's expert presented data that suggested the plaintiff's damages had amounted to $490,000, while conceding that they might be as low as $420,000. The defendant's expert, regardless of the model used, presented data suggesting that the most likely figure for damages was $35,000, but he conceded that the model could not rule out damages of up to $105,000.

63. There was no statistically significant difference in the ratings given the experts on persuasiveness or trustworthiness.

64. The correlation between the juries' mean predeliberation awards and their final verdicts was .54; for median predeliberation awards it was .62. For a jury's highest predeliberation award it was .24; and for the lowest predeliberation award it was .20.

65. The correlation between the foreperson's predeliberation awards and final jury awards was .44 across jury verdicts, while the correlation of final verdicts with the awards made by other members of the jury was .22.

66. The correlation between the preferences of the foreperson and final jury verdicts is .57 for forepersons with some postgraduate education and a course in statistics and .36 for forepersons who had neither of these qualifications.

67. The contrary implication that one may draw from the Schumann and Thompson study may result from the fact that their simulated jurors were a relatively homogenous group or that they had few subjects who had studied statistics. Thompson's description of that study, on which I have relied, does not describe the demographics of their simulated jurors. See "Are Juries Competent to Evaluate Statistical Evidence?"

68. Diamond and Casper, "Blindfolding the Jury," p. 558.

69. The possibility that jurors, when faced with a conflict of experts, simply endorse the views of one of them is a suggestion made by Raitz and others, who looked at the implications of expert economics testimony in a mock age-discrimination case. Allan Raitz and others, "Determining Damages: The Influence of Expert Testimony on Jurors' Decision Making," *Law and Human Behavior*, vol. 14 (August 1990), pp. 385–95. As a general matter, the findings of Raitz and his colleagues simply do not hold up in the face of the methodologically superior work of Diamond and Casper. See "Blindfolding the Jury." Raitz and his coauthors presented subjects with a 150-word summary of a trial and a 200-word "transcript" of testimony relating to damages in their "no expert" condition. The "plaintiff's expert only" condition added 200 words and included the examination and cross-examination of the plaintiff's expert, while the two-expert condition added an additional 400 words and the examination and cross-examination of a defense economics expert.

One cannot, however, on the basis of the work by Diamond and Casper rule out the possibility that jurors use an "endorsement strategy" when conflicting experts use the same methodology, although the *W. R. Grace* case shows jurors reacting in the opposite way by acknowledging that they are unable to decide. Nor is there necessarily anything wrong with an endorsement approach if the endorsement is based on a reasonable assessment of the credibility of the opposing experts, as may have occurred in *Johns Manville*. Also, if only one side presents expert evidence, endorsement of the expert's views may be a natural response, as seems to have occurred in *Pennzoil*.

70. See, for example, Edith Greene and Elizabeth F. Loftus, "When Crimes Are Joined at Trial," *Law and Human Behavior*, vol. 9 (June 1985), pp. 193–207; and Sarah Tanford, Steven Penrod, and Rebecca Collins, "Decision Making in Joined Criminal Trials: The Influence of Charge Similarity, Evidence Similarity, and Limited Instructions," *Law and Human Behavior*, vol. 9 (December 1985), pp. 319–37. For a review of this research, see Kenneth S. Bordens and Irwin A. Horowitz, "Joinder of Criminal Offenses: A Review of the Legal and Psychological Literature," *Law and Human Behavior*, vol. 9 (December 1985), pp. 339–53.

71. Hans and Doob, "Section 12 of the Canada Evidence Act"; Saul M. Kassin and Lawrence S. Wrightsman, "Coerced Confessions, Judicial Instruction, and Mock Juror Verdicts," *Journal of Applied Social Psychology*, vol. 11 (November–December 1981), pp. 489–506; Roselle L. Wissler and Michael J. Saks, "On the Inefficacy of Limiting Instructions: When Jurors Use Prior Conviction Evidence to Decide on Guilt," *Law and Human Behavior*, vol. 9 (March 1985), pp. 37–48; and Casper, Benedict, and Perry, "Juror Decisionmaking, Attitudes, and the Hindsight Bias," pp. 291–310.

72. Irwin A. Horowitz and Kenneth S. Bordens, "The Effects of Outlier Presence, Plaintiff Population Size, and Aggregation of Plaintiffs on Simulated Jury Decisions," *Law and Human Behavior*, vol. 12 (September 1988), pp. 209–29.

73. Researchers who have investigated the "just world" paradigm report that the greater the harm suffered by a victim, the greater the tendency to blame the victim. This is attributed to a psychological need to feel in control, which is undermined if people are seen to be suffering excessively through no fault of their own. Melvin J. Lerner, *The Belief in a Just World: A Fundamental Delusion* (Plenum Press, 1980).

74. Shari Seidman Diamond, "Order in the Court: Consistency in Criminal-Court Decisions," in C. James Scheirer and Barbara L. Hammonds, eds., *The Master Lecture Series: Psychology and the Law*, vol. 2 (Washington: American Psychological Association, 1983).

75. Jeffrey R. Rice and Neil Vidmar, "Non-Economic Damage Awards in Medical Negligence: A Comparison of Jurors and Arbitrators," unpublished manuscript, 1992.

76. In a later article using the same stimulus tape, the authors investigated the effect of bifurcating and trifurcating trials on damage awards. Irwin A. Horowitz and Kenneth S. Bordens, "An Experimental Investigation of Procedural Issues in Complex Tort Trials," *Law and Human Behavior*, vol. 14 (June 1990), pp. 269–85. The article is important for those interested in how juries deal with complex cases because it studies a variation that exists in such cases and suggests that the decision to bifurcate or trifurcate a verdict can have substantial consequences. It adds little, however, to what the first study suggests about the jury's capacity to handle complex litigation. Assuming that the jury's task is easier when it hears evidence on one issue and then decides that issue than when it hears evidence on all issues together and decides the issues seriatim, the study does not suggest that juries do worse when their task is more complex. First, there is no a priori reason to suppose that one pattern of verdicts represents a more rational outcome than another pattern. To the extent that verdict consistency across juries is such a standard, unitary trials produce more consistent verdicts. To the extent that a normative judgment is possible, the verdicts of the unitary juries appear more normative, for they are more likely to find for the plaintiffs on the liability issue, and an expert panel of two law professors and a lawyer who reviewed the evidence thought the liability evidence favored the plaintiff. Second, when a trial lasts only four hours, even if some evidence is complex and boring, presenting evidence on only one issue may not simplify the jury's task. Indeed, the longer trial may present a simpler decision problem if evidence allocated to one issue has some relevance on another, for additional evidence may make a case less close and a decision

easier rather than harder. An overlap in the implications of evidence may be one reason why the unitary juries studied by Horowitz and Bordens were more consistent with one another and more pro-plaintiff in deciding the issue of causality. The causality evidence was the only evidence subset that the expert panel saw as ambiguous rather than pro-plaintiff. Perhaps when the implications of other evidence for causality were considered, the task of deciding the causality issue became simpler, and this led to greater consistency. Alternatively, one might agree that sympathy or other factors that should not affect decisions on causality motivated pro-plaintiff decisions on this issue. But sympathy at least does not seem to have motivated the unitary jurors in this study. Sympathy should be a response to the plaintiff's damage claim; separated juries that heard liability evidence first, rendered a verdict, and then heard causal but not damage evidence, had a verdict pattern much like that rendered by the unitary jury deciding the liability and causal issues in the same order. In both cases the causal decision may reflect a desire to punish the defendant, but it is at least as plausible to suppose that the causal link between the presence of a chemical and the illness of a plaintiff becomes more likely when one knows that a defendant has been discharging the chemical where the plaintiff can encounter it. The authors also observed that once a jury decided for a side, consistency on the verdict among the members of a jury was "remarkable."

77. Richard O. Lempert, "Uncovering 'Nondiscernible' Differences: Empirical Research and the Jury-Size Cases," *Michigan Law Review*, vol. 73 (March 1975), pp. 643–708.

78. *Williams* v. *Florida*, 399 U.S. 78 (1970). Lempert, "Uncovering 'Nondiscernible' Differences." The experiment was Asch's line experiment in which experimental subjects were induced by group pressure to misidentify the larger of two lines. Misidentifications disappeared if one group member gave a true answer. The Court suggested that the proportion of group members giving true answers was important.

79. Michael J. Saks and Richard Van Duizend, *The Use of Scientific Evidence in Litigation* (Williamsburg, Va.: National Center for State Courts, 1983).

80. See, for example, *People* v. *Collins*, 438 P.2d 33 (1968).

81. *State* v. *Schwartz*, 447 N.W. 2d 422 (Minn. 1989).

82. *State* v. *Carlson*, 267 N.W. 2d 170 (Minn. 1978).

83. *U.S.* v. *Massey*, 594 F.2d 676 (8th Cir. 1979); *U.S. ex Rel. Di Giacomo* v. *Franzen*, 680 F.2d 515 (7th Cir. 1982); for a critique of these cases see Stephen E. Fienberg, ed., *The Evolving Role of Statistical Assessments as Evidence in Courts* (Springer-Verlag, 1989), pp. 60–67.

84. Fienberg, *Evolving Role of Statistical Assessments*, pp. 60–67.

85. Compare *U.S.* v. *Yee*, vol. 129, *Federal Rules Decsisions* (West), p. 629 (N.D. Ohio 1990) with *State* v. *Despain*, Superior Court of the State of Arizona in the County of Yuma, No. 15589, Feb. 12, 1991.

86. See, for example, *Ethyl Corp.* v. *Environmental Protection Agency*, 541 F.2d 1 at 67 (D.C. Cir. 1976); and *International Harvester Workers* v. *Ruckelhaus*, 478 F.2d 615 at 651 (D.C. Cir. 1973). Many of the text's examples of misunderstanding come from appellate judges, whose errors and bewilderment are more accessible because their opinions are generally published and they cannot disguise their difficulties by simply finding facts without describing the basis of their reasoning. While there is some reason to believe that trial judges are structurally better able than appellate judges to gain an understanding of difficult scientific facts, there is no reason to believe that their structural advantages eliminate problems of understanding. As individuals, most appellate judges are likely to be more capable than most of the judges who sit in the nation's trial courts. See Richard O. Lempert, "'Between Cup and Lip': Social Science Influences on Law and Policy," *Law and Policy*, vol. 10 (April–July 1988), pp. 167–200.

87. Heuer and Penrod, "Trial Complexity."

88. Richard Nisbett and Lee Ross, *Human Inference: Strategies and Shortcomings of Social Judgment* (Prentice Hall, 1980); and Amos Tversky and Daniel Kahneman, "The Framing of Decisions and the Psychology of Choice," *Science*, vol. 211 (January 30, 1981), pp. 453–58.

89. Richard E. Nisbett and Timothy D. Wilson, "Telling More Than We Can Know: Verbal Reports on Mental Processes," *Psychological Review*, vol. 84 (May 1977), pp. 231–59.

90. In the day-to-day evidentiary rulings at trial, Farris's rulings, particularly at the beginning of the trial, favored the defense on such mundane matters as objections to leading questions and hearsay. See Petzinger, *Oil and Honor*.

91. Bermant and others, *Protracted Civil Trials*, p. 39.

92. Harry Kalven, Jr., and Hans Zeisel, *The American Jury* (Little, Brown, 1966); and Christy A. Visher, "Juror Decision Making: The Importance of Evidence," *Law and Human Behavior*, vol. 11 (March 1987), pp. 1–17.

93. E. Donald Elliott, "Managerial Judging and the Evolution of Procedure," *University of Chicago Law Review*, vol. 53 (Spring 1986), pp. 306–36.

94. Peter H. Schuck, *Agent Orange on Trial: Mass Toxic Disasters in the Courts* (Harvard University Press, 1986); Peter H. Schuck, "The Role of Judges in Settling Complex Cases: The Agent Orange Example," *University of Chicago Law Review*, vol. 53 (Spring 1986), pp. 337–65; and Judith Resnik, "Managerial Judges," *Harvard Law Review*, vol. 96 (December 1982), p. 374.

95. I do not mean to suggest that the jury will always be impartial and the judge not. An inadequate voir dire or prejudices too subtle to spot may lead to a biased jury in situations where the judge is unbiased. The right to jury trial itself, however—at least in criminal cases—is an element of due process, which suggests that the possibility of benefiting from certain kinds of jury biases is in some measure an element of due process.

I also recognize that due process is not considered to be violated in settings where it is permissible to dispense with a jury—suits in equity are an example. As a formal matter this is certainly true since due process is in large measure historically defined. Yet even in equity, if bias could be proved, due process would be violated by using a partial judge. Bias can be hard to demonstrate, however. In *Pennzoil*, for example, Judge Farris was challenged on the basis of the $10,000 campaign contribution from Jamail, which was the largest single contribution he had received and amounted to about 10 percent of his reelection funds. The judge who heard the challenge, however, ruled there was no cause for disqualification. Totally apart from the issue of bias, the point of the Seventh Amendment is that in civil actions at law brought in the federal courts the process due includes the right to a jury trial if one party requests it.

96. Joe S. Cecil, Valerie P. Hans, and Elizabeth C. Wiggins "Citizen Comprehension of Difficult Issues: Lessons from Civil Jury Trials," *American University Law Review*, vol. 40 (Winter 1991), pp. 727–74; Christine Durham, "Taming the 'Monster Case': Management of Complex Litigation," *Law and Inequality*, vol. 4 (May 1986), pp. 123–35; Michael A. McLaughlin, "Questions to Witnesses and Notetaking by the Jury as Aids in Understanding Complex Litigation," *New England Law Review*, vol. 18 (Summer 1983), pp. 687–713; Donald Olander, "Resolving Inconsistencies in Federal Special Verdicts," *Fordham Law Review*, vol. 53 (April 1985), pp. 1089–1106; William W Schwarzer, "Techniques for Identifying and Narrowing Issues in Antitrust Cases," *Antitrust Law Journal*, vol. 51, no. 2 (1982), pp. 223–29; Thomas E. Willging, *Court-Appointed Experts* (Washington: Federal Judicial Center, 1986); James R. Withrow and David L. Suggs, "Procedures for Improving Jury Trials of Complex Litigation," *Antitrust Bulletin*, vol. 25 (Fall 1980), pp. 493–512; and Robert P. Taylor and others, "Charting a New Course for Complex Cases: A New Manual for Complex Litigation," *Antitrust Law Journal*, vol. 54 (July 1985), pp. 417–55.

97. Durham, "Taming the 'Monster Case'"; Schwarzer, "Techniques for Identifying Narrow Issues"; Wayne D. Brazil, "Special Masters in Complex Cases: Extending the Judiciary or Reshaping Adjudication?" *University of Chicago Law Review*, vol. 53 (Spring 1986), pp. 394–423; Wayne D. Brazil, Geoffrey C. Hazard, Jr., and Paul R. Rice, *Managing Complex Litigation: A Practical Guide to the Use of Special Masters* (Chicago: American Bar Foundation, 1983); and Wayne D. Brazil, "Special Masters in the Pre-Trial Development of Big Cases, Potential and Problems," *ABF Research Journal*, vol. 1982 (Spring), pp. 287–374.

98. Convincing experimental research on rewriting jury instructions had been done by 1981. See, for example, Charrow and Charrow, "Making Legal Language Understandable." It indicated that legal instructions could be rewritten to enhance jury comprehension considerably. Most states have not acted to revise their jury instructions; among the states that have done so, only a few have rewritten their jury instructions with this research in mind. See Tanford, "Law Reform by Courts, Legislatures, and Commissions."

99. Vicki L. Smith, "The Feasibility and Utility of Pre-Trial Instruction in the Substantive Law: A Survey of Judges," *Law and Human Behavior*, vol. 14 (June 1990), pp. 235–48; and Smith, "The Psychological and Legal Implications of Pretrial Instruction in the Law," Ph.D. dissertation, Stanford University, 1987.

100. Kassin and Wrightsman found that mock jurors who were pre-instructed on the presumption of innocence and the need to prove guilt beyond a reasonable doubt in a criminal case gave lower estimates of guilt both during the presentation of the evidence and after all the evidence was in than did mock jurors who were instructed only after the evidence was in or who received no instructions at all. The latter jurors were in their judgments very much like those jurors who were instructed only after all the evidence was in. Kassin and Wrightsman provide an information-integration model for their findings, arguing that the pre-instructed mock jurors began deliberations with a lower prior probability of guilt, which affected their judgments of the defendant's likely guilt as they assimilated the evidence offered at trial. Saul M. Kassin and Lawrence S. Wrightsman, "On the Requirements of Proof: The Timing of Judicial Instructions and Mock Juror Verdicts," *Journal of Personality and Social Psychology*, vol. 37 (October 1979), pp. 1877–87. Recent work by Pennington and Hastie on "story models" calls the adequacy of information integration models into question, however. Nancy Pennington and Reid Hastie, "Explaining the Evidence: Further Tests of the Story Model for Juror Decision Making," *Journal of Personality and Social Psychology*, vol. 62 (February 1991), pp. 189–206; Pennington and Hastie, "A Cognitive Theory of Juror Decision Making: The Story Model," *Cardozo Law Review*, vol. 13 (November 1991), pp. 519–57; Pennington and Hastie, "Explanation-Based Decision Making: Effects of Memory Structure on Judgment," *Journal of Experimental Psychology: Learning, Memory and Cognition*, vol. 14 (July 1988), p. 521; and Pennington and Hastie, "Evidence Evaluation in Complex Decision Making," *Journal of Personality and Social Psychology*, vol. 51 (August 1986), pp. 243–58. An alternative explanation consistent with more general findings in cognitive psychology is that the early instructions affected the way in which the mock jurors encoded the information they received (as more consistent with innocence) so that at each point they remembered the evidence as less probative of guilt than did the jurors who had not been pre-instructed. From an encoding perspective, instruction after all the evidence was in would not be expected to have a substantial effect because the evidence received would have been already encoded and so would be remembered in a way more consistent with guilt. This explanation is consistent with research suggesting that instructions to disregard or limit evidence will be relatively ineffective and with research on the timing of opening statements. Casper, Benedict, and Perry, "Juror Decisionmaking, Attitudes, and the Hindsight Bias"; Hans and Doob, "Section Twelve of the Canada Evidence Act"; and

Gary L. Wells, Lawrence S. Wrightsman, and Peter K. Miene, "The Timing of the Defense Opening Statement: Don't Wait Until the Evidence Is In," *Journal of Applied Social Psychology*, vol. 15, no. 8 (1985), pp. 758–71. Reid Hastie, "Final Report to the National Institute for Law Enforcement and Criminal Justice," Northwestern University, 1983; and Sales, Elwork, and Alfini, "Improving Comprehension for Jury Instructions," also examined the effects of pre-instructions, finding relatively few effects and none that seem to justify strong reliance on them.

101. It was apparently left to the judge to decide what to pre-instruct on, and they did not report on this. Thus, we do not know for a given judge or for the mix of cases whether the pre-instructions given contained general instructions, case-specific substantive instructions, or a mixture of the two. Larry Heuer and Steven D. Penrod, "Instructing Jurors: A Field Experiment with Written and Preliminary Instructions," *Law and Human Behavior*, vol. 13 (December 1989), pp. 409–30.

102. There was no difference between the effects of pre-instruction in more or less complex cases, where complexity is operationalized by the length of the trial. My hunch, however, is that the Wisconsin trials that Heuer and Penrod studied probably included few if any that would qualify as complex in the sense that I have been using that term in this paper.

103. As Diamond points out in her chapter in this volume, Heuer and Penrod only tested comprehension of general instructions so they could use their instrument across trials. This performance measure may not have been sensitive to the advantages of trial-specific written instructions.

104. A true random sample was not achieved in the Wisconsin field study because attorneys refused to go along with the experimental assignment in some cases. This happened most frequently with respect to written instructions, which, at the time of the study, were required in Wisconsin. Defense attorneys in particular were reluctant to waive their right to have the jury furnished with written instructions. This is the best testimony to their popularity.

105. Heuer and Penrod, "Increasing Jurors' Participation in Trials," and Heuer and Penrod, "Trial Complexity."

106. Two thousand judges were originally contacted. While two-thirds of the 314 judges who returned a questionnaire saying why they declined to participate indicated they were no longer hearing jury trials, the participation rate is still so low that the sample does not allow one to be certain that the results of this study would generalize to the federal courts as a group. The most important reason to have reservations about generalizing from Heuer and Penrod's sample is that participating judges probably had more interest in the experimental procedures than nonparticipating judges. Without an interested judge, the effects that the authors observe might be different. Furthermore, participating judges may be more capable than nonparticipants, and the capacity of a jury in a complex case seems in part to be a function of the capacity of the judge presiding at the trial.

107. The length of the trial in hours was related to both the complexity of the evidence and, somewhat less strongly, to the quantity of the evidence as measured by the number of pages of documents in evidence, the number of items of evidence submitted, and the number of parties. The study indicates that long trials tend to involve masses of evidence and that at least some of the evidence is more complex than that found in most trials.

108. Questioning occurred in only fifty-one of seventy-one trials in which question-asking was allowed, according to a preliminary report of the data. American Judicature Society, *Toward More Active Juries: Taking Notes and Asking Questions* (Chicago, 1991). Heuer and Penrod, "Increasing Jurors' Participation in Trials," report seventy-four cases in which question-asking was allowed. While Heuer and Penrod do not address the issue specifically, they seem to have compared trials based on whether question-asking was

allowed and not on whether it actually occurred. This analytical decision is in keeping with the design of the experiment, which is concerned with the effects of allowing judges to ask questions rather than with the effects of questions asked.

109. With respect to both comments and special verdict forms, I have ignored a significant association with the perceived helpfulness of the plaintiff-prosecutor because I do not think it is as important as the dimensions I cite, and I do not know precisely what to make of it. I am also ignoring significant interactions involving those variables that were not experimentally varied. There are a number of such interactions, but they are at times directionally inconsistent, and given the lack of experimental control, their interpretation is problematic.

110. Since there are fewer responses from judges than from jurors, one possible reason why juror responses are significantly associated with procedural variations while judicial responses are not is the relative lack of power in the analyses that deal with judges' reactions. This possibility is difficult to evaluate since comparable statistics are not presented for judges and jurors. Given the small amount of variance that the procedural measures uniquely explain when judicial satisfaction is dependent, however, it is probably a mistake to attribute the lack of significance of these measures to a problem of power. Relative differences in power are more plausible as an explanation of why certain interactions are significant when the jurors' views are dependent but not when the judges' attitudes are.

111. Heuer and Penrod, in a survey that elicited 553 responses, find that judges report allowing note-taking in about one-third of their trials. Only 37 percent of judges say they have never allowed juror note-taking. One would expect that judges who sometimes allow note-taking are more prone to allow it as case complexity increases. Larry Heuer and Steven D. Penrod, "Some Suggestions for the Critical Appraisal of a More Active Jury," *Northwestern Law Review*, vol. 85 (Fall 1990), pp. 226–39.

112. Leonard B. Sand and Steven A. Reiss, "A Report on Seven Experiments Conducted by District Court Judges in the Second Circuit," *New York University Law Review*, vol. 60 (June 1985), pp. 423–97.

113. Heuer and Penrod, "Increasing Jurors' Participation in Trials"; and Heuer and Penrod, "Instructing Jurors: A Field Experiment with Written and Preliminary Instructions."

114. Steven J. Friedland, "The Competency and Responsibility of Jurors in Deciding Cases," *Northwestern Law Review*, vol. 85 (Fall 1990), pp. 190–225.

115. In their Wisconsin field experiment, Heuer and Penrod did not find any evidence that this occurred. Heuer and Penrod, "Increasing Jurors' Participation in Trials."

116. Franklin D. Strier, "Through the Jurors' Eyes," *American Bar Association Journal*, vol. 74 (October 1988), p. 78.

117. Shannon, *Texaco and the $10 Billion Jury*.

118. Heuer and Penrod, "Trial Complexity."

119. C. Hawkins, "Interaction and Coalition Realignments in Consensus-Seeking Groups: A Study of Experimental Jury Deliberations," Ph.D. dissertation, University of Chicago, 1960; and Hastie, Penrod, and Pennington, *Inside the Jury*.

120. Kassin and Wrightsman, "On the Requirements of Proof."

121. Richard O. Lempert, "Jury Size and the Peremptory Challenge: Testimony on Jury Reform," *Law Quad Notes*, vol. 23, no. 1 (1978), rprt. in Owen Fiss and Robert Cover, eds., *The Structure of Procedure* (Mineola, N.Y.: Foundation Press, 1979).

122. I support the creation of a fund that would drastically increase the payment jurors receive in any trial that extends past fourteen trial days. To pay for such a fund, I would "tax" the payments made to lawyers in long cases where money damages are sought or where litigation involves a commercial matter. For example, in long cases the parties might be charged 1 percent of all lawyer's fees paid for pre-trial work and 3 percent of the fees paid for work during the trial. This proposal should not unduly discourage contingent-fee

representation since there would be no fees to be taxed if the plaintiff lost. It would also not discourage litigation over noncommercial matters disputed as issues of principal since no fees would be taxed in such cases. The exact trigger for payment could be adjusted to take account of party responsibility for lengthening the trial. In some small measure the tax should encourage pre-trial settlements and the shortening of cases that go to trial.

123. Pennington and Hastie, "Explaining the Evidence"; Pennington and Hastie, "Cognitive Theory of Juror Decision Making"; Pennington and Hastie, "Explanation-Based Decision Making"; and Pennington and Hastie, "Evidence Evaluation in Complex Decision Making."

124. W. Lance Bennett and Martha S. Feldman, *Reconstructing Reality in the Courtroom: Justice and Judgment in American Culture* (Rutgers University Press, 1981); John B. Black, James A. Galambos, and Stephen J. Read, "Comprehending Stories in Social Situations," in Robert S. Wyer, Jr., and Thomas K. Srull, eds., *Handbook of Social Cognition*, vol. 3 (Hillsdale, N.J.: L. Erlbaum Associates, 1984), chap. 2, pp. 45–86; James A. Holstein, "Jurors' Interpretations and Jury Decision Making," *Law and Human Behavior*, vol. 9 (March 1985), pp. 83–100; and Roger C. Schank, *Tell Me A Story: A New Look at Real and Artificial Memory* (Scribner's, 1990).

125. Petzinger, *Oil and Honor*, p. 371.

126. Diamond and Casper, "Blindfolding the Jury."

127. Horowitz and Bordens, "Experimental Investigation of Procedural Issues in Complex Tort Trials."

CHAPTER SEVEN

Attitudes toward the Civil Jury: A Crisis of Confidence?

Valerie P. Hans

Is THERE A crisis of confidence in the civil jury? Recent critical commentary about the civil jury might lead observers to say yes. Civil juries have been charged with resembling a random lottery rather than a competent and predictable dispute resolution tribunal, with misunderstanding the often complex evidence in civil trials, with penalizing wealthy corporations, and with undermining American competitiveness.[1] It is not only academic scholars who voice concerns about the civil jury. Lawyers, judges, litigants, business executives, and even the general public have criticized the jury in a variety of formats, including books, newspaper articles, letters to the editor, trade publications, and speeches. The anecdotal quality of much of the criticism makes it difficult to obtain a clear and accurate picture of attitudes toward the civil jury.

This paper examines the question of whether there is a crisis of confidence in the civil jury system by subjecting common perceptions of and attitudes toward the jury to systematic scrutiny. What are the sources of information about the civil jury? What views of the civil jury are held by the general public, judges, attorneys, litigants, and potential litigants? And what impact are these views of the civil jury likely to have?

There are several justifications for exploring the perceptions and attitudes that various groups hold about the civil jury. First, because the jury represents the public's voice in court, citizens' attitudes toward the jury deserve examination. The jury's primary function is to infuse community values into the legal system by interpreting legal standards

Some of the data reported here were collected under National Science Foundation grant SES-8822598 to Valerie P. Hans. I wish to thank Rob MacCoun, Tom Tyler, and Neil Vidmar for comments on an earlier draft, and Judyth Pendell for information about data collected for Aetna.

and specific factual patterns according to changing community norms of conduct and justice. In addition, legal institutions must have the consent of the citizenry if they are to function effectively.[2] If such institutions are not supported and are perceived to be unfair, their decisions are not likely to be widely accepted.[3] It is therefore important to know whether the community considers trial by jury to be a fair and equitable procedure for the resolution of civil disputes.

There is a second major justification for studying judgments about the civil jury. As this chapter will demonstrate, whether they are accurate or inaccurate, people's perceptions of the jury influence the operation of the entire civil justice system.[4] Plaintiffs decide whether or not to press or settle their claims based in part on how they think juries will react. Attorneys, insurance claims adjusters, and arbitrators base their settlements and decisions to go to trial on assumptions about the likely outcomes of trial by jury. At least in part, judges decide what evidence to allow and what instructions or guidance to provide based on their views of the jury and its competence. When businesses make decisions about whether to pursue innovative new technology, they sometimes take into account how juries might ultimately decide liability claims based on the technology.[5] Thus, studying the views of the jury held by the participants in the legal system can go a long way toward illuminating basic civil justice processes.

This essay addresses a number of issues. I first consider the sources of information that citizens and legal actors have about the civil jury. Then I explore the nature of the public's attitudes toward and perceptions of the civil jury, focusing on several key questions. How do people evaluate the civil jury? What factors create support for or opposition to the civil jury? Do general trust and confidence in the courts relate to support for the civil jury? How does the widespread perception that there has been a litigation explosion influence the way people see the role of the civil jury? I also explore the possibility that support for the civil jury varies among demographic subgroups. After examining these issues with respect to the public, I evaluate them for judges, attorneys, and litigants.

My assessment of contemporary opinion about the civil jury draws on responses not only to the civil but also to the criminal jury, in part because of the research that is available. Although several recent studies have focused specifically on the civil jury, there is a larger group of research studies on attitudes toward the courts, the jury as an institution, and the criminal trial jury. An assessment of the civil jury can benefit from this broader knowledge. It is also of interest to compare the various reactions to civil and criminal juries. The U.S. Supreme Court, for instance, has held that the criminal jury is more deserving of constitutional protection than the civil jury. Does public opinion provide a parallel distinction?

The final section of the paper points out the limitations and gaps in the knowledge researchers have been able to provide about attitudes toward the civil jury and speculates on why people hold the attitudes they do. I conclude with a judgment about whether the information presented indicates a crisis of confidence in the civil jury.

Sources of Knowledge about the Civil Jury

Preliminary issues to consider are the sources and nature of information available to the public about the civil jury. What people learn about the civil jury will shape their overall favorability to it as an institution.

The potential for direct participation creates the possibility that many citizens gain their knowledge of the civil jury through jury service. Such participation may have a salutary effect on people's evaluations of the justice system.[6] Yet, because only a small proportion of the public has ever served on a jury (either criminal or civil), most people will not learn about the jury directly or even indirectly, by talking to others who have served. In one national survey, just 6 percent of the respondents mentioned jury service as the source from which they learned the most about courts. Instead, the media and formal education, in that order, are the major sources of the public's information about law, justice, and the courts.[7]

Scholars have examined the nature and extent of media coverage of crime and criminal law. The conclusion from a host of such studies is that the media present a distorted picture of the realities of crime and justice, highlighting violent and sensational crimes, law enforcement, and the early stages of the criminal justice process.[8] Although there has been little systematic examination of how the media treat civil justice generally and the civil jury in particular, it is not unreasonable to assume that these topics are covered in much the same way as criminal justice. If the coverage given criminal justice is any indication, most of the reports can be expected to focus on high awards, unusual cases, and sensational verdicts, all of which are likely to excite the public imagination and sell newspapers. Just as minor crimes are underrepresented in the media, the routine and often tedious business of civil litigation is likely to be slighted. Early results from an ongoing archival analysis of media coverage of civil jury verdicts confirms these assumptions.[9]

One recent and popular theme of media coverage of civil justice has been the alleged "litigation explosion." During the 1980s, insurance companies undertook an advertising campaign criticizing the civil jury for its role in fostering an explosion of litigation and spiraling costs. Many media stories also picked up on this theme, buttressed by Vice President J. Danforth Quayle's speech on excessive litigation at the 1991 American Bar Association (ABA) convention.[10] Yet a good deal of scholarly research indicates both that the media coverage (including insurance advertising) presents an unrealistic picture of the tort system and that the charges of a litigation explosion are exaggerated.[11]

Nevertheless, such media coverage may well influence the public's views of the civil jury and the appropriateness of its awards. The "availability heuristic" refers to a well-known psychological phenomenon: the more readily instances of an occurrence can be brought to mind, the more frequently people assume they occur.[12] To the extent that the media disproportionately cover high awards and unreasonable jury verdicts, the more easily accessible or "available" these events will be in memory, and the more likely people will be to assume that they are frequent incidents.

Other aspects of media coverage and advertising campaigns must also be considered. Because stories and advertising are more influential and persuasive when they involve the reader personally, advertisements that point out the increased insurance costs or other negative personal consequences of large jury awards are likely to be particularly effective.[13] Several recent insurance industry advertising campaigns have taken just this tack in calling for tort reform. To examine the influence of tort reform advertising, one experiment used two groups of mock jurors, one that had been exposed to an insurance company tort reform advertisement and one that had not. The group that had been exposed to the advertising gave lower awards.[14] In another study that employed post-trial interviews with jurors in business cases, jurors frequently mentioned the litigation explosion and the need to hold down awards as justifications for reducing the amount of a plaintiff's damages.[15]

A related source of information about the jury is direct or indirect knowledge of specific jury verdicts. How do these verdicts, including those that are at odds with public sentiment, influence future juries? Jury verdicts and awards may serve as a lightning rod for all that is perceived to be wrong with the civil justice system. After all, they are highly visible and may be easier to blame than the more obscure aspects of the civil litigation system, such as pre-trial negotiation, confidential agreements between the parties, or judicial decisions about procedural matters. An instructive example comes from the Rodney King police brutality trial. In that case, a jury acquitted white Los Angeles police officers on all but one of the charges relating to the videotaped beating of black motorist Rodney King, creating a public outcry and provoking the subsequent riots. According to news coverage and opinion polls following the verdict, people blamed the jury for an incorrect verdict first and foremost. More technical details that might have had greater relevance to insiders, such as the judicial instructions, defense strategies, and prosecutorial tactics, were given less weight.[16]

As courtroom regulars, lawyers have additional sources of information about the civil jury. And, in contrast to the public at large, they are likely to have greater direct experience with civil juries. Where do lawyers obtain information about juries? Marc Galanter has listed a number of potential sources, including personal knowledge, other lawyers, appellate courts and official reporting, jury verdict reporting services, trade media (such as lawyers' publications, handbooks, and continuing education seminars), jury consultants, mass media, popular culture, and research.[17] However, even though litigators can obtain accurate information about the civil jury, their knowledge is likely to be incomplete. One study of Wisconsin attorneys indicates that the vast majority rely primarily on other attorneys at their own law firms for advice about how to evaluate potential jury cases.[18] Few lawyers reported obtaining the kind of systematic information about the jury decisionmaking process that is available in jury verdict reporters or through scientific research.[19]

Like lawyers, litigants, particularly repeat players, have the opportunity to consult additional sources of information about the civil jury and its likely behavior. Business executives are avid readers not only of weekly news magazines but also of business publications such as *Business Week*, *Fortune*, *Forbes*, and the *Harvard Business Review*, all of which carry articles pertinent to the legal environment of business.[20] In addition, a business may have a long history of litigation resulting in jury decisions in the local community, and through opinion polling and direct contact may have good insight about the firm's reputation in different geographical areas of the country.

Yet, like lawyers, litigants are likely to possess incomplete or biased information. For example, a systematic content analysis of articles about wrongful discharge appearing in personnel journals and law reviews reveals that the personnel journal articles significantly overstate the threat of wrongful discharge. Such articles also commonly state that the jury's sympathy is with the plaintiffs alleging wrongful discharge, suggesting a largely hostile environment for businesses in wrongful discharge litigation. Yet systematic analysis of wrongful discharge cases reveals no such pattern.[21] Further, even if businesses can draw on prior experience with litigation in the community, it must be remembered that only a small fraction of cases ever go to jury trial—and those tend to be unusual and nonrepresentative. And the extent to which a litigant's personal reputation in the community translates into the jury's receptivity to specific facts in a case is not clear. For both repeat and one-time litigants, it is likely to be hard to separate the jury's attitude toward the litigant from other aspects of a case.

Judges' opinions and perceptions are of considerable interest. Unlike the litigants, their vision is less likely to be influenced by strong partisan leanings. They participate in a larger number of trials than other court-room actors, so their opinions are likely to be based on greater direct information. They may also have a better sense than other trial participants of the types of issues and evidence that civil juries find most challenging. Of course, they preside only over their own trials in a specific jurisdiction and do not have direct access to the inner workings of the jury.[22]

This brief assessment of the sources of knowledge about the jury indicates that, with the exception of judges and some frequent litigators, most people do not have direct access to relevant information. The public is at a decided disadvantage. Given the modest rate of jury service, citizens depend almost entirely on the media for information about the jury. Yet even insiders are likely to have imperfect knowledge about how a jury functions. With these caveats in mind, I turn to a consideration of the existing data.

Public Attitudes toward the Civil Jury

We can learn a good deal about attitudes toward the civil jury by examining not only public views of the civil jury itself, but also lay knowledge and opinions of the courts, the criminal jury, and the civil litigation system. This material supplements the relatively small number of specific studies on opinions of the civil jury, and helps to put findings on attitudes toward the civil jury into a broader context.

Public Opinion about the Courts and the Criminal Jury

Before addressing the civil jury specifically, it is worthwhile to provide some context for the public's general views, attitudes, and knowledge of the courts. National surveys reveal that citizens lack direct or extensive knowledge of the courts and know very little about their operation. One national survey of attitudes toward the courts, conducted in 1977 by Yankelovich, Skelly, and White, Inc., includes the general public, judges, lawyers, and community leaders. The survey indicates that many people have little direct contact with the courts but a good deal of concern about their functioning. The public expressed dissatisfaction with the courts, believing that they do not do a good job of protecting society or administering justice competently, fairly, and equally. Twenty-three percent believed that there is a great need for court reform, while 25 percent saw the need as only moderate.[23]

The Yankelovich study finds that knowledge about the courts is directly related to demographic variables. Whites, high-income respondents, and those with substantial education were more familiar with the courts than blacks and those with less education and income. The majority of respondents (61 percent) knew that all courts in their state did not have juries. Disturbingly, confidence in the courts was higher among those with little knowledge.[24]

One purpose of the Yankelovich survey was to determine whether court reforms in different states have any impact on public opinion. This question is relevant to an inquiry about the civil jury because many states have passed or are considering tort reforms. Do such reforms have the potential to enhance public opinion about the courts and the civil justice system? To answer this question, the researchers compared the responses of citizens in states that had undergone sweeping court reforms with responses from states that had not. They found no greater knowledge that the laws had changed in the states with extensive reforms.[25]

The Hearst Corporation sponsored a national survey on Americans' knowledge of and attitudes toward the court system that included questions on both civil and criminal juries. Like the Yankelovich study, the Hearst survey reveals that the public lacks knowledge about many aspects of the legal system but appears to be better informed about the jury. Substantial majorities of the respondents, for example, know that some court cases are not heard before juries, can define a hung jury, are aware that lawyers may exclude prospective jurors, and know that jury verdicts and awards may be overturned by judges. These findings should be contrasted to those indicating that 50 percent of the general public believes that it is up to the accused to prove his or her innocence and 45 percent that it is the district attorney's job to defend accused criminals who cannot afford lawyers.[26]

It is interesting to speculate about why people's knowledge about the jury appears higher than their knowledge about other components of the trial process. It is possible that this is an artifactual result of the types of questions asked about different aspects of the trial process; perhaps the questions about the jury are inherently easier to answer. But it is also conceivable that the public focuses more on the jury than on other elements of the justice system. The jury may be more visible and accessible, or people may find it easier to identify with the jurors. In addition, people may attend to information about juries because they anticipate someday being called for jury duty.

In addition to these more general surveys of attitudes toward law, justice, and the courts, several surveys have explored public attitudes toward the criminal jury. The criminal trial, a kind of morality play pitting the forces of the government against an individual accused of wrongdoing, may be a better known and more compelling entity to the public. It is of interest to see whether similar patterns are displayed in public support for the criminal and civil juries.

In 1978, Herbert McClosky and Alida Brill conducted an ambitious national survey of the public, community leaders, and legal elites such as judges, lawyers, and police officials.[27] The researchers asked several questions about the jury but no specific questions pertaining to the civil jury. Eight out of ten respondents in all of the samples rated the right to a public trial by jury as "extremely important," and most of the rest of the respondents rated it as "important."[28] Only a small number of respondents thought that the right to trial by jury "is overrated because juries can so often be swayed by a clever lawyer."[29] Support for the criminal jury was somewhat higher for those respondents who expressed greater endorsement of civil liberties.[30]

Robert MacCoun and Tom Tyler conducted a more focused public opinion survey of 130 adults in Cook County, Illinois, asking them a number of questions about their support for the criminal jury and their procedural preferences concerning jury size and jury unanimity. Virtually all respondents endorsed the institution of the jury, with 97 percent describing it as "somewhat" or "very" important as a national institution. Nine out of ten respondents rated the jury system as "somewhat" or "very" fair. A similar number were satisfied with specific jury verdicts they had heard about. Respondents saw juries as likely to produce accurate verdicts in the substantial majority of cases.[31]

MacCoun and Tyler asked their respondents to compare the jury with its most likely alternative, the judge. The sample showed a strong preference for the jury. By a two-to-one margin, respondents perceived the jury as more accurate, fairer, and more likely to minimize bias than the judge. The jury was also seen as better able to represent minorities. Although respondents acknowledged that trial by jury is more expensive, the jury was still the decisionmaker of choice in a serious case such as murder.[32]

MacCoun and Tyler also examined the respondents' attitudes toward jury procedures and size. The elements that respondents considered most significant in evaluating the fairness of various jury procedures were verdict accuracy, thoroughness, minimization of bias, and representation of minorities. Compared with six-person juries and those with majority decision rules, the twelve-person unanimous jury was perceived most positively on a number of significant attributes related to justice, fairness, and accuracy: most accurate (63 percent), most thorough (62 percent), fairest (59 percent), most likely to represent minorities (67 percent), most likely to minimize bias (41 percent), and most likely to listen to holdouts (36 percent). In a serious case such as murder, respondents thought that a twelve-person unanimous jury was highly preferable, but in a minor case such as shoplifting, smaller and nonunanimous juries were preferred. The twelve-person unanimous jury was also believed to be the most expensive form of jury trial (91 percent).[33]

In 1977, the Law Reform Commission of Canada sponsored a Gallup Poll of approximately 1,000 Canadians on their attitudes toward the criminal jury trial.[34] The poll revealed that about 5 percent of Canadian adults had served on a jury and that an additional 29 percent knew at least one other person who had served. Men and older people were more likely to have served. Respondents were asked whether judges or juries are more likely to arrive at a just and fair verdict. Fifty-four percent thought that judge and jury are equally likely to arrive at a just and fair verdict. Of those who differentiated between the two, however, about four times as many favored the jury (37 percent) over the judge (9 percent). Women were more likely than men to say that judge and jury are equally likely to arrive at a fair and just verdict. Interestingly, those who had served, or who knew someone who had served, were significantly more likely than those with no direct or indirect contact to believe that the jury is more likely to arrive at a just and fair verdict. In fact, it appears that jury service makes people more favorable to the institution of the jury. A companion questionnaire study with actual Canadian jurors showed that about 95 percent had favorable views of the jury system both before and after jury duty.[35] Like the MacCoun and Tyler study, the Canadian Gallup poll shows that support for trial by jury and for the requirement of unanimity is strongest for the most serious criminal cases.

In sum, even though the public expresses a good deal of negativity over the failings of the criminal justice system at large, public opinion studies of the courts and the criminal trial process show strong public support for the jury as an institution.

Public Opinion about Civil Litigation and the Civil Jury

More direct information about public attitudes toward the civil jury may be derived from opinion surveys about reactions to the civil justice system. These surveys, all conducted since the mid-1980s, show that citizens believe there has been an explosion of civil litigation.

One of the most useful surveys was conducted in 1986 by Louis Harris and Associates for Aetna Life and Casualty. The firm surveyed 2,130 Americans by telephone, including small samples of civil defendants and accident victims.[36] According to the survey, three-quarters of Americans believe that the civil justice system enables those who suffer injuries to obtain adequate compensation from those who are responsible. But, while the majority thought that the system fairly balances the rights of plaintiffs and defendants, many respondents perceived that more people bring lawsuits than should. Majorities also felt that, over the past decade, the number of personal injury lawsuits has been growing faster than the population, and the size of awards faster than inflation. Forty-five percent of the sample found most awards in personal injury cases "excessive," compared with 28 percent who found the awards "about right" and just 16 percent who said they are "not enough."[37]

Respondents were provided with a list of ten possible reasons for the increase in the "overall cost of lawsuits" and asked to rank each reason as major, minor, or not a reason at all. Fifty-six percent cited "juries which hand out awards that are too big" as a major reason, while 31 percent cited it as minor, making it seventh in importance among the possibilities. Litigant behavior appeared to be a more significant factor for respondents: topping the list of reasons for the rise in lawsuit costs was "people who figure they can make a lot of money from such suits," cited as a major reason by 79 percent of those surveyed.[38] Insurance companies "that hold out or aren't willing to settle claims fairly and promptly" were cited as a major reason by 60 percent of the sample.[39]

Many respondents endorsed changes in the civil justice system that would make it more efficient and less costly. The Harris poll explored reactions to several reforms of jury decisionmaking. Thirty-nine percent of respondents found "very acceptable" a proposal that the judge give jurors specific guidelines on the size of damage awards in particular cases, and an additional 34 percent found it "somewhat acceptable." There was also some support for a more radical proposal that the jury decide on liability and the judge on the amount of damages. Twenty-nine percent of respondents found this division of labor between judge and jury to be "very acceptable," and another 33 percent found it "somewhat acceptable."[40]

The Harris poll found that demographic factors influenced judgments of the civil justice system. Generally, educated and well-off individuals, professionals, business proprietors, and older people found the most fault with the civil justice system.[41] No demographic data were presented for the questions that focused specifically on the jury, so it is difficult to know whether concerns about the civil jury varied across demographic subgroups in the same way as confidence about the civil justice system. The authors note that, although it is unusual to find high-status respondents most disaffected with the status quo, it is possible that these groups are more likely than others to be informed about the workings of the civil justice system or to believe that they are more likely to be sued.[42]

The jury consulting firm Metricus conducted a national opinion survey of over 500 jury-eligible adults. The study is proprietary and the detailed methodology and results have not been released to the public. However, the consultants distributed a press release giving some of the major findings and also wrote a descriptive piece for a practitioner's journal.[43] Several of the major findings converge with those of the Harris survey. For example, 68 percent of the respondents agreed that "juries today are awarding too much money," and three-quarters of the sample disagreed with the statement that "when juries award a lot of money in legal disputes, it has no effect on me." These results hint that the public might respond negatively to plaintiff claims. Yet a majority in the sample (64 percent) endorsed the notion that the side with the most resources has the best chance of winning, and 60 percent agreed that "to a big company, being forced to pay a million dollars in a legal dispute is just a slap on the hand." It appears that the public has some cynicism about civil litigants on both sides.

The *Public Pulse* reported similar concerns among Americans about the alleged litigation explosion. Like the findings of other research studies, a majority of the respondents in the *Pulse* survey believed that the current system encourages companies and individuals to act more responsibly in order to avoid being sued, and 40 percent said that it offers just compensation to victims. However, 46 percent believed that they are personally affected by large jury awards in product liability cases and medical malpractice lawsuits. The public favored limiting monetary awards such as those for pain and suffering and punitive damages. Between 40 percent and 50 percent of the public even supported limits on compensation for lost income and medical expenses.[44]

The *Public Pulse* study suggests that public perceptions of the cause of the litigation crisis focus more on the litigants and lawyers than on the jury. For example, 62 percent asserted that the reason the number of lawsuits has gotten out of hand is that people always look for a culprit when something bad happens, and 70 percent stated that the primary result of liability lawsuits is that lawyers make more money than they deserve.[45]

A recent telephone opinion poll conducted among 450 Delaware residents included both general questions about civil litigation and specific questions on the role of the jury. The same perception of a litigation crisis reflected in other studies was found in the Delaware survey. Ninety-one percent of respondents agreed that "there are far too many frivolous lawsuits today," although about half believed that "most people who sue have legitimate grievances," suggesting that citizens may think that frivolous lawsuits are brought by only a minority of plaintiffs. Fifty-seven percent believed that the media exaggerate the number of high jury awards, and 47 percent agreed that juries do a good job of determining the outcomes of lawsuits and assessing damages. Six out of ten believed that jury damage awards are too high. The sample was evenly divided in its reaction to a statement that most awards are reasonable and justified: 38 percent agreed and 39 percent disagreed.[46]

To explore the determinants of attitudes toward the jury, the responses to relevant items were correlated with a variety of demographic and other attitudinal measures of the survey participants. When answers to several items on the jury were related to respondents' general confidence in the courts, for instance, the findings showed that people expressing more confidence in the courts as a whole were more supportive of the jury system. Similarly, people expressing more confidence in lawyers expressed more support for the jury.[47] How these views are causally related is unclear. The perceived general legitimacy of the courts could bolster support for the jury, or, alternatively, concern about the actions of juries could undermine confidence in the courts.

As expected, public opinion about the litigation explosion was linked to more specific views about the competency of the civil jury. People who believed that there are far too many frivolous lawsuits today also asserted that most jury awards are too high; those who believed that people are too quick to sue claimed that the jury awards in civil cases are too large; those who worried that the number of lawsuits show that our society is breaking down were more likely to disagree that most jury awards are reasonable and justified. The correlations among such attitudes are statistically significant but modest. Although respondents' perceptions of the jury are linked to broader assessments of the failures and successes of the civil justice system, these broader assessments cannot account for all of the support or opposition to the civil jury as an institution.[48]

Interestingly, the study revealed some significant relationships between demographic variables and support for the civil jury. Age was a prominent factor in judgments about the amount of awards, with older respondents expressing greater concern over high monetary awards.[49] Compared with nonwhites, whites were more likely to agree that the money damages juries award in civil cases are too large.[50] Seventy-one percent of men but only 58 percent of women agreed with the same question.[51]

Religious preferences were also correlated with responses to several questions. For example, Catholics were more likely than Protestants and those who expressed other religious preferences or none at all to agree that jury awards are too large. Respondents with religious preferences other than Catholic or Protestant or none at all were most likely to disagree.[52] Catholics were also the most likely to disagree that the majority of jury awards are reasonable and justified.[53]

Marital status, education, political liberalism, income, and lack of full-time employment appeared to be unrelated to attitudes toward the jury. Yet the prevalence of significant relationships of gender, race, age, and religion suggests that there are important life experiences that relate to support for the jury and that these experiences differ for various demographic subgroups. Future research must examine why these relationships occur.

The chapter by Shari Seidman Diamond in this volume deals directly with the attitudes and opinions of jurors, and so we will not review that literature here. However, it is worth noting that surveys show that jurors, who have direct experience with the institution, display the same positive regard for the jury that is found in public opinion surveys. In many instances this regard increases after jury service.[54]

Taking the results of the public opinion surveys as a whole, I conclude that most citizens solidly support both the civil and the criminal jury as institutions and believe that both fulfill their basic functions reasonably well. Larger concerns about a civil litigation explosion and the failure of the criminal courts to control crime undoubtedly influence judgments of the civil as well as the criminal jury. Indeed, there is some evidence that belief in a litigation crisis is linked to concern about the civil jury. Although support for the jury is widespread, it tends to be higher among citizens who also express confidence in lawyers and the courts. Men, whites, and older respondents voice the greatest concern over what they perceive as high damage awards.

One point to keep in mind is that the Delaware survey and many other recent projects that have examined public opinion toward civil litigation have included items about the civil jury within a series of questions about the alleged litigation explosion. Thus, people responded to items about the civil jury within the context of the litigation crisis. By making the possibility of erroneous jury verdicts more salient, this technique could have encouraged people to respond more negatively than they would have otherwise. In addition, the surveys have all been conducted within a relatively short time span, making it impossible to know whether the concerns expressed about the civil jury are unique to the past decade.

Opinions of Trial Participants

Perceptions of the jury can influence decisions about civil litigation. Thus it is useful to consider the attitudes toward the jury of those who see it up close. I will assess the opinions of three significant groups of observers: trial judges, attorneys, and litigants.

Judges

Perhaps the most significant observer of the jury is the judge. Presiding over jury trials, judges have the greatest opportunity to see the civil jury in action. In addition, their views may be influenced less than those of other trial participants by the possibility that the jury may favor one side in a case. All the surveys of judges' attitudes toward the civil jury show virtually unanimous support for the institution.

The earliest study of judicial views of the civil jury was Kalven and Zeisel's pioneering work in the 1950s.[55] Surveying judges who presided over civil jury trials, Kalven and Zeisel found them in agreement with four out of every five verdicts reached by civil juries. On average, the damage awards were about 20 percent higher than those the judges themselves would have given.

The national poll of state and federal judges conducted in 1987 by Louis Harris and Associates for Aetna Life and Casualty constitutes the most comprehensive study to date of judicial attitudes toward the civil jury.[56] This extensive survey discovered that the vast majority of state and federal judges are strongly supportive of the jury system, including the civil jury. For example, three-quarters agreed that "for routine civil cases, the right to trial by jury is an essential safeguard which must be retained," and virtually all believed that "jurors usually make a serious effort to apply the law as they are instructed." Only a minority thought that "too often jurors fail to apply the law because they are not able to understand the law" (24 percent of federal and 31 percent of state judges) or that "the feelings jurors have about the parties often cause them to make inappropriate decisions" (18 percent of federal and 26 percent of state judges). Despite their very strong support for the civil jury, 63 percent of federal and 68 percent of state judges endorsed the idea that "a serious study should be made of alternatives to trial by jury for certain types of cases." However, even though the judges expressed a willingness to study the issue, there were few specific alternatives to trial by jury that the majority of judges were willing to support.[57]

Because of general concerns over juror competence in certain types of litigation, the Harris survey specifically addressed judicial opinions about the jury in complex cases with scientific and technical evidence.[58] Over half the judges (60 percent federal and 55 percent state) agreed that "it is difficult for jurors with differing levels of education to be effective when dealing with complex civil cases," and the majority (66 percent federal and 62 percent state) believed that "in complex civil cases, the jurors need more guidance than they usually get." But approximately the same percentages (58 percent federal and 66 percent state) rejected a minimum education requirement for jurors in complex cases. Both federal and state judges were split (53 percent versus 46 percent and 51 percent versus 46 percent, respectively) on the question of whether a trial before a panel of experts would be preferable to jury trial in some complex cases.[59] Remarkably, there was more support for limiting the use of juries in minor cases involving small sums of money (52 percent federal and 71 percent state) than in complex civil cases (44 percent federal and 39 percent state) or in very complicated business cases (38 percent federal and 40 percent state). Judges believe it is important to preserve juries in complex cases and those dealing with business matters, perhaps because such cases reflect significant social and political values. The social and political values of cases involving minor civil matters, on the other hand, may be less obvious.[60]

As for specific civil jury reforms, virtually all judges at both the federal and state levels rejected the suggestion that, in all civil cases, judges should decide on damages after the jury reaches its verdict on liability. Significant minorities (41 percent federal and 32 percent state) favored having judges determine damages in some civil cases.[61] These percentages might usefully be compared with the public's opinions, which are much more supportive of having the judge decide on damages.[62]

A Federal Judicial Center study interviewed both judges and lawyers in a sample of federal jury trials that lasted longer than nineteen trial days and included many complex factual and other issues. These protracted trials present perhaps the greatest challenge to the lay jury. Yet the researchers found that "judges and lawyers were uniformly complimentary of the diligence of the juries in these cases; with slightly less unanimity, they also affirmed the validity of the juries' deliberative processes."[63]

In 1987, the *National Law Journal* polled a random sample of 348 state trial court judges and 57 federal district and circuit court judges on their views of the civil jury. The results of this poll converge with other findings showing that judges are very supportive of the civil jury. The judges in the *National Law Journal* poll were asked what percentage of the time they disagreed with jury verdicts in the civil cases over which they presided. Of those judges who expressed an opinion, more than three-quarters said they disagreed with no more than 10 percent of civil jury verdicts. A majority rejected the proposal to alter the Seventh Amendment to the U.S. Constitution to permit excluding juries in some complex cases. There was little indication that judges were strongly critical of the size of jury awards; just 3 percent of the judges listed excessive jury awards as the most important problem facing the U.S. legal system, and only 6 percent thought jury damage awards had been excessive "in many cases."[64] Again, these numbers are valuably contrasted with the substantial percentage of the public that believes there are many excessive awards.[65]

One interesting study was conducted by Georgia law professor R. Perry Sentell, Jr., who sent questionnaires to Georgia judges along with information about the Kalven and Zeisel research.[66] Sentell asked the judges to indicate how their experiences with juries in negligence cases compared with the earlier Kalven and Zeisel work. An initial question informed the judges of Kalven's findings that "in 79 percent of all jury trials of negligence, the trial judge and jury agreed as to which party (either Plaintiff or Defendant) should win the case," and asked whether the judge's agreement rate was about the same, significantly higher, or significantly lower. Eighty-seven percent of the judges said about the same, while another 10 percent indicated that their agreement rate was significantly higher. Only three judges indicated that their own agreement rate was significantly lower. While a substantial number of judges (60 percent of those responding) reported that their rate of agreement with the amount of damages awarded by juries was comparable to Kalven's percentages, the rest indicated that, in general, their rate of agreement would have been either higher or lower than Kalven's.

Other results fleshed out the generally positive regard that the Georgia judges showed for the civil jury. Ninety-four percent of the Georgia judges believed that the jury generally experiences no difficulty in understanding a negligence case; 89 percent thought that the jury can follow judicial instructions.[67] Asked how their support for the civil and criminal jury systems compared, 71 percent of the judges indicated that their support was comparable, while another 11 percent said they approved of the civil jury more than the criminal jury. Surprisingly, 86 percent of the judges rejected the common wisdom that juries are more pro-plaintiff than judges.[68] Yet opinion was divided on the question of whether the defendant's identity influences the jury. About half the judges thought that the defendant's identity does play a role, with many judges asserting that corporate defendants, particularly large corporations, elicit less sympathy and pay larger damage awards than other defendants. Overall, 57 percent of the judges rated civil jury performance as "thoroughly satisfactory," and another 41 percent found the civil jury "satisfactory with changes." Just 2 percent called it unsatisfactory. Trouble spots identified by the judges included damage assessments and judicial instructions.[69]

Judicial behavior provides another means of assessing judges attitudes toward the civil jury. If judges disagree with jury decisions, they have the prerogative to overturn jury verdicts and awards. How often do they exercise this right? Not very often, it seems. In the Harris poll, only one in twenty judges had reduced jury damage awards more than five times in the previous three years.[70] A Rand Corporation study of post-trial adjustments to jury awards in Cook County (Illinois) and California found that 80 percent of the jury verdicts were unchanged after trial. While post-trial processes led to lower awards in about 15 percent of the cases, two-thirds of these reduced payments resulted from settlements between the parties, not court orders.[71] Many reductions were made because of a defendant's inability to pay the full amount rather than judicial concern over unfair awards; courts reduced awards in just 6 percent of the cases overall.[72] These findings converge remarkably well with the Harris poll data showing that judges did not find jury awards excessive in most cases and adjusted awards infrequently.

Attitudinally and behaviorally, judges are a strong source of support for the civil jury. They agree with jury verdicts and awards in the vast majority of cases, and only small numbers of judges favor major reform of the civil jury system. It is something of a paradox that judges are even more supportive of retaining the civil jury's powers than the public, since the jury's role is to represent the public in the courtroom.

Attorneys

Examining trial attorneys' perceptions of the civil jury is especially worthwhile, since in the vast majority of potential court cases, attorneys are the key actors who decide whether to proceed with, fight, or settle a claim. They select the decisionmaker—judge, jury, or alternative dispute resolution mechanism. In the civil system, the parties have the right to request or waive a jury trial, so the attorneys' perceptions of the jury can be critical.

The results vary from study to study, but in general, lawyers express more skepticism than judges about the civil jury. This may in part reflect a general preference for the greater predictability of settlement over the uncertain process of factfinding. (See the chapter by Judith Resnik in this volume.) As well, in contrast to judges, lawyers' perceptions that a jury will or will not be favorable to their side may be a more critical factor in their evaluation of its behavior. Attorneys also appear to have significant gaps in their understanding of and many misperceptions about the tendencies of civil juries.

Given the value of obtaining a complete picture of lawyers' views of the civil jury, it is unfortunate that no comprehensive studies on the subject exist. For my analyses of both judges and the public, I was able to draw on national opinion surveys, but that is not the case for lawyers.[73] A few more focused projects have included assessments of attorneys' opinions on the jury. Several recent studies have obtained lawyers' perceptions of trial by jury in the context of evaluating arbitration programs. Although the results cannot be taken as representative of all lawyers and may be skewed by the lawyer's recent involvement in an arbitration, it is interesting to examine them.

The Federal Judicial Center studied ten pilot programs of court-sponsored arbitration.[74] Lawyers whose cases had been selected for arbitration were contacted after the cases had closed and asked to participate in a survey of their reactions to the pilot program. About 75 percent of the lawyers contacted agreed to participate in the study. The attorneys were asked whether, considering time, cost, and fairness, they would prefer to have their cases decided by a judge, a jury, or by arbitration, or whether the decisionmaker would make no difference. About 15 percent said that the decisionmaker made no difference to them, while 43 percent selected arbitration, 20 percent the jury, and another 23 percent the judge as the preferred decisionmaker. Most attorneys said they were satisfied with their arbitration. Understandably, those who thought that the outcome of the arbitration proceedings had been unsatisfactory or that the hearing had been unfair were much more likely to endorse trial by jury or judge than arbitration.[75]

In one of the Federal Judicial Center pilot programs, the researchers took an in-depth look at attorneys' perceptions of the judge, the jury, and arbitration.[76] Lawyers were asked to compare the three types of decisionmakers on a number of factors, including which of the three would be most likely to understand their point of view, come up with a decision that was fair to everyone, and apply the law correctly. Not surprisingly, 72 percent of the attorneys thought that a judge would be most likely to apply the law correctly (5 percent selected the jury and 20 percent said that it would make no difference). About a third of the attorneys thought that there would be no difference between judge, jury, or arbitrator in understanding their point of view and coming up with a decision that was fair to everyone. Another 40 percent believed that a judge would be best on both of these counts. Just 17 percent of the lawyers believed that a jury was most likely to understand their point of view, and only 12 percent felt that a jury was most likely to reach a decision that was fair to everyone.[77]

A Rand Corporation study took a similar approach to examining the responses of litigants and their attorneys in personal injury cases arising from automobile accidents that were settled by arbitration. The project found greater attorney endorsement of the jury than did the Federal Judicial Center study.[78] Trial by jury was selected as the fairest procedure by 49 percent of the plaintiffs' and 47 percent of the defendants' attorneys, compared with 2 percent and 12 percent for bench trials and 49 percent and 41 percent for arbitration (which the attorneys had just experienced). Attorneys in this study believed that arbitration is much more efficient than either a jury or bench trial.[79]

Respondents in the Rand study who knew the details of their arbitration awards were asked to speculate on the possibility that the liability verdict and award would have been different in a jury trial. About two-thirds of all the attorneys believed the liability judgment would have been about the same, but, consistent with the popular view that juries favor personal injury plaintiffs, the plaintiffs' attorneys believed that a jury would have given a more generous award than the arbitrator. Defense attorneys were about as likely to expect a similar award (41 percent) as they were an award more favorable to them (44 percent).[80]

I have mentioned the widespread stereotype that portrays juries as sympathetic to personal injury plaintiffs. Do lawyers share that view, and if so, what impact does it have on their choice of trial mode? Kevin M. Clermont and Theodore Eisenberg, who conducted informal surveys, found that attorneys appear to hold strong assumptions about the proclivities of the civil jury.[81] Clermont and Eisenberg asked law professors, dispute experts, and law students to indicate typical success rates before judge and jury in product liability, medical malpractice, and contract trials. Participants were significantly more likely to predict that the plaintiff would have success before juries in product liability and medical malpractice cases. For example, law professors predicted that the plaintiff would win in 63 percent of product liability jury trials but in only 44 percent of product liability bench trials. However, juries were not seen as more or less favorable in contract cases: the predictions for plaintiff success in contract cases were 49 percent for juries and 50 percent for judges.[82]

The idea that a jury favors plaintiffs in particular kinds of cases can influence settlement strategies and the rate of winning at trial. Under

most circumstances, Clermont and Eisenberg argue, the likelihood that
a jury will favor one side in a case becomes a factor in settlement practices
by both sides. This should produce a "win ratio," or the relative
frequency of winning at a bench trial versus a jury trial, of around 1.0.
But systematic inaccuracies and misperceptions about the tendencies of
a jury or judge can lead to departures from that rate.[83] Comparing the
win rates in federal civil trials before judges and juries, Clermont and
Eisenberg discovered significant differences before judge and jury in six
of thirteen categories of cases. First of all, attorneys selected jury over
judge trials in the vast majority of personal injury cases.[84] However, in
two categories in which it is widely believed that juries are pro-plaintiff—
product liability and medical malpractice—plaintiffs were significantly
more likely to prevail before judges than before juries.[85] The researchers
explain these outcomes as the result of both the choice of a judge rather
than a jury trial and small differences in the way judge and jury treat
cases in these different categories. The popular stereotype about the jury,
particularly in product liability and medical malpractice cases, led litigants
and their attorneys to choose a jury trial unwisely.[86]

Although the lack of national surveys about attorneys' perceptions
precludes presenting a comprehensive picture of their views of the civil
jury, the findings above reinforce the point that these views are significant
factors that deserve systematic examination.

Litigants

The final group to consider comprises the litigants themselves. What do
they think about trial by jury? Certainly the writings and advertisements of
business and insurance representatives reflect the concerns of these
potential defendants about the impact of high jury awards on their
enterprises. Perhaps the most frequently expressed concern involves the
unpredictability of jury awards. The publications of the Conference
Board, a business information service for senior executives, regularly
focus on the civil litigation system and provide some interesting insights
into the way business executives view civil litigation and the role of the
jury. In one publication, E. Patrick McGuire summarized responses
from CEOs about the impact of product liability law on their businesses:
"Given the nature of the U.S. jury system, there is simply no way to
predict what is likely to happen, some CEOs feel. A tool company
president, for example, says, 'the likelihood of a runaway jury verdict,
along with judges' discretion in imposing sanctions, prompts settlements

at levels which are out of all proportion to the contribution a manufacturer makes to a plaintiff's injuries. "'87

Whether the perceptions of potential litigants are accurate is another question. For example, one study of medical doctors in South Carolina revealed that many doctors believe there is a crisis in the tort system. A comparison of their views with actual data on South Carolina tort cases, however, shows that they dramatically overestimate the typical tort award in both product liability and medical malpractice cases.[88]

Aside from such samplings of opinion of potential defendants, there are only a few studies of litigants' opinions about the civil jury. The Aetna survey of public attitudes toward the civil justice system determined whether respondents had been injured in an accident or had been a defendant in a lawsuit during the last ten years. Twenty-one percent of the sample had been in an accident, but only about a quarter of these individuals had retained a lawyer. Just 5 percent of the general population sample had been defendants, so the researchers oversampled defendants to obtain a clearer picture of their views.

Those who had been defendants in lawsuits held more negative views of the civil justice system than the general population. For example, 80 percent of civil defendants thought that more people bring lawsuits than should, compared to 68 percent of the overall population. And 58 percent of defendants believed that jury awards in personal injuries were excessive, compared with 45 percent of the population.

Respondents who had been injured in an accident but did not retain lawyers tended to have views similar to those of the general population. Those accident victims who did retain lawyers were inclined to see the system as more miserly toward plaintiffs. For instance, just 29 percent of the injured who had retained lawyers agreed that the size of jury awards was excessive, compared with 45 percent of the general population and 58 percent of defendants. Fully 60 percent believed that it was too difficult to recover damages, compared with 45 percent of the public and 37 percent of defendants. It seems that personal experience in litigation as either a defendant or an injured party seeking redress makes a significant contribution to people's views of the civil jury and the civil justice system. But the respondents' answers to these general questions do not allow us to separate the impact of the jury from the many other factors present during the resolution of a dispute.[89]

Do litigants consider trial by jury more or less fair than other dispute resolution mechanisms? One recent study interviewed tort litigants whose cases had been resolved through trial (ninety-five of the ninety-nine were jury trials) or bilateral settlement.[90] Even though litigants in both types of cases expressed satisfaction with the outcomes, litigants whose cases had been decided at trial were more satisfied with the procedural aspects than were litigants whose cases had settled. Compared with litigants who settled, trial litigants were more likely to see their proceedings as dignified and careful, and to report that they understood and participated in them.[91] This is an important result, even though the data do not reveal to what extent the jury is a crucial element in promoting this view of procedural justice. Would a judge have produced the same increase in satisfaction?

Another tactic that can be used to assess litigants' attitudes toward the jury is to ask those who have experienced one type of proceeding how another sort might compare, as was done in the attorney studies described in the previous section. In the Rand study of the postarbitration responses of litigants and their attorneys in personal injury cases arising from automobile accidents, 66 percent of plaintiffs and 68 percent of defendants chose arbitration as the fairest procedure. Just 24 percent of plaintiffs and 17 percent of defendants selected jury trial as the fairest procedure. Like their attorneys, litigants believed arbitration was much more efficient than either a jury or bench trial.[92] It is an interesting comment on the issue of fairness that attorneys expressed more support for trial by jury than the litigants they represented. This could conceivably be due to the different experiences litigants and attorneys have with jury trials.

Along with their attorneys, the Rand study litigants who knew the details of their arbitration awards were asked if they believed the liability verdict and award would have been different with a jury trial. Similar percentages of litigants thought they would have received the same liability judgment (42 percent) or a more favorable decision (48 percent). As for damages, 60 percent of the plaintiffs believed that a jury would have given them a higher damage award than the arbitrator had.[93] Of course, their recent experience with an arbitration proceeding may have influenced their comparisons of arbitration, bench trial, and jury trial.

The Federal Judicial Center study of ten pilot programs on court-annexed arbitration also surveyed litigants after arbitration. However, there were substantial sampling problems in obtaining the cooperation of the litigating parties, leading the researchers to be cautious about generalizing the results. Most of the parties who responded to the survey were sophisticated users of the civil justice system and had prior litigation experience. Just one-third were individuals; the remainder were corporations or people suing or being sued in their public or business capacity. Eight out of ten respondents agreed that their arbitration hearing had been fair. Half said that, considering time, cost, and fairness, they preferred to have their case decided by an arbitrator. A judge was the preferred decisionmaker of another 22 percent and the jury of 17 percent; the remainder said that the decisionmaker made no difference to them.[94]

The arbitration surveys are difficult to interpret in terms of overall support for jury trial, because the litigants were not representative and had been influenced in unknown ways by their personal experience with arbitration. Yet taken together with the other measures of litigant perceptions of trial by jury, the surveys indicate that parties to cases react in understandable ways to their experiences with civil litigation. If litigants are satisfied with the treatment of their cases, they endorse the procedure by which their cases were resolved. People with experience as civil defendants see juries as too generous, while injured people who have sought compensation respond in the opposite manner. Yet the Rand study comparing those who went through a trial with those whose cases settled provides the important information that, even if the outcome of a jury trial is unfavorable, the litigant is impressed with the procedural justice of trial by jury.

Conclusion

It is time to take stock. I began by arguing that views of the civil jury were important both to the legitimacy of the civil justice system and to their central role in influencing other stages of the civil justice process. What has been learned about attitudes toward and perceptions of the civil jury?

In light of the significance of public support for the jury, it is fortunate that public opinion surveys show quite strong endorsement of the institution. Recent surveys indicate that the public believes that the civil justice system fulfills its broad functions of providing compensation and deterrence reasonably well. However, the public also believes there has been a litigation explosion, that awards have increased in recent years, and that civil justice costs are high. Some of these general views can be correlated with attitudes toward the civil jury. For example, those who believe that there has been a litigation explosion are more likely than those who do not to find jury awards excessive. While members of the public express concern about high jury awards, they rank other factors (such as undeserving plaintiffs and insurance companies that will not settle deserving claims) above the jury as major reasons for the rising costs of litigation. Support for the civil jury is linked to confidence in lawyers and the courts, suggesting the significant role the jury plays in maintaining the legitimacy of the justice system.

Citizens' attitudes toward the jury are developed within a context of low information. What happens when people gain additional knowledge is worth exploring. Compared to the general public, those who serve on juries have more positive views about the jury as an institution. Yet national surveys of attitudes toward the courts indicate that greater knowledge of the justice system is sometimes accompanied by less confidence in it. Are these findings the result of demographic differences or of the type of knowledge? Does greater information and respect for expertise create negativity toward the common voice represented by the jury?

Because citizens' views of the civil jury are inextricably linked to general judgments about the efficacy of the civil litigation system, it is worthwhile to speculate about why people are concerned about the problems of our civil justice system. Surveys indicate that only a minority of citizens have served on a jury or been a party to a civil case. Most members of the public obtain their information about the courts and the jury primarily from the media rather than from direct experience such as jury duty or a lawsuit. Certainly, then, media coverage might be responsible for some of the public's concerns, especially if it is true that media coverage overrepresents extreme awards and unusual or unreasonable jury verdicts. Steven Daniels makes the argument that media stories and insurance industry advertising are part of a concerted effort by business and insurance companies to promote tort reforms beneficial to them. He points out that anecdotes about even a few outrageous jury decisions can have a powerful impact in shaping public perceptions about the civil jury as an institution, even in the face of research studies showing the stability and reasonableness of most jury verdicts.[95]

The media's biased presentation of jury verdicts is not the whole story, however. Why is the public drawn to such information in the first place? Robert Hayden maintains that anecdotes about outrageous tort cases hold particular shock value because they violate important principles of American culture related to individual responsibility, equality, and redistribution. Hayden argues that when plaintiffs use the courts to obtain compensation for personal injury, they violate all three of these principles. Bringing the court into a dispute between an injured individual and another party represents an effort to avoid personal responsibility for the injury and departs from the concept of equality by putting the state on the side of the plaintiff. Compensating a person who has not "earned" the money is also at odds with Americans' dislike of financial redistribution by government action, as evidenced by public hostility toward welfare.[96]

There is another cause for public concern. Like high crime rates, high rates of litigation represent the breakdown of the social contract that signifies a smoothly functioning society—a point likely to be most salient when plaintiffs sue authorities for redress. All of these factors probably combine to create worries about civil litigation in the minds of the public.[97] Yet it should be reassuring that the existence of the civil jury provides a mechanism for injecting these public norms, values, and concerns about the legitimacy of lawsuits into the civil justice system.

We could clearly benefit from gathering more differentiated information about people's perceptions of the civil jury. It has long been maintained that the existence of the jury promotes the overall legitimacy of the justice system, and I found some evidence of this while doing my review. This assumption deserves more systematic exploration. It is unclear how perceptions of the civil jury are influenced by judgments about specific jury verdicts or integrated into views of the overall legitimacy of the system of civil litigation. Are attitudes toward the civil jury strongly correlated with perceptions that juries reach accurate and just verdicts, or is there an appreciation of the broader significance of the jury that goes beyond its factfinding role? It is also important to determine the extent to which the jury's role as the decisionmaker (as distinct from the trial itself) is essential in promoting legitimacy and a sense of procedural justice. Studies like the MacCoun and Tyler project on the criminal jury, which examines the significance of different aspects of the jury, such as accuracy, fairness, and the ability to represent all segments of the community, might be usefully replicated with the civil jury. In particular, issues related to the links among the civil jury, proposed jury reforms, and legitimacy should be examined.

Trial Judges

National and regional surveys of trial judges show widespread endorsement of the civil jury. Judges agree with civil jury verdicts and awards in the vast majority of cases, modifying jury awards only in a small number of trials. Only a few judges favor major reform of the civil jury system, although many are open to the idea of studying various options in trial procedures. Judges point to judicial instructions and guidance in damage awards as areas needing examination.

Some jury critics have questioned whether civil juries are capable of handling disputes that involve complex technical, scientific, and business issues. While recognizing the challenges that these cases pose for the lay jury, judges report that, in protracted civil trials, juries perform well. The majority of judges endorse the continuation of trial by jury in complex cases. Indeed, judges are more willing to limit the right to jury trial in minor cases involving small sums of money than in complex civil trials or very complicated business cases.

Attorneys

Despite the central importance of lawyers' perceptions of the jury to the civil litigation system, there is little systematic information about their views. Attorneys often appear to have incomplete information or to be misinformed about the tendencies of civil juries. In particular, they share the widespread belief that the civil jury is pro-plaintiff in tort cases. There is evidence that these mistaken perceptions are detrimentally affecting settlement strategies, indicating the need for more precise information about the way civil juries make their decisions.

Litigants

There are few systematic studies of litigants' opinions about the civil jury. The attitudes of litigants and potential litigants toward the civil jury vary significantly, with some surveys showing endorsement of trial by jury and others showing a divergence of opinion. The writings and advertisements of business and insurance representatives reflect the concerns of these potential defendants about unpredictable and unreasonable jury awards. In contrast, those who have been injured and who have retained a lawyer are more likely to believe that it is too difficult to recover damages and that jury awards are insufficient. However, it appears that trial by jury has an advantage over settlement in that litigants perceive the trial as more procedurally just.

Summary

Although there are some significant gaps in our knowledge of the subject, there does not appear to be a serious crisis of confidence in the civil jury. Judges report that, in general, they agree with jury verdicts and strongly support the civil jury's soundness as an institution. Although they see the benefits of a systematic study of tort reform, they do not believe that there are major weaknesses in the civil jury as an institution. Most members of the public have little direct experience with the civil jury either as jurors or litigants but also endorse the institution of the jury. Recent surveys indicate that many people believe there is too much civil litigation and find jury awards too high. Media reporting may have heightened public concern about the civil justice system, for it appears that direct experience as a juror or a potential plaintiff lessens the perception that jury awards are excessive. Finally, the views of potential defendants and attorneys deserve more scrutiny because of the importance of these key players in determining the kind of conflict resolution mechanism chosen to resolve civil disputes—and because these views appear to include significant misperceptions of the civil jury.

Notes

1. For summaries of criticisms of the civil jury, the reader is referred to Steven Daniels, "The Question of Jury Competence and the Politics of Civil Justice Reform: Symbols, Rhetoric and Agenda-Building," *Law and Contemporary Problems*, vol. 52 (Autumn 1989), pp. 269–310; and Valerie P. Hans, "The Jury's Response to Business and Corporate Wrongdoing," *Law and Contemporary Problems*, vol. 52 (Autumn 1989), pp. 177–203.

2. Tom R. Tyler, *Why People Obey the Law* (Yale University Press, 1990).

3. People evaluate institutions by focusing on their procedures and whether the procedures appear to be fair, assuming that institutions with fair procedures will generally produce just outcomes. On the importance of fair procedures for political institutions, see generally E. Allan Lind and Tom R. Tyler, *The Social Psychology of Procedural Justice* (Plenum Press, 1988).

4. Marc Galanter, "Jury Shadows: Reflections on the Civil Jury and the 'Litigation Explosion'" in Morris S. Arnold and others, *The American Civil Jury: Final Report of the 1986 Chief Justice Earl Warren Conference on Advocacy in the United States* (Roscoe Pound-American Trial Lawyers Foundation, 1987), pp. 15–42.

5. The effects of the liability system on innovation are discussed in Peter W. Huber and Robert E. Litan, eds., *The Liability Maze: The Impact of Liability Law on Safety and Innovation* (Brookings, 1991).

6. Studies of actual jurors show that they typically become more favorable to the institution of the jury and to the justice system after jury service. See the chapter by Shari Seidman Diamond in this volume.

7. Yankelovich, Skelly, and White, "Highlights of a National Survey of the General Public, Judges, Lawyers, and Community Leaders," in Theodore J. Fetter, ed., *State Courts: A Blueprint for the Future* (Williamsburg, Va.: National Center for State Courts, 1978), pp. 5–69. For sources of information about the courts, see p. 19, table I.13.

8. See generally Valerie P. Hans and Juliet L. Dee, "Media Coverage of Law: Its Impact on Juries and the Public," *American Behavioral Scientist*, vol. 35 (November–December 1991), pp. 136–49. See also Doris Graber, *Crime News and the Public* (Praeger, 1980); and Ray Surette, ed., *Justice and the Media: Issues and Research* (Springfield, Ill.: C. C. Thomas, 1984).

9. Robert MacCoun and Daniel Bailis are currently undertaking a systematic study of newspaper coverage of civil jury verdicts by analyzing the frequency and content of stories of civil jury awards in major national publications, including the *New York Times*, *Wall Street Journal*, *Time*, *Newsweek*, *Fortune*, *Forbes*, and *Business Week* during the years 1980, 1985, and 1990. Although the analysis has yet to be completed, MacCoun has reported that "there is no question that the media focus on a handful of really big cases," supporting the analysis in this chapter that the media are likely to overreport high awards and sensational verdicts. Personal communication, Robert MacCoun, August 5, 1992.

10. Vice President J. Danforth Quayle, "Remarks at the Meeting of the American Bar Association," Atlanta, Georgia, August 13, 1991. Available through the Office of the Vice President.

11. Daniels, "Jury Competence and Politics"; Marc Galanter, "Reading the Landscape of Disputes: What We Know and Don't Know (and Think We Know) about Our Allegedly Contentious and Litigious Society," *UCLA Law Review*, vol. 31 (October 1983), pp. 4–71; and Michael J. Saks, "Do We Really Know Anything about the Behavior of the Tort Litigation System—And Why Not?" *University of Pennsylvania Law Review*, vol. 140 (April 1992), pp. 1147–1292.

12. Daniel Kahneman, Paul Slovic, and Amos Tversky, *Judgment under Uncertainty: Heuristics and Biases* (Cambridge University Press, 1982).

13. Edith Greene, "Media Effects on Jurors," *Law and Human Behavior*, vol. 14 (October 1990), pp. 439–50, especially pp. 445–46.

14. Elizabeth Loftus, "Insurance Advertising and Jury Awards," *American Bar Association Journal*, vol. 65 (January 1979), pp. 68–70.

15. Valerie P. Hans and William S. Lofquist, "Jurors' Judgments of Business Liability in Tort Cases: Implications for the Litigation Explosion Debate," *Law & Society Review*, vol. 26, no. 1 (1992), pp. 85–115.

16. The tendency for people to blame the person rather than the situation, a well-known phenomenon in social judgment, may encourage the public to blame the jury rather than other aspects of the trial. For discussion of the jury in the Rodney King beating case, see Terry McMillan, "This Is America," *New York Times*, May 1, 1992, p. A35; Timothy P. O'Neill, "Wrong Place, Wrong Jury," *New York Times*, May 9, 1992, p. 23; Janny Scott, "What Swayed the Jury?" *Los Angeles Times*, May 2, 1992, pp. A1, A28; and Amy Stevens and Sarah Lubman, "Deciding Moment of the Trial May Have Been Five Months Ago," *Wall Street Journal*, p. A6.

Many newspaper accounts focused particularly on the racial composition of the jury, which contained no blacks. A *Time*/CNN national public opinion poll taken on April 30, 1992, showed that fully 64 percent of the whites and 89 percent of the blacks believed that the verdict would have been different had there been blacks on the jury (Richard Lacayo, "Anatomy of an Acquittal," *Time*, May 11, 1992, pp. 30–32). Racial composition may be a very salient feature of the jury, as Supreme Court Justice Clarence Thomas observed in his concurrence in *Georgia* v. *McCollum*, 112 S.Ct. 2348 (1992) at 2360: "The public, in general, continues to believe that the makeup of juries can matter in certain instances.

Consider, for example, how the press reports criminal trials. Major newspapers regularly note the number of whites and blacks that sit on juries in important cases. . . . A computer search, for instance, reveals that the phrase 'all-white jury' has appeared over two hundred times in the past five years in the *New York Times*, *Chicago Tribune*, and *Los Angeles Times*."

17. Marc Galanter, "The Civil Jury as Regulator of the Litigation Process," *University of Chicago Legal Forum*, vol. 1990, pp. 201–71. For discussion of sources of attorney knowledge, see pp. 232–41.

18. The unpublished study is described in Galanter, "Civil Jury as Regulator," pp. 232–33.

19. Jury verdict reporters have their own problems in communicating accurate information about jury decisions. The verdict reporters oversample high award cases and tort cases. See Galanter, "Civil Jury as Regulator," p. 236. For an excellent analysis of additional factors that limit attorney knowledge of juries, see Michael Saks, "Do We Really Know Anything."

20. Patricia Bonfield, *U.S. Business Leaders: A Study of Opinions and Characteristics* (New York: Conference Board, 1980). Nine out of ten of the top business executives surveyed reported reading *Forbes*, *Fortune*, and *Business Week* regularly; about half read the *Harvard Business Review* (p. 23).

21. Lauren B. Edelman, Steven E. Abraham, and Howard S. Erlanger, "Professional Construction of Law: The Inflated Threat of Wrongful Discharge," *Law & Society Review*, vol. 26, no. 1 (1992), pp. 47–83, especially pp. 65–66.

22. Kalven and Zeisel justified the use of trial judges' opinions about the jury in their classic work by noting that the judge is in the best position to observe how juries function. Critics of their study pointed out that judges might rely on stereotypes of juries in assessing their behavior. See Harry Kalven, Jr., and Hans Zeisel, *The American Jury* (Little, Brown, 1966). For a review of the criticisms of the Chicago Jury Project, including its reliance on judicial perceptions, see Valerie P. Hans and Neil Vidmar, "*The American Jury* at Twenty-Five Years," *Law and Social Inquiry*, vol. 16 (Spring 1991), pp. 323–51.

23. Yankelovich, Skelly, and White, "Highlights of National Survey."

24. Ibid., p. 10, table I.2; p. 13, table I.5; and p. 16, table I.9.

25. Sixty-seven percent of the public respondents reported that they were unaware of any changes in the court system. The percentage was not significantly different for states that had or had not undergone substantial change. Yankelovich, Skelly, and White, "Highlights of National Survey," p. 15, table I.8.

26. Frank A. Bennack, Jr., "The Public, the Media, and the Judicial System: A National Survey on Citizen Awareness," *State Court Journal*, vol. 7 (Fall 1983), pp. 4–13, especially pp. 8–9. Bennack summarized and presented the highlights of the survey of 983 U.S. adults who were interviewed by telephone during 1983.

27. Herbert McClosky and Alida Brill, *Dimensions of Tolerance: What Americans Believe about Civil Liberties* (New York: Russell Sage Foundation, 1983). In 1978 the researchers undertook a cross-section sample of the general population of adults from 300 U.S. communities (N = 1,993), and two specialized elite samples from the same communities: community leaders (N = 1,157) and attorneys, judges, and police officers (N = 734).

28. Ibid., p. 162, table 4.6. In the public sample, 79 percent rated the right to trial by jury as "extremely important," and another 17 percent rated it "important." In the sample of community leaders, legal elites, and police officials, from 82 percent to 87 percent rated trial by jury as "extremely important" and 11 percent to 15 percent judged it to be "important." Thus in all samples support for trial by jury was striking. McClosky and Brill cite similar data from a public opinion survey by Chandler showing that 82 percent of the public supports the criminal trial jury (p. 162). Chandler's question was, "In most

criminal cases, the judge conducts the trial and a jury decides innocence or guilt. Instead of the jury, would it be better if the judge alone decided innocence or guilt?" Just 14 percent responded yes, and 82 percent no, with the rest undecided or not responding. Robert Chandler, *Public Opinion: Changing Attitudes on Contemporary Political and Social Issues*, CBS News Reference Book (R. R. Bowker, 1972).

29. McClosky and Brill, *Dimensions of Tolerance*, p. 162, table 4.6. Fourteen percent of the general public endorsed this statement, compared with 9 percent of community leaders, 8 percent of legal elites such as judges and attorneys, and 13 percent of police officials.

30. Ibid., pp. 168–70, table 4.8.

31. Robert J. MacCoun and Tom R. Tyler, "The Basis of Citizens' Perceptions of the Criminal Jury: Procedural Fairness, Accuracy, and Efficiency," *Law and Human Behavior*, vol. 12 (September 1988), pp. 333–52.

32. Ibid., p. 338, table 2. For shoplifting trials, judges were slightly preferred to juries.

33. Ibid., p. 339, table 3; p. 338, table 1.

34. Anthony N. Doob, "Public's View of the Criminal Jury Trial," in Law Reform Commission of Canada, *Studies on the Jury* (Ottawa, Ontario, 1979), pp. 1–26.

35. Doob, "Canadian Juror's View of the Criminal Jury Trial," Ibid., pp. 29–82.

36. Humphrey Taylor and others, *Public Attitudes toward the Civil Justice System and Tort Law Reform*, report of survey conducted for Aetna Life and Casualty (New York: Louis Harris and Associates, March 1987). (Hereafter Louis Harris and Associates, *Public Attitudes.*) The Harris analyses of public opinion are based on 2,008 interviews. An additional 122 civil defendants were oversampled to permit subgroup analyses. Their data are presented in a later section.

37. Ibid., pp. 11, 10, 13, 14, tables 1-2, 1-1, 1-3, and 1-4, respectively.

38. This is somewhat at odds with another finding in the Harris survey. Just 28 percent of the respondents said that when people take legal action, it is too easy to recover damages, compared with 45 percent who said that it is too difficult. Ibid., p. 17, table 1-6.

39. Ibid., p. 17, table 1-6.

40. Ibid., p. 26, table 3-1. This suggests that the public would be quite supportive of proposals such as that for damages scheduling, advanced by Peter H. Schuck in his chapter in this volume.

41. The exact age cutoffs vary with different questions. For example, the majority of respondents over 50 think that the civil justice system needs fundamental change. Furthermore, 21 percent of people aged 50-64, and 28 percent of those over 64, agree that "the civil justice system has so much wrong with it that we need to completely rebuild it." Louis Harris and Associates, *Public Attitudes*, p. 23.

42. Ibid., p. 24. However, recall that the Yankelovich, Skelly, and White survey ("Highlights of National Survey") also found that more informed respondents were less confident about the courts, indicating that there may be a generally negative relationship between knowledge and confidence.

43. Jeanne J. Fleming and Leonard C. Schwarz, "Juror Opinion Survey Reveals Obstacles for Litigators," *Inside Litigation*, vol. 5 (December 1991), pp. 21–24.

44. "To Sue or Not to Sue? Public Backs Liability Reform," *Public Pulse* (August 1991), p. 6.

45. Ibid., p. 6.

46. The survey, designed by Valerie P. Hans and funded by National Science Foundation grant SES-8822598, was conducted by a professional survey research group at the University of Delaware during the fall of 1991. The results are unpublished.

47. Confidence in the courts was significantly and positively correlated with judgments that juries do a good job of deciding outcomes and assessing damages ($r = .23$, $p < .01$); agreement that most awards were reasonable ($r = .23$, $p < .01$); and negatively associated

with statements that awards were too high ($r = -.11$, $p < .05$). Similar patterns held for confidence in lawyers. Hans, unpublished data.

48. The correlation between statements that there are far too many frivolous lawsuits today and the assertion that most jury awards are too high was .18, $p < .01$; statements that people are too quick to sue and that the money that juries award in civil cases is too large were correlated with an r of .28, $p < .01$; and statements that the number of lawsuits show our society breaking down and that most jury awards are reasonable and justified were negatively correlated, $r = -.14$, $p < .01$. Hans, unpublished data.

49. $R = .14$, $p < .01$.

50. Whites: 66 percent agreement; nonwhites: 52 percent agreement. Chi-square (2 $d.f.$) = 6.00, $p < .05$.

51. Chi-square (2 $d.f.$) = 8.55, $p < .01$.

52. Chi-square (4 $d.f.$) = 14.25, $p < .01$.

53. Chi-square (4 $d.f.$) = 12.39, $p < .02$.

54. Comparisons of the responses of civil jurors in tort cases and public opinion survey participants from the same county revealed that civil jurors appeared to be more positive about the civil jury system than the general public. For example, 39 percent of tort jurors but 65 percent of the public agreed that jury damage awards are too large. Similarly, 57 percent of jurors agreed that "juries do a good job determining the outcomes of lawsuits and assessing damages," compared with 48 percent of the general public. Valerie P. Hans, "Studying the Civil Jury's Treatment of Corporate Defendants: A Comparison of Different Methodological Approaches," paper presented at a Roundtable Discussion, Methodological Approaches to Jury Research, Law and Society Association meetings, Philadelphia, May 30, 1992.

55. Harry Kalven, Jr., "The Dignity of the Civil Jury," *University of Virginia Law Review*, vol. 50 (October 1964), pp. 1055–75.

56. Louis Harris and Associates, *Judges' Opinions on Procedural Issues: A Survey of State and Federal Judges Who Spend at Least Half Their Time on General Civil Cases* (New York, 1987). The study included two representative samples—800 state judges and 200 federal judges—who spent more than half of their time on general civil cases, including torts, contracts, and personal injury cases. Chapter 10 is devoted to an analysis of judges' opinions about the jury system.

57. Ibid., pp. 79–80, tables 10.1, 10.2.

58. For general assessments of the ability of the civil jury in complex cases, see Joe S. Cecil, Valerie P. Hans, and Elizabeth C. Wiggins, "Citizen Comprehension of Difficult Issues: Lessons from Civil Jury Trials," *American University Law Review*, vol. 40 (Winter 1991), pp. 727–74; and Richard Lempert's chapter in this volume.

59. Louis Harris and Associates, *Judges' Opinions*, pp. 81–82, tables 10.3, 10.4.

60. George Priest argues that juries spend only a minority of their time fulfilling their political function of expressing community values. In an interesting analysis of Cook County, Illinois, juries, Priest shows that juries spend a substantial amount of their time deciding auto accident cases and assessing damages for routine injuries. In these cases, he argues, the jury's political role is not paramount. George L. Priest, "The Role of the Civil Jury in a System of Private Adjudication," *University of Chicago Legal Forum*, vol. 1990, pp. 161–200.

61. Louis Harris and Associates, *Judges' Opinions*, table 10.7, p. 85.

62. See text accompanying note 40.

63. Gordon Bermant and others, *Protracted Civil Trials: Views from the Bench and the Bar: A Report to the Subcommittee on Possible Alternatives to Jury Trials in Protracted Court Cases* (Washington: Federal Judicial Center, 1981), especially p. 52.

64. Ellen L. Rosen, "The View from the Bench: A National Law Journal Poll," *National Law Journal*, August 10, 1987, pp. S1–S19, especially pp. S-6, S-8.

280 / *Valerie P. Hans*

65. See text accompanying notes 36-54.

66. R. Perry Sentell, Jr., "The Georgia Jury and Negligence: The View from the Bench," *Georgia Law Review*, vol. 26 (Fall 1991), pp. 85–178. Questionnaires were mailed to 180 Georgia judges, and 101 returned completed questionnaires.

67. Ibid. Judge-jury agreement on verdicts is presented on pp. 97–100 and p. 116, table 1. Judge-jury agreement on damages may be found on pp. 102–05. Results for jury understanding of the case are found on p. 113 and p. 117, table 4; results for jury adherence to judicial instructions are presented on p. 126 and p. 138, table 7.

68. Ibid., p. 110; and p. 117, table 3.

69. Ibid., pp. 132–37, and p. 139, table 8; p. 138, table 5; and pp. 140–42 and p. 167, table 9.

70. Louis Harris and Associates, *Judges' Opinions*, p. 87, table 10.9.

71. Michael G. Shanley and Mark A. Peterson, *Posttrial Adjustments to Jury Awards* (Santa Monica, Calif.: Rand Institute for Civil Justice, 1987). The authors surveyed plaintiff and defense attorneys in a large sample of cases and asked about the final payment. Most changes were reductions in the payment to the plaintiff. The larger the jury award, the smaller the proportion of it that was paid.

72. Ibid., p. xi. Shanley and Peterson reported that in 25 percent of cases defendants paid smaller amounts. Of that number, courts made the final decision in 23 percent.

73. One national survey of 900 attorneys on their perceptions of the civil justice system focused on other matters (such as transaction costs and delay) and did not include questions about the civil jury. Humphrey Taylor and Gary L. Schmermund, *Procedural Reform of the Civil Justice System*, study conducted for the Foundation for Change (New York: Louis Harris and Associates, March 1989).

74. Barbara S. Meierhoefer, *Court-Annexed Arbitration in Ten District Courts* (Washington: Federal Judicial Center, 1990).

75. Ibid. See pp. 71–72, table 19, for attorneys whose cases were arbitrated, and pp. 73–74, table 20, for attorneys in all cases. Similar preferences are reflected in both tables, although attorneys whose cases were arbitrated were somewhat more likely to endorse the jury (24 percent) and less likely to prefer arbitration (37 percent) than all attorneys (20 percent and 43 percent for jury and arbitration preferences respectively). See also p. 72, table 19.

76. See Barbara S. Meierhoefer and Carroll Seron, *Court-Annexed Arbitration in the Northern District of California* (Washington: Federal Judicial Center, 1988).

77. Ibid., pp. 22–23.

78. Robert J. MacCoun and others, *Alternative Adjudication: An Evaluation of the New Jersey Automobile Arbitration Program* (Santa Monica: Rand Corporation, 1988).

79. Ibid., p. 58, table 4.7.

80. Ibid., p. 59, table 4.8.

81. Kevin M. Clermont and Theodore Eisenberg, "Trial by Jury or Judge: Transcending Empiricism," *Cornell Law Review*, vol. 77 (July 1992), pp. 1124–77.

82. Ibid., p. 1128, notes 11, 12.

83. "If the parties perceive the adjudicator to be favorable to the plaintiff, but the adjudicator turns out not to be, then the apparently close cases would turn out to be losers and the win rate would drop. Similarly, if the adjudicator appears to be neutral, but turns out to be unfavorable to the plaintiff, then the win rate would drop. Imagined biases or unperceived biases therefore affect win rate." Ibid., "Trial by Jury or Judge," p. 1131.

84. Personal injury cases were much more likely to be heard by juries than were nonpersonal injury cases. Clermont and Eisenberg found that, across various categories of trials, the percentage of personal injury trials heard by judges ranged from 9 percent to 35 percent, while the percentage of judge trials in nonpersonal-injury categories ranged from 52 percent to 76 percent. Ibid., p. 1141, table 4.

85. Ibid., p. 1137, table 3. Two other categories, negotiable instruments and motor vehicle, also showed significantly greater plaintiff success before judges than juries. In contrast, cases involving federal employers' liability and marine personal injury showed greater plaintiff success before juries than judges. The remaining seven categories showed comparable win rates before judges and juries.

86. Ibid., p. 1126.

87. E. Patrick McGuire, "Impact of Product Liability," *Corporate Board* (November–December 1988), pp. 18–24; quotation from p. 18. For more extensive information about how business managers respond to product liability issues, see Nathan Weber, *Product Liability: The Corporate Response* (New York: Conference Board, 1987).

88. Donald R. Songer, "Tort Reform in South Carolina: The Effect of Empirical Research on Elite Perceptions Concerning Jury Verdicts," *South Carolina Law Review*, vol. 39 (Spring 1988), pp. 585–605.

89. Louis Harris and Associates, *Public Attitudes*, p. 11, table 1-2 (too many lawsuits); p. 14, table 1-4 (jury awards excessive); p. 22, table 2-2 (difficulty in recovering damages).

90. E. Allan Lind and others, "In the Eye of the Beholder: Tort Litigants' Evaluations of Their Experiences in the Civil Justice System," *Law & Society Review*, vol. 24 (November 1990), pp. 953–96.

91. Ibid., "Tort Litigants' Evaluations," pp. 966–68.

92. MacCoun and others, *Alternative Adjudication*, p. 58, table 4.7.

93. Ibid., p. 59, table 4.8.

94. For discussion of the sampling problems, see Meierhoefer, *Court-Annexed Arbitration*, pp. 53–57. For results of the survey, see p. 66, table 16; and p. 70, table 18.

95. Daniels, "Jury Competence and Politics," pp. 269–310.

96. Robert M. Hayden, "The Cultural Logic of a Political Crisis: Common Sense, Hegemony and the Great American Liability Insurance Famine of 1986," *Studies in Law, Politics, and Society*, vol. 11 (1991) pp. 95–117.

97. A lively discussion at a session on "The Three Faces of Torts" (May 29, 1992, presented at the annual meeting of the Law and Society Association, Philadelphia) provided much food for thought about why the public persists in seeing a litigation explosion in the face of mixed or contrary evidence. Bob Kagan noted the similarity of public reactions to rising crime rates and rising litigation rates. Marc Galanter observed that litigation against those in authority might be particularly disturbing to the public and that cases of this kind have increased substantially over the last several decades. See Marc Galanter, "The Life and Times of the Big Six; or, The Federal Courts Since the Good Old Days," *Wisconsin Law Review*, vol. 1988 (November–December), pp. 921–54.

CHAPTER EIGHT

What Jurors Think: Expectations and Reactions of Citizens Who Serve as Jurors

Shari Seidman Diamond

RECENT DEBATE ABOUT the civil jury centers on three primary questions: first, is the jury competent to understand complex testimony and judicial instructions? Second, is the jury biased in its evaluation of testimony and application of relevant legal standards? Finally, is the civil jury an expensive and unnecessary fixture justified in the American legal system only by tradition and constitutional mandate?[1] These questions have stimulated assessments of the jury as a decisionmaker, with a particular emphasis on its ability to comprehend and recall testimony and legal instructions, and on its reactions to particular types of defendants.[2]

Although research on the civil jury is still quite limited, particularly when compared with research on the criminal jury, most researchers who have studied decisionmaking by the civil jury have been impressed by the jury's performance.[3] That does not mean that all civil or criminal jury verdicts meet with universal approval; moreover, some juries do reach verdicts that appear contrary to the evidence. But such outcomes are to be expected from any human decisionmaker dealing with a complex judgmental task, and no research has demonstrated that the average judge is a better factfinder than the average jury.[4] In addition, as Herbert Jacob and others have suggested, the jury verdicts of disinterested amateurs

Some of the work reported in this chapter received support from the American Bar Foundation and the Social Sciences Program of the National Science Foundation (grant SES-8922582). I am grateful to Jonathan D. Casper and Scott Barclay for their constructive suggestions on the manuscript.

may have a legitimacy that the decision of a single judge does not possess.[5]

In this paper I take a somewhat different approach to the analysis of jury performance. Rather than focusing solely on verdicts, I look at what citizens have told researchers about their experiences as jurors. Although relatively few studies have collected systematic information on juror reactions to courthouse and courtroom experiences, a comparison of juror surveys with studies of jury performance suggests several possible ways to improve jury service and jury decisionmaking.

Part one outlines the reasons why discussions about the performance of the civil jury and its future should take into consideration what jurors have to say about their experiences. Part two provides an overview of juror expectations and reactions to the experience of being a juror. Part three explores what we know about the factors that account for juror reactions. Part four focuses on the reactions of the trial jury, assessing the extent to which the demands placed on jurors conflict or are consistent with jurors' actual abilities and describing potential opportunities for improving both the experience of serving as a juror and jurors' performance. Finally, part five proposes two general strategies for enhancing the experience of jury service for the substantial number of citizens called for jury duty.

Why Care What Jurors Think?

Why, in considering the future of the civil jury, should anyone be concerned not only with the verdicts that jurors produce but also with juror reactions to their experience? The most obvious reason is that jury service is an involuntary obligation imposed by the government on citizens. To justify that imposition, a legal system should be required to maximize the usefulness of its citizens' contributions and minimize the negative experiences that may accompany the obligation. Thus, negative juror reactions are appropriate cause for concern. But there are, in addition to this normative reason for considering juror reactions, three more pragmatic justifications.

First, jurors who have negative experiences in court are likely to make every effort to avoid service in the future and will undoubtedly share their unfavorable impressions with friends and neighbors. Despite its power to require citizens to serve on juries, in practice the ability of the legal system to maximize representativeness in its jury pool depends on its ability to elicit cooperation from the jurors themselves. For example, the shift in many jurisdictions to systems that require jurors to serve only one day unless they are chosen for trial ("one day/one trial" systems) eases the burden of jury service and apparently also increases the diversity of jurors reporting for jury duty.[6]

Second, the impressions left by jury service can have crucial implications for citizen support for the legal system. Scholars studying the jury identify a political role for jury verdicts in legitimating governmental resolution of conflict.[7] These scholars generally ignore the direct role that jury service can play in promoting or reducing support for the legal system from the jurors themselves. Jury duty represents for many citizens their first and only direct contact with the legal system. Reporting for jury service provides the opportunity either to confirm the negative impression many have about the court system or to arrive at a more favorable one. Jury duty can thus create fallout that extends beyond satisfaction with the jury itself.

And third, many of the sources of juror dissatisfaction point to remediable flaws in the justice system. Jurors are generally conscientious in their efforts to perform an extraordinarily challenging task, and their complaints and observations provide important signals that, if responded to, can enhance the performance of future juries.

Anticipating and Reacting to Jury Service

De Tocqueville saw jury service as an unparalleled opportunity for citizen education, and many people look forward to the experience. When a jury summons arrives, some are curious and intrigued by the possibility of serving as jurors; others, however, are not enthusiastic about the prospect of jury duty. Some are merely reluctant to put aside their usual activities. Some expect jury duty to be a waste of time, since they believe they will never avoid rejection by all parties. Many are apprehensive about their ability to perform adequately as jurors.[8] What happens to these reluctant trial participants? John Richert studied the reactions of New Jersey jurors after they received their jury summonses. Nearly half of them wrote letters to the court asking to be excused. Yet many jurors ended up serving despite this initial reluctance: only 25 percent of those who requested an excuse were granted one.[9]

The prospective jurors Richert studied in 1974–75 were summoned for four weeks of jury service. Most jurisdictions today have shorter terms that appear to have reduced unwillingness to serve.[10] But even when jury terms are significantly shorter, some people who ultimately serve as jurors report that they were not eager to serve when first contacted by the court. The Roscoe Pound Foundation surveyed 286 jurors who served in thirty-eight civil trials in Philadelphia. Twelve of the trials occurred in federal court, where the term was two weeks; the remaining twenty-six trials took place in a state court using the one day/ one trial system. Jurors were asked, "When you were first notified to report for jury service, were you looking forward to it or wanting to get out of it?"[11] Thirty-eight percent of the federal jurors and 42 percent of the state jurors reported that they had initially wanted to get out of jury duty. Although this number may be inflated because the forced-choice format of the question did not permit jurors to give a neutral response, the result suggests that, even among citizens who ultimately serve as jurors, a substantial number do not initially welcome a jury summons.[12]

What kind of jurors do these reluctant trial participants make? No study has yet evaluated whether jurors who initially express a desire to avoid jury service perform differently from those more willing to serve, although some critics have suggested that jurors may retaliate—for example, by failing to pay attention in court or participating only superficially in deliberations—if they are forced to render involuntary service.[13] Concern about this possibility might be greater were it not for evidence that the experience of becoming a juror modifies initially negative attitudes. By the end of their service, the vast majority of jurors, even those who never serve in trials, have favorable attitudes toward jury service and confidence in the jury system. In a survey by Janet T. Munsterman and her colleagues of 8,468 jurors in sixteen federal and state courts, a substantial majority of respondents reported having favorable attitudes toward jury duty after serving. And according to the jurors, this positive attitude was in part a result of their experiences during jury duty; 63 percent said their impression of jury service was more favorable after serving than before.[14] Of course, the credibility of such retrospective reports depends on jurors' ability and willingness to remember and report accurately how they felt before jury service. Unfortunately, only the study by James L. Allen has measured juror satisfaction both before and after jury service. It found no change, possibly because satisfaction with the prospect of jury service among the particular group of jurors studied was unusually high at the beginning of their term (23.2 on a 29-point scale).[15]

Both this study and the only other "before and after" survey of juror reaction did reveal another important positive shift in juror attitudes. The jurors Allen studied became more positive in their assessments of the justice and equity of the legal system following jury service. Similarly, Paula Consolini found that following jury service, jurors were more likely to report that the U.S. jury system is working well and more likely to see the courts as fair.[16] Moreover, Joyce E. Tsongas, Barry F. Anderson, and Arthur D. Monson found in a postservice survey that 76 percent of the jurors had a more favorable impression of the court system after jury duty. In addition, 81 percent agreed that if they were involved in a trial, they would feel confident having their case tried by a jury.[17]

The positive reaction of jurors to the court system following jury service is particularly striking in view of the relatively negative reactions of citizens who come into contact with courts in other ways. Reviewing surveys of such reactions, Austin Sarat reports that "support for the courts is eroded by experience with or knowledge about them."[18] Similarly, a national survey found that citizens who had some experience with state or local courts were more likely to see a need for substantial court reform than those who reported no court experience.[19] Thus, if jury service fosters citizen support for the court system, in planning for the future it is worth understanding how jury experience achieves this legitimizing effect—and why it sometimes fails.

Explaining Juror Reactions

Juror surveys have done a fair job documenting the generally positive attitude of jurors following jury duty. They have been less successful in explaining *why* a majority of jurors come away feeling positive about jury service and the court system, while some jurors are disappointed or remain unimpressed.

Traditionally, one of the primary dissatisfactions voiced by jurors is that their time has been wasted. Surveys of juror response and personal testimonials written by jurors for the popular press reveal the deep indignation of citizens who arrive at a courthouse prepared to be jurors, wait to be called, and never see a courtroom or a litigant.[20] Modern juror management has done much to reduce the waiting time involved in jury service. Many courts have shifted to one day/one trial systems, or allow jurors serving longer terms to call in to see whether they are likely to be needed. At thirteen of the sixteen courts Munsterman and her colleagues studied, a majority of the jurors reported spending less than half their time waiting. At those three courts where jurors said they waited more than half the time, jurors spent an average of only 1.70 days in the courthouse (the average for the remaining thirteen courts was 3.45 days in court). Even when waiting occupied a substantial portion of the time spent on jury duty, it rarely amounted to the weeks of idleness that used to be common.[21]

In a broader examination of the determinants of juror satisfaction, the same researchers investigated the potential role played by structural variables (for example, fees, length of term), experiences (lost days of work, service as a trial juror), and preservice expectations. They found few items that accounted for much variation. The factor most strongly related to the satisfaction of the jurors was their perception of the way in which they were processed—and it accounted for only 1/2 of 1 percent of the variability in satisfaction ratings.[22]

One explanation for the generally positive shift in jurors' attitudes after serving is that jurors who actually sit through a trial and deliberate (trial jurors) are more likely than nontrial jurors to say their impression of jury duty improved with service. The Munsterman research found that 72 percent of trial jurors reported becoming more favorable toward jury service, while 55 percent of nontrial jurors became more favorable.[23] Contrary to popular belief, there is no evidence that trial and nontrial jurors differ in ways that might be related to their satisfaction with jury duty. The more likely reason for the difference in satisfaction reported by trial and nontrial jurors is that something in the trial experience itself promotes juror satisfaction.

The simplest explanation for the more favorable reaction of trial jurors to jury service is that participation stimulates a commitment to specific jury and its verdict that is powerful enough to include the system as a whole. The influence of participation on satisfaction is well established. Early studies of group participation during World War II, for example, show the effect of participation on behavior. During meat rationing, Kurt Lewin attempted to encourage homemakers to purchase less popular meats such as liver and kidneys.[24] A nondirective discussion proved far more effective in encouraging the purchase of the specialty meats than a lecture format. Later research showed that participative decisionmaking facilitates both behavioral change and increases in satisfaction.[25] A "halo effect" from participation, however, cannot account for the textured reaction of jurors. Although jurors come away from the experience with a generally favorable attitude, they are not uncritical about some aspects of the jury system and court activity. As a review of the evidence indicates, jurors respond positively to some aspects of their experience but express frustration and disappointment with others. While little research has attempted directly to assess the connection between variations in trial procedures and juror satisfaction, we do have some data on juror reactions to various aspects of the trial process.

The Experience of Being a Trial Juror

Because the vast majority of jurors are motivated to do a good job, they often express dissatisfaction when they feel that some aspect of the trial or court procedure has impaired their ability to perform adequately. Thus, many juror reactions to experiences at trial suggest areas for potential changes in trial procedures that could not only increase juror satisfaction, but may also enhance juror performance. Nonetheless, we cannot depend entirely on juror assessments of what is difficult and what is helpful. Like other decisionmakers, jurors do not always know why they behave as they do and may not recognize when their performance is impaired. For this reason, we need to compare what jurors say helps and hurts their jury performance with what we know from other sources about how they actually perform.

Jury Selection

The process of jury selection is a potentially daunting experience for jurors. During the voir dire, or jury selection process, they are called upon to describe themselves and their private beliefs before a courtroom of strangers so that the attorneys and the judge can decide if they should be seated on the jury.[26] As a result, jurors may be reluctant to disclose attributes they believe are undesirable.[27] Do jurors resent the voir dire process, perceiving the occasion as an inappropriate invasion of their privacy? Juror surveys suggest that most jurors accept voir dire as a necessary part of jury selection, although some resent the intrusion. Forty percent of the jurors surveyed by Tsongas and her colleagues thought that jury selection took too long,[28] and 20 percent thought that the questions focused too much on private or personal matters.[29] The voir dire examination for jurors in the Tsongas research was generally conducted by judges and may have been less intense than the typical attorney-conducted examination.[30] Consolini, however, obtained a comparable result from jurors in state courts hearing criminal cases, where attorneys examined the jurors. Two-thirds of these jurors expressed neutral or positive attitudes toward the questioning.[31] Similarly, when jurors in New Mexico were asked if the questioning of prospective jurors was too personal, about right, or not personal enough, over 80 percent said the questioning was about right, and more found it too impersonal than found it too personal.[32]

One explanation for this generally accepting attitude toward intrusive public questioning is that jurors both expect it and understand its purpose.[33] Jurors are not as well prepared for some other aspects of the trial process (for example, recesses during the trial) and often see no reasonable explanation for them. The result is that unexpected and unexplained aspects of the trial may cause unnecessary juror frustration and resentment and in turn impair jury performance.

Presentation of Evidence

The presentation of evidence is also an area that greatly concerns jurors.

REPETITION AND REDUNDANCY. Jurors sometimes complain about the repetition and redundancy of trial testimony.[34] Although Federal Rule of Evidence 403 attempts to protect against excessive repetition by authorizing the judge to exclude evidence to prevent "undue delay, waste of time, and needless presentation of cumulative evidence,"[35] some redundancy probably is unavoidable and may even be desirable. The presentation of evidence during a trial violates normal rules of story presentation that require the story to unfold in chronological order. In a trial, this order is sacrificed to meet the constraints imposed by the courtroom setting. Witnesses may testify in the rough order selected by the attorney to fit the presentation of one side of the case, but limitations imposed by scheduling needs, time constraints, witness availability, and a constantly changing script often alter the sequence. Such an out-of-order presentation of evidence makes it more difficult for jurors to form a coherent picture of what actually transpired.[36] Although the alert juror may become impatient with redundancy, repetition can facilitate comprehension and recall, potentially improving juror performance. While further research is needed to evaluate the trade-offs between the benefits of repetition and the attention losses induced by boredom, it may be possible to reduce juror frustration with repetition by explaining why it occurs and why the legal system tolerates it.

OMISSIONS AND LIMITATIONS. As jurors listen to the testimony in a trial, they try to evaluate the credibility of the witnesses and develop a story consistent with the evidence.[37] The rules of evidence are designed to focus the jury's attention on relevant evidence and to exclude from consideration information that is irrelevant or carries more prejudicial than probative weight. Jurors are expected to attend passively only to what is in the testimony and exhibits, not to speculate on gaps or omissions, and to ignore any limitations in the completeness of the information presented.

Yet studies of jury behavior reveal that jurors are not passive. In fact, they are active information processors who bring expectations and preconceptions with them to the jury box, filling in missing blanks and using their prior knowledge about the world to draw inferences from the evidence they receive at trial.[38] The testimony they hear may in fact appear incomplete, containing curious references to persons involved in the matter at issue who never appear as witnesses. Although jurors are instructed to base their decisions only on the evidence presented in court, it can be difficult for them to avoid speculating about matters they view as omissions or limitations. Fifty-one percent of the jurors surveyed in the Pound study said they wondered why certain people who were mentioned during the trial didn't testify. One-fourth (27 percent) said they "held it against the side that didn't call certain people to testify who might have added important information."[39] In another survey, 75 percent of the jurors said they thought that some evidence ruled inadmissible on legal grounds should have been allowed in order to help the jury make a decision.[40]

Although the rules of evidence require the exclusion of some information that attorneys might wish to put before the jury, ignoring the potential effects of juror assumptions and speculations can introduce into the decisionmaking process some of the very distortions that the rules of evidence seek to avoid. Thus, jurors may erroneously assume that one of the parties in a trial is insured, or they may mistakenly believe that they understand how interrogatories will be used.[41] If they are incorrect in their assumptions, a wild card is introduced into the decisionmaking process, leaving the court with no opportunity to influence the way the jury uses that misinformation. Judge Schwarzer has argued that the courts should "level" with jurors as much as possible. As an example of what can happen when jurors are misinformed, he describes what a juror told him after an antitrust case in which the court, following the recent trend, did not tell the jurors that their damage award would automatically be tripled under the antitrust statute. The juror had heard from his law student daughter that the jury's damage award would be quadrupled, not tripled, by the court.[42] Because the court never mentioned the tripling provision to the jury, the court lost the opportunity to describe it accurately, explain its purposes, and provide guidance on how that information was to be treated.

A recent simulation by Jonathan Casper and I tested the effects of providing jurors with various types of information about trebling in an antitrust price-fixing case.[43] The results indicated that a simple instruction and admonition will not suffice to inform jurors about automatic trebling and at the same time induce them not to drop their award to avoid a plaintiff windfall. Jurors who were also told about the reasons for the statutory trebling provision, however, gave awards that were almost identical to the awards given by jurors who had no knowledge or misinformation about the trebling provision. Thus, treating the jurors as collaborators rather than as passive receivers avoided the possibility that uncontrolled sources of information could infect the decisionmaking process and provided a means of inducing the jurors not to subvert the intent of the statute.

How shall we know when jurors are concerned about the nature of the evidence they receive? Although research can uncover some of the recurring issues and experiment with methods of control, many issues will be case specific. One potential way to detect juror concerns that need to be addressed is to allow jurors to submit questions during the trial. Heuer and Penrod have shown, in a study of civil and criminal jury trials, that allowing jurors to ask questions produces none of the disruptions that some critics predicted would occur if questions were permitted.[44] In the thirty-three trials in which questions were permitted, jurors submitted eighty-eight questions to the judge (2.7 per trial). Fifteen of the questions were objected to by one of the parties; the remainder were asked. The result was that these jurors were more satisfied with the questioning of the witnesses, less inclined to feel that witnesses needed more thorough questioning, and more satisfied that the jury had received sufficient information to reach a responsible verdict than jurors who were not allowed to ask questions. Although the study did not find that jurors assigned to trials in which questions were permitted had less difficulty reaching verdicts or were more satisfied with the trial itself, it appears that allowing questions did offer a reasonable way to monitor their concerns. Jurors, it seems, generally favor the idea.[45]

EXPERTS. Experts appear as witnesses in a growing number of trials involving a wide variety of issues, including antitrust violations, trademark infringements, deceptive advertising, race and gender discrimination in employment, medical malpractice, and products liability.[46] One concern raised about expert testimony in jury trials is whether jurors, impressed by an expert's credentials, will uncritically accept or give too much weight to the expert's message. Do jurors ascribe, as one court has suggested, a "mystical infallibility" to scientific evidence?[47]

In examining juror reaction to expert testimony, it is worth remembering Richard Lempert's admonition that any assessments of jury performance should be informed by comparisons with judicial performance.[48] While little systematic evidence is available on judicial reactions to expert testimony, some of what does exist raises the same concerns that are raised about jury reactions.[49] Moreover, as work by Bermant and his colleagues has shown, attorneys tend to present more complex evidence when a judge rather than a jury is the factfinder; thus, jurors may face a less difficult task than the lone judge.[50] Faced with technical and scientific testimony, judges as well as jurors are generally novices.

Juror surveys reveal that jurors generally find expert testimony useful. Two-thirds of the criminal court jurors in the Grisham-Lawless survey said that expert testimony usually or always helped them reach a decision.[51] And nearly three-fourths of the jurors in the Tsongas survey agreed that the testimony of expert witnesses helped them understand the facts.[52] Since experts are permitted to testify only if the court finds they are in a position to assist the trier of fact, these survey responses do not indicate whether jurors are inordinately receptive to expert testimony. Some additional data, however, provide evidence that jurors anticipate that expert testimony will have to be closely scrutinized, since impartial testimony cannot be expected from a "hired gun" put on the stand by a party in the case.

In our antitrust study, the jurors heard testimony from two experts, one testifying for the plaintiff and one for the defendant. Before the simulated trial, however, the jurors answered some background questions, including items that assessed their expectations about expert testimony. The jurors on average anticipated that the experts would be competent, but also expected them to be somewhat biased, giving testimony that would favor the side that paid them.[53] These expectations were significant predictors of juror reactions to the experts in the case. Those who anticipated greater competence from the experts gave higher ratings of expertise to both experts (r = .20 and r = .15, p < .001). Similarly, jurors who expected most experts to favor the side that paid them tended to rate both experts in the case as less trustworthy (r = .14 and r = .16, p < .001).

The jurors in our study also revealed a critical attitude when it came to evaluating the positions advocated by the experts. The jurors were asked to determine the damages caused by a price-fixing conspiracy. They were told that an earlier trial had found the defendants liable for price fixing and that the jury's task in this case was to decide on damages. The two experts who presented damage estimates provided the central testimony in the case, and the jurors had to decide how to weigh that testimony. One expert presented a complex statistical model based on the past pricing experienced by the plaintiff, while the other expert presented a more homely and concrete damage model based on a comparison of prices experienced by another company in a market not affected by price fixing.

Half the jurors heard the plaintiff's expert present the statistical model and the defense expert present the concrete model. For the remaining jurors, the damage models were reversed: the plaintiff's expert presented the concrete model and the defense expert presented the statistical model. If the complex statistical model had overwhelmed the jurors, as Lawrence Tribe might have predicted,[54] we would have found higher awards when the plaintiff's expert presented the statistical model. Instead, we found no difference and this result apparently occurred because jurors were influenced by both the perceived expertise and the clarity of the statistical expert. The statistical expert was rated higher on expertise but lower on clarity. The expert's perceived lack of clarity, rather than impressing and overwhelming the jurors, made them less likely to find his testimony persuasive.[55]

On the assumption that the adversary process distorts the expert testimony presented at trial,[56] some have advocated the use of court-appointed experts to alleviate the pressures that are believed to produce distortion.[57] Concern has been expressed, however, that jurors who are appropriately skeptical of expert testimony presented in an adversarial context might uncritically accept the testimony of a court-appointed expert.[58] Empirical research examining jury reaction to court-appointed experts is sparse, but recent work by Nancy Brekke and her colleagues finds that jurors may attend less to testimony given by a nonadversarial expert than to testimony given by an adversarial expert; no evidence suggests that jurors give greater weight to nonadversarial expert testimony.[59]

Complex and difficult testimony taxes any decisionmaker, and it is not clear that juries face a unique challenge in deciding how to weigh expert testimony. In some important respects, however, experts do have special qualities that jurors may not recognize. For example, only experts are regularly permitted to express their opinions under the rules of evidence, and this latitude dramatically affects their presentations. Nonetheless, researchers have not assessed whether jurors approach the testimony of experts differently than they do the testimony of other witnesses. Attorneys generally remind jurors that experts are paid to testify, but no researcher has investigated the impact of such reminders on jurors' evaluations of expert testimony. Finally, although jury researchers have conducted a number of studies testing juror reactions to expert testimony, no specific attention has been given to ways of enhancing the critical skills of jurors in assessing it. With the increasing use of experts in civil litigation, we need to learn more about assisting the jury in evaluating such testimony.

EXHIBITS. Jurors report that the exhibits commonly used in civil trials are often very useful. Eighty-three percent of the jurors surveyed in the Pound study said that an exhibit helped them to reach a decision. Three-quarters of those who reported having some exhibits in the jury room said that at least one was important.[60] In the Federal Judicial Center's study of jurors in protracted trials, 11 percent of the jurors who were asked how the attorneys could make a similar case easier to understand suggested using more visual aids.[61]

A jury can, however, be left adrift in a sea of exhibits if too many are used, their significance is not clearly explained, or they are not organized so the jurors can make use of them. In one of the complex cases studied by the Litigation Section of the American Bar Association, jurors were faced with 291 mostly undated exhibits randomly placed in boxes, with no indication as to author or intended recipient. After struggling to locate and identify documents, the jurors became exasperated and in the end made very little use of the exhibits.[62] If attorney discretion cannot be relied upon to keep the flow of paper to a manageable level, it is up to the judge to step in. Suggestions for the future of the civil jury, at least in long and complex trials, should include finding acceptable ways for judges to ensure that exhibits given to jurors are reasonably organized and that the volume of paper sent back to the jury room is not excessive.

Judicial Instructions and Guidance on Standards

A telling inconsistency emerges from jury surveys in which jurors are asked about judicial instructions. Jurors in one survey were asked to indicate whether they had understood most of the law in the judge's charge, part of it, or not very much of it. Eighty-seven percent said they had understood most of it, while less than 1 percent said they did not understand much of it.[63] Similarly, in a second survey, 81 percent of the jurors agreed that they found the judge's instructions easy to understand.[64] Even in protracted civil trials in which the instructions are likely to be most taxing, 70 percent of jurors rated the instructions they received as easy to understand.[65] Yet when the jurors in one of these same surveys were asked about the understanding of their *fellow* jurors, 45 percent indicated that they thought fellow jurors did not understand the instructions.[66]

Respondents in surveys typically report more socially desirable characteristics about themselves than they do about others, but particular aspects of the jury experience may amplify the gap between jurors' self-reported understanding and their perceptions of understanding by others. Judicial instructions contain a mixture of unfamiliar legal concepts (such as proximate cause) and apparently familiar words that take on special meanings in a legal context (such as consideration). Even jurors who realize they are having difficulty understanding the meaning of the unfamiliar phrases may nonetheless be unaware that they are confused about the familiar words. During deliberations, jurors have an opportunity to learn how others have interpreted the instructions; if there is a disagreement, a juror may conclude that the other jurors are the ones who have misunderstood.

The extensive literature on juror comprehension of instructions reveals that jurors do indeed have difficulty understanding many of the instructions in current use.[67] In many cases, the difficulty appears to lie not in conceptual barriers to understanding but in the way the instructions are written. Efforts to revise and clarify instructions to make them more comprehensible appear to hold some promise for reducing juror confusion.[68] A few states have systematically modified their jury instructions in response to concerns about comprehensibility (for example, Pennsylvania, Alaska, Arizona, Florida). Moreover, a recent decision by the California Supreme Court suggests that some courts may be receptive to challenges that confusing legal terminology can have a prejudicial effect on the rights of litigation. The court disapproved the traditional California Pattern Jury Instruction on proximate cause[69] commonly used in cases of negligence to specify the causal connection that must be shown between the defendant's action and a plaintiff's injury. The court reached its decision based in part on evidence that the instruction was confusing to jurors. Relying on the 1979 research by Robert P. Charrow and Veda R. Charrow, the court concluded that the instruction was grammatically confusing and conceptually misleading and banned its further use in favor of a clearer "substantial factor" instruction.[70]

Much of the previous work on jury instructions has focused on concepts used in criminal proceedings, so that little research is available on the comprehensibility of civil jury instructions. Even if courts are receptive to efforts aimed at improving juror comprehension of instructions, reform will require developing empirical evidence that shows not only how well jurors understand current instructions but how changes will enhance that comprehension.

Complex and unfamiliar language, awkward linguistic structure, and convoluted sentences are not the only aspects of instructions that seem designed to defeat the most diligent juror. In many jurisdictions, jurors retire to the jury room without a written copy of what the judge has told them about the law they are expected to apply. Surveys indicate that jurors given written copies of instructions find them very useful,[71] although in their experimental work on the impact of written instructions, Larry Heuer and Steven Penrod found that written instructions had no effect on either juror satisfaction or performance.[72] Since the primary objection to written instructions is logistic,[73] and judges willing to try giving jurors a written copy of the charge have found it feasible, this low-cost mechanism for offering assistance to the jury deserves consideration.

A more controversial effort to aid the jury involves preinstruction, or instructing the jury on the law prior to as well as after the evidence is presented. Although the jurors studied by Heuer and Penrod appeared to like preinstruction, and judges expressed less surprise at jury verdicts when it was used,[74] Reid Hastie has suggested that the potential virtues of preinstruction are also potential dangers.[75] By giving the jurors a legal framework for the evidence, preinstruction may induce jurors prematurely to decide the case and engage in a hypothesis-confirming search.[76] To ensure that preinstruction does not impair some aspects of jury functioning in the course of facilitating others, research is needed specifically to assess its effects on the timing of judgments and the resistance of those judgments to countervailing evidence introduced late in the trial.[77]

In civil cases, jurors report that determining damages is more difficult for them than is deciding on liability. They find the guidance that is given to them on how to compute damages to be minimal and agree with legal analysts that the law itself provides precious little guidance for assessing damages.[78] Here the jurors are pointing not to a potential instruction problem, but to a possible legal problem. Because of the absence of legal standards in this area, providing jurors with further guidance would require legal changes rather than just adjustments in jury instructions. One reason the law may be unclear, of course, is that it is difficult to identify appropriate standards for such damages as "pain and suffering" or "loss of consortium" that will be applicable across cases (or indeed in any particular case). With no realistic external standard, it may be appropriate to ask a group of laypersons to place monetary value on these intangibles.

Thus, although jurors generally express satisfaction with the judicial instructions they are given, their performance indicates that instructions often fail to guide the jury. There is room for improvement as well as the need for research to guide changes.

Deliberations

The conventional wisdom from research on the jury in criminal cases is that deliberations have little impact on outcomes and that the majority viewpoint before deliberations begin generally becomes the jury's verdict.[79] Recent research on the civil jury suggests that deliberations may play a more important role in civil litigation. Thirty percent of jurors questioned in the Pound survey, for example, reported that the verdict reached by the jury was not the one favored by a majority at the start of deliberations.[80] Deliberations may play a larger role in civil cases in part because a variety of viewpoints and extensive avenues for compromise are available when damages are involved; an initial majority may exist only on the issue of liability.[81]

Jurors questioned about deliberations generally report that their fellow jurors were extremely conscientious,[82] and helped them to remember what occurred during the trial. Simulation studies find the same patterns. For example, Phoebe Ellsworth found that mistakes in factual statements tended to be corrected during deliberations and that jurors who deliberated performed better on comprehension measures than those who did not.[83] Moreover, although a foreperson is selected quickly and apparently casually, this selection is not random. There is some evidence that, in addition to preferring males with managerial or professional backgrounds, jurors select colleagues whose skills mesh with case characteristics or volunteer themselves if they have the attributes. For example, if a juror has taken a statistics course he or she had an increased likelihood of being chosen as foreperson in a price-fixing case that required the jury to set damages based in part on statistical evidence.[84]

If jurors are satisfied with deliberations and with each other, that does not mean that deliberations are easy or always harmonious. In particular, there is usually some ambiguity about how to organize matters at the beginning of deliberations. Some juries begin by discussing the evidence; others take an initial straw vote, either open or secret. Hastie and his colleagues called the first type of jury "evidence-driven" and the second type "verdict-driven."[85] They found that discussion was more thorough in evidence-driven juries; as a result, some have suggested that juries be encouraged to discuss the evidence before taking any votes.[86] Although the suggestion is plausible, the Hastie juries chose their own method of deliberation. Before recommending that courts impose delays in voting, it would be advisable to see the results of experimental research that gauge jury response to an assigned method of deliberation. The more general point is that, if deliberations generally end up producing full debate, we should be hesitant about recommending directives on how deliberations should be structured.

Facilitating Jury Performance and Enhancing the Benefits of Jury Service

From the juror's point of view, the civil jury is functioning well. The positive response of trial jurors is most clearly revealed in a study by the Federal Judicial Center that questioned jurors who served in trials lasting more than twenty days. Willingness to serve again was high: 85 percent who served in long trials (compared with 93 percent who served in short trials) said they would be willing to serve again.[87] And even a majority of those not selected for a trial leave jury service with a favorable view. Yet there is still room—and opportunity—for improvement.

A Collaborative Approach

While jurors come away from jury service generally pleased with the experience and impressed by the jury system, they also report sources of dissatisfaction and frustration. Juror surveys reveal that there is a pattern to juror criticism. First, jurors are dissatisfied when they do not feel they are being treated with respect. Thus, higher rates of dissatisfaction are not associated with the actual length of the trial; they emerge when a trial lasts much longer than expected.[88] Although the jury is asked to make the ultimate decision, jurors themselves are often treated as passive and compliant subjects who need only absorb the evidence and law presented in the courtroom and produce a verdict. When they are given no explanations for their treatment and no warnings about what is to come, their dignity and sense of fairness suffer. And because jurors are not passive, they may search for and find inaccurate answers to their questions or develop legally unacceptable solutions.

A collaborative model for juror treatment can address most of these problems. Such a model acknowledges that jurors are active and responsive and views them as partners of the litigants, attorneys, and court personnel in the production of trial verdicts. Collaborating with the jurors means providing full disclosure when research indicates that doing so will not be detrimental, giving warnings and explanations when delays or exclusions are inevitable, and furnishing opportunities for jurors to voice their concerns. These strategies offer the promise of minimizing juror frustrations and maximizing juror performance.

An Educational Opportunity

Numerous studies have shown that most Americans lack basic knowledge about the workings of the judicial system.[89] Jury service provides an opportunity to at least partially improve this situation. De Tocqueville called the jury "one of the most effective means of popular education at society's disposal."[90] Moreover, it is an educational opportunity that currently touches a significant portion of the population as a growing number of citizens are called for jury duty. Some 45 percent of Americans aged eighteen and over say they have been called, up from 35 percent in 1984; 17 percent of adults say they have served as jurors through an entire trial.[91]

Jurors appear to agree that the jury experience provides an opportunity for learning. The majority (68 percent) of both trial and nontrial jurors surveyed by Consolini reported that they learned something positive or factual while on jury duty.[92] Although it is not clear precisely what jurors learn, they say they learn more about state and local courts from jury duty than from any other source. Citizens without jury experience report that the media is their major source of information.[93] Since television is one of the public's major sources of information about the courts, and fictionalized television accounts are often false, jury experience offers a powerful opportunity to correct misinformation.[94]

As we think about the future of the civil jury, we need to know what jurors learn about civil justice and the legal system in the course of their service. Armed with information about what the courts teach and fail to teach jurors, we can begin to identify the educational paths not yet taken.

Notes

1. See, for example, "Is the Jury Competent?" in Neil D. Vidmar, ed., *Law and Contemporary Problems*, vol. 52 (Autumn 1989); Audrey Chin and Mark A. Peterson, *Deep Pockets, Empty Pockets: Who Wins in Cook County Jury Trials* (Santa Monica: Rand Corporation, 1985); and George L. Priest, "The Role of the Civil Jury in a System of Private Litigation," *University of Chicago Legal Forum*, vol. 1990, pp. 161–200.

2. See, for example, Valerie P. Hans and M. David Ermann, "Responses to Corporate Versus Individual Wrongdoing," *Law and Human Behavior*, vol. 13 (June 1989), pp. 151–66; and Valerie P. Hans and William S. Lofquist, "Jurors' Judgments of Business Liability in Tort Cases: Implications for the Litigation Explosion Debate," *Law & Society Review*, vol. 26, no. 1 (1992), pp. 85–115.

3. For reviews of research on jury comprehension and performance, see Joe S. Cecil, Valerie P. Hans, and Elizabeth C. Wiggins, "Citizen Comprehension of Difficult Issues: Lessons from Civil Jury Trials," *American University Law Review*, vol. 40 (Winter 1991), pp. 727–74; and Robert J. MacCoun, *Getting Inside the Black Box: Toward a Better Understanding of Civil Jury Behavior* (Santa Monica: Rand Corporation, 1987).

4. See Shari S. Diamond, "Order in the Court: Consistency in Criminal-Court Decisions," in C. James Scheirer and Barbara L. Hammonds, eds., *Psychology and the Law: The Master Lecture Series*, vol. 2 (Washington: American Psychological Association, 1983), pp. 123–46. Table 1 presents examples of interjudge inconsistency in complex human judgments for a variety of judgment tasks ranging from physical diagnosis by physicians to the evaluation of job applicants by interviewers.

5. Herbert Jacob, *Justice in America: Courts, Lawyers, and the Judicial Process* (Little, Brown, 1965), p. 157. See also Theodore L. Becker. *Comparative Judicial Politics: The Political Functioning of Courts* (Rand McNally, 1970), pp. 320–26. Becker discusses evidence for the frequently presented propositions that "jury service, as a method of direct citizen participation in the governmental process, engenders a sense of efficacy among the citizenry," (the efficacy hypothesis) and that "when a case is controversial the citizenry is more likely to accept the verdict of a jury than of a judge alone" (the legitimacy hypothesis). Becker finds little convincing evidence for or against the efficacy hypothesis and only slight support for the legitimacy hypothesis.

6. Jurors selected for a trial serve until the trial ends. David E. Kasunic, "One Day/ One Trial: A Major Improvement in the Jury System," *Judicature* vol. 67 (August 1983), pp. 78–86.

7. See, for example, James P. Levine, *Juries and Politics* (Brooks/Cole, 1992).

8. Holly G. VanLeuven asked trial jurors if they felt apprehensive, duty-bound, positive, neutral, or negative when they first received a summons for jury duty. Forty-

four percent said they were apprehensive. VanLeuven, "In Decision: An Analysis of Some Social Dynamics in the Decision-Making Process of the Jury," unpublished manuscript, 1975.

9. John P. Richert, "Jurors' Attitudes toward Jury Service," *The Justice System Journal*, vol. 2 (Spring 1977), pp. 233–45.

10. William R. Pabst, Jr., G. Thomas Munsterman, and Chester H. Mount, "The Value of Jury Duty: Serving Is Believing," *Judicature*, vol. 61 (June–July 1977), pp. 38–42.

11. John Guinther, *The Jury in America* (Facts on File Publications, 1988), p. 305.

12. In two other studies jurors were asked at the end of jury duty if they had requested an excuse or asked to have their jury duty delayed. In Paula M. Consolini's study of jurors at three courts in California, 7 percent of the jurors said they had requested an excuse; an additional 32 percent said they had either asked for a delay or received one earlier. Consolini, "Learning by Doing Justice: Jury Service and Political Attitudes," Ph.D. dissertation, University of California, Berkeley, 1992. In a national survey of jurors in sixteen courts, Janet T. Munsterman and others found that 15 percent of jurors had asked to be excused, and an additional 20 percent had sought a deferral. Munsterman and others, *The Relationship of Juror Fees and Terms of Service to Jury System Performance* (Arlington, Va.: National Center for State Courts, March 1991), p. 29.

13. Richert, "Jurors' Attitudes," p. 244.

14. Munsterman and others, *Jury System Performance*, appendix C. The percentage of jurors agreeing varied from 72 percent to 90 percent. The percentage of jurors who said their impression of jury service improved varied from 58 percent to 86 percent. Caroline K. Simon found that jurors serving in civil court reported becoming more favorable to jury service, while jurors in criminal court showed no net change in their attitudes. Simon, "The Juror in New York City: Attitudes and Experiences," *American Bar Association Journal*, vol. 61 (February 1975), pp. 207–11. When William R. Pabst, Jr., G. Thomas Munsterman, and Chester H. Mount, asked jurors in twenty-eight state and federal courts, "After having served, what is your impression of jury duty?" more than two-thirds said they had either become more favorable or stayed favorable. Pabst, Munsterman, and Mount, "The Myth of the Unwilling Juror," *Judicature*, vol. 60 (November 1976), pp. 164–72.

15. James L. Allen, "Attitude Change Following Jury Duty," *Justice System Journal*, vol. 2 (Spring 1977), pp. 246–57.

16. Consolini, "Learning by Doing Justice," p. 155, table 5.4.

17. Joyce E. Tsongas, Barry F. Anderson, and Arthur D. Monson, "The Ninth Circuit Courts: A View from the Jury Box," unpublished manuscript, 1986.

18. Austin Sarat, "Studying American Legal Culture: An Assessment of Survey Evidence," *Law & Society Review*, vol. 11 (Winter 1977), pp. 427–88; especially p. 439.

19. Six percent of those in one survey (13 percent of those who reported some court experience) said they had served as jurors. The report does not indicate how the jurors felt about the need for court reform, but among those with court experience, jurors were least likely to report an unfavorable reaction to their court experience. Theodore J. Fetter, ed., *State Courts: A Blueprint for the Future* (Williamsburg, Va.: National Center for State Courts, 1978), p. 24, table II.3.

20. See, for example, Ellen W. Egger, "Jurors Also Serve, but Mostly They Sit and Wait," *Washington Post*, Sept. 19, 1985, p. DC2.

21. Munsterman and others, *Jury System Performance*, p. D-6.

22. Ibid., pp. 28–37, especially pp. 30–31. This index gauged juror reaction to the manner in which the court processed jurors between arrival and going to court, as well as to the processes of selecting jurors to serve on a particular case and determining which days the juror would be called in to appear.

23. Ibid., p. 35.

24. Kurt Lewin, "Studies in Group Decision," in Dorwin Cartwright and Alvin Zander, eds., *Group Dynamics: Research and Theory* (Evanston, Ill.: Row, Peterson and Co., 1953), pp. 287–301.

25. See, for example, Edward E. Lawler III and J. Richard Hackman, "Impact of Employee Participation in the Development of Pay Incentive Plans: A Field Experiment," *Journal of Applied Psychology*, vol. 53, no. 6 (1969), pp. 467–71.

26. In a study of the effects of voir dire on jury decisions, jurors who were excused as a result of peremptory challenge were retained to constitute a shadow jury. These alternate jurors consistently referred to themselves as the rejects and expressed the view that they had "failed" voir dire. This experiment is reported in Hans Zeisel and Shari Seidman Diamond, "The Effect of Peremptory Challenges on Jury and Verdict: An Experiment in a Federal District Court," *Stanford Law Review*, vol. 30 (February 1978), pp. 491–531.

27. Dale W. Broeder, "Voir Dire Examinations: An Empirical Study," *Southern California Law Review*, vol. 38, no. 4 (1965), pp. 503–28.

28. Some courts take a similar view and have introduced pre-trial questionnaires designed to reduce the number of questions that must be asked during voir dire.

29. Tsongas and others, "The Ninth Circuit Courts," p. 16.

30. But note that there is also evidence that jurors are less inclined to disclose to the higher-status judges than they are to attorneys. Thus, the experience of being questioned by an attorney may be less threatening to jurors. Susan E. Jones, "Judge- Versus Attorney-Conducted Voir Dire: An Empirical Investigation of Juror Candor," *Law and Human Behavior*, vol. 11 (June 1987), pp. 131–46.

31. Consolini, "Learning by Doing Justice," p. 256.

32. Thomas L. Grisham and Stephen F. Lawless found that 6 percent of potential jurors said the questions asked by the attorneys were too personal; 11 percent said they were not personal enough (p. 354). Grisham and Lawless, "Jurors Judge Justice: A Survey of Criminal Jurors," *New Mexico Law Review*, vol. 3 (May 1973), pp. 352–63.

33. It is unclear whether jurors respond similarly to voir dire in civil and criminal cases. The Consolini and Grisham-Lawless surveys questioned jurors who served in criminal cases. In the Tsongas survey, 40 percent of the jurors had served only in civil cases, but the study did not report whether juror evaluations differed by type of case.

34. See, for example, Joe S. Cecil, E. Allan Lind, and Gordon Bermant, *Jury Service in Lengthy Civil Trials* (Washington: Federal Judicial Center, 1987), pp. 30–31; and Guinther, *Jury in America*, p. 313.

35. *Landis* v. *North American Co.*, 299 US 248, 254 (1936).

36. Nancy Pennington and Reid Hastie, "Explanation-based Decision Making: Effects of Memory Structure on Judgment," *Journal of Experimental Psychology: Learning, Memory, and Cognition*, vol. 14 (July 1988), pp. 521–33.

37. Reid Hastie, Steven D. Penrod, and Nancy Pennington, *Inside the Jury* (Harvard University Press, 1983); and Nancy Pennington and Reid Hastie, "Evidence Evaluation in Complex Decision Making," *Journal of Personality and Social Psychology*, vol. 51 (August 1986), pp. 242–58.

38. See Shari Seidman Diamond, Jonathan D. Casper, and Lynne Ostergren, "Blind-folding the Jury: Is the Jury Competent?" *Law and Contemporary Problems*, vol. 52 (Autumn 1989), pp. 247–67.

39. Guinther, *Jury in America*, p. 313.

40. Grisham and Lawless, "Jurors Judge Justice," p. 356.

41. According to Guinther, 54 percent of the jurors said they thought that the defendant carried insurance; 60 percent of the jurors who sat on a jury that awarded damages to the plaintiff said they discussed whether some of the plaintiff's losses were already covered by

insurance; and 95 percent of jurors on cases that used interrogatories said they understood how their answers would be used. Guinther, *Jury in America*, pp. 299, 330, and 324 respectively.

42. William W Schwarzer, "Reforming Jury Trials," *University of Chicago Legal Forum*, vol. 1990 (1990), pp. 119–46, especially p. 134. See also chapter 12 in this volume.

43. See Shari Seidman Diamond and Jonathan D. Casper, "Blindfolding the Jury to Verdict Consequences: Damages, Experts, and the Civil Jury," *Law & Society Review*, vol. 26, no. 3 (1992), pp. 513–63.

44. Larry Heuer and Steven Penrod, "Increasing Jurors' Participation in Trials: A Field Experiment with Jury Notetaking and Question Asking," *Law and Human Behavior*, vol. 12 (September 1988), pp. 231–61.

45. Guinther found that 80 percent of the jurors said they would have liked to question some of the witnesses themselves, either directly or by having the judge ask the questions for them. Guinther, *Jury in America*, p. 310.

46. Neil Vidmar, "Assessing the Impact of Statistical Evidence, A Social Science Perspective," in Stephen E. Fienberg, ed., *The Evolving Role of Statistical Assessments as Evidence in the Courts* (Springer-Verlag, 1989), pp. 279–319; and Michael J. Saks and Richard Van Duizend, *The Use of Scientific Evidence in Litigation*, (Williamsburg, Va.: National Center for State Courts, 1983).

47. *U.S.* v. *Addison*, 498 F.2d 741, 744 (D.C. Cir. 1974).

48. Richard O. Lempert, "Civil Juries and Complex Cases: Let's Not Rush to Judgment," *Michigan Law Review*, vol. 80 (November 1981), pp. 68–132.

49. See Vidmar, "Assessing the Impact of Statistical Evidence," p. 300.

50. Gordon Bermant and others, *Protracted Civil Trials: View From the Bench and Bar* (Washington: Federal Judicial Center, 1981).

51. Grisham and Lawless, "Jurors Judge Justice," p. 358.

52. Tsongas and others, "The Ninth Circuit Courts," p. 19.

53. 4.55 on a 7-point scale on which 1 = strongly agree most expert witnesses in court cases are highly competent and 7 = strongly disagree, and 3.08 on a 7-point scale on which 1 = strongly agree that most expert witnesses in court cases will give testimony that favors the side that paid them to come to court. Diamond and Casper, "Blindfolding the Jury to Verdict Consequences."

54. Laurence H. Tribe, "Trial by Mathematics: Precision and Ritual in the Legal Process," *Harvard Law Review*, vol. 84 (April 1971), pp. 1329–93.

55. The Special Committee on Jury Comprehension of the American Bar Association's Section of Litigation studied four complex cases, observing the alternates deliberate and interviewing the trial jurors, attorneys, and the judge. The authors of the Committee Report concluded that jurors were not unduly influenced by the expert testimony presented in these cases. In one case, the jurors rejected the testimony of an expert they found confusing; one of the attorneys confessed that he was also unable to follow this expert's testimony (p. 41). See Chairman Daniel H. Margolis and others, *Jury Comprehension in Complex Cases: Report of the Special Committee of the ABA Section on Litigation* (Chicago: The Committee, 1990).

56. See, for example, Michael J. Saks and Roselle L. Wissler, "Legal and Psychological Bases of Expert Testimony: Surveys of the Law and of Jurors," *Behavioral Sciences and the Law*, vol. 2 (Fall 1984), pp. 435–49.

57. See, for example, Theodore I. Botter, "The Court-Appointed Impartial Expert," in Melvin D. Kraft, ed., *Using Experts in Civil Cases* (Practicing Law Institute, 1977), pp. 53–85.

58. Lacking the adversarial signal that systematic processing is required, jurors might assume that the court-appointed expert's conclusions can be trusted without detailed evaluation.

59. Nancy J. Brekke and others, "Of Juries and Court-Appointed Experts: The Impact of Nonadversarial versus Adversarial Expert Testimony," *Law and Human Behavior*, vol. 15 (October 1991), pp. 451–75.

60. Guinther, *Jury in America*, pp. 295, 302.

61. Market Facts, Inc., *Final Report of an Evaluation of Jurors' Trial Experience*, unpublished report to Federal Judicial Center, Washington, 1981.

62. ABA Litigation Section, *Jury Comprehension in Complex Cases*, p. 31.

63. Guinther, *Jury in America*, p. 296.

64. Tsongas, Anderson, and Monson, "The Ninth Circuit Courts," p. 9.

65. Market Facts, Inc., *Evaluation of Jurors' Trial Experience*, table 17. In contrast, 90 percent of the jurors in short trials said the instructions were easy to understand.

66. Tsongas, Anderson, and Monson, "The Ninth Circuit Courts," p. 9.

67. See, for example, Amiram Elwork, Bruce D. Sales, and James J. Alfini, "Juridic Decisions: In Ignorance of the Law or in Light of It?" *Law and Human Behavior*, vol. 1, no. 2 (1977), pp. 163–89. Alan Raifman, Spencer M. Gusick, and Phoebe C. Ellsworth, "Real Jurors' Understanding of the Law in Real Cases," *Law and Human Behavior*, vol. 16 (December 1992), pp. 539–54; and Joseph O'Mara and Rolf von Eckartsberg, "Proposed Standard Jury Instructions—Evaluation of Usage and Understanding," *Pennsylvania Bar Association Quarterly*, vol. 48 (October 1977), pp. 542–56.

68. See, for instance, Lawrence J. Severance and Elizabeth F. Loftus, "Improving the Ability of Jurors to Comprehend and Apply Criminal Jury Instructions, *Law & Society Review*, vol. 17, no. 1 (1982), pp. 153–97; and Robert P. Charrow and Veda R. Charrow, "Making Legal Language Understandable: A Psycholinguistic Study of Jury Instructions," *Columbia Law Review*, vol. 79 (November 1979), pp. 1306–1374.

69. *Mitchell* v. *Gonzales*, 819 P.2d 872 (Ca. 1991) Proximate cause is variously interpreted as meaning cause-in-fact.

70. That is, whether the defendant's conduct was a substantial factor in bringing about the injury. Note that "legal cause" was rejected as an alternative based on evidence from the Charrow and Charrow study that a number of jurors would interpret it as meaning the opposite of an "illegal cause."

71. See, for example, Market Facts, Inc., *Evaluation of Jurors' Trial Experience*, p. 30. Ninety-eight percent of the jurors who received written copies of the instructions said they were helpful; 73 percent said they were very helpful; 76 percent of the jurors agreed that judges should always give jurors written instructions to use during deliberation. Tsongas, Anderson, and Monson, "The Ninth Circuit Courts," p. 9.

72. Note, however, that the performance measure may not have been sensitive to the advantages of a written instruction. The measure tested comprehension of general instructions, selected so that it could be used across different trials. See Larry Heuer and Steven D. Penrod, "Instructing Jurors: A Field Experiment with Written and Preliminary Instructions," *Law and Human Behavior*, vol. 13 (December 1989), pp. 409–30.

73. An additional objection occasionally raised is that jurors given a written copy of the instructions will focus on a part of the instruction as opposed to the entire instruction. See Leonard B. Sand and Steven Alan Reiss, "A Report on Seven Experiments Conducted by District Court Judges in the Second Circuit," *New York University Law Review*, vol. 60 (June 1985), pp. 423–97. No evidence has been found to support this contention, but no research has addressed this issue.

74. Heuer and Penrod, "Instructing Jurors," p. 426.

75. Reid Hastie, "Final Report to the National Institute for Law Enforcement and Criminal Justice," Northwestern University, 1983.

76. See, for example, Mark Snyder and William B. Swann, Jr., "Hypothesis Testing Processes in Social Interaction," *Journal of Personality and Social Psychology*, vol. 36 (November 1978), pp. 1202–12.

77. Work on preinstruction in criminal cases suggests that fears about overpowering preinstructions may be largely unfounded. Vicki L. Smith, "Prototypes in the Courtroom: Law Representations of Legal Concepts," *Journal of Personality and Social Psychology*, vol. 61 (December 1991), pp. 857–72. Smith found no effect of preinstruction on jurors' naive representations of crime categories.

78. Harry J. Kalven, Jr., "The Jury, The Law, and the Personal Injury Damage Award," *Ohio State Law Journal*, vol. 19, no. 1 (1958), pp. 158–78.

79. Harry Kalven, Jr., and Hans Zeisel, *The American Jury* (Little, Brown, 1966). For a discussion of social decision schemes that model this transformation process, see, for example, Garold Stasser, Norbert L. Kerr, and Robert M. Bray, "The Social Psychology of Jury Deliberations: Structure, Process, and Product," in Norbert L. Kerr and Robert M. Bray, eds., *The Psychology of the Courtroom* (Academic Press, 1982), pp. 221–56.

80. Guinther, *Jury in America*, p. 326.

81. Diamond and Casper, "Blindfolding the Jury to Verdict Consequences."

82. Tsongas and others, "The Ninth Circuit Jurors," p. 20. Some 82 percent rated fellow jurors as serious about serving as jurors, while 76 percent said they received help.

83. Phoebe C. Ellsworth, "Are Twelve Heads Better Than One?" *Law and Contemporary Problems*, vol. 52 (Autumn 1989), pp. 205–24.

84. Diamond and Casper, "Blindfolding the Jury to Verdict Consequences."

85. Hastie and others, *Inside the Jury*, pp. 163–64.

86. Guinther, *Jury in America*, p. 85.

87. This difference was not statistically significant. Cecil and others, *Jury Service in Lengthy Civil Trials*, p. 23.

88. Ibid., p. 25.

89. See, for example, Yankelovich, Skelly, and White, "Highlights of a National Survey of the General Public, Judges, Lawyers, and Community Leaders," in Theodore J. Fetter, ed., *State Courts: A Blueprint for the Future* (Williamsburg, Va.: National Center for State Courts, 1978), pp. 5–69.

90. *Democracy in America*, trans. George Lawrence (Doubleday, 1969), p. 275.

91. Research & Forecasts, Inc., "The Defense Research Institute's Report on Jury Service in the United States," unpublished manuscript, 1990.

92. Consolini, "Learning by Doing Justice," p. 123. Consolini found some increases in knowledge about due process principles among jurors who served in criminal court.

93. Thirteen percent of respondents with court experience obtained it from serving as a juror, while 8 percent of respondents with court experience said they learned most about court from their jury service. Thus 61 percent (8/13) of jurors reported that jury service was their most important source of information about courts. Fetter, *State Courts*, pp. 19, 21.

94. The new Courtroom Television Network, carried nationwide on cable, may also serve this function. It broadcasts substantial portions of actual trials, providing a new and potentially powerful educational source. Bill Carter, "TV in the Courtroom: 2 Plans to Capture Real Trials' Drama," *New York Times*, June 19, 1991, C11.

CHAPTER NINE

Mapping the Debate on Jury Reform

Peter H. Schuck

CONTROVERSY ABOUT THE civil jury is probably as old as the institution itself. The jury has changed in many ways since its beginnings. Remarkably, however, few of these changes have been structural.[1] Instead, it is the social functions and context of the jury that have changed. Functionally, the jury has moved from fact-reporting to factfinding; from deciding both the law and the facts to deciding only the facts; and from being utterly controlled by the judges to being relatively independent of them.[2] Contextually, it now operates in a milieu of declining institutional authority, sharpened social divisions, and more complex factual and normative disputes.

The contemporary debate over the jury is also one in which the ultimate prize is public opinion ("the thirteenth juror," as some have put it). Law's growing prominence and complexity, its penetration into the interstices of daily life, have galvanized public attention.[3] Articles about "hyperlexis," novel claims, soaring insurance rates, declining availability of coverage, overwhelming judicial caseloads, high legal costs, complex litigation, and interminable trials are common fare in the mass media. Some of this commentary is accurate; much of it is false or misleading.[4] At the center of the contending arguments, however, is the question of the jury's contribution to these conditions.

Calls to reform the jury abound. The proposals for change range from limiting or abolishing the jury to enhancing its authority, independence, and jurisdiction. Because advocates on both sides often argue from quite different factual and normative premises and do not always articulate

I wish to thank John Langbein, Judith Resnik, and Michael Saks for their comments on an earlier draft, and Bill Malley and Margo Schlanger for their assistance with citations.

these premises or understand their implications, the issue of reform has seldom been squarely joined in a way that crystallizes the right questions. At a minimum, a coherent debate over jury reform requires agreement on a precise definition of the problem so that relevant evidence can be adduced, sifted, and appraised.

A consensus on how to define the problem now seems more possible than ever before. Aided by more sophisticated theories about juries, researchers have gathered richer data on how they perform.[5] Legislatures have adopted a number of reform strategies, and some of these changes have been appraised. The rhetoric of crisis surrounding civil litigation generally and the tort system in particular has lent urgency, along with some risk of hyperbole and distortion, to the inquiry.

This chapter attempts to clarify the arguments for and against reform of the civil jury. I first distinguish four quite different ways of defining the "problem" posed by the civil jury: irrationality of jury decisions; the jury's undesirable effects on the behavior of others; the jury system's administrative costs, quite apart from the quality of its decisions; and the jury's effects on the overall structure of litigation. Because each of these problem definitions implies a different remedial approach, I turn in the next part to four principal strategies for jury reform: enhancing jury efficiency; restructuring the jury; constraining jury discretion; and diverting disputes to nonjury forums. For each strategy, I discuss a number of specific policy options. Finally, I speculate about the future of jury reform, concluding that the only proposals likely to find much support are quite modest, though certainly worth instituting.

Before turning to the analysis, I wish to underscore three points that must frame any discussion of jury performance. First, the importance of juries transcends the tiny proportion of civil disputes that they actually decide. In fiscal year 1991, for example, of the cases terminated in federal district courts by settlement, withdrawal, or conclusion, only 4 percent ever reached trial (a fraction that has declined over time). Of the 4 percent, 51 percent were tried to a jury. Thus, only 2 percent of civil cases go to juries.[6] In most state courts, jury trials comprise an even smaller share, although the lay public probably believes that jury trials are far more common.[7] In any event, the most significant function of juries is to shape the parties' predictions about what will happen *if* the case goes to trial. These predictions in turn drive the complex screening process that determines the mix of the cases that are initiated, the pattern of pre-trial settlements, and the mix of the cases that go to trial.[8]

The second point follows closely upon the first. The cases that do reach jury trial are the closest ones, those most nearly balanced on the facts and the law; hence they are the hardest cases for lawyers to predict and for juries to decide.[9] Michael Saks's recent description is highly pertinent to any discussion of jury performance:

> How would any rational decision-maker decide such cases? Answer: randomly. If the cases going to trial were so close as to be toss-ups, rational decisions about them would resemble coin tosses. Thus, seemingly random and unpredictable verdicts might merely reflect a highly effective filtering of cases through the settlement process, allowing only the insoluble, too-close-to-call cases to proceed to trial.[10]

Third, this chapter emphasizes the jury's role in *tort* cases. This orientation merits comment, for although the current public debate over the jury does indeed focus on its effect on the tort system, individual tort claims have not been increasing very rapidly in recent years. Instead, the fastest growing categories of litigation involve contract claims among businesses and real property disputes, some of which are also tried to juries.[11] My focus on how juries perform in tort cases begins to make more sense, however, when one considers that such cases constitute most of the relatively small number of civil jury trials.[12] But the linkage between tort litigation and the jury goes well beyond this fact. Tort cases and the jury both arouse populist sentiments and David-and-Goliath imagery in the public mind, and both instantiate a characteristically American individualistic ethos. Tort cases, moreover, often involve personal injuries of tragic dimensions; they tend to be more dramatic and evocative than most other disputes tried to juries. Finally, the protracted struggle over tort reform has political overtones that inevitably resonate in the controversy over the jury's role even though the issues in the two debates only partly overlap.

Defining the "Problem"

Objections to the use of juries fall into four major categories.

Jury Decisions Are Irrational

One type of objection to the jury is based on the claim that it tends to make irrational decisions. This irrationality could derive from systematic bias, from unsystematic errors, or from both.

SYSTEMATIC BIAS. It is often said, and many practicing lawyers and other commentators presume, that juries tend to be more sympathetic to the interests of some categories of litigants than to others.[13] The supposedly favored categories include seriously injured plaintiffs in tort cases and police officer defendants and witnesses.[14] In contrast, large corporations (especially those located in other states), governmental entities, insurance companies, and other "deep pockets" are thought to arouse little sympathy, or even to elicit hostility, from juries.[15] Another common assumption is that juries are more or less likely to believe witnesses who exhibit certain characteristics, such as self-confidence, even if those characteristics are not obviously correlated with credibility or legal justification.

We cannot readily determine the truth of these generalizations. We can begin, however, by distinguishing jury sympathy from systematic bias. Suppose that despite the efforts of defense counsel to screen out biased jurors during the voir dire, some jurors begin with a sympathy (perhaps natural or social in origin) for those who have suffered injuries severe enough to induce them to initiate litigation.[16] From these initial sympathies, however, it would not necessarily follow that jurors would render biased verdicts in favor of plaintiffs. Defendants' lawyers might succeed in neutralizing these initial sentiments by evoking countervailing sympathies for their clients. Judges' instructions emphasizing the importance of juror impartiality might have a similar effect. The jury's own deliberations over the evidence might mute any initial sympathies one way or the other. In short, we need to know how the ethos of the courtroom and the persuasiveness of arguments and evidence affect initial sympathies (assuming that they exist) and how these sympathies are then transformed into decisions.

Unfortunately, reliable data bearing on decision bias are hard to come by because the notion of bias is so difficult to define. Unless jurors identify themselves as biased, which is most unlikely given both the screening performed by the voir dire and people's perceptions of themselves as fair-minded, an accurate determination of bias depends on finding an objective standard for unbiased decisions to which the jury's decision can be compared. Because such a standard is elusive, no satisfactory solution to this problem seems likely.[17]

The most ambitious studies of jury bias have sought to address this problem by comparing the jury's decision to the judge's views of the same case.[18] This approach, of course, begs the question of whether judges have their own systematic biases. The answer is clearly yes. In terms of social status, wealth, political activity, peer group, professional training, socialization, and many other characteristics that surely affect one's attitudes toward the resolution of legal disputes, judges do not constitute a random sample of the population.[19] Judicial attitudes, then, are almost certainly different from those of juries. And although some of those attitudes may be conducive to rational decisions in legal disputes, they nevertheless qualify as biases under any intelligible definition of the term.

These judicial biases should be perhaps even more troubling than those that juries harbor. First, judicial biases are precisely the kind that the Framers appear to have had in mind when they adopted the Seventh Amendment guarantee of a jury trial in most civil cases.[20] Moreover, as Richard Lempert has argued, judges' systematic biases (because of which they may well have been appointed or elected) are more objectionable than juries' random biases, which will tend to negate each other over a series of cases or perhaps even over the group in a single case. Indeed, Lempert suggests that the jury may represent a "minimax" solution to the institutional problems posed by the great variation in the quality and impartiality of judges.[21]

Since judges also have biases, we lack any unbiased decisionmaker who could serve as the gold standard of rationality, a circumstance that might seem fatal to any attempt to assess the jury's performance objectively along this dimension. This conclusion, however, is somewhat palliated by the findings of a number of studies conducted over a long period of time suggesting that judges and juries would decide the same disputes the same way in a high percentage of the cases. More precisely, the percentage of cases on which they would agree compares quite favorably with the level of agreement observed among members of specialized professional decisionmaking groups who are presented with the same problem.[22] Perhaps even more striking in this regard is the finding in the classic study by Harry Kalven and Hanz Zeisel: in cases that juries and judges would have decided differently, there appeared to be no systematic biases that could account for those differences. Indeed, the study found that the decisionmakers in those cases were about equally likely to decide in favor of plaintiff or defendant.[23] Although the Kalven-Zeisel study has been criticized on a number of grounds, these findings are supported by other studies that suggest both that jury decisions are closely correlated with the strength of the evidence adduced in the cases and that jury awards are not excessive.[24]

Thus, although the conceptual and methodological difficulties inherent in defining and measuring systematic jury bias are formidable, the next best evidence—comparisons between outcomes in jury trials and in bench trials—indicates that whatever jury bias may exist is either shared by judges or somehow fails to affect jury decisions. The shared-bias hypothesis tends to be negated by the fact, noted above, that judges differ from juries in so many important respects. The possibility remains, however, that these jury-judge differences, while profound, either do not involve the kinds of attitudes that affect decisions in civil cases or cancel each other out.

This leaves us with the hypothesis that juries' biases, while perhaps different from judges' biases, still do not affect their decisions systematically. This interpretation, if correct, is even more striking when one considers the fact—explained by the "selection effect" theorists and stressed in the passage by Saks quoted earlier—that the cases that reach juries are likely to be the most evenly balanced. Since these cases are precisely the ones in which even a small amount of jury bias could tip the balance of decision in the direction of bias, the conclusion that the decisions are unaffected by systematic jury bias would seem to reveal an impressive degree of self-discipline on the part of jurors, a remarkably successful determination to subdue their own biases in the interests of fairness.

UNSYSTEMATIC ERRORS. Even if jurors do not favor one or another category of litigant, their decisions may nevertheless be irrational if those decisions are arbitrary and thus often inaccurate. Their irrationality, in short, could be more or less random rather than systematically biased.

A variety of reasons inherent in the jury's *process and structure* could contribute to irrational jury decisionmaking. Juries are not obliged to provide formal written or oral justifications for their decisions.[25] By being freed of any duty to rationalize their judgments—indeed of any duty to be accountable in any form—juries are deprived of constraints that in many other situations are thought to be conducive to fair, accurate decisions. Juries, moreover, are constituted on an ad hoc, one-time basis; thus they lack specialization, expertise, and experience, attributes that would enhance consistent decisionmaking. Perhaps most important, the law systematically denies them any information about decisions by other juries in prior cases. Hence they are guided neither by precedents (except to the extent that earlier decisions have crystallized into legal rules) nor by other information that could help them to treat like cases alike.

It would not be surprising if these features of the jury encouraged irrational decisions. In particular, we should expect that the ad hoc, one-time nature of their decisions would produce some variation among

312 / Peter H. Schuck

different juries deciding similar types of cases. Empirical evidence relating to jury awards of personal injury damages, especially for pain and suffering, tend to support this prediction, although not conclusively. A recent study of jury verdicts in Florida and Kansas City between 1973 and 1987 found, as one would hope, that severity of injury measured along a nine-level scale explained a substantial amount of the variation among awards—one index of rationality.[26] The authors assert, however, that the variations *within* each severity level were so large—a six-fold spread, for example, between the awards in the top and bottom quartiles of the "permanent significant" level—that the variations could not be explained by factors for which the authors could not control, such as how the injury occurred.[27] (On the other hand, it is not clear how the authors could support such an assertion about variables that they neither controlled for nor measured but that surely had *some* effect on awards.) A more recent study, still preliminary and unpublished, indicates even greater disparities in awards to seriously injured children.[28]

Issues concerning damages may indeed be the ones about which jury irrationality is most likely. A given jury—as distinct from a large number of juries over time—does not possess any special information or competence in assessing nonpecuniary damages. Ordinarily, this is an issue to which neither an appraisal of the plaintiff's character nor general community knowledge is particularly relevant. George Priest's analysis of jury cases in Chicago, which finds that juries spend a disproportionate amount of their time assessing the value of routine injuries, fortifies this point.[29] Assessment of damages, moreover, lends itself to systematic treatment based on the accumulation and analysis of objective data about injury costs and about awards in similar cases in the past. In England, where juries have been removed from the consideration of most personal injury cases, judges have adopted a number of techniques for facilitating such assessments.[30]

Critics often charge that juries are incompetent to decide some types of disputes. Juries' alleged incompetence arises from their lack of technical expertise (for example, in cases involving complex scientific evidence or business transactions), their susceptibility to cognitive errors (for example, overvaluation of eyewitness testimony or confusion about judges' instructions), or their unrepresentativeness (for example, as a result of their reduced size and the composition of the venire from which they are selected). For such critics the judge is usually the implicit or explicit standard of comparison, as with claims of systematic bias, but sometimes a reconstituted or specialized jury is the model.

Jury Decisions Affect Litigants' Behavior

Another major category of objections to the jury centers on how the jury affects the behavior of various participants in the legal process. These objections do not claim that juries are biased or prone to error, but rather that they emit liability signals that are inevitably confusing, inconsistent, arbitrary, and generally noisy. The jury's signals, in this view, convey little useful information about actual legal norms. Coupled with the unusually unregulated, generous system of damage awards, jury decisions generate widespread uncertainty, anxiety, and aversion to risk in those who must respond to them.[31]

Jury decisions affect the behavior of six groups of participants in the legal process, although in varying degrees. These groups include insurers; the media; primary actors (that is, people or organizations in general); trial lawyers (of whom insurance lawyers are of course an important subset); judges; and other policymakers.

INSURERS. One assumes that insurers, the real parties in interest in a significant proportion of civil cases, observe and analyze jury verdicts more obsessively and rigorously than any other group of legal actors. The reductions in the availability of liability insurance and the sharp rise in premiums that occurred during the mid-1980s constituted genuine crises at the time. In the face of uninsurable liability risks, many activities that were both socially valued and (in some cases) not notably dangerous were curtailed, abandoned, or transformed. Some activities that were seriously affected were medical care, product distribution, corporate directorships, activities that altered the environment, automobile driving, general aviation, pharmaceuticals, day care, after-school athletics, and local government programs.[32]

Although the availability and cost of insurance were undeniably affected, however, the true sources, nature, and consequences of the convulsions that produced these effects remain controversial.[33] One influential school of thought ascribes much of the responsibility to new legal uncertainties that have arisen because over-eager juries have applied principles of open-ended liability and damages elaborated by reform-minded courts. According to this view, these uncertainties made it increasingly difficult for insurers accurately to predict claims and losses, to define risk pools, and to establish efficient premium schedules.[34] This actuarial indeterminacy is surely compounded by the relatively small number of cases that go to trial and the even smaller number in which juries make awards.[35]

Insofar as this theory is based on the premise that juries have increased their awards dramatically during the period in question, the argument rests on uncertain data.[36] Other commentators offer different diagnoses that exculpate the jury. Some ascribe the changes in cost and availability to insurers' anti-competitive conduct.[37] Others attribute it to a distinctive insurance pricing cycle, perhaps reflecting the interaction of imprudent investment practices by insurers and swings in interest rates.[38] Although strong empirical evidence supports the former view, the more relevant point here is that even those who advance it place most of the blame on misguided courts, not on the juries that implement their principles.[39]

MEDIA. The mass media often report on jury verdicts, and these reports are perhaps the most important vehicles through which the general public gains information about jury decisionmaking. The media do not analyze meaningful samples of jury verdicts, of course; instead, they report on a small number of verdicts, and these verdicts are almost always either very large—for example, the recent $105 million verdict against General Motors that was front-page news[40]—or linked to important public figures or events. Because these media reports are highly selective and disproportionately involve large recoveries, they are bound to create in the public mind impressions that are misleading—and in one direction. This distortion is magnified by the fact that the media, having reported on a jury verdict, are not as likely to report on post-trial developments that substantially reduce the amount of these large recoveries. Yet such reductions are common, especially in libel actions and awards of punitive damages.[41]

PRIMARY ACTORS. What difference does it make to primary actors that a jury (as opposed to a judge or some other arbiter) will decide disputes that may arise out of their decisions somewhere down the road? The answer almost certainly is, not much. Although we lack data directly responsive to this question, we know that primary actors are influenced in their decisions by many factors: perceptions of costs and benefits, substantive law, psychological factors, and various other behavioral motives and constraints. We have seen, moreover, that the public's knowledge of jury decisionmaking is extremely fragmentary and that the fragments—the particular decisions on which the media happen to report—constitute a decidedly unrepresentative sample of the whole.

Also mediating between juries and the public is the insurance system. As we have seen, this system significantly affects decisions to undertake activity and to exercise care by setting premium levels and coverage limits. But those levels and limits, like the primary conduct that they shape, depend on much more than jury decisions. Compared with all of the other factors that influence actors' decisions, the marginal effect of juries on those decisions must be quite small.

TRIAL LAWYERS AND JUDGES. Like insurers, trial lawyers are a highly specialized audience for whom the pattern of jury decisions is a high-stakes issue. Their ability accurately to value claims for settlement determines the integrity of the claims settlement process, which in turn is essential to the integrity of the litigation process. One would therefore expect lawyers to attain a high degree of proficiency in predicting how juries will decide issues involving liability and damages.[42]

This expectation, however, may be false. Experimental evidence on lawyers' evaluations of the same case suggests, in Marc Galanter's words, "persistent and sizable variability and error."[43] Michael Saks agrees, pointing out that insurance claims adjustors vary widely in their valuations of the same case; that on average lawyers do not settle auto and plane crash cases for less than the successful trial awards, as the clairvoyant lawyer hypothesis would predict; that the few jury decisions that the lawyer sees comprise an inadequate data base for predicting how juries will decide any particular claim; and that even judges, who can base their predictions of jury decisions on a relatively large sample of observations, consistently err by a wide margin, predicting higher awards than juries actually render.[44]

Some of Saks's points are arguable. For example, lawyers' access to services reporting jury verdicts extends their data base beyond the cases that they personally try, although the data reported by the services are also deficient in important respects.[45] Furthermore, we should not necessarily expect tried cases to have higher values than settled ones; after all they are different populations of cases. Although settlement amounts are presumably discounted to reflect the higher costs and risks of going to trial, the tried cases (as Saks himself notes) are more closely balanced than the settled ones, and the uncertainty surrounding predictions affects the amount of the settlement. How lawyers resolve these conflicting effects remains unclear. Still, the data on judges' erroneous predictions are telling: if judges systematically misperceive jury decisions, perhaps we should not be surprised that lawyers are also prone to err.

If lawyers are poor at predicting juries' decisions, they may also predict judges' decisions incorrectly. Again, Galanter cites empirical evidence that this is true, and he suggests that lawyers' errors in this regard may be due to factors other than the jury's performance.[46] This possibility casts George Priest's recent analysis of the problem of delays of civil trials in Chicago in a somewhat different light. Priest claims that the jury impedes settlements by increasing the uncertainty of outcomes even in routine cases and that shifting such cases to judges would increase predictability and thus the rate of settlement.[47] But the rate of settlement is not simply a function of the objective certainty of judges' verdicts relative to that of juries' verdicts. The rate also reflects the relative accuracy with which lawyers perceive and predict both sets of verdicts, yet Priest presents no data on either of these factors. Thus, even if he is correct that judges' verdicts are more certain than juries' verdicts, lawyers' inaccurate predictions may well neutralize this theoretical advantage of bench trials. We cannot be certain how these two factors cut in practice and on balance. Finally, the assumption in Priest's settlement model that uncertainty of outcome always impedes settlement may be too broadly stated. Under some circumstances or within a range, uncertainty may actually *encourage* settlement.[48]

One can imagine some other ways in which jury decisions might affect the behavior of lawyers and judges. For example, Peter Huber argues that the critical consideration in assessing juries' effects on lawyers' settlement strategies in complex scientific disputes is the mean, rather than the median award. If even one outlier jury returns a large enough verdict, the mean may be much higher than the median; the Bendectin litigation is an example.[49] On the other hand, Huber does not explain why rational, profit-maximizing lawyers would stray so far from the expected return by making such an obvious statistical error. Another example is my speculation that juries' unexplained verdicts may, by diffusing accountability for the consequences of new rules of law, encourage judges to innovate.[50]

POLICYMAKERS. The discussion so far indicates that we know remarkably little about how the patterns of jury decisions actually affect the behavior of the various groups that the law seeks to influence. Perhaps more important, the discussion also suggests that much of what we *think* we know about this question may well be wrong, and further, that it may be impossible to devise a methodology that can improve our understanding of these matters very much.

This ignorance, however, has not prevented legislators and bureaucrats from adopting potentially far-reaching reforms based on the premise that jury decisions are irrational and perversely affect the participants in certain categories of disputes. Antijury reforms have been particularly conspicuous, of course, with respect to personal injury cases.[51] But such reforms have also been adopted for some types of contract and property disputes, for example, which arbitration and other nonjury techniques for resolving disputes are being encouraged or mandated.[52]

These critiques of the jury have an important but easily overlooked implication for policy. If the critiques are correct, then many reforms that seek to improve the rationality or behavioral effects of legal decisions may be futile unless they also exclude the jury from those decisions. If juries are indeed biased, error-prone, or magnify uncertainty, then doctrinal changes—those aimed at altering the legal standards that juries apply—are likely to be particularly feckless so long as those characteristics persist and the jury's decisionmaking process remains the black box that it is.

A final point about the interaction between juries and policymakers relates to the political cover that juries provide for courts. Michael Saks has observed that juries are often a lightning rod, attracting much of the criticism from politicians that might be directed at judges if judges rendered the factual verdicts instead of juries.[53] Stephen Yeazell makes a somewhat different but equally pertinent point—that jurors' temporary, nonofficial status makes them virtually exempt from criticism and therefore capable of facilitating legal changes that policymakers might not otherwise endorse.[54]

Jury Trials Are Expensive

The third major category of objections to the jury concerns not the intrinsic truth of its decisions or the effect of those decisions on the behavior of others, but the administrative costs imposed by the jury system. These include the costs to litigants of waiting for jury trial; the costs associated with the longer duration of jury trials; and the costs of recruiting, screening, selecting, and paying jurors, including the opportunity costs to the jurors themselves.[55] There may be additional categories of administrative costs. For example, if jury trials result in more appeals than bench trials (which seems unlikely since a judge's written decisions, explaining her reasons are easier to challenge than a jury's general, unexplained verdicts), the costs of additional appeals would also be relevant to an objection based on administrative cost.

In evaluating the jury's administrative efficiency, of course, the absolute magnitude of these costs is less important than the jury's *marginal* costs over and above those generated by some benchmark decisionmaker of acceptable administrative efficiency, presumably a judge. Data on these parameters would also need to control for the likelihood that the kinds of cases tried by juries are different from those tried by judges.

Although such data are lacking, the longer duration of jury trials probably does make them more costly. Still, it is hard to imagine that these marginal administrative costs of the jury system are large enough to affect significantly the debate over jury reform. Some of these costs have surely been reduced by the trends toward smaller juries and nonunanimous verdicts, although these changes have almost certainly produced costs of their own, especially greater variability of verdicts and perhaps (if Huber is correct about lawyers being too influenced by mean verdicts) also distortion of settlement decisions. Some of these costs, moreover, may plausibly generate offsetting benefits. For example, although Priest's analysis strongly suggests that the social value of civic education through jury service is greatly exaggerated, he does not suggest that it is zero. Jurors evidently find their own service rewarding.[56]

Juries Affect the Overall Structure of Litigation

A fourth way to define the "problem" posed by the civil jury constitutes what may be the most fundamental criticism of all. In this view, the jury's most far-reaching consequence relates to its implications for the deeper structure of litigation, particularly the structure of the trial and hence of the pre-trial activities of lawyers and adjudicators. This only constitutes an objection to the jury, of course, if one views the structure that it entails as problematic.

The comparative law scholar Arthur von Mehren has argued convincingly that the crucial divide between procedural systems is not, as is generally supposed, whether they are adversarial or inquisitorial. Instead, the decisive factor that shapes almost everything else about a system's procedure is whether its trials are continuous (concentrated) or discontinuous. The common law, von Mehren observes, "had to concentrate trials because of the jury. (Courts of equity, which did not utilize juries, did not require a concentrated trial.) The presence of a jury makes a discontinuous trial impractical."[57] But as von Mehren also points out, a concentrated trial in turn entails a number of other procedural elements: extensive pre-trial proceedings to minimize the problem of surprise; a high degree of lawyer control over the evidentiary and case-shaping processes; a related emphasis on party presentation and party prosecution; and a problem of delay at the pre-trial rather than at the trial stage.

Regardless of the nature of the trial, moreover, a jury affects litigation in other important respects. For example, it necessitates a relatively complex law of evidence and alters the way in which expert witnesses are used.

An analysis, like von Mehren's, that emphasizes—and criticizes— these momentous consequences of using a traditional jury is clearly important and deserves the most careful attention. But precisely because a jury's existence shapes the legal system fundamentally rather than marginally, the normative assumptions of such a critique are so basic and its implications so far-reaching that they can only be evaluated at a highly abstract level. Such an evaluation is far beyond the scope of this paper. In addition, there is little likelihood that the jury will be seriously altered, much less eliminated. Accordingly, my discussion of remedial alternatives will not deal with this option.

Finding a Remedy

The four types of objections to the civil jury—based on its putative irrationality, its behavioral effects, its administrative costs, and the litigation structure that it entails—are obviously quite different. Although some of these objections appear to be more persuasive than others, none of them seems clearly sustainable on the basis of the current data. Here, as elsewhere, one's conclusion about the need for reform may well depend on who one thinks should bear the burden of proof.

Whatever the resolution of this question, these very different critiques might be thought to imply a wide variety of remedial responses. I distinguish five discrete strategies. Moving from the most incremental to the most radical strategies, they are to: (a) improve jury comprehension; (b) reduce administrative costs; (c) restructure the jury; (d) constrain jury discretion; and (e) divert disputes to nonjury forums. I discuss a number of specific jury reforms that might be used to implement each of these strategies. Some of these specific reforms, of course, are consistent with more than one strategy.

Improve Jury Comprehension

The problem of jury misunderstanding of evidence, arguments, and instructions has received considerable attention from reformers. Since a number of the contributors to this volume have summarized the empirical evidence concerning jury misunderstanding and analyzed some possible reforms, I have nothing to add except to note that the effectiveness of many of the changes to the jury that I do consider below depends on a solution to this comprehension problem.[58]

Reduce Administrative Costs

Strategies aimed at reducing administrative costs would retain the jury's current functions and structure because of the social benefits that the jury confers and because of its political support, but they would seek to reduce the costs of operating the jury system. One option—directed not so much at reducing the magnitude of these costs as toward changing their distribution—is to raise the fees for parties who demand a jury. As Judge Posner has noted, existing fees for the use of the courts are trivial, far below the level necessary to cover the full net social costs and private benefits of even a bench trial, much less a jury trial.[59] If the fees were raised to cover a greater part of the net social costs and private benefits of a jury trial, the demand for both jury and bench trials would decline and settlements would become correspondingly more attractive. At the margin, moreover, jury trials would be demanded less often, and society would gain whatever administrative cost advantages attach to bench trials. Special provision should be made, however, to ensure that low-income disputants enjoy continued access to the courts.

Some reform proposals, primarily advanced as ways to improve jury comprehension, would also reduce the cost of jury trials by expediting them. These include techniques to streamline the voir dire, to present deposition evidence more efficiently, to impose time limits on the lawyers, and to narrow the issues before trial.

The critical question in evaluating reforms aimed at reducing administrative costs is the extent to which they can be instituted without also changing the substantive outcomes of cases by altering the balance of litigation advantage in ways that go beyond mere cost reduction. At the margin, of course, every cost change will affect the propensity to litigate (indeed, cheaper jury trials will encourage parties to demand more of them) and will also affect the parties differently. The fact that a reform might alter the balance of advantage need not be a decisive objection to it if there is no good reason to concede privilege to the procedural status quo. But such reforms should be justified, if at all, in terms of those advantages and disadvantages, and not on the supposedly neutral ground of cost reduction.

Restructure the Jury

Two features of the jury's current structure—size and composition—appear to impair jury rationality, to contribute to undesirable behavior by other participants in the legal process, and to affect administrative cost. (I do not discuss here a third feature, the degree of unanimity required, which interacts strongly with the size factor.) A restructuring strategy would seek to improve the jury's performance by altering its size, its composition, or both, without necessarily changing the questions that are put to it or the ways in which it operates.

Commentators have pointed out that the move to smaller civil juries has reduced their representativeness while increasing the likelihood of bias and other sources of irrational behavior. Smaller juries are generally thought to produce somewhat greater variability and thus unpredictability in their verdicts.[60] Some evidence shows that reduced size impairs juries' collective memory.[61] By impeding the settlement process, smaller juries have probably increased the number of trials and necessitated greater resort to remittitur and other techniques for controlling and modifying outlier jury verdicts, perhaps dissipating the administrative savings from reduced size.[62] An obvious response to these changes would be to increase the jury's size. This should not be accomplished by enshrining in the Seventh or Fourteenth amendments any particular number of jurors. Instead, it should result from a process of experimentation that better informs us about the relevant effects and trade-offs of jury panels of different sizes.

The jury's composition also affects the rationality of its decisions and the behavior of other actors. In addition to the likelihood that greater diversity among jurors increases the variability of decision outcomes, there is the irony noted by Paul Carrington: recent developments encouraging greater diversity and representativeness, including statutory requirements for more broadly based jury venires and growing judicial control of the voir dire, have occurred at precisely the time that other developments—the reduction in jury size, longer trials, new forms of evidence, and more complex litigation—have rendered representativeness both harder to achieve and more of a barrier to juries capable of rational decisions in certain kinds of cases.[63] This latter concern has led to controversial proposals to select juries in complex disputes from among individuals possessing special expertise in the relevant subject, and for judges to screen scientific testimony more rigorously before it goes to a jury.[64] The earlier discussion of the degree of agreement between decisions a jury would reach and those that judges and other more expert decisionmakers would reach is relevant to, albeit not dispositive of this controversy. Again, more experimentation will help us to understand fully the implications of such a change.

Constrain Jury Discretion

The next, more radical strategy moves beyond the kinds of procedural tinkering and structural changes that I have been discussing. It seeks instead (or in addition) to impose significant limitations on the jury's discretion in the hope of improving its rationality, providing clearer liability signals to others, and reducing administrative costs. These limitations may take at least four different forms.

ASK THE JURY DIFFERENT SUBSTANTIVE QUESTIONS. One group of reforms that will constrain discretion appeals to the principle of institutional competence. These reforms emphasize that since jurors can answer some questions more readily than others, the law should only ask jurors the kinds of questions for which they possess the requisite expertise, information, and cognitive capacities. As legal disputes become more complex, the legal doctrines that frame their resolution should be altered to take account of jurors' limited competence.

Some advocates of this approach emphasize the goal of improving jury rationality. The continuing controversy over the test for design defect in strict product liability law is an important example. The Second Restatement's test provides the jury with an open-ended criterion and little guidance.[65] Some other formulations, like Dean John Wade's seven-factor test, go too far in the other direction, prescribing tests based on numerous factors that are hard for the jury to balance and apply.[66] In response, George Priest has urged that the doctrine return to a standard that asks whether in a given case an alternative design existed that might have avoided the accident in a cost-effective manner.[67] Guido Calabresi and Jon Hirschoff, in contrast, have proposed a strict liability test that does not inquire on a case-by-case basis into the result of the cost-benefit analysis. They argue that juries are poorly equipped to perform this scrutiny and that such consideration would be costly. Instead, they would have the jury decide which of the parties was in the best position both to conduct this analysis and to implement it so as to minimize accident costs, a determination that will usually turn on the distribution and costs of information about risks, benefits, and alternatives.[68]

The effectiveness of reforms that would alter substantive legal doctrine in order to reformulate jury questions depends on how deeply the critiques of jury rationality cut. If juries are in fact as biased or prone to error as their most thoroughgoing critics assert, their answers to the new questions may not be much better than their answers to the old ones. In that event jurors' ability to answer Dean Wade's questions correctly may not be much greater than their ability to answer those posed by Priest or even by Calabresi and Hirschoff.

Many jury critics, however, would find more categorical, discretion-constraining doctrines attractive even if such doctrines had little effect on jury bias or rates of error. These critics emphasize that a doctrine's substantive content may be less important than the clarity and determinacy of its rules. This possibility is particularly great in those contexts in which potential risk-bearers, confronted with a bright-line rule, can reallocate risks among themselves at low cost. If people know about a rule, can predict how it will apply to their conduct, and can easily bargain about who should bear the risk under what circumstances and at what cost, they can produce a risk allocation that is more efficient for them than the one prescribed by the doctrine.[69] Juries can also apply such rules at lower cost and with greater accuracy and predictability. An example is the common-law rule categorically denying liability for pure economic loss caused by negligence.

These conditions are usually satisfied in contract situations; they are sometimes also satisfied in certain areas of accident law where many contractual relationships have increasingly been subjected to tort liability principles, as noted in the next section. But even where the primary actors may not be well positioned to allocate risk at low cost, clear rules may be valuable if their transparency facilitates insurance and reduces appeals without increasing jury error. The California Supreme Court's landmark decision in *Rowland* v. *Christian* is an interesting example of precisely the opposite strategy. There the court substituted a single, open-ended reasonableness standard of occupier liability for the three more determinate (albeit admittedly artificial) categories on which liability had turned for centuries.[70]

INCREASE THE JURY'S DEFERENCE TO OTHERS' DECISIONS. We have seen that the jury's discretion can sometimes be constrained by formulating new doctrines that present it with more tractable, hopefully more useful, questions. But reformers can also limit jury discretion by reinvigorating old doctrines that require the jury to defer to decisions already made by others, especially in tort law. In this category, two important sources of external norms might be used to confine jury decisions in tort cases: contract and regulation. Both, however, are highly controversial when courts invoke them for this purpose.

I have already noted that contemporary courts increasingly apply tort principles to transactions and relationships that are also governed—some used to be *exclusively* governed—by contract principles. Some examples of this extension include liability for pure economic loss, manufacturer and distributor liability to purchasers for defective products, landlord liability to tenants, wrongful discharge of employees, insurer liability for failure to pay claims, and medical malpractice liability even in organized care settings where provider contracts are actually negotiated.[71] Even workplace injuries in settings in which workers compensation is supposed to be the exclusive remedy against employers have increasingly become the province of tort law.[72]

In tort disputes arising in such situations, courts could bind juries with the norms adopted in these contractual transactions and relationships. They could do so in several ways. The most conventional approach would be to resuscitate the defense of assumption of the risk (or informed consent, in the health-care context). I say "resuscitate" because the doctrine of assumed risk has fallen into some desuetude in recent decades as courts in many different contexts have overridden even explicit contractual risk allocations, allowing the jury to find for the plaintiff. These courts typically rely on a number of grounds—consumer ignorance, unequal bargaining power, and a catch-all category called "public policy." For example, an appellate court in New York refused to enforce a contract in which the plaintiff had waived his right to sue a university dental clinic for malpractice in exchange for receiving services at half the normal fee.[73] It is possible, however, that courts are becoming more hospitable to the doctrine. Several cases pending in leading state supreme courts point in that direction, but it remains unclear how representative they are of current judicial attitudes.[74] To the extent that the doctrine is reinvigorated, the ambit of jury decisionmaking would decrease.[75]

Juries cannot be so easily confined, however, in those cases in which defendants cannot rely on an express contract but must instead argue that a risk allocation was implicit in the contract or that the plaintiff made a noncontractual, informed, consensual decision to accept the injury-producing risk. Such cases surely compose the vast majority of those in which the assumed-risk defense is invoked. Juries in product liability cases, for example, must often decide whether the warning accompanying a product adequately informed the user about the risk that resulted in the injury. The only practicable ways to constrain jury discretion in cases of this kind are to broaden the assumed-risk defense with clear rules, or to move the dispute out of the tort system, a strategy that I discuss below.

The second major source of external norms to which reformers might require juries to defer is administrative regulations. The traditional legal doctrine holds that the jury is the best and ultimate judge of whether a particular course of conduct complies with the standard of reasonableness, nondefectiveness, or normative criteria to which parties in civil liability litigation are held. Even regulations directed at controlling the very same risks that are at issue in the tort case do not ordinarily bind the jury. Thus, although defendants' failure to comply with such regulations almost invariably operates to establish liability, those who comply with the regulations may also be held liable.

Some commentators have sharply criticized this doctrine. They point to the importance of expert judgment on such technical issues, the advantages of regulatory analysis over ad hoc jury decisions in making the socially relevant trade-offs between risk and benefits, the confusion that tort law's rejection of regulatory standards sows in the private sector, and other problems with the traditional rule. They have called for courts to recognize a regulatory compliance defense in one form or another that would prevent the jury from second-guessing the regulators and imposing liability in such situations.[76]

LIMIT THE JURY'S ABILITY TO DETERMINE DAMAGES. As noted earlier, jury discretion is at its height in the determination of damages, and the resulting variability of awards in cases that in objective terms seem quite similar is large enough to be disturbing. Quite apart from its unfairness, this variability has undesirable effects on the behavioral incentives of primary actors and on settlement decisions. If it can be reduced without unduly sacrificing other important values, justice requires that we try to do so.

A number of reformers have proposed to narrow, though not eliminate this jury discretion by awarding damages according to established schedules.[77] These schedules could be similar to those used in workers compensation and similar social insurance programs, but they might be made considerably more flexible by taking into account a variety of factors relevant to measuring the plaintiff's loss. In most damage scheduling schemes, the jury would make findings that would enable the court to classify the injury according to the categories established by the damage schedule. The classifications could be defined narrowly or broadly, depending on the amount of jury discretion desired, and the jury might also be permitted to vary the amount of the award within a given classification.

A flexible system of damage schedules, however, might nevertheless fail to attract the necessary public support (for example, few of the participants in this symposium other than academics seemed willing to endorse it). Even so, it should be possible to improve the determination of damages by measures short of scheduling. For example, the jury might be informed about a range of previous awards without being confined to that range, or it might be informed about a range but be allowed to award outside that range as long as it gives reasons for doing so. Alternatively, its discretion might be informed by data on the distribution in past cases of the ratios of out-of-pocket losses to total damage awards or of the ratios of compensatory to punitive damages.[78]

Analogous reforms are common enough in other areas of social life; the law, after all, is not the only domain to face the necessity of somehow reconciling the uniqueness of the individual case with the goals of equal treatment, predictability, ahd administrative efficiency. In addition to social insurance, the medical profession—yielding to the pressure of insurance rules, cost controls, and malpractice litigation—is increasingly constrained by treatment norms and reimbursement categories (for example, Medicare's "diagnostically related groups") even though it values individualization of care at least as much as the law cherishes individualization of justice.

REQUIRE THE JURY TO RENDER SPECIAL VERDICTS. Another way to control jury discretion would be to require the jury to submit verdicts in a specific form instead of (or as well as) in a general form. To critics (or even friends) of the jury, this approach, which is authorized by Rule 49 of the Federal Rules of Civil Procedure, possesses numerous advantages. It would simplify the jury's task by posing specific questions for it to answer; focus the jury's attention on the critical factual issues; obviate the need for the judge to instruct the jury on the law; highlight any inconsistent findings by the jury; and facilitate appellate review by rendering more transparent the factual premises underlying the jury's verdict and animating the judge's application of the law.

These are considerable virtues, which makes it even more important to know why special verdicts are not used very often. Apparently, the reasons have to do with lawyers' tactical opposition to special verdicts and with judges' fears about erring in the formulation of the questions, calling attention to jury inconsistencies (which may be more widespread than we like to think), and inviting more intensive appellate review of jury verdicts.[79] Whether these problems are tractable to legal reforms, of course, is another question.

Divert to Nonjury Forums

Historically, the most far-reaching response to the perceived defects of the civil jury has been to divert to nonjury forums disputes that would otherwise be tried to a jury. In most but not all diverted cases, the reallocated factfinding function remains subject to at least limited judicial review.

Generally speaking, diversion may take three forms. One category consists of a varied group of relatively informal techniques commonly referred to collectively as alternative dispute resolution (ADR). A large theoretical, descriptive, and evaluative literature on ADR now exists, which I shall not attempt to summarize here.[80] ADR is the least radical of the diversion strategies because most ADR techniques are consensual; they are available to disputants who wish to use them in lieu of a jury trial, but jury trial ordinarily remains as the default option. To the extent that ADR functions as an add-on to the jury system rather than replacing it—to the extent that ADR simply creates an additional layer of cost and delay while only settling cases that would eventually have settled before trial anyway–its cost-effectiveness will be reduced.[81] In that event, ADR's other putative advantages (for example, greater satisfaction by participants or fairer outcomes) would have to be large indeed to justify the system.[82]

A second type of diversion reform—what Jeffrey O'Connell calls the "neo-no-fault" approach—involves somewhat more legal regulation of the parties' access to jury trial than does ADR. O'Connell has imaginatively crafted a variety of neo-no-fault schemes, tailoring them to the special characteristics of different areas of tort law and tort litigation.[83] These versions have two pertinent features in common. First, they encourage a potential defendant to make to a potential plaintiff a preaccident offer to defray certain categories of cost (usually out-of-pocket expenses) that the offeree may incur as a result of certain actions by the defendant, in return for the offeree's waiver of a tort claim. (These plans also encourage postaccident, prelitigation offers). Second, they provide that if such an offer is rejected, the issues that may be raised in the subsequent litigation, and the burdens of proof that will then apply, will be governed by rules that are more disadvantageous to the offeree than those that would otherwise apply. It is in this sense that the neo-no-fault approach is more coercive than most ADR reforms.

A third reform model would replace (partly or completely) jury trials of particular categories of claims with bench or administrative agency trials of such claims. For example, most damage actions against governments in the United States can only be tried to judges. In England, Canada, Australia, and New Zealand, judges hear almost all civil actions. The workers compensation system, which usually includes exclusive remedy provisions designed to supplant all common law claims by workers against their employers, is perhaps the most important example of the administrative agency model.[84] Environmental protection agencies have displaced some private environmental litigation that would have been tried to juries, although the environmental statutes often preserve damage remedies for nuisance, which may be tried to juries.

Diversion reforms, whatever their merits, probably reached their high-water mark some time ago and may have already begun to retreat. The evidence from some contemporary reform debates indicates strongly that the political obstacles to adopting such reforms are enormous, perhaps insuperable. To a lesser degree, much the same might be said of all of the other reform strategies, except for some of the proposals aimed at reducing administrative costs.

Looking to the Future of Jury Reform

If the recent past is prologue, the prospects for reform of the civil jury are dim. The politics of jury reform are daunting. Virtually all of the important groups with stakes in the system of civil litigation favor retaining the jury. Trial lawyers' veneration of the jury is almost religious in its fervor: their missionary zeal and the satisfying experiences of many former jurors appear to have won many converts among the general public, which expresses great confidence in the jury. When queried about the value of the jury, judges almost invariably praise it.[85] From a purely institutional perspective, judges have many reasons to favor juries. As has already been noted, juries shoulder some of the judges' responsibility for adjudication and diffuse their public accountability for decisions. Jury verdicts can insulate judges' rulings at trial from effective appellate review. Juries, moreover, help to legitimate the judicial process as a whole.

The jury exercises a strong symbolic hold over the public mind. As Roscoe Pound observed, the jury seems to vindicate our fantasy that *any* citizen, not simply legal experts, can administer justice.[86] It also reifies some extraordinarily powerful, even mythic themes: that ordinary citizens can get their day in court and are entitled to be judged by their peers; and that lay jurors serve as a shield preventing the government from oppressing the individual—a "democratic counterforce to state authority." [87]

Given the broad array of public and special interest support for the jury system, one would not expect politicians to show much interest in jury reform. It is an issue on which the narrow economic interests of two powerful groups, trial lawyers and insurance companies, are in sharp conflict. Politically speaking, however, the two sides are ordinarily poorly matched in battles over jury reform. The trial lawyers, who defend the status quo, are well represented in state legislatures, contribute large amounts of money to campaigns, have the support of labor unions, and can appeal to populist rhetoric and civic ideals in their defense of the jury. The insurers and their agents also contribute much money to campaigns, of course, but they ordinarily are less well represented in the legislatures, are singularly unpopular with the voting public, and are viewed (along with their corporate allies) as wholly self-interested. [88] In this setting, those who would change the jury system are highly vulnerable to accusations that they serve corporate interests and are hostile to the public interest. Jury reformers normally are voices crying in the political wilderness.

I say "normally" in recognition of the fact that this political inertia favoring the status quo with respect to juries can be overcome in unusual circumstances. The insurance crisis of price and availability in the mid-1980s is the most important example. The spasm of reform activity that followed in its wake, was unusual for both its intensity and its legislative success: almost all states imposed some restrictions on jury awards— typically with respect to pain and suffering, punitive damages, joint and several liability, or the treatment of collateral sources. [89] Yet this episode in fact demonstrates the political marginality of jury reform efforts. Despite the political tide propelling tort reform in virtually every state in the 1980s, few changes to the jury were actually adopted and those were decidedly incremental. [90] They succeeded in chipping away at the edges of jury discretion but neither invaded its core nor altered the jury's structure or essential functions.

Two more recent developments—the continuing effort to amend the Federal Employers' Liability Act of 1908 (FELA) and the extension of jury trials to claims of sex and disability discrimination—are even more revealing about the current political limits on jury reform. Both developments suggest that public attitudes, far from supporting reforms that would restrict juries, strongly favor *preserving and expanding* the scope of their authority. [91]

The FELA established a negligence-based, jury trial liability regime for work-related injuries to railroad workers. The original statute, which has never been amended, contains many pro-plaintiff provisions, generates high transaction costs, and produces recoveries, especially for seriously injured workers, that far exceed awards in similar cases under the workers compensation systems that apply to virtually all other workers in the United States. More than five years of vigorous campaigning by the railroad industry to convert FELA into a workers compensation system with awards determined by an administrative agency rather than by juries has utterly failed; indeed only one congressional hearing has ever been held on this issue.[92]

In the Civil Rights Act of 1991, Congress amended Title VII of the Civil Rights Act in a number of respects, partly in order to overrule a series of Supreme Court decisions unfavorable to plaintiffs in employment discrimination cases under Title VII.[93] The right to jury trial had previously been limited to claims of racial and religious discrimination. The most controversial of these fiercely contested amendments extended that right to claims of sex discrimination. (In a similar spirit, the Americans with Disabilities Act of 1990 provided jury trials for discrimination claims based on disability.)[94] Although a statutory cap on jury awards for such claims was part of the compromise that made passage of the 1991 act possible, these caps may soon be removed.[95]

Additional evidence of the jury's political invulnerability can be seen in the conspicuous failure of no-fault reforms to win enactment in recent years. Federal no-fault legislation is a dead letter, state no-fault plans have made little headway since the 1970s, and all of the plans that have been adopted preserve the option to sue in tort, including jury trial. Although the court system is groaning under the unprecedented burden of asbestos-related tort claims, no legislation to replace jury trials with an administrative compensation scheme has even been seriously considered.[96] The status quo enjoys manifestly powerful political support insofar as the civil jury is concerned; diversion-type reform, in contrast, is a cause without a constituency.

In itself, this is not particularly troubling. The evidence so far suggest that both the alleged vices of the jury and the supposed virtues of its alternatives are exaggerated. No one would suggest, of course, that the jury is an ideal institution; its critics raise many important concerns. If true, the claim that jury unpredictability inhibits settlements even in relatively routine cases should be especially worrisome. But the jury's critics have not yet substantiated their most salient claims; still less have they made a compelling case for abolishing the jury. The overwhelming pro-jury sentiment among the participants in this symposium confirms that the jury's future is secure not only with the politicians and the lay public, but also with those who study it at close hand.

The case for experimenting with some of the more incremental reforms that I have discussed, however, stands on a much stronger footing. Many of these reform options aimed at improving jury comprehension and reducing administrative costs deserve to be tried. They promise to improve jury performance without threatening the values of due process; indeed, they seem likely to advance those values. States should also consider experimenting with a return to larger juries in the hopes of enhancing the rationality and representativeness of juries. Any additional costs of larger juries might be defrayed by increasing the fees for jury trials to more realistic levels, a reform that can stand on its own merits quite apart from the issue of jury size.

The strategy of constraining jury discretion is and ought to be more controversial. Even the most attractive of the reform options entail some genuinely difficult value conflicts. Of the options for reform, some attempt to rationalize the way in which damages for nonpecuniary losses are assessed probably offers the greatest promise of meeting the legitimate concerns of the jury's critics. (Candidly, most of the symposium participants were far less receptive to this reform than are academics.) Such damages are the subject over which the jury's discretion is most unconstrained, the variability of its decisions most objectionable, and the effects on settlements most troubling. In this area, moreover, our experience with social and private insurance systems, which use such schedules, can provide good information about the likely consequences of this approach. Finally, such reforms do not require that the jury be abolished (which, as we have seen, is politically unrealistic in any event), but demand only that jury decisions on damages be guided, informed, and possibly constrained in the interests of more equal treatment of similar cases and greater predictability of outcomes. On the primacy of these values, at least, the debate on jury reform should be able to reach a firm consensus.

Notes

1. The major exception has occurred during the past two decades, when many jurisdictions reduced the standard size of the jury.

2. Maryland and Indiana still permit their juries to interpret the law. See Valerie P. Hans and Neil Vidmar, *Judging the Jury* (Plenum Press, 1986), p. 31. The contrast with the situation in England, where judges have always exercised much greater control over both lawyers and juries, is instructive. John H. Langbein, "The Criminal Trial before the Lawyers," *University of Chicago Law Review*, vol. 45 (Winter 1978), pp. 284–300.

3. For a general discussion of some of these issues, especially legal complexity, see Peter H. Schuck, "Legal Complexity: Its Causes, Consequences, and Cures," *Duke Law Journal*, vol. 42 (October 1992), pp. 1–52.

4. For notorious examples of such controversy, compare Peter W. Huber, *Liability: The Legal Revolution and its Consequences* (Basic Books, 1988), with Joseph A. Page, "Deforming Tort Reform," *Georgetown Law Journal*, vol. 78 (February 1990), pp. 649–97, which reviews Huber, and Marc Galanter, "The Debased Debate on Civil Justice," Working Paper DPRP 10-10 (University of Wisconsin, Madison Law School: Institute for Legal Studies, February 1992), debunking exaggerated claims about the cost of the tort system and the magnitude of civil litigation.

5. See Valerie P. Hans and Neil Vidmar, "The American Jury at Twenty-Five Years," *Law and Social Inquiry*, vol. 16 (Spring 1991), p. 342.

6. Director of the Administrative Office of the U.S. Courts, *Annual Report*, table C4 (1991). The fraction of cases reaching trial that are tried by a jury is *not* declining over time. The statements about trends are based on a survey of Director of the Administrative Office annual reports since 1970. Indeed, Albert W. Alschuler, drawing upon Raymond Moley's imagery of more than sixty years ago, has referred to "the vanishing civil jury." Albert W. Alschuler, "The Vanishing Civil Jury," *University of Chicago Legal Forum*, vol. 1990, p. 1. Invoking another metaphor, he views the civil trial as "on its deathbed, or close to it" (p. 5).

7. According to the National Center on State Courts, 9.2 percent of the civil cases were "disposed of at trial" in the state courts in 1988 (the most recent year in which these data were gathered), and 12.5 percent of these dispositions were jury trials. Thus, only 1.2 percent of the civil cases reached a jury. National Center on State Courts, *State Court Caseload Statistics: Annual Report* (Williamsburg, Va.: 1988), text table 8, p. 60.

8. See, for example, George L. Priest and Benjamin Klein, "The Selection of Disputes for Litigation," *Journal of Legal Studies*, vol. 13 (January 1984), p. 1; and Theodore Eisenberg, "Testing the Selection Effect: A New Theoretical Framework with Empirical Tests," *Journal of Legal Studies*, vol. 19 (June 1990), p. 337. See also Peter W. Huber, "Junk Science and the Jury," *University of Chicago Legal Forum*, vol. 1990, pp. 279–81, maintaining that plaintiff lawyers' exploitation of outlier jury verdicts ("right-field slouch") disproportionately influences the decisions of insurers and defendants.

9. See Priest and Klein, "Selection of Disputes for Litigation."

10. Michael J. Saks, "Do We Really Know Anything about the Behavior of the Tort Litigation System—and Why Not?" *University of Pennsylvania Law Review*, vol. 140 (April 1992), p. 1233.

11. National Center on State Courts, *State Court Caseload Statistics: Annual Report* (Williamsburg, Va.: 1989), pp. 43–49. The federal court filings show an even more striking growth in contract cases during the 1980s. Marc Galanter and Joel Rogers, "A Transformation of American Business Disputing? Some Preliminary Observations," Working Paper DPRP 10-3 (University of Wisconsin: Institute for Legal Studies, 1990).

12. This is particularly true in the state courts, where the percentage of jury trials that are tort cases sometimes exceeds 80 percent. See discussion and statistics in Marc Galanter, "The Civil Jury as Regulator of the Litigation Process," *University of Chicago Legal Forum*, vol. 1990, pp. 212–14. Galanter notes that *federal* courts hear a disproportionately high percentage of the civil jury trials in the United States and that the proportion of tort

cases in the federal jury trial caseload has fallen dramatically in recent decades. Even so, over 55 percent of the federal jury trials in 1980 were tort cases.

13. Some evidence on this point is cited in Kevin M. Clermont and Theodore Eisenberg, "Trial by Jury or Judge: Transcending Empiricism," *Cornell Law Review*, vol. 77 (July 1992), pp. 1127–28, which discusses "the popular view."

14. See, for example, Huber, *Liability*; "Suing the Police in Federal Court," *Yale Law Journal*, vol. 88 (March 1979), p. 781; and Jon O. Newman, "Suing the Lawbreakers," *Yale Law Journal*, vol. 87 (January 1978), p. 447.

15. Richard Neely, *The Product Liability Mess: How Business Can Be Rescued from the Politics of State Courts* (Free Press, 1988), p. 63. For this reason, Rule 411 of the Federal Rules of Evidence excludes evidence of whether a defendant carries liability insurance if offered to prove that the defendant acted negligently or otherwise wrongfully. State courts have traditionally applied the same rule. See *American Jurisprudence*, 2d ed., vol. 29, "Evidence," § 404 (Rochester: Lawyers Co-Operative Publishing Co.) (discussing state court decisions about the admissibility of evidence of liability insurance). There is some empirical support for this expectation. The studies are discussed in Saul M. Kassin and Lawrence S. Wrightsman, *The American Jury on Trial: Psychological Perspectives* (Hemisphere Publishing, 1988), pp. 162–63.

16. The voir dire, so important in U.S. litigation, apparently is seldom used in other Anglo-American law jurisdictions such as the United Kingdom and Canada. Hans and Vidmar, *Judging the Jury*, chap. 4.

17. Rand researchers have identified five common criteria: verdicts in similar jury trials, judicial statements on the deliberation process, public attitudes on the issue at trial, the decision that a judge would reach in the same case, and the judge's instructions in the case. They note that each of these criteria is problematic. Molly Selvin and Larry Picus, *The Debate over Jury Performance: Observations from a Recent Asbestos Case*, R-3479-ICJ (Santa Monica: Rand Institute for Civil Justice, 1987).

18. Selvin and Picus, *Debate over Jury Performance*, chap. 9.

19. Indeed, they may not even be representative of the legal profession in these respects.

20. Akhil Reed Amar, "The Bill of Rights as a Constitution," *Yale Law Journal*, vol. 100 (March 1991), pp. 1183–86.

21. Richard O. Lempert, "Civil Juries and Complex Cases: Let's Not Rush to Judgment," *Michigan Law Review*, vol. 80 (November 1981), p. 95. Although Lempert's point is made in the context of a discussion of complex cases, it would seem to apply more generally.

22. These studies are summarized in two recent articles. See Clermont and Eisenberg, "Trial by Jury or Judge," pp. 1151–55; and Saks, "Do We Really Know Anything," pp. 1232–37, especially note 316. See also Michael J. Saks, "Enhancing and Restraining Accuracy in Adjudication," *Law and Contemporary Problems*, vol. 51 (Autumn 1988), pp. 246–354.

The findings of Clermont and Eisenberg in their recent study—that plaintiffs actually have a higher win rate and higher mean recoveries before judges than before juries in certain categories of personal injury cases (especially medical malpractice and product liability)—are not necessarily inconsistent with the earlier studies, although they may be. The authors explain these findings by supposing that (1) litigants misperceive differences between the judge and the jury by failing to perceive real differences or by perceiving differences that do not in fact exist (or both); (2) these misperceptions affect the case mixes that survive the settlement process and go to each trial mode; and (3) this selection effect produces the observed pattern of win rates and recoveries.

Unfortunately, the persuasiveness of this explanation would seem to depend on the ability of the authors' data to distinguish between the two types of misperceptions above, yet their data cannot do so. It is hard to imagine available data that could. Moreover, the authors do not really refute (although they do reject) some alternative explanations of litigants' choice of trial mode, such as relative cost and requisite lawyering skills. Clermont and Eisenberg, "Trial by Jury or Judge," pp. 1148–49. Finally, they acknowledge an objection to their explanation—that any such misperceptions, and thus their effect on outcomes, should be eliminated by the keen-eyed observations by legions of trial lawyers of actual outcomes over time—which seems highly plausible rather than being merely "theoretical" (p. 157).

23. Harry Kalven, Jr., and Hans Zeisel, *The American Jury* (Little, Brown, 1966), p. 64.

24. See, for example, Michael Walsh, "The American Jury: A Reassessment," *Yale Law Journal*, vol. 79 (November 1969), p. 142; George Priest, "The Role of the Civil Jury in a System of Private Litigation," *University of Chicago Legal Forum*, vol. 1990, pp. 163 and 194, note 6. See also Theodore Eisenberg and James A. Henderson, Jr., "Inside the Quiet Revolution in Products Liability," *University of California Law Review*, vol. 39 (April 1992), pp. 785–86, and the sources cited there.

25. Of course, they may decide to explain their reasons to others after the trial.

26. Randall R. Bovbjerg, Frank A. Sloan, and James F. Blumstein, "Valuing Life and Limb in Tort: Scheduling 'Pain and Suffering,'" *Northwestern University Law Review*, vol. 83 (Summer 1989), pp. 919–24, concludes that the severity of the injury explained two-fifths of the variation. Mark Peterson's reanalysis of award data from Cook County found that severity explained 51 percent of the variation. "Compensation of Injuries: Civil Jury Verdicts in Cook County," R-3011-ICJ (Santa Monica: Rand Institute for Civil Justice, 1984), pp. 87–94. See also W. Kip Viscusi, "Pain and Suffering in Product Liability Cases: Systematic Compensation or Capricious Awards," *International Review of Law and Economics*, vol. 8 (December 1988), p. 203.

27. Viscusi, "Pain and Suffering," pp. 923–24. In the most serious injury category, the spread was between $147,000 and $18,100,000. Viscusi's study, which provided "only a very limited test of the rationality of the process" and which concluded that awards generally reflected injury severity and were "not entirely random," did find "striking" evidence of irrationality in the large pain-and-suffering awards for fatal injuries. See pp. 213–14.

28. David Baldus, John MacQueen, and George Woodworth, "Regulating the Quantum of Damages for Personal Injuries Through Enhanced Additur-Remittitur Review," paper prepared for the annual meeting of the Law and Society Association, May 1992. Table 1 shows that median awards for nonpecuniary damages at the 10th and 90th percentiles within the highest of five severity categories were $382,000 and $6,548,000, respectively.

29. Priest, "Role of the Civil Jury," pp. 196–99.

30. See J. R. Spencer, ed., *Jackson's Machinery of Justice*, 8th ed. (Cambridge University Press, 1989), p. 395. For a summary history of England's abolition of the civil jury in most cases, see p. 72.

31. A very recent comparison between the liability and compensation regimes in the United States and ten other developed countries concludes that although liability rules in the United States are usually not particularly generous, American damage awards appear to be much larger and less predictable. Werner Pfennigstorf and Donald G. Gifford, *A Comparative Study of Liability Law and Compensation Schemes in Ten Countries and the United States* (Oak Brook, Ill.: Insurance Research Council, 1991), pp. 156–57.

32. For discussion of the behavioral effects in many of these areas, see many of the chapters in Peter H. Schuck, ed., *Tort Law and the Public Interest: Competition, Innovation, and Consumer Welfare* (Norton, 1991). For perhaps the most tendentious account of these changes, see Huber, *Liability*. For a critique of Huber's analysis, see Page, "Deforming Tort Reform."

33. See, for example, Scott Harrington, "Liability Insurance: Volatility in Prices and in the Availability of Coverage," in Schuck, ed., *Tort Law and the Public Interest*, pp. 47–49.

34. George L. Priest developed this argument most elaborately with respect to products liability; "The Current Insurance Crisis and Modern Tort Law," *Yale Law Journal*, vol. 96 (June 1987), p. 1527. Priest's argument is challenged in Steven P. Croley and Jon D. Hanson, "What Liability Crisis? An Alternative Explanation for Recent Events in Products Liability," *Yale Journal on Regulation*," vol. 8 (Winter 1991). Priest responded to the challenge in "Can Absolute Manufacturer Liability Be Defended?" *Yale Journal on Regulation*, vol. 9 (Winter 1992), pp. 237–64. Kenneth Abraham makes a similar argument with respect to environmental risk insurance in "Environmental Liability and the Limits of Insurance," *Columbia Law Review*, vol. 88 (June 1988), pp. 942–88.

35. Michael J. Saks points out, for example, that in Minnesota and several neighboring states, only twenty medical malpractice settlements were awarded to plaintiffs over a six-year period in the mid-1980s. Letter from Michael Saks, July 21, 1992.

36. See, for example, Stephen Daniels, "The Question of Jury Competence and the Politics of Civil Justice Reform: Symbols, Rhetoric, and Agenda-Building," *Law and Contemporary Problems*, vol. 52 (Autumn 1989), pp. 300–04.

37. See, for example, Jay Angoff, "Insurance against Competition: How the McCarran-Ferguson Act Raises Prices and Profits in the Property-Casualty Insurance Industry," *Yale Journal on Regulation*, vol. 5 (Summer 1988), pp. 397–415.

38. Ralph A. Winter, "The Liability Crisis and the Dynamics of Competitive Insurance Markets," *Yale Journal on Regulation*, vol. 5 (Summer 1988), pp. 455–99; and Angoff, "Insurance against Competition."

39. See, for example, Harrington, "Liability Insurance"; and Glenn Blackmon and Richard Zeckhauser, "State Tort Reform Legislation: Assessing Our Control of Risks," in Schuck, ed., *Tort Law and the Public Interest*, pp. 272–300. The evidence on the effect of tort reform statutes on plaintiff success rates and award levels is equivocal. Eisenberg and Henderson, "Inside the Quiet Revolution in Products Liability," pp. 774–78, 781–83, conclude that statutes reduced the success rates but had no effect on the awards. On the competitive behavior of insurers, compare Ian Ayres and Peter Siegelman, "The Economics of the Insurance Antitrust Suits: Toward an Exclusionary Theory," *Tulane Law Review*, vol. 63 (May 1989), pp. 971–97, with George L. Priest, "The Antitrust Suits and the Public Understanding of Insurance," *Tulane Law Review*, vol. 63 (May 1989), pp. 999–1044. Elsewhere, I have argued that there is an intimate connection between judicial innovation and jury decisionmaking. Peter H. Schuck, "The New Judicial Ideology of Tort Law," in Walter Olson, ed., *New Directions in Liability Law* (New York: Academy of Political Science, 1988), pp. 11–12.

40. Peter Appelbome, "G.M. Is Held Liable over Fuel Tanks in Pickup Trucks," *New York Times*, February 4, 1993, p. A1.

41. Eric Schnapper, "Judges against Juries: Appellate Review of Federal Civil Jury Verdicts," *Wisconsin Law Review*, vol. 1989 (March–April 1989), pp. 237, 247. Schnapper found that federal appellate courts reversed jury verdicts in 49 percent of the cases in which the verdicts were challenged, based on a study of 208 appellate opinions published in 1984–85. See also Michael Rustad, *Demystifying Punitive Damages in Products Liability Cases: A Survey of a Quarter Century of Trial Verdicts* (Washington: Roscoe Pound Foundation, 1991). For a very critical account of the media's coverage of scientific issues involved in litigation, see Peter W. Huber, *Galileo's Revenge: Junk Science in the Courtroom* (Basic Books, 1991), chap. 4.

42. For a very recent analysis adopting this assumption, see Eisenberg and Henderson, "Inside the Quiet Revolution in Products Liability," pp. 744–45, 756.

43. Galanter, "Civil Jury as Regulator," pp. 242–45, describes the studies.

44. Saks, "Do We Really Know Anything," pp. 1223–24. Judges' predictions of what juries would award are not necessarily inconsistent with the findings in Clermont and Eisenberg, "Trial by Jury or Judge," that judges in bench trials tend to award damages different from those that juries award—sometimes higher, sometimes lower.

45. For criticism of both the Jury Verdicts Research (JVR) data and the uses often made of it, see Saks, "Do We Really Know Anything," pp. 1245–46; and Daniels, "Question of Jury Competence," pp. 300–02.

46. Galanter, "Civil Jury as Regulator," pp. 250–54, describes studies and suggests other explanations.

47. Priest, "Role of the Civil Jury."

48. See, for example, Peter H. Schuck, "The Role of Judges in Settling Complex Cases: The Agent Orange Example," *University of Chicago Law Review*, vol. 53 (Spring 1986), pp. 352–53, in which I conclude that the uncertainty that increased the pessimism on both sides encouraged settlement; and Cynthia Fobian and Jay J. Christensen-Szalanski, "Ambiguity and Liability Negotiations: The Effects of the Negotiators' Role and the Sensitivity Zone," in *Organizational Behavior & Human Decision Processes* (forthcoming 1993), cited in Saks, "Do We Really Know Anything?" p. 1215, note 231 (evidence from simulation).

49. Huber, "Junk Science and the Jury." American Bar Foundation research suggests that this situation may be typical. See Daniels, "Question of Jury Competence," pp. 301–02, pointing out that 88 percent of plaintiffs' awards in Cook County were lower than the mean.

50. Schuck, "The New Judicial Ideology of Tort Law," pp. 11–12. See also *Duncan v. Louisiana*, 391 U.S. 145, 187 (1968). Justice Harlan dissenting, ruled that the jury "eases the burden on judges by enabling them to share a part of their sometimes awesome responsibility." Paul Carrington suggests that the large role played by judges in our polity may make this diffusion of responsibility desirable in "The Seventh Amendment: Some Bicentennial Reflections," *University of Chicago Legal Forum*, vol. 1990, p. 42.

51. See George L. Priest, "The Current Insurance Crisis and Modern Tort Law," *Yale Law Journal*, vol. 96 (June 1987), pp. 1587–88, cataloging tort reform legislation enacted by forty-two states during the mid-1980s, much of which aimed to reduce juries' discretion to grant large damage awards.

52. For a recent review of such reforms, see Robert J. MacCoun, E. Allan Lind, and Tom R. Tyler, "Alternative Dispute Resolution in Trial and Appellate Courts," in Dorothy K. Kagehiro and William S. Laufer, eds., *Handbook of Psychology and Law* (Springer-Verlag, 1992), p. 95.

53. Saks, "Do We Really Know Anything?" pp. 1230–31.

54. Stephen C. Yeazell, "The New Jury and the Ancient Jury Conflict," *University of Chicago Legal Forum*, vol. 1990, pp. 111–17.

55. George Priest reports an estimate that more than six years is required to move a civil case from initiation to jury trial. He does not report the analogous period for bench trials. Priest, "Role of the Civil Jury," p. 193, note 85. For a discussion of delay costs in the special context of asbestos litigation, see Peter Schuck, "The Worst Should Go First: Deferral Registries in Asbestos Litigation," *Harvard Journal of Law and Public Policy*, vol. 15 (1992), pp. 558–59. According to estimates published in 1959, a jury trial is roughly 40 percent longer than a bench trial of the same case. Hans Zeisel, Harry Kalven, Jr., and Bernard Buchholz, *Delay in the Court*, 2d ed. (Little, Brown, 1959), chap. 6. Judge Posner notes that federal jury trials in 1983 consumed twice as much time on average as federal bench trials. Richard Posner, *The Federal Courts: Crisis and Reform* (Harvard University Press, 1985), p. 130, note 1. He does not attempt to control for type of case. One study estimated the aggregate social cost, including juror opportunity costs, of using all jurors

at somewhere between $129 million and $338 million in 1962. Most of this cost was borne by jurors rather than by taxpayers. Donald L. Martin, "The Economics of Juror Conscription," *Journal of Political Economy*, vol. 80 (July–August 1972), pp. 700–01.

56. Priest, "Role of the Civil Jury," pp. 187–91. See sources cited in Galanter, "Civil Jury as Regulator," p. 203, note 16.

57. Arthur Taylor von Mehren, "The Significance for Procedural Practice and Theory of the Concentrated Trial: Comparative Remarks," in Norbert Horn, ed., *Europaisches Rechtsdenken in Geschichte und Gegenwart: Festschrift für Helmut Coing*, vol. 2 (Munich: C. H. Beck, 1982), pp. 361, 364. I thank my colleague John H. Langbein for directing me to this important article. Langbein's own article, "The German Advantage in Civil Procedure," *University of Chicago Law Review*, vol. 52 (Fall 1985), pp. 823, 830, provides a detailed comparison of American and German procedure.

58. See the chapters by MacCoun, Diamond, Casper, Lempert, and Sarokin and Munsterman in this volume. See also William W Schwarzer, "Reforming Jury Trials," *University of Chicago Legal Forum*, vol. 1990, p. 119.

59. See Posner, *The Federal Courts*, pp. 10–11, 131; and Martin, "Economics of Juror Conscription," p. 700. The desired level is *net* social costs since, as Posner recognizes, litigation does generate some social benefits.

60. See, for example, Michael J. Saks, *Jury Verdicts: The Role of Group Size and Social Decision Rules* (Lexington Books, 1977). A recent empirical study in California found no difference between eight-person and twelve-person juries on the accuracy of verdicts (measured by the conformity of liability findings to the views of the judges) and reliability (measured by their acceptance), but did find a difference in the size of awards. G. Thomas Munsterman, Janice T. Munsterman, and Steven A. Penrod, *A Comparison of the Performance of Eight- and Twelve-Person Juries* (Williamsburg, Va.: National Center for State Courts, April 1990).

61. See, for example, Nancy Pennington and Reid Hastie, "A Cognitive Theory of Juror Decision Making: The Story Model," *Cardozo Law Review*, vol. 13 (November 1991), pp. 519–57.

62. See, for example, the discussion and sources cited in Carrington, "Seventh Amendment," pp. 53–54; and Hans and Vidmar, *Judging the Jury*, chap. 11.

63. Carrington, "Seventh Amendment," pp. 62–73.

64. See, for example, Note, "The Case for Special Juries in Complex Civil Litigation," *Yale Law Journal*, vol. 89 (May 1980), p. 1155, and sources cited there at note 9. This proposal is sufficiently controversial that the American Law Institute has so far declined to take a position on it. See American Law Institute, "Complex Litigation Project," tentative draft 1, April 14, 1989, p. 5, note 9. See also Huber, *Galileo's Revenge*, chap. 11.

65. See comment g to Section 402A: a defective condition is one "not contemplated by the ultimate consumer, which will be unreasonably dangerous to him."

66. John W. Wade, "On the Nature of Strict Liability for Products," *Mississippi Law Journal*, vol. 44 (November 1973), pp. 837–38. His test was adopted in, for example, *Camacho* v. *Honda Motor Co., Ltd.*, 741 P. 2d 1240, cert. dismissed, 485 U.S. 901 (1988). For a similar type of test, see *Barker* v. *Lull Engineering Co., Inc.*, 20 Cal. 3d 413, 573 P.2d 443 (1978).

67. See George L. Priest, "Products Liability Law and the Accident Rate," in Robert E. Litan and Clifford Winston, eds., *Liability: Perspectives and Policy* (Brookings, 1988), pp. 220–21.

68. Guido Calabresi and Jon T. Hirschoff, "Toward a Test for Strict Liability in Tort," *Yale Law Journal*, vol. 81 (May 1972), p. 1055.

69. This, of course, is an important teaching of the Coase theorem. Ronald H. Coase, "The Problem of Social Cost," *Journal of Law and Economics*, vol. 3 (October 1960), p. 1.

70. 69 Cal.2d 108, 443 P.2d 561 (1968). For an economic analysis of the types of rules involved in this decision, see Jason S. Johnston, "Uncertainty, Chaos, and the Torts Process: An Economic Analysis of Legal Form," *Cornell Law Review*, vol. 76 (January 1991), pp. 379–82.

71. See Schuck, "The New Judicial Ideology of Tort Law," pp. 6–8.

72. Paul C. Weiler, "Workers' Compensation and Products Liability: The Interaction of a Tort and a Non-Tort Regime," *Ohio State Law Journal*, vol. 50 (October 1989), pp. 825–54.

73. *Ash* v. *New York University Dental Center*, 164 A.D.2d 366, 564 N.Y.S.2d 308 (1st Dept. 1990).

74. Gail Cox, "Assumption of Risks," *National Law Journal*, October 28, 1991, p. 1, discusses cases.

75. Peter Huber is perhaps the most energetic voice lamenting the decline of the assumed-risk doctrine and calling for its revival. See Huber, *Liability: The Legal Revolution and its Consequences*. For a sharp critique of Huber's analysis, see Page, "Deforming Tort Reform."

76. See, for example, Peter Huber, "Safety and the Second Best: The Hazards of Public Risk Management in the Courts," *Columbia Law Review*, vol. 85 (March 1985), pp. 332–35; Peter H. Schuck, *Agent Orange on Trial: Mass Toxic Disasters in the Courts*, enlarged ed. (Harvard University Press, 1987), p. 291; and American Law Institute, "Compensation and Liability for Product and Process Injuries," proposed final report, council draft 1, November 5, 1990, chap. 16.

77. For one such proposal, see Bovbjerg and others, "Valuing Life and Limb." For a critique of that proposal, see Peter H. Schuck, "Scheduled Damages and Insurance Contracts for Future Services: A Comment on Blumstein, Bovbjerg, and Sloan," *Yale Journal on Regulation*, vol. 8 (Winter 1991), p. 213. Damages scheduling bears a superficial resemblance to the federal guidelines on criminal sentencing, which have recently come under withering criticism on a variety of grounds. See, for example, Albert W. Alschuler, "The Failure of Sentencing Guidelines: A Plea for Less Aggregation," *University of Chicago Law Review*, vol. 58 (Summer 1991), pp. 901–51. The analogy, however, is a poor one. Unlike juries assessing damages, sentencing judges with or without guidelines possess a great deal of information and experience about how others have performed the task in the past. The sentencing guidelines are mandatory, whereas damage schedules, as noted in the text, could be merely informative or precatory. The criminal process is far more complex than the civil process, providing numerous points at which discretion is exercised in ways that can vitiate or distort the effects of the guidelines in unanticipated, undesirable directions. Hence the defects of the sentencing guidelines should not be used to stigmatize damages scheduling, especially in the flexible forms that I propose.

78. I am indebted to Judith Resnik and Judge William Schwarzer for this suggestion.

79. See Pamela J. Stephens, "Controlling the Civil Jury: Towards a Functional Model of Justification," *Kentucky Law Journal*, vol. 76, no. 1 (1987), pp. 81–165.

80. For some recent examples, see MacCoun, Lind, and Tyler, "Alternative Dispute Resolution in Trial and Appellate Courts," and the articles by Wayne Brazil, Deborah Hensler, and Diane Wood in the symposium on the civil jury published in *University of Chicago Legal Forum*, vol. 1990, pp. 303–456. See also American Bar Association, Standing Committee on Dispute Resolution, *Alternative Dispute Resolution: An ADR Primer* (Chicago, 1989).

81. Add-on ADR bears a discouraging resemblance to the add-on automobile no-fault

reforms, adopted in about half of the states, which simply add no-fault benefits to the tort system rather than constituting a genuine alternative to that system, and which have tended to exacerbate the very conditions that led to the initial calls for reform. See sources cited in Marc A. Franklin and Robert L. Rabin, eds., *Tort Law and Alternatives: Cases and Materials*, 5th ed. (Westbury, N.Y.: Foundation Press, 1992), p. 772.

82. For a cautionary tale about one form of ADR, medical liability screening panels, see Jona Goldschmidt, "Where Have All the Panels Gone? A History of the Arizona Medical Liability Review Panel," *Arizona State Law Journal*, vol. 23 (Winter 1991), pp. 1013–1109. This points out that experience invalidated all the factual assumptions underlying the reform, leading to its repeal.

83. See, for example, Jeffrey O'Connell, "A 'Neo-No-Fault' Contract in Lieu of Tort: Preaccident Guarantees of Postaccident Settlement Offers," *California Law Review*, vol. 73 (May 1985), p. 914 (athletic programs); Jeffrey O'Connell, "Balanced Proposals for Products Liability Reform," *Ohio State Law Journal*, vol. 48 (Spring 1987), p. 321; O'Connell, "RX for Governments' Skyrocketing Insurance Rates," *Current Municipal Problems*, vol. 16 (1989), pp. 150–56 (governmental liability); and O'Connell, "A Draft Bill to Allow Choice Between No-Fault and Fault-Based Auto Insurance," *Harvard Journal on Legislation*, vol. 27 (Winter 1990), p. 144.

84. They have not always succeeded in achieving this exclusive remedy goal. See Weiler, "Workers' Compensation and Product Liability," pp. 834–38. Dissatisfaction with the jury, however, was not a principal reason animating the adoption of workers compensation schemes. Laurence W. Friedman and Jack Ladinsky, "Social Change and the Law of Industrial Accidents," *Columbia Law Review*, vol. 67 (January 1967), pp. 65–69.

85. See the chapter by Hans in this volume with reference to attitudes of both lawyers and the general public.

86. Roscoe Pound, "The Causes of Popular Dissatisfaction with the Administration of Justice," *American Bar Association Reports*, vol. 29 (1906), p. 395, in *Federal Rules Decisions*, vol. 35 (West, 1964), p. 241.

87. Priest, "Role of the Civil Jury," p. 170. Priest shows, however, that very few of the jury trials in Chicago involved issues bearing on these themes. Nevertheless, this was the Framers' vision of the jury, even in civil cases. See Amar, "Bill of Rights as a Constitution," pp. 1182–99.

88. For a recent account of the insurance industry's political ineffectiveness, see Stephen D. Sugarman, "California's Insurance Regulation Revolution: The First Two Years of Proposition 103," *San Diego Law Review*, vol. 27 (May–June 1990), pp. 684–92.

89. For an overview of these reforms, see Franklin and Rabin, *Tort Law and Alternatives*, pp. 710–15. See also Glenn Blackmon and Richard Zeckhauser, "State Tort Reform Legislation," p. 272.

90. Indeed, that is the term used by Franklin and Rabin, *Tort Law and Alternatives*, p. 710, to describe these reforms.

91. A similar expansion of judicial review of administrative action has occurred despite widespread criticism of its adverse effects on policy development. See Jerry L. Mashaw, "Improving the Environment of Agency Rulemaking: An Essay on Management, Games, and Legal and Political Accountability," *Law and Contemporary Problems*, (forthcoming).

92. See, for example, Gary Taylor, "Is FELA a Runaway Train?" *National Law Journal*, April 30, 1990, p. 1; W. John Moore, "Knocking the System," *National Law Journal*, November 23, 1991, p. 2848; and *Federal Employers' Liability Act*, Hearings before the Subcommittee on Transportation and Hazardous Materials of the House Committee on Energy and Commerce, 101 Cong. 1 sess. (Government Printing Office, November 1, 1989).

93. P. L. 102-66.

94. P. L. 101-336, 104 Stat. 327, codified at 42 U.S.C. §§ 12101-213 (1992).

95. The statutory caps depend on the size of the employer's work force. On repeal of the caps, see Kitty Oumas, "Senators Target Damages Caps in Sex Discrimination Suits," *Congressional Quarterly Weekly Report*, March 14, 1992, p. 620, which discusses bipartisan support.

96. See Lester Brickman, "The Asbestos Litigation Crisis: Is There a Need for an Administrative Alternative?" *Cardozo Law Review*, vol. 13 (April 1992), pp. 1819–89.

CHAPTER TEN

Improving the Quality
of Jury Decisionmaking

Stephen A. Saltzburg

T HE RIGHT TO TRIAL BY JURY is one of the fundamental rights claimed by Americans and has been since the adoption of the Constitution. Article III provided the right to jury trial in criminal cases even before the adoption of the Bill of Rights.[1] The Sixth Amendment right to jury trial in criminal cases and the Seventh Amendment right to jury trial in actions at law when the amount in controversy exceeds $20 demonstrated the importance the framers and the states approving the amendments placed on trial by jury.[2] State constitutions traditionally have also recognized this fundamental right.[3] And even in those states that do not extend the right as far as it is extended by other states and the federal government, the decision of the Supreme Court in *Duncan* v. *Louisiana*, which has been clarified in subsequent cases, requires states to afford persons accused of serious crimes a jury trial.[4]

Despite its pedigree, the jury has come under attack in both civil and criminal cases. Perhaps no case has caused more concern about the jury system than the trial of four white Los Angeles police officers for the beating of an African-American arrestee, Rodney King. The prosecutor relied upon a videotape taken by a bystander that depicted the officers' conduct. Although the Chief of Police in Los Angeles called this conduct "excessive," his comments were not published until after the jury had acquitted three defendants on all charges and could not decide on one charge against a fourth officer, who will be retried. The riots that followed sent a chill throughout all parts of the nation. Although the jurors in the case sought to justify or explain their verdict, the African-American community in Los Angeles was outraged that they had not convicted the officers.

This celebrated case does not stand alone. When former District of

Columbia Mayor Marion Barry was charged with possession of cocaine and with lying to a grand jury, his jury acquitted or could not agree on all charges except one misdemeanor, despite the government's videotape showing the then mayor smoking cocaine in a pipe. Later, the trial judge criticized the jury in comments made at the Harvard Law School.[5] At the 1992 annual judicial conference for the District of Columbia Circuit, the issue of jury nullification was a prime topic of discussion—a choice that suggests concern about the way the jury functions in modern courts.

The institution of the civil jury has also been attacked. Claims have been made that jurors return inflated verdicts and decide cases without an adequate understanding of the legal principles they are required to apply to the evidence. Suggestions have been made that America should follow the English lead and do away with juries in all or almost all civil cases.[6] Much of the discussion of civil juries has concerned complex cases, with some advocates arguing that jury trials in such cases result in injustice because the jurors cannot comprehend the evidence.[7] Arguments have also been made that judges need to do more to make juries work more effectively in complex cases.[8] While some jury advocates argue that the jury system works satisfactorily even in complex cases, dissatisfaction exists, and it is not confined to complex cases.[9] Insurers complain that the system of judging tort, or wrongful injury, cases—including trial by jury—has run amuck and that reforms are needed. If the English can run a civil justice system without juries in most cases, this argument runs, Americans can do the same.

Respective Advantages of Judges and Juries

My view is that the institution of the civil jury is as important today as it ever was, perhaps more so. It is necessary to explain why I hold this view before turning to ways the jury decisionmaking process can be improved.

Even before addressing the function juries serve, it may be useful to make a point about alternative dispute resolution. Potential litigants have the opportunity in some cases to contract with one another for an option other than the traditional judicial resolution of disputes. For example, two corporations contemplating a joint venture might choose to select arbitration as their preferred method of resolving disputes, designating rules and even the forum for their arbitration proceedings. Such a choice is likely to be respected by the courts.

Not all potential litigants can opt for an alternative to traditional litigation before a dispute arises. In many instances they cannot know who their potential adversaries will be or what their dispute will be about. Drivers of automobiles, for example, cannot contract for alternative dispute resolution with an adversary before an accident. But once the accident has occurred, the participants can choose to resolve any dispute by some means other than traditional litigation. As long as one litigant believes, however, that having a neutral third party hear the case is the best method of resolving the dispute, a trial will be required. A plaintiff may sue and decline invitations to participate in alternative forms of dispute resolution and may in fact have no other recourse but to sue if the defendant wants a trial.

The trial system in the United States essentially affords two choices, trial by judge or trial by jury. The advantages of trial by judge are many:

—the judge is presumed to know the law, which may eliminate some of the need for trial attorneys to devote part of the their opening statements and closing arguments to legal matters and to submit proposed jury instructions;

—the judge is a single decisionmaker who can indicate more readily than a jury whether he or she is confused and can ask questions with knowledge as to what questioning is permissible and impermissible and what evidence is admissible;

—the judge can deliberate alone, eliminating the possibility of a hung jury;

—the judge often has experience in sifting through evidence, which may help in resolving disputed issues of fact;

—the judge is likely to be more consistent in deciding cases than a group of juries.

The advantages of a jury are perhaps more numerous:

—jurors, who come to each case without the baggage of having heard similar cases, are more likely than a judge to keep open minds and not prejudge a case simply because it bears some resemblance to earlier cases;

—the jury has the benefit of input from a number of people, all of whom have heard the same evidence and analyzed it from their different perspectives, while the judge deliberates alone;

—the jury hears only the evidence the judge has ruled admissible, whereas a judge in a bench trial often hears inadmissible evidence and must perform the difficult task of ignoring that evidence;

—jurors do not speak directly to lawyers, and thus any hostility that might develop in a case between lawyers and the judge will not prejudice the jury's factfinding;[10]

—a jury selected from a cross section of the community is likely to have members whose biases or prejudices cancel or neutralize each other, but nothing cancels or neutralizes those of a judge;

—a representative jury offers the possibility that at least some of its members will be from a social class which a litigant can view as a peer group, while a judge may not be perceived as a peer;

—a jury is by definition drawn from all parts of a community and therefore is in touch with community standards, but a judge may have experience with only a small part of the community.

There are cases in which both sides prefer trial by judge for the reasons just given. A preference for a bench trial may also be a preference for a quicker, somewhat less expensive trial or for a particular judge regarded as especially good in handling certain kinds of cases. When both parties prefer a bench trial, usually they can and should have one.[11] But when at least one side prefers a jury trial, generally no bench trial will be required; a jury will be preferred.

There is a final aspect of trial by jury that makes the jury preferable to a judge in many cases. Federal judges are appointed for life and are, therefore, totally independent. Such independence is essential if they are to make difficult judgments on important questions, particularly those involving sensitive constitutional issues. But it does create a unique problem: independent judges may take on a regal air that makes litigants feel that judges do not think about things the way "ordinary people" do. Moreover, this independence means that, even if lawyers and litigants frequently have little confidence in the decisionmaking ability of a presiding judge, they have no remedy other than appeal from questionable decisions. Appeals are costly, and the deference appellate courts show to trial court decisions means that truly questionable decisions may be affirmed.

Few state court judges have life tenure. Some are appointed; others are elected. Those who are elected may face opposition in future elections, or they may run on their records. Whether judges are appointed or elected, and whether they face opposition or run on their record, the danger exists that they may be inclined to make decisions which may help them continue in office. Unpopular decisions may lead to challenges[12] and to public criticism by influential news media.[13] Even a jury that has been fairly selected may feel pressure from the public.[14] But the system has ways—sequestration, for example—to minimize such pressure and insulate jurors before they reach a decision. And jurors do not run for reelection or seek reappointment, of course.

For these reasons, juries offer advantages that judges cannot. It is difficult to imagine any other institution that could provide these advantages.[15] But the extent to which the juries do their job well depends in part on whether judges and lawyers participate in jury trials in ways that enhance or diminish the jurors' capacity to understand a case and render a proper verdict. While impartiality and insulation from political pressure are features inherent in the jury system,[16] the other advantages of juries can be affected by the procedures judges use in handling jury trials and the approaches lawyers take in offering evidence. The remainder of this article discusses how judges and lawyers can help juries perform the functions assigned to them.

The Quality of the Jurors

For juries to provide the advantages described above, it is important that all segments of the community be represented in the jury pool, or venire. Litigants will not have a reasonable chance of finding that their peers are represented on the jury unless these peers are represented in the venire. It is important that doctors, lawyers, bankers, teachers, and members of other professions be represented, along with retirees, blue collar workers, unemployed persons, and people who work in the home.

Many communities have realized the importance of making certain that the venire is drawn from a true cross section of the community. They have eliminated most exemptions from jury service and instead consider only individual claims of hardship. This is a step in the right direction. It goes without saying that, in some complicated commercial cases, a jury might well function better if at least some of its members have some experience in dealing with complicated business ventures, just as a jury might well function better in a case involving an altercation between white police officers and an African-American arrestee if there is minority representation on the jury. To the extent that the spectrum of life experiences on a jury can be broadened, the jury will benefit from the additional input.

There are two principal problems with expanding the jury pool in a meaningful way. First, a number of people will make strong claims that they cannot be absent from their jobs or their homes for long trials.[17] It can be an enormous burden on a juror to be away from work or out of the home for a long period of time, and the daily juror fee is no substitute for the income many jurors lose. As nice as it might sound to a judge to tell prospective jurors that service is their civic responsibility, even public-spirited individuals have reason to be concerned about the demands of jury duty. Jurors who are forced to serve under circumstances they regard as unfair might well pay less attention and be more concerned with deciding a case quickly than with reaching a fair verdict. Finding ways to shorten trials and minimize some of the burdens of service should enable more potential jurors to serve and broaden the spectrum of representation at the practical as well as the theoretical level.

The second problem is the use of peremptory challenges, which require no justification and which may be used to keep a group of people off a jury even though the group is represented in the pool. Cases such as *Batson* v. *Kentucky* (now extended to federal civil cases) bar the exclusion of jurors on racial grounds, and some courts have extended *Batson* to other classes of individuals.[18] But it is clear that peremptory challenges may also be used in an effort to keep more- or less-educated jurors from serving and to eliminate jurors because they are quite properly associated with a certain group.

There are three ways to prevent peremptory challenges from interfering to an undesirable extent with the ability of groups of jurors to serve. One is to assure that litigants do not have an overabundance of such challenges. If each side is limited in the exercise of these challenges, the possibility of excluding blocks of jurors diminishes. A second method is to broaden the jury pool as described earlier to produce more jurors from all segments of the community and make excluding entire groups more difficult. A final way is to provide better information to litigants and their counsel concerning individual jurors.

Years ago I made the point that, because parties in most cases want to win, only in extreme instances of racism or sexism will a litigant risk losing by choosing to eliminate jurors on the basis of race or gender rather than on the basis of their usefulness to the case.[19] Attorneys and litigants who use stereotypes in the exercise of peremptory challenges do so because they have little choice. Possessing scant information about potential jurors, they use rough guidelines they probably would not use if they had better information.

The use of juror questionnaires has been suggested elsewhere.[20] It makes good sense. Jurors can answer their questions in writing as a group, before they are brought to the courtroom, eliminating the delay associated with long individual voir dire, or preliminary, examinations. Three copies of their answers can be made for both sides and the judge. Challenges for cause, which require that the challenging party give a reason for wanting to eliminate a juror, will then probably be easier to make, because jurors are likely to reveal information in writing that they would not reveal in open court in the presence of others. All parties to the case would benefit, and peremptory challenges would be used to screen potential jurors who appear likely to be biased because of the nature of the case rather than because of affiliation with a certain group.[21]

Judge William Schwarzer has also suggested two possible procedures that could result in "more intelligent" jurors for complicated cases. The first is to permit each side to select a given number of jurors following the voir dire examination and then allow peremptory challenges and challenges for cause against those selected.[22] Another idea is for the trial judge to select a sufficient number of jurors based on their education and experience, then to meet in chambers with the attorneys in the case to discuss challenges, and then to select a jury.[23]

The first idea might well improve the quality of juries, depending on the number of peremptory challenges available and the jury pool itself. The second might guarantee a more intelligent jury, provided that the trial judge has the right to reject certain peremptory challenges and decide on minimum qualifications.[24] The second idea raises an issue that cannot be ignored: will a jury do a better job if less-educated jurors are totally excluded?

There is no ready answer to this question. One writer observes that conflict exists between the requirement that a jury represent a cross section of the community—a rule intended to guard against the exercise of arbitrary power—and the requirement that a jury's decisions be accurate if they are to be fair. He reasons that "while the cross-section requirement ensures that the jury is representative of the community and has the full moral weight of the community behind it, if juries were composed of specially qualified individuals or groups—for example, those selected on different grounds, such as intelligence—a jury decision arguably would be more accurate."[25] This supposed conflict between representativeness and accuracy may or may not be real; it depends on how people view the kinds of decisions jurors are called upon to make in trials. Are more intelligent jurors better at judging the credibility of witnesses? Are more intelligent jurors better at assessing the amount of money that should be paid as punitive damages when the conduct of a defendant has been found to be willful and wanton? I know of no way to answer these questions on the basis of the empirical information currently available.[26]

It is tempting for lawyers and judges to assume that well-educated jurors will be more accurate than less-educated jurors.[27] After all, lawyers and judges are college and law school graduates and tend to regard themselves as better able to resolve problems than most people. It is a small leap of faith to conclude that other highly educated individuals are probably better able than those with less education to resolve disputed issues accurately. But the decisions that jurors are called upon to make require deciding whether to believe the evidence the lawyers are putting before them and whether to be persuaded by the arguments lawyers make about such evidence. Their judgments may be more accurate than those lawyers and judges make, because jurors may look beyond the jargon with which lawyers and judges become comfortable and draw upon their own experiences. Some of those experiences may be more relevant to resolving disputed issues of fact than the education provided by the finest colleges and universities.

Moreover, I confess to doubting whether anyone would be able to agree on what constitutes a complicated case. For example, is a case complicated simply because it involves statistical evidence, or is it complicated only for those who are not mathematically inclined? Is it more difficult for a jury to decide damages in an antitrust case than it is to assess how much a defendant should pay for abusing a child? These questions cannot be answered on the basis of any data that now exist. My speculation is that judges and lawyers, using all the tools available to them, can make any case that is triable to a judge or to a group of so-called "experts" understandable to a jury, provided that the jury is not drawn exclusively from the worst-educated portion of the community. The tools that should be used to make a case clear are discussed later in the chapter.

Moreover, it seems doubtful to me that an accountant is necessarily better at understanding medical testimony than a midwife who may have less education. And, although it does seem intuitively obvious that accountants would have an easier time dealing with accounting issues in a case, this fact does not mean that they would be more accurate or fairer than other jurors. Suppose a plaintiff sues an accountant for malpractice or negligence. Would a jury of accountants be fairer and more likely to be accurate than a jury of ordinary people, some of whom use accountants to assist them in filing a tax return?

The evidence does not persuade me that a blue-ribbon jury is necessary or desirable, even in complex cases. There is reason to believe, however, that including more educated jurors might contribute to any jury's capacity to deal with difficult issues.[28] For instance, there is evidence that better-educated people score higher on tests evaluating understanding of jury instructions than jurors with poorer educations—the fact of the matter is that jury instructions are too often confusing to everyone, including those who are highly educated.[29] A better solution than imposing a minimum education requirement for a particular case would be to improve instructions or to rely more on special verdicts, two of the suggestions considered below.

Judicial Techniques to Improve Jury Trials

It is possible for the judiciary to reform the process for selecting jurors and trial procedures to broaden the venire and make jury service less burdensome. Such reform would eliminate some of the criticism now leveled against the civil jury.

Expanding the Pool of Jurors Able and Willing to Serve

I have emphasized the importance of drawing all segments of the community into the jury pool to improve the quality of jury decisionmaking. The judicial system can do this in two ways.[30] First, it is possible to eliminate almost all automatic exemptions from jury service so that everyone will actually be called to appear in court; hardship claims can be made there. Second, it is possible to eliminate many of the hardship claims by establishing the presumption that everyone should be prepared to serve as a juror every few years for one week (or possibly two weeks) without complaining of undue burdens.[31]

Individuals who have professional obligations or whose employers cannot readily replace them can be excused from trials expected to last longer than a week or two. Potential jurors can indicate on a questionnaire whether a long trial would pose a great hardship, and why. The court will then have two lists, one to be used for all cases expected to last less than two weeks and another for longer cases.[32] Under this system, no group of individuals is totally excused. Both highly educated jurors and those with less education would be on the first list and would therefore be available for most civil trials.

It is likely that potential jurors engaged in various professions or holding important employee positions might frequently seek to be excused from longer cases on the basis of hardship. If the longer cases are generally more complex than the shorter cases, this could cause a shortage of highly educated jurors for complex cases. Some may conclude that this is inevitable and that there are too few of these longer cases to worry about. It is also possible, however, to contemplate some additional steps that might increase the availability of highly educated jurors for all cases.

I recommend consideration of the following five steps for all cases. Each promises to expand the pool of willing and available jurors.

—Jurors should be asked to set aside a designated period of one week or more for possible jury service, and firm trial dates should be set and kept. Courts should work to develop a system in which judges back each other up, when necessary, so that cases are not postponed because judges are unavailable. Only the number of jurors reasonably expected to be needed on a given day should be called. Those who are selected serve as jurors; those who are not should be excused, unless it appears that another trial may begin and be completed during the designated period, in which case the jurors should be recalled for jury selection on the date the trial is to begin. All jurors should be paid for each day they attend court or are on call. This proposal will reduce the burdens associated with the uncertainty of not knowing exactly when jury service will begin and end or how long it will take.[33]

—Trial judges should consider imposing deadlines on the parties for presentation of evidence in order to fit the vast bulk of cases into the presumptive time period described above.[34] This will make it more likely that jurors represent a cross section of the community, because the venire will not be limited to people who have large blocks of free time and little else to do.[35] If both sides of a case oppose being held to the presumptive time period, the judge understandably may want to reconsider whether such a period is sufficient for a fair trial. But if one side seeks the benefit of a broadened jury pool, there is reason for the trial court to strain to provide it. This tactic involves a trade-off: less time is allotted for the presentation of evidence in return for a broader jury pool. It would be wrong to pretend that a trial which should take six weeks under ideal conditions can be tried in five days, but it would be just as wrong to pretend that a trial that might take eight days cannot be shortened to five.[36]

—Consideration should be given to segregating discrete issues for trial and to the possibility of trying these issues to different juries.[37] Judge Schwarzer has noted that bifurcation, which allows jurors to decide the issue of liability first and then set a damage award, "can produce economies except where much of the evidence must be produced at both trials."[38] If separate juries can be used, then long cases can be broken into several short trials, and it is possible that the separate jury pools will be more representative than one would have been for a single long trial.

—Efforts should be made to schedule a trial so that it begins at 4:00 p.m. and continues until 8:00 p.m. for as long the trial takes if this will increase the representativeness of the jury pool. If such a trial schedule is imposed, the financial hardship on highly paid individuals may be considerably reduced, and employees who operate on a flex-time schedule may find it easier to serve on the jury. It can be argued that jurors who work during the day and then attend court will be tired. But jurors who attend court during the day and then hurry home to take care of many of the tasks that cannot be ignored while a trial goes on may also be tired. The trial judge will be burdened with a trial that concludes at 8:00 p.m. each working day for several weeks—a problem for a judge conducting other judicial business (perhaps even other trials) during the earlier part of the day. Judges should not be expected to try cases on this schedule except when a trial cannot be completed within a week or two and the jury pool will not be sufficiently representative of the community if the trial goes forward during the usual daytime hours.

It may be possible to adopt a hybrid schedule that allows a case to be tried for a week or two (the presumptive time for jury service) and finished on the evening schedule just described. The point is to find a way to remove unacceptable burdens on those asked to perform jury service.

—In some cases, jurors can be given exhibits and even videotape depositions to view at home over a weekend in order to reduce the time required in court. Such a procedure carries with it the risk that jurors will not do their homework. But even when exhibits are presented in court, it is never possible to be sure that all jurors are paying attention. If jurors were required to certify to the court that they had read or watched what was presented to them, sufficient incentive might exist for jurors to do what they are asked. Assuming that jurors absorb material at differing rates—depending on their education, experience, mental agility, and interest—it seems that giving jurors some flexibility in dealing with exhibits might provide them with the opportunity to take as much or as little time as they need to understand the material. And to the extent that trial time can be reduced with this technique, the jury pool might be broadened.

Identifying the Issues in Dispute

One of the most common complaints jurors make is that lawyers bore them by putting forward more evidence and making cases more complicated than necessary.[39] In my experience as well, it is not uncommon for lawyers to put forward unnecessary evidence and for both sides to repeat evidence. Part of the problem is that documents in a case are often due weeks before the trial so that careful attorneys decline to ask to have certain facts admitted, list more witnesses than they ever really expect to call, and set forth lists of exhibits that are overinclusive in case something is forgotten and might be precluded during the trial. Simply by asking to have certain facts "admitted," as I will show, can spare jurors much time and frustration.

In theory, Federal Rule of Civil Procedure 36 provides an opportunity for one side to put the other in the position of having to state whether or not it "admits" that certain facts in a case cannot really be disputed. The problem is that such facts are usually "admitted" during the pre-trial disclosure of facts, or discovery process, and attorneys are not always sure which facts are most important and which they want to have admitted so early in the proceedings. Moreover, a party to a case may sense a tactical advantage in offering proof of a fact rather than simply acknowledging its validity. When one side does ask to have certain facts admitted, the other side theoretically must admit those which are not reasonably in dispute, or face a penalty if they are proved at trial.[40] But it is common knowledge that most cases settle before a trial verdict is reached, so a failure to admit to fact, in most cases, will never reach the penalty stage. A party challenged to admit or deny a fact can also claim that insufficient information is available to make such a determination, which means that asking to have facts admitted early in the pre-trial discovery process is likely to be ineffective.[41] And when the time allotted for this process runs out (as it does in those jurisdictions that impose a time limit for discovery), the chance to make such requests may disappear.

My recommendation to trial judges is that they permit or even require that certain facts be admitted after the pre-trial disclosure of facts. Many orders by federal courts (issued under Federal Rule of Civil Procedure 16) require final pre-trial statements, a listing of exhibits, and a statement of agreed-on facts. But, my experience is that the agreed-on facts rarely encompass all or even most of those that are not genuinely disputed. Again, this may be because the final statements are often filed well before the trial date. And since most cases settle, efficient attorneys may wisely conclude that spending large amounts of time seeking to agree on facts for a pre-trial statement would be wasteful. In theory, time spent talking about undisputed facts could lead to settlement discussions, but in practice settlement discussions often do not reach fruition until the trial is on the immediate horizon—possibly because attorneys do not have time to think about a case until the trial is in the offing, or because clients choose not to focus on settlement until they face the alternative of trial and an all-or-nothing verdict.

Whatever the reason, the reality is that when the trial becomes a reality, lawyers must decide which issues they will actually contest and which they will forgo. This is the time when "admissions" of fact should be sought. Thus, I suggest that trial judges permit or require the attorneys for each party in a case to file, ten days prior to trial, a request for admissions. The judge should urge the admission of as many facts as possible. Both sides will have three to five days to respond, and at trial time, no other response should be permitted. Either side can be held responsible for facts it denies during the final pre-trial process and later tries to establish or concede. In addition, the trial judge should be permitted to instruct the jury as follows: "The purpose of seeking admissions is to spare you, the jury, from having to take time to consider evidence on matters that are not really in dispute and to permit both sides to try a case fairly without being surprised as to what is and is not disputed. When a party denies a fact shortly before trial, and at trial it is clear that the fact is really not in dispute, you may consider this conduct in assessing the weight to be given that party's evidence."

There are two other remedies that ought also to be available to the trial judge. If it appears that a party to a case has engaged in a pattern of denials of facts not really disputed and that this pattern has delayed the trial, the judge should be able to limit the offending party's evidence as a penalty. And, after the jury has returned a verdict, the judge should be able to hold a hearing and to consider sanctions such as those imposed by Federal Rule of Civil Procedure 11 which include monetary penalties imposed upon parties, their counsel, or both.[42]

As indicated, the court should either permit or require requests for admission of facts. In a voluntary system, the advantages of such requests accrue only to the attorney who takes the trouble to make requests. In a mandatory system, the advantages accrue in all cases. To make a mandatory system work, the trial judge must use the two remedies suggested in the preceding paragraph—limiting the presentation of evidence and imposing sanctions—if attorneys do not make reasonable efforts to have facts admitted.

This procedure promises to promote pre-trial preparation, shorten trials, clarify the disputed and undisputed issues, and in the end to make cases clearer to jurors by forcing attorneys to focus on all the facts before presenting a case to a jury.

Experts and Undisputed Issues

A procedure similar to the one described above can be used in cases involving expert witnesses. Each side should be permitted or required to request admissions of fact concerning issues undisputed by experts. The same type of schedule can be used and the same remedies made available in the event of noncompliance. The one addition that I would suggest is that experts sign, along with the attorneys, both the form requesting the admissions and the response. It is important to get experts involved in ferreting out the undisputed issues rather than leaving the entire task to attorneys who may later attribute any breakdown in the process to their lack of expertise rather than to an intent to subvert the process.[43]

Alternate Jurors and Jury Size

A trial judge has discretion over the seating of alternate jurors in many jurisdictions. Even before the Federal Rules of Civil Procedure were amended in 1991 to eliminate alternate jurors, Judge Schwarzer observed, "Although that rule [47(b)] provides that alternates shall replace regular jurors in the order in which they are called, it does not by its terms preclude seating a jury of more than six in lieu of designating alternates."[44] He added that "many judges now use this method, rather than designating alternates at the outset, reasoning that when none of the jurors regard themselves as supernumeraries likely to be excused before deliberations begin, they will all be more attentive and responsible." Federal Rule of Civil Procedure 48, as amended in 1991, provides that "[t]he court shall seat a jury of not fewer than six and not more than twelve members and all jurors shall participate in the verdict unless excused from service by the court pursuant to Rule 47(c)."[45]

This approach of not identifying alternates makes eminent good sense.

Indeed, it is difficult to see any advantage to telling jurors at the outset of a case that some constitute the official jury while others are reserves. In jurisdictions without the equivalent of Rule 48, when a case is submitted to the jury, the judge should be able to excuse jurors if the parties and the court believe that six is the correct number—or all jurors could be allowed to deliberate. Juries of eight are likely to be more representative of the community and probably should be preferred.[46] And letting all jury members who hear a case deliberate will eliminate the frustration and disappointment that can be anticipated when a member who has listened carefully to all the evidence discovers that he or she is being excused prior to deliberations.[47]

Jury Instructions

It is easy to say that jury instructions should be written so they can be comprehended by lay persons and that they should not be full of legal jargon. It is hard, however, to make judges give such instructions. In some jurisdictions, judges are required to use certain approved instructions, and those instructions are not well written. Judges in other jurisdictions who have choices tend to prefer instructions that have been upheld when tested on appeal. It is difficult to persuade judges to take a risk on a new set of instructions.

There are books and articles that describe how better instructions can be written.[48] But there is little evidence to suggest that improved instructions are in fact being written. I have collaborated with Dean Harvey Perlman and Professor Jo Potuto, both of the University of Nebraska College of Law, in writing jury instructions in plain language for federal criminal trials.[49] But even when we have been able to convince some judges that our instructions are clearer and more likely to be understood than others, in several circuits the existence of pattern instructions (those approved by one of the federal courts) discourages federal judges from taking a chance on new ones. We also found that some judges stick with instructions that have withstood appeal, even if the judges acknowledge that jurors have had trouble understanding the language.

Some criminal defense lawyers have told us they believe that our "plain language" instructions favor the government. After asking for explanations and considering them, my conclusion is that these lawyers can have only one reason for saying this. Our revised instructions remove the gibberish from what juries are told, but some defense attorneys want the gibberish, which they hope will confuse the jury about the law in cases where there is no very good defense.

Dean Perlman and I wrote civil jury instructions for the state of Alaska more than a decade ago. We worked with a committee of lawyers and judges to produce a product that addressed more aspects of civil law than we had seen covered in any other instructions. We discovered that one reason new jury instructions are hard to sell is that, properly written, they force courts and lawyers to confront the meaning of legal doctrines which the old instructions, embedded in jargon, leave unconfronted. An amazing number of times, we found that the law was unclear to the judges and lawyers themselves. More than a few times, these judges and lawyers indicated they were concerned that our new instructions seemed to change the law. What they really meant was that our instructions actually confronted issues, and no one could be sure whether these instructions changed anything because no one knew what the old instructions really meant.

This is a major problem in writing new jury instructions, but it must be confronted if juries are expected to decide cases properly. Trial courts understandably hesitate to risk having a decision reversed on the basis of an untested instruction that clarifies language so that there can be no mistake about what a jury is asked to do. The risk might be more worth taking if appellate courts wrote opinions that not only affirmed or reversed decisions on the basis of questions concerning jury instructions but provided nontechnical language to be used in subsequent jury trials. Cases of appellate courts engaging in this effort are not easy to find. Thus, trial judges may conclude that, if they take the risk of clarifying an instruction, not only might their decision be reversed, but the appellate court could reverse it in an opinion that only condemns the innovative instruction without offering any improvement thus leaving the judge with little recourse but to rely upon a "standard" instruction, no matter how confusing it actually is. The parties to a case also may favor a standard instruction, even if it is ambiguous, because they bear the costs if a case is reversed and must be retried. Thus, the choice of a standard instruction makes some sense. For jury instructions to be improved, appellate courts and trial judges must work together to make the risks of clarity worth taking at the trial level.

There are some suggestions trial judges should consider that fall short of actually rewriting instructions. I propose that all traditional instructions regarding the credibility of witnesses be eliminated and the following instruction substituted: "You are to decide who and what to believe.

The weight to be given any testimony or other evidence is solely for you to decide." Eliminating unnecessary instructions focuses the jury on the heart of the case.

I also suggest eliminating instructions that set forth legal terms which are defined only in subsequent instructions. For example, it is not necessary to tell the jury that the plaintiff must prove negligence by a "preponderance" of the evidence and then define a preponderance. It is shorter and clearer to say to the jury, "You must decide whether it is more likely than not that. . . ." It is not even necessary to tell the jury that it must decide whether or not the defendant was negligent and then define negligence. It is shorter and clearer to add words to the instruction just given, so that it reads, "You must decide whether it is more likely than not that the defendant failed to exercise reasonable care under the circumstances."

It is important, I believe, that jury instructions be as case specific as possible. Thus, if the plaintiff's theory of negligence is that a defendant failed to stop at a traffic light, the instruction previously given could be made case specific by the addition of a few words, so that it reads, "You must decide whether it is more likely than not that the defendant failed to exercise reasonable care under the circumstances because he drove his car through a red light."

It is also important not to define terms after telling jurors to disregard them. For example, it is common in many courts for the judge to define both direct and circumstantial evidence but to tell the jury that one type of evidence is not necessarily more probative than another.[50] It would be less confusing to say nothing to the jury about types of evidence and to rely on the one simple instruction that I have previously set forth.

In long or complicated cases, trial judges may want to give preliminary instructions before the evidence is heard. These instructions have been called "the logical corollary to the lawyers' opening statements."[51] There are good reasons for the court to require attorneys to submit their proposed instructions before the case begins. The judge is then in a position to know which legal doctrines the attorneys believe the jury needs to know about and can decide what the jurors should be told at the outset of the case.

In jurisdictions that permit the trial judge to give final instructions prior to the closing arguments, for example, Federal Rule of Civil Procedure 51, the instructions to the jury should be given before the attorneys argue their cases. This permits the lawyers to address their arguments about the evidence to the specific language the judge has used in the instructions. After the arguments, the judge should reinstruct if necessary to correct any misimpression that may have been created. It makes good sense to give the jury a written or recorded copy of the instructions.[52] In many courts, exhibits that are admitted as evidence go to the jury room, and jurors have an opportunity to review or to re-review them. Jurors also ought to have an opportunity to review what the judge has said, particularly as their deliberations focus on aspects of evidence they may view differently from the lawyers.

If the instructions are clear and uncluttered, if the jury is given preliminary instructions in a long or complicated case, if the judge instructs the jury before closing arguments, and if the jury is provided with a copy of the instructions, the judge will have done a great deal to promote juror comprehension.

Some judges believe that they can be more helpful to the jury if they not only instruct on the law but also marshal the evidence in the instructions in order to make the connection between the evidence and the instructions more readily apparent.[53] If the judge instructs before the closing arguments, an effort to marshal the evidence and help the jury may work well. It is important, however, that the trial judge indicate clearly when the jury is bound by the instructions—that is, when the judge is setting forth a legal rule that must be followed—and when the lawyers are free to disagree with the judge about the evidence presented and the jurors permitted to reach their own conclusion about who is correct.

Juror Questions and Note-taking

Suggestions have been made recently that jurors should be invited to ask questions in writing when they are confused about evidence or believe that some fact that has not been elicited is important.[54] One judge who has for a decade permitted juries to ask questions reports that "most lawyers who have been exposed to jury questioning in my court have either dropped their initial resistance or become active supporters of the procedure."[55] This judge raises the issue of jury questioning with the attorneys at the outset of a case, because in some cases there may be reasons why questions should not be asked—for instance, in a criminal case when significant evidence has been suppressed, or in a civil case when substantial videotape deposition testimony will be used. If questions are to be permitted, the judge instructs the jury that, after each witness testifies, any juror may submit a written question. The judge consults with the attorneys on each question to see if they have any objections, and if they do not, the question is asked. If an objection is made, a question may be revised or rejected. If a question is asked, each side is permitted to ask follow-up questions. Counsel who object to a juror's question may make a record of an objection at the next recess outside the hearing of the jury to avoid any direct clash between counsel and the juror.

Jury questions have long been permitted in the military but are not common in most courts.[56] It seems intuitively obvious that juries are likely to render more informed decisions and lawyers to understand better when jurors are confused if the jurors are permitted to actively participate by asking questions.

Interestingly, the state judge whose procedure is described above requires jurors who wish to ask questions to raise their hands and request pencil and paper. This implies that the jurors are not otherwise permitted to take notes. It is arguable that people cannot listen and take notes at the same time; if this argument is accepted, however, classes in most universities and law schools would have to be taught much differently than they now are. Most of us cannot imagine being expected to remember all the things we are told, sometimes over a period of days, without being permitted to make some notes. Research on note-taking indicates that it improves memory and recall and improves the performance of the notetakers.[57] An experiment conducted by the Federal Courts Committee of the Philadelphia Bar Association involved note-taking in thirty civil and nine criminal trials. Note-taking was optional, and various techniques were used to protect the privacy of each juror's notes. Jurors found taking notes to be helpful, and it did not appear to interfere with factfinding.[58]

My recommendation is that jurors be permitted to take notes and to ask questions in writing. I would modify the procedure for questioning, however, by telling jurors to write down questions if they are confused and to keep their written questions for the end of the witness's testimony, by which time the matter may have been cleared up and the written questions can be discarded. If the confusion persists or a concern remains, the written question can be submitted to the court. In some cases, after consulting with the attorneys, the trial judge may conclude that the confusion will dissipate following the introduction of additional evidence. The trial judge can also ask later in the trial whether any of the jurors are still uncertain, leaving it to the attorneys to decide whether to address the problem through evidence or argument.[59]

There is always the danger that jurors will be disappointed when their confusion is not resolved or their questions are not asked. The judge can do a great deal to soften this disappointment by explaining that there are rules governing the sort of evidence courts may receive and the type of questions that can be asked—and that jurors are not expected to be aware of or to anticipate those rules.

Verdicts and Deliberations

In complicated cases, there is much to be said for special verdicts. Federal Rule of Civil Procedure 49, which provides for special verdicts, allows the trial judge to "require a jury to return only a special verdict in the form of a special written finding upon each issue of fact," or the court to "submit to the jury, together with appropriate forms for a general verdict, written interrogatories upon one or more issues of fact the decision of which is necessary to a verdict." The history of special verdicts has demonstrated that they are controversial because they threaten to guide or control the jury's decisionmaking process and thus, to some extent deprive the jury of its role as the conscience of the community.[60] For this reason, Supreme Court Justices Hugo L. Black and William O. Douglas opposed the use of special verdicts in civil cases.[61] Another eminent jurist, Judge Jerome Frank, was a strong supporter of them.[62]

The special verdict as permitted by Federal Rule of Civil Procedure 49(a) promises to save judicial time in crafting instructions, provided that the trial judge bears the burden of identifying the factual issues the jury must decide. Surely it is easier for jurors to understand that they are being asked to decide whether it is more likely than not that the defendant drove through a red light than for them to master the law of negligence and apply it to the facts of a case. The special verdict, particularly the fact verdict, permits jurors to find facts without mastering the law. It also permits the trial judge and appellate courts to see how the jury reached a decision, something that may be important when a number of complicated issues are presented. Some courts have used special verdicts when they have been concerned that jurors might be disinclined to apply a technical rule of law to a case.[63] Other courts have recognized the advantage of being able to ensure that jurors adhere to the legal framework governing a case.[64]

The advantages of having jurors focus on the facts are obvious. Focusing on the facts eliminates the need for complicated instructions on the law, simplifies invocation in subsequent cases of the doctrine of issue preclusion (a doctrine that permits a decision in one case to be controlling when the same issue arises in a subsequent case), and allows for monitoring of the jury's adherence to law. It may also ensure a truly unanimous jury on important points and can facilitate appellate review. The disadvantages all relate to the question of how much control judges should have over jury deliberations and the fear that the jury's independence may be compromised.

There is every reason to favor special verdicts, particularly fact verdicts, in complicated cases. By definition, difficult cases are the ones in which efforts to assist a jury ought to be most welcome, because they are the cases in which the judge must find some way of communicating to the jury its role in the case. Perhaps in some cases it is better not to know how the jury reached a conclusion. But in complicated cases in which parties and the judicial system invest substantial resources, the following point seems especially apt: "[W]hen the jury is unable to determine the normal application of the law to the facts of a case and reaches a verdict on the basis of nothing more than its own determination of community wisdom and values, its operation is indistinguishable from arbitrary and unprincipled decisionmaking."[65]

It may be possible to combine separation of the issues with a special verdict. Such a combination would reduce the number of questions a jury would have to decide with respect to a part of a case. It is also possible for the trial judge to ask the jury to decide some questions of fact before others are submitted. Suppose, for example, in a products liability case, the court believes that causation is much in doubt. The court can ask the jury to answer questions relating to causation before any other questions are submitted. If the jury finds no causation, the judge can enter judgment and no further deliberations will be required. This procedure can save substantial time in some complicated cases.

It can be argued, however, that the judge should submit all issues to the jury, increasing the odds that no new trial will be needed if an appellate court disagrees with the verdict.[66] In some cases, having a jury decide all issues even after it decides one that resolves the case is more efficient than terminating deliberations once such a decision is made. A middle ground would be for the judge to submit an issue such as causation to the jury and, if that issue is decided in a way that resolves the case, to submit all other issues to the jury without requiring lengthy deliberations. If the jury reaches agreement rapidly on additional questions, it is more efficient to obtain the jury's answers than to end the case. To the extent that the jury has difficulty with additional issues, it makes sense to terminate the case.

Whether a general or special verdict is used, there is much to commend a unanimity rule.[67] When a jury is required to reach a unanimous verdict, the jurors must deliberate with each other. Any rule that permits a majority to prevail raises the possibility that the majority will not listen to a minority once sufficient votes exist to return a verdict.[68] One exception to the unanimity rule might be recognized, however. After a jury has deliberated for what the trial judge regards as a sufficient period of time to demonstrate that a unanimous verdict is unlikely, the trial judge can submit one additional interrogatory to the jury in the following language: "Since you have not been able to reach unanimity, I must decide whether to order a new trial or to permit you to return a verdict on the basis of a divided vote. You have the benefit of knowing the basis on which you disagree. My question is whether you believe that justice would be better served by my accepting a less than unanimous verdict or by ordering a new trial. You may answer this question by a less than unanimous vote. Please return your verdict form with an indication of how you divide[69] together with your answer to this question."[70]

The answer to this question will give the court a sense of whether the jury believes that it has addressed the issues seriously and that any other jury will also have difficulty reaching unanimity, or whether some jurors simply regard others as unreasonable. Looking at the vote and the evidence presented at trial, the trial judge can be empowered to enter a judgment based on a nonunanimous verdict.[71]

Some commentators urge the judge to provide some guidance to the jury on how to go about its deliberations—for instance, how to elect a foreperson and when to vote.[72] Although this suggestion may raise the specter of judicial interference with juries, I believe it has much to commend it. Most jurors have no idea of how to proceed, and it makes little sense for them to waste time wondering about how to begin deliberations.

Finally, Judge Schwarzer has suggested that it may be time to reconsider the typical jury instruction that forbids jurors to talk to each other about the case until they actually begin deliberations.[73] He questions whether jurors can adhere to this instruction and whether it is worth seeking to require them to do so. With so much attention being paid to opening statements in cases, and with defense attorneys aware of the importance of a powerful opening early in a case, there is reason to believe that jurors can talk about a case without prejudicing their final deliberations. Indeed, it may well be that jurors can educate the court about common areas of confusion if they are permitted to speak with one another about the case during the trial. As long as the trial judge reminds the jurors that they should not close their minds until all the evidence is in, jurors who use recesses and periods in which they are excused from the courtroom to talk about the case may be better prepared for final deliberations than they would be under the current procedure.

There is a caveat to be offered about midtrial deliberations. The jury should be told that its discussions should only take place in the jury room. There is reason to worry about some jurors becoming too cozy with one or two others and forming a block based on contact outside the courthouse. This can be controlled to a large extent if all discussions take place in the jury room.

Expert and Scientific Evidence

One suggestion about expert and scientific evidence that is extremely appealing involves having a trial judge utilize Federal Rule of Evidence 403 to ensure that evidence is submitted in a form that actually assists a jury in understanding a case.[74] Rule 403 allows a judge to exclude certain evidence that could confuse the jury rather than help it reach a decision. I submit that the trial judge should consider whether expert or scientific evidence is being submitted in a form he or she understands and whether in this form, it can be effectively applied to the case. If the judge cannot understand the evidence or has difficulty deciding how to relate it to the disputed issues, the judge should assume that the jurors will have the same problems.

Although the jury is entitled to assess how much, if any, weight to give specific evidence, the judge is responsible for assuring that what is proffered satisfies the rules of evidence. It is possible that a jury will be better able than a judge to understand unfamiliar and specialized material and that items a judge finds confusing could nevertheless assist the trier of fact and satisfy Federal Rule of Evidence 702, which requires that expert testimony assist the factfinder.[75] But if the judge is confused and not assisted by the evidence, the presumption should be that the jury would also be confused.

Many courts have been concerned in recent years that some expert opinion not adequately grounded in science has been admitted. At one time, the Frye test required that expert opinion be based on generally accepted principles and techniques, but while some courts adhere to this test, others have relaxed or modified it.[76] Recently, the New Jersey Supreme Court in two cases concluded that:

> The admissibility of such testimony depends on the expert's ability to explain pertinent scientific principles and to apply those principles to the formulation of his or her opinion. Thus, the key to admission of the opinion is the validity of expert's reasoning and methodology. . . . In resolving these issues, the trial court should not substitute its judgment for that of the relevant scientific community. The court's function is to distinguish scientifically sound reasoning from that of the self-validating expert, who uses scientific terminology to present unsubstantiated personal beliefs.[77]

This approach appears to strike a fair balance between the need to screen out unreliable evidence and judicial intrusion into matters outside a judge's area of expertise. It also provides a standard that should guide judges in deciding what evidence really helps a jury. Evidence can help a jury only if the jurors can understand the expert's reasoning and methodology and, in addition, see clearly how his or her opinions or ideas fit into the case. This additional factor is the guarantee against confusion.

It is wrong for a trial judge simply to admit evidence for what it is worth. As one federal court of appeals stated, "Our message to our able trial colleagues: it is time to take hold of expert testimony in federal trials."[78] By taking hold, trial judges can promote jury understanding and increase the probability of just verdicts in cases involving important expert testimony or scientific evidence.

How Trial Lawyers Can Promote Comprehension

All the suggestions made thus far are intended to improve the quality of the jury's decisionmaking process in civil cases, and most are equally applicable to criminal cases. I have reserved for last a discussion of what lawyers can do to promote juror comprehension and improve the quality of jury verdicts.

The Relative Importance of Lawyers' Contributions to Comprehension

Placing this subject last indicates my view that lawyers can do a good deal to make their presentations more interesting, even though ultimately they have less control over juror comprehension than the judge has. Moreover, the techniques that lawyers choose to use are likely to be less important to juror comprehension than the procedures just discussed, because adversarial attorneys in our system do not always have an incentive to make things clear and to promote understanding. There are times when confusion and ambiguity promote the odds of one party's prevailing. This is not to say that promoting confusion ought to be deemed a worthy goal for any litigant. But the reality is that litigants want to win, and attorneys adopt methods that increase the odds of winning *to the extent that the methods are permitted under the governing rules.* The italicized clause is important, because it explains why the rules and the judge's enforcement of them are crucial to juror comprehension. Lawyers can be compelled to be clear, but they cannot be depended on to be clear in all cases. Even if one side in a case makes heroic efforts to educate the jurors about all disputed issues, the other side may strain to muddy the water.

Visual Evidence

The single most important thing lawyers can do to help jurors understand is to rely on visual evidence that demonstrates principles, depicts events, explains the relationship of various pieces of evidence, and presents people, places, and things that are important to a case. The table of contents of the leading work on visual evidence lists videotape evidence (including depositions), computer-generated evidence, and in-court exhibitions, demonstrations, and experiments as the most common forms of visual evidence.[79]

This treatise makes it clear, however, that the decision to use visual evidence is a tactical one. Consider the following passage, for example:

The principal characteristic of videotape is that it provides a much fuller representation of testimony than a written transcript. It captures important indicia of testimonial trustworthiness—e.g., appearance, demeanor, inflection, facial expressions, nervous mannerisms—that are lost in a transcript. A transcript is a great equalizer. Widely discrepant degrees of witness sincerity and persuasiveness are homogenized in that bland ennui which is induced by a third person's reading of a deposition transcript into the record. Videotape invites discrimination.[80]

This analysis suggests that videotape evidence will convey more information to a jury than a transcript of testimony read by an attorney or witness. In some cases, more is better, and videotape evidence should be preferred. In other cases, the transcript probably conveys sufficient information and involves less presentation time because it is easier to edit and requires no equipment.

Just as the decision to call a witness or pursue a certain line of questioning involves tactical judgments, so does the decision to use certain types of visual evidence. Videotape and other forms of visual presentations have the capacity to bring more information before jurors in ways that are likely to be more memorable than mere oral testimony. Because the parties make judgments concerning the tactics that will best serve their cases before the trial starts and for most purposes, outside the province of the court, the evidence available at trial will be largely a function of tactical decisions made along the way.

Videotape Evidence

The use of videotapes should be encouraged by courts. Photographic evidence has been a powerful form of proof for years (the cases in which gruesome photographs are admitted in a criminal prosecution are legion). Videotape evidence is similar, except that the movement and sound make it more interesting and real to a jury.[81]

I believe that courts should encourage videotape depositions of important witnesses. If a witness is unavailable, the videotaped testimony is likely to be more helpful to a jury than a written transcript. And if a witness gives testimony that is inconsistent with a deposition, the videotape can help the jury decide whether the inconsistency can be explained on acceptable grounds (such as nervousness, fear, or inability to understand the question) or whether the trial testimony is suspect.

If one party wants a videotape deposition and can successfully prove the witness's importance, the court should routinely order such a deposition. To the extent that the opponent of a videotape raises cost as an objection, the judge should have the discretion to allocate the cost of the taping and of making copies to the party requesting the deposition.

The fact that one party might have a tactical reason to prefer less significant evidence is not a factor that any judge should look upon with favor. To reiterate a point made earlier, one side in a case may have an incentive to leave matters ambiguous, but a judge ought not to encourage such tactics when the other side is attempting to explain the issues fairly.

Judges should encourage the use of videotape evidence whenever it saves time and conveys a more accurate sense of a scene than still photographs. Suppose, for example, an accident takes place in a plant. To the extent that a jury needs to understand where various equipment was and where individual workstations were in relation to the equipment, a videotape will almost certainly provide a better understanding of the plant and will do so more quickly than a series of still photographs. Videotape and still photographs are not mutually exclusive evidence, however. Used together, they can educate jurors about general scenes and highlight particular items, places or people. A blowup of a certain piece of equipment may add to the general overview provided by the videotape and may be an extremely valuable piece of evidence.

Videotape evidence can also be useful in demonstrating how things work—a machine in a plant, for instance. A visual demonstration of this kind can often save time and is much clearer than oral testimony. But videotape and oral testimony also are not mutually exclusive, for oral testimony can explain a tape and answer questions it raises.

Further, videotape evidence can be useful to recreate events.[82] The concern, however, is that in some instances in which there are enormous differences of opinion about the facts, a videotape recreation may convey a sense of reality that gives one side an undue advantage. A recreation can also involve conditions so different from those that existed at the time of a relevant event that it is not of great probative value.[83]

Videotape evidence can be used effectively and fairly to demonstrate injuries to items or to people. Although some courts once viewed "day in the life" films as unduly prejudicial, a videotape that accurately depicts the hardships an injured person must endure may convey probative and necessary information to a jury.[84] Where testimony would be admitted and videotape evidence accurately portrays facts more completely, it should be preferred.

Courts should permit attorneys to take videotape depositions in classrooms or work areas so that witnesses can have access to diagrams, charts, or equipment while being questioned. It makes sense to admit portions of these depositions, even though witnesses are available, rather than to require witnesses to bring diagrams, charts, or equipment to the courtroom. Witnesses can adopt the deposition testimony as trial testimony and be cross-examined on it.

Courts should also encourage videotape depositions of expert witnesses and consider rules that permit admitting such tapes without proof that the witness is unavailable. Because not all trial dates are firm, and because in the course of a trial there may be unforseen delays, it can be costly for parties to have expert witnesses waiting to be called to testify. Moreover, some experts do not want to be involved in trials because of the disruption to their schedules. By permitting videotape depositions of experts, courts can save parties to a case money and provide an incentive for some experts who are currently unwilling to become involved in trials to do so.

Computer-Generated Evidence

All kinds of computer-generated evidence are possible. Some involve basic business records that are admissible when a foundation is laid according to rules such as Federal Rule of Evidence 803 (6) (exception to the rule regarding hearsay evidence) and properly authenticated under rules like Federal Rule of Evidence 901 (basic requirement that a foundation be presented to put evidence in context). Such evidence poses no great difficulty for courts. More difficulty is raised when computers are used to recreate events such as airplane crashes.

The basic rule that trial judges should use in dealing with computer-generated reenactments is similar to that used in connection with videotape: such evidence should be admitted if it illustrates and explains to the jury a party's case and is grounded in admissible evidence. Like videotapes, computer-generated evidence can save time and promote understanding. Courts should require that both computer-generated evidence and videotape experiments be disclosed prior to trial and that an adversary have the opportunity then to learn how the evidence was created and what assumptions were used in creating it. Furthermore, to the extent that software is involved, an adversary should have access to it under an appropriate protective order.

When litigants and their attorneys can use computer-generated demonstrations to illustrate and explain their case, such exhibits ought to be encouraged, particularly now that the cost of preparing them is dropping. Cost may, however, be a factor a court should consider in deciding whether evidence will assist a jury in deciding a case fairly. If one side has vast resources and the other few, the side with more resources may be able to fund impressive exhibits that create an unfair advantage. One of the interesting aspects of trials is that, except for demonstrative evidence and expert testimony, parties generally take the evidence as they find it. Less wealthy litigants may even have more impressive witnesses than wealthy litigants. But, it remains true that wealthy litigants can afford experts and demonstrative evidence that others can only envy.

Determining the point at which the use of demonstrative evidence becomes unfair is not easy. My preference is for evidence that helps a jury understand a case, provided that certain rules are followed prior to trial. A proponent of "fancy" evidence will regret spending a fortune if an opponent can demonstrate that the evidence distorts the facts rather than illustrates them.

Other Equipment

All kinds of equipment are available today to assist witnesses, particularly experts, in testifying. Experts using illustrators draw information from computer disks or videotapes and then use a highlighter to explain the information to a jury, much as sports broadcasters do when explaining a videotaped highlight. Documents can be read by scanners and stored on worm disks.[85] These documents can then be shown to a jury via a large-screen television set. Such equipment can speed up a trial, highlight important information, and help a jury understand. Portions of videotape depositions can also be stored on disks and shown on a television screen to demonstrate similarities or differences among witnesses or to highlight portions of depositions.

Depending on how it is used, this equipment can retard a jury's understanding as well as advance it. In some simple cases, using expensive machines is excessive. The costs outweigh the benefits, and the use of such equipment may lengthen a trial and confuse matters that could be explained with old-fashioned exhibits and oral testimony. The general rule of thumb for trial attorneys should be that the equipment must fit the case. The fact that advanced technology is available does not mean that it will assist the trier of fact in every case.

General Propositions

There are four general propositions that I would offer with respect to videotapes, computer-generated evidence, and other technological advances. First, judges should encourage attorneys to use rules (such as

Federal Rule of Evidence 1006) that permit summaries in lieu of massive amounts of documents or information. Judges can even explain to jurors that the court has encouraged summaries as a likely means of promoting understanding and saving time. Second, judges should encourage attorneys to use videotapes, computer-generated evidence, and demonstrative evidence in opening statements and closing arguments as well as during a case. Such evidence, when used properly and early on, can make the case come alive in a vivid and understandable way from the outset. It can also be effective in summarizing the case. Third, judges should require litigants who plan to use videotape, computer-generated evidence, or other equipment to indicate their intent prior to trial so that objections can be heard and arrangements made for the equipment to be properly installed in order to maximize its advantages. Fourth, when powerful demonstrative evidence is offered that rests on flawed assumptions, the judge should consider excluding it outright rather than admitting it so that the jury can determine its weight, unless it is clear that the jury would know how to properly discount the evidence if necessary.[86]

Videotaping the Trial

When all courts are equipped with video equipment, the issue will arise of whether trials should be videotaped and jurors given access to the tapes during their deliberations. Just as television viewers often benefit from instant replays that clarify action it may have been hard to see, jurors can benefit from access to a tape of all testimony. If jurors are permitted access to tapes, the next question is whether they should be able to take a tape of a day's proceeding home to review at their leisure. This would lessen the need for note-taking and provide jurors with an opportunity to study the film, much like football or basketball analysts.

The complaint can be made that a jury might view a witness out of context. A jury should, however, have the power to decide what to review. Giving jurors a chance to review a tape of any part of a trial they choose can promote understanding and juror confidence. It is a radical idea that warrants some consideration. To the extent that a tape exists, it can also aid appellate review on some issues that are currently beyond effective appellate supervision, such as nonverbal behavior by the trial judge. Further, a tape would assist an appellate court in understanding precisely the tone and circumstances in which evidence was admitted or excluded. This would not directly improve juror comprehension but might indirectly cause trial attorneys and trial judges to be more careful in dealing with evidence—and thus improve the quality of their presentations to jurors.

Conclusion

To improve the quality of jury trials, it is essential to broaden the jury pool, encourage citizens to serve on juries, and eliminate the burdens associated with jury service. Trial judges can adopt a number of measures to ensure that the parties address the issues really in dispute and that expert testimony does the same. Lawyers can use visual evidence to save time and enhance the quality of their evidence, although they have incentives in some cases not to do so. Jurors yearn to reach correct decisions. Lawyers yearn to prevail. Thus, in the end it will fall to the makers of rules and the judges to permit and require practices that promote jury comprehension.

Notes

1. "The trial of all crimes, except in cases of impeachment, shall be by jury; and such trial shall be held in the State where the said crimes shall have been committed; but when not committed within any State, the trial shall be at such place or places as the Congress may by law have directed." U.S. Constitution, Article III, Section 2.

2. Amendment VI states, "In all criminal prosecutions, the accused shall enjoy the right to a speedy and public trial, by an impartial jury of the State and district wherein the crime shall have been committed, which district shall have been previously ascertained by law." Amendment VII asserts, "In suits at common law, where the value in controversy shall exceed twenty dollars, the right of trial by jury shall be preserved, and no fact tried by a jury, shall be otherwise re-examined in any court of the United States, than according to the rules of the common law."

3. See, for example, Article I, Section 8, of the Virginia Constitution, which states that "in criminal prosecutions a man . . . shall enjoy the right to a speedy and public trial, by an impartial jury of his vicinage."; Article I, Section 11, adds that "in controversies respecting property, and in suits between man and man, trial by jury is preferable to any other, and ought to be held sacred."

4. *Duncan* v. *Louisiana*, 391 U.S. 145 (1968). The right to jury trial for offenses punishable by more than six months' imprisonment has been established in *Bloom* v. *Illinois*, 391 U.S. 194 (1968); and *Baldwin* v. *New York*, 399 U.S. 66 (1969).

5. The court of appeals upheld a resentencing by the trial judge and concluded that the trial judge was not obliged to recuse himself, since his comments, based on what he had observed during the trial, were similar to comments he made when he first sentenced the defendant. *United States* v. *Barry*, 960 F.2d 260 (D.C. Cir. 1992).

6. Edward J. Devitt, "Federal Civil Jury Trials Should be Abolished," *American Bar Association Journal*, vol. 60 (May 1974), p. 570.

7. Joseph C. Wilkinson, Frank D. Zielinski, and George M. Curtis III, "A Bicentennial Transition: Modern Alternatives to Seventh Amendment Jury Trial in Complex Cases," *University of Kansas Law Review*, vol. 37 (Fall 1988), pp. 62–105.

8. Roger W. Kirst, "The Jury's Historic Domain in Complex Cases," *Washington Law Review*, vol. 58 (December 1982), pp. 1–38.

9. Joe S. Cecil, Valerie P. Hans, and Elizabeth C. Wiggins, "Citizen Comprehension of Difficult Issues: Lessons from Civil Jury Trials," *American University Law Review*, vol. 40 (Winter 1991), pp. 727–74.

10. It is possible that the jury may perceive hostility between attorneys and the judge in some instances. In some cases, the jury even may perceive the basis of the hostility—for instance, when an attorney makes a vigorous objection and is overruled by a judge who appears to resent the vigor with which the attorney argues. In such cases, the jury may be affected by its perception of hostility between the court and counsel, but the effect is only indirect. Nothing personal has occurred between the attorney and the jurors.

11. In some cases, the trial judge may still want additional input from community members and may try a case with an "advisory" jury.

12. Following the verdict in the prosecution of the police officers charged with assaulting Rodney King, the *Los Angeles Times* reported that a state trial judge's reelection race received more attention than any judicial election since the 1986 election in which former Chief Justice Rose Bird was defeated in her bid for reelection to the California Supreme Court. The story described the trial judge's "controversial decision to grant a Korean-born grocer probation in the killing of 15-year-old Latasha Harlins." Harlins was an African-American youth. Sheryl Stolberg, "Judge Karlin's Race Is Closely Watched," *Los Angeles Times*, May 27, 1992, p. B1.

13. Again, see *Los Angeles Times*, May 27, 1992, p. B6.

14. We know this from the reaction to the verdict in the trial of the officers charged with assaulting Rodney King. A fictitious view of how jurors might deal with various influences in a small community is offered in John Grisham, *A Time to Kill* (Wynwood Press, 1989).

15. For a sociological study of jurors, which concludes that they generally perform well, see Valerie P. Hans and Neil Vidmar, *Judging the Jury* (Plenum Press, 1986).

16. They are inherent if jurors are selected randomly and not on the basis of their affiliation with public officers, and if they serve for only a brief time, until new jurors take their place.

17. Under federal law, district courts have the discretion to exempt certain groups from jury service if it can be proved that it will cause "undue hardship or extreme inconvenience." 28 U.S.C. 1863 (b)(5). Some courts have excused doctors, lawyers, and other professionals routinely and have been upheld on appeal. See, for example, *United States* v. *Van Scoy*, 654 F.2d 257, 262-63 (3rd Cir. 1981). Employees who hold key positions in organizations may also find it difficult to be away from work for long periods. The burden jury service imposes on highly salaried individuals may greatly exceed the financial burden imposed on most jurors.

18. *Batson* v. *Kentucky*, 476 U.S. 79 (1986); and *Edmonson* v. *Leesville Concrete Co.*, 112 S. Ct. 2077 (1991). Sex-based exclusion has been held unconstitutional in a case remanded for a determination of whether a prosecutor removed men from a jury in a discriminatory manner. *People* v. *Mitchell*, 228 Ill. App, 3d, 593 E. 2d 882 (Ill. App. 1992).

19. Stephen A. Saltzburg and Mary Ellen Powers, "Peremptory Challenges and the Clash between Impartiality and Group Representation," *Maryland Law Review*, vol. 41 (Summer 1982), p. 337.

20. William W Schwarzer, "Reforming Jury Trials," *Federal Rules Decisions*, vol. 132 (West, 1991), p. 581.

21. There is a considerable difference of opinion as to the advantages and the fairness

of "scientific" jury selection. Compare Hans and Vidmar, *Judging the Jury*, pp. 79–89, with Eric M. Acker's book review of *Judging the Jury*, *Michigan Law Review*, vol. 85 (April–May 1987) p. 1241. I believe that questionnaires like those recommended here can provide advantages for all parties in civil cases with little burden on the courts and little invasion of juror privacy.

22. Schwarzer, "Reforming Jury Trials," p. 580. Judge Schwarzer further proposes that each side select a number equal to one-half the number of jurors and alternates from the remaining pool. It seems that if each side were compelled to exercise its peremptory challenges, and if a party were permitted to add a juror to replace any juror excused for cause, the exact number of jurors required to try the case plus alternates could be obtained.

23. Judge Schwarzer reports that Chief Judge John F. Grady of the Northern District of Illinois has used this procedure with the consent of the parties. Although he notes that it is questionable whether such a procedure should be used without such consent, Judge Schwarzer concludes that even in such cases the procedure might have sufficient merit to warrant its adoption as an experiment. Schwarzer, "Reforming Jury Trials," p. 581.

24. There is some evidence that one side of a case may be more inclined to strike well-educated jurors than the other. See Douglas W. Ell, "The Right to an Incompetent Jury: Protracted Commercial Litigation and the Seventh Amendment," *Connecticut Law Review*, vol. 10 (Spring 1978), pp. 775–800. The assertion has been made by an experienced antitrust lawyer that the defense in antitrust cases is more likely to strike well-educated jurors than the plaintiff. Robert P. Furth and Robert Emmett Burns, "The Anatomy of a Seventy Million Dollar Sherman Act Settlement—A Law Professor's Tape-Talk with Plaintiff's Trial Counsel," *De Paul Law Review*, vol. 23 (Spring 1974), pp. 880–81. For an argument that abolishing peremptory challenges in civil cases would promote justice, see Eric D. Katz, "Striking the Peremptory Challenge from Civil Litigation: "Hey Batson, Stay Where You Belong!" *Pace Law Review*, vol. 11 (Winter 1991), pp. 357–409.

25. Steven I. Friedland, "The Competency and Responsibility of Jurors in Deciding Cases," *Northwestern University Law Review*, vol. 85 (Fall 1990), pp. 190, 195–96.

26. Fifth Circuit Judge Patrick B. Higginbotham, frequently mentioned as a possible nominee to the United States Supreme Court, has observed that juries have been able to deal with complex and difficult issues. Patrick E. Higginbotham, "Continuing the Dialogue: Civil Juries and the Allocation of Judicial Power," *Texas Law Review*, vol. 56 (December 1977), pp. 47–60.

27. It is not surprising, therefore, that the suggestion has been made that a separate jury wheel should be established with the names of jurors who have earned a bachelor's degree from an accredited college or university. William V. Luneburg and Mark A. Nordenberg, "Specially Qualified Juries and Expert Nonjury Tribunals: Alternatives for Coping with the Complexities of Modern Civil Litigation," *Virginia Law Review*, vol. 67 (June 1981), pp. 942–50.

28. For an argument in favor of using "special juries" in complicated cases, see Rita Sutton, "A More Rational Approach to Complex Civil Litigation in the Federal Courts: The Special Jury," *University of Chicago Legal Forum*, vol. 1990, p. 575. For another conclusion that "knowledgeable jurors take the lead in jury deliberations, thereby strengthening the group's overall ability," see Cecil and others, "Citizen Comprehension of Difficult Issues: Lessons from Civil Jury Trials," p. 773.

29. See David U. Strawn and Raymond W. Buchanan, "Jury Confusion: A Threat to Justice," *Judicature*, vol. 59 (May 1976), p. 483.

30. In some jurisdictions, the court itself may have the authority to take some of the actions described here. In other jurisdictions, legislation may be required to change statutes that already exist and provide various exemptions from jury service.

31. Average lengths of trials may vary among jurisdictions. The courtroom operations

manager for the United States District Court for the Northern District of California states that the average trial length is five days in that district but that each year five to seven jury trials exceed a month. Dennis Bilecki, "A More Efficient Method of Jury Selection for Lengthy Trials," *Judicature*, vol. 73 (June–July 1989), pp. 43–47.

32. Bilecki, "A More Efficient Method of Jury Selection for Lengthy Trials," reports that the Northern District of California uses questionnaires before the voir dire process to screen prospective jurors in lengthy cases.

33. It is impossible to know how long a jury will deliberate. Most deliberations are unlikely to take several days, but jurors can be told that their week might be extended by a day or two if necessary. Alternatively, in some cases it is possible to have the jury return to deliberations in the evening after jurors have had an opportunity to work or perform other obligations.

34. Judge Schwarzer has pointed out that "judges have imposed time limits, often without objection, and occasionally even with the approval of counsel, by giving each side a specified number of trial days to present its case. To prevent prejudice to a side from its opponent's excessively long cross-examination, it is better to allow each side a specified number of hours to use, for both direct and cross-examination, as it sees fit." Schwarzer, "Reforming Jury Trials," p. 579.

35. See Joe S. Cecil, E. Allen Lind, and Gordon Bermant, *Jury Service in Lengthy Civil Trials* (Washington: Federal Judiciary Center, 1987), pp. 19–21.

36. For an argument that Federal Rule of Evidence 611 and similar state rules can be used as the authority for imposing time limits, see Howard Ross Cabot, "Breaking the Siege: Protecting the System through Rule 611" *Arizona Attorney*, vol. 27 (May 1991), p. 18.

37. Judge Howard T. Markey has concluded that the "ordering of a separate trial of the [patent] infringement issue under Rule 42(b), and entering judgment for the defendant when that trial results in a determination of noninfringement, would greatly simplify those patent trials in which a patentee did not carry its burden and would have no serious effect on the conduct of those patent trials in which the patentee did carry its burden." Markey, "On Simplifying Patent Trials," *Federal Rules Decisions*, vol. 116 (West, 1987), p. 383.

38. Schwarzer, "Reforming Jury Trials," p. 595, citing both William W Schwarzer, *Managing Antitrust and other Complex Litigation: A Handbook for Lawyers and Judges* (Charlottesville: Michie, 1982) pp. 47–51; and Hans Zeisel and Thomas Callahan, "Split Trials and Time Savings: A Statistical Analysis," *Harvard Law Review*, vol. 76 (June 1963), p. 1609.

39. Judge Schwarzer has written that "post-trial interviews with jurors invariably disclose complaints about the lawyers' prolixity and tendency to present too much evidence." Schwarzer, "Reforming Jury Trials," p. 578. One recent analysis of trial strategy argues that the cost of overtrying a case involves more than boring or confusing the jury; it also involves a risk of undermining the evidentiary significance of probative evidence. Robert H. Klonoff and Paul L. Colby, *Sponsorship Strategy: Evidentiary Tactics for Winning Jury Trials* (Charlottesville: Michie, 1990), p. 44.

40. See Fed. R. Civ. P. 37 (c), which provides for an award of expenses for a failure to admit the genuineness of a document or the truth of a matter that is proved at trial unless the court makes certain findings.

41. Many lawyers with whom I have worked have indicated that they rarely succeed in having their adversaries admit important facts during discovery. This is not surprising in light of the practical and tactical reasons why a party might prefer not to admit facts early in a case.

42. It should be noted that many lawyers are unhappy with the way in which judges have used Rule 11. Proposals to modify it have been under consideration by the Advisory Committee on the Federal Rules of Civil Procedure. The sanction suggestion which I make

comes into play only in cases that are tried and could be extremely important in avoiding waste in our courts. If it did not work as intended, it (like Rule 11) could be reconsidered or rewritten to provide a more elaborate procedural framework for a judge to follow.

43. The trial judge could also appoint a special master, under Federal Rule of Civil Procedure 53, or a court-appointed expert, under Federal Rule of Evidence 706, in the event that the parties' experts needed help in addressing the issues on which they agree.

44. Schwarzer, "Reforming Jury Trials," p. 581. See also *Hanson* v. *Parkside Surgery Center*, 872 F.2d 745, 748 (6th Cir. 1989), which finds no reversible error in such a procedure.

45. Schwarzer, "Reforming Jury Trials," p. 582.

46. The literature on juries suggests that juries of twelve are preferable to juries of six. It seems too late in the day, especially in view of the burdens many courts face, to persuade courts to return to juries of twelve in all courts. One benefit of the approach to alternates discussed here is that it increases the size of the jury on the basis of a rationale that is difficult to dispute. See Hans and Vidmar, *Judging the Jury*, pp. 65–76.

47. A system in which some jurors are excused carries the danger that prospective jurors, realizing this, will listen less carefully to the evidence than they otherwise would, since they have reason to believe they may only be alternates.

48. See, for example, Amiram Elwork, Bruce D. Sales, and James J. Alfini, *Making Jury Instructions Understandable* (Charlottesville: Michie, 1982); and Robert P. Charrow and Veda R. Charrow, "Making Legal Language Understandable: A Psycholinguistic Study of Jury Instructions," *Columbia Law Review*, vol. 79 (November 1979), p. 1306.

49. Josephine R. Potuto, Stephen A. Saltzburg, and Harvey F. Perlman, *Federal Criminal Jury Instructions*, 2d ed. (Charlottesville: Michie, 1991).

50. See, for example, Committee on Model Jury Instructions, Ninth Circuit, *Manual of Model Instructions for the Ninth Circuit* (West, 1985), p. 39.

51. Schwarzer, "Reforming Jury Trials," p. 583.

52. One federal circuit experimented with giving juries copies of instructions, and the results were largely favorable. *Report of the Committee on Juries of the Judicial Council of the Second Circuit* (August 1984), p. 76.

53. See, for example, Jack B. Weinstein, "The Power and Duty of Federal Judges to Marshall and Comment on the Evidence in Jury Trials and Some Suggestions on Charging Juries," *Federal Rules Decisions*, vol. 118 (West, 1988), pp. 161–88.

54. Mark A. Frankel, "A Trial Judge's Perspective on Providing Tools for Rational Jury Decisionmaking," *Northwestern University Law Review*, vol. 85 (Fall 1990), pp. 221–25; and Friedland, "The Competency and Responsibility of Jurors," p. 190.

55. Frankel, "A Trial Judge's Perspective," p. 222.

56. Stephen A. Saltzburg, "The Unnecessarily Expanding Role of the American Trial Judge," *Virginia Law Review*, vol. 64 (February 1978), pp. 1–81; and Larry Heuer and Stephen D. Penrod, "Some Suggestions for the Critical Appraisal of a More Active Jury," *Northwestern University Law Review*, vol. 85 (Fall 1990), pp. 226–39 (surveying experienced judges), respectively.

57. Kenneth A. Kiewra, "Notetaking and Review: The Research and Its Implications," *Instructional Science*, vol. 16, no. 3 (1987), p. 234.

58. The study is discussed in Friedland, "Competency and Responsibility of Jurors," pp. 212–13.

59. For a proposed model evidence rule governing juror questions, see the student comment, "Standardized Procedures for Juror Interrogation of Witnesses," *University of Chicago Legal Forum*, vol. 1990, p. 557.

60. The history is set out well in Mark S. Brodin, "Accuracy, Efficiency, and Accountability in the Litigation Process—The Case for the Fact Verdict," *University of Cincinnati Law Review*, vol. 59 (Summer 1990), pp. 15–111.

61. "Minority Statement Opposing the 1963 Amendments to the Federal Rules of Civil Procedure," 374 U.S. 865, 967-68 (1963).

62. Jerome Frank, *Courts on Trial: Myth and Reality in American Justice* (Princeton University Press, 1949), p. 116. Judge Frank blamed the general verdict for many of the problems assigned to civil juries. *Skidmore* v. *Baltimore & O.R.R.*, 167 F.2d 54, 56 (2d Cir.), *cert. denied*, 335 U.S. 816 (1948).

63. A trial judge has decided that a claim was time barred on the basis of the special interrogatory to jury. *Beard* v. *J.I. Case Co.*, 823 F.2d 1095, 1097 n.2 (10th Cir. 1987).

64. The court has directed use of special interrogatories on retrial of defamation. *Sunward Corp.* v. *Dun & Bradstreet, Inc.*, 811 F.2d 511 (10th Cir. 1987).

65. *In re Japanese Elec. Prod. Antitrust Litig.*, 631 F.2d 1069, 1085 (3rd Cir. 1980).

66. Thus, if the appellate court concludes that causation was proven to such an extent that no jury could reasonably have found that it did not exist, a verdict for the plaintiff could be ordered, provided that the plaintiff prevailed on all other issues. The fact is that there is no guarantee that a reversal will not require a new trial even if the jury completes all issues. The typical reversal does not occur on the ground that the jury should have decided a case the opposite way; after all, an appellate court has to find that both the jury and the trial judge who denied a judgment as a matter of law were not reasonable in order to reverse a judgment on this ground. More typically, reversals occur because of procedural or evidentiary rulings. Such rulings may affect more than one issue in a case, and a new trial can be required on some or all issues, no matter how many questions a jury answers.

67. Federal Rule of Civil Procedure, 48 states that the verdict "shall be unanimous".

68. Psychologists have concluded that unanimous juries are more likely to deliberate. Saul M. Kassin and Lawrence S. Wrightsman, *The American Jury on Trial: Psychological Perspectives* (Hemisphere, 1988). For an argument against unanimity premised on political theory, see Gary J. Jacobson, "The Unanimous Verdict: Politics and the Jury Trial," *Washington University Law Quarterly*, vol. 1977 (Winter), pp. 39–57.

69. By comparing the verdict form with the vote on the unanimity question, the judge might be better informed about the jury's confidence in a less than unanimous judgment.

70. In jurisdictions that require unanimity, legislation or rule changes would be required before such an instruction could be given.

71. Of course, an evenly divided jury vote would not provide any support for a judgment.

72. Kassin and Wrightsman, *American Jury on Trial*, pp. 214–15.

73. Schwarzer, "Reforming Jury Trials," pp. 593–94.

74. The suggestion is made in Kenneth R. Kreiling, "Scientific Evidence: Toward Providing the Lay Trier with the Comprehensible and Reliable Evidence Necessary to Meet the Goals of the Rules of Evidence," *Arizona Law Review*, vol. 32 (Fall 1990), pp. 915–83.

75. This is more likely if the jury members include people who have specialized training they can share with other jurors.

76. Stephen A. Saltzburg and Michael M. Martin, *Federal Rules of Evidence Manual: A Complete Guide to the Federal Rules of Evidence*, 5th ed. (Charlottesville: Michie, 1990), pp. 61–63.

77. *Landrigan* v. *Celotex Corp.*, 605 A.2d 1079, 1084 (N.J. 1992). *See also Caterinicchio* v. *Pittsburgh Corning Corp.*, 605 A.2d 1092 (N.J. 1992).

78. For one case that states this explicitly, see *In re Air Crash Disaster*, 795 F.2d 1230 (5th Cir. 1986). See also ibid. at 1234.

79. Gregory P. Joseph, *Modern Visual Evidence* (New York: Law Journal Seminars Press, 1984).

80. Joseph, *Modern Visual Evidence*, chap. 2, p. 5.

81. Videotape evidence is similar to motion picture film, but videotape is more portable.

It can be used in a variety of conditions and can be immediately edited and played back; the original will not be damaged in editing. See John C. Buchanan, Carole D. Bos, and Fred I. Heller, *How to Use Video in Litigation: A Guide to Technology, Strategies, and Techniques*, (Prentice Hall, 1986), p. 81; and Saltzburg and Martin, *Federal Rules of Evidence Manual*, pp. 192–94.

82. A trial judge's rulings that films prepared by an auto manufacturer were more probative than prejudicial were affirmed in *Szeliga* v. *General Motors Corp.*, 728 F.2d 566 (1st Cir. 1984). Filmed reenactment of the start-up of an auto was permitted in *Conti* v. *Ford Motor Co.*, 578 F. Supp. 1429 (E.D. Pa. 1983), *rev'd on other grounds*, 743 F.2d 195 (3rd Cir. 1984), *cert. denied*, 470 U.S. 1028 (1985).

83. A court of appeals has said that a videotape admitted in a first trial should be excluded in the second trial of the case. *Gladhill* v. *General Motors Corp.*, 743 F.2d 1949 (4th Cir. 1984).

84. Introduction of such a film has been upheld in *Bannister* v. *Town of Noble*, 812 F.2d 1265 (10th Cir. 1987).

85. These are write once, read many times disks. The information can be retrieved many times but cannot be edited.

86. This is not always easy to do. In one case in which an economist colleague and I participated, our adversary used a multiple regression analysis that was replete with errors. Because of the mistakes, it would have been impossible, without redoing the regression, for anyone to know which numbers were correct. Notwithstanding this fact, the trial judge admitted the evidence so that the jury could assign it any weight it chose. In that case, the regression was used to calculate damages in a bid-rigging case. In the end, the jury found liability but zero damages and thus rejected the regression analysis. Although the particular result—the jury's rejection of the model—could be used to bolster the case that juries can deal with complicated evidence, it cost our client a fortune to demonstrate the problems with the evidence and to educate the jury on why the problems rendered the model useless. This client could afford to make the showing, and that particular jury understood it.

There undoubtedly exist cases in which a jury can "eyeball" small defects with computer-generated numbers and raise or lower the numbers. But, when statistical analysis is extraordinarily complicated (and dozens of factors may be considered in a regression analysis), mistakes may make it impossible for even experts to "eyeball" the errors and determine what effect they have on the numbers. If experts cannot do it, juries surely cannot.

CHAPTER ELEVEN

Recent Innovations in Civil Jury Trial Procedures

H. Lee Sarokin and G. Thomas Munsterman

Despite THE TITLE of this chapter, what is discussed here may be neither recent nor innovative. The procedures we present are original and borrowed; some have been tried, but others have not. Many have not received widespread attention because of the lack of a central forum for exchanging views. Thus, what we consider to be new and unique may be old. Further, to call something an innovation implies that it will bring about an improvement. We obviously believe that all the ideas presented here fall into that category, although few have received appellate or academic scrutiny. In any event, we have tried to submit a group of proposals, based on current trends and practices, that will improve the effectiveness of juries and help ensure fair, informed, well-reasoned verdicts.

The method we used to select the procedures to be discussed was very informal: we have both been in positions that allowed us to observe, implement, or review new procedures.[1] The list presented in this chapter is hardly exhaustive, and the techniques to be discussed are applicable to most civil jury trials. Those particularly applicable to complex trials or notorious cases are not included, although many are equally useful in more routine trials.

The innovations are discussed in the order in which they would be used during an actual trial. They are offered as methods of improving jury selection, juror comprehension, and final deliberations in the hopes of improving this important exercise in citizenship.

Our concern for innovations, or the lack thereof, is supported by a 1987 survey (published in 1989), of state and federal trial judges who spend at least half of their time on general civil cases.[2] The judges strongly support the use of civil juries but conclude that there should be some limitation on the use of juries in minor cases involving small sums of money. When the judges were asked, "What do you think is the most important change, if any, that should be made to the jury system?" they gave few responses. Since the issues of eliminating or limiting juries had been the subjects of previous questions, it is not surprising that the most frequent response to this question was the suggestion (made by 12 percent of the federal and 16 percent of the state judges) that juries be eliminated in complex cases. The second most frequently suggested change was the need for improved instructions. Other innovations, such as reduced terms of service, better pay, smaller juries, nonunanimous verdicts, more communication with juries, and improved treatment were cited by less than 6 percent of the judges who did not identify an urgent need for change. It is therefore reasonable to expect innovative judges to be isolated and the innovations themselves to be accepted very slowly.

As noted, the procedures to be presented are those applicable to most civil jury trials. The world of mass tort and complex litigation has its own set of needed innovations beyond those we will discuss. However, that world has indirectly provided many of the innovations cited, for when civil juries are pushed to handle these cases, many judges look to new procedures for help. For instance, it should be helpful in all cases for jurors to take notes; not being permitted to take notes in trials lasting months, with a vast array of witnesses, depositions, and exhibits seems at odds with our desire that the juror be able to recall the evidence presented.

Among the techniques not discussed are the following:

—Daily trial schedules that permit jurors, judges, and attorneys to take part in other ongoing activities;

—Test case jury verdicts in which the verdicts and awards in a group of jointly tried cases are used as the basis for awards in similar cases;

—Provisions for jurors who miss portions of the trial for reasons such as illness or personal problems to watch video recordings in lieu of actual attendance;

—Sequential verdicts on separate issues, with new instructions for each verdict;

—Separate juries for different portions of the trial to reduce the burdens on any one jury;

—Joint state-federal trials;

—Multitribunal trials combining the jury trial with OSHA, workers' compensation, or other administrative law proceedings;

—Videotaped case introductions so that successive panels of prospective jurors receive the same information;

—Summaries of depositions;

—Mock and shadow juries; and

—Special or expert juries.

In his recent thesis, Judge B. Michael Dann examines the role of the jury through history. He states, "There is no question but what the colonies received a jury model premised on almost total juror passivity."[3] In fact, before arriving on the shores of this country, the jury had already shifted from an active to a passive role as control of the institution passed into the hands of attorneys and judges. Judge Dann also turns to the works of educators and social scientists to develop a behavioral model of the jury that would permit jurors to learn in the most effective way. Not surprisingly, this model requires active participation to enhance learning and is at odds with the passive legal model of the jury. To arrive at an effective model for a well-educated jury able to comprehend the evidence and arrive at an informed decision, Judge Dann proposes many techniques that will result in greater juror participation. Interestingly, the techniques he proposes closely parallel many of those discussed in this paper. Because most of these techniques limit the extent to which attorneys and judges can control the jury, opposition is expected to such concepts as permitting jurors to ask questions. If the jury is to perform its duties more effectively, however, giving up some control may be necessary.

Pre-trial Innovations

A number of innovations have been introduced into the jury system that have affected the composition of juries by promoting greater diversity. More than half the states now use sources other than the voter registration list to identify potential jurors. Thus, although voter registration has declined, lists of registered drivers provide access to well over 90 percent of the adult population.[4] Using lists of drivers also reduces the possibility that people will not register to vote in order to avoid the possibility of juror service.[5] In addition, the exemptions from jury service that were automatically granted to certain professionals, such as doctors, lawyers, and ministers, have been greatly reduced. As of 1992, twenty-six states have no professional exemptions, and nine have very limited exemptions. In 1991 the New York Bar Association studied the need to exempt lawyers from jury service. Based on responses from lawyers who had served and their fellow nonlawyer jurors, the study found no reason why lawyers should not serve. A lawyer's chances of being selected for jury service were about the same as for nonlawyers.[6]

While many people are excused from jury service because of hardship, that number has also been greatly reduced through various innovative administrative changes, including reducing the term of jury service to the minimum possible. The "one trial/one day" concept, which allows those who report for jury service to complete their obligation by serving on one jury or, if they are not selected, by being available in the courthouse for only one day, now pertains to about 25 percent of the U.S. population.[7] In addition, people summoned for jury service at an inconvenient time can, in most courts, select a more convenient date.

The fees paid to potential jurors and jurors in the courts in the United States vary from nothing at all to $50 per day. The average is about $10 per day, hardly enough to pay for lunch and parking in many cities. In a national survey of juror satisfaction and hardship, researchers found that the average out-of-pocket expenses for meals and parking were $9.18 in state and $11.69 in federal courts, and these expenses more than doubled if child care expenses were included.[8] A new approach to juror fees instituted in Massachusetts in 1982 requires employers to pay their employees for the first three days of jury service; after three days, these jurors are paid $50 per day. The unemployed are paid up to $50 per day in expenses.[9] Because Massachusetts courts use the one trial/one day concept, only those selected as jurors serve beyond the first day, and most trials are completed within three days. This approach has resulted in fewer potential jurors being excused for reasons of financial hardship, as well as in a net reduction in juror fees. Similar versions of this fee structure are used in Colorado, Connecticut, and several cities.[10]

The result of these innovations, now codified in the American Bar Association's *Standards Relating to Juror Use and Management*, is that more people are eligible and able to serve, improving the representativeness of the venire, or jury pool, and distributing both the positive experience and the economic burden of jury service across the greatest possible proportion of the population.[11] This broadening of jury duty to all segments of the population is one of the most desirable innovations to the jury system.

Innovations in Jury Selection

Selecting a jury can be a drawn-out and frustrating process for everyone involved, owing to the lengthy questioning and peremptory challenges. We suggest two innovations—the use of questionnaires and the elimination of peremptory challenges—that can significantly improve the jury selection process. Both deserve more study.

Juror Questionnaires

In many cases, and certainly in complex or notorious cases with extensive pre-trial publicity, it can be anticipated that a number of potential jurors will be challenged for cause. Here the use of juror questionnaires can be very helpful. A panel of potential jurors can be given the questionnaires to complete in a single day; the attorneys in the case can then review the questionnaires and indicate to the judge those individuals they wish to challenge for cause. The judge can then review the proposed challenges for cause, rule on them, and bring in the remaining jurors for final selection.

Despite the use of questionnaires, attorneys and litigants still want and are entitled to the opportunity to see and hear from the jurors for some brief follow-up questioning in open court. However, the questionnaires are a considerable timesaving device and serve to excuse those individuals challenged for cause from further needless reporting at the court each day. In some less notorious cases, the questionnaires can be completed in the morning when the jurors report. When the jurors are called, the parties and attorneys will already have in their possession background information on them, and the time spent on voir dire, or preliminary examination, can be substantially reduced.[12] Furthermore, a questionnaire is much more apt to elicit all the more detailed information the lawyers seek. The questionnaire most often can be developed by the attorneys themselves, without the judge's intervention; however, the judge should exercise some control over the scope and content of the questions in order to ensure that the privacy of the individual is not violated.[13] Procedures should be established to prevent public disclosure of information furnished by prospective jurors that is likely to embarrass the prospective juror or invade his or her privacy.[14]

Peremptory Challenges

The time may have come to consider the elimination of peremptory challenges, which permit a lawyer to excuse prospective jurors without providing a reason. There are many arguments for retaining these challenges, but current decisions may have furnished the catalyst to reexamine this practice and perhaps even to abandon it.

Recent rulings of the U.S. Supreme Court and appellate courts on the abuse of peremptory challenges recognize what trial judges and lawyers have always known—that discrimination in selecting jurors has been practiced systematically for decades, with the knowledge and acquiescence of the courts.[15] Lawyers use peremptory challenges to obtain a partial jury, not an impartial one. The fact that an impartial jury may result because challenges based upon bias offset each other does not alter the underlying rationale behind their use. Lawyers seek to exclude those potential jurors they believe will not find in their client's favor and to retain those who will. Their decisions are most often based on stereotypes and assumed prejudices.

If asked privately to articulate their reasons for excluding or not excluding certain jurors, attorneys will candidly say such things as "Jews and Italians are generous; bankers and engineers are not" or "persons of the same race, religion, or nationality as the party on trial are more likely to identify with, and thus rule for, that party." The myths abound, and advocacy guides have even been published codifying such supposed criteria.

Under the recent Supreme Court decisions, in a growing number of cases, attorneys who appear to be engaged in discriminatory practices will be required to provide a nondiscriminatory justification for excusing certain classes of jurors.[16] We respectfully submit that this requirement will not end the objectionable practices but will merely compel lawyers to be more creative in finding reasons for excluding potential jurors. The only change will be the improved ingenuity of the attorneys who must justify their actions, and the court will be placed in the awkward and untenable position of judging the credibility and the good faith of trial lawyers.

The answer to the dilemma may be to consider abolishing peremptory challenges entirely, at least in civil cases.[17] This should be done not only as a matter of principle (because it will end this institutionalized condoning of discrimination in our judicial system) but as a practical consideration.[18] Three practical reasons for abolishing peremptory challenges are discussed below.

First, an entire matter may be tried and decided, only to have an appellate court require a second trial because a peremptory challenge was improperly used before the trial began, rather than because of some substantial error during the trial. If discriminatory selection has been practiced, a new trial may be required.

Second, peremptory challenges are expensive and time-consuming. In federal court, at least sixteen jurors may be called and excused in criminal cases, and at least six in most civil cases. Many more may be challenged in multidefendant cases, both criminal and civil. Multiply that number in every court throughout the country by the number of trials, and the total of those peremptorily challenged and thus excluded from service is staggering. Each prospective juror must spend at least a day in court, be paid the required fee, and lose the equivalent amount of productive work time. This process involves thousands of people and millions of dollars each year.

Third, the strength of our judicial system is predicated and dependent on the public's confidence in the courts. That confidence is weakened when people are summoned to court, and, after having been required to leave their work and other responsibilities, excused without reason. Many may be relieved to be excused, but an equal number may be insulted, and justifiably so.[19]

What could be fairer than a group of jurors drawn by lot from a panel that represents a fair cross section of the community and subject only to valid challenges for cause? Many of the methods previously cited are used by the courts to try to ensure that the panel of prospective jurors is representative of the population (for example, reducing the term of service, using multiple source lists, eliminating exemptions from jury service, and making jury fees more realistic). But the demographic balance achieved through these efforts can be easily destroyed by only a few discriminatory peremptory challenges. It is evident that no one can predict how a juror will decide a particular case, and participants in our judicial system should not be permitted to do so when those predictions are based upon unfounded assumptions of bias or prejudice.[20]

In the search for a fair and impartial jury, the means for attaining it should not be tainted by assumption of bias or prejudice based solely upon race, nationality, gender, religion, or occupation, even if the attributed characteristic is favorable rather than unfavorable. A bias is still a bias, even where tendered in the form of a compliment. Recognizing that there are valid arguments for retaining peremptory challenges, at a minimum we strongly recommend that the idea of abandoning them be considered and that it be supported by study and an open dialogue. This would allow both for determining whether or not peremptory challenges should survive, and for deciding what changes in voir dire and challenges for cause might be required.

Innovations in Trial Procedure

The following innovations in trial procedure should be considered.

Elimination of Alternates

The need to address the problems presented by alternate jurors is a pressing one. To permit jurors to serve and not deliberate is annoying and frustrating for them. It is more than an annoyance to litigants and attorneys when a designated alternate is not attentive, despite the court's instructions. Any reasonable means of including alternates in the deliberations, or, at a minimum, deferring the designation of alternates until deliberations begin, is preferable. Several practices have been utilized:

—Selecting alternates by lot from the jury just prior to giving instructions;

—Not disclosing the names of the alternates until just prior to instructing the jury (a practice which some judges and jurors might properly find offensive); and

—Permitting additional peremptory challenges to be used to strike a juror just prior to instructing the jury (these peremptories are in addition to the usual challenges), a technique that exacerbates the concerns already expressed.

The best solution appears in Federal Rule of Civil Procedure 48 and has been used in Pennsylvania for years.[21] The jury must have at least six persons and not more than twelve. The verdict must be unanimous (in Pennsylvania five out of six jurors must agree). Under this procedure, there are no alternates. Jurors can be dismissed during the trial for reasons as is now done. The jurors remaining at the time of deliberation, provided there are at least six, then proceed to deliberate and deliver their verdict.[22] The concept is an excellent one for civil trials, because it ensures that all remaining jurors will participate in the deliberations.

Opening Statements to the Entire Panel of Prospective Jurors

It has been suggested that jurors do not know enough about a case during the selection process to recognize whether they have or may have any particular bias, prejudice, or former experience that might affect their impartiality. Delivering opening statements to the entire panel would avoid this problem, since prospective jurors would then be more fully informed on the issues and facts to be presented and could respond to questions during voir dire more intelligently. This procedure is much more likely to elicit responses that might truly reflect a juror's impartiality or lack of it.

This technique obviously requires more time from the entire panel of prospective jurors. The efficient use of juror time must be balanced against the goal of a more effective voir dire by allowing discretion in its use. If other judges are also waiting to select juries, then a quick screening might eliminate those jurors ineligible because of the length of trial, employment, or personal acquaintances, and the remaining prospective jurors could hear the opening statements, thus freeing up at least a portion of the panel.

Pre-trial Instruction and Charge

At a Third Circuit judicial conference, one session, called "Jurors Speak," was devoted to the observations of those who had served on a jury. One former juror related that, after summations and the charge had been given, another juror began putting on her coat and preparing to leave, since she believed that her service on the case had been concluded. This may be an extreme example of lack of communication, but an inexcusable error is committed when jurors are not told from the outset what is expected of them. Not only should they be informed about the nature of the case and the way in which it is to proceed, but they should also be given some idea of the scope of their responsibility and of the issues they will be called upon to decide. It may be extremely difficult to do this at the beginning of a case, when the facts and issues have not been defined by the evidence. However, the lawyers (preferably by agreement) should furnish the court with a brief statement of the factual and legal issues to be presented, so that the court can outline for the jury what it is they will be called upon to decide—subject, of course, to final instructions on those issues that remain at the end of the trial. An experiment in the U.S. District Courts in the Second Circuit with this procedure had very positive results.[23]

Note-taking

No judge would sit through a bench trial without taking notes and, after days or weeks of testimony, expect to be able to render an opinion.

It is ironic that jurors are told they must rely on what they remember in making their decision yet are denied the opportunity to refresh their memories, as both judges and attorneys do. With appropriate instructions as to the role and function of note-taking, jurors should routinely be given notebooks and be permitted to make whatever notations they deem appropriate.[24] The potential problems can be addressed, but those dangers and concerns should not deny the jurors the opportunity of doing what others require under identical circumstances. Jurors should be advised that they should not attempt to take verbatim notes but should jot down what they think is significant; that the better notetakers should not dominate the proceedings; and that their notebooks are confidential and will not be shown to anyone.

Note-taking by jurors is one area that has received serious consideration by the courts and researchers. Note-taking is common in many courts, and as judges become increasingly aware of the procedure, many more can be expected to adopt it. Two studies demonstrated very positive results with juror note-taking, one in the Federal District Court, Eastern District of Pennsylvania, and another in the Second Circuit courts.[25] Six judges in eighteen civil and fourteen criminal trials permitted jurors to take notes. The participants approved of the use of note-taking to help jurors and did not find the note-taking disruptive.

Under the auspices of the Wisconsin Judicial Council, Steve Penrod and Larry Heuer conducted an experiment on juror note-taking, using sound methodological conditions. The results supported the use of note-taking.[26] The authors conducted a similar experiment nationwide, working with 103 judges in thirty-three states.[27] The findings were drawn from 160 actual trials. A set of advantages and disadvantages to juror note-taking was developed for the study.

The advantages were cited as follows:

—Juror notes serve as a memory aid.

—Juror note-taking increases juror satisfaction with the trial, the judge, and the verdict.

The disadvantages were cited as follows:

—Jurors overemphasize the evidence they have noted at the expense of evidence they did not record and produce a distorted view of the case.

—Notetakers cannot keep pace with the trial.

—Note-taking jurors distract other jurors.

—Notetakers have an undue influence over nonnotetakers.

—Juror notes are an inaccurate record of the trial.

—Note-taking favors either the prosecution or the defense.

—Note-taking consumes too much time.

While the researchers were unable to substantiate the advantages, they were able to prove that none of the disadvantages they had postulated became a concern. This does not mean that the note-taking does not offer these hypothetical advantages, but rather that they could not be verified in this study.

Exhibit Notebooks

Most trial witnesses are shown documents and questioned about them, but the jury often has no idea what the documents are or what they say. In every case, jurors should be given copies of documents received in evidence, or some form of overhead projection should be used so that the jurors can follow and understand the testimony. Notebooks of exhibits for the jurors offer a convenient solution to the problem of presenting evidence to a jury.[28] Not only does an exhibit book give the jury the opportunity to follow the testimony and understand the exhibit as the witness testifies, but it serves the added purpose of providing jurors with a copy of the exhibits for their deliberations. It is important that an index be included and that the documents be tabbed so that the jurors will not have to search through the exhibit books during the trial. Pictures of the witnesses, which have been found to be a considerable aid to jurors in recollecting the testimony and attributing it to the appropriate individuals, can also be included. Although an exhibit book may contain documents that are not yet received in evidence, an appropriate instruction from the judge can inform jurors that they should not examine any document until the court gives them permission to do so; alternately, copies of the documents can be handed to the jurors after they are received as evidence.

Premarked Exhibits

Premarked exhibits are an absolute must in expediting trials. All exhibits, even those that will not be offered as evidence, should be premarked. Not one minute of any trial should be taken up with such extraneous activities as having court personnel mark exhibits, handing exhibits to opposing attorneys, or allowing documents to be passed from juror to juror.

Projection of Simultaneous Testimony

Certain technological innovations can be incorporated into the court-room, one of which is the simultaneous projection of testimony. A jury is much more apt to recall testimony that can be read at the same time that it is heard. In fact, educators tell us that comprehension is increased when people have the text to follow as opposed to simply hearing it read. This technique also saves considerable time by reducing or eliminating the need to have testimony read to the jury. Some claim that the projected testimony is distracting, but this has not been the experience of most courts utilizing it.

Mini-Summations and Statements on the Relevance of Evidence

Mini-summations may serve a useful purpose in long trials. They can aid the jury by providing a summary of what has transpired to date and explaining the significance of the evidence.[29] Indeed, it seems to make extremely good sense to accompany every document offered in evidence with a brief explanation (one or two sentences) of what the evidence purports to demonstrate; the opposition should be given the same opportunity to comment on its relevance. One of the great failings of our trial procedures is the absence of an effective means of conveying the relevance of testimony or exhibits to jurors, who are left to guess as to the purpose, usually until final argument. There should be some method to advise jurors about the relevance of an exhibit so that they can place the evidence in context when it is admitted, rather than at some time in the future. One method is to give each side a certain amount of time or number of opportunities to comment on the evidence that could be used by the attorneys at their discretion—like chits to be cashed in during the trial.[30]

Identifying Lawyers and Parties

Because the attorneys and parties to a case are introduced only briefly at the beginning of a trial, jurors frequently do not know who the lawyers are or whom they represent. Names can be complex and unusual, and yet the jury often does not have access to the name except as it is first pronounced (or mispronounced). At least in cases involving multiple parties, place cards should be utilized to identify the lawyers and the parties.

Video Technology

Video technology is being used in the courtroom in many innovative ways.[31] It is difficult to envision a more boring moment in a trial than the reading of deposition testimony. Videotaped deposition testimony, now less costly, has become so commonplace that it should be utilized whenever possible, in preference to having the testimony simply read, if witnesses cannot appear to testify.

Video technology is also an excellent resource for re-creation and simulation, although the validity of such demonstrations must be carefully scrutinized. The potential for abuse is the same as it is for expert testimony, and the risks may be multiplied by the fact that visual presentations have a greater impact than oral testimony. However, such technology affords an inexhaustible means of educating jurors.

Juror Questions

There is an understandable reluctance to permit jurors to ask questions from the jury box. A question may be improper; it may disclose the juror's thinking; it may be something not yet addressed for strategic reasons. However, it seems nonsensical not to satisfy a juror who has a pertinent and relevant question. The safer course would be to advise jurors that, if a question has not been asked, it should be put in writing so the judge can discuss it with the attorneys to determine whether it is appropriate.[32] Whether or not this instruction should be given if the jury does not specifically inquire about asking questions is debatable. In most cases, a judge would not want to encourage questions from the jury, but on the other hand, questions should not be discouraged.

The experiments in the Second Circuit courts included juror questions.[33] Six judges tried the procedure in twenty-six trials, and all of the judges giving an opinion favored the technique as being helpful. The same national study that examined note-taking also examined the procedure of permitting jurors to submit questions.[34] Again, certain advantages and disadvantages to permitting jurors to ask questions were hypothesized and examined in the study.

The advantages of asking questions were postulated as follows:

—Juror questions promote the jury's understanding of the facts and issues.

—Juror questions help in finding the truth.

—Juror questions alert attorneys to issues that require more extensive development.

—Juror questions increase the satisfaction of both jurors and lawyers with the trial, the judge, and the verdict.

The disadvantages of asking questions were postulated as follows:

—Jurors do not know the rules of evidence and therefore ask inappropriate or impermissible questions.

—Trial lawyers are reluctant to object to inappropriate juror questions.

—If an attorney objects to a juror's question, the juror is embarrassed or angry.

—If the attorney objects, and the objection is sustained, the jury draws inappropriate inferences from unanswered questions.

—In assuming duties not properly theirs, jurors become advocates rather than neutral factfinders.

—Jurors overemphasize their own questions and answers at the expense of other evidence presented during the trial.

—Juror questions have a prejudicial effect.

Only the first advantage—that juror questions promote the jury's understanding—was verified, but all the disadvantages were disproved. As with the note-taking study, the lack of verification of the advantages does not necessarily mean that they do not exist, but rather that the study could not statistically verify them.

Bifurcated Trials

Many states provide defendants with the right to a bifurcated trial when punitive damages are sought and greater use should be made of this method of simplifying trials, which allows jurors first to decide the issue of liability and then set a damage award. But frequently even issues of liability can be separated and dealt with sequentially. An adverse determination on a liability issue can eliminate the need to present certain evidence concerning other claims, and, of course, a failure to succeed on all liability issues eliminates the need for any testimony regarding damages. Decisions on certain issues may also promote the settlement of any remaining issues.

Limitations on Time and Number of Witnesses

The shorter a case, the easier it is for a jury to understand; the longer a case, the more difficult it becomes. Therefore, we must consider whether or not it is appropriate to put limitations of time or number of witnesses on the parties. Surprisingly, courts that have experimented with limitations on presentations of each side's evidence or witnesses have found that the parties involved have little difficulty in complying and, indeed, do so with few complaints.[35] At a minimum, the court should be able to control the number of expert witnesses. Controlling other witnesses or limiting the amount of time they may testify obviously poses greater difficulties and raises questions of due process. Therefore, any limitations should be agreed to by all parties to a case rather than being set by the judge.

Juror Discussions during the Trial

Asking jurors not to discuss the evidence until all of it has been presented runs contrary to the normal decisionmaking process. This prohibition is intended to keep jurors from making decisions early in a trial and to ensure that testimony presented early on does not receive more attention or credibility than subsequent evidence. When complex testimony is received over weeks or months, social scientists have noted that the jurors' decisionmaking process is impaired by the rule of silence. A few innovative judges (with appropriate admonitions) permit jurors to discuss the case among themselves throughout the trial.[36] In this way any problems or misconceptions that develop early in the trial can be discussed and corrected, and the information can be handled in a far more normal manner. Permitting jurors to discuss the evidence is in keeping with the previously discussed innovations involving the use of mini-summations and explanations throughout the trial.

It is now recognized that jurors suffer from postverdict trauma. Although primarily associated with criminal cases, this trauma provides another reason for permitting jurors to discuss a case throughout the trial. Psychiatrists who have conducted postverdict sessions with jurors following difficult decisions or distressing testimony or exhibits report that not permitting the jurors to engage in discussions of this evidence causes or exacerbates stress.[37] The normal reaction of people to stress (and the frequent recommendation of therapists) is to "get it out" by talking.

The rationale for prohibiting jurors from discussing a case during a trial is powerful. The restriction, however, may be imposing an unnatural and frustrating burden on the jurors, who certainly think about the case as it progresses. Consideration should be given to whether allowing jurors to discuss a case in progress is as harmful as we have always assumed.

Innovations in Jury Instructions and the Deliberation Process

As jury instructions have become more complex we have not adapted our techniques to help the jury contend with this complexity.

Furnishing Copies of Instructions

Here again, it is totally unrealistic to believe that jurors can absorb and understand highly complex legal jargon without receiving the judge's instructions in writing. A better practice is to have instructions handed out to the jurors so that they can follow along as the judge reads. In addition, the jury will then have copies for use in the jury room. Jury instruction should not be a test of the jurors' memories.

A less desirable alternative to written instructions is a tape recording made while the judge reads. The recorder and tape are given to the jury to take into the deliberation room.

All of this presupposes that the instructions will be submitted to the jury in a clear and concise manner. The mere fact that they are in writing does not eliminate the fundamental difficulty juries often have with them—namely, that they are not understandable because courts insist on using formalized language that jurors do not hear in their everyday lives. Some strides have been made in making jury instructions understandable.[38] A great deal of the fault with jury instructions lies with trial judges, who fear that if they do not adopt language that has been approved by the appellate courts, a verdict in a long and complex trial may be reversed.

Use of Interrogatories or Process Instructions in Special Verdicts

To a large extent, the need to provide instructions for a jury can be substantially reduced, and in some cases even eliminated, with better use of fact interrogatories.[39] In other words, if the factual issues are properly framed for a jury, there is no need for an extensive discourse on the law. The judge can mold the verdict once the jury makes the necessary factual determinations. For instance, in a fraud case, a jury can be asked whether or not the evidence presented corresponds to the elements of the case as given in the jurors' instructions without any explanation as to what the law of fraud is and what must be proven in order to establish fraud. With rare exceptions, the same can be done in almost every case.

Witness Transcripts

Technology has now made it possible for a court reporter using a computer to transcribe testimony, automatically eliminating all side-bar conferences (conferences held at the bench out of hearing of the jury) from the record. This saves time when the jury requests that testimony be reread, and every court should make certain that its court reporter has the capability to produce such transcripts in the event that they are needed by the jury.

Reclosing the Case

In fourteen states and the federal courts, jury verdicts in civil cases must be unanimous. The probability of a hung jury is obviously greatest where unanimity is required. One innovative solution to the problem of hung juries has been tried. In a civil case involving alleged police brutality, the deliberating jury arrived at a partial verdict and sent out a message: "We seem to be at an impasse. Have been for some time, any suggestions?"[40] The presiding judge, Stewart A. Newblatt, asked the jurors which subjects the jury wished the attorneys to address. The jury sent out a note listing several areas. The parties were then permitted to reargue based on this response from the jury. In his memorandum opinion, Judge Newblatt notes, "It is surprising that no reported case that I have found has utilized this procedure, which to me makes eminent good sense. It is clear that the plaintiff has not been prejudiced by the procedure, which I find to be within the general discretionary power of the court over oral argument."[41]

Judge Dann discusses the above technique and presents the results of its use in a murder case being tried for the third time.[42] After six days of deliberation, the jury sent out a note saying it was deadlocked and asking for suggestions. The same technique described above was used, with each side given an hour to respond to the jury's concerns. Although the jury remained deadlocked and a mistrial was declared, the jurors praised the technique in post-trial interviews. (Defense attorneys, however, did not like the technique. They preferred the mistrial.) Judge Dann argues that cases should be reopened for further evidence or instructions, as they are for omitted or overlooked evidence. For civil cases, this innovation appears to be a useful technique to aid the jurors in making a decision.

Postverdict Innovations: Post-trial Interviews

To a large extent, the prohibition on or reluctance to conduct post-trial interviews of jurors is predicated on the fear that the judge will learn something it might be better not to know, or that lawyers conducting the interviews will seek to find something that will discredit the verdict if they are dissatisfied with it. However, the postverdict interview with the jurors, when conducted by the presiding judge, is a most revealing process.[43] Every judge, from time to time, should invite jurors into chambers just to chat with them about how well the system is working and what can be done to improve it. Jurors sometimes make the most extraordinary and obvious suggestions, and it pays to take heed. Such an interview is also an invaluable opportunity to personally express the importance of and need for jury service. Jurors enjoy and appreciate this opportunity to meet informally with the judge.

Conclusion

The foregoing suggestions may be accepted or rejected; they may succeed or fail. They are submitted for the reader's consideration, discussion, and trial, if deemed appropriate.

Whether any of these innovations is truly needed or useful is open to debate. What is not debatable is the need for a forum to exchange and evaluate such ideas. Those who work within the judicial system share a common goal: to present cases to juries in a clear and meaningful way so that jurors can render fair, just, and reasoned verdicts. That goal is best served by sharing techniques which serve that purpose. We hope, in some small measure, we have aided in the progress toward that goal.

396 / H. Lee Sarokin and G. Thomas Munsterman

Notes

1. Judge Sarokin has written and delivered presentations on civil trial procedures and has implemented many himself. He edited a column in *Chambers to Chambers* (published by the Federal Judicial Center) on trial techniques. Munsterman, by virtue of his writings and teaching assignments, has become an important source of information on jury trials. The *Center for Jury Studies Newsletter* and the column in the National Center for State Courts' *Report* (published from 1979 to 1984) contain many of the techniques described.

2. Louis Harris and Associates, "Judges' Opinions on Procedural Issues: A Survey of State and Federal Trial Judges Who Spend at Least Half Their Time on General Civil Cases," Study 874017 (New York, 1989); also published *Boston University Law Review*, vol. 69 (May 1989), pp. 731–63.

3. B. Michael Dann "'Learning Lessons' and 'Speaking Rights': Creating Educated and Democratic Juries," thesis, Graduate Program for Judges, School of Law, University of Virginia, March 1992, p. 11.

4. G. Thomas Munsterman and Janice T. Munsterman, "The Search for Jury Representativeness," *Justice System Journal*, vol. 11 (Spring 1986), pp. 59–78.

5. Stephen Knack, "The Voter Participation Effects of Selecting Jurors from Registration Lists," working paper 91-10, Department of Economics, University of Maryland, April 1991. To be published: *Journal of Law and Economics*, April 1993.

6. *Ensuring a Jury of One's Peers! The Need to Eliminate Occupational Exemptions from Jury Service in New York State Courts* (New York State Bar Association, Commercial and Federal Litigation Section, October 7, 1991).

7. *Methodology Manual for Jury Systems* (Williamsburg, Va.: National Center for State Courts, 1981), pp. 6-1–6-6.

8. Janice T. Munsterman and others, *The Relationship of Juror Fees and Terms of Service to Jury System Performance*, WPO-029 (Arlington, Va.: National Center for State Courts, Washington Project Office, 1991).

9. *Massachusetts General Laws Annotated* (West, 1986), Chapter 234A.

10. *Connecticut General Statutes Annotated* (West, 1985), *Title* 51-217. *Colorado Revised Statutes 13–71* (Denver: Bradford, 1987).

11. American Bar Association, "Standards Relating to Juror Use and Management," revised draft, Chicago, 1992.

12. G. Thomas Munsterman and Janice T. Munsterman, *Supplement to the Methodology Manual for Jury Systems* (Arlington, Va.: National Center for State Courts, 1987), pp. 34–36.

13. Timothy R. Murphy, Genevra Kay Loveland, and G. Thomas Munsterman, *A Manual for Managing Notorious Cases*, R-130 (Williamsburg, Va.: National Center for State Courts, 1992), pp. 59–66; and Dennis Bilecki, "A More Efficient Method of Jury Selection For Lengthy Trials," *Judicature*, vol. 73 (June–July 1989), pp. 43–47.

14. *Copley Press Inc.* v. *San Diego County Superior Court*, 223 Cal. App. 3d 994 (1990); see also 228 Cal. App. 3d 77 (1991).

15. *Kentucky* v. *Batson*, 476 U.S. 79 (1986); *Edmonson* v. *Leesville Concrete Co. Inc.*, 111 S.Ct. 2077 (1991); *Hernandez* v. *New York*, 111 S.Ct. 1859 (1991); *Powers* v. *Ohio*, 111 S.Ct. 1364 (1991); *Georgia* v. *McCollum*, 91-372 (decided June 18, 1992); and *U.S.* v. *DeGross*, 960 F.2d 1433 (1992).

16. *Kentucky* v. *Batson* at 17.

17. Civil jury trials are used in England (Queens Bench) only for libel, slander, malicious prosecution, and false imprisonment, and there is no right to peremptory challenges in such cases. *Halsbury's Laws of England*, vol. 26, 4th ed (London: Butter-Worths, 1979), para 624.

18. If the use of experts continues and expands, it will give the litigant another advantage (through the exercise of peremptory challenges)—assuming such experts can predict any juror's vote.

19. Albert W. Alschuler, "The Supreme Court and Jury: Voir Dire, Peremptory Challenges, and the Review of Jury Verdicts," *University of Chicago Law Review*, vol. 56 (Winter 1989), pp. 153–233.

20. True, there will be the occasional juror whose presence on the jury troubles an attorney for reasons that cannot be determined or articulated. But Judge Sarokin who regularly meets with jurors in his chambers after trial, is constantly amazed and uplifted by their conscientiousness and dedication to their duties. Furthermore, every lawyer has an anecdote about a juror who, it was certain, would decide one way but in fact did just the opposite.

21. *Federal Rules of Civil Procedure* (West, 1992); and *Purdon's Pennsylvania Consolidated Statutes Annotated* (West, 1981), Title 42, Section 5104.

22. It can be argued that the plaintiff's task of convincing six persons is easier than convincing seven, eight, or even twelve, and that unanimity should not be required as the number of jurors increases.

23. Leonard B. Sand and Steven Alan Reiss, "A Report on Seven Experiments Conducted by District Court Judges in the Second Circuit," *New York University Law Review*, vol. 60 (June 1985), pp. 423–97.

24. *Toward More Active Juries: Taking Notes and Asking Questions* (Chicago: American Judicature Society, 1991).

25. Fay A. Siles, "Juror Notes: Say They Aid Fact-Finding," *ABA Journal*, vol. 72 (March 1986), pp. 20–21; and Sand and Reiss, "Report on Seven Experiments."

26. Larry Heuer and Steven Penrod, "Increasing Jurors' Participation in Trials: A Field Experiment with Jury Notetaking and Question Asking," *Law and Human Behavior*, vol. 12 (September 1988), pp. 231–61.

27. Larry Heuer and Steven Penrod, "Juror Notetaking and Question Asking during Trials: A National Field Experiment," State Justice Institute, Alexandria, Va., 1991.

28. John V. Singleton and Miriam Kass, "Helping the Jury Understand Complex Cases," *Litigation*, vol. 12 (Spring 1986), pp. 11–13.

29. Dann, "Creating Educated and Democratic Juries," pp. 44–45.

30. Pierre N. Leval, "*Westmoreland* v. *CBS*," *Litigation*, vol. 12 (Fall 1985), p. 7.

31. See the chapter by Stephen Saltzburg in this volume.

32. American Judicature Society, *Toward More Active Juries: Taking Notes and Asking Questions* (Chicago, 1981).

33. Sand and Reiss, "Report on Seven Experiments."

34. Heuer and Penrod, "A National Field Experiment."

35. Leval, "*Westmoreland* v. *CBS*."

36. William W Schwarzer. "Reforming Jury Trials," *Federal Rules Decisions*, vol. 132 (West, 1991), pp. 575–96.

37. Theodore B. Feldmann and Roger A. Bell, "Crisis Debriefing of a Jury after a Murder Trial," *Hospital and Community Psychiatry*, vol. 42 (January 1991), pp. 79–81.

38. J. Alexander Tanford, "The Law and Psychology of Jury Instructions," *Nebraska Law Review*, vol. 69 (Winter 1990), pp. 71–111; Edward J. Imwinkelried and Lloyd R. Schwed, "Guidelines for Drafting Understandable Jury Instructions: An Introduction to the Use of Psycholinguistics," *Criminal Law Bulletin*, vol. 23 (April 1987), pp. 135–50; Walter W. Steele, Jr., and Elizabeth G. Thornburg, "Jury Instructions: A Persistent Failure to Communicate," *North Carolina Law Review*, vol. 67 (November 1988), pp. 77–119; and Amiram Elwork, Bruce D. Sales, and James J. Alfini, *Making Jury Instructions Understandable* (Charlottesville, Va.: Michie, 1982).

39. David U. Strawn and others, "Reaching A Verdict, Step By Step," *Judicature*, vol. 60 (March 1977), pp. 383–89.

40. Mark S. Brodin, "Accuracy, Efficiency, and Accountability in the Litigation Process—The Case for the Fact Verdict," *University of Cincinnati Law Review*, vol. 59 (Summer 1990), pp. 15–111; and *William Withers v. Julie Ringlein, et. al*, 89-40085. United States District Court, Eastern District of Michigan, Southern Division.

41. *William Withers*, p. 4.

42. Dann, "Creating Educated and Democratic Juries," p. 66.

43. Judge Sarokin meets with jurors after every case. He does not inquire as to their deliberations and, indeed, instructs them not to disclose anything concerning their verdict. However, he learns a great deal about what they consider important and is able to ascertain whether they feel the process has been helpful and where we are failing or can improve.

CHAPTER TWELVE

The Modern American Jury: Reflections on Veneration and Distrust

William W Schwarzer and Alan Hirsch

T HE JURY is one of America's venerated institutions. It is seen as a barrier against abuse of governmental and judicial power, a guaranty that citizens will be judged by their peers, a means to temper justice with other community values, and a bridge between the citizenry and its courts. Some see it as the ultimate emblem of popular justice and believe it affords an almost mystical vindication of individual rights. Although from time to time questions are raised about its relevance to contemporary civil litigation—especially in complex cases—there has been no serious effort to alter the constitutional guaranty of trial by jury.

Thus civil juries are entrusted with decisions of often staggering difficulty and vast importance. While many jury cases are routine, increasingly they affect large numbers of people; they can jeopardize the survival of major enterprises, carry profound social and political implications, and bring about far-reaching transfers of wealth. Yet at the same time, the trials in which these kinds of decisions are made are tightly bound by rules and conventions that bespeak a fundamental fact: the justice system does not fully trust jurors. This distrust is pervasive. It is evident in the practice of prohibiting them from taking notes, asking questions, and discussing the case among themselves during trial,[1] and the tendency to keep them in the dark about much of what goes on during the trial.[2] Perhaps most importantly, it is reflected in the rule that keeps evidence from them on the basis of subjective, ad hoc, and sometimes arbitrary judgments and in the attempt generally to insulate their decisionmaking process from reality.

We are grateful to Russell Wheeler, Gordon Bermant, Joe Cecil, and Diane Sheehey for their comments and suggestions.

The justification for this tradition-bound choreography of the jury trial is obvious: to ward off influences that may lead to an unfair (or seemingly unfair) verdict. The irony is that sentiment, more than reason and logic, is a driving force behind many jury decisions—or, if not sentiment, the jury's independent sense of the "equities." As Stephen Yeazell has put it:

> Even those who have made careers and fortunes presenting cases to juries will always be somewhat wary of the jury because it is unaccountable and unpredictable. In such a view the jury is a regrettable experiment in sentimentality freed from the restraints of accountability. But common sense and adjustment of individual equities have equally persuasive defenders. A society that depends on compromise and the blurring of sharp differences will have use for an institution so well suited to this function.[3]

Whatever side of the argument one takes, therefore, the reason is not that jurors are expected to parse the law carefully and diligently sort out and weigh the relevant facts. That this may at times occur is undeniable; that jury cases are tried in the expectation that it will occur surely is not.

The jury trial thus presents the justice system with a dilemma. The jury exercises great power with little accountability, yet is virtually untouchable. At the same time, distrust of the way that jurors exercise this power has led to some arbitrary and potentially counterproductive restraints.

The contradiction between veneration and distrust that besets the jury system[4] has been exacerbated as jury trials have become more complex and protracted and their economic, social, and political impact more critical. In this paper, we reflect on ways in which the contradiction plays itself out and consider, in a preliminary way, whether changes in the way civil juries are selected may help resolve the contradiction.

The Exclusion of Relevant Evidence

The jurors' function in the trial is, as they are told in the standard instruction, to be the judges of the facts. They are to find the facts from the evidence the lawyers offer and the judge receives into the record. Rule 401 of the Federal Rules of Evidence defines relevant evidence, in substance, as evidence tending to prove the existence of a material fact.

All relevant evidence is admissible except as otherwise provided in the rules.

Some rules require or permit the exclusion, for public policy reasons, of relevant evidence such as subsequent remedial measures, payment of medical expenses, and offers of compromise. Rule 403 permits a judge to exclude evidence, though relevant, "if its probative value is substantially outweighed by the danger of unfair prejudice, confusion of the issues, or misleading the jury, or by considerations of undue delay, waste of time, or needless presentation of cumulative evidence." (Probative value is the tendency of evidence to prove facts in dispute.) Policy reasons favoring the expeditious and economical resolution of cases justify the exclusion of "needless . . . cumulative evidence" and of evidence that would result in "undue delay [or] waste." But no such justification is available for excluding relevant evidence the judge believes may confuse or mislead the jury or result in unfair prejudice.

What is the rationale for authorizing judges to deprive jurors of relevant evidence on the ground that it may result in unfair prejudice or may confuse or mislead the jury? Significantly, the provision for excluding misleading evidence is explicitly limited to juries. And while Rule 403 does not specifically limit the exclusion of prejudicial or confusing evidence to jury trials, it is generally considered inapplicable to bench trials.[5] This is partly a practical matter—judges must look at the evidence in order to rule on an objection. But more broadly, judges are trusted to segregate in their minds the probative component of evidence from its prejudicial, confusing, or misleading features, presumably because judges are expert at assessing evidence. That reasoning, however, is at war with the fundamental notion underlying jury trials, which rejects the need for expertise in assessing evidence in all other respects, including evidence of the most complex and technical nature. If jurors cannot be trusted to determine what is unfairly prejudicial, they can scarcely be trusted to decide cases turning on highly complex evidence such as recombinant genetic engineering.

Of course, Rule 403 does not authorize a court to exclude proffered evidence solely because there is a risk of unfair prejudice or confusion. The court must find that this risk substantially outweighs the probative value of the material. While relevant evidence is that which makes a disputed fact in the case more or less probable, probative value refers to the *extent* that the evidence does so. Assessing the extent to which evidence proves a party's case is at the core of the jury's function. For a court to exclude relevant evidence in part because it isn't impressed with the probative value of the evidence seems to involve a direct incursion into the jury's turf.

Traditionally, Rule 403 has been concerned primarily with evidence that might be considered inflammatory, such as a bloody shirt or photographs of a shocking scene. Today, the rule seems to be gaining a more powerful and controversial role. As evidence, principally expert testimony, becomes more technical and complex, Rule 403 is sometimes used as the basis for its exclusion. There is, however, no discernible consistency in its application from case to case and no objective standard for prospective guidance. By what standards does the judge assess whether prejudice is unfair? Probative evidence is always prejudicial to the opponent; when does it become "unfairly" prejudicial? Similarly, it is odd to say that evidence is too confusing for a jury to hear in a trial on issues that are confusing by their nature, such as the causal relationship between toxic substances and the disease of a particular plaintiff. Prejudice and confusion are in the beholder's eye, and lawyers and judges have never found a principled basis for the application of these exclusionary rules.

The objection, of course, is not to rules of evidence. They are a part of the legal framework within which factfinding should take place. Rule 403, however, is less a component of an ordered legal structure than a very elastic leash on the jury. It reflects distrust rather than principle and is a manifestation of the contradiction of the jury system. While the consequences of eliminating the rule could be worse than those of keeping it, it is important to recognize the contradiction out of which it arises and perhaps consider the advisability of taking a critical look at whether it should be retained in its present form.

The Blindfolding of Jurors

The distrust that pervades the jury system is evidenced by other rules and practices designed to blindfold jurors, keeping from them information for fear that it might adversely affect their decisionmaking process. Examples include information about parties' insurance coverage, treble damages in antitrust cases, attorneys' fees, taxability of awards, settlement offers, and actual settlements involving some of the parties. Though well intentioned, the effort to insulate jurors from the real world is often futile and potentially counterproductive.

Jurors bring with them both information and misinformation that forms the mix known as juror "common sense and experience." Jury instructions call on jurors to make determinations, such as evaluating circumstantial evidence, "in the light of reason, common sense and experience."[6] Even when jurors are not specifically referred to their common sense and experience, these attributes are often their only refuge in a sea of confusing evidence and legal jargon.

Common sense and experience quickly tell most jurors struggling through the trial that information is being withheld from them. Aside from feeling chagrined at being treated like children, jurors may be tempted to fill in blanks—speculating, for example, about insurance. Insurance is common currency in the discourse of the average citizen. Few jurors can be expected to come to jury service without some awareness of insurance; consciously or subconsciously, this knowledge is likely to enter into their deliberations. In a recent study of thirty-eight jury panels, half the jurors assumed that defendants were covered by insurance, nearly a third assumed that plaintiffs had insurance or some other form of compensation, and many acknowledged that these assumptions influenced their decisions.[7] Yet reference to insurance at trial remains taboo.

It is bad for jurors to speculate about insurance; it is worse when they come to an incorrect conclusion. Jurors may incorrectly assume that a party's loss is covered by insurance or that the policy limits cover the loss when they do not. The study mentioned above indicated that a number of jurors were led to reduce damage awards on the assumption that the plaintiff had insurance, unaware of the insurance company's right to recover from the wrongdoers what it paid its insured.[8]

The risk to parties from jurors' speculations about insurance resembles the risk to a defendant from the privilege against self-incrimination, for just as it is difficult to know whether a defendant who chooses not to testify is better off having the jury instructed on the privilege or having nothing said, so it may seem difficult to decide how best to handle the question of insurance. But since keeping the jury ignorant about parties' insurance coverage does not guarantee that the issue will have no impact on the verdict, much is to be said for candor. It seems preferable to level with jurors by giving them a fair explanation of how they should treat insurance in their deliberations.[9]

The blindfolding of jurors has other implications. In criminal cases, for example, jurors are normally told that punishment is not their concern.[10] Yet many jurors will have seen news stories about sentences imposed by judges and formed views on the subject. Although in theory punishment is irrelevant to the finding of guilt, it would be risky to assume that jurors will always be indifferent to what they believe (correctly or incorrectly) will be the penal consequences of their verdict. Postverdict interviews, not surprisingly, reveal a high degree of interest in the sentence the defendant faces.[11]

Blindfolding remains firmly entrenched. A recent illustration is the Civil Rights Act of 1991[12] which extends jury trials to employment discrimination cases under Title VII. In the Act, Congress set caps (keyed to the size of the defendant's work force) on compensatory and punitive damage awards, but directs that jurors not be told of the caps. There can be no reason for keeping this information from jurors other than the assumption that they cannot be trusted to assess damages fairly if they know that the amount plaintiff can recover is limited by law.

It may be argued that there is no reason why jurors should know of the caps. However, some jurors may well have heard about them (given the amount of publicity this legislation received), and may describe them to fellow jurors (correctly or incorrectly); thus the jury may be influenced in reaching a verdict. Such things occur. In one antitrust case, for example, a juror reported in a postverdict interview that he had learned from his daughter, a law student, that damage verdicts are quadrupled. In fact, the law provides for triple damages, but appellate decisions have generally barred trial judges from instructing juries on this point.[13]

The attempt to insulate jurors from matters about which they may well be informed or misinformed stems from the same distrust of jurors that leads to the exclusion of prejudicial, confusing, and misleading evidence. This assumption that jurors cannot be trusted to accept explanations and follow appropriate instructions concerning the real-world circumstances of a case ought to be acknowledged and reevaluated.[14]

The Selection of Jurors

This brief overview indicates that practices founded on distrust of jurors can be troublesome and counterproductive. Revising the practices discussed above, however, would not eliminate the distrust from which they stem. This distrust of the individuals who constitute the jury stands in stark contrast to the veneration in which the jury as an institution is held. Recognition of this contradiction raises the question of whether it can be resolved by changing the way in which jurors are selected. Conceivably, selecting more qualified jurors could reduce distrust (and might lead to a rethinking of the rules and practices founded on distrust).

The selection process used today is a part of the jury trial's tradition-bound choreography and is based more on appearances and sentiment than on substance. Pretending to select what is referred to as a "fair and impartial" jury, the participants seek those jurors who appear most sympathetic to their respective causes (or at least fit no disfavored stereotype), attempting in the process to checkmate the opponent's choices. Competence is rarely a factor.

Earlier sections discussed jurors' alleged difficulties with relevant evidence that is deemed confusing, misleading, or prejudicial, as well as with extraneous information and assumptions, both true and false, not relevant to the issues in the case but potentially influential. It may be that a jury selected with an eye toward competence would be better able to sort out such evidence and extraneous matters and to comprehend complex evidence generally. This intuitively credible proposition remains unproven, making research and study about the issue clearly desirable. Meanwhile, so is consideration of possible ways to improve the process of civil jury selection. While important values in the existing process need to be preserved, the process should not be assumed to be beyond improvement—especially in complex cases.

The Context of Jury Trials

Some contend that since the process by which civil juries are selected has proved itself by producing competent juries, it is best to leave well enough alone. Those taking this position rely heavily on Harry Kalven and Hans Zeisel's findings, based on a study conducted in the 1950s, which show that judges agreed with jury verdicts in about 80 percent of the cases reviewed.[15] Of course, a 20 percent rate of disagreement is not necessarily an endorsement; moreover, the study showed that jury awards averaged 20 percent more than the amounts judges would have granted. But whatever the weight to be given this study at the time it was made, drastic changes in the intervening years call into question its relevance to current conditions.

Though juries continue to decide simple tort and contract cases, the jury docket today (particularly in the federal courts) increasingly consists of product liability, racketeering, environmental, high-technology patent, and other complex litigation. These cases involve voluminous and complicated evidence, often have many parties, and call for the application of standards that are usually vague, elusive, and foreign to a juror's experience. The decisions in such cases, moreover, can have far-reaching and devastating consequences. As described by Peter Schuck,

> Today, the law books abound with tort cases, especially in the product liability area, that involve not a few individuals but large aggregations of people and vast economic and social interest. These cases are not preoccupied with corrective justice between individuals concerned solely with past events. Instead, they concern the public control of large-scale activities and the distribution of social power and values for the future. The court and jury in these cases do not simply prescribe and apply familiar norms to discrete actions; they function as policy-oriented risk regulators, as self-conscious allocators of hard-to-measure benefits and risks, and as social problem solvers.[16]

At the time of the study by Kalven and Zeisel, the jury's task generally was to decide disputes that could be resolved by reference to community standards of prudent conduct that could be derived from a background of common experience. Those kinds of issues are far removed from what is involved in determining, for example, the causal relationship between the ingestion of Bendectin and an individual's birth defects.

Drastic changes have also taken place in the population from which juries are drawn. Jury selection procedures in the past, though often invidiously exclusionary, probably resulted in juries composed of relatively educated jurors. Courts now go to great lengths to ensure that the jury pool comprises a true cross section of the community; in most jurisdictions, practically any nonfelon who votes or drives can serve.[17] As a result, numerous persons with limited education (and often a precarious command of English) serve on juries.

The essence of a trial is communication. Yet today, a growing proportion of the population speaks and understands English poorly. Recent census data indicate that in New York City, for example, 41 percent of residents speak a foreign language at home and nearly half of them said they do not speak English well. In Miami, nearly 75 percent of the residents speak a foreign language at home and 67 percent of them said they do not speak English well.[18] Not all of these residents would be eligible for jury duty, but judges selecting juries regularly encounter jurors who are not comfortable with English. Such jurors are unlikely to comprehend at least some of the more complex evidence.

Though jurors today will often be unfamiliar with the subject matter of cases they hear and may have trouble understanding the language as well, they will likely have accumulated much more information and misinformation than jurors in the past. Constant exposure to the mass media imprints a variety of messages on jurors' minds that could influence their decisionmaking process. Few jurors, for example, will not have seen television shows such as "L.A. Law" that serve as powerful molders of attitudes toward law and lawyers. Media coverage of ecological disasters and harmful substances is common and pervasive. A constant drumbeat of controversy fills the air, raising not only issues of public policy but also of individual values; few citizens can be expected to enter the jury room with a tabula rasa on issues such as the environment, race, gender, and public safety, to name a few. This could lead to the worst of both worlds: biased or predisposed jurors who lack competence.

These and other elements of change in the context in which the jury system operates challenge the assumption that the jury today is the institution it was forty years ago–and even then, of course, confidence in jury competence was tempered by the restrictions and constraints discussed earlier. Questioning that assumption could lead to questioning the way juries are selected and utilized, the manner in which cases are presented to juries, and the kinds of issues that are appropriate for decision by juries.[19] We have singled out for discussion the jury selection process. There may be better alternatives, or at least improvements in the process, that could be reconciled with the important values underlying the jury system.

The Competence Problem

The demands on jurors today are greater than ever: Trials are longer and more complex, decisions more difficult and their impact greater. Yet the selection process remains fixed on random selection from a cross section of the population, usually derived from voter registration and driver's license lists. There is no way of ensuring that a jury will be competent in terms of education, experience, and capacity to exercise judgment. The contradiction of the system thus becomes more acute: distrust increases as juror responsibility and power increase without a corresponding increase in juror competence.

Could this trend toward greater distrust be ameliorated by tinkering with the jury selection process—for instance, by utilizing procedures that encourage or promote the selection of the best-educated and most experienced members of the venire?

The present random selection process is intended to produce "representative" juries. Even if a representative jury is desirable in the abstract, randomness cannot be equated with representativeness; six- to twelve-person juries cannot be expected to reflect anything even approaching a cross section of the community.[20] They are more likely to reflect the lower end of the spectrum of education and experience, partly as a result of pre-trial excuses, and partly because of peremptory challenges.

Attorneys have little power to seat competent and experienced jurors. Challenges for cause, which are confined to concerns about impartiality, do not serve this purpose. Peremptory challenges can be used to eliminate unqualified jurors, but there is no assurance that replacements will be more qualified. The jury is picked by a process of elimination (seating those left after challenges are exercised) rather than in an effort to find qualified jurors. Whether attorneys will even seek competence depends on the merits of the case and trial strategy. Educated and experienced jurors are often eliminated because they may be too influential. The purpose of seating jurors, however, is not simply to fill the chairs or to please the parties, but rather to select factfinders. Interest in the integrity of the process counsels selecting persons sufficiently qualified so that they may be trusted to handle relevant evidence and other important information properly.

The current selection process concerns itself almost exclusively with eliminating potentially biased jurors. This is a quixotic effort, since it is impossible to identify (as opposed to guess about) deeply imbedded bias or predisposition.[21] The process of voir dire spots obvious areas of potential bias arising from interest or association, but it cannot effectively probe the recesses of prospective jurors' hearts and minds for hidden or unconscious bias, tacit assumptions, and personal values. Everyone operates from philosophical premises—notions about justice, self-reliance, social and individual responsibility, distribution of risk in society—that influence our evaluation of evidence. No selection process can eliminate this human element. But while no person's mind is a blank slate, those able to understand the issues and manage the evidence may have less need to resort to preexisting mindsets, prejudices, or intellectual shortcuts.

Various modifications of the factfinding process in certain trials have been suggested, including using juries of experts or specialized factfinders whose report would be presented to the jury at trial.[22] It is not necessary to go that far; even within the existing system, the most competent members of the venire can be selected without abandoning the random selection process by which the venire itself is formed. One might, for example, permit each party to select a number of prospective jurors from the venire, subject only to challenges for cause by the opposing party. Or judges can be authorized to establish objective minimum standards for service on the case,[23] such as high school graduation or perhaps college attendance, or to strike the least qualified prospective jurors from the venire. Judges can also be authorized to select from the venire a few jurors with the relevant education or business, scientific, or technical experience.[24]

Would such changes in the selection process produce jurors better able to cope with the problems discussed in earlier sections and be conducive to increased trust in the jury system? Presumably, more educated and experienced jurors are less susceptible to being confused or misled by evidence; whether such jurors are also better able to cope with the danger of unfair prejudice and the kinds of extraneous information against which jurors are now blindfolded is less clear (though, again, perhaps intuitively credible). These questions are surely worthy of study and informed debate.

A selection process that affirmatively seeks more qualified jurors seems particularly worth considering for complex cases. Whether it is appropriate in other civil cases is an open question. It can be argued that the selection procedures discussed above would deprive some citizens of an opportunity to serve—but for reasons sounder than the stereotypical justifications that now influence peremptory challenges.[25] Moreover, potential jurors not selected in one case would remain eligible for others, particularly criminal cases.[26]

Consideration needs to be given to how such procedures might be implemented: by agreement of the parties, by statute or rule, or simply at the judge's discretion.[27] The permissible range of judicial action under the Seventh Amendment, as well as other constitutional issues, must also be taken into account.[28] These questions are worth addressing, however, if a more rational selection process can be devised that will preserve the essential values of the jury system while helping to resolve its contradiction by building trust in the jury.[29]

Conclusion

This discussion may not be universally welcomed, since the jury system's status quo is widely deemed acceptable. But we have vested enormous power in the jury, and though it alone among our institutions of government is without ambition, it is also unaccountable and need give no explanation for its actions.[30] To distrust (as reflected in the rules and practices discussed) those who have been given such power is disquieting; to do nothing about it may be unwise.

These reflections may be criticized as elitist and undemocratic. But it is not unreasonable to ask whether education and experience are not as relevant to jurors' tasks as they are to most professional tasks. Embracing the jury system does not require ignoring its contradiction, long part of the system but perhaps easier to tolerate in simpler times. The drastic changes in the landscape of litigation during recent years have exacerbated the contradiction and made it harder to ignore.

Over its long history, the common-law jury has been a flexible institution able to adapt to changing needs and conditions. Openness to change may in the end be the key to the survival of the American civil jury. No institution should be viewed as incapable of benefiting from occasional searching examination; no assumptions about an institution should be beyond questioning. The civil jury is no exception.

Notes

1. Steven I. Friedland notes that "paternalistic limitations on the jury . . . imply that the jury is unable to shoulder the responsibility of governing the decisionmaking process." Friedland, "The Competence and Responsibility of Jurors in Deciding Cases," *Northwestern University Law Review*, vol. 85 (Fall 1990), p. 192.

2. See William W Schwarzer, "Reforming Jury Trials," *Federal Rules Decisions*, vol. 132 (West, 1991) pp. 575–96.

3. Stephen C. Yeazell, "The New Jury and the Ancient Jury Conflict," *University of Chicago Legal Forum*, vol. 1990, p. 106.

4. Mark S. Brodin notes that "the jury has become part of the national folklore," yet fears persist "regarding decision-making by amateurs," and he quotes Judge Learned Hand (in "The Deficiencies of Trials to Reach the Heart of the Matter," in *Lectures on Legal Topics, 1921–22*, vol. 3 [MacMillan Company, 1926], p. 89, as saying that we "trust Jurors as reverently as we do, and still surround them with restrictions which, if they have no rational validity whatever, depend upon our distrust." Brodin, "Accuracy, Efficiency, and Accountability in the Litigation Process: The Case for the Fact Verdict," *Cincinnati Law Review*, vol. 59 (Summer 1990), p. 16.

5. See, for example, *Gulf States Util.* v. *Ecodyne Corp.*, 635 F.2d 517, 519 (5th Cir. 1981).

6. See Committee on Model Jury Instructions, Ninth Circuit, *Manual of Model Criminal Jury Instructions for the Ninth Circuit* (West, 1989), p. 6.

7. John Guinther, *The Jury in America* (Facts on File, 1988), pp. 298–99, 342–43.

8. Ibid., p. 98.

9. Jurors can be instructed not only that insurance is irrelevant and that they should

not guess about it, but also *why*. It can be explained to them that an insurance company is entitled to the same fair treatment as the parties themselves, that even an insured loss is a loss, and that losses paid out by the insurer will likely be collected through higher premiums.

10. See *Manual for the Ninth Circuit*, p. 91.

11. Here consideration might be given to satisfying jurors' natural curiosity and countering their tendency to speculate by telling them the statutory sentencing range.

12. P.L. 102-66, 105 Stat. 1071.

13. An instruction might read, "The antitrust laws require that whatever damage verdict you return must be tripled. Congress has made a policy decision to triple damages in order to discourage violations of the antitrust laws. If you adjust your verdict because of the fact that it will be tripled by the court, you will defeat Congress' purpose. It is your duty simply to determine the amount of damages plaintiff suffered."

14. Various studies support the view that juries often disregard admonitions to disregard certain facts. See citations and summaries of the studies by J. Alexander Tanford, "The Law and Psychology of Jury Instructions," *Nebraska Law Review*, vol. 69 (Winter 1990), pp. 86–87; and Jonathan D. Casper, Kennette Benedict, and Jo L. Perry, "Juror Decision Making, Attitudes, and the Hindsight Bias," *Law and Human Behavior*, vol. 13 (September 1989), pp. 291–310. However, an ongoing study suggests that jurors are likely to follow such instructions if they come accompanied by an explanation. See Shari Seidman Diamond, Jonathan D. Casper, and Lynne Ostergren, "Blindfolding the Jury," *Law And Contemporary Problems*, vol. 52 (Autumn 1989), pp. 247–67. Note 13 offers an example of an explanation that could accompany the instruction.

15. See Harry Kalven, Jr., and Hans Zeisel, *The American Jury* (Little, Brown, 1966). Evidence of jury competence in the more complex kinds of cases that have become common today is limited and inconclusive. See, for example, Joe S. Cecil, Valerie P. Hans, and Elizabeth C. Wiggins, "Citizen Comprehension of Difficult Issues: Lessons from Civil Jury Trials," *American University Law Review*, vol. 40 (Winter 1991), pp. 750–64.

16. Peter Schuck, *Agent Orange on Trial: Mass Toxic Tort Disasters in the Court* (Harvard University Press, 1987), p. 4.

17. The eligibility criteria for federal jury service are residence in the judicial district, U.S. citizenship, age (18), literacy, the absence of mental or physical infirmity, and the lack of a criminal record. 28 U.S.C. § 1865.

18. See Barbara Vobejda, "America's Many Tongues," *Washington Post*, April 16, 1992, p. A1. For further indication of the prevalence of foreign language in the population generally, see the *Annual Report of the Administrative Office of the United States Courts, 1989* (p. 76), which notes that interpreters were used in more than 46,000 federal cases in the previous year alone.

19. See, for example, Schwarzer, "Reforming Jury Trials"; William W Schwarzer, Alan Hirsch, and David J. Barrans, *The Analysis and Decision of Summary Judgment Motions: A Monograph on Rule 56 of the Federal Rules of Civil Procedure* (Washington: Federal Judicial Center, 1991), pp. 13–37.

20. Federal law does not require that each jury be a representative cross section of the community. See *Frazier* v. *United States*, 335 U.S. 497, 507 (1948).

21. Lawyers make such guesses in exercising their peremptory challenges. The continuing viability of the peremptory challenge is doubtful. *Batson* v. *Kentucky*, 476 U.S. 79 (1986), and its progeny, in which the Supreme Court rejected the use of peremptories to eliminate members of protected groups, opened most challenges to challenge themselves, inviting controversy and delay. Moreover, permitting jurors to be excused on the strength of the remaining permissible stereotypes or lawyers' hunches is of little value to the system and exacts some cost. From the point of view of prospective jurors, peremptory challenges may be insulting and offensive. More generally, permitting each side to dismiss jurors

without cause encourages a view of jurors as pawns to be manipulated by the parties, not as responsible decisionmakers. Thus peremptory challenges reinforce the aura of distrust of jurors.

22. See, for example, Peter Huber, "Junk Science and the Jury," *University of Chicago Legal Forum*, vol. 1990, pp. 301–02; Dan Drazan, "The Case for Special Juries in Toxic Tort Litigation," *Judicature*, vol. 72 (February-March 1989), p. 292; and William V. Luneberg and Mark A. Nordenberg, "Specially Qualified Juries and Expert Nonjury Tribunals: Alternatives for Coping with the Complexities of Modern Civil Litigation," *Virginia Law Review*, vol. 67 (June 1981), pp. 887–1007.

23. See Richard O. Lempert, "Civil Juries and Complex Cases: Let's Not Rush to Judgment," *Michigan Law Review*, vol. 80 (November 1981), pp. 119–20; and Luneberg and Nordenberg, "Specially Qualified Juries," p. 900.

24. See *In re Richardson-Merrell "Bendectin" Products Liability Litigation*, 624 F.Supp. 1212, 1217 (S.D. Ohio 1985), *aff'd* in part and *vacated* and *remanded* in part, 857 F.2d 290 (6th Cir. 1988), *cert. denied*, 488 U.S. 1006 (1988). There the court "discussed with counsel selecting a jury composed of persons knowledgeable in the field or a jury of those persons having the most formal education available in the jury panel," but plaintiff's counsel would not consent, so the procedure was not used.

25. See note 21.

26. Jury selection in criminal cases is beyond the scope of this essay. We note, however, that because the criminal jury plays a unique role as a buffer between the state and the citizenry, increasing judges' discretion in the jury selection process in the manner suggested in this essay may be inappropriate.

27. Jury selection in federal cases is governed by the Jury Selection and Service Act of 1968, 28 U.S.C. §§ 1861-74. Section 1861 states a policy of obtaining juries "selected at random from a fair cross section of the community." Section 1862 prohibits exclusion based on race, color, religion, sex, national origin, or economic status, and section 1863 requires each district court to implement a random selection plan to achieve the objectives of sections 1861 and 1862. Specifically, it requires that the jury plan provide "detailed procedures to be followed by the Jury Commission or clerk in selecting names from the sources [of prospective jurors] . . . to ensure the random selection of a fair cross section of persons residing in the community." Section 1865 lists the only grounds for disqualification from the jury pool (see note 17). These provisions appear to be aimed at providing a cross section of the community in the venire and preventing discrimination based on the enumerated classifications; arguably they do not rule out modification of random selection *from* the venire. Section 1870 confers on each side three peremptory challenges and challenges for cause to be determined by the court. The statute neither specifically authorizes nor precludes an affirmative role for judges in the selection process.

28. In *Fay* v. *People of State of New York*, 332 U.S. 261 (1947), the Court upheld a New York statute against due process and equal protection but not Seventh Amendment challenges, creating a special jury pool limited to property owners judged "intelligent, of sound mind and good character, well informed, and able to read and write the English language understandingly." See pp. 266–67. A trial court could resort to the special pool on application of either party on a showing that "the importance or intricacy" of the case warranted it. The court found in the same case that "each of the grounds of elimination is reasonably and closely related to the juror's suitability for the kind of service the special panel requires or to its fitness to judge the kind of cases for which it is most frequently utilized" (p. 270). See also *United States* v. *Hawkins*, 566 F.2d 1006, 1012 (5th Cir.), *cert. denied*, 439 U.S. 848 (1978) ("the right to a jury 'selected at random' is a statutory creation . . . not a constitutional command"); and *United States* v. *Henderson*, 298 F.2d 522 (7th Cir.), *cert. denied*, 369 U.S. 878 (1962) (upholding constitutionality of statute limiting jury pool to persons with formal eighth grade education).

29. As noted, it is conceivable that if more competent jurors were selected, some of the rules reflecting distrust could be relaxed. For example, the exclusion of probative evidence because of its tendency to confuse or mislead jurors would be harder to justify.

30. See Stephen C. Yeazell, "The New Jury and the Ancient Jury Conflict," *University of Chicago Legal Forum*, vol. 1990, pp. 105–06.

CHAPTER THIRTEEN

Restructuring the Traditional Civil Jury: The Effects of Changes in Composition and Procedures

Jonathan D. Casper

MORE THAN forty years ago, Judge Jerome Frank forcefully expressed his reservations about the structure and procedure of trials, pointing out the many disjunctions between the theory of the trial process and the reality experienced by litigants, lawyers, jurors, and judges.[1] Frank and other "fact-skeptics" focused on a central underpinning of traditional jurisprudence—the notion that the facts of a case can be clear and accessible to judges and juries—while the so-called "rule skeptics" questioned traditional assumptions that legal norms are clear and unambiguous.[2] His indictment of the "fight" theory on which Anglo-American trial courts are based pointed out that trials inevitably produce uncertainty about the facts at issue in litigation, as the two sides are encouraged to provide self-serving and divergent accounts of what happened. If some version of objective truth is the goal of the factfinding process, Frank argued, the adversary system is not well designed to achieve it. Much of his criticism was leveled at the jury, which he described as laboring under the burden of a counterproductive system of evidence presentation; arcane, ambiguous, and complicated legal instructions; and the general shortcomings of laypersons asked to decide difficult and sometimes technical questions. In one of his judicial opinions, Frank offered the following assessment of juries and the general verdict:

> We come, then, to this position, that the general verdict . . . confers on the jury a vast power to commit error and do mischief by loading it with technical burdens far beyond its ability to perform, by confusing

I am indebted to Shari Seidman Diamond and Scott Barclay for their advice and assistance.

it in aggregating instead of segregating the issues, and by shrouding in secrecy and mystery the actual results of its deliberations. . . . In short, the general verdict is valued for what it does, not for what it is. It serves as the great procedural opiate . . . draw[ing] the curtain upon human errors and sooth[ing] us with the assurance that we have attained the unattainable.[3]

Thirty years later, in the early 1980s, we witnessed another period of intense criticism of the ability of juries to decide adequately the cases they are called upon to hear. Much of the criticism stemmed from a sense that changes in the character of civil litigation—a proliferation of large and complex cases involving vast amounts of documentary evidence and highly technical expert testimony presented over the course of trials that last months and sometimes years—were rendering the jury incapable of effective participation in a substantial number of cases. Indeed, a conflict developed among federal circuit courts on the question of whether an exception should be made to the Seventh Amendment guarantee of the right to a jury trial in federal civil cases when such a trial promises to be extremely lengthy and complex.

Although very complex cases make the issue of jury competence more immediate, the question itself involves a broad range of concerns that have long been in dispute among supporters and detractors of the traditional civil jury. In a particularly thoughtful discussion of the criticisms of the civil jury, published in the early 1980s, Lempert urged that we not "rush to judgment" on the fate of the civil jury.[4] Rather, he argued, the controversy over jury competence could be better addressed by careful thought and research on several fronts: clarification of the goals and appropriate baselines against which to measure jury performance; consideration of the potential impact of reforms within the jury system itself; and, most importantly, serious empirical research examining both the effectiveness of the traditional jury and proposed alternatives to it. A decade has passed since this call for further consideration and research, and it now seems an opportune time to ask whether the passage of time has helped in the evaluation of the desirability of alternatives to the traditional civil jury.

The purpose of this paper is to review some of the proposed modifications in the structure and procedures of the traditional civil jury. With one exception, I will not treat alternatives that differ radically from the traditional jury, including alternative dispute resolution (ADR) processes such as mediation or arbitration and the development of neighborhood-based courts. The exclusion of ADR is based on two considerations: first, the literature on the subject is so extensive that it is beyond the limits of what I can handle here; and second, although there are suggestions that ADR processes might be useful in the complex cases that are of such concern to critics of the traditional civil jury, much of the literature focus on more common types of disputes. My exclusion of neighborhood courts, on the other hand, is related to the lack of any substantial literature on their operation, as well as to the fact that, even more clearly than ADR procedures, these courts are not designed for complex litigation. The one "radical" change from the traditional civil jury that I will discuss is the proposal to abandon the jury altogether in very complex cases.

The remainder of the introductory section will discuss criticisms that have been leveled against the civil jury and the criteria that can be used to assess its performance. The following section discusses the appropriate benchmarks against which to measure jury performance, particularly the question of whether comparisons of judge and jury provide the only appropriate baseline. I will turn next to a discussion of the proposed modifications, including the "complexity exception" to the right to a jury trial in federal courts, the use of special or "blue-ribbon" juries in place of traditional civil juries, modifications to jury verdict procedures (special verdicts and special interrogatories), and procedural changes in the ways in which juries hear testimony (pre-instruction, note-taking, rewriting judicial instructions to make them clearer to jurors, and court-appointed experts). In each section, I will review substantive proposals and available evidence about their likely effects on jury performance.

Criticisms of the Traditional Civil Jury

One critical feature of the traditional civil jury is its selection procedure. Selection begins with a relatively random sample of the adult population of the jurisdiction (for example, drawn from lists of registered voters or those with drivers' licenses). Selection of petit juries from this venire stresses procedures designed to preserve the representativeness of juries. Thus, although not all juries mirror the attributes of the community, over a large number of juries, no groups definable by gender, race, religion, ethnicity, or socioeconomic status should be systematically underrepresented. The "traditional" civil jury is passive during testimony, receives instructions at the end of the presentation of arguments and evidence, and renders a general verdict in the case. Although civil juries in some jurisdictions may no longer have all of these defining characteristics, I take these attributes to be central to the traditional civil jury in this country and to remain the most common among juries in state and federal courts.

Now, let me turn to some of the most frequent criticisms of the traditional civil jury.

ABILITY TO GET THE FACTS STRAIGHT. A long-standing concern with jury decisionmaking deals with jurors' ability to get the facts straight. Errors may emerge from a variety of sources, including the confusion caused by the adversary system, with its two competing accounts of events; the inability to understand certain types of testimony because of lack of education or appropriate training; and the tendency to give disproportionate weight to certain types of testimony.[5] Concerns over the jury's ability to sort out and make sense of the testimony in a case has grown as the complexity of evidence has increased.

ABILITY TO GET THE LAW STRAIGHT. In addition to concerns about jurors' ability to sort out the facts that emerge from the testimony, their ability to understand and apply appropriate legal principles has often been questioned. These principles are frequently complex and subtle, and appropriate jury decisionmaking often depends on a series of contingent judgments. For example, in a relatively simple negligence case the jury must decide whether the defendant committed the act or omission; if so, whether the act or omission constituted negligence; if so, whether the negligent act was a proximate cause of the occurrence; if so, whether the plaintiff contributed to the occurrence; and, finally, how much damage was suffered by the plaintiff. Even in a simple accident case, the critical terms are not clear and must be defined, often in difficult language. As a case becomes more complex, the legal instructions may become even more difficult to understand.

INEFFICIENCIES IN JURY TRIALS. Jury trials have been criticized because the mechanics of jury selection and deliberation make them longer than bench trials. Moreover, presenting testimony that is understandable and persuasive to a lay jury may require more time than is involved in presenting the same issues to a judge. Finally, it is asserted that attorneys in jury trials are likely to take up excessive amounts of time with posturing, presentation of arguments, and oral testimony that could be submitted in written form.

JURORS AND COMMUNITY VALUES IN DECISIONMAKING. A point of recurring tension in the discussion of juries is the role of the community values jurors bring to legal proceedings. Even when juries fully understand the testimony and the legal rules they are instructed to apply, they may not produce the decision that an "objective" observer concludes is legally appropriate. Sometimes their decisions are the product of conscious nullification by citizens whose sense of justice is offended by the legally appropriate conclusion. Examples of such nullification are more common in the criminal than the civil arena, perhaps because community values are more often implicated in cases where liberty and life are at stake, but they occur in the civil context as well.

Juries are often said, for example, to give larger damage awards in tort suits when they believe that the defendant is insured, despite an instruction to disregard this factor, on the theory that equity is better restored when the defendant can afford to pay the claim.[6] Juries tend to assign greater responsibility to corporations in negligence suits and to give larger awards to plaintiffs suing corporations than to those suing individual defendants, either because they believe that organizations should be better able to foresee the consequences of their actions or because of a sense of fairness or mercy.[7] In private antitrust cases, it is often asserted that jurors informed of the treble damage rule will reduce awards below the true compensation level in order to avoid giving a windfall to the plaintiff.[8] In using the principle of comparative negligence, which allows the jury to find the plaintiff partially responsible and still grant damages, concern is often expressed about informing jurors that any plaintiff whose share in the negligence is found to be 50 percent or more can receive no damages. Jurors who know this, many believe, may adjust their findings so that the plaintiff's share in the negligence is less than half, allowing damages to be awarded.[9]

Of course, one person's jury nullification is another's tempering of justice with equity. Such behavior can be condemned as an inappropriate usurpation of legislative authority by juries that have run amok. Or it may be viewed as an example of the democratic and populist role of the jury in shaping the application of legal rules to the living norms of the community.

UNPREDICTABLE AND ERRATIC DECISIONMAKING. Putting together all these concerns, many observers argue that the decisions juries make tend to be unpredictable and erratic. The random quality often seen in jury decisions may be due in part to jurors' misunderstanding of factual testimony or legal instructions. Also, to the extent that decisions are influenced by sympathy, a sense of rough justice, or conscious nullification of unpopular policies, the decisions of juries across similar cases may be quite different. As with many issues about juries, this unpredictability is a two-sided coin. On the one hand, predictability is desirable because it enables citizens to order their affairs and make decisions knowing the likely consequences of their acts. Moreover, increased predictability presumably promotes the settlement of disputes before suits are filed (or before the suits go to trial). On the other hand, if unpredictability is the inevitable concomitant of a system whose verdicts are more "just" because juries bring community values to bear on the application of legal rules, it may be viewed as a virtue rather than a vice.

Criticisms of the civil jury are numerous and diverse, and they often involve basic questions about both the values the jury system is expected to promote and the way juries actually behave.

Criteria for Evaluating Changes to the Traditional Jury

Assessing alternatives to the traditional composition and procedures of juries requires criteria for measuring jury performance.[10] Moreover, some criteria may be viewed as more important than others, and achieving some may make it more difficult to achieve others.[11]

THE SEARCH FOR TRUTH. Clearly much of the impetus for seeking alternatives to the traditional civil jury is motivated by a desire to increase the truth-seeking capacity of juries. Much of the critical and reformist literature proceeds from the premise that the decisionmaker, whether judge or jury, should be able to reach a "correct" decision, with "correct" defined as following the intentions of the lawmakers by applying the rules appropriately to the "facts" as they would be understood by objective outside observers. In a price-fixing case, for example, the jury should be able to understand the often technical testimony by statisticians and economists about the extent of the damage suffered by the plaintiff and arrive at an amount close to "true compensation."[12] In a toxic tort case in which the possibility that the plaintiff will suffer harm in the future is a matter of dispute between the parties, the jury should understand complex epidemiological evidence about risks and not be swayed by concerns about the ability of the defendant to pay an award. While this notion of comparing decisions to absolute truth involves, to be sure, an abstract ideal that is never reached in practice, it also suggests that the relative performance of alternative decisionmaking systems should be measured against a standard of truth-seeking.

SPEED AND EFFICIENCY. Alternatives to traditional jury procedures should be evaluated in terms of their ability to help jurors make decisions in the minimum amount of time and at the least cost to the parties and the state. When proposed changes are speedier or cheaper, all other things being equal, they are typically thought to be preferable.

REPRESENTATIVENESS AND BIAS. It is important that jurors bring to their task an appreciation of the diversity of views in the community. Moreover, they should not be selected in ways that produce systematic bias toward one side of the other in the disputes they hear. There are considerations in favor of these goals quite independent of constitutional requirements or normative principles.

As discussed later in this chapter, juries whose members come from diverse backgrounds may have more accurate collective recall of testimony and instructions and more nuanced understanding of the behavior of parties than juries more homogenous in education or socioeconomic status. Thus conceived, representativeness may be justified in terms of increasing truth-seeking itself.

Proposals that consciously change selection criteria—so-called "blue-ribbon juries," for example—exclude or include individuals on the basis of such attributes as education. Such compositional changes may affect, and perhaps produce unintended consequences for, who wins and who loses. Thus, concerns about representativeness implicate issues not only of truth-seeking but of systematic bias in outcomes.

LEGITIMACY. The decisionmaker should enjoy the respect of community members and a concomitant sense that its decisions are appropriate, legitimate, and authoritative. As Judge John Gibbons put it in his dissent to a decision upholding a complexity exception to the right to a jury trial, "In the process of gaining public acceptance for the imposition of sanctions, the role of the jury is highly significant. The jury is a sort of ad hoc parliament convened from the citizenry at large to lend respectability and authority to the process. . . . Any erosion of citizen participation in the sanctioning system is in the long run likely . . . to result in a reduction in the moral authority that supports the process."[13] In the context of particular decisions, this legitimacy may be a critical determinant of compliance and finality.[14] In a broader systemic sense, the legitimacy of decisionmakers at the trial court level may contribute to respect for and deference to decisions not only of the legal system but of the political system as well.[15]

Thus, there are a variety of criteria against which jury performance may be measured. Arguments against or in favor of an innovation should not be restricted to a comparison of the traditional civil jury and the altered version on a single dimension such as truth-seeking or efficiency.

Rather, such arguments should attempt to comprehend the range of goals and values that the jury serves and the ways in which maximizing one may adversely affect another. Finally, not only must alternatives to the traditional jury be compared to current practices, but both must be measured against some benchmark of adequacy. The most commonly applied standard asks whether the jury has made the same decision a judge would make in the same case. This plausible suggestion requires more reflection. We need to examine whether judges are more competent at all tasks than jurors, how jury performance can be improved, and how effective either is in comparison to more objective standards of performance before it can be sensibly decided whether judge or jury is the preferred decisionmaker.

Baselines for Assessing Jury and Judge Performance

Judgments about whether to retain the traditional civil jury in its current form, to modify it, or to abandon it in some types of cases require some benchmark against which to measure jury performance. Kalven and others have insisted that the only appropriate benchmark is the performance of the judge:

> When one asserts that jury adjudication is of low quality, he must be asserting that jury decisions vary in some significant degree from those a judge would have made in the same cases. If he denies this and wishes to include the judge, he has lost any baseline, and with it any force, for his criticism. . . . Trial by judge is the relevant and obvious alternative to trial by jury. To argue against jury trial is, therefore, to argue for bench trial.[16]

While judicial performance is a clear and appropriate baseline against which to measure jury performance, it is not the only one. The use of simulated cases and mock jurors permits researchers to measure jury performance against a more objective standard as well. To discover whether juries understand complex expert testimony or arcane judicial instructions, researchers can assess comprehension against a level of truth that is quite independent of any judicial decision. Indeed, judicial performance can be assessed as well.

Measuring the relative performance of judges and juries is clearly important to policy-making, for the bench trial is the most likely available alternative to the traditional civil jury in the short run. But applying a more absolute standard is also important. Given the symbolic and legitimizing roles that jury trials play in the civil justice system, it is important to ask not only whether judges or juries are "better" at various tasks, but whether juries are performing so poorly that the costs associated with limiting their use are justified. While Kalven and Zeisel's first study of jury performance included data on both civil and criminal cases, most of the published work from the later Chicago Jury Project dealt with criminal cases.[17] In the very brief published accounts of the civil jury data, Kalven reported relatively high rates of agreement between judges and juries in several thousand civil trials.[18] The methodology involved surveying judges about recent jury trials over which they had presided, asking them questions about the cases (including the performance of the attorneys and of the jury), and, finally, asking them how they would have decided the case if it had been heard as a bench trial. Judges reported agreeing with civil juries on the issue of liability in four out of five cases (79 percent, with both deciding for the plaintiff in 44 percent and for the defendant in 35 percent).[19] In the remaining cases, the patterns of disagreement were evenly divided (in 10 percent the jury found for the defendant when the judge would have found for the plaintiff, and in 11 percent the reverse pattern occurred). Thus, the overall frequency of agreement was high, and neither one side nor the other was favored when disagreement occurred.

Kalven reported more substantial rates of disagreement on the size of awards in cases in which both jury and judge found for the plaintiff. In this group of cases, the jury gave higher awards than the judge slightly over half the time (52 percent); the judge gave a higher award 39 percent of the time; and both agreed in the remaining 9 percent of the cases. Overall, jury awards averaged 20 percent higher than those given by judges.[20] Citing data from the study of criminal juries which suggested that disagreements between the judge and jury did not appear to be the product of juror misunderstanding of the case, Kalven asserted that there was no reason to doubt that a similar finding would emerge from analysis of the civil jury data. He concluded that juror misunderstanding of evidence and instructions was probably not as significant a problem in civil cases as had sometimes been suggested.

The sample of civil cases studied by Kalven and Zeisel did not focus on those with particularly complex evidence or legal principles. Evidence gathered since the Kalven and Zeisel study suggests a more measured conclusion about such complex cases. Simulation studies[21] and post-trial interviews with judges and jurors[22] suggest that jurors have substantial difficulties with traditional judicial instructions and complex expert testimony. In general, the findings suggest that jurors do a reasonably good job, compared with either judges or more objective standards of correct recall, in getting the facts straight; their ability to understand and appropriately apply judicial instructions seems weaker.

The assumption implicit in the arguments of many who support the complexity exception—that judges are better decisionmakers in complex trials than juries—basically rests not on an empirical foundation but on simple asservation. Presumably, this assumption is based on the fact that judges have higher levels of education than jurors, as well as legal training and prior experience with similar issues. In terms of understanding legal instructions, the argument seems plausible, since judges' training and experience make it likely that they are better able to understand the instructions than are lay jurors. Two caveats are in order here, though. First, pattern instructions are written by committees and designed to cover wide ranges of fact situations and legal principles. The language used is therefore the result of compromise that often renders it abstract and general. Although it would be very surprising if their comprehension levels were not higher than those of jurors who hear them delivered, it would be useful to find out whether judges fully understand their own words. This would be useful not only for its titillation value, but as potential ammunition in the effort to persuade judges to present their instructions in language which is more accessible to lay jurors.[23]

The assumption that judges have a better understanding of complex technical evidence seems even more problematical. Although judges are in general more highly educated than typical jurors, most judges do not have training in the various fields relevant to understanding expert testimony, such as statistics, economics, epidemiology, physics, medicine, and psychiatry. Moreover, as suggested in a recent study of judges' responses to statistical testimony, the tension between the quest for certainty that infuses much legal training and practice and the probabilistic basis of much statistical evidence may cause judges to misunderstand and sometimes misuse such evidence.[24]

In addition, the jury has the advantage of being a group, not a single person. In a group of six or twelve jurors, the likelihood that one or more will have education or experience relevant to the case may be increased, making the jury better able than the judge to understand complex evidence or testimony.[25] Moreover, the group deliberation process—during which collective recall and understanding may prove more effective than that of any individual member—also gives juries a strength that individual judges do not possess. Michael J. Saks argues, for example, that Kalven and Zeisel's evidence on judge/jury agreement suggests that "a group of presumably less skilled and certainly less experienced individuals can, when combined into a group, perform a legal fact-finding task at approximately the same level of competence as a judge."[26]

A smattering of the research emerging from interviews with judges and examination of their written opinions suggests that even judges do not always get the facts straight in complex cases. The NAS Panel on the Use of Statistical Evidence in the Courts examined the testimony of statistical experts and its interpretation by judges in a range of cases, including such diverse areas as antitrust litigation, job discrimination, the use of formaldehyde in insulation, and identification of hair samples. Citing problems arising from the adversary mode of presentation, the complexity and unfamiliarity of statistical evidence, and the quest for certainty alluded to above, the overall conclusion of the panel was that judges "do not ordinarily handle cases well when a significant portion of the evidence, or crucial evidence, is statistical in nature." This is the product of "a lack of fit between judicial dispute resolution procedures and the quality of statistical procedures and evidence."[27] In a review of court decisions dealing with novel forensic evidence, John W. Osborne examined a series of judicial decisions dealing with voiceprint evidence, the psychological stress evaluator (a device designed to detect deception by examining spoken words), and the paraffin gloves used for establishing whether firearms have been used by a specific individual.[28] He argued that the decisions were flawed by a variety of misunderstandings of scientific evidence as well as by the judges' reliance on earlier decisions that were subsequently discredited by new evidence. Although he was not sanguine about the prospects that jurors will do better than judges in similar matters, his analysis does suggest significant limitations on judicial ability to understand and appropriately apply complex technical evidence.

Thus, the scanty evidence available suggests that there may be relatively high levels of agreement between judges and juries in run-of-the-mill cases and cause for concern about the capacity of either to deal with complex technical evidence. Before prescribing remedies, however, a good deal more research needs to be done on juries that explores not only the types of evidence they find difficult but also the sources of their misunderstanding. Are they bowled over by what seems authoritative because it is hard to understand?[29] Or do they inappropriately discount testimony that is difficult and adopt the views of experts whose examples are homely and easy to understand?[30]

By the same token, studies of judges' ability to understand complex evidence and testimony ought to be undertaken as well. A simple strategy might involve asking judges who have presided over complex cases to assess their own levels of understanding as well as those of attorneys and jurors. Such evidence could be complemented by interviews with expert witnesses and lawyers about their assessments of judges' competence, for they are in a strong position to assess how much judges actually understand. Questions judges ask witnesses, their discussions with attorneys about lines of inquiry, and their instructions and special interrogatories all provide opportunities for developing a sense of how well they have handled the material and what they have found most difficult to comprehend. Written opinions can be analyzed to supplement and assess the accuracy of judgments made by other courtroom participants.

Knowing more about capabilities of juries and judges is important not only in making decisions about policies such as the complexity exception, but also in understanding the likely effects of innovations designed to improve jury performance. The potential trade-offs between maintaining competence and accuracy in decisionmaking and allowing for the inclusion of community values that help establish legitimacy mean that policy choices should be based on adequate (and not currently existing) evidence about the relative performance of juries and judges under both current and improved procedures.

Some Proposals to Improve Jury Performance

Given the concerns that have been raised about the competence of juries and the goals and baselines against which to measure jury performance, I turn now to a discussion of some of the alternatives that have been proposed to improve jury performance. The first, the so-called complexity exception, suggests that juries should not be employed in particularly complex cases. Other, less radical proposals, include specially qualified juries for some classes of cases, modifying the structure of jury verdicts by use of special interrogatories or special verdicts, and a series of procedural modifications designed to assist the jury with its tasks. I will describe the various proposals, assess the evidence about their likely impact, and suggest lines for further research.

The Complexity Exception to the Right to a Jury Trial

Concerns about the relative abilities of judges and juries have led to a discussion of whether the protection of the right to a jury trial offered by the Seventh Amendment at the federal level and in many state constitutions should be interpreted to permit an exception for complex cases. If a complexity exception is created, certain cases would be heard and decided by judges acting alone or with the assistance of special masters, or using other factfinding procedures. Discussion of the complexity exception has extended beyond the academic literature; some courts have endorsed such an exception, while others have rejected it.

The debate in the lower federal courts, which has yet to be resolved by the Supreme Court, involves doctrinal and empirical issues. The first is the problem of justifying and crafting such an exception. The empirical issues deal with the ability of judges and juries to understand evidence and testimony in complex cases. Two major legal arguments have been offered to justify the policy of restricting the right to a jury trial in complex cases. One turns on the different procedures followed in trying cases under a court's law or equity jurisdiction.[31] Under established legal principles, if juries cannot understand the evidence and render a fair decision, courts cannot hear a case under their law jurisdiction. Thus, the argument for a complexity exception runs, cases in which juries cannot understand the testimony must be heard as equity cases, and in equity cases there is no constitutional right to a jury trial.[32] A footnote in the Supreme Court's *Ross* decision suggests that one factor to be used in determining whether a case should be tried under law or equity is "the practical abilities and limitations of juries."[33] The second and more general argument for the complexity exception notes the tension between the due process clause of the Fifth Amendment and the Seventh Amendment's right to a jury trial. If due process requires that a case be decided by a rational decisionmaker on the basis of the evidence and legal principles presented, and juries are incapable of doing so, the argument runs, then the right to a jury trial must be set aside.[34] Federal District Courts have differed on whether such an exception exists, as have the Circuits.[35]

The importance of *empirical* issues in these cases can be seen in the following observation by the Ninth Circuit in the *U.S. Financial Securities Litigation*: "We do not believe any case is so overwhelmingly complex that it is beyond the abilities of a jury."[36] This reliance by a court on an unsupported assertion highlights the importance of developing and employing adequate empirical evidence in the debate over the competence of juries. The sanguine but equally unsupported assertions by courts and commentators about the abilities of judges to handle material said to be beyond the capacity of juries provide another example.

The discussion in the preceding section suggests that current knowledge about jury and judge performance is quite fragmentary. What is known about the operation of juries under current practices certainly casts doubt on the assertion that no case is so complex that a jury cannot understand it, but available evidence suggests that judges have similar difficulties. To the extent that the policy question turns on such empirical issues, there is as yet no way to make an adequately informed choice. My own reading of the research developed in the last decade suggests that juries are probably better at understanding complex cases than many proponents of the complexity exception have asserted.[37] Interview and simulation studies suggest that juries do possess significant capacities to sort out even complex testimony, to evaluate expert testimony in sensible ways, and to think about apportioning damages across categories when appropriately instructed.

Developments in court practice and research caution against deciding on the complexity issue prematurely. The courts themselves are experimenting with procedures such as special verdicts, innovative interrogatories, pre-instruction, note-taking, and restrictions on evidence, all of which are designed to assist juries in complex cases. The evidence suggests that these procedures may have an impact on the behavior of the jury, sometimes intended and sometimes unintended. While further research and experimentation is clearly called for, it seems evident that the appropriate "jury" to employ when deciding whether to grant an exception to the right to a jury trial is not the traditional jury but one that has been given the advantage of using procedures designed to maximize its capabilities. Given that the complexity exception carries with it potential costs in terms of legitimacy[38] and community values, as well as difficulties in specifying the class of cases for which such an exception might be granted,[39] and given the lack of adequate knowledge about how much better judges are likely to perform than jurors, Richard O. Lempert's advice to not rush remains wise counsel.[40] Moreover, the impediments to the complexity exception raised by the Seventh Amendment and many state constitutions ensure that there is little possibility of rushing even if the evidence in favor of this reform were more persuasive.

The Special Jury

Perhaps the most common proposal designed to deal with concerns about jury competence, particularly in complex cases, is the empaneling of special or "blue-ribbon" juries. If the traditionally selected jury lacks appropriate education or training, the argument runs, then selection criteria should be modified to insure that jurors possess the skills and knowledge necessary to understand the evidence and legal rules:

> A jury composed of particularly qualified individuals could understand sophisticated concepts that might be beyond the abilities of either a judge or a traditional jury. Jury confusion would be less of a problem than it is with jurors who are unfamiliar with the technical, financial, and legal issues involved in much of today's complicated litigation. There also would be less likelihood of an irrational verdict because the jurors would be able to make a reasoned decision based on their understanding of the facts and the law.[41]

Proponents of special juries point to a long tradition of such juries in England. Such accounts often cite the practice in fourteenth-century London of employing juries composed of fishmongers and cooks to hear cases alleging the sale of bad food,[42] and proponents often cite James B. Thayer's description of the development of the jury in English jurisprudence: "As among eligible persons, there seems always to existed the power of selecting those especially qualified for a given service. . . . What we call the 'special jury' seems always to have been used."[43]

Some seventeen states have passed legislation authorizing the use of special juries, and in 1947 the Supreme Court upheld the use of a special jury in a New York case involving the conviction of union officials on criminal charges of extortion and conspiracy.[44] A New York statute authorized trial courts in certain types of cases involving "important, intricate, or widely-publicized" issues to empanel special jurors drawn from the general jury lists.[45] The jury commissioner selected the jurors after they had been questioned about their qualifications and fitness for such service. In upholding the scheme, the Supreme Court relied heavily on the absence of evidence showing that the statute authorized the exclusion of citizens on the basis of traits such as race or occupation, as well as on the general reasonableness of the selection criteria. The four dissenters urged that such special juries denied defendants the right to a trial by a jury representative of a cross section of the community. The New York statute survived later constitutional challenges but was repealed in 1965 after a campaign based on concerns about representativeness.[46] At the federal level, impediments to the use of special juries were imposed by a provision of the 1968 federal Jury Selection Act requiring that jurors be selected "at random from a fair cross section of the community,"[47] and a subsequent amendment specifically prohibiting use of special juries.[48] Thus, in federal courts, current statutes would have to be amended before special juries could be used.

In general, proposals urging more widespread use of special juries suggest that selection criteria should be based on education and relevant experience. Some put forward relatively simple and easily verifiable criteria such as a college degree,[49] while others argue for more specific qualifications related to the case itself.[50] Proponents argue that special juries have a better understanding of factual testimony and legal issues than traditional juries and, at the same time, retain the representativeness and advantages of group decisionmaking that are absent from bench trials.

Extensive experience with the use of special juries and research on their impact are lacking. There is an intuitive plausibility to the argument that jurors with a certain level of education or experience might fare better at understanding complex evidence and legal rules than a traditional jury. But there are also countervailing considerations and research findings.

The view that jurors with high education levels will understand difficult testimony is somewhat at variance with evidence about the cognitive limitations of even those who are likely to be chosen for special jury service. In their work on cognitive biases, Daniel Kahnemann, Amos Tversky, and Paul Slovic find evidence that many people make fundamental mistakes when trying to understand basic principles of probability and statistics.[51] Such mistakes are quite common among highly trained groups, including students in statistics courses, as well as among those with little or no exposure to the relevant training. Another example comes in a recent report on the advice physicians give to their patients about the risks of developing breast cancer and problems associated with various treatment options. The study revealed very widespread and fundamental misunderstanding among physicians of relatively straightforward principles of statistical inference.[52] Thus, when it is suggested that traditionally selected juries are not qualified to understand epidemiological or statistical evidence but that "special juries made up of scientific and medical experts from many fields" could do better, skepticism may be in order.[53]

Special qualification procedures could affect both individual and group decisionmaking. Excluding individuals who lack certain attributes—for example, a certain educational level, special training, or relevant experience—may produce unintended consequences for case outcomes. Specially selected individuals may better understand the evidence or judge's instructions than those excluded from service, but they may also have individual biases that incline them toward a party less likely to be favored by those who have excluded. Jurors with a high socioeconomic status may be more favorably disposed to large corporations than low SES/low income jurors, for instance. Moreover, the types of behavior considered appropriate by jurors may vary substantially across socioeconomic and ethnic groups. Thus, at the individual level, special juries may differ from traditional juries in terms of the predispositions their members bring to the deliberation process.

Studies comparing college-educated jurors to those with lower educational levels typically find that the better educated jurors participate more actively in discussions, devote more of their comments to issues of procedure and legal rules, and are more effective at changing the minds of other jurors.[54] Reid Hastie and others also found that high educational levels are also associated with greater accuracy on measures of recall of instructions and testimony. Shari Seidman Diamond and Jonathan D. Casper have found in a study currently in progress that jurors with higher educational levels are more accurate in their recollection of complex expert testimony and judicial instructions than less educated jurors.[55]

In addition to its effect on the individual juror, the use of special qualifications may affect the quality of group decisionmaking as well. Special juries are less diverse at least in terms of the selection criteria, and the degree of homogeneity among jury members may affect the outcome of their deliberations. Proponents of special juries tend to characterize their increased homogeneity as desirable, since highly educated jurors are expected to understand evidence and instructions well and produce a reasoned and rational decision. Alternatively, however, heterogeneity may be of value in the deliberative process. Varied life experiences, perspectives, and values in the group may result in a more wide-ranging discussion and increased understanding of the behavior of the parties involved.

As I have noted, the available evidence does tend to suggest that education is associated with more accurate individual recall of instructions and testimony, as well as with greater attention to the relationship between legal and factual issues. But this observation does not mean either that *all* members of a jury must have a high educational level to enjoy the benefits associated with greater educational attainment or that juries with greater diversity may not perform better in areas other than recall. Thus, the critical issue is not the effect of homogeneity or diversity at the *individual* level, but their impact on the group's decision. Reid Hastie, Steven D. Penrod, and Nancy Pennington found that the numbers of issues generated and the relationship between factual and legal issues were not significantly related to the overall educational level of juries. Thus, the lower levels of recall associated with lower education levels may not, on a traditional and diverse jury, produce less effective recall at the group level.[56]

In a simulation study of the effects of homogeneity on jury deliberations, Claudia L. Cowan, William C. Thompson, and Phoebe C. Ellsworth studied the effects of "death qualification" procedures in capital cases. In cases in which the death penalty may be imposed, prospective jurors are asked about their attitudes toward the death penalty, and those who say they would never impose it can be excused for cause. Cowan, Thompson, and Ellsworth varied the homogeneity of juries in terms of their members' willingness to consider giving the death penalty.[57] Postverdict interviews showed that jurors whose juries included both death qualified and "excludable" jurors (that is, those who would have been dismissed in a real case because of their opposition to the death penalty) were more critical in their evaluations of all witnesses, regardless of whether the juror was individually predisposed toward the prosecution of the defense. Based on this finding, the authors argue that heterogeneity promotes livelier debate, more contention, and a greater likelihood that someone on the jury will question or point out flaws in the testimony of witnesses. They suggest that "homogeneity may hush the voice of a dissenting minority, whose criticisms of the majority viewpoint would have fostered the careful scrutiny of all relevant issues."[58] Moreover, members of heterogenous juries recalled testimony more accurately than homogeneous panels, though they were no better at recall of jury instructions.

These studies examine criminal rather than civil cases, and the issues of technical complexity that are often cited as reasons for employing special juries were not at issue. Yet the evidence they present does suggest caution in embracing the assumption that juries with special attributes will necessarily perform more effectively than those with a greater diversity of background and experience. To the extent that the jury's task is to understand not only complex fact patterns or legal instructions, but also to make sense of the behavior of the parties and to judge them against the appropriate legal standards, diversity may be a strength rather than a weakness.

For example, in a serious automobile accident case in which defendant negligence is at issue, there may be substantial variation across communities in beliefs about the appropriate uses of the public streets. Urban areas may have norms encouraging the use of streets as areas for play or general congregating that are uncommon in affluent suburban areas. An awareness of such subcultural differences may be important in making judgments about the plaintiff's negligence. The capacity of a blue-ribbon jury to make sensible judgments on issues of negligence may be seriously eroded in such a case, even if its ability to deal with statistical evidence about future wage loss or the testimony of forensic experts in accident reconstruction is enhanced. In an analogous situation in a criminal case, Hastie, Penrod, and Pennington report that, in the murder case they studied, jurors varied greatly in their interpretation of the fact that the defendant was carrying a knife when a fight with the victim began. Jurors who lived in communities similar to the defendant's were able to persuade others that, in the community in which the defendant and victim lived, carrying a knife was not uncommon, and thus was not as indicative of an intent to harm, as those from more affluent communities were inclined to believe. These members of heterogeneous juries were reported to influence the choice of a verdict category in helpful ways.

As with many issues discussed here, plausible but contradictory views of the effects of a reform on the behavior of juries make clear the need for careful research to assess which of the views is consistent with actual behavior of juries.

Alternatives to the General Verdict

The traditional general verdict has long been criticized as an impediment to rational decisionmaking in civil cases. Two related concerns lie at the center of most of these critiques. The first focuses on the fact that juries are often called on to make several legally discrete decisions on the basis of different evidence. By asking the jury for a single answer, the general verdict procedure fails to assist the jury in organizing the evidence and legal principles in appropriate ways. Second, the general verdict in civil cases is often said to promote compromise verdicts, conflating legally separate issues and producing results that may appear just to jurors but that are inconsistent with the policies of the legislatures or appellate courts fashioning the legal rules. Thus, in a tort case in which the evidence on issue of causation or liability is perceived by the jury to be slightly in favor of the defendant, but the injuries to the plaintiff are substantial, a jury may decide to award damages but discount them because of the ambiguity in defendant responsibility. This compromise flies in the face of legal principles, but the general verdict does not reveal to trial or appellate judges the basis for the verdict. In the civil context, the sense of equity or justice that may have motivated such decisions—but is masked by the general verdict—is typically decried, even though it may be characterized as a strength in many criminal cases.[59]

Such concerns about the general verdict have led to many suggestions for modifying the jury's tasks, some experimentation with such innovations, and a small body of research assessing the consequences of such change. Three alternatives have been most frequently discussed: special verdicts, bifurcated verdicts, and general verdicts with interrogatories.

SPECIAL VERDICTS. Both special verdicts and interrogatories are authorized by Rule 49 of the Federal Rules of Civil Procedure. Under a special verdict procedure, the judge submits to the jury a series of specific questions dealing with factual issues and requires the jury to deliberate and provide answers to them.[60] The judge then applies the law to these findings to decide the case. In a negligence case, for example, the judge might instruct the jury to decide whether the defendant committed the act, whether negligence was involved, whether the act caused the harm to the plaintiff, and what damages should be awarded. The questions the jury answers often involve some mixture of law and fact, for they require the application of legal concepts such as negligence, but the decisions are made separately, and it is usually suggested that jurors not be told the consequences of their verdicts.[61]

Several variants of the special verdict procedure have been suggested and sometimes used in complex trials.[62] In the highly publicized libel suit filed by Israeli Defense Minister Ariel Sharon against *Time* magazine, the district judge presented the jury with a series of special verdict questions to be answered after all the testimony had been completed.[63] The questions covered the issue of defamation, the truth or falsity of the allegations about Sharon's role in the massacre of civilians in Beirut refugee camps, and, finally, the problem of whether *Time* had knowingly and maliciously printed a falsehood. The jury was instructed at the end of the trial to deliberate on each verdict and to announce its special verdicts as each was reached. The judge employed the technique to avoid a single set of long and complex instructions and to facilitate the jury's ability to organize the facts and legal rules.

An alternative has been called the "periodic, segmented special verdict." Under this procedure, judges can separate various questions that are at issue in the case, allowing the jury to hear testimony and reach a special verdict on each at the conclusion of each segment of the trial.[64] In one complex antitrust case, the district court divided the presentation of evidence into three stages.[65] The first involved the issues of antitrust violation and lost profits, the second, losses based on marketing practices, and the third, the value of an exclusion claim. After each stage, the jury returned a special verdict. As a result, evidence about claims rejected in prior segments did not have to be presented in subsequent segments. The trial judge concluded that the format promoted organized consideration of evidence and decreased the likelihood of a retrial.[66]

BIFURCATED TRIALS. Under the special verdict procedures described above, the judge retains the authority to decide the case, employing the jury's special verdicts to reach the ultimate decision. A closely related procedure is the bifurcated or split trial. In a typical criminal case involving a capital offense, for example, the jury first hears evidence about the defendant's guilt or innocence. If the defendant is found guilty, the jury then serves in a separate penalty hearing in which further evidence is presented on whether the defendant should receive the death penalty. In the civil context, for example, a procedure was employed in the Northern District of Illinois in the 1960s that allowed jurors in tort cases to first hear evidence and bring in a verdict on liability; only if liability were found would evidence on damages be presented, and the jury would then render a second verdict. Such bifurcated verdict procedures are very similar to the periodic, segmented special verdict procedure described above, except that the judge retains decisionmaking authority in the special verdict procedure, while the jury returns the final verdict in a bifurcated trial. Both methods are aimed at making the jury's task easier by segregating the issues they must consider.

GENERAL VERDICTS WITH SPECIAL INTERROGATORIES. A closely related procedure involves retaining the general verdict but adding special interrogatories that require the jury to make additional specific factual determinations.[67] Like special verdict procedures, these interrogatories permit the judge to insure that the jury's verdict is the product of appropriate factual determinations and provide a way for the jury to structure its deliberations. Under this procedure, the jury reaches its general verdict, but the judge oversees the process by examining the relationship between the jury's factual findings and its decision.

Advantages of Alternative Verdict Procedures

Proponents of such modifications to jury verdict procedures cite a variety of advantages they may provide when compared with the traditional general verdict.

ORGANIZING AND SIMPLIFYING JURY TASKS. As some of the examples cited above suggest, special verdicts or special interrogatories may provide a useful framework within which the jury can organize testimony, particularly when the facts and law are complex.

> [Special verdicts] operate to improve the reliability of jury decisionmaking through the recognized psychological impact specific questions have in concentrating jury attention on certain matters to the exclusion of others. Special verdicts are thus used to encourage jurors to focus on the discrete issues which are critical to the lawsuit. This is particularly important in those categories of cases where jurors' sympathy for the alleged victim may overpower their willingness to enforce legal doctrine.[68]

Moreover, when special verdicts or interrogatories are submitted during a trial that involves large numbers of witnesses and exhibits, they may improve jurors' ability to recall testimony.

SIMPLIFYING JUDICIAL INSTRUCTIONS. Special verdicts or interrogatories may simplify judicial instructions in a least two ways. If the periodic, segmented special verdict is employed, jurors will receive judicial instructions and the accompanying verdict questions in smaller packets delivered at intervals during the testimony. A small amount of difficult material can then be presented and discussed more effectively than the numerous judicial instructions traditionally presented together at the end of the trial. Some proponents have also claimed that jury instructions are likely to be simpler when special verdicts are employed because fewer legal concepts will have to be accurately conveyed to the jury:

> The special verdict eliminates complicated instructions which so often plague courts using general verdicts. The special verdict records only

the jury's factual findings, eliminating explanations of legal issues or hypothetical instructions demonstrating how to apply the law to the facts.[69]

It is clear from prior research that understanding judicial instructions is one of the most difficult tasks faced by the traditional jury.[70] But the frequent assertion that special verdicts will solve this problem may be too optimistic. Because special verdicts typically involve mixed issues of fact and law, legal concepts must be conveyed in order to facilitate appropriate verdicts. If a special verdict asks about negligence or causation, for example, these concepts must be explained to the jury and understood before the special verdict question can be adequately answered.[71]

ENCOURAGING SETTLEMENTS AND REDUCING THE LENGTH OF TRIALS. Special verdicts may increase the willingness of parties to settle cases during a trial. If a special verdict question is answered in a way that clearly favors one side—if, for example, a defendant is found liable— this interim result may encourage the losing party to seek a settlement rather than continue the trial. Since the burden of proof requirement often demands that plaintiffs prevail on a variety of sequential points, a decision by the jury that the plaintiff has failed on an early point can terminate the trial well before all the evidence has been presented, again reducing the length of time required for trial.

EFFECTIVE SUPERVISION OF JURIES BY TRIAL AND APPELLATE JUDGES. By requiring juries to make specific factual determinations during the trial itself or at the end, special verdicts or interrogatories can facilitate the ability of judges to monitor how well juries comply with legal principles. Trial judges can discern inconsistencies in jury responses to special verdicts or between answers to special interrogatories and jury verdicts that may require further deliberation or a new trial. There may be advantages at the appellate level as well. Instead of having to speculate about the grounds for a jury decision, an appellate court will have direct answers to special verdict or interrogatory questions. Moreover, "the special verdict enables errors to be localized so that the sound portions of the verdict may be saved."[72] As Jerome Frank observes, the special verdict may "enable the public, the parties, and the court to see what the jury has really done."[73]

AVOIDING COMPROMISE VERDICTS. Special verdicts or interrogatories may also reduce the possibility of compromise verdicts. If jurors are not informed of the legal consequences of their answers to special verdict or interrogatory questions, and if the questions are sufficiently opaque that their implications are not readily discernible by the jurors, legal principles may be more appropriately applied. Thus, for example, if jurors remain unaware that a decision which finds the plaintiff's negligence is greater than 50 percent precludes the awarding of damages, the jury will not be able to evade this outcome by adjusting its finding to 49 percent and discounting the damage award:

> Opponents argue that representing the claim as a series of separate and independent facts is misleading. The jury may not know who has won and may be bitterly disappointed when the effects of its answers cause the less favored party to prevail. This result is actually the beauty of the special verdict: the jury cannot be swayed by emotions and prejudices, which can cause a compromise verdict.[74]

This very "beauty," however, is held out by others as a serious deficiency of special verdicts and interrogatories.

Disadvantages of Alternative Verdict Procedures

The list of advantages must be weighed against a series of concerns about the intended and unintended consequences of special verdicts and interrogatories.

JUROR EVALUATION OF WITNESSES. Juror judgments about the credibility and persuasiveness of witnesses are presumably formed over the course of the whole range of testimony. These judgments depend on the testimony and demeanor of the witness during testimony, as well as on the statements and credibility of other witnesses who testify later in the trial. The early closure caused by the requirement of a series of special verdicts over the course of the trial may inappropriately affect the ability of jurors to evaluate witnesses and their testimony. Witnesses may testify in more than one segment, and judgments jurors make about their credibility may change as further direct and cross-examination occurs.[75]

SYSTEMATIC BIASES ASSOCIATED WITH SPECIAL VERDICTS. Richard O. Lempert and others discuss a number of unexplored but plausible systematic biases that could be associated with the move from the general verdict to special verdicts, some operating against the plaintiff and some against the defendant. In terms of possible bias against the plaintiff, two important elements stand out: the requirement that the jury find for the plaintiff on all issues and the increased number of decisions that special verdicts require the jury to make. Lempert notes, "As the number of issues that the factfinder considers increases and the evidence on each issue becomes closer, it becomes likely that chance will at some point lead the factfinder mistakenly to hold for the defendant."[76] Posing another possibility, Lempert suggests that a majority that has prevailed over a minority on several issues may eventually defer to the minority on a later issue in a spirit of compromise, inadvertently causing the defendant to win. This possibility could, of course, be prevented if the jurors were informed before deliberations of the legal consequences of their answers to special verdict or interrogatory questions; however, as noted above, many of the proponents of special verdicts argue against providing such information.[77]

Elizabeth C. Wiggins and Steven J. Breckler suggest that the move to special verdicts might have unfavorable consequences for the defendant as well. They argue that in cases with multiple claims or alternative theories, special verdicts give the plaintiff greater opportunities to prevail because jurors are more likely to compromise when the evidence is seen as relatively even across the two sides.[78]

Thus, plausible a priori theorizing suggests that special verdicts may produce unintended bias in favor of either plaintiffs or defendants. Below I describe the available evidence about which, if any, of these effects may actually characterize jury behavior when special verdict procedures are employed.

DIFFICULTIES IN FORMULATING SPECIAL VERDICT QUESTIONS. There are also questions about the actual task of the jury in a case employing special verdicts or special interrogatory questions. Advocates of such techniques cite the advantages of simplifying the tasks of the jurors by segmenting and organizing their efforts and, in particular, by reducing their need to deal with arcane legal concepts. In practice, though, questions of this sort are not easy to frame. The following special interrogatories (the final two of a total of four) were submitted to the jury in the widely publicized toxic tort case involving the contamination of the drinking water in Woburn, Massachusetts. The questions had been the subject of extensive negotiations among the parties during the trial.

Have the plaintiffs established by a preponderance of the evidence that the substantial contribution to the contamination of Wells G and

H prior to May 22, 1979, by chemicals disposed of on the Grace site after October 1, 1964 was caused by negligence of Grace, that is, the failure of Grace to fulfill any duty of due care to the plaintiffs—with respect to [the following list of chemicals]? (Only answer with respect to a chemical as to which you answered "Yes" on question 1.)

If you have answered "yes" to any part of question 3, what, according to a preponderance of the evidence, was the earliest time at which the substantial contribution referred to in question 3 was caused by the negligent conduct of this defendant—with respect to [the list of chemicals]?

(If, on the evidence before you, you are unable to determine by a preponderance of the evidence the appropriate date, write "ND" for Not Determined).[79]

After the jury had deliberated and answered the special verdict questions, the trial judge found their answers ambiguous and contradictory and ordered a new trial. Post-trial interviews suggested the jurors had been unable to understand the interrogatories.[80] The point is not to criticize the judge, but to suggest that special interrogatory and verdict questions in complex cases often involve mixed issues of fact and law, making such questions difficult to formulate; in addition, many of the problems with judicial instructions in general may plague special verdict or interrogatories as well.

Mark S. Brodin suggests a distinction between questions of "actual" and "ultimate" fact to be found by juries.[81] Actual facts deal with the occurrence of certain events; ultimate facts involve a mixture of actual facts with legal concepts. Thus, in a toxic tort case, a question of actual fact to be decided by the jury might be: "Did the defendant dump a chemical into a river during 1989?" An ultimate fact issue might require a decision about whether the defendant's dumping of the chemicals into the river was done in a negligent fashion and was the cause of particular harms to the plaintiff.

Brodin argues for a return to the type of "fact" verdict that Frank originally urged, with jury questions focused more directly on simpler factual issues and the judge applying legal principles. Thus, for example, in an employment discrimination case claiming wrongful dismissal on the basis of sexual preference, Brodin approvingly cites a series of special verdict questions such as the following:

(1) Are you satisfied by a preponderance of the evidence that the decision to terminate the plaintiff was motivated at least in part by her admitted homosexuality?

(2) If so, are you satisfied by a preponderance of the evidence that the plaintiff would have been terminated anyway for other reasons? If your answer is "yes," state the other reasons.

(3) Are you satisfied by a preponderance of the evidence that in their decision to terminate the plaintiff, the defendants treated her differently than heterosexual employees because of her sexual preference?[82]

Whether it is feasible to use this approach in dealing with the issues in much complex litigation is an open question, but the discussion does suggest that the distinction between fact and legal issues may be much cleaner in theory than in the actual trying of cases.

THE JURY AS REPRESENTATIVE OF COMMUNITY VALUES. Special jury verdicts or interrogatories may reduce the ability of the jury to bring its own sense of justice, rightness, or equity to its decision. Indeed, as I have noted, the specificity of special jury questions is said to guard against such a role by allowing judges to check for discrepancies in jury behavior. Other commentators argue that checking the jury's power in this way is not a virtue but a vice. Many complex cases involve allegations that large institutions have seriously harmed individuals. These cases can also involve acts or practices people tend to view unfavorably, large sums of money, or strongly contested public policy issues that pit environmental protection versus business efficiency, for example, or workers' rights versus the right to accrue private wealth. Thus, there are strong arguments for the idea that, in the civil as well as the criminal sphere, reducing the role of the jury as a representative of community values may not be desirable. As one federal judge noted in his decision to tell jurors in a comparative negligence case that their award to the plaintiff would be reduced proportionately if he were found to have behaved negligently:

The jury is not to be set loose in a maze of factual questions to be answered without intelligent awareness of the consequences. One of the purposes of the jury system is to temper the strict application of law to facts, and thus bring to the administration of justice a common sense lay approach, a purpose ill-served by relegating the jury to a role of determining facts *in vacuo*, ignorant of the significance of their findings.[83]

The use of special interrogatories along with a general verdict may appear to offer the best of both worlds: a technique that focuses jurors on the critical issues while still allowing the jury's sense of justice to play a role in its verdict. This does not, however, appear to be the aim of those urging the use of special interrogatories along with general verdicts. Much emphasis is placed on the use of jury responses as a means of overturning the verdict when their responses to interrogatories and their general verdict appear inconsistent. Proponents of interrogatories, like proponents of special verdicts, stress both the need to control the jury's impulse to introduce its own sense of justice and the importance of insuring that legal instructions are followed.

The Effects of Changes in Verdict Structure

The available empirical evidence on the effects of changes in verdict structures remains quite small but intriguing. The sketchy anecdotal evidence from practitioners who have employed innovative verdict procedures and from post-trial interviews with jurors conducted by journalists and academics is quite mixed.[84] Judges who have employed special verdicts or interrogatories tend to find that they were helpful, while evidence from jurors suggests that problems with comprehension and organization of testimony and legal rules are not always solved. Systematic evidence suggests that the ways in which verdicts are structured may affect jury decisions. An early study by Hans Zeisel and Thomas Callahan examined the effects of unitary versus bifurcated trials in tort cases in federal courts in northern Illinois. The study was aimed primarily at assessing the effects of the new trial structure on trial delay, and the design did not involve random assignment to the two trial procedures. The data presented do permit examination of the overall win rates for plaintiffs and defendants in unitary and bifurcated trials (in which jurors first decided the issue of liability and then set a damage award).[85] The results are striking, with defendants prevailing in 42 percent of the unitary trials and 79 percent of the bifurcated trials. Because they were focused on another question, the authors did not speculate on the cause of this difference, but it has generally been interpreted as indicating that in unitary trials jurors employ evidence about the extent of damages in making decisions about liability, thus advantaging plaintiffs.[86] In bifurcated trials, in which jurors do not hear evidence on damages until they have already decided the liability issue, this spillover effect cannot occur, and the hurdle of proving liability proves harder for plaintiffs to jump.

In a recent study of the effect of special verdict procedures, Elizabeth C. Wiggins and Steven J. Breckler examined the effects of both special and general verdicts in a simulation study of juror decisions in a defamation case.[87] The verdict procedure had no effect on decisions about the defendant's liability, with some two-thirds of all jurors in both verdict conditions finding for the plaintiff. Jurors making special verdicts gave significantly higher compensatory damage awards than those making only general verdicts, although there were no differences in the size of punitive awards or in total awards.

In another recent study, Irwin A. Horowitz and Kenneth S. Bordens used a simulated toxic tort case to examine the effects on jury decisionmaking of variations in trial structure (unitary and separate verdicts on several issues); order of presentation of issues (causation first, liability second, and vice versa); and the number of decisions to be made by the jury.[88] Like Zeisel and Callahan, they observed that plaintiffs are more likely to prevail on issues of liability and causation in unitary than in separated trials; found that unitary trials produce lower compensatory damage awards than special verdict trials; and they observed a significant interaction among trial structure, order of presentation, and number of decisions to be made.

The story Horowitz and Bordens tell suggests that changing the verdict structure of trials produces a number of unintended consequences. They argue that separation can have both positive and negative results for defendants. It does appear to produce fewer verdicts against defendants, giving them the advantage on the first issue. If, however, a jury using the special verdict procedure does find for the plaintiff, the awards are significantly higher than those given by juries operating under the general verdict procedure. The researchers' analysis of tapes made during deliberations supports their theory that evidence about damages was employed by jurors in unitary trials to resolve the issues of liability and causation. Such spillover effects were not possible under the special verdict procedure, for the liability and causation issues were decided prior to hearing evidence on damages. This differentiation in the character of testimony had an impact on jury verdicts:

A greater proportion of the evidence heard by separated juries would have contained testimony less favorable to the plaintiffs than the unitary structure. In fact, only 25 percent of the juries in the separated condition hearing only causation evidence . . . found for the plaintiffs, whereas 87.5 percent of the unitary trial juries, which only decided causation (but heard all of the evidence), found for the plaintiffs. Thus, the unitary juries, with their unified representation of all of the trial evidence, are more sympathetic to the plaintiff's cause.[89]

In their discussion of the higher awards for compensatory damages that resulted from separated verdicts, Horowitz and Bordens argue that juries able to overcome the initial hurdles of finding liability and especially causation (the most ambiguous issue in the trial) must have been relatively pro-plaintiff and thus went on to award particularly large damage awards. However, their explanation depends in part on whether jurors are fully informed about the ramifications of potential awards when they make their decisions. In the unitary trial, for instance, juries setting compensatory awards had already been instructed that they would be awarding both compensatory and punitive damages. In the separated verdict trial, jurors awarding compensatory damages had not yet heard instructions about the possibility of punitive damages. Thus, the separated verdict juries may have given larger compensatory awards than the unitary juries, who were aware that they could go on to make a subsequent award if they wished.[90]

A somewhat different process might also account for the larger damage awards in separated trials when both liability and causation are found. Under the special verdict procedure, jurors must make several separate unfavorable judgments about the defendant before they set damages. But in unitary trials, juries may make awards on the basis of more global judgments that combine issues of liability and harm. The former procedure may not only give defendants the advantage by making it harder to find against them but lead to assigning more blame if liability is found.

Finally, on the issue of the relationship between verdict structure and juror comprehension, Wiggins and Breckler did not find that alternative structures had a strong effect on jurors' ability to understand the evidence and testimony.[91] On the burden of proof issue, special verdict jurors recalled the instructions more accurately, perhaps simply because the information was provided to them twice (in the judge's instructions and by the special verdict questions). However, when Wiggins and Breckler tested juror understanding of the appropriate relationship between answers to special verdict questions and a finding for the plaintiff or defendant, they found no difference across the verdict procedure conditions and very low accuracy rates overall.

There is clearly much still to be learned about the effects of changes in verdict procedures. Many quite plausible consequences have been advanced, and the early work done thus far to examine how variations in verdict procedures play out suggests that the consequences are likely to be quite complex and unpredictable.

Making the Jury's Task Easier

In addition to modifications in verdict procedures, a number of other procedural alterations that might improve juror performance have been suggested, implemented, and sometimes evaluated.

NOTE-TAKING. Jurors in complex cases are called on to sit through long stretches of testimony and to recall it accurately after a substantial period of time has elapsed. Taking notes is common as an aid to memory, and it has often been suggested that jurors be permitted or encouraged to take notes during trial testimony.[92] The most common objections to the procedure have focused on several possibilities: that better notetakers will dominate jury deliberations, that notes will not always be accurate but will be given greater weight than recollections because they are in writing, and that jurors may fail to pay adequate attention to testimony because they are busy taking notes. A number of studies have examined the impact of note-taking, some based on post-trial interviews with jurors and some employing experimental designs in field or laboratory settings.[93] The cases examined included criminal and civil trials but did not focus on long trials or those with particularly complex evidence. The overall results do not suggest that note-taking improves juror recall of evidence or testimony. Evidence about the effects of note-taking on juror satisfaction is mixed, but there seems to be general enthusiasm for the policy on the part of judges and attorneys.

MAKING JUDICIAL INSTRUCTIONS CLEARER. Jurors seem to understand factual testimony relatively well, particularly in comparison to their ability to understand and accurately recall judicial instructions. Most jurisdictions use pattern instructions, written by committees and designed to be used across a wide range of cases, that often employ highly complex circumlocutions, arcane language and concepts, and elaborate series of contingent judgments. As a result, these instructions are sometimes difficult for even those trained in law to understand, and they are certainly difficult for juries.[94]

The extent of the difficulty has been demonstrated in a variety of ways. Laurence J. Severance and Elizabeth F. Loftus document the fact that juries often interrupt their deliberations to ask the judge to clarify instructions.[95] In an experimental study, Amiram Elwork, Bruce D.

Sales, and James J. Alfini found no differences in decisions between jurors who received no instructions on how to decide the issue of negligence and those who were given the Michigan pattern instructions.[96]

These projects and others also demonstrate that rewriting instructions can make them easier for jurors to understand.[97] If simpler words and formulations are substituted for arcane legal terms and phrases, and the structure is made simpler and redesigned to highlight the contingent judgments that must be made, jurors appear to be able to understand legal principles better than they do using typical pattern instructions. Again, it is important to note that the difficulties in simplifying instructions may be especially great in the complex litigation about which concern over jury competence is most often expressed. But there does seem to be reasonable hope that clearer instructions will mean substantial improvement in jury performance.[98]

PRE-INSTRUCTIONS. Traditionally, the jury first hears arguments and evidence and is instructed about the relevant legal principles by the judge only just prior to deliberations. Offering the jurors instructions prior to the hearing of evidence may have several advantages. First, pre-instruction may give jurors a framework that helps them make sense of the testimony, alerting them to important factual and legal issues whose significance they otherwise might not recognize. As a result, they may be more likely to encode and be able to recall evidence that otherwise might seem of little importance. Second, pre-instruction may also increase jurors' comprehension of legal rules simply because the rules are heard twice, facilitating their ability to employ the legal principles appropriately in reaching a decision. Juries able to recall testimony and legal principles accurately may be more likely to reach appropriate verdicts.

Studies designed to test the effects of pre-instructions have typically used the experimental design, in either field or laboratory contexts. The results are somewhat mixed. Some studies suggest pre-instructed jurors better recall testimony,[99] while others report no such effect.[100] There is little definitive evidence that pre-instruction improves jurors' ability to recall judicial instructions. In terms of its effect on overall verdicts, the evidence is also mixed. In their study of a criminal case, Saul W. Kassin and Lawrence S. Wrightsman argue that pre-instruction produces more not guilty verdicts because it predisposes jurors to favor the defendant. Hastie found that pre-instructions had no effect on patterns of overall verdicts in criminal trials but did observe that pre-instructed jurors spent about twice as much time discussing the presumption of innocence and reasonable doubt than juries that had not been given preinstructions.[101]

Larry Heuer and Steven D. Penrod argue that their field experiment pre-instruction did improve the ability of their jurors (who heard both civil and criminal cases) to "evaluat[e] the evidence according to correct legal guidelines."[102] Finally, Vicki Smith found that, in a simulated criminal case, jurors who were instructed before and after evidence presentation were "better able than other jurors to integrate the facts with the law . . . and more likely to defer their verdict decisions until after the [evidence]."[103]

Finally, it is worth noting that none of the research suggests that there are serious costs associated with the procedure. Fears that pre-instruction might be logistically burdensome, promote premature decisionmaking, or encounter opposition from judges or attorneys do not appear to be borne out. Indeed, it appears that jurors are more satisfied with their experience when given pre-instructions and that judges and attorneys are pleased with the procedure. The evidence, however, does not come from complex cases. Under conditions of greater complexity, the efficacy of repetition and of a framework that facilitates jurors' ability to comprehend information might be expected to be greater. Given the general enthusiasm with which jurors, judges, and attorneys generally appear to greet the pre-instruction procedure, it seems worthwhile to employ it and to evaluate its efficacy further.

COURT-APPOINTED EXPERTS. It has often been argued that the battle of experts that often occurs in complex trials confuses jurors and works against their ability to understand technical evidence. An alternative frequently advocated but only occasionally employed involves the use of court-appointed experts. Such experts, called in by the trial judge, may offer objective testimony about technical matters that are at issue in the trial, provide a framework for jurors to understand the critical issues, and perhaps even assess the qualifications of the experts brought into the case by the parties.[104] Such experts may be considered balanced and accurate in their evaluations of the scientific evidence, and jurors may be less likely to dismiss the technical evidence as inevitably impossible to analyze because every expert has an axe to grind. Moreover, experts may prefer to work for the court rather than for the parties to a trial, because pressure to slant or temper their views will be reduced. Finally, court-appointed experts could reduce imbalances in resources between the parties.

The major objections to this proposal include concerns that jurors could be too easily swayed by these experts because of their impartial status. Additionally, lawyers may lose some control over the proceedings, and the practice could entail additional expense for the parties, who would have to help pay for the court's expert as well as their own.[105]

As is true for nearly all the innovations discussed here, evidence about the effects of court-employed experts is rather fragmentary. It appears that judges tend to think them a good idea but don't use them very much.[106] Preliminary results from a study by Thomas Willging and Joe Cecil suggest that court-appointed experts appear to dominate trial outcomes when they are used in federal courts.[107] In a simulation study of juror decisionmaking in a trial that turned on the credibility of eyewitness testimony, Brian L. Cutler, Hedy R. Dexter, and Steven D. Penrod found that, when compared with the same evidence presented by opposing experts hired by each side, the testimony of a court-appointed witness was perceived as more credible and caused jurors to be more skeptical about the accuracy of eyewitness testimony. With the court-appointed expert, however, jurors were less sensitive to the conditions under which the defendant was observed.[108]

In the most elaborate simulation research employed thus far, Nancy J. Brekke and others examined the effects on nondeliberating jurors and juries of both court-appointed and adversarial expert witnesses in a rape trial. The researchers found no evidence that court-appointed experts dominated the decisionmaking process, although jurors tended to have better recall of evidence and instructions when the court-appointed expert was used. But they also found that deliberating jurors had better recall of and were more responsive to the content of expert testimony when experts hired by parties to the trial rather than court-appointed experts were used.[109]

These simulation studies suggest that using a court-appointed expert can result in both positive and negative effects. A court-appointed expert appears to reduce some of the distrust engendered by the battle of experts in an adversarial setting. At the same time, the fact that an expert is court-appointed may raise his or her perceived credibility so much that jurors pay less attention to the actual content of the testimony. This finding is somewhat speculative in both studies and may be conditioned in important ways by deliberation. But both studies suggest that the testimony of court-appointed experts may be overweighted by the jurors because of the status conferred by their selection by the judge.

The National Academy of Sciences Panel on Statistical Assessments as Evidence in the Courts has adopted a recommendation suggesting that "judges have been unduly reluctant to appoint statistical experts to assist the court and [we] recommend the increased use of court-appointment procedures such as those provided by Rule 706 of the Federal Rules of Evidence."[110] The recommendation seems a reasonable one, assuming that it is accompanied by research designed to measure the impact of such testimony on jury understanding of complex evidence.

SUMMARY. A number of procedural changes, including allowing jurors to take notes, providing clearer instructions, pre-instructing juries, and using court-appointed experts, have been suggested to make the jury's tasks easier in complex cases. These procedures have been used in several jurisdictions and appear to meet with general approval from jurors, judges, and attorneys.[111] Theoretically, they might be expected to have quite useful effects on the ability of jurors to handle the tasks at which they are typically said to do poorly. Although these suggestions have been made for many years, and implemented in a spotty fashion for a decade or so, the systematic evidence about their effects is sparse and of very recent vintage. The dearth of research should make us wary about reaching closure on the utility of these innovations. The available evidence on the effects of these procedures comes primarily from examination of typical criminal and civil cases that lack the large bodies of evidence, long trials, and complex testimony often conjured up in the debate over the role of civil jury. Given the lack of sufficient evidence and our societal bias in favor of using juries whenever there are not overriding reasons to abandon their use, it would seem prudent both to employ these more procedures widely in complex cases and to encourage serious evaluation of their effects.

Conclusion

Three major points seem to me to stand out in the debate over alternatives to the traditional civil jury. The first emphasizes the need to be clear about the parameters of the problem being addressed. The second involves the underlying tension between rationality (and its concomitant predictability) and community values in jury decisionmaking. The third is that further research is needed before sensible choices can be made.

Kalven and Zeisel's study of the rates of agreement between judges and juries in civil trials is more than twenty-five years old, but it remains our single best piece of evidence about the relative abilities of these decisionmakers to understand evidence and decide civil cases in appropriate ways. The very high rates of agreement suggest that juries seem to perform quite well on a wide range of cases when measured against the benchmark of judicial decisionmaking. Is there reason to believe that this is no longer true?[112] For run-of-the-mill civil cases, there seems little reason to believe that the situation has changed markedly. To the extent that the nature of civil cases has changed in the intervening years, however, perhaps the study's sanguine conclusion may be in need of some revision. The development of toxic tort litigation, the movement of government and courts into race and gender discrimination in schools and the workplace, a possible return to more vigorous enforcement of antitrust laws all suggest that the caseloads, particularly in federal courts, may involve increasing proportions of suits with complex legal and factual issues, as well as technical evidence and testimony by expert witnesses. According to a recent report, the number of trials lasting more than ten days in federal District Courts rose from 1.4 percent in 1960 to nearly 4 percent in 1987; the number of such protracted trials involving civil juries rose from 1.6 percent in 1960 to more than 6 percent in 1987.[113]

There is certainly reason to be concerned about the ability of both juries and judges to deal with law and evidence in many complex cases. But these cases remain relatively few, and solutions should be tailored to the problems actually presented. I do not believe that at this stage the evidence for jury incompetence is sufficient to justify excluding complex cases from the right to trial by jury. Moreover, as noted earlier, the impediments to the complexity exception imposed by both the Seventh Amendment and many state constitutions would make this reform difficult to implement even if the evidence in its favor were more compelling. As a result, I believe that attention ought to be focused on procedural changes that can improve the performance of both judges and juries. Such experience may provide persuasive grounds for choosing policies that maximize the various goals of the civil justice system.

My second point deals with the general purposes of the jury system. Discussions of the deficiencies and virtues of the civil jury seem to me often to turn not only on imperfect data but also on unexamined assumptions about the values that should be promoted in the factfinding process. Critics of the civil jury assert the importance of a distinction between factfinding and application of legal principles. Their implicit view is that the problem is harnessing the jury so that it proceeds in a rational and predictable way. This seems to me to be implausible, both descriptively and prescriptively.

The tasks before the decisionmaker in a civil trial—whether a jury or a judge or a special magistrate–inevitably involve facts, law, and values. Concepts such as negligence, foreseeability, prudence, due care, and the "reasonable person," are not simply state of nature questions. Rather, they involve a number of complex decisions about a variety of matters: who did what; interpretations of how human beings behave or should behave; what it is reasonable to expect others to do or not do; and what motivations lead to what types of behavior. They also involve judgments about the consequences of deciding a case one way or the other—for example, who will be helped or harmed or what types of behavior will be encouraged or discouraged by certain outcomes. The urge to separate factfinding from law or policy is a natural one, for it seems to promote the predictability that is a cornerstone of a legal order. Yet there are clear limits to what may be achieved in this domain.

This emphasis upon predictability, consistency, and rationality lurks in the background of arguments against the civil jury as an undiscussed but assumed premise. On other occasions, such as discussions of using "science courts" in cases involving complex technical issues, the notion of separating factfinding from other tasks becomes more explicit.[114] This argument is reminiscent of the age-old distinction in the literature of public organizations between policy and administration.[115] According to this view, which dominated discussions of public administration for the first third of this century, policymaking functions are the province of the legislature, while bureaucratic agencies should restrict themselves to administering or implementing those policies rather than influencing the results of such policies. Given the obvious difficulties in formulating rules to cover all contingencies, it is evident that the distinction between policy and administration is bound to be chimerical.[116]

Similarly, the notion that juries can simply apply the law to the facts they find is problematical as well. Inevitably, uncertainty exists about the facts in any case, and not surprisingly this uncertainty is most prominent in the very cases that cause most concern to critics of the civil jury. Making decisions about the relationship between the defendant's behavior and plaintiff's injury or about whether the motives that caused a defendant's behavior are appropriate or inappropriate are what makes complex litigation complex. There is also the inevitable ambiguity in the rules themselves, for they are by definition designed as general principles to cover a wide variety of human behavior.

The drive toward rationality and predictability is certainly understandable, but it cannot govern our choices totally, for it is an unattainable goal, whether the decisionmaker is a judge, a jury, or some other institution. Moreover, as normative propositions, rationality and predictability are not the only goals of the civil justice system. The sense of justice that emerges from the community is also critical to a civil justice system that is likely to endure and produce outcomes acceptable to the community at large. In the criminal context, the notion of community values leavening the application of outdated or unpopular laws certainly causes some discomfort but is generally recognized as one of the strengths of the jury system.[117]

Because there is less concern in civil than in criminal cases about the consequences of error or the need to protect individuals against governmental tyranny, the uncertainty introduced by the impact of community values is clearly viewed with greater suspicion. As I have noted, however, the stakes are high in many complex cases, and these cases often involve contests in which individuals or groups with few resources are pitted against large and powerful institutions. As a result, many of the arguments favoring a role for juries in shaping legal rules to contemporary standards seem to me to have pull in the civil context as well.

I am not saying that irrational decisions made by jurors who have not understood the testimony are desirable. Rather, the debate over the fate of the civil jury ought to deal more explicitly with the conflict in values that I believe lies behind much of the prescriptive literature. Moreover, it ought to proceed on the basis of a much clearer understanding of the nature of the "problem" that is supposed to be solved, not on the basis of idealized juries that decide only "fact issues" or the notion that the typical civil jury is a group of unintelligent, uninformed citizens driven only by an ideological commitment to punish those with deep pockets.

This brings me to my last observation. Calls for more research—particularly when they are made by those of us who make our living doing research—are often a matter of skepticism and sometimes of ridicule. Yet this is what is needed in the debate over the future of the civil jury. This is a time for serious evidence to be brought to bear on policymaking, not for symbolic politics or quick fixes suggested by some of the proposals I have discussed. Such "fixes" may be directed at problems that do not exist, at least not in the magnitude imagined, wasting resources and compromising important values. Restricting the right to a jury trial is a very important step that goes to the heart of our legal culture. Unless it can be proved that no alternatives providing satisfactory decisionmaking are available, it is a step that should not be taken.

Relatedly, quick fixes may produce unintended consequences. In a project on jury decisionmaking, Shari Seidman Diamond and I are exploring the policy of not telling jurors about the treble damage rule in private antitrust cases. As I have indicated, denying jurors such information is typically justified on the ground that, if they are told, they will lower their award below the "true compensation" amount in order to avoid giving the plaintiff a windfall. Of course, in the absence of evidence, it is equally plausible to suppose that jurors not told about the trebling rule will add amounts to their award for deterrence and punishment, thus exceeding true compensation. One reasonable proposal for dealing with this problem suggests that judges tell jurors to award only the amount necessary to compensate the plaintiff and not to increase awards as punishment or deterrence, but that the *judge* would add such amounts if he or she felt it was appropriate in the case.[118] Thus, judges could acknowledge the jurors' instinct to punish and deter but remove any motive to raise or lower awards. In our simulation study, which uses adults called for jury service and a videotaped antitrust trial, we found to our surprise that jurors given such an instruction made the highest damage awards of all jurors, including those who had been told about trebling, those given no information, and those given a completely open-ended instruction that asked them to select a "fair and appropriate" amount. The explanation for this behavior appears to lie in the issue of framing: by informing jurors that punishment and deterrence may be appropriate values to consider in such a case, the behavior of the defendants was framed and perceived by jurors as more serious and blameworthy. Moreover, because this instruction fails to provide jurors with a clear and certain mechanism assuring them that such concerns will be effectively dealt with in the final award, jurors took it upon themselves to make sure that the plaintiff's award was very substantial.[119]

This is an example of the type of unintended consequences that could result from adoption of policies without sufficient prior empirical research on their likely consequences. Urging that such research be done before innovations are adopted is not a temporizing strategy designed to delay change forever. Rather, developing a systematic understanding of the nature of problems and the likely effect of proposed solutions is an appropriate activity for the legal profession and social science community in carrying out their responsibility to protect the complex set of values at the heart of our legal institutions.

Notes

1. Jerome Frank, *Courts on Trial: Myth and Reality in American Justice* (Princeton University Press, 1949).

2. See, for example, Karl M. Lewellyn, *The Common Law Tradition: Deciding Appeals* (Little, Brown, 1960).

3. *Skidmore* v. *Baltimore & Ohio Railroad Company*, 167 F. 2d 54 (1948), at 61.

4. Richard O. Lempert, "Civil Juries and Complex Cases: Let's Not Rush to Judgment," *Michigan Law Review*, vol. 80 (November 1981), pp. 68–132.

5. For example, jurors may give too much credence to eyewitness testimony. Elizabeth F. Loftus, "Reconstructing Memory: The Incredible Eyewitness," *Psychology Today*, vol. 8 (December 1974), pp. 116–19. They may also be persuaded by expert testimony that is difficult to understand because its complexity makes it seem more authoritative. See Laurence H. Tribe, "Trial by Mathematics: Precision and Ritual in the Legal Process," *Harvard Law Review*, vol. 84 (April 1971), pp. 1329–93. Or they may dismiss such testimony *because* of its complexity. See Michael J. Saks and Robert F. Kidd, "Human Information Processing and Adjudication: Trial by Heuristics," *Law & Society Review*, vol. 15, no. 1 (1980-81), pp. 123–60. Jurors can also be swayed more by witness demeanor than by other indicators of credibility, discount testimony on the basis of personal experience or bias, and make decisions on the basis of irrelevant or excluded evidence, including pre-trial publicity.

6. Dale W. Broeder, "The University of Chicago Jury Project," *Nebraska Law Review*, vol. 38 (May 1959), pp. 744–60.

7. Valerie P. Hans and M. David Ermann, "Responses to Corporate Versus Individual Wrongdoing," *Law and Human Behavior*, vol. 13 (June 1989), pp. 151–66.

8. *Pollock and Riley, Inc.* v. *Pearl Brewing Company*, 498 F.2d 1240 (5th Cir. 1974). See also Shari Seidman Diamond and Jonathan D. Casper, "Blindfolding the Jury to Verdict Consequences: Damages, Experts, and the Civil Jury," *Law & Society Review*, vol. 26, no. 3 (1992), pp. 513–63.

9. See, for example, "Informing the Jury of the Legal Effect of Special Verdict Answers in Comparative Negligence Actions," *Duke Law Journal*, vol. 1981 (November 1981), pp. 824–52, p. 829; and "Informing the Jury of the Effect of Its Answers to Special Verdict Questions—the Minnesota Experience," *Minnesota Law Review*, vol. 58 (April 1974), pp. 903–32.

10. Any evaluation of alternatives also must involve constitutional issues as well, given the Seventh Amendment and the constraints on states that may be imposed by the Fourteenth Amendment's due process clause. These constitutional issues will not be treated in detail here.

11. For a somewhat different list of criteria for jury performance and a useful review of what we know about jury decisionmaking, see Robert J. MacCoun, *Getting Inside the Black Box: Toward a Better Understanding of Civil Jury Behavior* (Santa Monica: Rand Institute for Civil Justice, 1987).

12. Diamond and Casper, "Blindfolding the Jury."

13. *In re Japanese Electronics Products Antitrust Litigation*, 631 F.2d 1069 (1980), at 1093.

14. See, for example, William K. Muir, *Prayer in the Public Schools: Law and Attitude Change* (University of Chicago Press, 1967); and Tom R. Tyler, *Why People Obey the Law* (Yale University Press, 1990).

15. See, for example, Tom R. Tyler, Jonathan D. Casper, and Bonnie Fisher, "Maintaining Allegiance toward Political Authorities: The Role of Prior Attitudes and the Use of Fair Procedure," *American Journal of Political Science*, vol. 33 (August 1989), pp. 629–52.

16. Harry Kalven, Jr., "The Dignity of the Civil Jury," *Virginia Law Review*, vol. 50 (October 1964), pp. 1055–75, 1063. It is worth noting that this is a particularly American perspective. In several European legal systems, mixed tribunals that include both professionals and laypersons have been employed in both criminal and civil contexts. Moreover, even in the American context, the growing use of arbitration procedures is providing an alternative to judge or jury.

17. Harry Kalven, Jr., and Hans Zeisel, *The American Jury* (Little, Brown, 1966).

18. Kalven, "The Dignity of the Civil Jury"; Harry Kalven, Jr., "The Jury, the Law, and the Personal Injury Damage Award," *Ohio State Law Journal*, vol. 19 (1958), pp. 158–78.

19. Similar rates of agreement were found in the companion study of criminal cases, which employed the same methodology of asking judges how they would have decided jury trials over which they presided.

20. Kalven, "The Dignity of the Civil Jury," p. 1065.

21. Reid Hastie, Steven D. Penrod, and Nancy Pennington, *Inside the Jury* (Harvard University Press, 1983); Phoebe C. Ellsworth, "Are Twelve Heads Better Than One?" *Law and Contemporary Problems*, vol. 52 (Autumn 1989), pp. 205–24; and William C. Thompson, "Are Juries Competent to Evaluate Statistical Evidence?" ibid., pp. 9–41. A somewhat more sanguine account of jurors' capacity to understand and use the evidence provided by experts in the context of "social-framework testimony" can be found in Neil J. Vidmar and Regina A. Schuller, "Juries and Expert Evidence: Social Framework Testimony," ibid., pp. 133–76.

22. Alan Reifman, Spencer M. Gusick, and Phoebe C. Ellsworth, "Real Jurors' Understanding of the Law in Real Cases," *Law and Human Behavior*, vol. 16 (December 1992), pp. 539–54; Chairman Daniel H. Margolis and others, *Jury Comprehension in Complex Cases*, Report of the Special Committee of the ABA Section on Litigation (Chicago: The Committee, 1990); Molly Selvin and Larry Picus, *The Debate over Jury Performance: Observations from a Recent Asbestos Case* (Santa Monica: Rand Institute for Civil Justice, 1977).

23. In a recent appeal of a death sentence, a central issue in the case involved the question of whether the Illinois pattern instructions for death penalty cases can be comprehended by jurors. Because of my personal involvement in one stage of the case, I was able to observe several highly educated and experienced attorneys struggle among themselves to comprehend what, indeed, the instructions meant. Whether judges who have the occasion to deliver the pattern instructions are better able to follow them seems to me an open question.

24. Stephen E. Fienberg, ed., *The Evolving Role of Statistical Assessments as Evidence in the Courts* (Springer-Verlag, 1989), pp. 78–79.

25. This assumption may, of course, be undermined if selection strategies pursued by the judge or the parties are consciously designed to eliminate jurors with knowledge or experience about the issues at hand.

26. Michael J. Saks, "Small-Group Decision Making and Complex Information Tasks" (Washington: Federal Judicial Center, 1981).

27. Fienberg, *The Evolving Role of Statistical Assessments*, p. 73. The case studies are primarily directed at trial court proceedings, but do include some appellate court decisions as well. There seems little reason to believe, however, that appellate courts—with more extensive clerk resources and collegial decision processes—would do worse at the relevant tasks than trial judges.

28. John W. Osborne, "Judicial/Technical Assessment of Novel Scientific Evidence," *University of Illinois Law Review*, vol. 1990 (Spring 1990), pp. 497–546.

29. As suggested by Laurence Tribe, "Trial by Mathematics." For evidence that jurors

may be more discriminating in their treatment of complex expert testimony, see Diamond and Casper, "Blindfolding the Jury," pp. 539–44.

30. See, for example, Michael J. Saks and Robert F. Kidd, "Human Information Processing and Adjudication"; Zvi Ginossar and Yaacov Trope, "The Effect of Base Rates and Individuating Information on Judgments about Another Person," *Journal of Experimental Social Psychology*, vol. 16 (May 1980), pp. 228–42.

31. In deciding disputes, courts may exercise principles of law or equity. In exercising equity jurisdiction, a court employs the body of principles and precedents which have been developed historically to deal with certain issues not directly covered by common-law writs. Such equity cases typically involve violations of rights or interests whose remedies are injunctive rather than monetary.

32. See *In re U.S. Financial Securities Litigation*, 75 F.R.D. 702 (S.D. Cal. 1977), rev. *In re U.S. Financial Securities Litigation*, 609 F.2d 411 (9th Cir. 1979).

33. *Ross* v. *Bernhard*, 396 U.S. 531 (1970), fn. 10, at 538.

34. For a discussion of this point, see Ninth Circuit opinion *In re U.S. Financial Securities Litigation*, at 427-431. See also Lempert, "Let's Not Rush to Judgment," pp. 86–97.

35. Decisions upholding the striking of a jury trial request include *In re Boise Cascade Securities Litigation*, 420 F. Supp. 99 (W.D. Wash. 1976); *Bernstein* v. *Universal Pictures, Inc.*, 79 F.R.D. 59 (S.D.N.Y. 1978); *ILC Peripherals Leasing Corp.* v. *International Business Machines*, 458 F.Supp 423 (N.D.Cal. 1978); and *In re U.S. Financial Securities*. Trial court rulings rejecting motions to strike a demand for a jury trial include *Radial Lip Mach. Inc.* v. *Intern. Carbide Corp.*, 76 F.R.D. 224 (N.D. Ill, 1977); and *In re Japanese Electronic Products Antitrust Litigation*, 478 F. Supp. 889 (E.D. Pa. 1979), rev. *In re Japanese Electronic Products Antitrust Litigation*, 631 F.2d 1069 (1980).

36. 609 F.2d 411 (1979), at 432.

37. For a useful recent review which describes the complex ways in which jurors reach damage award decisions, See Edith Greene, "On Juries and Damage Awards: The Process of Decisionmaking," *Law and Contemporary Problems*, vol. 52 (Autumn 1989), pp. 225–46.

38. Adoption of this policy has the potential of suggesting that juries are for less significant cases, while important cases involving large stakes need not go before lay decisionmakers.

39. The Third Circuit opinion overturning a trial court ruling and holding that a complexity exception ought to be created attempted to define the appropriate set of cases as follows: "A suit is too complex for a jury when circumstances render the jury unable to decide in a proper manner." *In re Japanese Electronics Products Antitrust Litigation*, 631 F.2d 1069 (1980), at 1079. The tautological quality of this "definition" is somewhat meliorated by a later statement which suggests that the circumstances which are likely to prevent a jury from rational decisionmaking include "long trial periods and conceptually difficult factual issues" (Ibid.) But it is clear that definition of the appropriate class is difficult and that concerns about creating exceptions which threaten to swallow the rule must be taken seriously.

40. Lempert, "Civil Juries and Complex Cases."

41. "The Case for Special Juries in Complex Civil Litigation, *Yale Law Journal*, vol. 89 (May 1980), p. 1159. See also William V. Luneberg and Mark A. Nordenberg, "Specially Qualified Juries and Expert Nonjury Tribunals: Alternatives for Coping with the Complexities of Modern Civil Litigation," *Virginia Law Review*, vol. 67 (June 1981), pp. 887–1007; and Dan Drazan, "The Case for Special Juries in Toxic Tort Litigation," *Judicature*, vol. 72 (February–March 1989), pp. 292–98.

42. "The Case for Special Juries," p. 1163.

43. James B. Thayer, "The Jury and Its Development," *Harvard Law Review*, vol. 5 (February 1892), pp. 295–319, quotation on p. 300.

44. *Fay* v. *New York*, 332 U.S. 261 (1947).

45. Luneberg and Nordenberg, "Specially Qualified Juries," p. 906.

46. Ibid., p. 909.

47. The Jury Service and Selection Act of 1968, 28 U.S.C. § 1861–1874.

48. 28 U.S.C. § 1865(a) 1970.

49. Luneberg and Nordenberg, "Specially Qualified Juries."

50. "The Case for Special Juries"; Drazan, "The Case for Special Juries in Toxic Tort Litigation"; and Nancy A. Friley, "Blue Ribbon Juries," *Florida Bar Journal*, vol. 64 (February 1990), pp. 10–13.

51. Daniel Kahneman, Paul Slovic, and Amos Tversky, *Judgment under Uncertainty: Heuristics and Biases* (Cambridge University Press, 1982).

52. Sandra Blakeslee, "Faulty Math Heightens Fears of Breast Cancer," *New York Times*, March 15, 1992, p. A1.

53. Drazen, "The Case for Special Juries in Toxic Tort Litigation," p. 294.

54. Rita James, "Status and Competence of Jurors," *American Journal of Sociology*, vol. 64 (1959), pp. 563–70; Hastie, Penrod, and Pennington, *Inside the Jury*, p. 145.

55. Hastie, Penrod, and Pennington, *Inside the Jury*; and Diamond and Casper, "Blindfolding the Jury."

56. Hastie, Penrod, and Pennington, *Inside the Jury*, p. 136.

57. Claudia L. Cowan, William C. Thompson, and Phoebe C. Ellsworth, "The Effects of Death Qualification on Jurors' Predisposition to Convict and on the Quality of Deliberation," *Law and Human Behavior*, vol. 8 (June 1984), pp. 53–79.

58. Ibid., p. 60.

59. Even in the civil context, though, critics of such "compromise verdicts" based on a sense of justice sometimes recognize their utility. Thus, the tendency of juries operating under contributory negligence rules to "overlook" a very small degree of a plaintiff's responsibility has often been characterized as an appropriate response to an unreasonable rule.

60. "Special Verdicts. The court may require a jury to return only a special verdict in the form a special written finding upon each issue of fact" (Fed R. Civ. P. 49). For useful discussions of special verdicts in criminal cases see Verla S. Neslund, "Comment: The Bifurcated Trial: Is It Used More Than it is Useful?" *Emory Law Journal*, vol. 31 (Spring 1982), pp. 441–87; Robert M. Grass, "Bifurcated Jury Deliberations in Criminal Rico Trials," *Fordham Law Review*, vol. 57 (April 1989), pp. 745–63.

61. "Informing the Jury of the Effect of Its Answers to Special Verdict Questions."

62. These examples are drawn from Elizabeth A. Faulkner, "Using the Special Verdict to Manage Complex Cases and Avoid Compromise Verdicts," *Arizona State Law Journal*, vol. 21 (Spring 1989), pp. 297–325, especially pp. 316ff.

63. *Sharon* v. *Time, Inc.*, 599 F. Supp. 538 (S.D. N.Y. 1984).

64. Lempert, "Civil Juries and Complex Cases," pp. 112–13.

65. *SCM* v. *Xerox*, 463 F. Supp. 983 (D. Conn. 1978), *aff'd* 645 F.2d 1195 (2d Cir. 1981), *cert. denied*, 455 U.S. 1016 (1982), *reh'g denied*, 456 U.S. 985 (1982).

66. Because special verdicts early in the trial made it unnecessary to present certain evidence that would have been presented if a general verdict had been used, the length of the trial was presumably decreased. It did, however, require fourteen months of trial and thirty-eight days of deliberation!

67. "General Verdict Accompanied by Answer to Interrogatories. The court may submit to the jury, together with appropriate forms for a general verdict, written interrogatories upon one or more issues of fact the decision of which is necessary to a verdict." Fed R. Civ. P. 49.

68. Mark S. Brodin, "Accuracy, Efficiency, and Accountability in the Litigation Process–the Case for the Fact Verdict," *University of Cincinnati Law Review*, vol. 59, no. 1 (1990) pp. 15–111, especially pp. 63–64.

69. Faulkner, "Using the Special Verdict to Manage Complex Cases," p. 314.

70. Hastie, Penrod, and Pennington, *Inside the Jury*; and Ellsworth, "Twelve Heads Are Better Than One"; and Reifman and others, "Real Jurors' Understanding of the Law."

71. Elizabeth C. Wiggins and Steven J. Breckler, "Special Verdicts as Guides to Jury Decision Making," *Law and Psychology Review*, vol. 14 (Spring 1990), pp. 1–41; and Brodin, "Accuracy, Efficiency, and Accountability."

72. Brodin, "Accuracy, Efficiency, and Accountability," p. 60, quoting from Edson R. Sunderland, "Verdicts, General and Specific," *Yale Law Journal*, vol. 29 (January 1920), pp. 253–69, especially p. 259.

73. *Skidmore* v. *Baltimore & Ohio Railroad Company*, 167 F.2d 54, at p. 65.

74. Faulkner, "Using the Special Verdict to Manage Complex Cases," p. 323.

75. Lempert, "Civil Juries and Complex Cases," p. 113.

76. Ibid., p. 113; and Amiram Elwork, Bruce D. Sales, and James J. Alfini, *Making Jury Instructions Understandable* (Charlottesville, Va.: Michie Co., 1982).

77. "Informing the Jury of the Legal Effect of Special Verdict Answers."

78. Wiggins and Breckler, "Special Verdicts as Guides," p. 9.

79. Mitchell Pacelle, "Contaminated Verdict: Don't Blame the Jury for Its Incoherent Verdict in the W. R. Grace Toxic Tort Trial," *American Lawyer*, vol. 8 (December 1986), pp. 75–80, extract on p. 77.

80. Ibid., pp. 75–76.

81. Brodin, "Accuracy, Efficiency, and Accountability," p. 85.

82. Ibid., pp. 92–93.

83. *Porche* v. *Gulf Mississippi Marine Corp.*, 390 F. Supp. 624 (E.D. La. 1975) at 632.

84. See, for example, Mitchell Pacelle, "Contaminated Verdict"; and Selvin and Picus, *The Debate Over Jury Performance*.

85. Hans Zeisel and Thomas Callahan, "Split Trials and Time Saving: A Statistical Analysis," *Harvard Law Review*, vol. 76 (June 1963), pp. 1606–25, especially p. 1612.

86. The advantages to plaintiffs of having the liability issue decided after testimony on damages is presented may be the product of two rather different processes: the increased blame jurors assign to the defendant after hearing damages-related testimony may spill over and influence the liability judgment, and evidence about injuries to the plaintiff may lead jurors to lower their standard of proof for the liability judgment in order to make it possible to compensate a needy plaintiff. See Sally Lloyd-Bostock, "Attributions of Cause and Responsibility as Social Phenomenon," in Jos. Jaspars, Frank D. Fincham, and Miles Hewston, eds., *Attribution Theory and Research: Conceptual, Developmental, and Social Dimensions* (Academic Press, 1983), pp. 261–92.

87. Wiggins and Breckler, "Special Verdicts as Guides."

88. Irwin A. Horowitz and Kenneth S. Bordens, "An Experimental Investigation of Procedural Issues in Complex Tort Trials," *Law and Human Behavior*, vol. 14 (June 1990), pp. 269–85.

89. Ibid., p. 282.

90. This explanation does not appear to account for the similar finding in the Wiggins and Breckler study. Jurors using special verdicts were informed on their verdict sheets that they were entitled to make both compensatory and punitive damage awards.

91. Wiggins and Breckler, "Special Verdicts as Guides."

92. The procedure was, indeed, endorsed by the Judicial Conference on the Jury System in 1960. See Judicial Conference Committee on the Operation of the Jury System, "The Jury System in the Federal Courts," *Federal Rules Decisions*, vol. 26 (West, 1960), pp. 409–24.

93. See, for example, Victor Eugene Flango, "Would Jurors Do a Better Job if They Could Take Notes?" *Judicature*, vol. 63 (April 1980), pp. 436–43; Larry Heuer and Steven Penrod, "Increasing Jurors' Participation in Trials: A Field Experiment with Jury Notetaking and Question Asking," *Law and Human Behavior*, vol. 12 (September 1988), pp. 231–61; Larry Heuer and Steven Penrod, "Juror Notetaking and Question Asking during Trials: A National Field Experiment," unpublished manuscript, Barnard College, 1992; and Reid Hastie, *Final Report to National Institute Law Enforcement and Criminal Justice*, unpublished manuscript, Northwestern University, 1983.

94. For a review of some of the literature, see Valerie P. Hans and Neil Vidmar, *Judging the Jury* (Plenum Press, 1986), pp. 120–27. See also Reifman and others, "Real Jurors' Understanding of the Law."

95. Laurence J. Severance and Elizabeth F. Loftus, "Improving the Ability of Jurors to Comprehend and Apply Jury Instructions," *Law & Society Review*, vol. 17 (November 1982), pp. 153–97.

96. Elwork and others, *Making Jury Instructions Understandable*.

97. Robert P. Charrow and Veda R. Charrow, "Making Legal Language Understandable: A Psycholinguistic Study of Jury Instructions," *Columbia Law Review*, vol. 79 (November 1979), pp. 1306–74.

98. Margolis and others, *Jury Comprehension in Complex Cases*.

99. Amiram Elwork, Bruce D. Sales, and James J. Alfini, "Juridic Decisions: In Ignorance of the Law or in Light of It?" *Law and Human Behavior*, vol. 1, no. 2 (1977), pp. 163–89.

100. Saul W. Kassin and Lawrence S. Wrightsman, "On the Requirements of Proof: The Timing of Judicial Instruction and Mock Juror Verdicts," *Journal of Personality and Social Psychology*, vol. 37 (October 1979), pp. 1877–87; Larry Heuer and Steven D. Penrod, "Instructing Jurors: A Field Experiment with Written and Preliminary Instructions."

101. Hastie, *Final Report*.

102. Heuer and Penrod, "Instructing Jurors," p. 426.

103. Quoting from a summary in *Jury Comprehension in Complex Cases*, p. 617, reporting findings presented in Vicki Smith, "The Psychological and Legal Implications of Pretrial Instruction in the Law," paper presented to Law & Society Meeting, 1988.

104. See, for example, Theodore I. Botter, "The Court-Appointed Impartial Expert," in Melvin D. Kraft, ed., *Using Experts in Civil Cases* (New York: Practising Law Institute, 1982), pp. 53–85; Fienberg, "The Evolving Role of Statistical Evidence"; Nancy J. Brekke, Peter J. Enko, Gail Clavet, and Eric Seelau, "Of Juries and Court-Appointed Experts," *Law and Human Behavior*, vol. 15 (October 1991), pp. 451–75.

105. For an excellent review of the legal literature on court-appointed experts, as well as a discussion of more general issues involving expert testimony, see Samuel R. Gross, "Expert Evidence," *Wisconsin Law Review*, vol. 1991 (November–December 1991), pp. 1113–1232, especially pp. 1187–1208.

106. Michael J. Saks and Richard Van Duizend, *The Use of Scientific Evidence in Litigation* (Williamsburg, Va.: National Center for State Courts, 1983).

107. Brekke and others, "Juries and Court-Appointed Experts," p. 454, citing evidence from a study in progress by Thomas E. Willging and Joe S. Cecil.

108. Brian L. Cutler, Hedy R. Dexter, and Steven D. Penrod, "Nonadversarial Methods for Sensitizing Jurors to Eyewitness Evidence," *Journal of Applied Social Psychology*, vol. 20 (August 1990), pp. 119–207.

109. Brekke and others, "Juries and Court-Appointed Experts," pp. 469–70.

110. Fienberg, *The Evolving Role of Statistical Assessments*, p. 14.

111. Another proposed innovation allowing jurors to question witnesses seems to arouse greater resistance from the parties. See generally, Joe S. Cecil, Valerie P. Hans, and Elizabeth C. Wiggins, "Citizen Comprehension of Difficult Issues: Lessons from Civil

Jury Trials," *American University Law Review*, vol. 40 (Winter 1991), pp. 727–74, p. 769 and sources cited there. In their field experiment, Heuer and Penrod report that jurors allowed to ask questions were more satisfied, but the technique had little impact on juror decisions. Other courtroom participants were skeptical about the procedure prior to their experience with it but reportedly found that it caused them few significant problems. Heuer and Penrod, "Increasing Jurors' Participation in Trials."

112. The recent national study of juror note-taking by Heuer and Penrod provides evidence on rates of agreement between judges and juries in a sample of roughly 150 criminal and civil cases and generally finds rates of agreement comparable to those found by Kalven and Zeisel more than thirty years ago. Heuer and Penrod, "Juror Notetaking and Question Asking during Trials."

113. Elizabeth C. Wiggins and Steven J. Breckler, "The Management of Complex Civil Litigation," in Dorothy K. Kagehiro and William S. Laufer, eds., *The Handbook of Psychology and Law* (Springer-Verlag, 1992), p. 78.

114. David L. Bazelon, "Coping with Technology through the Legal Process," *Cornell Law Review*, vol. 62 (June 1977), pp. 817–32.

115. "Political functions group themselves naturally under two heads . . . the action of the state as a political entity consists either in operations necessary to the expression of its will, or in operations necessary to the execution of that will. . . . These two functions of government may for purposes of convenience be designated respectively as Politics and Administration." Frank Johnson Goodnow, *Politics and Administration* (Macmillan Company, 1900), pp. 9, 17.

116. See Herbert Alexander Simon, *Administrative Behavior: A Study of Decision-Making Processes in Administrative Organization*, 2d ed. (Macmillan, 1957), pp. 52–57.

117. To be sure, the recent and shocking verdict in the Rodney King police brutality trial makes one a bit queasy about blanket endorsements of the importation of community values to leaven the impact of the law.

118. "Controlling Jury Damage Awards in Private Antitrust Suits," *Michigan Law Review*, vol. 81 (January 1983), pp. 693–713.

119. Shari Seidman Diamond and Jonathan D. Casper, "Blindfolding the Jury."

CHAPTER FOURTEEN

Jury Service and Community Representation

Barbara Allen Babcock

M Y FATHER, who liked to call himself a country lawyer, once took in lieu of fee a nineteenth-century print entitled *Gentlemen of the Jury*. Twelve white men are in the box. Several whisper, one scowls, another dozes; not one face is friendly, receptive, or even intelligent. I've always wondered what the client, an elderly black lady, made of this possession, which had hung in her parlor for many years.

Most American juries looked much like that old print until well into the twentieth century. In 1957, the popular movie *Twelve Angry Men* (Caucasian) valorized juries. In that movie, the defendant was white. But when a black man was on trial, the prototypical American jury became the ugly, unjust villain in a classic film made in 1962, *To Kill a Mockingbird*.

The picture of an African American before a jury from which the state has "expressly excluded every man of his race" is a powerful negative image in the United States.[1] The force of that image spilled out into the Los Angeles riots of 1992, following the acquittal of white policemen accused of assaulting an African American named Rodney King (who later became more defendant than victim in the case). Voices from the public, as well as the legal profession, proclaimed that had the jury included African Americans, the response to the verdict, if not the verdict itself, would have been different.[2]

I gratefully acknowledge my Stanford research assistants, whose help was made possible by a bequest from the Dorothy Redwine estate: Laura Gomez, Joanna Grossman, and Lauren Willis. Mary Erickson also provided valuable research support. My civil procedure colleagues, Janet Cooper Alexander and Janet Halley, as well as Jamie Kogan, made many helpful suggestions on an earlier draft. As always, Thomas Grey provided a very high order of intellectual and editorial support.

In the Rodney King case, the defense lawyers, after winning a change of venue to a predominately white jurisdiction, used peremptory challenges to shape a jury that matched the defendants racially.[3] More usually, in criminal cases, the state strikes people of color in order to prevent a jury from resembling the defendant. Consequently, minority defendants often must face all-white juries.

Driven by this negative image, the Supreme Court has, starting with *Batson* v. *Kentucky* in 1986, delivered six full-dress opinions dealing with the use of peremptory challenges.[4] The Court's immediate goal is to make it impossible for litigants to engineer all-white juries through the use of peremptory challenges. Ultimately, however, the Court has embarked on a mission to eliminate racial bias in the selection of jurors.

These cases are astonishing both in reach—potentially to every jury trial in every county, state, and federal courthouse—and in remedy— automatic reversal of criminal convictions and civil judgments. In the cases regulating the use of the peremptory challenge, the Court invoked the extreme remedy of reversal without any evidence that racial bias affects the decisions of juries.[5] The cases went back for new trials with new juries that would look better to the litigants, the people in the courtroom, and those watching from the outside.

The peremptory challenge cases provide a unique study of community and its representation on juries. So far the Supreme Court cases have considered only the strikes of minority men—mostly African Americans—and thus have focused on the image of exclusively white juries that first impelled them on this course. But some day soon, the Court must decide whether female gender (or perhaps either gender) can be a legitimate basis for removing individuals from the panel. The decision on gender will likely consummate the remarkable line of cases.

I will start by examining the uses of the peremptory challenge and then turn to the cases that have so heightened its actual and symbolic place in the ritual of jury selection. Here is my main point: although the *Batson* cases originated out of concern for the rights of the black accused, they have, from the beginning, also considered the harm inflicted on the excluded jurors. Protecting those people summoned to serve, once a secondary concern, has now moved to the center of the analysis.

In effect, the Court has reframed the image of the black accused before the white jury so that the striking of the individual juror is the critical moment. In light of this shift in emphasis, one must ask whether the strikes of women because of their gender should be prohibited, just as the strikes of blacks for their color were in *Batson*. Equal protection analysis, illuminated by feminist theory and women's legal history, points to an affirmative answer.

Opponents of this view contend that adding gender as a *Batson* category will make the peremptory impossible to administer. And some of its proponents agree, urging abolition of the peremptory, as a result. In the final section of this chapter, I briefly outline changes that would help preserve the peremptory while also making the whole process of jury selection more efficient and fair.

These conclusions are very similar to the ones drawn in another article I wrote long before *Batson* was decided. At the time I thought I was writing about voir dire and merely using the peremptory as a vehicle to argue that parties must be made equal in their abilities to learn about potential jurors (and thus enabled to exercise their peremptories). But the part of the article most frequently cited was my description of the uses of the peremptory. Now as I address that issue explicitly, I wonder at how things change and how they stay the same.[6]

Unspeakable Reasons and Unexplained Challenges

The jurors who stand and swear to "do justice in this cause" between the plaintiff and defendant, or between the state and the accused, have passed four possible elimination points. Originally summoned from lists that typically exclude, for example, the criminally convicted, the homeless, and the unregistered voter, each juror then had a chance to offer a personal excuse (a sick child, inventory-time in a small business) for not serving. Later, potential jurors were called to a courtroom set for trial and questioned by the judge or by counsel about their fitness to serve in the individual case. After this "voir dire" examination, the judge removed some among them for cause, and finally lawyers for each side struck others without giving a reason—peremptorily.

While the details of administration vary, this is the basic system for jury selection followed, or at least mandated, everywhere in the United States. We now understand, after many years of constitutional interpretation and statutory reform, that the goal of all these procedures is to achieve representative and impartial juries.[7] On the surface at least, the peremptory challenge seems ill-suited for this purpose.

The practical operation of the peremptory challenge is not always an uplifting sight. In hundreds of appellate cases—an index to thousands more that left no record—we see the peremptory used to remove people of color from juries. Many African Americans, for instance, who have made it to the jury lists and been summoned, and neither excused for a personal reason nor struck for cause, have, in the end, been rejected without ceremony, articulation, or outward regard for impartiality or fairness.[8] Worst were the cases in which the public prosecutor purposefully removed all members of the defendant's own race from the jury that would try him.

The constitutionality of this worse-case scenario was affirmed in 1965 by the Supreme Court. In *Swain* v. *Alabama*, the prosecutor struck all African Americans from a capital jury that tried a black man accused of raping a white woman.[9] Even though disapproving in theory a pattern of racially based challenges, the Court upheld the practice in the extreme situation before it. As translated in the courts below, *Swain* stood for acceptance, even endorsement, of open season on minority juror service. Prosecutors in many courts continued their regular, unabashed removal of people of color from juries, especially those that shared the same race as the accused.[10]

During the sixties I was a public defender in the District of Columbia, where the free-wheeling use of peremptories was common practice on both sides. I used my strikes to eliminate white men and middle-class black men, assuming that both groups would be unsympathetic to my usual client, a young African American man. The people my client and I wanted for his jury were African American women—any age would do. In trying to produce a white majority on the jury, the prosecutor often challenged the black women.

What chaos it seemed was present in those scenes: people making choices on the basis of intuition, stereotype, and prejudice. The fifty-year-old black janitor I struck from the jury that would have tried my twenty-year-old African American client for armed robbery might indeed have resented him. But he might also have seen himself or his son or the whole suffering race and felt the deepest empathy for the accused. Similarly, the prosecutors who dismissed African American women might have mistakenly deprived the People's jury of stern protectors of law and order.[11]

None of us doing the choosing in routine cases knew much about the people we rejected. The wealthy or well-connected litigants who could buy jury-investigation services and other experts to assist them in looking beneath the stereotypes knew more. But even they did not often have the kind of information necessary to reveal the individual behind the pigmentation and the gender.[12]

Many years later, after reflecting on these experiences, I wrote about jury selection from an academic viewpoint. I argued for expanding the pool of information available to everyone by enlarging and supplementing the voir dire procedures. Seeking to turn *Swain* into a silk purse, I argued that because the peremptory challenge had been elevated to near-Constitutional status, both parties needed more information to use it effectively. Citing William Blackstone, I explained that the peremptory allows the litigant to dismiss "those he fears or hates the most, so that he is left with 'a good opinion of the jury, the want of which might totally disconcert him.'"[13]

I noted other important functions of the peremptory as well, such as shielding the exercise of the challenge for cause. When voir dire questioning has alienated a juror without necessarily establishing a basis for removal, the litigant turns to the peremptory as insurance against bias. But the most cited argument in that old piece about the unique functions of the peremptory challenge was my attempt to deal directly with the effect of race on its exercise.

> Common human experience, common sense, psychosociological studies, and public opinions polls tell us that it is likely that certain classes of people statistically have predispositions that would make them inappropriate jurors for particular kinds of cases. But to allow this knowledge to be expressed in the evaluative terms necessary for challenges for cause would undercut our desire for a society in which all people are judged as individuals and in which each is held reasonable and open to compromise.[14]

My thesis was that it would be unseemly and unfair to openly express the idea, for example, that older African American men holding low-paying jobs would be prejudiced against my young black client who gave no signs of having worked hard, or at all. Or for the prosecutor to state the belief on which he acted: that African American women would not convict young men who might be their sons or brothers. Instead of speaking the searing words that identified this fear, each side might simply strike from the jury the object of his concern. I celebrated the evolution of the peremptory challenge as a method for dealing covertly with such assumptions, avoiding the ugliness and embarrassment that would arise from expressing them. "The peremptory, made without giving any reason, avoids trafficking in the core of truth in most common stereotypes . . . [It] allows the covert expression of what we dare not say but know is true more often than not."[15]

What I failed to recognize was that, even though no words were spoken, the same tides of racial passion swept through the courtroom when the peremptory challenges were exercised. Everyone could see what was happening—*voir* dire. Perhaps the silence harbored thoughts worse than those that might have been spoken. In the years after *Swain*, this possibility became more apparent, partly because of developments in the process of jury selection that were ostensibly unrelated to the common practice of race-based peremptories.

First, many more minorities were summoned for potential service. The civil rights movement ushered in the Federal Jury Selection Act of 1968.[16] Widely copied in the states, the new act sought to make juries more representative by increasing the diversity of the pools from which they were drawn. But people of color—and white women—arrived at the courthouse in new numbers only to be peremptorily ejected from particular courtrooms where their kind was on trial. "Why bother to call us down to these courts," wrote an African American man, who with all others of his race was peremptorily struck from a jury, "we could be on our jobs or in schools trying to help ourselves instead of in courthouse Halls being Made Fools of."[17] His experience was unusual only because he protested it to the chief prosecutor.

Other developments in jury trial administration heightened the unfairness of race-based peremptory challenges. The shape of the jury changed, scaled down to eight or even six in many places.[18] Most jurisdictions, when reducing juries, did not simultaneously cut the statutory number of peremptory challenges. Thus, though not deliberately intended, it became easier to remove *all* members of any racial minority from actual service.[19]

Another change that unexpectedly decreased minority participation on juries was the abandonment in many places of the requirement of jury unanimity.[20] Thus, even if one or two African Americans, for example, remained on a jury, they would not necessarily be taken seriously because the decision could be 6-2, or 5-1. The litigant could effectively have her all-white verdict without an all-white jury.

These and other trends brought the *Swain* issue back to the Supreme Court on a tide of unease that had been rising for twenty years. The case, *Batson* v. *Kentucky*, was not unusual. A prosecutor had used his challenges to remove the only four blacks from the venire in a routine criminal case. But this time the Court outlawed racially based peremptories by prosecutors in criminal cases.[21] Five years later it did the same for civil litigants on both sides of the case.[22] Last term in *McCollum* v. *Georgia* (1992), the Court applied its ruling to strikes by criminal defendants as well.[23]

In *McCollum*, as in the Rodney King case, white men were accused of assaulting African Americans.[24] In ruling that these criminal defendants must also give neutral, nonracial reasons for their strikes, the Court took another major step toward transforming jury selection. Now no one may lawfully remove jurors for racial reasons; nor may anyone hide his motives in a reverberating silence, but must, when called upon, give reasons that rise above prejudice and its surrogate: stereotype.

For a time at least, these procedures could result in further veiling (behind barely plausible pretexts) of race hatred.[25] Yet even this result, which I will argue need not follow, would be better than the open but unarticulated racism often practiced earlier. A central credo of contemporary culture is that the expression of thoughts and feelings ultimately helps to heal divisions. As Justice Anthony Kennedy, the chief architect of the new procedures, says, "The quiet rationality of the courtroom makes it an appropriate place to confront race-based fears or hostility by means other than the use of offensive stereotypes."[26]

Although the result in *McCollum* was certainly predictable, a strong argument existed for allowing defendants to continue their unfettered exercise of the peremptory challenge. A substantial body of scholarship supported the peculiar importance to the defendant of the peremptory challenge.[27] In its *McCollum* amicus brief, for example, the National Association of Criminal Defense Lawyers put the matter bluntly, "The defendant's interest . . . outweighs the concerns of the rejected juror or the community polarized along racial lines. The juror is not at risk of losing life or liberty, and will perceive the defendant's strike as the defensive gesture it is by one stripped to a position of almost total powerlessness."[28]

But in this whole case line, the Court has not balanced competing rights but blended them—in the name of national progress toward "multiracial democracy."[29] Thus, the African American defendant's right to a jury of his peers is blended with the juror's right not be excluded from juries; and over both of them, as well as over the community they share, the Court has thrown a mantle of equal protection. Whether women's rights (with attendant gender concerns) should now be included in the mix is the next question. The answer, in turn, depends on understanding how the rights of the accused became intermingled with those of the potential jurors and how the analysis shifted to equal protection of the laws.

The Democratic Jury

Having lived through the Civil War and the passage of the Fourteenth Amendment, the Supreme Court Justices saw the black defendant before the white jury and asked rhetorically: "How can it be maintained that compelling a colored man to submit" to a jury "from which the State has expressly excluded every man of his race . . . is not a denial to him of equal legal protection?"[30] More than one hundred years of equal protection later, the Court followed *Strauder* exactly in finding the picture still unacceptable, though this time the state had used its peremptory challenges, rather than a statute, to exclude every member of the defendant's own race from his jury.[31]

Following *Strauder* exactly meant, first, that the *Batson* Court said that the black defendant's equal protection was violated. It meant as well that the *Batson* majority was concerned with discrimination against the excluded juror. The Court cited with approval this famous passage from *Strauder*: "The very fact that colored people are singled out and expressly denied [the right to serve as jurors] is practically a brand upon them (affixed by law), an assertion of their inferiority, and a stimulant to that race prejudice which is an impediment to securing . . . equal justice."[32] Finally, both *Strauder* and *Batson* found that the harm from "selection procedures that purposefully exclude black persons from juries" affects the entire community, undermining "public confidence in the fairness of our system of justice."[33]

Though *Strauder* is a venerable and impressive case, the Court's central reliance on it in *Batson* was startling. The grant of certiorari had not mentioned equal protection nor had Batson's counsel urged any such ground. Both had referred instead to cases dealing with the defendant's right to a jury drawn from a fair cross section of the community: Sixth Amendment cases.[34]

This was the doctrine that, after it was applied to the states in 1968, became the chief vehicle for ensuring representative juries.[35] Especially in light of *Swain*'s approach to equal protection, criminal defendants who attacked race-based peremptories had come to rely almost exclusively on the Sixth Amendment or its state-constitutional analogs.[36] The leading cases under the Sixth Amendment invoked "the American concept of the jury trial [that] contemplates a jury drawn from a fair cross section of the community" and added that the exclusion of distinctive groups from jury service was "at war with our basic concepts of a democratic society and a representative government."[37] As the image of the all-white jury and the black accused rose once more before the Supreme Court in *Batson*, language like this would lend itself to a new effort to regulate the peremptory challenge.

But there were significant problems in applying the Sixth Amendment cases to the situation of the jury stripped of African Americans by the prosecutor's peremptory strikes. Most notably, the cases on fair cross section, with their language of representation, all dealt with the sum-moning of the entire venire, not with the jury of an individual defendant. In a multiracial society, which even includes multiracial individuals, it could be difficult to determine what exactly would constitute a representa-tive jury for a particular case.[38]

The timing of *Batson* was especially poor for applying the Sixth Amendment fair cross section requirement to the petit jury, moreover, because *Lockhart* v. *McCree* was under consideration at the same time. Petitioner McCree had argued that the process of removing those potential jurors doubtful about imposing the death penalty violated the requirements for a fair cross section. In that context, the Court would resoundingly reject extension of the requirement to actual trial juries as "unworkable and unsound."[39]

Doubtless for these and other reasons, the Court did not openly follow the obvious Sixth Amendment path.[40] Instead, it imported its concerns that the jury be representative of the community into the allusive and diffused equal protection doctrine taken from *Strauder*.[41] The crucial passage in *Batson* explained:

> Racial discrimination in selection of jurors harms not only the accused whose life and liberty they are summoned to try. Competence to serve as a juror ultimately depends on an assessment of individual qualifications and ability impartially to consider evidence presented at trial. See *Thiel* v. *Southern Pacific Co.*, 328 U.S. 217, 223-224 (1946). A person's race simply "is unrelated to his fitness as a juror."[42]

The next sentence is one of the many references to the mother case of this opinion: "As long ago as *Strauder* . . . the Court recognized that by denying a person participation in jury service on account of his race, the State unconstitutionally discriminated against the excluded juror."[43]

But the *Thiel* citation is the handwriting on the wall of the *Batson* opinion.[44]

Translated, it revealed that concern for the jury as an institution had become the centerpiece of the analysis, which, in peremptory challenge cases, means that the rights of excluded jurors rather than those of litigants are paramount. One has only to study *Thiel* briefly to understand how it signals the Court's switch from defendant to juror as the object of its concern for equal protection purposes.

Out of his "normal mind," Thiel threw himself from the window of a moving train. He sued the railroad and lost before a jury chosen largely from a group of "business men and their wives."[45] On appeal, he argued that there should have been more daily wage earners in the pool, though he did not urge that members of this class were more likely to respond to his claim. Indeed, five apparently unsympathetic daily wage earners had been among the jurors who decided against him.[46]

Yet the Court reversed the judgment in the exercise of its supervisory power in order to reassert "high standards of jury selection."[47] Decided the year after the Second World War ended, *Thiel* rings with affirmations of the jury as fundamental to a democratic society. Selection procedures should draw "every stratum of society" into jury service and treat "jury competence . . . [as] an individual rather than a group or class matter."[48] It finds essential to the jury's (somewhat mysterious) functioning that it be inclusive of all elements of the community. When some identifiable group has been excluded, reversal, according to *Thiel*, is the only remedy that will "guard against the subtle undermining of the jury system."[49]

In the same year as *Thiel*, 1946, the Court decided a similar case, *Ballard* v. *United States*, this one involving male criminal defendants who objected to the lack of women in the jury pool.[50] Again the Court acted under its supervisory power to reverse the conviction because the exclusion of women "deprives the jury system of the broad base it was designed . . . to have in our democratic society."[51] *Ballard* was the second major case the Court cited in *Batson* for its blending of defendant's rights with those of the excluded juror.[52]

What should we make of the centrality of these two old cases—*Thiel* and *Ballard*—in the new peremptory challenge case line that started with *Batson*? A great deal, I suggest. In a strictly doctrinal sense, they are the cases that join the Sixth Amendment concerns for a fair cross section with *Batson*'s analysis of equal protection for excluded jurors. The major Sixth Amendment opinions cite and use these cases in exactly the same way that *Batson* does.

First, as we have already seen, the focus is on the jury as an institution and on the experience of those summoned to serve. Second, *Thiel* and *Ballard* are about the interest of the whole community in diverse juries. Finally, the old supervisory cases found that the remedy for exclusion was reversal of the judgment and the impanelment of a new jury for the cause. These three propositions (and their logical corollaries) are at the core of the equal protection mission the Court took up in *Batson*: to reclaim the jurybox as the microcosm of representative democracy.[53]

The first case after *Batson* allowed a white defendant "to object to the discriminatory use of peremptory challenges" against blacks, thus separating concern about the all-white jury from the image of the black accused.[54] *Powers*, though a criminal case, harks back to *Thiel*, where a salaried employee raised the rights of daily wage earners, and to *Ballard*, where men objected to the lack of women in the venire. The next case in the peremptory challenge line, *Edmonson v. Leesville Concrete Co.*, dealt directly with civil practice.[55] Thaddeus Edmonson was an African American construction worker suing for injury on his job. Lawyers for the defendant concrete company struck all members of his race from the jury. Finding explicitly that removal of African Americans on the basis of race would violate *their* equal protection rights, the Court reversed the judgment. To reach this result, it not only held that Edmonson could raise the rights of the excluded jurors (not such a stretch after *Powers*) but also that the lawyers for the concrete company must be statesmen in the exercise of their peremptory challenges; they could not strike jurors with only their client's narrow interest in mind. Engaging in jury selection transformed these insurance defense lawyers into representatives of the state, exercising its power, and thus charged them with the duty not to discriminate.[56]

Edmonson explicitly rejected the main argument offered initially against the *Batson* line of cases that its extension would impair the peremptory challenge, whose ancient role is to promote the litigant's acceptance of the jury as his own. "If race stereotypes are the price for acceptance of a jury panel as fair, the price is too high," said the *Edmonson* Court. On the road to "progress as a multiracial democracy," they added, we "must recognize that the automatic invocation of race stereotypes retards that progress and causes continued hurt and injury."[57] In the interest, then, of the jury's appearance, other systemic concerns are rendered strictly secondary: in *Edmonson*, preservation of the peremptory challenge; in the next case, *McCollum*, the peculiar needs of the criminally accused in relation to the jury.[58]

Swept aside as well in the *Batson* line are the usually cherished goals of repose and finality of judgments. Reversal for a new trial with a new jury is the remedy for the improper exercise of peremptory challenges. In *Thiel* and *Ballard*, decided under the supervisory power of the Supreme Court and in the Sixth Amendment cases, *Taylor*, for example, this was the remedy. But again, these cases do not deal with the selection of a particular petit jury. For this situation, we might have expected that the Court would require some showing of prejudice before ordering reversal.

For comparison, consider the application of equal protection doctrine to cases on voting rights. If African Americans, for instance, are wrongfully excluded from the polls, the Court does not call off the election and set a new one.[59] Yet this in effect is what happened in the *Batson* cases when the judgments were reversed. Reversal does attract attention and sharpen efforts for compliance. And courtrooms are unlike the polls in terms of the Court's control over them and special interest in making them fair places. Arguably, without the remedy of reversal, the Court's words about race-based peremptories might be dismissed as merely idealistic or hortatory.

Yet this Court has required a showing of prejudice before reversal in many other constitutional contexts.[60] And in interpreting the *Batson* line for purposes of habeas corpus, the Court has held that racial bias in the exercise of the peremptory challenge does not automatically affect the jury's truth-finding function.[61] Thus, it is odd that the Court does not demand proof of harm to the decisionmaking of the jury before reversing judgments on the direct appeal of *Batson* cases.

The remedy of reversal, taken over wholesale from the other lines of jury selection cases, is one key to the meaning and thus the outer boundaries of the *Batson* doctrine. What the Court holds when it reverses is that something is terribly amiss with the process itself, something so serious that the result cannot stand. Reversals are an acknowledgement of an unarticulable evil, an unprovable loss. Only reversal, said the *Thiel* court, over Justice Felix Frankfurter's dissent, will prevent the "subtle undermining of the jury system," in ways not subject to measurement.[62]

The idea that we cannot measure the effects of exclusion on the jury's functioning was most famously expressed by Justice Thurgood Marshall in *Peters* v. *Kiff*. "When any large and identifiable segment of the community is excluded from jury service, the effect is to remove from the jury room qualities of human nature and varieties of human experience, the range of which is unknown and perhaps unknowable."[63] Note again that he spoke in a case in which a white man contested the exclusion of blacks from his jury. He added, "It is not necessary to assume that the excluded group will consistently vote as a class in order to conclude, as we do, that its exclusion deprives the jury of a perspective on human events that may have unsuspected importance in any case that may be presented."[64]

Similar views about the damage to decisionmaking caused by removal of certain jurors appear most notably in two other cases: *Ballard* v. *United States* and *Taylor* v. *Louisiana*, both involved the exclusion of women from jury service.[65]

Women And Juries

At the trial of black political activist, Angela Davis, only one black woman was in the venire. Her removal was later described by a juror who served in the case: "When [the prosecutor] announced, 'The People will excuse and thank Juror Number 9, Mrs. Hemphill,' [there were] murmurs . . . and hisses. . . . We all knew she was going to be excused. She knew it. We were all embarrassed and saddened that Mrs. Janie Hemphill had to suffer another insult."[66]

Many women have responded to the court's summons, as Mrs. Hemphill did, only, like her, to be rejected upon arrival at the entrance to the jury box. The ones I felt for most when I was a defender were the sweet-faced white ladies with their walking shoes and hardcover books. Defense lawyers in the District of Columbia struck them first. Sometimes I would convince my client that we should keep one of these women simply because "she will love me." But usually, the African American men I represented preferred their own mothers to mine on the jury that would determine their liberty. These, the prosecutor struck.

I am certain that the women who spent their jury duty being struck from criminal cases, and from big money civil cases too, suffered injury much like that of the black men who are most often the subject of the *Batson* line of cases. The Court has identified such injury as "a profound personal humiliation heightened by its public character," and held that citizens must not be called to serve and then abused in this way.[67]

By shifting its equal protection concern largely to the effect of the peremptory on the stricken juror, the Court necessarily rendered gender-based challenges against women illegal.[68] In this section, I will show why the long, sad history of discrimination against women in the courtroom and on juries makes any other result insupportable.[69] We can see this most vividly in the situation of African American women.

In fact, the difference in the standard of equal protection for racial and for gender difference was born out of disregard for black women. When the Fourteenth Amendment conferred citizenship on the former slaves, only men attained the (all too formal) right to vote and to serve on juries—in any functional sense, only men became African *Americans*. The great post-Civil War movement for legal equality omitted half the black population. *Strauder*, the case on which *Batson* is modeled, found abhorrent the picture of a black man on trial before a jury from which members of his own race had been excluded. But this great case explicitly said those black jury members need not be women.[70] Discrimination against women, even those who were former slaves, did not violate equal protection.

Historical incongruity is heightened when a modern litigant strikes an African American woman and justifies the rejection in terms of gender. In one case, a black man was on trial for murder, and the prosecutor explained a challenge by saying, "It's been my experience women are not good jurors in capital cases. They feel more sympathetic than men. They go in there and feel like a mother."[71] Perhaps in this case the prosecutor was striking all women to reach his stereotypical ideal for a capital jury—white males. Yet these words, spoken in response to a *Batson* challenge, also make gender a proxy for race.

The use of gender as a pretext may explain why most of the cases arguing for the extension of *Batson* deal with strikes of minority women.[72] Not only may gender be used as a cover for race prejudice, but in the case of minority women, allowing gender strikes subjects them to the most virulent double discrimination: that based on a synergistic combination of race and sex.[73] Noting that minority women have been "largely invisible in the debate about the use of the peremptory challenge," Shirley Sagawa wrote that they "will be the first to be excluded from the jury if *Batson* does not cover gender. We can well surmise the message this will communicate; that Black women are the most prejudiced of jury members, the least qualified to serve."[74]

Eliminating woman-based peremptories is the only way to enforce the purposes of *Batson* and to offer, finally, some measure of equal protection to minority women. Perhaps, though, the Court might distinguish between white women and those of color when it requires that peremptory challenges be justified.[75] This result would deny history and demean the equal protection principles on which jury selection jurisprudence now stands.

White women abolitionists like Susan Anthony, Lucy Stone, the Grimke sisters, and many others sought freedom for all black slaves and equal rights for themselves at the same time. It was not until after the Civil War that the causes of former slave men and white women were divorced from each other. How this happened is a complicated piece of history, with conflicting accounts of who was a fault in splitting the coalition. It is clear that the early woman suffrage movement itself broke apart over the refusal of Anthony and Elizabeth Cady Stanton to support the Fourteenth Amendment because it restricted the word "citizen" with the word "male" for the first time in the Constitution.[76]

The former female slaves did not figure into the rhetoric of the Republicans and reformers who turned the white women away from the phrase, "It is the Negro's hour." To which Elizabeth Cady Stanton angrily responded, "May I ask . . . just one question based on the apparent opposition in which you place the Negro and woman. My question is, Do you believe the African race is composed entirely of males?"[77] Sojourner Truth, virtually the only black woman's voice from this early period said, "There is a great stir about colored men getting their rights, but not a word about the colored women and if colored men get their rights, and not colored women theirs, you see the colored men will be masters over the women, and it will be just as bad as it was before."[78]

The woman suffrage movement was born in the dawn of the realization that unless they were forced into it, neither politicians nor statesmen would ever go beyond the enfranchisement of black men. It took fifty-two years, roughly fifty national campaigns, and almost one thousand state campaigns, the whole adult life of many earnest women, to win the vote. From the beginning, their struggle was also about the right to serve on juries. The two causes were the twin indicia of full citizenship both in the minds of woman suffragists and in the attitudes of American society.[79]

The force of this history has borne in on me lately as I have studied the seemingly endless petitions and debates, conventions and marches, bill-drafting and lobbying, that consumed the times of Clara Shortridge Foltz, a pioneer suffragist and the first woman lawyer on the Pacific Coast. Using one important year of her life for illustration—the year before *Strauder*, I want to show first that the arguments against women in public life was fused. Whether it was the vote, jury service, or entry to the professions that women sought, they met the same contentions about their rightful roles, and they found each rejection rooted in "an assertion of their inferiority."[80]

In the years 1878 and 1879, Foltz with other suffragists, including notably Laura Gordon, the second woman lawyer in California, pursued rights for themselves and other women in every conceivable public forum. They started in the legislature where they lobbied for woman suffrage and the amendment of the California code section that limited the legal profession to white men.

They met the constant refrain that voting, its attendant right to serve on juries, and being a lawyer, would "unsex" women–a charge as dire then as it would be today. Its force appears in the following verse from a popular magazine, printed at the moment Foltz and Gordon were campaigning for access to the ballot and to the jury box:

Shame unto womanhood! The common scold
Stands railing foul-mouthed in the public street;
And in the mart and 'fore the justice seat
Her shallow tale of fancied wrongs is told.
No woman these such as our hearts enfold,
Mothers and wives are cast not in this mold.[81]

The apparent fear was that public woman would no longer have time for the domestic rounds that were her higher and finer calling. Time spent "fore the justice seat" would, moreover, be a pollutant for women who were supposed to inhabit an ideal world of nurturance and tender feeling. By the very nature of their personalities and training, women were unfitted for "all the nastiness of the world which finds its way into courts of justice, all the unclean issues . . . sodomy, incest, rape, seduction, fornication, adultery . . . libel and slander of sex, impotence, divorce" and many more "among the nameless catalogue of indecencies." This quotation is from an opinion read in its entirety by Clara Foltz's opponent who argued in 1879 that though she had been admitted to practice law, she should not be allowed to study it at California's newly established Hastings College of the Law. The opinion was from a Wisconsin judge denying Lavinia Goodell the right to practice law and holding, "Reverence for all womanhood would suffer in the public spectacle of women so engaged."[82]

Woman defiled was a common rhetorical trope used against all forms of equal rights, and jury service was its prime example. For instance, when Clara Foltz, Laura Gordon, and the other suffragists lobbied the California constitutional convention of 1879 to include woman suffrage, the chief opponent, assuming the vote would bring with it jury service, argued that women would lose their purity by hearing all the terrible evidence in court and then being sequestered with male strangers to decide the case. This idea of women relating to men as fellow jurors was seen as singularly lewd. In exasperation, one of the women's supporters finally made the relevant comparison to crude racist arguments: he said that when the great abolitionists Gerritt Smith and Wendell Phillips spoke, "There were . . . these old whited sepulchers, asking us: 'Do you want your daughter to marry a nigger?' . . . Now these same fossilized ideas are presented to an intelligent audience. 'Do you want your daughter locked up in a jury room?' . . . Ha ha."[83]

The third standard argument by opponents was that women would skew the process. They would vote only for handsome men, whether at elections or on juries. Women lawyers, through their seductive wiles, would cause juries to acquit the guilty and reward the undeserving.[84] Whether as lawyers or as jurors, women would not be able to sustain the mental labor and intensity of the work and would constantly fall ill, thus causing mistrials and other inefficiencies in the system.[85]

Although the arguments against women in public life were joined, winning the vote and right to practice law did not automatically carry with it access to jury service in every state.[86] Women who had counted on the vote to solve the major problems of discrimination now waged a separate battle for equal jury representation. In this renewed struggle, women lawyers were in the forefront speaking, writing, lobbying, petitioning, and briefing cases.[87]

Like the suffrage crusades, the campaign for jury service was arduous and long. The law reports of many states, and federal courts as well, reflect the second wave of women's quest for political equality.[88] Perhaps the best known state case is the old law school chestnut that held, even after women were enfranchised, that the word "voter" in a jury eligibility statute referred solely to males.[89] In the Supreme Court, *Hoyt* v. *Florida* held, in 1961, that a state could, without violating equal protection of the laws, automatically exclude women from jury service unless they voluntarily registered.[90] It was not enough for Gwendolyn Hoyt to show that of 46,000 registered women voters in the county, only 220 had volunteered (over a period of many years) as jurors. Nor was the Court appalled by the sight of a woman on trial before an all-male jury. Instead of resonating with equal protection concerns (like *Strauder*) the opinion invoked the standard stereotype of "woman as the center of home and family life" and found it reasonable that the state's interest in enabling her presence there superseded all others.[91]

But *Hoyt* is, in some sense, an outlier among Supreme Court cases treating gender and jury service. Many of the Court's most far-reaching jury cases deal with women, including those that rendered *Hoyt* obsolete by requiring that there be a fair cross section of the community in jury pools.[92] Moreover, in holding that the "systematic and intentional exclusion of women, like the exclusion of a racial group," violated a federal statute whose purpose was to make juries representative, the Court wrote words whose ring has yet to be fully realized: "The truth is that the two sexes are not fungible . . . the subtle interplay of influence one on the other is among the imponderables. . . [a] flavor, a distinct quality is lost if either sex is excluded."[93]

To recapitulate the history—women sought jury service as one facet of a greater struggle for recognition in the public life of the community. Arguments that it would be unseemly, inappropriate, and harmful for women to be jurors were joined with the contentions that they were incompetent to vote or practice law. In the end, recognition as jurors proved hardest to achieve because special legislative exemptions (like that in *Hoyt*) made it unlikely that women would actually serve even when they had the right. Now that these kinds of exemptions have largely disappeared, the remaining point at which women may effectively be excluded from jury service is in the exercise of the peremptory challenge.

The denouement of the whole jury selection story came down to the peremptory challenge for African Americans too, resulting in the *Batson* line of cases. Because the story of women's exclusion from jury service is not only analogous to the history of racial exclusion—it is the *same* story growing out of the same historical period and events—the conclusion must also be the same. What the Supreme Court said of the African Americans who were peremptorily struck in *Edmonson* is equally true of women: they should not now be "required by summons to be put at risk of open and public discrimination as a condition of their participation in the justice system."[94]

Opponents of the extension of *Batson* will argue that the implications of woman-based strikes are different from racial peremptories. There is less humiliation and stigma, they will say, when gender rather than race is the reason for the peremptory challenge. Yet to those watching in the courtroom, at the counsel tables, in the newspaper and appellate record, the strike of a woman for no apparent reason other than her gender carries a message far different than the strike, say, of a lawyer from the jury, even (or especially) a woman lawyer. The message is one that comes from the long history of sex discrimination in this country and is based strongly "in archaic and overbroad generalizations."[95]

The unexplained strike of a woman says that she does not belong on the jury—that she could not be impartial or that she is incompetent. The crude stereotypical message is summed in the trial manuals and jury selection tracts that typically include such advice as "women are more suspicious of other women, especially as plaintiffs in civil cases or defendants in criminal cases" and "women are more likely than men to be influenced by the physical attractiveness and personality traits of witnesses."[96] Striking individual women on the assumption they hold such views because of their sex is "practically a brand upon them, affixed by the law, an assertion of their inferiority"—to return to the words of Strauder.[97]

Again, opponents will declare that all peremptory challenges are the acting out of stereotypes, the expression of intuitive class biases. When a postman or Presbyterian is struck, unpleasant stereotypes are also at work—so goes the refrain.[98] But in the case of the postman or the Presbyterian, the same ancient stereotypes about their competence and predispositions have not been used to prevent them from voting or being summoned for juries, pursuing their chosen professions and vocations, and otherwise participating in public life and discourse.

Though women are now becoming lawyers in unparalleled numbers, voting, and holding office, sex discrimination still exists and the courtroom, in particular, remains in many places a white male arena. Gender bias task forces in more than half the states have documented the unequal, and comparatively bad, treatment of women attorneys, witnesses, and parties in the courtroom.[99] The open and unjustified striking of women from juries only adds to the chill. Not surprisingly, women lawyers are once again in the forefront of the final phase of the movement to win equal access to jury service.[100]

Preserving the Peremptory

The Supreme Court leaves the translation of large edicts like those in the Batson line to the offices and officers of the courts below. Some critics would find the peremptory challenge too much like the offending right hand, and heeding the biblical injunction, simply cut it off.[101] Others would forbid the use of the peremptory challenge on the basis of race alone.[102] Still others, with whom I agree, would use the occasion to rework and revitalize jury selection so that it better suits all its purposes, one of which is to help ensure the acceptance of verdicts.[103]

Critics and dissenters have warned (or perhaps threatened) that, whatever the intent, the *Batson* line will make the peremptory challenge so difficult to administer that its abolition must quickly follow.[104] To forbid gender-based strikes would simply be the last straw under this view. Somewhat paradoxically, though, the *Batson* dissenters have in the course of their argument, elevated the peremptory from an ordinary (if old) procedural device to near Constitutional status. In *Holland*, for instance, the majority wrote that "the tradition of peremptory challenges . . . was already venerable at the time of Blackstone, was reflected in a federal statute enacted by the same Congress that proposed the Bill of Rights, was recognized in an opinion by Justice Story to be part of the common law of the United States, and has endured through two centuries in all the States."[105] Repeatedly, the Supreme Court and lower courts have praised the peremptory challenge as well designed to ensure that juries are impartial and that they seem so to the litigants and to society. Thus, any effort to abolish peremptories would rouse due process objections, as well as Sixth or Seventh Amendment claims about the nature of the jury that is guaranteed.

Aside from the difficulty of doing it, elimination of the peremptory challenge is a bad idea. It would focus jury selection entirely on the challenge for cause. Thus, the judge alone—in a series of highly discretionary, practically unreviewable decisions—would then shape the jury in every case. But under the Constitution, jury trial is guaranteed because our tradition is not to trust judges acting alone.[106] In particular, the jury is meant to offset the class bias and elitism of the judiciary, yet we can hardly expect judges to find "cause"—that is, incipient bias—in jurors who are like themselves in background or outlook.

Not only would the increased importance of the cause challenge heighten the judge's power, but abolition of the peremptory would make it more difficult for the litigant to lay the groundwork for a cause challenge. Vigorous questioning may antagonize and hence prejudice a potential juror. The peremptory challenge is the insurance that makes genuine inquiry into juror bias possible.[107]

Most important, the peremptory gives the litigant a role in the process and so promotes in Blackstone's words "a good opinion of the jury the want of which might totally disconcert him."[108] Although the Supreme

Court disallows race as a reason for striking jurors, and should also forbid female gender as a rationale, it does not follow that litigants must relinquish all sense of choice over their shared juries.

The peremptory is important enough that instead of gearing up legislatures to abolish it, we should seize the occasion of the Supreme Court's intervention to enact modern jury selection statutes—statutes that will aid our "progress toward a multiracial democracy."[109] This essay concludes by outlining some of the elements a statute might include, but many of the suggestions could as well be implemented by trial judges or by appellate courts through their supervisory powers.[110]

A comprehensive statute would start by broadening the juror pool beyond voter registration lists to include licensed drivers, utility users, and the city directory.[111] Jurors to be summoned should each receive, as they often do now, a questionnaire covering items relevant to their basic fitness to serve. (This initial questionnaire can go on the back of the summons to jury service.)

The statute would forbid racial and gender discrimination in the exercise of peremptory challenges. It would also reduce peremptories where they are excessive in relation to jury size in the jurisdiction.[112] In light of the history of the peremptory challenge and of the greater significance of the jury verdict to the criminally accused, legislation might award more challenges to the defense.

The voir dire process can be changed to facilitate the exercise of peremptory challenges on a basis other than race or gender. Juror questionnaires can be supplemented by questions designed case-by-case to probe the attitudes of potential jurors toward sensitive issues that are likely to arise.[113]

Such tailored questionnaires can help the parties base their arguments for cause challenges and their exercise of peremptories on suspected race prejudice rather than on the color of the potential juror's skin. And though they cannot substitute for some public procedures—to see and to hear is, after all, the point of voir dire—the questionnaires can provide grounds for open inquiry that neither humiliates the potential juror nor rouses the ire of the others in the venire.[114]

In order to explore prejudiced attitudes more effectively and efficiently, the parties might give their opening statements to the whole venire and then inquire afterward for both cause and peremptory challenges. Potential jurors would then understand how and where their answers fit into the theory of the case and the evidence that will be presented.[115] Once procedures are in place that allow parties to act on intimations of actual bias, rather than on the crude proxy of race or gender, then the requirement for making a prima facie case by letting one or two strikes pass before objecting would no longer be necessary.[116]

Expanding the information available from voir dire responds to the concerns of those who fear that modifying the peremptory challenge will destroy the mystique—or science—of jury selection. Automatic strikes of white women and people of color are not only unnecessary to the art but detract from it. When that legendary jury lawyer Clarence Darrow spoke in a much-cited passage of "the knowledge of life, human nature, psychology and the reactions of the human emotions" that a lawyer must bring to jury selection, he was looking at juries that contained no racial minorities and few white women.[117] Rather, in shaping the jury he examined "nationality, business, religion, politics, social standing, family ties, friends, habits of life and thought; the books and newspapers he likes and reads and many more matters that combine to make a man."[118] These qualities will still count in exercising challenges after the *Batson* line of cases is complete.

Litigants should be able to point to attitudes that, when held by an individual, would make for bias in a particular case, and to devise procedures for uncovering them. Recently, for instance, professional football players sued to terminate a contractual system in which they allegedly could not market their services freely.[119] They submitted affidavits from sports psychologists about the biases of "highly identified sports fans" and sought a tailored questionnaire, individual voir dire, and extra peremptory challenges in order to identify and eliminate such fans.[120] Special procedures for exploring attitudes and experience might also be appropriate to sexual harassment cases, for another example, rather than the present crude system in which one side strikes women and the other, men.[121]

Finally, the actual routine of exercising challenges can be revised to ease the stigma of rejection. One attractive suggestion is a form of "affirmative selection," in which, after voir dire and cause strikes, each party designates, in preferential order, those venire persons who should sit on the jury.[122] Jurors who appear on both lists are seated, and then alternating between lists until the number of peremptories is reached for each side, the court will either seat or strike a juror who appears on only one list. If the juror is a white woman or a person of color, a neutral explanation would be required. At the least, courts should ensure, as many already do, that the explanations for strikes are offered out of the potential juror's presence.

The *Batson* line of cases establishes three kinds of challenges: cause, peremptory, and modified peremptory, that is, those for which some explanation is required.[123] In many jurisdictions, practices regulating and enabling a modified peremptory are already in effect and can serve as models for statutory, as well as discretionary, procedural change.[124] Although its administration takes time at jury selection and still generates new issues for appeal, *Batson* has not, by any account, created the chaos some critics suggested it would. And less than a decade has passed since the case was decided—not very long in legal history. There is, finally, much we can do procedurally to ease the burden of making jury selection actually and symbolically representative of our best collective selves.

Conclusion

I have been subject to warring impulses in writing this piece. At heart, I will always be a criminal defense lawyer—one of that peculiar breed who look to the jury for their clients' salvation and their own. Thus though it has been twenty years since I tried a case, I cannot view with academic detachment the picture of a jury that includes somebody the defendant hates or fears—even for irrational, or unpopular, reasons. That picture could materialize were the peremptory abolished.

However, as I study American women's history through the experiences of a singular lawyer, I see how prejudice cripples lives and extinguishes hopes. When Clara Foltz, who could not vote or serve on juries, appeared in court, she often had to defend herself before she could reach her client's cause. The accusation was always, in one form or another, simply that she was a woman. Through Foltz's struggles, I have learned that acceptance of the phrase "She is a woman" as explanation for any exclusion denies equal protection of the laws. That sort of unfair discrimination, exacerbated when women of color are rejected, occurs now and will continue if women may be peremptorily removed for their gender alone.

In attempting to reconcile these oppositions, I suggest that jury selection procedures be expanded and elevated to preserve the peremptory challenge while eliminating its excesses. This is a conclusion that reconciles competing claims, widens the context, embraces what is, and rejects only rigid dichotomies: thus it is feminist in method as well as in effect.

Notes

1. *Strauder* v. *West Virginia*, 100 U.S. 303, 309 (1880).
2. There were ten whites (five women and five men), one Latino, and one Asian American woman on the jury. See generally David Margolick, "As Venues Are Changed, Many Ask How Important a Role Race Should Play," *New York Times*, May 23, 1992, p. 7; Erwin Chemerinsky, "How Could the King Jury Do That?" *Legal Times*, May 11, 1992, p. 18 (instead of having a racially mixed jury pool with a sense of the city's police problems, the jury pool was virtually all white and dominated by a conservative law-and-order mentality); Marcia Chambers and Sua Sponte, "It Is Always Difficult to Convict a Cop, Especially in the Suburbs," *National Law Journal*, May 18, 1992, p. 13 (no doubt that moving the case from ethnically diverse Los Angeles to Simi Valley had a dramatic impact on outcome); Timothy P. O'Neill, "Wrong Place, Wrong Jury," *New York Times*, May 9, 1992, p. 23; Joseph Kelner and Robert S. Kelner, "The Rodney King Verdict and Voir Dire," *New York Law Journal*, May 26, 1992, p. 3 (the "ethnic, philosophical and social predilections for Ventura County's residents predictably provided jurors with a penchant for finding reasonable doubt of guilt despite the police brutality"); Barry Scheck, "Following Orders," *New Republic*, May 25, 1992, pp. 17–19 (the result "surely would have been different if there were blacks on the jury, or the jurors were less homogeneous"). But compare Roger Parloff, "Maybe the Jury Was Right?" *American Lawyer*, vol. 14 (June 1992), p. 7, suggesting that a jury that represented a more accurate cross section of the community would, in the end, likely have come to the same legal conclusions as the Simi Valley jury. Parloff admits, however, with hindsight, that an acquittal in a case like this tried before a jury with no blacks could "never command public confidence." Ibid., p. 80.
3. The numbers of African Americans in the pool of potential jurors had been drastically reduced before the challenge stage by the change of venue from Los Angeles to Ventura county. *Powell* v. *Superior Court*, 283 Cal. Rptr. 777, 780 (2d Dist. 1991) (reversing the trial court's refusal to change venue for pre-trial publicity, emphasizing the "political turmoil and controversy" surrounding the case). No other change of venue had been granted in Los Angeles county since 1973 because of the diverse pool of 3.5 million jurors on which the county draws. Sheryl Stolberg, "Judge Offers to Move Trial of 4 Officers," *Los Angles Times*, June 19, 1991, p. A1.
  Ventura county has 2 percent African Americans in its population, and that same percentage was among the 264 prospective jurors in the case. A number of blacks were struck for cause after acknowledging bias against the defendants. Three were struck peremptorily.
  Legislative responses to the verdict followed in several states, including California, New York, New Jersey, and Florida, altering venue statutes to require judges considering change to take into account the similarity of the transferee district in its racial, gender, and economic composition.
4. *Batson* v. *Kentucky*, 476 U.S. 79 (1986) (black defendant may challenge prosecutor's use of peremptory challenges against racial minorities); *Powers* v. *Ohio*, 111 S. Ct. 1364 (1991) (white defendant has standing to object to prosecutor's strike of racial minorities); *Edmonson* v. *Leesville Concrete Co.*, 111 S. Ct. 2077 (1991) (prohibiting private civil litigants from exercising peremptory challenges to exclude jurors solely on the basis of race); *McCollum* v. *Georgia*, 112 S. Ct. 2348 (1992) (prohibiting criminal defense counsel from exercising race-based peremptory challenges); *Holland* v. *Illinois*, 493 U.S. 474 (1990) (white defendant may not base claim that prosecutor struck blacks on Sixth Amendment); *Hernandez* v. *New York*, 111 S. Ct. 1859 (1991) (explanations for peremptory challenges

to Hispanics were sufficiently neutral, that is, free from racial bias; trial court's determination should be reviewed under the deferential abuse of discretion standard).

5. The Court has come very close to holding explicitly that mistakes in a jury's composition do not undermine the accuracy of its findings (and thus the conviction). *Allen* v. *Hardy*, 478 U.S. 255 (1986). In finding *Batson* not retroactive, the Court stated that the opinion has no "fundamental impact on the integrity of factfinding." Ibid., p. 259. *Teague* v. *Lane*, 489 U.S. 288, 315 (1989).

See the text accompanying note 62 for an explanation of why the use of race-based peremptory challenges is considered reversible error. Compare the use of the remedy of reversal in the misused peremptory challenge cases, based on equal protection and on ideals of jury representation, with the refusal to reverse when a party's loss of his peremptory challenge was at issue. See, for example, *Ross* v. *Oklahoma*, 487 U.S. 81 (1988) (no denial of due process when capital defendant was forced to use one of his nine peremptories to cure the erroneous refusal by the court to excuse a juror for cause); see also *McDonough Power Equipment, Inc.* v. *Greenwood*, 464 U.S. 548 (1984) (no reversal in case where counsel would have stricken juror if questionnaire responses had been accurate without a corresponding showing that a correct response would have supported a valid challenge for cause). Compare also *Ham* v. *South Carolina*, 409 U.S. 524 (1973) (ordering reversal for failure to inquire into racial bias on voir dire where there were special circumstances threatening the fundamental fairness of the trial); but see *Ristaino* v. *Ross*, 424 U.S. 589 (1976) (confining *Ham* to its facts and finding no constitutional error where the trial judge questioned veniremen about general bias and prejudice but refused to question them specifically about racial prejudice).

6. Barbara Allen Babcock, "Voir Dire: Preserving 'Its Wonderful Power'" *Stanford Law Review*, vol. 27 (February 1975), pp. 545–65. I think often of Jay Spears, my brilliant research assistant on that piece and how he would have engaged the turn things have taken. Jay died of AIDS in 1986.

7. See Valerie P. Hans and Neil Vidmar, *Judging the Jury* (Plenum Press, 1986), pp. 47–61, for an excellent description of the American ideal of jury representativeness and the tendency to blame unsatisfactory verdicts on the composition of the jury.

The Supreme Court has relied on the presumption that the composition of the jury critically influences the outcome of a case in its case line establishing the right to a jury drawn from a fair cross section of the community. Derived from the Sixth Amendment guarantee of an impartial jury, the "fair cross section" cases deal with the constitutional understanding of how impartial juries are assembled. A representative jury is one drawn from a pool in which no distinctive community group is underrepresented owing to systematic discrimination in the selection process. *Duren* v. *Missouri*, 439 U.S. 357, 364 (1979).

However, the notion of representativeness has never included a Sixth Amendment restriction on the use of peremptory challenges. In *Lockhart* v. *McCree*, the Court expressly declined to invoke the principle of a fair cross section to "invalidate the use of either for-cause or peremptory challenges to prospective jurors, or to require petit juries, as opposed to jury panels or venires, to reflect the composition of the community at large." 476 U.S. 162, 173 (1986).

For a case presenting differing views on what the requirement for a fair cross section entails, see *Holland* v. *Illinois*, 493 U.S. 474, 480 (1990). The majority in *Holland* asserts that the defendant cannot challenge the prosecutor's discriminatory use of peremptory challenges under the Sixth Amendment because the requirement for a fair cross section does not apply to petit juries. Rather, the Sixth Amendment requirement of a fair cross section on the venire "is a means of assuring, not a *representative* jury (which the Constitution does not demand), but an *impartial* one (which it does)." Based on this belief, the majority concludes that the traditional understanding of the fair cross section requirement has "never included the notion . . . that initial representativeness cannot be diminished by allowing both the accused and the State to eliminate persons thought to be inclined against their interests." Compare Justice Stevens's view in dissent, that, although the petit jury is not subject to a guarantee of representativeness, the exercise of race-based peremptory challenges is a violation of the Sixth Amendment because it manipulates the fair chance of producing a representative jury.

8. Trial manuals candidly advised striking minorities because they were likely to feel sympathy with the defendant, and prosecutors spoke among themselves of the duty to ensure convictions by arranging all-white juries. There was nothing covert, nothing irregular, nothing cabined, or contained about the practice in most places. See, for example, Frederick L. Brown, Frank T. McGuire, and Mary S. Winters, "The Peremptory Challenge as a Manipulative Device in Criminal Trials: Traditional Use or Abuse? *New England Law Review*, vol. 14, no. 2 (1978), p. 224.

9. *Swain* v. *Alabama*, 380 U.S. 202, 225 (1965) (accepting as true that no black person had served on a jury in Talledega County since 1950).

10. Justice Byron White, *Swain's* author, later wrote that despite the "warning" language of his original opinion, "[i]t appears . . . that the practice of peremptorily eliminating blacks from petit juries in cases with black defendants remains widespread. . . ." *Batson* v. *Kentucky*, 476 U.S. 79, at 101 (White, J., concurring).

Prior to *Batson*, some states under their own constitutions or statutes, and the Second Circuit under the Sixth Amendment, sought to regulate the practice. See, for example, *People* v. *Wheeler*, 22 Cal.3d 258, 583 P.2d 748, 148 Cal. Rptr. 890 (1978) (holding it unconstitutional for a party to exercise its peremptory challenges to remove prospective jurors based solely on group bias); *Commonwealth* v. *Soares*, 377 Mass. 561, 387 N.E.2d 499, *cert denied*, 444 U.S. 881 (1979) (finding prosecutor's use of peremptory challenges to strike twelve of thirteen blacks on the venire to violate state constitutional right to a petit jury that "is as near an approximation of the ideal cross-section of the community as the process of random selection permits"); *McCray* v. *Abrams*, 750 F.2d 366 (2d Cir. 1984) (holding that prosecutor's use of peremptory challenges to strike all black jurors violated the cross-sectional requirement of the Sixth Amendment). See also Justices Brennan and Marshall dissenting from the denial of *certiorari* in *McCray* v. *New York*, 461 U.S. 961 (1983) and calling for reexamination of *Swain*.

Only one case, *Carter* v. *Jury Commission*, 396 U.S. 320 (1970), a civil case against the jury commissioners for a pattern of discrimination, directly took up the Court's invitation in *Swain* to focus on showing a trend case of race-based peremptories. But it was obviously too great a burden to raise the equal protection rights of excluded jurors in jurisdiction after jurisdiction and aside from the pressing interest of a particular case.

11. Numerous empirical studies support the notion that jurors of a certain age, race, ethnicity, religion, or occupation are predisposed to react a certain way to evidence or defendants of a certain sort, despite their individual attempts to be fair and impartial. Though such studies establish neither the rightness nor the need for peremptory challenges, they help explain why lawyers on both sides are prone to exercise them based on group, rather than individual, characteristics. William T. Pizzi, "*Batson* v. *Kentucky*: Curing the Disease but Killing the Patient," *The Supreme Court Review* (1987), pp. 97, 129–35; see also Peter Perlman, "Jury Selection," in D. Lake Rumsey, ed., *Master Advocates' Handbook* (St. Paul: National Institute of Trial Advocacy, 1986), pp. 59, 77–78; Jeffrey L. Kestler, *Questioning Techniques and Tactics*, sec. 3.20 (McGraw-Hill, 1982), p. 98; and Jon M. Van Dyke, *Jury Selection Procedures: Our Uncertain Commitment to Representative Panels* (Ballinger, 1977).

Although the tenets of social psychology also hold that jurors, like everyone else, tend to evaluate ingroup members (shared identity) more positively than outgroup members, former Supreme Court Justice Thurgood Marshall, drawing from his life experience as well as social science studies, observed that some members of minority groups "respond to discrimination and prejudice by attempting to disassociate themselves from the group, even to the point of adopting the majority's negative attitudes." *Casteneda* v. *Partida*, 430 U.S. 482, 503 (1977). More pungently to the same point, in response to a question about whether his replacement should be an African American, he responded, "There is no difference between a white snake and a black snake. They'll both bite." See Thurgood Marshall, press conference on Supreme Court Retirement, quoted in Neil A. Lewis, "Marshall Urges Bush to Pick 'The Best,'" *New York Times*, June 29, 1991, p. A8; see also Barbara D. Underwood, "Ending Race Discrimination in Jury Selection: Whose Right Is It, Anyway?" *Columbia Law Review*, vol. 92 (May 1992), pp. 725, 728 (arguing that there is no satisfactory way to explain how "race-based jury selection discriminates against the defendant, as distinct from the jurors").

12. Pizzi, "*Batson* v. *Kentucky*," p. 129. Albert W. Alschuler, "The Supreme Court and the Jury: Voir Dire, Peremptory Challenges, and the Review of Jury Verdicts," *University of Chicago Law Review*, vol. 56 (Winter 1989), pp. 153–233 (attacking the use of social science techniques in selecting juries).

13. William Blackstone, *Commentaries on the Laws of England*, vol. 4 (Garland Publishing Company).

14. Babcock, "Voir Dire," p. 533.

15. Babcock, "Voir Dire," p. 553.

16. The Federal Jury Selection and Service Act of 1968, codified at 28 U.S.C. §§ 1861-1869, is designed to ensure that juries are "selected at random from a fair cross section of the community in the district or division wherein the court convenes." Ibid. at §1861. Specifically, the act provides that the exclusion from service as a juror "on account of race, color, religion, sex, national origin, or economic status" is prohibited. Ibid. at §1862. I use the paradigmatic example of the African American defendant and the white jurors. But the Court has extended its cognizable categories for equal protection and fair cross section analysis to other groups. See, for example, *Hernandez* v. *Texas*, 347 U.S. 475 (1954) (equal protection clause prohibits discrimination on bases other than race, such as national origin); *Lockhart* v. *McCree*, 476 U.S. 162, at 175 (1986) (class of prospective jurors fervently opposed to the death penalty does not constitute a distinctive group for purposes of a fair cross section).

17. Anonymous letter from excluded juror, quoted in Amicus Curiae Brief for Elizabeth Holtzman, district attorney, Kings County, at 81, in *Batson* v. *Kentucky* 476 U.S. 79 (1986). See also Underwood, "Ending Race Discrimination in Jury Selection," (arguing that the real harm in racially motivated jury selection is incurred by the excluded jurors and the stigmatized group to which they belong).

18. *Williams* v. *Florida*, 399 U.S. 78 (1970) (upholding the constitutionality of six-person juries in state criminal trials); *Colgrove* v. *Battin*, 413 U.S. 149 (1973)(upholding the constitutionality of six-person juries in federal civil cases); *Ballew* v. *Georgia*, 435 U.S. 223 (1978) (holding that a jury of five substantially threatens the guarantees of the Sixth and Fourteenth Amendments concerning a fair cross section of the community).

19. Pizzi, "*Batson* v. *Kentucky*," p. 147, in discussing various proposals to abolish the peremptory challenge or otherwise curtail its use, argues that by abolishing the system of peremptories, we would be able to "eliminate the use of social science experts and psychologists in jury selection," thereby countering "the impression that it is the composition of the jury and not the evidence presented that is fundamental to the determination of guilt or innocence at trial" (p. 144). Second, petit juries would more often actually represent a fair cross section of the community (pp. 144–45). Finally, trial time devoted to jury selection would be greatly diminished (p. 145).

20. *Apodaca* v. *Oregon*, 406 U.S. 404 (1972) (upholding less-than-unanimous jury verdicts in state criminal trials against Sixth and Fourteenth Amendment challenges).

21. 476 U.S. 79 (1986).

22. *Edmonson* v. *Leesville Concrete, Inc.*, 111 S. Ct. 2077 (1991).

23. *Georgia* v. *McCollum*, 112 S. Ct. 2348 (1992) (holding that the equal protection clause prohibits criminal defendants from engaging in purposeful discrimination on ground of race in exercise of peremptory challenges).

24. Before jury selection began, the prosecution, expecting to show that the victims' race was a factor in the assault, moved to prohibit the defendants' counsel from exercising its peremptory challenges to remove all African Americans from the jury. The prosecution argued that if a statistically representative jury panel was assembled it would contain eighteen African Americans—all of which the defendants' counsel would be able to strike with its twenty allotted peremptory challenges. The trial judge denied the prosecution's motion and the Supreme Court of Georgia affirmed the ruling. *State* v. *McCollum*, 261 Ga. 473, 405 S.E.2d 688 (1991).

25. The Supreme Court has never fully addressed the issue of the circumstances under which an explanation is either permissibly race-neutral or impermissibly a proxy for racial bias. *Hernandez* v. *New York*, 111 S. Ct. 1859 (1991) upheld the strikes of Spanish-speaking jurors where the prosecutor was able to show a nexus between the jurors' bilingualism and their possible approach to the trial. For a sample of the issues being presented to lower courts in the application of *Batson*, see generally *United States* v. *Bishop*, 959—F.2d 820 (9th Cir. 1992) (holding that the prosecution's explanation that a black juror lived in a predominantly low-income, black neighborhood and was therefore likely to believe that "the police pick on black people" was not race neutral); *United States* v. *Mitchell*, 877 F.2d 294 (4th Cir. 1989) (accepting the prosecutor's explanation based on the residence of the jurors—though acknowledging that the reason given could be pretextual because of a lack of discriminatory intent); *United States* v. *Briscoe*, 896 F.2d 1476 (7th Cir. 1990) (no discriminatory motive in residence-based peremptory, because the prosecutor made specific allegations that the jurors had lived extremely close to the defendant). Justice Marshall, concurring in *Batson* v. *Kentucky*, expressed early concern about the difficulties of assessing prosecutorial motive in peremptory challenge cases. He anticipated that the problem of prosecutors lying about their motives, as well as simply subconsciously incorporating their own racism into their decisions about which jurors to strike, could very possibly disable the protections erected by the Court in *Batson*. 476 U.S. 79, 106-07.

26. *Edmonson* v. *Leesville*, 111 S. Ct. at 2088.

27. Katherine Goldwasser, "Limiting a Criminal Defendant's Use of Peremptory Challenges: On Symmetry and the Jury in a Criminal Trial," *Harvard Law Review*, vol. 102 (February 1989), pp. 808-40; Susan Bandes, "Taking Some Rights Too Seriously: The State's Right to a Fair Trial," *Southern California Law Review*, vol. 60 (May 1987), pp. 1019-57; E. Vaughn, "Discrimination by the Defense: Peremptory Challenges after *Batson* v. *Kentucky*," *Columbia Law Review*, vol. 88 (March 1988), pp. 358-61. My own view is that the best reading of the history and meaning of the peremptory challenge would be to consider it a defendant's right under the Sixth Amendment, following the analysis of Toni M. Massaro in "Peremptories or Peers? Rethinking Sixth Amendment Doctrine, Images, and Procedures," *North Carolina Law Review*, vol. 64 (March 1986), pp. 501-64.

28. Amicus Curiae Brief for National Association of Criminal Defense Lawyers, in support of Respondent, *Georgia* v. *McCollum*, 112 S. Ct. 2348 (1992) (arguing against the extension of *Batson* to prohibit the exercise of race-based peremptory challenges by the defense in a criminal case).

29. *Edmonson* v. *Leesville*, 111 S. Ct. at 2088.

30. *Strauder*, 100 U.S. at 309. In striking down an 1873 statute that limited jury service to white males, the Court found the black accused entitled to a jury chosen without the

exclusion of his race and without "discrimination against them." Ibid. The Court also noted that the West Virginia statute was an example of what might be anticipated when "those who had long been regarded as an inferior and subject race" were "suddenly raised to the rank of citizenship." The Court said it took "little knowledge of human nature" to expect "that State laws might be enacted or enforced to perpetuate the distinctions that had before existed." Ibid, at 306.

31. *Batson* v. *Kentucky*, 476 U.S. 79 (reversing a conviction where the prosecutor exercised his peremptory challenges to strike all blacks from the jury).

32. *Strauder* v. *West Virginia*, 100 U.S. 303, at 308 (1880), cited in *Batson* v. *Kentucky*, 476 U.S. 79, at 87 (1986).

33. Ibid., at 87; see also *Strauder*, 100 U.S., at 308.

34. See Brown, McGuire, and Winters, "The Peremptory Challenge"; see also *Taylor* v. *Louisiana*, 419 U.S. 522 (1975) (holding that the Sixth Amendment entitles every defendant to object to a venire that is not designed to represent a fair cross section of the community, whether or not the systematically excluded groups are groups of which the defendant is a member). But while the jury must be drawn from a pool that is a representative cross section of the community, there is no absolute right to fair representation on the jury panel itself. The Court in *Taylor* expressly declined to impose a requirement that petit juries actually chosen must mirror the community and reflect the various distinctive groups in the population. Ibid. at 363–64. The Supreme Court has recently reaffirmed its belief that this Sixth Amendment right does not include "the notion that, in the process of drawing the jury, that initial representativeness cannot be diminished by allowing both the accused and the State to eliminate persons thought to be inclined against their interests." *Holland* v. *Illinois*, 493 U.S. 474, 480 (1990); see also *Lockhart* v. *McCree*, 476 U.S. 162 (1986) (refusing to invoke the principle of a fair cross section to invalidate the use of either for-cause or peremptory challenges, or to require petit juries, as opposed to venires, to reflect the composition of the community at large).

35. *Duncan* v. *Louisiana*, 391 U.S. 145, 149 (1968) (extending the Sixth Amendment right to a trial by a jury guaranteed to defendants in criminal cases in federal courts to the states through the Fourteenth Amendment).

36. See note 10. Such were the grounds on which Batson's counsel and various amici urged reversal in his case. Such were also the grounds on which state courts and two federal circuits had outlawed the peremptory removal of minorities from the jury. We can see the logical and precedental force of these arguments in Justice Stevens's opinion in *Holland* v. *Illinois*. Holland was a white man who objected to the peremptory removal of all blacks from his jury. Chary of the equal protection argument, partly because of the Court's repeated references in *Batson* to the defendant's own race being the same as the excluded jurors, Holland based his claim exclusively on the Sixth Amendment right to an impartial jury drawn from a fair cross section of the community.

See also note 27. Massaro, "Peremptories or Peers?" who argued while *Batson* was *sub judice* that it should be decided on Sixth Amendment rather than equal protection grounds. Identifying government, community, and defendant interests in how a jury "looks," Massaro dissected the Court's attempts to regulate jury appearance through interpretations of the constitutional word "impartial" and the definitions: "fair cross section of the community" and "a jury of peers."

37. *Taylor* v. *Louisiana*, at 527 (1975) (citing *Smith* v. *Texas*, 311 U.S. 128, 130 (1940)) (holding unconstitutional a state provision that required women, but not men, to file a written declaration before they were placed in the jury pool).

38. Alschuler, "The Supreme Court and the Jury," pp. 153–233, outlines what he sees as seven major problems in the administration of *Batson*. Although I argue that most of these have not come to pass, his detailing of the difficulties that might result from having juror selection or de-selection depend on a correspondence of race with the defendant

shows conclusively that such a requirement would never work. See also *Holland* v. *Illinois*, 493 U.S., at 507 (Stevens, J., dissenting) (arguing that a requirement that the defendant share the same race with the challenged juror is inconsistent with the equal protection clause and unworkable as a standard).

39. 476 U.S. 162, 174 (1986). See Pizzi, "*Batson* v. *Kentucky*," p. 119 (arguing that the approach of ensuring a fair cross section is a myth: our system of jury selection has never been designed to assure defendants "a demographically representative cross section on the jury"). See also Justice William Rehnquist's dissent in *Batson*, 476 U.S., at 134.

40. Explanations for why the Court relied instead on equal protection (of the *Strauder* allusive brand) are varied: ranging from the vulgar (there were not enough votes for boldly enlarging the rights of the criminal defendant), to the instrumental (the Court hoped it could establish a limited principle applicable only to the prosecutorial practice of striking minority members from the juries of minority defendants). Alschuler, "The Supreme Court and the Jury," pp. 186–88, speculates that the *Batson* majority relied on equal protection in order to circumvent the concepts of standing articulated in *Peters* and *Taylor*, and to limit its holding to the exclusion of blacks. The focus on *Strauder* lends itself to this latter explanation because the Court there said the equal protection it had in mind was only for "colored men" and went on to add somewhat gratuitously that states could, of course, continue to exclude others from its juries: women, propertyless people, and the uneducated among other examples. 100 U.S, at 310.

41. The Sixth Amendment never gets direct mention in *Batson's* equal protection discourse, and yet, in the words of Justice Stevens in a later case, the "requirement of impartiality is, in a sense, the mirror image of a prohibition against discrimination." *Holland* v. *Illinois*, 493 U.S. 474, 506 n. 4 (Stevens, J., dissenting). Justice Rehnquist in his dissent in *Duren* v. *Missouri*, 439 U.S. 357 (1979) acknowledges that the equal protection arguments have been imported into the Sixth Amendment, and he rails against it. 439 U.S. 359, 371 (1979) (Rehnquist, J., dissenting).

42. *Batson*, 476 U.S., at 87 (quoting *Thiel* v. *Southern Pacific Co.*, 328 U.S. 217, 223-24 (1946)).

43. Ibid.

44. See 5 Daniel 25 (King James ed.).

45. *Thiel*, 328 U.S., at 219, 222.

46. According to the Brief of the Petitioner, Thiel himself, though salaried, was a "humble wage earner," and the daily wage earners who actually served on the jury all had some personal or business connection to Respondent.

47. 328 U.S., at 225.

48. Ibid., at 220.

49. Ibid., at 227. (Frankfurter, J., dissenting). Many of the frequently quoted *bon mots* were from Justice Felix Frankfurter's opinion where he spoke of the need to maintain the "broad representative character of the jury . . . as assurance of a diffused impartiality." Ibid. Despite his language on the importance of representative juries, Justice Frankfurter dissented, objecting to the extreme remedy of reversal when "no constitutional issue is at stake." Ibid. On the merits, he found it "too large an assumption . . . that those workers who are paid by the day have a different outlook psychologically and economically than those who earn weekly wages." Ibid. at 230.

50. *Ballard* v. *United States*, 329 U.S. 187 (1946).

51. Ibid., at 195.

52. *Batson* v. *Kentucky*, 476 U.S., at 87 ("The harm from discriminatory jury selection extends beyond that inflicted on the defendant and the excluded juror to touch the entire community. Selection procedures that purposely exclude black persons from juries undermine public confidence in the fairness of our system of justice") (quoting *Ballard* v. *United States*, 329 U.S., at 195).

53. See *Edmonson* v. *Leesville Concrete*, at 111 S. Ct. at 2088 (arguing that *Batson* and its progeny are necessary in order to ensure "progress toward a multiracial democracy" by preventing the invocation of racial stereotypes that inevitably cause profound hurt and injury); compare *Georgia* v. *McCollum*, 112 S. Ct. 2348 (Scalia, J., dissenting) (chastising the court for using the Constitution to compromise the right of criminal defendants to exercise peremptory challenges in pursuit of a jury they perceive to be fair in the interest of "promoting the supposedly greater good of race relations in the society as a whole").

54. *Powers* v. *Ohio*, 111 S. Ct. 1364, 1368, 1373 (1991). Though acknowledging "the emphasis in *Batson* on racial identity between the defendant and the excused prospective juror," the majority in *Powers* interpreted *Batson* as serving multiple ends: to prevent black defendants from being tried by a jury from which all members of his race have been excluded, but also to protect excluded jurors and the community at large from being harmed by the prosecutor's discriminatory use of peremptory challenges. The latter purpose is fully served only if white defendants, as well as black defendants, are able to challenge the exclusion of blacks from the petit jury. Compare Justice Scalia's dissent in *Powers*, which argues that "no defendant except *one of the same race as the excluded juror* is deprived of equal protection of the laws," by the use of racially discriminatory peremptory strikes. Ibid., at 1376.

55. 111 S. Ct. 2077 (1991). In the time between *Powers* and *Edmonson*, the Supreme Court heard another case challenging the discriminatory use of peremptory strikes, *Holland* v. *Illinois*, 493 U.S. 474 (1990). *Holland*, however, was analyzed as a Sixth Amendment case, rather than under the equal protection clause. See notes 4, 7.

56. "When private litigants participate in the selection of jurors, they serve an important function within the government and act with its substantial assistance. If peremptory challenges based on race were permitted, persons could be required by summons to be put at risk of open and public discrimination as a condition of their participation in the justice system. The injury to excluded jurors would be the direct result of governmental delegation and participation." *Edmonson*, 111 S. Ct., at 2087 (1991).

57. Ibid., at 2088.

58. Ibid., at 2088. See notes 27, 28, and accompanying text. In *Georgia* v. *McCollum*, the Court further excluded the Batson doctrine, holding that the criminal defendant (this time a white seeking to exclude blacks from jury service) also acted for the state and thus must not discriminate in his use of peremptory challenges.

59. See, for example, *Harper* v. *Virginia Board of Elections*, 383 U.S. 663 (1966) (declaring poll tax unconstitutional); *Kramer* v. *Union Free School District*, 395 U.S. 621 (1969) (invalidating New York law that restricted school district election to residents who owned property in the district or had children enrolled in the schools); *Reynolds* v. *Sims*, 377 U.S. 533 (1964) (remedy for malapportionment that violates the equal protection clause is mandatory reapportionment); *South Carolina* v. *Katzenbach*, 383 U.S. 301 (1978) (upholding order to suspend literacy tests and similar devices for a period of five years in order to remedy voting discrimination).

60. See, for example, *Strickland* v. *Washington*, 466 U.S. 668 (1984) (on an ineffective assistance of counsel claim, a defendant must show that, but for the counsel's deficiencies, there is a reasonable probability that the result of the proceeding would have been different); *Brady* v. *Maryland*, 373 U.S. 83 (1963) (in challenging the prosecutor's duty to disclose evidence, the defendant must show that if it were made available the withheld evidence would tend to exculpate him or reduce the penalty); *United States* v. *Agurs*, 427 U.S. 97 (1976) (defendant must show, upon an assessment of the whole record, that there is a strong likelihood that the undisclosed evidence would have affected the outcome).

61. *Allen* v. *Hardy*, 478 U.S. 255, 259 (1986) (holding that the new rule laid down in *Batson* was designed to serve multiple ends and that it does not have such a fundamental impact on the integrity of factfinding as to compel retroactive application); *Teague* v.

Lane, 489 U.S. 288 (1989) (reaffirming that new rules of criminal procedure should generally not be applied retroactively to cases on collateral review unless the likelihood of an accurate conviction is seriously diminished without the new procedures).

62. Compare Justice Antonin Scalia's view in *Powers*, where he railed against the remedy of reversal by finding it to be "a reprise, so to speak, of *Miranda* v. *Arizona*, in that the Court uses its key to the jail-house door not to free the arguably innocent, but to threaten release upon the society of the unquestionably guilty unless law enforcement officers take certain steps that the Court newly announces to be required by law." 111 S. Ct., at 1381 (citation omitted). He further argued that in *Miranda*, the rule applied at least to the defendant's rights, if not to his guilt, whereas *Batson* relates to neither—the defendant is set free because even though the fairness of the trial was not affected, the jurors at this trial were denied equal protection of the laws.

Justice Scalia assumes that the reversal remedy vindicates the rights of the excluded jurors. It serves this purpose, of course, which could not be done by any method other than reversal. But as I argue in the text, the extremity of the remedy derives from the importance we place on the way in which a jury is composed. Compare counsel's remarks in *Eiland* v. *Maryland*, note 71, in which the prosecutor struck women on the basis of gender: "The jurors suffered an unconstitutional act. . . . The Supreme Court has held that the defendant stands in the shoes of the jurors to vindicate the harm that has been done to them. The only remedy is reversal." "Keeping Women Off Jury May Torpedo Convictions," *Legal Times*, November 23, 1992, p. 21 (Steven Reich, defense counsel).

63. *Peters* v. *Kiff*, 407 U.S. 493, at 503 (1972) (Marshall, J.).

64. Ibid., at 503-04. Pre-*Batson* and in pluralities of three, the Court found the practice of striking blacks from the jury unacceptable. The doctrinal basis of *Peters* is difficult to discern, though Justice Thurgood Marshall relied on equal protection and federal statutes and read due process as prohibiting trials by illegally constituted juries. The case also has a strong Sixth Amendment flavor, though it had been litigated before *Duncan* had applied that amendment to the states. See Underwood, "Ending Race Discrimination in Jury Selection," pp. 739–42, which argues that Justice Byron White's opinion (also for three Justices) also has a Constitutional basis, though in due process rather than equal protection.

65. *Ballard* v. *United States*, 329 U.S. 187, at 193–94 (claiming that "a flavor, a distinct quality, is lost if either sex is excluded"); and *Taylor* v. *Louisiana*, 419 U.S. 522, at 530 (1975) (excluding "identifiable segments playing major roles in the community cannot be squared with the constitutional concept of jury trial").

66. Mary Timothy, *Jurywoman: The Story of the Trial of Angela Y. Davis* (Palo Alto, Calif.: Emty Press, 1974), pp. 27–29.

67. *Powers* v. *Ohio*, 111 S. Ct. 1364, at 1372 (1991).

68. There is currently a split among the Circuits on the issue of gender-based peremptories. See *U.S.* v. *Hamilton*, 850 F.2d 1038 (4th Cir. 1988), *cert. denied*, 493 U.S. 1069 (1990) (holding that *Batson* does not apply to restrict the use of gender-based peremptory challenges); *U.S.* v. *DeGross*, 913 F. 2d 1417 (9th Cir. 1990), reheard en banc, 960 F.2d 1433 (1992) (extending *Batson* to prohibit gender-based peremptory challenges by either prosecutors or defense counsel in criminal cases, and by both parties in civil cases); *U.S.* v. *Nichols*, 937 F.2d 1257 (7th Cir. 1991), *cert. denied*, 112 S. Ct. 989 (1992) (holding that strikes against black women were racially motivated).

Several states have spoken on the issue of gender-based peremptories as well. The leading state cases have all concluded that *Batson* does not apply to gender-based strikes. See generally *Daniels* v. *State*, 581 So. 2d 536 (Ala. Crim. App.) (holding that the state did not violate *Batson* by removing a black woman from the jury), *cert. denied*, 112 S. Ct. 315 (1991); *People* v. *Crowder*, 515 N.E. 2d 783 (Ill. App. 1987) (holding that male defendant lacks standing to challenge the exclusion of women on *Batson* grounds), *appeal denied*, 119 Ill. 2d 562 (1988); *Hannan* v. *Commonwealth*, 774 S.W.2d 462 (Ky. App. 1989);

State v. *Adams*, 533 So. 2d 1060 (La. Ct. App. 1988) (noting that U.S. Supreme Court had the opportunity to extend *Batson* to gender, but declined to do so), *cert. denied*, 540 So. 2d 338 (1989); *State* v. *Pullen*, 811 S.W.2d 463 (Mo. Ct. App. 1991) (holding that precedent dictates that *Batson* applies only to race—despite the court's own logical inclination to extend the doctrine to gender); *State* v. *Clay*, 779 S.W.2d 673 (Mo. Ct. App. 1989) (rejecting the extension of *Batson* to instances other than race discrimination); *State* v. *Culver*, 233 Neb. 228, 444 N.W.2d 662 (1989); *State* v. *Oliviera*, 534 A.2d 867 (R.I. 1987); *Mowbray* v. *State*, 788 S.W.2d 658 (Tex. Ct. App. 1990). But compare *People* v. *Irizarry*, 560 N.Y.S.2d 279 (1988) (holding that *Batson* applies to gender-based peremptories).

The issue of gender-based peremptory challenges has been the subject of a great deal of law review commentary. For the leading, though somewhat outdated, article, see Shirley S. Sagawa, "*Batson* v. *Kentucky*: Will It Keep Women on the Jury?" *Berkeley Women's Law Journal*, vol. 3 (1987), pp. 14, 48, arguing that any benefits of allowing unexplained gender-based peremptories are clearly outweighed by "the negative effects to women, to defendants, and to the entire community." Most recent is Note, "Beyond *Batson*: Eliminating Gender-Based Peremptory Challenges," *Harvard Law Review*, vol. 105 (June 1992), pp. 1920–39 (gender-based peremptories should be abolished because of history of sex discrimination and of equal protection doctrine). See also Susan McCoin, "Sex Discrimination in the Voir Dire Process: The Rights of Prospective Female Jurors," *Southern California Law Review*, vol. 58 (July 1985), pp. 1225–59. See also Alan Raphael, "Discriminatory Jury Selection: Lower Court Implementation of *Batson* v. *Kentucky*," *Willamette Law Review*, vol. 25 (Spring 1989), pp. 293–349 (arguing that the impact of *Batson* on limiting discrimination in jury selection turns on the level and kind of scrutiny applied in evaluating the reasons given to support peremptory challenges); Paul H. Schwartz, "Equal Protection in Jury Selection? The Implementation of *Batson* v. *Kentucky* in North Carolina," *North Carolina Law Review*, vol. 69 (September 1991), pp. 1533, 1577 (arguing that the equal protection clause and the peremptory challenges "are inherently contradictory"); S. Alexandria Jo, "Reconstruction of the Peremptory Challenge System: A Look at Gender-Based Peremptory Challenges," *Pacific Law Journal*, vol. 22 (July 1991), pp. 1305–31 (arguing that *Batson* should be extended to gender-based peremptory challenges). See also Laura Gaston Dooley, "Sounds of Silence on the Civil Jury," *Valparaiso University Law Review*, vol. 26 (Fall 1991), pp. 405–18 (questioning whether juries can ever truly be representative institutions when the traditional binary model of jury decisionmaking in civil cases prevents women jurors from affecting outcomes); Deborah L. Forman, "What Difference Does It Make? Gender and Jury Selection," *UCLA Women's Law Journal*, vol. 2 (Spring 1992), pp. 35–83 (rejecting *Batson* in favor of system of proportional representation to ensure gender equality in jury selection by focusing on inclusion rather than exclusion).

69. It does not follow inevitably, however, that challenges must be free from all gender considerations. If we want to preserve the unexplained peremptory challenge, the line could be drawn to exclude nonminority men from protection. Certainly, the history of discrimination that comprises the foundation for equal protection of the *potential jurors* has not similarly affected white men. However, there is still a strain of litigant's rights in these cases, and there are instances in which the gender-based strikes of white men from a white male litigant's jury arguably violates this aspect of the equal protection analysis. *Dias* v. *Sky Chefs, Inc.* 919 F.2d 1370 (9th Cir. 1990) (defendant challenged plaintiff's use of peremptory challenges to strike men, achieving an all-woman jury in a sexual harassment case), vacated and remanded for reconsideration in light of *Edmonson* v. *Leesville Concrete*, 111 S. Ct. 2077 (1991). On reconsideration, the court found that the issue had not been timely raised in the trial court. 948 F.2d 532 (9th Cir. 1991), *cert. denied*, 112 S. Ct. 1294 (1992).

70. *Strauder* v. *West Virginia*, 100 U.S. at 310 (explaining that despite its holding that blacks could not be expressly excluded from jury service, states could certainly confine jury selection to "*males*, freeholders, to citizens, to persons within certain ages, or to persons having educational qualifications") (emphasis added).

71. *Fisher* v. *State*, 587 So. 2d 1027, 1037 (Ala. Crim. App. 1991), *cert. denied*, 112 S. Ct. 1486 (1992). In *Eiland* v. *Maryland*, 607 A.2d 42 (Md. App. 1992) black men were on trial for murder; the state used 80 percent (sixteen) of its strikes against women, fourteen strikes removed black women. The prosecutor gave as his race-neutral explanation the fact of their gender. As of this writing, the case was on certiorari from the Court of Appeals, no. 87 September Term, set for en banc argument in January 1993.

72. Of the four gender-based peremptory cases that have reached the federal circuit courts, all have involved the striking of minority women, as have most of the state cases. See notes 68, 71.

73. See, for examples of scholarly treatment of the intersection of race and gender, Angela P. Harris, "Race and Essentialism in Feminist Legal Theory," *Stanford Law Review*, vol. 42 (February 1990), pp. 581–616; Marlee Kline, "Race, Racism and Feminist Legal Theory," *Harvard Women's Law Journal*, vol. 12 (Spring 1989), p. 115; Elizabeth Spelman, "Gender and Race: The Ampersand Problem in Feminist Thought," in Elizabeth V. Spelman, *Inessential Woman: Problems of Exclusion in Feminist Thought* (Beacon Press, 1988); Kimberle Crenshaw, "Demarginalizing the Intersection of Race and Sex: A Black Feminist Critique of Antidiscrimination Doctrine, Feminist Theory, and Antiracist Politics," *University of Chicago Legal Forum*, vol. 1989, p. 139; and Judith Scales-Trent, "Black Women and the Constitution: Finding Our Place, Asserting Our Rights," *Harvard Civil Rights-Civil Liberties Law Review*, vol. 9 (Winter 1989), pp. 9–44.

74. Sagawa, "*Batson* v. *Kentucky*," pp. 36–37. This early article is both prescient and perceptive. In a long footnote supporting her assertion that minority women have been excluded from the debate about peremptory challenges, she notes that "when white commentators write about women as jurors, it is often clear that they mean *white* women only." She goes on to cite examples of the stereotypes surrounding women as jurors, almost all applying to white women only. Sagawa also notes and documents how seldom the dual discrimination against minority women enters the discourse, despite the plethora of academic writing on the subject of jury discrimination. Ibid. at n. 162. See also Ian Ayres, "Fair Driving: Gender and Race Discrimination in Retail Car Negotiations," *Harvard Law Review*, vol. 104 (February 1991), pp. 817, 819 (concluding that in the process of negotiating for a new car, black women had to pay more than three times the markup of whites males, whereas white women paid only 40 percent more, and black men paid twice the markup of white males).

75. This is a line that has already been suggested. At the oral argument in *McCollum* v. *Georgia*, this exchange occurred:

Justice Kennedy: You are not suggesting that gender stereotypes are more valid than race stereotypes, are you?

Counsel: No. There has been a particular problem with invidious race discrimination, and there has not been a similar problem with gender discrimination. The Court has to draw the line somewhere if it is going to preserve the institution of peremptory challenge.

(Oral argument in *McCollum* v. *Georgia*, No.91-372; February 26, 1992). *Criminal Law Reporter*, March 4, 1992, p. 3183.

See *People* v. *Motten*, 704 P.2d 176 (Cal. 1985) at 178 (finding black women a discrete and cognizable group; overruling a trial judge who said to defense counsel's objection to striking of black women: "You have got women on the jury. What function does a Black woman fulfill that the White woman doesn't?")

76. On the early history of the women's movement, see Ellen C. DuBois, *Feminism and Suffrage: The Emergence of an Independent Women's Movement in America 1848-*

1869 (Cornell University Press, 1978); Ellen C. DuBois, "The Radicalism of the Woman Suffrage Movement: Notes toward the Reconstruction of Nineteenth-Century Feminism," in Kermit L. Hall, ed., *Women, the Law and the Constitution: Major Historical Interpretations* (Garland, 1987). Excellent standard accounts include William Chafe, *The American Woman* (Oxford University Press, 1972); Eleanor Flexner, *Century of Struggle: The Woman's Rights Movement in the United States* (Atheneum, 1968); Aileen Kraditor, ed., *Up from the Pedestal: Selected Writings in History of American Feminism* (Quadrangle Books, 1968), p. 243; Aileen S. Kraditor, *Ideas of the Woman Suffrage Movement 1890-1920* (Doubleday, 1971); William O'Neill, *Everyone Was Brave: The Rise and Fall of Feminism in America*, Rev. ed. (Quandrangle Books, 1975).

77. Theodore Stanton and Harriet Stanton Blatch, *Elizabeth Cady Stanton as Revealed in Her Letters, Diary and Reminiscences* (Harper and Brothers, 1922), pp. 266–69. See also William McFeely, *Frederick Douglass* (Norton, 1991), pp. 266–69.

78. Sojourner Truth, who took this name to replace that given her as a slave, was an important figure in the early woman's movement. Susan B. Anthony and Ida Harper, *History of Woman Suffrage*, vol. 2 (Fanter and Wells, 1881), p. 193. For a sense of the immediacy of the connection between women's rights and former slaves' rights, see Elizabeth Cady Stanton, Susan B. Anthony, and Matilda Joslyn Gage, eds., *History of Woman Suffrage* (in six volumes covering the years 1848–1920). Vols. 1–3 were edited by Elizabeth Stanton, Susan Anthony, and Mathilde Gage; vol. 4 by Anthony and Harper; and vol. 5 and 6 by Harper.

79. This is a recasting of the figures in Carrie Chapman Catt and Nettie Rogers Shuler, *Woman Suffrage and Politics: The Inner Story of the Suffrage Movement* (University of Washington Press, 1970), pp. 107–08. Jury service as a badge of full citizenship and a form of political participation was within the intent of the framers of the Sixth and Seventh Amendments. Akhil R. Amar, "The Bill of Rights as a Constitution," *Yale Law Journal*, vol. 100 (March 1991), pp. 1183–90. In 1848, de Tocqueville wrote about the jury "as the most effective way of establishing the people's rule and the most efficient way of teaching them how to rule." Alexis de Tocqueville, *Democracy in America*, ed. J. P. Mayer (Doubleday, Anchor, 1969). In the late nineteenth century, a legal scholar wrote of the purposes of jury service, numbering among them: "It makes a participation of the public in the administration of justice possible," and "it is the greatest practical school of free citizenship." Francis Lieber, *On Civil Liberty and Self-Government* (J. B. Lippincott, 1859), quoted in Paul D. Carrington, "The Seventh Amendment: Some Bicentennial Reflections," *University of Chicago Legal Forum*, vol. 1990, pp. 37–38. The modern Court has recognized explicitly that "with the exception of voting, for most citizens the honor and privilege of jury duty is their most significant opportunity to participate in the democratic process." *Powers* v. *Ohio*, 111 S. Ct.1364, 1369. Woman suffragists drew all these same connections between jury service and citizenship.

80. *Strauder* v. *West Virginia*, 100 U.S. 303, 308 (1880). I draw on the following published "chapters" of the biography I am writing on Foltz for the historical background presented here. "Reconstructing the Person: The Case of Clara Shortridge Foltz," in Susan G. Bell and Marilyn Yalom, eds., *Revealing Lives: Autobiography, Biography, and Gender* (State University of New York Press, 1990); "Clara Shortridge Foltz: 'First Woman,'" *Arizona Law Review*, vol. 30 (Fall 1988), pp. 673–717; and "Clara Shortridge Foltz: Constitution-Maker," *Indiana Law Review*, vol. 66 (Fall 1991), pp. 849–940.

81. Cited in Babcock, "Constitution-Maker," pp. 866, 907.

82. *Matter of Goodell*, 39 Wis. 232, 245-6 (1875) (denying Lavinia Goodell admission to the Bar), cited in Babcock, "First Woman," pp. 711–12.

83. *Debates and Proceedings of the Constitutional Convention*, (1879), p. 1367, cited in Babcock, "Constitution-Maker," p. 894.

84. Babcock, "First Woman," p. 680, n. 80 (citing *Sacramento Union*, January 11,

1878, p. 2) ("Impressionable male jurors" would "return a verdict of acquittal without leaving the box," and "the law and the facts would be simply ignored.") For another example of the attitudes of the time toward women as jurors, see "Women as Jurors," *Central Law Journal*, vol. 93, no. 4 (1921), pp. 57–58, concluding that one of the dangers of enfranchising women was imposing on them the additional "duties of citizenship hard for them to perform . . . none [of which] are more difficult for women than that of determining the issues in a case at law." The article continued by noting that "[t]here are many serious and embarrassing situations caused by a woman's presence on a jury and these embarrassments sometimes affect the woman herself and sometimes the case which she is called upon to decide. . . . They are sometimes very embarrassing to lawyers on both sides of a case who do not know the psychology of a woman's mind and are not sure which way she is going to jump." Ibid. Ironically, however, this same article, after cataloguing the reasons for excluding women from juries, went on to conclude that because "a woman's intuition will reach a just conclusion where frequently a man, who is unable or refuses to use his reason, will stumble into error," the influence of "women in the jury box cannot, on the whole, but prove wholesome and beneficial." Ibid., p. 58.

85. Wyoming, as territory and then as state, was first to grant women suffrage in 1869. See Grace Raymond Hebard, "The First Woman Jury," *Journal of American History*, vol. 7 (Associated Publishers of American Records, 1913), p. 1293 (noting that the Wyoming Women's Suffrage Act marked the first time that a government (the Commonwealth of Wyoming) derived its powers from "the consent of the governed" and not just from "a designated portion of those governed"). In the California constitutional debates of 1879, much was made of the experience in Wyoming, with opponents referring often to the mistrial caused after two weeks when a woman juror fell ill. *Debates and Proceedings of the [California] Constitutional Convention* (1879), pp. 1015–16.

86. See Barbara Babcock and others, *Sex Discrimination: Causes and Remedies* (Little, Brown, 1975), pp. 65–68 (comparing the effects of the Fifteenth and Nineteenth Amendments on rights attendant to suffrage, particularly jury service).

87. See, for example, Judge Florence Allen, "Tried and Approved—The Woman Juror," *Literary Digest*, vol. 70 (September 1922), p. 26 (Allen was an Ohio judge when she wrote this, among many such articles. Later she was the first woman appointed to a federal circuit court); "Women as Jurors," *Virginia Law Review*, vol. 7 (December 1921), p. 634 (Annette Abbot Adams, first woman assistant attorney of the United States, Florence Allen, and others). Burnita Shelton Matthews, "The Woman Juror," *Women Lawyers Journal*, vol. 15 (April 1927), pp. 15–16. (Matthews was later the first woman federal district court judge in Washington, D.C.). Grace H. Harte, "Women Jurors and the American Scene," *Women Lawyers Journal*, vol. 25 (January 1939), p. 9 (calling on women lawyers to fight for jury duty for women). For a comprehensive listing of the legal, scholarly, and popular materials capturing the struggle of women for full citizenship rights and responsibilities, including jury service, see Carole L. Hinchcliff, "American Women Jurors: A Selected Bibliography," *Georgia Law Review*, vol. 20 (Winter 1986), pp. 299–321.

Glasser v. *United States*, 315 U.S. 60 (1942) was one odd offshoot of the women's efforts to gain jury service rights. In one jurisdiction, only women who were members of the League of Women Voters (that is, responsibly civic) were eligible for service on juries. Three male criminal defendants challenged the exclusion of other women from the jury venire on Sixth Amendment grounds, even though the jury actually impaneled consisted of six women and six men. Though holding that the "deliberate selection of jurors from the membership of particular private organizations definitely does not conform to the traditional requirements of a jury trial," the Court held that the defendants had not presented sufficient evidence to support their claim that nonmembers of the League were excluded.

88. See discussion of women's historical exclusion from jury service in eliminating gender-based peremptories, note 68, at 1924-27, citing Carol Weisbrod, "Images of the Woman Juror," *Harvard Women's Law Journal*, vol. 9 (Spring 1986), pp. 59, 60–61.

89. *Commonwealth* v. *Welosky*, 276 Mass. 398, 177 N.E. 656 (1931).

90. *Hoyt* v. *Florida*, 368 U.S. 57 (1961).

91. *Hoyt* v. *Florida*, 368 U.S., at 62.

92. *Taylor* v. *Louisiana*, 419 U.S. 522 (1975). At issue in *Taylor* was a Louisiana statute that required women, but not men, to complete a written declaration to become eligible for jury service. As a result of this exemption for women, only 10 percent of the women in the county ended up in the jury pool, while 53 percent were eligible to serve. The Court held that women cannot be categorically excluded because of sex alone, and, the Court further found that exemptions for women resulted in juries that do not represent a fair cross section of the community, in violation of the Sixth Amendment guarantee of a fair jury trial. *Duren* v. *Missouri*, 439 U.S. 357 (1979) (invalidating a Missouri jury selection system that provided automatic exemptions for any women requesting them; resultant venires were less than 15 percent women). See also Rhonda Copelon, Elizabeth M. Schneider, and Nancy Stearns, "Constitutional Perspectives on Sex Discrimination in Jury Selection," *Women's Rights Law Reporter*, vol. 2 (June 1975), pp. 3–12 (arguing (before *Duren*) that the existence of automatic exemptions based on the notion that jury service is a particular hardship for women operates to drastically reduce the number of women serving on juries).

In addition to *Taylor's* specific ruling that domestic exemptions for women violate requirements for a fair cross section under the Sixth Amendment, the domestic exemption upheld in *Hoyt* was rendered obsolete by the Supreme Court's adoption of heightened scrutiny for all gender classifications. See generally *Frontiero* v. *Richardson*, 411 U.S. 677 (1973) (holding that classifications based on sex are subjected to strict scrutiny); *Craig* v. *Boren*, 429 U.S. 190 (1976) (settling on intermediate scrutiny as the official standard of review for gender classifications). Under intermediate scrutiny, the reasons advanced in *Hoyt* favoring the exemption would likely fail to meet the required showing that the exemption was substantially related to an important governmental interest. Administrative convenience has been rejected as a justification for gender classifications, as have laws which protect archaic and overbroad generalization. See, for example, *Wengler* v. *Druggist's Mutual Ins. Co.*, 446 U.S. 142 (1980) (invalidating automatic assumption of dependency of women on their husbands, but not vice versa for purposes of workers' compensation death benefits); *Schlesinger* v. *Ballard*, 419 U.S. 498, 508 (1975) (upholding differential treatment of women for purposes of tenure in the navy where women have fewer opportunities to complete the requisite number of tasks required for promotion). Under this heightened scrutiny, the desire to keep women as the center of home and family would definitely be struck down as a justification for a law that facially adverted to gender.

93. *Ballard* v. *United States*, 329 U.S. 187, 193-94 (1946), discussed in text at notes 50–53 (holding that women may not be systematically excluded from jury service in federal courts that sit in states allowing them to serve). The Court relied in this case on its supervisory power and on Judicial Code S.275, 28 U.S.C. S241.

94. *Edmonson* v. *Leesville Concrete, Inc.*, 111 S. Ct. at 2087 (1991). The Court made this observation in relation to its finding of state action. The paragraph quoted in the text continues: "The injury to excluded jurors would be the direct result of governmental delegation and participation." Ibid. *Edmonson* contains as well a paean to the importance of the civil jury that would be inconsistent with sex discrimination in its administration. Ibid. at 2082.

95. *Frontiero* v. *Richardson*, 411 U.S. 677 (1973) (holding it a denial of equal protection for women's military dependents to receive less than men's dependents). "What differentiates sex from such nonsuspect statuses as intelligence or physical disability, and aligns it with

the recognized suspect criteria, is that the sex characteristic frequently bears no relation to ability to perform or contribute to society. As a result, statutory distinctions between the sexes often have the effect of invidiously relegating the entire class of females to inferior legal status without regard to the actual capabilities of its individual members. Ibid. at 686–87. Counsel for petitioner in *State* v. *Eiland*, note 71 (arguing that the prosecutor's peremptory challenges of black women violate equal protection) point out that the Court in its most recent peremptory challenge case, *Georgia* v. *McCollum*, stated that "constitutional considerations militate against the divisive assumption—as a per se rule— that justice in a court of law may turn upon the pigmentation of skin, *the accident of birth*, or the choice of religion." Ibid. at 2539. The Court's reference to 'the accident of birth' clearly indicates that peremptory strikes aimed specifically at women are unlawful, for the Court has previously remarked that "sex . . . is an immutable characteristic determined solely by *the accident of birth.*" (citing *Frontiero* at 686; emphasis added). Brief of Petitioner, at 17.

96. Anne Rankin Mahoney, "Sexism in Voir Dire: The Use of Sex Stereotypes in Jury Selection," in Winifred L. Hepperle and Laura Crites, eds., *Women in the Courts* (Williamsburg, Va.: National Center for State Courts, 1978), pp. 118–21 (noting that predictions of how women jurors will behave receive particular attention in trial practice manuals); Solomon M. Fulero and Steven D. Penrod, "Jury Selection Folklore: What Do They Think and How Can Psychologists Help," *Forensic Reports* (July–September 1990), pp. 233, 236–37; and Weisbrod, "Images of the Woman Juror."

97. *Strauder* v. *West Virginia*, 100 U.S. at 308.

98. See *Holland* v. *Illinois*, 493 U.S. at 486 (Scalia, J.) (analogizing a white defendant's challenge to the strikes of blacks to a claim based on the exclusion of "postmen, or lawyers, or clergymen, or any number of other identifiable groups").

99. Karen Czapanskiy, "Gender Bias in the Courts: Social Change Strategies," *Georgetown Journal of Legal Ethics*, vol. 4 (Fall 1990), pp. 1, 1–3; Jeannette Swent, "Gender Bias at the Seat of Justice: An Empirical Study of State Task Forces," *Law & Society Review*, forthcoming (shows that the one universal finding of the completed reports is that the courtroom atmosphere is still decidedly chilly for women).

100. Judy Clarke, Mario Conte, and Sara Rapport, Brief of Amicus Curiae, National Association of Criminal Defense Lawyers on Rehearing En Banc, *U.S.* v. *DeGross*, 960 F.2d 1433 (1991) at 21-37. See note 68. See also Amicus Curiae Brief for Elizabeth Holtzman, *Batson* v. *Kentucky*, 476 U.S. 79 (1986). Marcia Greenberger and Myung Lee for the National Women's Law Center as Amicus Curiae in *Eiland* v. *Maryland*, notes 71, 95. In addition to litigating the issue of gender-based peremptory challenges, women are also the leading academic commentators on the subject. See, for example, Weisbrod, "Images of the Woman Juror"; Underwood, "Ending Race Discrimination in Jury Selection"; and Sagawa, "*Batson* v. *Kentucky.*"

101. *Batson* v. *Kentucky*, 476 U.S. 79, 107-08 (Marshall, J., concurring). Alschuler, "The Supreme Court and the Jury," pp. 199–211; Brent J. Gurney, "The Case for Abolishing Peremptory Challenges in Criminal Trials," *Harvard Civil Rights-Civil Liberties Law Review*, vol. 21 (Winter 1986), pp. 227–84; Clara L. Meek, "The Use of Peremptory Challenges to Exclude Blacks from Petit Juries in Civil Actions: The Case for Striking Peremptory Strikes," *Review of Litigation*, vol. 4 (Spring 1985), pp. 182–84.

102. "A careful examination of the Batson opinion, however, leads this Court to the firm conclusion that, in light of the important position of the peremptory challenge in our jury system, the Court intended Batson to apply to prohibit the exercise of peremptory challenges on the basis of race only." *United States* v. *Hamilton*, at 1042-43, quoted approvingly in *Eiland* v. *State*, 607 A.2d 42, 59 (Md. App.1992). See generally cases cited in note 68.

103. Underwood, "Ending Race Discrimination in Jury Selection," pp. 761–73; Robert

L. Harris, Jr., "Redefining the Harm of Peremptory Challenges," *William and Mary Law Review*, vol. 32 (Summer 1991), pp. 1027–64; Note, "Beyond Batson: Eliminating Gender-Based Peremptory Challenges," *Harvard Law Review*, vol. 105 (June 1992), pp. 1920–39.

104. *Batson*, 476 U.S 79, 127 (Burger, C. J., dissenting); *McCollum* v. *Georgia*, 112 S. Ct. 2348, 2367 (Thomas, J., dissenting); see also Irving Younger, "Unlawful Peremptory Challenges," *Litigation*, vol. 7 (Fall 1980), pp. 23, 56 (*Batson* line will result in elimination of peremptory altogether).

105. See *Holland* v. *Illinois*; and "We have acknowledged that this device [the peremptory challenge] occupies 'an important position in our trial procedures,' and has indeed been considered 'a necessary part of trial by jury.'" *Holland* v. *Illinois*, at 484.

106. Paul D. Carrington, "The Seventh Amendment: Some Bicentennial Reflections," *University of Chicago Legal Forum*, vol. 1990, pp. 33, 36–39. (reviewing history of jury trial).

107. See the text coinciding with notes 13-14. Underwood, "Ending Race Discrimination in Jury Selection," p. 771 (peremptory as a "margin of protection" for cause challenges).

108. See text accompanying note 13. This was written in the criminal context about the right to challenge peremptorily as "a provision full of that tenderness and humanity to prisoners for which our English laws are justly famous." Ibid.

109. *Edmonson*, 111 S. Ct. at 2088.

110. Many of the suggestions here were presented at the Conference on the Civil Jury from which this book springs. See especially the chapter by H. Lee Sarokin and G. Thomas Munsterman, and the one by Stephen A. Saltzburg in this volume.

111. See, for example, David Kairys, Joseph B. Kadane, and John P. Lehoczky, "Jury Representativeness: A Mandate for Multiple Source Lists," *California Law Review*, vol. 65 (July 1977), pp. 776–827.

112. Pizzi, "*Batson* v. *Kentucky*, pp. 147–51, suggests this change, while acknowledging the difficulties of statutory reform.

113. See, for example, Schwarzer, "Reforming Jury Trials," *Federal Rules Decisions*, vol. 132 (West, 1991), pp. 575, 581; see the chapter by Sarokin and Munsterman in this volume; Robert M. Takasug, "Jury Selection in a High-Profile Case: *United States* v. *DeLorean*," *American University Law Review*, vol. 40 (Winter 1990), pp. 837–46 (discussing the jury questionnaire in *United States* v. *DeLorean*, a highly publicized criminal case in which the defendant was acquitted). Questionnaires may not only provide a greater volume but also may raise the quality of information. See Robert W. Balch and others, "The Socialization of Jurors: The Voir Dire as Rite of Passage," *Journal of Criminal Justice*, vol. 4 (Winter 1976), pp. 271, 278 (reporting strong tendency of jurors in oral voir dire to provide answers they felt the questioner wanted or expected them to give).

114. *McCollum* v. *Georgia* holds that the third party standing which allows litigants to raise the rights of excluded jurors depends partly on the bond formed between attorneys and potential jurors at the voir dire. 112 S. Ct. 2348 (1992); see also *Powers* v. *Ohio*, 111 S. Ct. 1364, 1372 (1991); *Edmonson* v. *Leesville Concrete Co.*, 111 S. Ct. 2077, 2087 (1991). The public inquiry will better enable the establishment of such a bond if private questionnaires are first administered, allowing for better framing of questions, and perhaps on some sensitive issues, individual voir dire out of the presence of the other venirepersons. (This aspect of McCollum would also support attorney-conducted voir dire, which has recently become less frequent in federal jury trials. See FRCP 47 (a) allowing judge-conducted voir dire in the court's discretion.) For other suggestions on improving voir dire through a combination of attorney and judge conducted inquiry and questionnaires, see Barbara Babcock, "Voir Dire: Preserving Its Wonderful Power," *Stanford Law Review*, vol. 27 (Fall 1975), pp. 561–62.

Some provision for the confidentiality of jury questionnaires must be included in the statute or considered case by case. *In re South Carolina Press Ass'n.*, 946 F.2d 1037 (4th Cir. 1991) (limited public and press access to juror questionnaires that were described as "designed to examine the prospective jurors' possible racial prejudice, attitudes toward elected officials, concerns about 'sting' operations, efforts to bribe members of the General Assembly, use of undercover agents, possible entrapment, and may other sensitive areas.") Ibid., at 1028, n.2.

115. See the chapter by Sarokin and Munsterman in this volume; Judge Jim Corrigan (N.D. Colo.) reported successful use of this technique at the Charlottesville conference.

116. Noting that the purpose of *Batson* is to eliminate discrimination, not to minimize it, the New York Court of Appeals has, in effect, canceled the requirement of a prima facie case. *People* v. *Jenkins*, 554 N.E.2d 47 (1990). Mary Erickson, "Administering *Batson*," research memorandum (on file with author) finds that "fast forwarding" to the *Batson* inquiry is the trend but notes the importance of making a record on voir dire sufficient for review.

117. Clarence Darrow, "Attorney for the Defense," *Esquire*, May 1936, p. 35. Cited in Younger, "Unlawful Peremptory," p. 23.

118. Darrow, "Attorney for the Defense." Darrow did not use the male pronoun generically, since he advised striking any women who might be called.

119. *McNeil* v. *Nat'l. Football League* (D. Minn. 1992).

120. Under similar circumstances, in *Los Angeles Memorial Coliseum Commission* v. *NFL* 726 F.2d 1381 (9th Cir. 1984), the court administered a forty-eight page questionnaire, provided each party with ten peremptory challenges, and dismissed "jurors for cause if even the slightest doubt of prejudice was raised." Ibid., at 1400.

121. See, for example, *Franklin* v. *Gwinnett County Public Schools*, 112 S. Ct. 1028 (1992) (damages and jury trial mandated in a case in which a female student sought damages because of alleged sexual harassment by a male high school teacher).

122. See Tracey L. Altman, "Affirmative Selection: A New Response to Peremptory Challenge Abuse," *Stanford Law Review* vol. 38 (February 1986), pp. 781, 806; Hans Zeisel, "Affirmative Peremptory Juror Selection," *Stanford Law Review*, vol. 39 (May 1987), pp. 1165–72 (variations on the affirmative selection scheme); and Harris, "Redefining the Harm," pp. 1027, 1056–64 (endorsing and further refining the idea).

123. This designation is Barbara Underwood's in "Ending Race Discrimination in Jury Selection."

124. State courts in California, Massachusetts, and Florida have had more than a decade's experience in administering *Batson*-type rules. As Barbara Underwood points out, their "experience suggests that the cost of administering the rule need not be overwhelming." See "Ending Race Discrimination in Jury Selection," p. 769. See also Gerald I. Uelmen, "Striking Jurors under *Batson* v. *Kentucky*: Lessons from California," *Criminal Justice*, vol. 2 (Fall 1987), pp. 2–5; and Mary Erickson, "Administering *Batson*."

CHAPTER FIFTEEN

Finding the Factfinders

Judith Resnik

IN 1979, veterinarians employed by the University of California published a report that described the death of some 848 cows, owned by George Neary. The report concluded that the cattle had died from mismanagement, and not from the spraying of toxaphene, a chemical provided by health officials for the pregnant heifers who might have been exposed to scabies mite.[1]

George Neary sued the veterinarians and the university; he claimed that he had been libeled by the report. After a trial of more than four months, a jury awarded him seven million dollars. The defendants appealed, but then the parties informed the appellate court of their settlement—contingent upon action by that court. The *Neary* litigants agreed to settle *if* the intermediate appellate court dismissed the appeal, reversed or vacated the jury verdict, and ordered the dismissal with prejudice of the case.[2] In other words, the *Neary* litigants asked for a consent judgment, entered by an appellate court, instead of by a trial court, and justified the request on the basis of the litigants' need for "peace of mind."[3]

The intermediate appellate court said no: The Honorable J. Anthony

Copyright, Judith Resnik. This essay was written with the support of the American Bar Association's Litigation Section and the Brookings Institution. My thanks to Liz Atlee, Heidi Binford, Christine Carr, and Lee Seltman for their thoughtful research assistance, and to Dennis Curtis, John C. Coughenour, and Stephen Yeazell for helping me think about these issues.

I write about events in which I have participated. I have provided testimony on proposed amendments to the Federal Rules of Civil Procedure, provided an opinion letter to the California Supreme Court on the petition for review in *Neary* v. *Board of Regents of the University of California*, am a member of the ABA Litigation Section Task Force on the Civil Justice Reform Act, have consulted on some of the large-scale cases discussed, and served as an advisor to a subcommittee of the Federal Courts Study Committee.

Kline, writing for the court, concluded that while the parties were free to settle, they could not insist that an appellate court change a jury judgment as a part of that settlement. As he explained: "As imperfect as the process of trial may be, it is the way in which our society establishes legal truth. Because it is an adjudicative and not simply a dispositional act, the reversal of a judgment not thought to be legally erroneous simply to effectuate settlement would trivialize the work of the trial courts and undermine the integrity of the entire judicial process."[4] That decision sparked considerable controversy,[5] as has the decision of the California Supreme Court, which ordered the intermediate appellate court to grant the stipulated reversal.[6]

I will leave to others to consider the effects of *Neary* on the jury system.[7] I begin with *Neary* for another reason: It illustrates the interaction between attitudes toward settlement and attitudes toward trial and thus exemplifies the point of this essay. This symposium about changes—over the course of this century—in the role of the jury must consider the jury as but one instance of an activity done by judges or jurors: factfinding.[8] Whether by judge or jury, factfinding today is a deeply contested phenomenon, as is reflected in contemporary practice, procedure, and politics.

Below I bring together a range of developments, primarily about litigation in the federal courts, that point in the same direction: to declining interest in factfinding, to limiting roles for factfinders, and to the growing commitment to managed settlements in lieu of adjudication. The issues raised by *Neary* are questions of legal and social policy: how much adjudication (by judge or by jury) do we, as a polity, want to promote? Should we be urging changes in the modes of adjudication or alternatives to adjudication? What, after trial, is the import of decisions rendered by judge or jury? Are virtually all parties' agreements to conclude without adjudication acceptable, or are there limits on what agreements should be given the force of law? Should parties have the power to require (or request) that an appellate court obliterate a jury verdict that has not been challenged on any legally cognizable ground?

These questions are being answered, often *sub silentio*, via rule changes, legal doctrine, and policy arguments that are gaining currency. My purpose here is to push these questions into sharper focus and to link the changes in rules for bench trials and civil litigation—outside the context of the jury—to the concerns that are at the center of this symposium: the future of the jury trial. I believe that the question to be asked is about the future of factfinding itself.

Contemporary Alterations of Adjudication

In this section, I provide examples of the changing attitudes toward litigatory procedure. In legislation, in rule-making, and by proposed procedural innovations, policy makers are announcing preferences that are decidedly anti-trial.

Avoiding Trial and Changing Its Forms

My first example comes from the recently enacted Civil Justice Reform Act of 1990 (CJRA).[9] That legislation required that each of the ninety-four federal district courts develop plans to promote the reduction of "expense and delay" in civil litigation and to "ensure just, speedy, and inexpensive resolutions of civil disputes."[10] According to Congress, district court planners had to consider (and could implement) a series of "principles and guidelines"—including "differential treatment" (often called "tracking") of cases based on complexity or other characteristics; "early and ongoing control of the pretrial process through involvement of a judicial officer;" and "monitoring" of and limitations on discovery.[11]

Since the act, the chief judges of the federal district courts have formed the required advisory groups, which in turn have filed reports and made plans. In both the legislation and the documents written in its wake, the focus is not on adjudication—on trials either by jury or judge or on factfinding on the papers. The focus, instead, is on disposition by other means. The legislation itself provides the first example. Early drafts of the bill did not include discussion of adjudication; as enacted, the statute mentions adjudication once.[12] Juries are not mentioned at all; trial is mentioned only in the context of preparing for trial, setting firm trial dates (or being unable to do so because of a case's complexity), and bifurcating trial.[13] In contrast, settlement and alternative dispute resolution play prominent roles in the statute.[14]

The sponsors of the legislation should be pleased to learn that many of the district reports and plans echo the Civil Justice Act's orientation. Managerial judging, settlement, and alternative dispute resolution feature prominently in the reports; trials (by judge or jury) are less visible issues. For analyses of the more than thirty reports available as of this writing, I rely here primarily on memoranda prepared by members of the Civil Justice Reform Act Task Force, formed by the Section on Litigation of the American Bar Association (ABA).[15] These analyses examine the central elements of the local plans: judicial management, differential case management, pretrial motions, phased discovery, mandatory disclosure, discovery limits, and alternative dispute resolution.[16] I do not want to be read as overstating the case; the possibility of trial is not utterly ignored by the reports, but as the members of the CJRA Task Force of the ABA note, trial is not the centerpiece of any of the plans.[17] As George Beall put it: "there is very little discussion in the Plans at this point about trial procedure generally. . . ."[18]

Think about trying to learn—from reading these CJRA reports and plans—about how litigation is conducted in the federal courts of the United States in the early 1990s. One could fairly conclude that factfinding by trial—with either judge or jury—is not a central topic. Further, while it is possible that trial is so problem-free that it requires little additional attention,[19] the more plausible explanation is that trial is not a dominant concern, because the focus has shifted to stressing techniques that avoid trial.

Recent and proposed amendments to the Federal Rules of Civil Procedure provide another source of information about changing attitudes toward adjudication. The major rule changes in the 1980s promote managerial judging, with its concomitant control over the pretrial process and the pressures for dispositions without trial.[20] These changes are of a piece with the CJRA, pressing judges into managerial and settlement modes and continuing the shift of attention, begun with the 1938 Federal Rules of Civil Procedure, from the trial to the pretrial process.[21]

In addition to these changes in Rules 11, 16, and 26, all of which have been much discussed, recent (and in some sense "sleeper") proposals, about relatively low-visibility rules that have particular relevance to factfinding, also deserve attention. These proposals alter the mode of factfinding for judges by promoting the use of documentary rather than live testimony.

In 1989, the Advisory Committee on the Federal Rules of Civil Procedure recommended revision of Rule 63, which had been entitled "Disability of a Judge." That rule had provided that if "by reason of death, sickness, or other disability, a judge before whom an action has been tried" is unable to perform his or her judicial duties, another judge may step in, but only "*after* a verdict is returned or findings of fact and conclusions of law are filed."[22]

In contrast, the Advisory Committee proposed a new title—"Inability of a Judge to Proceed"—and a new rule: one judge should be authorized to substitute for another whenever a trial judge was "unable to proceed," even when that judge was in the midst of a "trial or a hearing."[23] The only predicates to substitution were that the substitute judge certify "familiarity with the record" and determine that the "proceedings in the case may be completed without prejudice to the parties." At his or her discretion, the substitute judge could also "recall any witnesses."[24] In the version that was promulgated by the Supreme Court and that became effective in December of 1991, parties gained the right to insist that a witness be recalled, if that witness had "material" testimony and was "available to testify again without undue burden."[25]

This amendment changed Rule 63 in two respects. First, it altered the *reasons* for substitution. Prior to the 1991 amendments, only "death, sickness, or other disability" justified substitution of a factfinding judge. Now, all that is required is a general inability "to proceed," explained in the Advisory Committee Note as appropriate mid-trial only for "compelling reasons."[26] Further, no preference for a hiatus in the trial, rather than the substitution of a judge, is expressed. Second, the revision altered the *timing* of substitution. Under the prior rule, substitution *during* a trial or hearing was not permitted. Under the new rule, a substitute judge can come in at any time and, in a bench trial, make findings of fact and conclusions of law—even if that judge has not heard the witnesses' oral testimony nor certified more than "familiarity" with the record.[27] As the Advisory Committee stated: "The revised text [of Rule 63] authorizes the substitute judge to make a finding of fact at a bench trial on evidence heard by a different judge."[28]

A second challenge to the privileged place of oral testimony came by means of another proposed rule amendment (first set forth in 1991 and then withdrawn in the spring of 1992[29]) to alter Rule 43, which governs the "Taking of Testimony." Rule 43 generally requires that "[i]n all trials the testimony of witnesses shall be taken orally in open court."[30] In August of 1991, the Advisory Committee proposed eliminating that requirement. Instead, in *non-jury* trials, the Committee proposed that the direct examination of expert or lay witnesses could be presented— by order of the trial court—by written report.[31] Cross-examination "in the traditional manner" (i.e., oral) would still have been permitted.[32] Whatever might come from the interruptions—to ask questions, to probe answers, and to clarify comments—that trial judges make when witnesses testify in bench trials, the initial proposal of the Advisory Committee was to grant judges the power to compel (even over parties' objections) the written word instead.[33] While the proposal was only for direct testimony in bench trials, its premises might well prompt other changes. If judges can read, why not let juries do the same? If oral direct testimony can be limited, why not cabin cross-examination to the written form as well?

Such a revision of Rule 43 would have had a similar effect to the new Rule 63—moving a part of the oral conversations of trial offstage and substituting written materials for interpersonal live exchanges.[34] That preference for written words is not dampened by the knowledge that much (all?) written testimonials provided to judges are authored by lawyers, and that the judicial time saved by conversion to the written process depends, in part, on a judge's capacity to skim (skip?) much of what is written. In short, these proposals would transform the judicial factfinder from a person who *listens* to a person who *peruses* and would make the federal civil process even more lawyer dependent than it currently is.

Amended Rule 63 raises constitutional issues,[35] but those questions are not my concern here. The changes in Rule 63 and those proposed for Rule 43 are of interest because of what they reflect about changing attitudes toward the factfinding process. Images of trials within the Western tradition—whether from Renaissance paintings or contemporary television dramas—place witnesses before factfinders. This image of trial is reflected in Supreme Court doctrine; in a case about the power of a trial judge to reassess issues decided by a magistrate judge (and which provides another example of the problem raised by the Rule 63 amendments[36]), Justice Marshall (in dissent) invoked the axiom: "[t]he one who decides must hear."[37] Embedded in this principle are views about accuracy, participation, interpersonal contact and responsibility, fairness, and the nature of the very activity of "trial."

To give oral testimony before one person and then have a decision rendered by another who has not heard that testimony (Rule 63) or to give written testimony (proposed Rule 43) challenges this definition of trial. The substitution of a different judge for the person who has heard earlier testimony alters, retrospectively, the value to the oral exchanges that predated the substitution. Absent repetition of oral testimony, the relevance of taking that testimony orally is diminished—as demonstrated by the suggestion of eliminating oral direct testimony completely in bench trials. If reading testimony is an appropriate basis for judgment, why take any oral testimony?

One answer to this question is that listening to witnesses does not enhance the capacity to assess the accuracy of their statements, and whatever other uses that listening has do not provide sufficient basis for preserving the oral exchanges of traditional trials. Contemporary theories of cognitive processes support such a view; psychologists have documented the disutility of reliance on demeanor evidence.[38] With these insights, Rule 63 and the tentative rewriting of Rule 43 mark the beginning of a recognition that factfinding-by-reading is as valuable as factfinding-by-listening, and that the era in which oral testimony is a privileged form is waning. These rules move toward a different model of adjudication, one more responsive to the phenomenon of longer trials and to the other demands on trial judges' time. Under this model, discussions about "dry" and "cold" records being insufficient bases for judgment would be replaced not only by claims of economy of time but also about the desirability of such "dry" transcripts. The proposed revisions could well mark a quiet but revolutionary challenge to the long-standing legal presumption in favor of live testimony.[39]

One response to that challenge might come from a view that the presentation of testimony orally is not only justified by the value of assessing witnesses' demeanor or enhancing accuracy but is also supported by a political theory about the source of legitimacy of judgments enforced by the state. One might conceive of a trial as a highly personal, immediate, and compelling event for participants (and, in the rare instances of televised trials, for more distant viewers as well). In a bench trial, one might understand the trial judge as in a continuing conversation with litigants and lawyers; the judge raises questions, makes judgments about permitting and limiting testimony, presses a particular witness, or determines that no additional information is needed. Under this vision, the trial is an intensely interactive dialogic process; the trial judge's personal role (ranging from active governance to a more umpirial style) is critical to the jurist's formation of a judgment. This line of argument insists on the personal exchange as a means for making judges more responsible decisionmakers which in turn protects citizens from the anonymity of the bureaucratic state.

The kind of debate I have just outlined—between critics of judgments founded on the demeanor of witnesses and proponents of trials at which witnesses testify orally—has not, unfortunately, accompanied the rule revisions. Relatively little attention is being paid to these potentially profound changes in the *mode* of factfinding. My thesis is that skepticism about the *need* for factfinding diminishes interest in whatever proposals are made to change how judges find facts. Case law such as *Neary*, the absence of discussion of factfinding in the CJRA and the plans it has spawned, and the delegation of factfinding to lower echelon judges (detailed below) all reiterate this contemporary disinterest in finding facts. The activity of factfinding—that messy, difficult task of sorting through conflicting claims of knowledge and right to construct descriptions that have the weight of legal "fact" and that have the force of law—moves into the shadows, as simply not central to the litigation world.

Changing Factfinders

Not only are the modes of decisionmaking in federal courts shifting away from trials (either by judge or jury), the people who do factfinding, to the extent there is any, are also changing. The desirability of adding a "fourth tier" to the federal court system has been much discussed; the fourth tier referred to in that debate is another set of appellate judges, sitting between the Supreme Court and the current Courts of Appeals.[40] However, that discussion misses that there already *is* a fourth tier—at the bottom of the hierarchy, at the trial level.

As of 1990, Congress had authorized the appointment of 575 Article III life-tenured trial judges,[41] who worked on a caseload of approximately 280,000 civil and criminal cases.[42] In addition, some 301 full-time and 156 part-time magistrates, newly renamed "magistrate judges,"[43] worked as delegatees of the district court. In 1987, federal magistrates presided over some 500,000 judicial proceedings; they conducted 134,000 preliminary hearings in felony cases, took references from Article III judges to consider 197,000 civil and criminal pretrial issues, considered 6,500 social security "appeals" and 27,000 prisoner filings, and "tried more than 95,000 misdemeanor and 4,900 civil cases on consent of the parties."[44] As a specially commissioned study by the Ninth Circuit described, "magistrates now possess the authority to handle, under appropriate circumstances, virtually any matter normally decided by district judges, except for felony trials and sentencing."[45]

Another three hundred "bankruptcy judges," sitting as "units" of the district court, preside over the more than 700,000 bankruptcy petitions filed annually.[46] Federal adjudication does not, however, only occur in the "federal courts." Agencies are a critical place in which factfinders make decisions on individual cases. For example, as of April of 1991, almost 1,100 people were administrative law judges (ALJs) in the Social Security Administration.[47] Those judges decide more than 250,000 claims annually.[48]

The powers of these Article III delegatees are currently disputed, but their authority over factfinding is growing. In the 1930s, when litigants challenged the authority of agency factfinders, the Supreme Court cautioned against the delegation of "essential attributes of judicial power."[49] While a deputy commissioner of the United States Employees' Compensation Commission could make certain kinds of factual decisions, it would be unconstitutional, said the Court, to permit too much delegation. Congress could not transfer from the federal courts all factfinding powers, for to do so "would be to sap the judicial power as it exists under the federal Constitution, and to establish a government of a bureaucratic character alien to our system."[50]

Since the 1930s, Congress has created and then increased magistrate judges' authority,[51] expanded the range of agency adjudication, and conferred new powers on bankruptcy judges; almost all of these legislative innovations have met with Supreme Court approval.[52] Moreover, contemporary proposals call for more powers to be conferred on these "other" federal judges. For example, Congress charged the Federal Courts Study Committee (FCSC) with developing "a long-range plan for the future of the Federal judiciary."[53] Concerned about the special role of Article III judges[54] and believing that it was critical to keep the number of such judges small,[55] the FCSC Report urged that, in a variety of federal civil statutory cases, more of the first-line adjudicatory work—factfinding and sometimes a first level of appellate review—be shifted away from Article III judges to others. Building on earlier proposals to exclude Social Security cases from Article III jurisdiction,[56] the FCSC Report called (over dissents from some members) for the creation of a special disability court, staffed with non-Article III judges, and of limited Article III review when "constitutional claims" and "pure questions of law" were at issue. In addition, the FCSC Report recommended administrative decisionmaking for cases under the Federal Employer Liability Act and the Jones Act; Article I status for Tax Court trial (but not appellate) judges; Article I decisionmaking in federal tort claims when the matter in controversy is under $10,000; and increased powers for bankruptcy judges and magistrate judges.[57]

The legal issue today is no longer whether judicial factfinding can be delegated but whether there are any limits on that delegation. The Supreme Court leaves murky the powers of bankruptcy judges to conduct jury trials,[58] and one federal courts scholar argues that the critical Article III ingredient is *not* factfinding but appellate review.[59] Implicit in the proposals of the FCSC Report is not only a return to a formalistic division between law and fact but also a devaluation of the task of factfinding. Given the Report's attitude that Article III judges are the key, elite cadre of decisionmakers, the Report's willingness to delegate factfinding elsewhere bespeaks a view that factfinding is not the "important" work of "important" judges. Interacting with litigants, lawyers, and witnesses—listening to differing versions of events and attempting to construct narratives—is for second-order judges and thus is second-order work.[60]

Changing the Scope of the Case to Be Adjudicated

One reason to shift factfinding away from Article III judges is a view that they have other—more "valuable"—work to do. What is that other work? Managing and settling cases, justified as saving time, takes time, and those activities are one source of the new definition of the work of the trial judge.[61] In addition, federal litigation is increasingly focused not on individual case adjudication but on large-scale litigation.

In the 1960s, federal rule drafters frowned on the use of class actions for mass torts. Rule drafters assumed that individual cases were the norm, and group litigation needed special justification. In the specific context of mass torts, rule drafters believed that the need for aggregation of cases was outweighed by an understanding of such torts as imposing individual, specific injuries, inappropriate for treatment under a common rubric.[62]

Over the past thirty years, that attitude has changed. The perceived usefulness of aggregation has fueled informal and formal changes to enable more group litigation—not only by class actions, but by multi-district litigation, consolidation, joinder, and a myriad of techniques developed by lawyers and judges to bring groups of litigants together.[63] Several proposals, including statutory changes to relax the requirements for diversity in certain kinds of mass torts, have been put forth to increase the possibilities of aggregation.[64] Enthusiasm within the legal community for changes to enable greater use of aggregative processing is substantial. While the Report of the ABA Task Force on Mass Torts did not garner the approval of the American Bar Association, the American Law Institute's ongoing Project on Complex Litigation is exemplary of efforts on the agendas of law reform groups, to reframe statutes and rules to enable additional group processes.[65] Mass torts are but one example of the growing interest in group processing; federal sentencing guidelines and administrative compensation schemes are others.

As multi-party, multi-claim litigation becomes ever-more commonplace, attitudes change about the appropriate scale of any given case. The pursuit of group-based, large-scale processes alters the perception of the utility, desirability, and value of responding to individual small cases. "Complex litigation" becomes the title of a law school course, and lawyers specialize in such work. But naming cases "small" or "large," "simple" or "complex," "routine" or "novel" comes not from absolute values but relative judgments.[66] As "large" cases become more frequently constructed and perceived as more "interesting" than "small" cases, adjudicating *individual* cases is viewed as less desirable. The pressures to settle or move such cases to alternative dispute resolution (ADR)— or out of the Article III courts altogether[67]—demonstrate an unwillingness to spend the time and money on and to devote the social resources to individual claims.

Where is factfinding in these increasingly common large-scale "litigations"? In a few instances, such lawsuits themselves go to trial, at least in part.[68] But the pressures to settle large cases are also great.[69] The prospects of gargantuan trials are unappealing—not only because of the legal, management, and logistical issues but also because of the size of the stakes. Those settlements, however, do not end all questions of fact. When monetary damages are involved, *disaggregation* is frequently required to disperse the funds. Sometimes, a preexisting formula is applied, in lieu of individual decisionmaking after settlement.[70] But often, questions about which plaintiff gets what amount of money remain.

To respond, these cases generate their own "claims facilities," which are in essence mini-agencies, created to implement a particular remedial scheme and to adjudicate as needed.[71] Just as in courts, the popular mode of decisionmaking in claims facilities is ADR.[72] But just as in courts, some small percentage of the individual cases require third-party resolution of disputed facts, and something called "trial" is often offered.[73] Those trials, however, may not look quite like what is available in courts.[74] Unlike courts, claims facilities are low-visibility places. Premises of ready public access do not necessarily apply; information about the facilities may be limited, and the persons who do factfinding may never be identified to the public at large.[75]

The Future of Factfinding

Let me clarify what I take to be the import of these recent procedural developments. For decades, most cases have ended—by being withdrawn, settled, or disposed of on the papers—before trial. As a consequence, trial has been and remains the *unusual* method of disposition. Thus, I am not making an argument that the general mode of case disposition has suddenly shifted away from trial.[76] Further, given the dispersion of factfinding to lower-tier judges, agencies, and claims facilities, quantifying the amount of factfinding and comparing it to prior eras is problematic. The ever-present issue of a baseline against which to measure and the minimal empirical information available preclude claims of more or less factfinding in the federal adjudicatory world, once it is redefined to include adjudication by non-Article III federal judges.

Instead, I am making an argument about change in the *value* attached to trials, to factfinding by either judge or jury and by either Article III judge or non-Article III judge. Recently enacted legislation, rule changes, pending civil justice proposals, and the delegation of factfinding powers away from the Article III judiciary all demonstrate that factfinding is viewed as not very desirable. The message that emerges—if you are a litigant or a judge—is that the polity would prefer that you avoid doing it.

If I am correct that there is a decline in appreciation for factfinding, questions emerge. What are the sources? Where will this orientation take us? Having documented the shift in emphasis, let me turn now to these issues. The many pressures to move away from adjudication to other means of disposition or resolution bespeak a shared distaste for and distrust of factfinding. Of course, one explanation is that the cost of factfinding (with the particularly expensive element of fees paid to lawyers to generate that factfinding) is simply too great. While astonishing costs are unquestionably a factor, I believe that there is more at work than costs. As I have described elsewhere, there is a deeper skepticism, a failing faith that adjudication generates results "worth" not only the expense but the social value accorded.[77] Belief in the value of adjudication is undermined by contemporary fact skepticism, by a sense of the frequent mismatch of resources in adjudication, and by views that the system of adjudication is laden with prejudice.

Those attitudes are both exemplified and fueled by proposed changes in legal doctrine. The Civil Justice Reform Act is not called the "Civil Speedy *Trial* Act,"[78] and does not reaffirm the value of factfinding; it invites alternative dispute resolution and consensual outcomes. While ADR embraces a range of activities and has a host of adherents, many of whom begin from differing world views, there is a common thread—that the outcomes achieved by ADR are not only cheaper and faster, but also *better* than those that are achieved after factfinding.[79] ADR consists of processes that, as compared to trial, are abbreviated; implicit in claims for ADR is a deep-seated hostility to the longer version of factfinding that is trial.[80] Proposed sanctions for failure to settle reiterate that it is wrong to insist on trial but wise to accommodate. The disinterest manifest in ADR in factfinding results in the reallocation of that task to other judges. Taking factfinding away from the most prestigious judges underscores that the idea that factfinding is not a task on which those judges should be spending their time.

If the current trends continue, the contours of litigation in the federal courts in the twenty-first century become predictable. Article III district court judges will move further away from the work of factfinding, which will itself move "down" to become the domain of lower-level, less visible federal judges, who themselves will read more documents than listen to witnesses. Article III district judges will preside over a tier of decisionmakers, most of whom will also press litigants to settle rather than try cases.[81] The current preference for ADR will become more insistent and aggressive.[82] Factfinding—especially of individual claims— will thus become an extraordinary event in Article III civil litigation, and will require special justification before it is permitted. While I hold no view that factfinding is an activity sacrosanct for Article III judges, those judges who are empowered in their stead by the state with the capacity to find fact deserve societal attention and respect, and they ought to be visible. Unfortunately, there is little current evidence that the transfer of factfinding and other tasks to lower-tier judges will be accompanied by concomitant commitments of either social resources or prestige equal to their expanded roles.[83]

If this description is plausible and these predictions prove true, what are we to think about these changes? One approach is to embrace this movement away from factfinding—as many have. An array of proponents (who range from evangelists to those who argue that current trends promise if not a good world, one that is better, or marginally better, than what we have) argue against factfinding.[84] Another approach is to decline to take sides. The history of adjudicatory procedure is filled with shifts in forms, from movements that empower judges at the expense of litigants to those that empower lawyers (at the expense of judges and perhaps of litigants as well).[85] The current trend could be understood as simply a shift in the balance, and as not a cause for either praise or alarm. A third approach is to worry—about what might be lost with the abandonment of factfinding. Since the contemporary debate is filled with the voices of many who heap praise on these reforms, let me sketch some of what "worrying" about the loss of factfinding by prestigious judges might entail.[86]

One concern is about the role of judges, both those who have Article III status and those who do not. The amendments to Rule 63 of the Federal Rules of Civil Procedure prove oddly prophetic; *substitution* of the judge is indeed what is happening, on a grand scale. "Inability to proceed" becomes defined as the undesirability of proceeding to find fact and to engage in adjudication. Judging itself moves from the courtroom to chambers, to conversations with lawyers or staff, and then to sub-judges, agencies, and claims facilities. Factfinding by Article III judges becomes deeply *impersonal*. While many criticize adjudication as already disengaged from litigants (the subject of decision) and disproportionately owned by the lawyers, contemporary reforms disengage adjudication from the adjudicator. The Article III trial judge as overseer and manager sees lawyers, not litigants. The demise of Article III factfinding and its movement elsewhere thus raises the problems that all liberal polities have with their decisionmakers: constraints and accountability become more difficult as the process of factfinding becomes more disengaged, closed, invisible, and unrecorded. For the "other" judges—the non-Article III bankruptcy, magistrate, and administrative law judges—yet another issue is the political value that will be attached to their work.

Let me be clear. Questioning current procedural trends away from factfinding does not require an argument that traditional factfinding was a perfect (or even a particularly good) process of ensuring accountable decisionmaking. (I am personally skeptical about some of the arguments that have been made about the benefits of open court processes.[87]) But unease about the success of factfinding does not mitigate unease about the absence of attention paid by proponents of managerial judging, ADR, and settlement to questions of legitimacy, accountability, public access, information, and the development of legal norms. Laura Macklin has described factfinding as "accessible" and "tenacious," and has argued that those attributes, coupled with the participation of opposing parties and the procedural framework that constrains factfinding, provide legitimacy for the decisions made.[88] Others may be less confident; the contemporary world of the courtroom is deeply contested, challenged as a race-biased and gender-biased world, and permeated with class advantages.[89] The verdict in the Rodney King beating confirmed many of the worst suspicions. But however painful the struggle to remake court-based factfinding, at least such a struggle is ongoing. Few admit that comparable problems must, inevitably, haunt alternative dispute resolution mechanisms and infect parties' negotiated agreements.[90]

A second concern is about the source of judicial authority—to act in both adjudicatory and non-adjudicatory modes. As judges become primarily settlers and managers, judges risk losing their distinct identity and becoming, instead, simply another set of players on a field that includes litigants, lawyers, insurance companies, arbitrators, special masters, and other facilitators of dispute resolution. But judges still retain a claim of specialness: what keeps judges distinct is that they have more *power*,[91] and it is that very power that is invoked to argue for the need to involve Article III judges, and not underlings, in case management and settlement.

Yet a problem emerges: what exactly is the basis of judicial authority to guide the parties to settlement, to oversee and sometimes to mandate ADR, and to endorse parties' agreements? The doctrinal answer is straightforward: The Civil Justice Reform Act, Rule 16 of the Federal Rules of Civil Procedure, other statutes and rules, as well as inherent court powers, confer such authority.

But the political answer is not quite so simple. Why should judges have such powers? If judges know nothing about the respective legal rights and obligations between the parties, what is the source of judicial wisdom to advise on appropriate or desirable outcomes? While Congress and the rulemakers can stipulate to such wisdom by enacting authorizing provisions, the judges who receive such grants of authority might be less welcoming of these changes.[92] Judicial authority has traditionally been justified by its labor-intensive specificity embedded in announcing rights in a particular case, by its visibility, and by the limits imposed from both process and appellate review. The stunning power that resides in individual judges[93] has many critics, and the Supreme Court has self-consciously constructed justiciability doctrines to protect against spending such powers unnecessarily.[94] Not only might the polity be nervous about how to constrain the managerial judge, but judges given those tasks might themselves pause to wonder what other changes in job descriptions were coming and whether those roles were ones to invite. One hundred years of "managerial judging" may not provide the basis for much respect for the Third Branch.

The problems of legitimating judicial exercises of authority are not limited to the situations in which judges act as ADR managers. Judges in adjudicatory roles may also face questions about what animates their rulings and the reach of their coercive powers. Given the increasingly frequent amalgam of some factfinding followed by consent, confusion has arisen about what was adjudicated by the judge and what was negotiated by the parties.[95] The fuzziness of judicial authority and party agreement may enable some "deals" that might have not occurred if factfinding had been required, but those consent judgments also preclude pronouncements of legal right. If no facts are found and no legal rights announced, exactly why should the state's authority flow to enforce the bargains struck?[96] Current doctrine documents that problem: consent is not always a basis equal to factfinding for purposes of coercive enforcement.[97] As the line between what is "law" and what is "contract" blurs, judges' capacity to enforce what they thought was predicated upon law diminishes.

A third issue is politics. According to Stephan Landsman, the movement from an inquisitorial to an adversarial mode over centuries in England did not occur with much design. "No one set out to build the adversary system."[98] The same cannot be said today. Procedural reform is plainly political, and interest groups are unabashed in their campaigns to modify procedural forms.[99] As Judge Jack Weinstein has put it, "The truth about the 'litigation explosion' is that it is a weapon of perception, not substance."[100] Thus, questions about the campaign against factfinding need to be asked: whose political interests are served and whose harmed by the diminished use of the Article III judiciary for factfinding and its transfer elsewhere?

To answer those questions one needs to pierce two claims frequently made of *civil* procedure—that it is neutral and that it is anonymous.[101] By "neutrality" I mean that in theory on the civil side, the Rules have no political content.[102] The assumption of "anonymity" is predicated on the interchangeability of civil litigants. The theory is that, in advance, one never knows who will be a plaintiff, who a defendant. Further, with trans-substantive rules, one never knows the kind of case to which a particular rule will be applied. Thus, even if rules can affect outcomes (and hence, are not really neutral after all), we all suffer them equally, sapping those rules of political content.

Neither the theory of neutrality nor the theory of anonymity turns out to be in true in practice. In practice, civil rights claimants are women and men of color and white women, and the defendants are governmental agencies and corporations regulated by anti-discrimination statutes. Although in some kinds of cases corporations may be either plaintiffs or defendants, in specified sets of cases, corporations understand themselves as possible or actual defendants. Although the divisions between plaintiff and defendant in civil procedure are more subtle than the divisions in the criminal law, identifiable plaintiffs and defendants exist. In a substantial category of cases, we know upfront the identity of those who will be plaintiffs and defendants. The question of whether a particular civil rule helps or hurts a set of litigants is thus more than plausible.[103] Once the assault on factfinding is recognized, the problem is to understand who fuels that aggression and for what perceived advantage.

Conclusion

I began with *Neary* v. *Board of Regents of the University of California*, and to it I return to conclude. *Neary* proves to be a landmark for the emerging contours of litigation with its growing "law of settlement."[104] The praise of settlement and of alternative dispute resolution affect our understanding of the value of factfinding. A diminished sense of the import of factfinding in turn prompts renewed pressures for its avoidance. Contemporary procedural rules suggest that factfinding is not the work of important people, and that its historic reliance on witnesses' oral statements is questionable. Developing legal doctrine prizes parties' consensual settlements over adjudication and presses for parties' consent. Given these views, how might one frame a coherent negative response to the veterinarians' plea that their "peace of mind" requires obliteration of a jury verdict? Since factfinding is a suspect activity, why insist on its longevity by preserving the jury verdict in *Neary*? If settlement is the most valued outcome at the trial level, why not similarly embrace it at the appellate level?

Of course, I can frame arguments to explain why the intermediate appellate court in *Neary* was correct–that once the parties had chosen to obtain adjudication, they had no power to demand its revision based solely on their desires that the outcome no longer exist and, further, that courts should not be shy in authoring rules that cabin parties and preclude deals predicated on certain court actions.[105] But making such arguments does not respond to the deeper challenges presented to factfinding by the myriad of changes I have reviewed above. It comes as no surprise that the California Supreme Court, with a lone dissent, created a strong presumption in favor of stipulated reversals, praising their efficiency and belittling "[h]omilies about 'judicial integrity.'"[106]

To consider the future of jury trials, one must think about the future of factfinding. That future looks dim in the absence of some theory that affirms the meaning of trials and the factfinding that results. My hope has been to show that an implicit theory about factfinding *is* imbedded in conversations about alternative dispute resolution, settlement, and managerial judging—that factfinding is not much socially desired. Those who have not only affection but also respect for that form of response to disputes and who believe in the utility of the imposition of decision in the name of the state must now understand that the burden is shifting. If factfinding is to continue to be a respected enterprise, if factfinders are to be understood as engaging in a critically useful activity, then support for the many procedural innovations that deprecate the activity of factfinding must be reevaluated.

Notes

1. See *Neary v. Regents of the University of California*, 3 Cal. 4th 273, 10 Cal. Rptr. 2d 859 (1992). See also *Neary v. Regents of the University of California*, 228 Cal. App. 3d 131, 133, 278 Cal. Rptr. 773, 774 (Cal. App. 1st Dist. 1991); *Neary v. Regents of the University of California*, 185 Cal. App. 3d 1136, 230 Cal. Rptr. 281 (1986) (reversing the trial court's grant of summary judgment on behalf of the defendants). Details of the case come not only from these opinions but also from the briefs of the petitioners and amici curiae, prepared for the California Supreme Court review of the 1991 decision.

2. *Neary*, 228 Cal. App. 3d at 133, 278 Cal. Rptr. at 774.

3. See "Brief of Amicus Curiae in Support of the Court of Appeal's Decision," p. 3 (the defendant veterinarians "look[ed] upon the judgment in this case as a conviction, as a finding of guilt"). See also *Neary*, 228 Cal. App. 3d at 134, 278 Cal. Rptr. at 775 (the parties claimed that "[u]nless the judgment is vacated, the veterinarians will not have achieved the peace they bargained for when they signed their settlement agreement").

4. *Neary*, 228 Cal. App. 3d at 138, 278 Cal. Rptr. at 778.

5. See, for example, Philip Hager, "Justices to Review Plea to Set Aside Libel Ruling," *Los Angeles Times*, May 24, 1991, p. A41; "Appeal Court Won't Erase Decision in Libel Lawsuit," *Los Angeles Daily Journal*, March 7, 1991, p. 3; and George Markell, "Court Scolds Lawyers in Post-Verdict Deal," *San Francisco Chronicle*, March 7, 1991, p. A10. See also California Academy of Appellate Lawyers, "Amicus Letter Supporting Grant of Review," May 15, 1991.

6. *Neary*, 3 Cal. 4th at 277, 10 Cal. Rptr. 2d 860 ("As a general rule, the parties should be entitled to a stipulated reversal to effectuate settlement absent a showing of extraordinary circumstances that warrant an exception."). See Stephen R. Barnett, "Judgments for Sale," *Los Angeles Daily Journal*, August 27, 1992, p. 6; Daniel B. Moskowitz, "Calif. High Court Enters Fight Over Wiping Rulings Off Books," *Washington Post*, August 31, 1992, p. 11. The most recent legal ruling in *Neary* is not the only controversial aspect of the case; see John Carmody, "The TV Column," *Washington Post*, November 22, 1982, p. D10 (discussion of the "60 Minutes" TV segment about Mr. Neary's conflict with the state about the cause of death of the cows).

Neary is one of several examples of setting aside jury verdicts at the behest of litigants to obtain a settlement. See Andrew Pollack, "Big Defendants Settle in Miniscribe Lawsuit,"

New York Times, February 19, 1992, p. C4 (as part of a settlement, a trial judge "signed decisions that said that the [jury] verdicts were 'not supported by sufficient evidence' and were 'contrary to the great weight and preponderance of the evidence'"). The *Times* quoted the judge as explaining that he struck the verdicts "only as a result of the settlement, not as an independent decision that the jury verdict was bad or anything." For discussion of other cases in which the same issue has emerged, see Stacy Goron, "Vanishing Precedents: Policyholders Can Get Better Deal—If Rulings Are Erased," *Business Insurance*, June 15, 1992, p. 1; Jill E. Fisch, "Rewriting History: The Propriety of Eradicating Prior Decisional Law through Settlement and Vacatur," *Cornell Law Review*, vol. 76 (March 1991), p. 589.

7. According to one of the briefs, as the settlement request was pending before the appellate court, George Neary himself had second thoughts. He wrote to the court that "[t]o reverse the decision would be an outrage to me and other victims and an affront to the jury system." Letter from George Neary, plaintiff and respondent in *Neary* v. *Regents of the University of California*, et al., February 8, 1991, as quoted by "Brief of Amicus Curiae in Support of the Court of Appeal's Decision," p. 4, n. 1.

8. For an overview of the issues addressed, see Theodore R. Tetzlaff, "Opening Statement: Four Urgent Questions," *Litigation*, vol. 18 (Fall 1991), p. 1, in which Tetzlaff calls for preservation of a "healthy jury system," and see Robert Litan's introduction to this volume.

9. P.L. 101-650, codified at 28 U.S.C. § 471 et seq., which was also called the "Biden Bill," because of the role Senator Joseph Biden played in promoting the legislation.

10. 28 U.S.C. § 471.

11. 28 U.S.C. § 473(a). The legislature is not the only branch in the business of "civil justice reform." See also Executive Order 12778, October 23, 1991, based on recommendations in a report, *Agenda for Civil Justice Reform in America* (Government Printing Office), made by the President's Council on Competitiveness (informally called the Quayle Commission). Under the Executive Order, which binds federal lawyers, the United States must attempt settlement and pursue alternative dispute resolution. Further, federal lawyers are to move "for summary judgment in every case where the movant would be likely to prevail, or where the motion is likely to narrow the issues to be tried." The Executive Order is similar to the congressional legislation in its focus on settlement and alternative dispute resolution. For analysis of the empirical bases (or lack thereof) for the proposals, see Deborah R. Hensler, "Taking Aim at the American Legal System: The Council on Competitiveness's Agenda for Legal Reform," *Judicature*, vol. 75 (February–March 1992), p. 244. In response, see Gregory Brian Butler and Brian David Miller, "Fiddling while Rome Burns: A Response to Dr. Hensler," *Judicature*, vol. 75 (February–March 1992), p. 251. For criticism that the Quayle agenda "ignores broader and more significant problems of our justice system as a whole—principally underfunding and inadequate access," see American Bar Association, *ABA Blueprint for Improving the Civil Justice System* (Chicago, 1992), p. xi.

Given the interest in civil justice expressed by the legislative, executive, and judiciary, we are in an era comparable to the 1930s, out of which emerged the major procedural reform embodied in the Federal Rules of Civil Procedure.

12. By May 17, 1990, the proposed legislation did include the goal of facilitating "deliberate adjudication of civil cases on the merits" in its list of purposes. See S. 2648, 101 Cong. 2 sess. (introduced May 17, 1990) § 471. In the preamble, Congress stated that the purposes of each civil justice plan "are to facilitate deliberate adjudication of civil cases on the merits, monitor discovery, improve litigation management, and ensure just, speedy, and inexpensive resolutions of civil disputes."

13. 28 U.S.C. § 473(a)(1); 28 U.S.C. § 473(a)(2)(B); 28 U.S.C. § 473(a)(2)(B)(i) and (ii); and 28 U.S.C. § 473(a)(3)(B).

14. One of the statute's "principles" is that a judicial officer "explores the parties'

receptivity to, and the propriety of, settlement" for all "complex and [in] any other appropriate cases." 28 U.S.C. § 473(a)(3)(A). Another principle is to provide "authorization to refer appropriate cases to alternative dispute resolution programs. . . ." 28 U.S.C. § 473(a)(6). Further, district plans may require that "each party be represented at each pretrial conference by an attorney who has the authority to bind that party" (28 U.S.C. § 473(b)(1)); that a "neutral evaluation program" be provided (28 U.S.C. § 473(b)(4)); and that courts could require that parties' representatives "with the authority to bind them in settlement discussions be present or available by telephone during any settlement conference" (28 U.S.C. § 473 (b)(5)).

15. The two co-chairs of the Task Force are Brad D. Brian (of Los Angeles) and Richard McMillan, Jr. (of Washington). Members include John P. Driscoll, Jr. (First Circuit); Patricia Hynes (Second Circuit); Edwin J. Wesely (Second Circuit); Kenneth C. Frazier (Third Circuit); John E. Sandbower II (Fourth Circuit); George Beall (Fourth Circuit); Barbara M. G. Lynn (Fifth Circuit); David C. Weiner (Sixth Circuit); Michael B. Hyman (Seventh Circuit); George F. McGunnigle, Jr. (Eighth Circuit); P. Arley Harrel (Ninth Circuit); Molly Munger (Ninth Circuit); Jimmy K. Goodman (Tenth Circuit); H. Thomas Wells, Jr. (Eleventh Circuit); Loren Kieve (D.C. Circuit); and myself, as a member at large. See generally *Report of the Task Force on the Civil Justice Reform Act* (Chicago: American Bar Association, July 1992). For additional discussion of the implementation of the act, see Carl Tobias, "Judicial Oversight of Civil Justice Reform," *Federal Rules Decisions*, vol. 140 (West, 1992), p. 49.

16. For analysis of the plans' treatments of these issues, see John P. Driscoll, Jr., and George F. McGunnigle, Jr., "Analysis of Expense and Delay Reduction Plans with Respect to Early and Ongoing Judicial Involvement," April 21, 1992, p. 1-2; David C. Weiner, "Differentiated Case Management," April 20, 1992; Thomas Wells and Ivey Horn, "Differential Case Management," April 7, 1992; Loren Kieve, "Time and Numerical Limits in Discovery," April 10, 1992; Kenneth C. Frazier and John E. Sandbower III, "Plan Provisions Relating to Pretrial Motions," April 17, 1992; Diane M. Sumoski and Barbara M. G. Lynn, memorandum of April 8, 1992, pp. 1–3; Edwin J. Wesely, "National Overview of Plan Provisions for Automatic Disclosure" (Winthrop, Stimson, Putnam & Roberts, March 9, 1992); and Molly Munger, Brenda A. Stanulevich, Michael B. Hyman, and Ellyn Lansing, "Comparison of Expense and Delay Reduction Plan Alternative Dispute Resolution Provisions," April 15, 1992. The ADR techniques discussed in the plans include settlement conferences, early neutral evaluation, mediation, arbitration, court-annexed arbitration, mini-trials, summary jury trials, and reference to a special master.

17. See, for example, P. Arley Harrel, "Memorandum: District Court Plans on 'Trial,'" subtopic, 'Bifurcation,'" April 15, 1992, p. 1. Mention of trial is made in relation to other issues; as part of case management, many plans recommend "early and firm trial dates." See Driscoll and McGunnigle, "Analysis," p. 2 (when such dates cannot be kept, some plans recommend "consideration of reassignment to other judicial officers for trial"). The plan proposals on "tracking" systems also include discussion of trial dates. In addition, some district plans do recommend "mini-trials" and "summary jury trials"—sometimes by order of the court—as alternative dispute resolution methods. See Munger, Stanulevich, Hyman, and Lansing, "Comparison of Expense and Delay," chart, p. 33-39. The plan from the Eastern District of New York suggests that the option to consent to "trial before magistrate judge" be more "widely publicized" (ibid. at p. 42). Further, some plans address—in the context of discovery as well as of trials—taking testimony of expert witnesses. See Jimmy K. Goodman, memorandum, April 23, 1992.

18. George Beall, "Memorandum: Trial," April 3, 1992. A few plans do address trial-related topics, and four mention issues specific to the jury, such as voir dire and instructions. See also Liz Atlee, memorandum to Judith Resnik, April 22, 1992, pp. 3–5 (District of Wyoming plan made recommendations that were not adopted about jury voir dire; the

District of Delaware recommended standard jury instructions; the Southern District of New York recommended provisions of jury instructions on computers to enable court editing, and the Southern District of Texas recommended visual aids to jury education).

19. See, for example, Beall, "Memorandum," p. 2, quoting the Advisory Group for the Western District of Texas: "the trial phase of the litigation process has not itself been a significant cause of unnecessary cost and delay in the Western District. Trials in the Western District are already among the most efficient in the nation, with the vast majority consuming fewer than three days."

20. See the 1983 amendments to Rule 16 of the Federal Rules of Civil Procedure and the series of rule changes governing discovery practice. See generally Judith Resnik, "Managerial Judges," *Harvard Law Review*, vol. 96 (December 1982), p. 374; Robert Peckham, "The Federal Judge as Case Manager: The New Role in Guiding a Case from Filing to Disposition," *California Law Review*, vol. 69 (May 1981), p. 770; and G. Heilman Brewing Co. v. Joseph Oat Corp., 871 F.2d 648 (7th Cir., en banc, 1989) (upholding the power to compel parties' attendance at settlement conferences).

Also of relevance, but not detailed here, are the doctrinal changes and proposed revisions of summary judgment rules. See *Celotex Corp. v. Catrett*, 477 U.S. 317 (1986); William Schwarzer, "Summary Judgment: A Proposed Revision of Rule 56," *Federal Rules Decisions*, vol 110 (West, 1986), p. 213; and Paul Carrington, "Making Rules to Dispose of Manifestly Unfounded Assertions: An Exorcism of the Bogy of Non-Trans-Substantive Rules of Civil Procedure," *University of Pennsylvania Law Review*, vol. 137 (June 1989), p. 2067.

21. See Stephen C. Yeazell, "The Unintended Consequences of Modern Civil Process" (draft manuscript, October 1992, on file with author).

22. See the former Federal Rule of Civil Procedure 63 (amended in 1987 to incorporate gender neutral language) (emphasis added).

23. See "Proposed Rules: Preliminary Draft of Proposed Amendments to the Federal Rules of Appellate Procedure and the Federal Rules of Civil Procedure," *Federal Rules Decisions*, vol 127 (West, 1989), pp. 237, 385–86. Compare Federal Rule of Criminal Procedure 25(a), which permits substitution of judges for "reason of death, sickness, or other disability," but only in *jury trials*, upon a certification of "familiarity with the record of the trial." If a trial judge is unable, "after a verdict or finding of guilt," to perform the duties (implicitly of deciding about post-trial bail and sentencing), then another judge may be substituted. If that substitute judge believes that such duties cannot be performed properly, that judge has the authority to order "a new trial." Federal Rule of Criminal Procedure 25(b).

This model of distinguishing between the liability and remedy phases was not adopted on the civil side, in which one might have permitted substitution if a phase of a trial, and the facts found therein, had concluded. See, for example, *Home Placement Service, Inc. v. Providence Journal Co.*, 819 F.2d 1199 (1st Cir. 1987).

24. "1989 Advisory Committee Proposal," *Federal Rules Decisions*, vol. 127 (West), p. 386.

25. "Amendments to Federal Rules of Civil Procedure," Fed. R. Civ. Pro. 63, as amended, 1991 (April 30, 1991), which became effective on December 1, 1991, *Federal Rules Decisions*, vol. 134 (West, 1991), pp. 525, 552–52.

26. 1991 Advisory Committee Note, 28 U.S.C.A. Rules, Federal Rules of Civil Procedure, Rule 63, p. 165 (1992). Under the original 1989 proposal, the revision had included permission for substitution if the original judge was unable to proceed "*for any reason.*" *Federal Rules Decisions*, vol. 127, p. 385 (emphasis added). The accompanying Advisory Committee Note offered no guidance on what reasons were appropriate. *Federal Rules Decisions*, vol 127, pp. 386–87. Compare *United States v. Lane*, 708 F.2d 1394, 1396-97 (9th Cir. 1983), concluding that another "commitment" is not an appropriate

reason for substitution of a judge under Rule 25 of the Federal Rules of Criminal Procedure, and which was included as a reference in Rule 63 as promulgated.

27. According to the *1990 Annual Report of the Director of the Administrative Office of the United States Courts*, p. 161, table C-7, in the twelve-month period ending June 30, 1990, there were 11,502 civil trials, of which 6,737 were bench trials and 4,765 jury trials. A total of 347 trials (unspecified as bench or jury) lasted from ten to nineteen days, and 85 trials lasted twenty days or more. See p. 163, table C-8. Such lengthy trials were cited in the 1991 Advisory Committee Note as animating the need for a rule change: "[t]he increasing length of federal trials" makes interruption more likely. "An efficient mechanism for completing these cases without unfairness is needed to prevent unnecessary expense and delay." 1991 Advisory Committee Note, 28 U.S.C.A. Rules, Federal Rules of Civil Procedure, Rule 63, at 165 (1992).

28. 1991 Advisory Committee Note, 28 U.S.C.A. Rules, Federal Rules of Civil Procedure, Rule 63, at 165.

29. See Proposed Amendments to the Federal Rules of Civil Procedure and the Federal Rules of Evidence, submitted to the Standing Committee on Rules of Practice and Procedure by the Advisory Committee on Civil Rules (May 1992) (no submission to revise Rule 43).

30. Fed. R. Civ. Pro. 43(a). Further, Rule 43(e) authorizes judges to hear oral testimony when evidentiary matters are at issue in motions.

31. Committee on Rules of Practice and Procedure of the Judicial Conference of the United States, "Proposed Rules: Preliminary Draft of Proposed Amendments to the Federal Rules of Civil Procedure and the Federal Rules of Evidence" (August 1991), *Federal Rules Decisions*, vol. 137 (West), pp. 53, 135.

32. *Federal Rules Decisions*, vol. 137, p. 71.

33. The proposal might have been an effort to sharpen the focus and fulfill the promise of cross-examination. Further, the shift of power to the lawyer-authors might have been welcomed as an antidote to the expanding powers of judges to control the questioning of witnesses in bench trials. Compare Stephan Landsman, "The Rise of the Contentious Spirit: Adversary Procedure in Eighteenth Century England," *Cornell Law Review*, vol. 75 (March 1990), p. 512: "Judicial interrogation of witnesses was a prominent feature of criminal courtroom procedure in Tudor and Stuart times. . . . Judicial inquisition is antithetical to an adversary approach."

34. Moreover, if Rule 43 had changed, it would have generated conditions that permit substitution of judges under the new Rule 63. One objection to substituting judges in the middle of a bench trial is that the oral proceedings might not be fully captured when transcribed. When a trial consists principally of a set of documents, that objection is greatly diminished, as the successor judge can reread all the materials that were before the first judge.

35. As the Advisory Committee noted, "The court would, however, risk error to determine the credibility of a witness not seen or heard who is available to be recalled" and cited *Anderson* v. *City of Bessemer City*, 470 U.S. 564, 575 (1985). 1991 Advisory Committee Note, 28 U.S.C.A. Rules, Federal Rules of Civil Procedure, Rule 63, at 165.

36. In *United States* v. *Raddatz*, 447 U.S. 667 (1980), the question was the constitutionality of 28 U.S.C. § 636(b)(1)(B), which permits trial judges to refer suppression motions to magistrates. After the magistrate rules, the statute provides that, upon objection of a party, the trial judge "shall make a de novo determination of those portions of the report or specified proposed findings or recommendations to which objection is made." Charged with illegal possession of a firearm, Raddatz moved to suppress statements given to agents of the Alcohol, Tobacco, and Firearms Bureau. After hearing testimony from the agents, a magistrate denied suppression, and Raddatz objected. The trial judge affirmed, having "considered the transcript of the hearing before the Magistrate," as well as the parties' arguments. The *Raddatz* majority interpreted the statutory "de novo determination" as

not requiring a de novo *hearing* in all cases. 447 U.S. at 675. Turning then to the constitutional question, the Court held that at a suppression hearing (a proceeding with "interests at stake . . . of a lesser magnitude than those in the criminal trial itself"), a trial judge could make a de novo determination without hearing the witnesses again. 477 U.S. at 679–80. However, the Court thought it unlikely that a trial court could reject magistrates' proposed dispositive credibility findings without hearing the relevant witnesses directly (at 681, n. 7).

37. *Raddatz*, 447 U.S. at 696 (Marshall, J., dissenting, quoting *Morgan* v. *United States*, 298 U.S. 468, 481 (1936)). In the context of the pre-1991 revisions of Rule 63, some appellate courts have required that a successor Rule 63 judge had to "readopt the findings of fact and conclusions of law previously made . . . [or] grant a trial *de novo*." See *In re Allied Supermarkets, Inc.*, 951 F.2d 718, 726-27 (6th Cir. 1991).

38. For a review of the literature supporting this thesis, see Olin Guy Wellborn III, "Demeanor," *Cornell Law Review*, vol. 76 (July 1991), p. 1075 ("According to the empirical evidence, ordinary people cannot make effective use of demeanor in deciding whether to believe a witness. On the contrary, there is some evidence that the observation of demeanor diminishes rather than enhances the accuracy of credibility judgments"). See also Michael J. Saks, "Enhancing and Restraining Accuracy in Adjudication," *Law and Contemporary Problems*, vol. 51 (Autumn 1988), p. 263 ("people are not good at sensing when someone is telling the truth") (citation omitted). Compare *Roman* v. *Abrams*, 822 F.2d 214, 228 (2d Cir. 1987), *cert. denied*, 489 U.S. 1052 (1989) (two co-defendants filed habeas petitions, raising the issue of exclusions of whites from juries; the appellate court concluded that the factual conclusions of the district judge who had viewed the demeanor of the witness were entitled to greater deference than the factual conclusions of another district court that had not conducted an evidentiary hearing).

39. Here, I part company with Professor Wellborn, who argues that "[r]ecognition of the weakness of demeanor evidence does not herald a revolution in trial procedure." Wellborn, "Demeanor," p. 1094. The growing challenge to demeanor evidence, when coupled with the other developments outlined above, do provide the basis for major transformations in trials.

40. In 1975, the Hruska Commission (named after its chair, Senator Roman Hruska) proposed the creation of a National Court of Appeals staffed with seven Article III judges who would hear cases referred to it by the Supreme Court or transferred by the Courts of Appeal. See Commission on Revision of the Federal Court Appellate System, "Structure and Internal Procedures: Recommendations for Change," 1975, reprinted in *Federal Rules Decisions*, vol. 67 (West), p. 195. For discussion of this and other proposals for restructuring, see Symposium, "The Federal Courts: The Next 100 Years," *South Carolina Law Review*, vol. 38 (Spring 1987), pp. 597–98, which provides a bibliography on the debate on an intercircuit panel.

41. *1990 Annual Report of the Director of the Administrative Office of the United States Courts*, p. 3. Article III judges are those judges appointed by the president, with the approval of the senate, and thus have life tenure and salary protections, under Article III of the United States Constitution. The actual number of sitting trial judges is larger because, upon taking senior status, an Article III judge opens up a position for a new appointee. As of April 1990, there were some 750 such judges. Administrative Office of the United States Courts, *United States Court Directory* (Washington, Spring 1990), pp. 3–42, 56–338.

42. *1990 Annual Report of the Director of the Administrative Office of the United States Courts*, pp. 6, 10–11, table 8 (217,879 civil cases and 48,904 criminal cases were filed).

43. The number of magistrate judges is provided by *United States Court Directory*, pp. 56–338; their new name comes from the *Judicial Improvements Act of 1990*, P.L. 101-

650 § 321, 104 Stat. 5089, 5117. According to the legislative history, the addition of the word "judge" was "designed to reflect more accurately the responsibilities and duties of the office." *Federal Courts Study Committee Implementation Act of 1990*, H. Rept. 1010-734, 101 Cong. 2 sess. (GPO, 1990), p. 31.

44. S. Rept. 293, 100 Cong. 2 sess. (GPO, 1988), p. 7, reprinted in *U.S. Code Cong. & Admin. News* (West, 1988), p. 5565.

45. Ninth Circuit Judicial Council's United States Magistrates Advisory Committee, *Study of Magistrates within the Ninth Circuit Court of Appeals* (April 15, 1990), p. 9, which recommended that magistrates gain additional powers.

46. In 1990, 725,484 bankruptcies were filed. *1990 Annual Report of the Director of the Administrative Office of the United States Courts*, p. 22.

47. John C. Holmes, "ALJ Update, A Review of the Current Role, Status, and Demographics of the Corp of Administrative Law Judges," *Federal Bar News & Journal*, vol. 38 (May 1991), p. 202.

48. *Background Material and Data on Programs within the Jurisdiction of the Committee on Ways and Means, House Committee on Ways and Means*, 101 Cong. 1 sess. (GPO, March 15, 1989), p. 51, reported 258,421 dispositions by ALJ's on disability determinations.

49. *Crowell v. Benson*, 285 U.S. 22, 51 (1932).

50. 285 U.S. at 57.

51. See P.L. 90-578 § 101, 82 Stat. 1108 (October 17, 1968), which initially created the magistrate system, and its amendments, including those in 1976, P.L. 94-577 § 1, 90 Stat. 2729 (October 21, 1976), and in 1979, P.L. 96-82 § 2, 93 Stat. 643 (October 10, 1979). See generally Linda Silberman, "Judicial Adjuncts Revisited: The Proliferation of Ad Hoc Procedure," *University of Pennsylvania Law Review*, vol. 137 (June 1989), p. 2131.

52. While *Northern Pipeline Construction Co. v. Pipe Line Co.*, 458 U.S. 50 (1982), struck the broadest reach of bankruptcy judges' power, a good deal remains, and the Court has had a difficult time agreeing about what constitutional limits existed. Since *Northern Pipeline*, the Court has upheld congressional grants of adjudicatory power to the Commodities Futures Trading Commission. See *Commodities Futures Trading Commission v. Schorr*, 478 U.S. 833 (1986).

53. *Federal Courts Study Act*, P.L. 100-702 § 102(a) (1988), codified as 28 U.S.C. § 331 (note), and § 102(b).

54. "[T]he federal judiciary is composed most importantly of the Article III judiciary." *Report of the Federal Courts Study Committee*, April 2, 1990, p. 69 (hereafter *FCSC Report*).

55. "1,000 [Article III judges] is the practical ceiling." *FCSC Report*, p. 8. These views match those of Richard Posner, who was a member of the Committee. See Richard A. Posner, *The Federal Courts: Crisis and Reform* (Harvard University Press, 1985); and Posner, "Coping with the Caseload: A Comment on Magistrates and Masters," *University of Pennsylvania Law Review*, vol. 137 (June 1989), pp. 2215, 2216 ("The federal courts were created to be small. . . . The natural limits of expansion were not reached until very recently"). See also the address by Justice Antonin Scalia to the fellows of the American Bar Foundation and the National Conference of Bar Presidents, (February 15, 1987), reprinted in *Federal Bar News & Journal*, vol. 34 (July–August 1987), p. 252 (concluding that it was important to keep the federal judiciary small); and Robert H. Bork, "Dealing with the Overload in Article III Courts," *Federal Rules Decisions*, vol. 70 (West), pp. 231, 234 (address delivered at the National Conference on the Causes of Popular Dissatisfaction with the Administration of Justice, the Pound Conference, April 1976), who argued: "Large numbers damage collegiality, lessen esprit, and diminish the possibility of interaction throughout the judicial corps."

Compare Erwin Chemerinsky and Larry Kramer, "Defining the Role of the Federal

Courts," *Brigham Young University Law Review*, vol. 1990, no. 1, pp. 67, 69–74, questioning many of the arguments against increasing size but recognizing the difficulties of a too large Article III bench; and Loren Robel, "The Politics of Crisis in the Federal Courts," *Ohio State Journal on Dispute Resolution*, vol. 7, no. 1 (1991), p. 115.

56. See, for example, H. Rept. 4647, 99 Cong. 2 sess. (1986); and Robert E. Rains, "A Specialized Court for Social Security? A Critique of Recent Proposals," *Florida State University Law Review*, vol. 15 (Spring 1987), pp. 1, 3 (discussing three bills, with the sponsorship of the Reagan administration, that sought to "remove all or almost all Social Security appeals" from Article III courts).

57. *FCSC Report* at 55, 62-64, 69-72, 81-83, 76, 79-81.

58. *Granfinanciera* v. *Nordberg*, 109 S. Ct. 2782 (1989). See also *In re Ben Cooper, Inc.*, 896 F.2d 1394 (2d Cir. 1990), *vacated and remanded*, 111 S. Ct. 425 (1990), *reinstated*, 924 F.2d 36 (2d Cir. 1991) (ruling that bankruptcy judges can preside at jury trials).

59. Richard Fallon, Jr., "Of Legislative Courts, Administrative Agencies, and Article III," *Harvard Law Review*, vol. 101 (March 1988), p. 915.

60. See generally Judith Resnik, "Housekeeping: The Nature and Allocation of Work in Federal Trial Courts," *Georgia Law Review*, vol. 24 (Summer 1990), pp. 909–64.

61. See generally Wolf Heyderbrand and Carroll Seron, *Rationalizing Justice: The Political Economy of Federal District Courts* (State University of New York Press, 1990), p. 1, who believe that "quiet revolution" has occurred consisting of changes in the "forms of case disposition," in the "growth in the range, variability, and complexity of demands on federal district courts as well as the addition of a host of new organizational actors, including court managers, computer experts, parajudges, and support staff." See also G. Thomas Eisele, "From the Bench: No to Mandatory Court-Annexed ADR," *Litigation*, vol. 18 (Fall 1991), pp. 3, 5 (discussing the fifty-four civil and criminal trials per judgeship in the Eastern District of Arkansas, in 1990, compared with seventeen, twenty-two, and nineteen trials per judgeship in three other districts, which have "taken the lead" in ADR; as of 1991, the number of trials in those three districts were thirteen, sixteen, and sixteen respectively).

62. See generally Judith Resnik, "From 'Cases' to 'Litigation,'" *Law and Contemporary Problems*, vol. 54 (Summer 1991), pp. 5, 6–22.

63. Resnik, "From 'Cases' to 'Litigation,'" pp. 22–45.

64. See *The Multiparty, Multiforum Act of 1990*, H. Rept. 3406, *Congressional Record*, vol. 136 (June 5, 1990), p. H3116, which passed the House but not the Senate and provided federal court jurisdiction only if several prerequisites were met, including that the cause of action arose "from a single accident," the parties were minimally diverse, and "at least 25 natural persons have either died or incurred injury in the accident at a discrete location." See generally Robert N. Kastenmeier and Charles Gardner Geyh, "The Case in Support of Legislation Facilitating the Consolidation of Mass-Accident Litigation: A View from the Legislature," *Marquette Law Review*, vol. 73 (Summer 1991), p. 535.

65. See ABA Commission on Mass Torts, Report 126, February 1989 (renumbered 116), and 58 LW 2109, August 22, 1989 (report not adopted), and American Law Institute, "Complex Litigation Project, Tentative Draft 1," April 1989; "Tentative Draft 2," April 1990; "Tentative Draft 3," March 1991 (Philadelphia).

66. See, for example, the exchanges among Geoffrey C. Hazard, Jr., "Authority in the Dock," *Boston University Law Review*, vol. 69 (May 1989), pp. 471–76; H. Lee Sarokin, "A Comment on Geoffrey Hazard's 'Authority in the Dock,'" *Boston University Law Review*, vol. 69 (May 1989), pp. 477–79; and Stephen C. Yeazell, "The Salience of Silence: A Comment on Professor Hazard's 'Authority in the Dock,'" *Boston University Law Review*, vol. 69 (May 1989), pp. 481–86.

67. See Bork, "Dealing with the Overload"; and *FCSC Report*.

68. See, for example, *In re DuPont Plaza* (fire at a hotel in Puerto Rico), described in

part *In re Allied Signal Corp*, 891 F.2d 974 (1st Cir. 1989), *cert. denied sub nom. ACW Airwall Inc.* v. *U.S. Dist. Ct*, 111 S.Ct. 2561 (1990), and also described in Marcia Coyle, "Both Sides Claiming Victory," *National Law Journal*, October 15, 1990, p. 3, in which some 2,000 plaintiffs sued more than 200 defendants, and representative trials were held in phases. In *Cimino* v. *Raymark Industries, Inc.*, 751 F. Supp. 649, 653 (E.D. Tex. 1990), appeal pending, 2,298 class members claiming asbestos injuries were divided into five disease categories, and sample cases were tried. The results, as modified, were then extrapolated to the rest of the class.

69. See, for example, *In re "Agent Orange" Product Liability Litigation*, 818 F.2d 145, 166 (2d Cir. 1987): "Indeed, a settlement in a case such as the instant litigation, dramatically arrived at just before dawn on the day of trial after sleepless hours of bargaining, seems almost as inevitable as sunrise." See generally Peter H. Schuck, *Agent Orange on Trial: Mass Tort Disasters in the Courts* (Harvard University Press, 1987). I know of no current quantification that provides a compilation of such cases to enable us to know settlement rates, compared with trial rates, of large-scale litigation. One obvious obstacle to such research is the difficulty of sorting and characterizing cases.

70. For example, in *DuPont Plaza*, settlement values for each of the more than 2,000 plaintiffs were negotiated individually with the Honorable Louis Bechtle, who worked as a settlement judge, while Judge Acosta presided over trials and related activities in Puerto Rico.

71. See generally Mark A. Peterson, "Giving Away Money: Comparative Comments on Claims Resolution Facilities," *Law and Contemporary Problems*, vol. 53 (Autumn 1990), p. 113; and Deborah R. Hensler, "Assessing Claims Resolution Facilities: What We Need to Know," *Law and Contemporary Problems*, vol. 53 (Autumn 1990), p. 175.

72. See, for example, "Trustees Approve Alternative Dispute Resolution; New Process Speeds Resolution of All Claimants," Claims Resolution Report: A Newsletter of the Dalkon Shield Claimants Trust, no. 11 (April 1992), p. 1 (hereafter *Dalkon Shield Newsletter*): "ADR is a win-win situation for everyone." For those claimants who reject settlement offers of $10,000 or less, made by the Dalkon Trust Claimants, they may use ADR but must in turn accept a "$10,000 cap on any award for . . . injuries. Once the election is made," claimants cannot choose to accept a settlement offer instead. Further, "[b]y electing ADR, she gives up her right to resolve her claim in fast-track arbitration, regular arbitration or a jury trial."

73. For example, the Dalkon Shield Claimants Facility reported an 80 percent acceptance rate on its offers to claimants under one of its tracks. Of the 1,700 who have rejected those offers, 39 have sought and been permitted trial, and the first trial was expected to occur in the spring of 1992. *Dalkon Shield Newsletter*, p. 4.

74. Again using the Dalkon Shield case as an example, the current procedures are governed by an "administrative order," which is also on appeal in the Fourth Circuit. Under that order, no punitive damages are available. Further, because the Trust has determined to "hold back" funds to preserve its corpus, all that a claimant "wins" at "trial" will not be paid immediately. *Dalkon Shield Newsletter*, pp. 8–9.

75. See the brief filed on behalf of the appellants for a description of the *in camera* proceedings conducted by the Dalkon Claims Facility in *Anderson* v. *Dalkon Shield Claimants Trust*, No. 91-1752 (4th Cir.). Appellants objected to the requirement that to be eligible for factfinding by either arbitration or trial, "certification" from the Trust of the completion of various procedural steps had occurred; argued that the "holdback" provisions were unsupported by the public record; and claimed that the Trust violates the statutory right of personal injury victims to jury trial available in bankruptcies.

The document depository of the Trust contains information produced by virtue of discovery by A. H. Robins before it filed for bankruptcy. However, "a claimant will not find documents by or about the Trust, including those concerning the claims valuation system or other claims." *Dalkon Shield Newsletter*, p. 9. The Dalkon Trust is the vehicle, created by the bankruptcy adjudication, to distribute funds to Dalkon claimants. As such, it is not clear why at least some of the documents in its possession are not viewed as court-generated materials, to which common law and constitutional rights of access apply. See, for example, *Nixon* v. *Warner Communications, Inc.*, 435 U.S. 589 (1978); and *Bank of America National Trust and Savings Association* v. *Hotel Rittenhouse Association*, 800 F.2d 339 (3rd Cir. 1986). Further, contemporary concern about "secrecy in the courts" has prompted some jurisdictions to limit parties' authority to seal records. See *Examining the Use of Secrecy and Confidentiality of Documents by Courts in Civil Litigation*, Hearing before the Subcommittee on Courts and Administrative Practice, Court Secrecy, 101 Cong. 2 sess. (GPO, 1990); New York Uniform Rules for the Trial Courts, Part 216.1, 22 NYCRR Part 216 (February 6, 1991) (limiting the power of courts to seal records); and George F. Carpinello, "Public Access to Court Records in Civil Proceedings: The New York Approach," *Albany Law Review*, vol. 54 (Fall 1989), p. 93.

76. There is some evidence of declining rates of trial. See generally Marc Galanter's chapter in this volume. According to the American Law Institute, *A Study of the Business of the Federal Courts, Part II, Civil Cases* (Philadelphia, 1934), which surveyed thirteen federal district courts, 71 percent ended without trial. In contrast, in 1980, the percentage of federal civil cases reaching trial was 6.5 percent. *1980 Annual Report of the Director of the Administrative Office of the United States Courts*, p. 391, table C-4A (of 154,985 civil cases, 6,171 were terminated during or after a bench trial and 3,920 were terminated during or after a jury trial). By 1990, that number was 4.3 percent. *1990 Annual Report of the Director*, p. 153, table C-4.

77. See Judith Resnik, "Failing Faith: Adjudicatory Procedure in Decline," *University of Chicago Law Review*, vol. 53 (Spring 1986), p. 494.

78. In contrast, see the *Speedy Trial Act of 1974*, P.L. 93-691, 88 Stat. 2076 (January 3, 1975), 18 U.S.C. § 3161 et seq.

79. See Carrie Menkel-Meadow, "Pursuing Settlement in an Adversary Culture: A Tale of Innovation Co-Opted or 'The Law of ADR,'" *Florida State University Law Review*, vol. 19 (Summer 1991), pp. 1, 7–11. Menkel-Meadow reviews the different "constituencies" of ADR, including those who believed it generated better outcomes, those who sought caseload reductions, those who sought to reduce legal costs of corporate enterprises, and those who argued that ADR was more efficient. Further, she argues that "outcomes derived from our adversarial judicial system or the negotiation that occurs in its shadows are inadequate" (p. 7) (footnotes omitted).

80. Because most cases do not end in trial, ADR programs may sometimes increase, rather than reduce, the amount of state-supported procedural opportunities available to litigants. For example, in those cases that would have terminated by settlement based upon bi-lateral negotiation but in which court-annexed arbitration occurs, the availability of ADR gives some litigants more process and more factfinding than would have occurred without it. In these cases, ADR programs may increase both time and costs, but might be justified as providing enriched process. For an example of such results, see the discussion of one ADR program by Robert J. MacCoun, E. Allan Lind, Deborah R. Hensler, David L. Bryant, and Patricia A. Ebener, *Alternative Adjudication: An Evaluation of the New Jersey Automobile Arbitration Program* (Santa Monica: Rand Institute for Civil Justice 1988). See generally Deborah R. Hensler, "Court-Ordered Arbitration: An Alternative View," *University of Chicago Legal Forum*, vol. 1990, pp. 399, 407: "Contrary to what many supporters and opponents of arbitration expected, court-ordered arbitration produces mixed results with regard to efficiency. . . . [I]n most instances, the arbitration process does not divert cases from trial, but rather provides an alternative to a settlement reached without hearing."

81. See, for example, *The Administrative Dispute Resolution Act*, P.L. 101-552, 104

Stat. 2736 (1990), which requires federal government agencies to develop plans to use alternative dispute resolution.

82. "Let us face the truth: From the court's point of view, coerced settlement is the primary objective of these compulsory ADRs, despite protests to the contrary." Eisele, "From the Bench," p. 5.

Again, bear in mind a distinction I am making, between a decline in factfinding and changes in adversarial activity. The rise of ADR entails a decline in factfinding but not necessarily a decline in adversarialism. For example, Carrie Menkel-Meadow notes "the omnipresence of the adversary model" in ADR. See Menkel-Meadow, "Pursuing Settlement," p. 17.

83. The renaming of magistrates as "magistrate judges" is instructive. While the legislation offers a name that (especially when shortened to "judge") would provide an illusion of authority equal to that of the Article III judiciary, the legislative history states that the new name was "not intended to affect the substantive authority or jurisdiction of . . . magistrates." *FCSC Implementation Act of 1990*, H. Rept. 5381, § 204, 101 Cong. 2 sess. (September 27, 1990). Similarly, when some proposed that bankruptcy judges be given Article III status, many in the Article III judiciary lobbied against that proposal. See Stuart Taylor, Jr., "The Free-for-All on the Bankruptcy Express," *New York Times*, March 2, 1984, p. 10; and "Chief Justice Opposes Bankruptcy Bill," *New York Times*, December 12, 1982, p. 21.

84. A related argument would be that, in a world in which all television viewers can see the same events and watch trials, fewer factfinding occasions are needed.

85. See Landsman, "The Rise of the Contentious Spirit," pp. 516–34, on the movement in English history from "judicial primacy" to party and lawyer control. Landsman discusses the rise of "adversarialism," which he links to political concerns about the legitimacy and fairness of adjudication (pp. 604–05). My focus here, in contrast, is on factfinding, which at least in theory is analytically distinct from adversarialism. Social investment in and attention paid to factfinding could occur in the presence of either an inquisitorial or adversarial process.

86. For others who worry as well, see Laura Macklin, "Promoting Settlement, Foregoing the Facts," *Review of Law and Social Change*, vol. 14 (Summer 1986), p. 575; and Owen Fiss, "Against Settlement," *Yale Law Journal*, vol. 93 (May 1984), p. 1073.

87. See Judith Resnik, "Due Process: A Public Dimension, in Conference: Procedural Due Process: Liberty and Justice," *University of Florida Law Review*, vol. 39 (Spring 1987), p. 405 (analyzing and questioning the arguments that access to courts protects a historical tradition and ensures public education, accountability, catharsis, control, and accuracy, and considering the role of public trials in developing debates about legal norms).

88. Macklin, "Promoting Settlement," p. 599.

89. More than thirty jurisdictions have questions of bias in the courts on their agendas. See Lynn Hecht Schafran, "Gender Bias in the Courts: An Emerging Focus for Judicial Reform," *Arizona State Law Review*, vol. 21 (Spring 1989), p. 237.

90. For one such analysis—of the problems women may face in mandatory mediation— see Trina Grillo, "The Mediation Alternative: Process Dangers for Women," *Yale Law Journal*, vol. 100 (April 1991), p. 1545. For suggestions that court-annexed arbitration be modified to strengthen its attention to such problems (but not to turn it into trial), see Hensler, "Court-Ordered Arbitration," pp. 419–20.

91. Precisely because of that power edge, a group convened by Senator Joseph Biden, the Foundation for Change, and the Brookings Institution, called for judges, and not magistrates, to manage cases, as part of their "judicial" functions. See *Justice for All: Reducing Costs and Delay in Civil Litigation*, Report of a Task Force (Brookings, 1989), p. 28. Similarly, some advocates of ADR argued specifically for the involvement of the Article III judiciary.

528 / Judith Resnik

92. Indeed, some members of the Article III judiciary objected to aspects of the *Civil Justice Reform Act of 1990*; they argued that Congress was inappropriately intruding on and managing the judiciary. See Stephan Labaton, "Business and the Law: Biden's Challenge to Federal Courts," *New York Times*, April 16, 1990, p. C2 (describing "heavy opposition from the bench"); Marvin E. Aspen (chair, National Conference of Federal Trial Judges), "The Biden Bill," *Judges' Journal*, vol. 29 (Fall 1990), pp. 23, 47 (the Judicial Conference "played a key role in opposing the Biden bill's provisions . . ." that stemmed from a "flawed committee report of the Brookings Institution . . . that [urged legislation to] micromanage civil litigation"); Diana E. Murphy, "The Concerns of Federal Judges," *Judicature*, vol. 74 (August–September, 1990), p. 112 (systemic delays were not demonstrated, and the legislative failed to consider issues related to the criminal docket; further, the mandatory nature of the proposed legislation was inappropriate).

In response to the legislative effort, the Judicial Conference approved a "14-point program to address the problems of cost and delay in civil litigation" and, like the Biden Bill, emphasized case management. See "Judicial Conference Approves Plan to Improve Civil Case Management," *Third Branch*, vol. 22 (May 1990), p. 1.

93. See Robert M. Cover, "Violence and the Word," *Yale Law Journal*, vol. 95 (July 1986), p. 1601.

94. Standing requirements and the prohibition on "advisory opinions" are justified in part by these concerns. Of course, the question is when such powers are necessarily deployed. Compare Alexander M. Bickel, "The Passive Virtues," *Harvard Law Review*, vol. 75, no. 1 (1961), p. 40; with Gerald Gunther, "The Subtle Vices of the 'Passive Virtues'—A Comment on the Principle and Expediency of Judicial Review," *Columbia Law Review*, vol. 64 (January 1964), p. 1.

95. Compare the majority opinion in *Martin* v. *Wilks*, 490 U.S. 755, 759 (1989), with Justice Stevens's dissent, 490 U.S. at 769 (disputing what the trial court's factfinding had been). See also *Rufo* v. *Inmates of Suffolk Country Jail*, 112 S. Ct. 748, 768 (1992) (Justice Stevens, joined by Justice Blackmun, dissenting, and arguing that the negotiated decree had to be understood in light of the fact that "litigation had established the existence of a serious constitutional violation").

96. For further questioning of the propriety of court entry of consent decrees, see Judith Resnik, "Judging Consent," *University of Chicago Legal Forum*, vol. 1987, p. 43.

97. For example, factual findings of discrimination may be critical to remedial rights. See *Firefighters Local Union No. 1784* v. *Stotts*, 467 U.S. 561 (1984); and Macklin, "Promoting Settlement," pp. 584–88. Further, in institutional reform cases, the Supreme Court has upheld a "flexible standard" under which parties may seek modification of consent decrees. See *Rufo* v. *Inmates of Suffolk Country*, 112 S. Ct. 748 (1992). While the holding is addressed to the question of consent decrees, some of the language of the opinion suggests that, in any institutional injunction, such flexibility may be appropriate. See also Justice O'Connor, concurring, 112 S.Ct. at 765. Moreover, as applied, the "flexible standard" continues to impose a significant burden on the party seeking change.

98. Landsman, "The Rise of the Contentious Spirit," p. 502.

99. Both the *Civil Justice Reform Act*, a part of Senator Biden's agenda, and the recommendations of the Quayle Commission exemplify Democratic and Republican views of the political utility of focusing on such "reform." A range of trade associations and institutional litigants provide commentary on proposed rule changes. See, for example, the comments of the Lawyers for Civil Justice on Proposed Amendments to the Federal Rules of Civil Procedure and Evidence, cover letter (Washington, November 7, 1991), which explains that the organization is a nationwide coalition of corporate and defense counsel," and its supplementary comments of February 7, 1992; and "Trial Lawyers for Public Justice Comments on the Proposed Amendments to the Federal Rules of Civil Procedure and Evidence" (February 14, 1992), p. 1, describing that organization as a "national public

interest law firm that specializes in . . . socially significant tort and trial litigation . . . [and] is dedicated to pursing justice for the victims of corporate and government abuses."

100. Jack B. Weinstein, "After Fifty Years of the Federal Rules of Civil Procedure: Are the Barriers to Justice Being Raised?" *University of Pennsylvania Law Review*, vol. 137 (June 1989), pp. 1901, 1909. See also Marc Galanter, "The Debased Debate on Civil Justice," Working Paper, Dispute Processing Research Program, February 10, 1992, p. 8 ("assertions are made about complex states of affairs without any sense of accountability to some body of reliable information. It seems to be assumed that in addressing the legal system, fibs and fables are acceptable").

101. In contrast, on the criminal side, there is an acknowledgement, upfront, of the political and social content of the Federal Rules of Criminal Procedure, some of which are directly aimed at protecting the power disequilibrium between prosecution and defense. See, for example, Federal Rule of Criminal Procedure 11, requiring judicial supervision of guilty pleas to attempt to ensure that one party—the defendant—has adequate information for consenting. No such requirement is applicable to individual civil litigants, although the trial judge is required in class actions to supervise consent. See Federal Rule of Civil Procedure 23(e).

102. Of course, such a claim is belied not only by contemporary debates but also by the history of civil rule drafting, which is replete with political and social visions. See Stephen C. Yeazell, *From Medieval Group Litigation to the Modern Class Action* (Yale University Press, 1987); Stephen B. Burbank, "The Rules Enabling Act of 1934," *University of Pennsylvania Law Review*, vol. 130 (May 1982), p. 1015; and Stephen N. Subrin, "How Equity Conquered Law: The Federal Rules of Civil Procedure in Historical Perspective," *University of Pennsylvania Law Review*, vol. 135 (April 1987), p. 909.

103. For efforts to ask such questions in the context of civil rules, see Carl Tobias, "An Independent Public Law," *Administrative Law Journal*, vol. 4 (Spring 1990), p. 143; and Robert L. Carter, "The Federal Rules of Civil Procedure as Vindicator of Civil Rights," *University of Pennsylvania Law Review*, vol. 137 (June 1989), p. 2179. For commentary on proposed amendments that focus on the impact of such amendments on "plaintiffs" and "defendants," see the comments of the Association of Trial Lawyers of America (ATLA) to the Standing Committee on Civil Rules, February 14, 1992. For efforts to "reform" the civil justice system from the vantage point of the insurance industry, see Insurance Information Institute, *Working toward a Fairer Civil Justice System* (New York, 1987), which "includes a summary of a Harris poll, conducted for Aetna Life & Casualty" about public attitudes toward the justice system.

104. See generally Symposium, "Consent Decrees," *University of Chicago Legal Forum*, vol. 1987, p. 43; and Samuel R. Gross and Kent D. Syverud, "Getting to No: A Study of Settlement Negotiations and the Selection of Cases for Trial," *Michigan Law Review*, vol. 90 (November 1991), p. 319.

105. And did. See Resnik letter to the Justices of the California Supreme Court re Petition for Review in *Neary* v. *Regents of the University of California*, April 30, 1991. For other commentary objecting to such settlements, see *Memorial Hospital* v. *United States Department of Health & Human Services*, 862 F.2d 1299 (7th Cir. 1988), which held that a court should decline parties' request to vacate a judgment, but that parties remained free to settle on other terms. Compare *National Union Fire Insurance Co.* v. *Seafirst Corporation*, 891 F.2d 762 (9th Cir. 1989), which imposed a balancing test to be applied when vacatur was requested, and *Nestle Co.* v. *Chester's Marker, Inc.*, 756 F.2d 280 (2d Cir. 1985), which granted vacatur without such a test. See generally Fisch, "Rewriting History," pp. 610–42, who argues that the costs of vacatur include altering the incentives and timing of settlements between parties and effecting legal doctrines of preclusion, which are costs "borne directly by third party litigants but shared by the public interest."

106. *Neary*, 3 Cal. 4th at 280, 10 Cal. Rptr. 2d at 862. Justice Stanley Mosk concurred "under the facts" but objected to the majority opinion and argued that the matter should reside "entirely to the discretion of the [intermediate] appellate court." 3 Cal. 4th at 286, 10 Cal. Rptr. 2d at 866. Justice Joyce L. Kennard's dissent stressed that a "judgment embodies an act of government" and criticized the purchasing of reversals without consideration of the "public value" of judgments. 3 Cal. 4th at 286-7, 10 Cal. Rptr. at 867. For discussion of the variety of docket clearing techniques recently embraced by the California Supreme Court, including precluding judicial review over a binding arbitration award that, on its face, was legally wrong, see Gail Diane Cox, "Innovation—or Just Court Triage," *National Law Journal*, October 5, 1992, pp. 1, 10 ("Stipulated reversals join a series of California innovations—including unjust-but-approved arbitrations, rent-a-judging, and decertification—that whatever else their value promise triage for the nation's busiest state appellate system").

Contributors

BARBARA ALLEN BABCOCK
Stanford Law School

JONATHAN D. CASPER
American Bar Foundation;
Northwestern University

SHARI SEIDMAN DIAMOND
American Bar Foundation

MARC GALANTER
Institute for Legal Studies,
University of Wisconsin-Madison

VALERIE P. HANS
University of Delaware

ALAN HIRSCH
The Federal Judicial Center

STEPHAN LANDSMAN
Cleveland-Marshall College of Law,
Cleveland State University

RICHARD LEMPERT
The University of Michigan Law
School

ROBERT E. LITAN
The Brookings Institution

ROBERT MACCOUN
The Institute for Civil Justice,
RAND

G. THOMAS MUNSTERMAN
National Center for State Courts

GEORGE L. PRIEST
Yale Law School

JUDITH RESNIK
The Law Center, University of
Southern California

STEPHEN A. SALTZBURG
The National Law Center, The
George Washington University

H. LEE SAROKIN
U.S. District Court, District of
New Jersey

PETER H. SCHUCK
Yale Law School

WILLIAM W SCHWARZER
The Federal Judicial Center;
U.S. District Court,
Northern District of California

Index

ABF. *See* American Bar Foundation

Ad damnum. *See* Plaintiffs

Addison, Alexander, 40

Adler, Stephen, 197

ADR. *See* Alternative dispute resolution

African Americans. *See* Racial issues

Aggregation. *See* Class action suits

Alexander, Janet Cooper, 89

Alfini, James J., 444–45

Allen, James L., 285, 286

Alternative dispute resolution (ADR), 18–19, 327, 342–43, 415–16, 502, 510, 511–12, 514

American Bar Association (ABA): case studies, 184, 185–86, 191–92, 204; Civil Justice Reform Act Task Force, 502–04; sexual harassment case, 185, 204; *Standards Relating to Juror Use and Management*, 381; Task Force on Mass Torts, 509; trade secrets case, 190, 194–95, 203, 227, 229

American Bar Foundation (ABF), 138, 148–49, 150

American Law Institute, 509

Americans with Disabilities Act (*1990*), 330

Anthony, Susan B., 474

Antitrust law: damages, 290–91, 404, 418, 452; trials, 63, 434

Appeals, 190, 317, 323, 324, 326–27, 344, 355, 356, 360, 361, 370, 404, 436, 462, 500–01, 507, 516

Apodaca et al. v. *Oregon* (*1972*), 161

Arbitration: comparison with trial verdicts, 154–65, 166, 213; opinions of, 266–67, 270–71; use of, 18, 317. *See also* Alternative dispute resolution; Negotiation

Assize, 26

Assumption of risk. *See* Risk

Attaint, 27, 28–29

Attorneys: case presentation, 352–54, 389–90, 505; case selection, 163, 165; case valuation, 315–16; characteristics, 74–75, 259, 292, 481; female, 478; instructions, 446; jury service of, 380; mistaken verdicts, 11, 203–04, 205, 214–15, 234; opening/closing statements, 19, 362, 370, 385–86; opinions of arbitration, 266–67; opinions of instructions, 355–56; opinions of judges,

217–18, 266–67; opinions of juries, 6, 12, 74–87, 151, 204, 217–18, 252, 265–68, 274, 315, 329, 355–56, 358, 400; opinions of trials, 82–83, 218, 270; peremptory challenges, 19–20, 383; recommendations for, 16, 19, 365–66, 369–70; settlements, 76, 81–86; statistical fallacies, 206–07; trial instructions, 221

Austin, Arthur, 184, 195

Automobile injury: awards, 9, 148, 149; claims, 119–20; juries, 124, 432; settlements, 73–74; win rates, 148, 165

Awards: automobile cases, 9, 148, 149; caps, 404; consolidated trials, 158, 510; corporations, 163–64, 165; effects of delays, 130; expected, 148; liability, 9, 148, 149, 150, 155; malpractice, 9, 148, 149; media exaggeration, 14; mean/median, 9, 148–50, 164, 166, 209–10, 316; million-dollar, 9, 77, 91, 149; over-estimation, 85; personal injury, 149–50, 158; public opinions of, 12, 258–59, 260, 261, 270, 275; reduced, 9, 149, 150, 314; review of, 125–26; scheduling, 18; variability, 17–18, 72, 81–86, 165, 293. *See also* Damages; Verdicts

Babcock, Barbara, 19, 20

Ballard v. *United States* (*1946*), 469–70, 471, 472

Ballew v. *Georgia* (*1978*), 161

Bar Associations, 359, 380. *See also* American Bar Association

Barry, Marion, 341–42

Batson v. *Kentucky* (1986), 346, 461–62, 465–66, 467, 468–69, 470–71, 472, 473, 477, 479, 481, 482

Beall, George, 503

Beattie, John, 31

Belli, Melvin, 151

Bench trials. *See* Trials, bench

Bermant, Gordon, 204–05, 217–18, 292

Bifurcation. *See* Trials, bifurcated

Black, Hugo L., 360

Blackstone, William, 30

Bordens, Kenneth S., 212, 214, 234, 442–43

Brazil, Wayne, 76